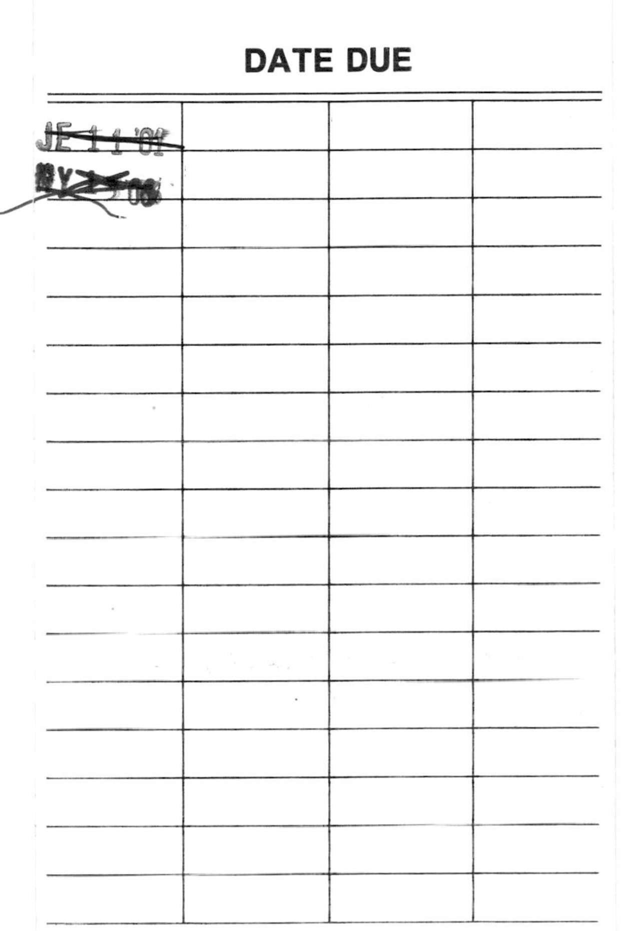
DATE DUE
JE 11 '01
DEMCO 38-296

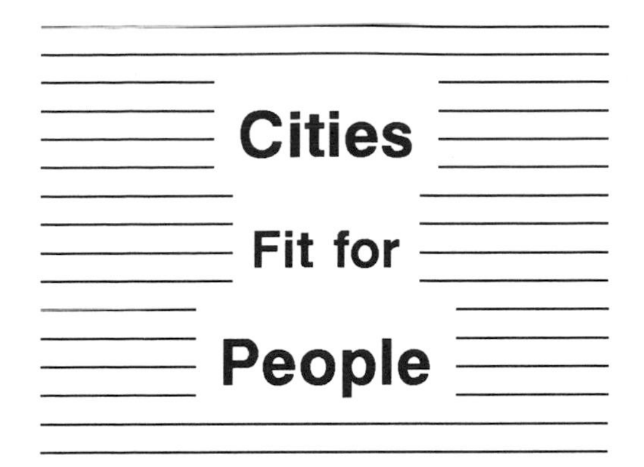
Cities
Fit for
People

R

Cities Fit for People

Edited by

Üner Kırdar

United Nations
New York
1997

The contents of this book do not necessarily reflect the views of the United Nations or of the United Nations Development Programme. The papers in this volume were contributed by authors in their personal capacities and they are solely responsible for their views.

United Nations Publications
United Nations
Room DC2-853
New York, NY 10017, U.S.A.

United Nations Publications
Palais des Nations
1221 Geneva 10
Switzerland

U.N. Sales No: E.97.III.B.12
ISBN 92-1-126072-8

Manufactured in the United States of America

Contents

Foreword

In the waning days of this century, we cannot look back at our era without being struck by the momentous social and demographic changes and the challenges they present for the century ahead.

Perhaps the most important change of our lifetimes has been the fact that the human race has ceased to be predominantly rural. This shift from agriculturally-based to industrial- and service-based economies has caused irreversible changes. One of the most visible is the phenomenal mass migration of people from rural areas to the cities—a migration fuelled primarily by the prospects of better living conditions and greater prosperity.

As the next millennium begins, the overwhelming majority of people in every country, rich or poor, will be living in urban areas. Cities will face an influx of vast new populations clamoring for jobs and housing. Great efforts must be made to prevent this influx from breeding poverty instead of peace and social unrest instead of greater prosperity. Considerable financial resources will be required to ensure adequate infrastructure and services. Cities will become the centers of economic, social, and ecological changes. A major challenge of the future, therefore, will be to make the cities safer, healthier, more sustainable, and more humane—more fit for people.

Cities fit for people must be the engine of progress and the source of culture, education, and wealth, where people's lives can be broadened and fulfilled; where people can find rewarding and renumerative jobs; and where they can acquire adequate housing. Cities fit for people should be places where new dynamic communities are created and where democratization, political participation, gender equality, and full partnerships are forged among neighbors and residents.

To promote these objectives and to ensure the necessary global commitment to their realization, the United Nations convened last year, in Istanbul, Turkey, the Second Habitat Conference—The City Summit—20 years after the first Habitat Conference in Vancouver, Canada.

Habitat II was truly a conference of partners, involving the active participation of all the constituents of the cities from national leaders to local authorities to people from every walk of life. The private and the public sectors, non-governmental organizations, professional organizations and associations, the academic and scientific communities, parliaments, trade unions, women's groups, coalitions of the young and elderly, and community representatives—all those who have a stake in improving cities were there.

The Istanbul Conference addressed the future of the cities in a comprehensive and integrated manner. Developing solutions for global urban problems, the City Summit was part of a remarkable series of UN conferences that have taken place during the 1990s. This series has led to the creation of a new UN economic and social agenda, a new social contract for building a more humane and more sustainable world for the new millenium.

Cities Fit for People, which grew out of the ideas presented at that conference, is a collaborative work of an eminent group of scholar citizens. It makes a lasting and valuable intellectual contribution to the advancement and realization of this new UN agenda by presenting knowledge, insights, and experiences at a critical time for the international community.

Kofi A. Annan
Secretary-General
United Nations

Introduction

This book addresses the most compelling social problems of contemporary urban life, offering ideas and suggestion on how to make our cities fit for people at the beginning of a new millennium. It provides realistic policy options and practical advice on what each of us—in our communities and in our homes—can do to make our habitats more livable, sustainable, and humane. In short, these pages are filled with the insight, knowledge, and viewpoints of key development actors with varying backgrounds: international and national policy makers, city administrators, and representative of civil society, academia, the media, and the private sector.

Changes in urban life are the result of two related phenomena—globalization and urbanization. Globalization encompasses economic liberalization, including liberalization of financial markets, and the growing capability to overcome barriers of space and time by applying the technological advances in the areas of transportation and communication. Globalization has many positive aspects. In many ways, it has created one world. But, it has also had negative consequences. For instance, while it generates cultural harmony and greater interconnectedness, it also leads to environmental degradation and social alienation.

Urbanization is a growing trend. Studies show that by the year 2000 more than half of humankind will live in urban areas; by 2025, that number will rise to three quarters. This urban explosion will result in more urban poverty, homelessness, unemployment, and social dissatisfaction and disintegration. Is it not then imperative that cities take the lead in eradicating poverty? That we work together for poverty-free cities? That we target the many walls—economic, social, cultural, psychological, and political—that today separate the "citadels of the rich" from the "ghettos of the poor?" Would it not be a win–win proposition for all—rich and poor, for urban and rural—to enter into a new compact of solidarity?

In seeking answers to these questions, *Cities Fit for People* argues for a new vision of world cities, a vision of equality, empowerment, justice, and hope. Today, poverty is growing very quickly; 13 to 18 million people die annually of its consequences. The gap between what is and what ought to be has never been greater. And, nowhere is that disparity more obvious, more palpable, than in our cities. As we approach the twenty-first century, large urban settlements are the most common scene of the human drama. Cities set the pacc, and the example. Cities are the epicenters, where the battle for world equality will be won or lost.

Cities are shaped by, among other factors, the way we "do development." When international trade emerged, many cities, such as Bombay, Mobasa, Hamburg, Rotterdam, Venice, Shanghai, and Hong Kong, gained prominence as harbors and commercial centers. When the Industrial Revolution occurred, factor halls and workers' settlements expanded city borders and smokestacks dominated skylines. Cities, such as Liverpool and Kanbur, are examples of that period. Then colonialism gave rise to such cities as New Delhi and Nairobi. When we entered the era of mass production and consumption, cars began jamming city streets and highways, skirted by shopping malls. Cities began to suffer from air pollution. Manila, Mexico City, and Los Angeles are just three examples of cities gasping for air.

Consider the recent trend of economic liberalization. We have made considerable progress in removing trade barriers, including barriers to foreign investment. Capital is moving freely across international borders. More and more enterprises are creating foreign subsidiaries. There is a growing demand for such services as communication, information, banking, investment, foreign currency exchange, stock markets, human capital formation, retraining, and research and development.

But today's open economies and societies place additional demands on all of us. Rapid developmental changes, and technological changes in particular, demand new capabilities, and, quite often, a basic rethinking of current patterns of production and consumption. Changes in attitudes and preferences are involved – to encourage public transportation rather than individual cars, recycling and energy saving, and the development of environmentally sound technologies.

Progress in the development of such technologies is vital to more humane and more sustainable cities. After all, many parts of today's most advanced cities are high-technology fantasy lands. So many of the toys of science fiction are now at our fingertips. Urban life in run on pentium chips and fiberoptic cables. The sun never sets on globalized financial markets from new York and Chicago and Rio to London, Hong King, Tokyo, Bombay, and Johannesburg. And yet, when we walk out into city streets, we see the battle for equality being lost. Within the unprecedented opulence, we see crushing poverty. We see shanytowns and pollution. We feel the burden of the urban poor, the refugees, and migrant workers, the street children, the AIDS victims – all surviving from day to day without adequate nutrition or shelter or healthcare, without jobs or sanitation or solace.

The world's cities are full of contradiction, disparity, and tension at a time when we need cities of empowerment, community, and solidarity. We need to build bridges within our cities. Democratic societies must be build on foundations of democratic cities. Any credible attack on world poverty must be led by our cities. And, in this question, we need to develop better cooperation:

- Cooperation that recognizes that economies exist for people, not people for economies;
- Cooperation that benefits the poor more than the rich;
- Cooperation not just with central governments, but with local governments, the private sector, and civil society;
- Cooperation that recognizes that the policy is as important as the economy;
- Cooperation that seeks growth, but growth with equality, empowerment, employment, and environment; and
- Cooperation, in short, for sustainable human development.

Broad agreement now exists for the argument that development should meet three criteria: it must be pro-growth, pro-people (in particular, pro-poor and pro-women), and pro-environment. Being pro-people will, most importantly, mean development that is participatory and inclusive. Pro-jobs and pro-equality means allowing all people access to the opportunities that development has to offer, including opportunities for peace and security.

To make cities fit for people, we must bring our new visions of development and policy goals to the local level, down to where people live, down to where people experience development, down to where developmental constraints and new avenues shape human lives, and down to where people themselves take initiatives to transform their own living conditions according to their means, hopes, and expectations.

We have also learned that for the next millennium we need cohesive, not fractured, globalization. We need cohesive, not fractured, cities. We need cities that ensure basic social services for all by investing in people; we need cities that provide jobs and sustain the natural resource base, on which the poor depend; we need cities that promote advancement and empowerment of women; and, we need cities in which the enabling environment is made up of macroeconomic policies and good governance.

I thank all of the contributors to *Cities Fit for People* for bringing their fresh, independent, and cutting-edge viewpoints to this critical dialogue. I express my highest appreciation to the government of Turkey for its generous financial support for this book and for its gracious hosting of the Marmaris Roundtable and the Habitat II Conference in Istanbul. Most of the ideas expressed in this book took shape at that conference.

Finally, a personal word of appreciation. With the editing of this book, Üner Kırdar is retiring from the United Nations after twenty-five years of dedicated service. As the author, contributor to, or editor of more than fifteen books, his legacy will continue to enhance the contribution of the UN as it prepares for the challenges of the new century. This is particularly true in the area he helped so effectively to pioneer – the human dimension of development. He originated the United Nations Development Study Programme, both in concept and organization. Üner Kırdar has been recognized as an outstanding and exceptional international civil servant in every respect. His initiatives have helped to place UNDP, as an organization, at the forefront of development thinking. We, his friends and colleagues, warmly thank him for his valuable contributions and services to the United Nations and to the international community at large, as we wish him our very best.

James Gustave Speth
Administrator
United Nations Development Programme

Recollections and Acknowledgments

Üner Kırdar

The making of this book is the last stop in my long, challenging, sometimes depressing, but mostly rewarding journey in the fascinating world of the United Nations. I will be retiring from the services of the secretariat of the United Nations, after having served there for a quarter of a century. I spent nearly forty years of my career—first as a scholar, then as a diplomat, and later as an international civil servant—dedicated to the advancement, greater understanding, and fulfillment of the UN's goals and objectives.

In the 1960s I published my first book, *Structure of United Nations Economic Aid*, which became a kind of textbook for development practitioners, diplomats, economists, students of international affairs, and others interested in the United Nations' economic activities. In this book, I argued that the most practical means of defeating the international economic difficulties was to end the "laissez-faire" attitude toward human welfare problems and to make the UN a powerful engine for promoting social justice among the members of the international community.[1]

As a diplomat, I took an active role in the formation of UNCTAD and also initiated several UN resolutions.[2] During this period of my life, I was privileged to work closely with, and benefited immensely from the vision and wisdom of, a series of great international civil servants and statesmen, such as Gunnar Myrdal, Raul Prebisch, Paul Hoffman, Saburo Okita, Perez Guerrero, Sidney Dell, Philippe de Seynes, Janez Stanovnik, and Gamani Correa, most of whom later became my colleagues when I joined the UN Secretariat.

As an international civil servant, I had the good fortune to serve on several exciting and challenging assignments and missions, which have enriched my career and my life.[3] On these assignments, I worked either under the guidance of or in collaboration with wonderful, remarkable, admirable, and truly global citizens. The list is enormous, but I feel obliged to mention a few by name: Bradford Morse, G. Arthur Brown, Kenneth K. Dadzie (all three of whom, unfortunately, are no longer among us), as well as Ismat Kittani, Richard N. Gardner, Enrique Peñalosa, Maurice Strong, James Gustave Speth, and Patrizio Civili. I am deeply grateful and indebted to these committed people for the trust, cooperation, and friendship that they have generously extended to me.

Among my assignments, I must mention one specific initiative that I undertook during 1981 – namely, the establishment of the UNDP Development Study Programme. During my work on reform at the United Nations, I became convinced that development must be seen as a process, rather than a static phenomenon, through which one lives, learns and participates. In the 1950s and 1960s, international development dialogue and negotiations were primarily based on the conventional wisdom that successful development could best be ensured mainly through a massive transfer of capital resources and the provision of technical assistance by developed countries to developing countries. The transfer of financial resources and technical knowledge, while essential, was certainly not the only critical factor. In most cases, the idea that individual people are at the core of all developmental efforts has been overlooked. Therefore, issues such as education, knowledge, the quality and level of skills, productivity, improvement of management, the capacity to respond to changing requirements, and cultural factors needed to receive equal, if not greater, attention during the development process. I became similarly convinced of the need for a closer interaction between the research and operational activities of the UN. To be successful, a voluntarily funded development organization of the UN needs an adequate intellectual and research base to provide a framework for its operations. When I joined the UNDP at the invitation of the late administrator, Bradford Morse, I shared these convictions and views with him. Morse encouraged me to develop them for consideration by the Governing Council. As a result, in 1981, I presented the blueprint of the UNDP Development Study Programme to the Council. The objective of the program was to promote a greater understanding of and to generate new ideas and innovative solutions for the problems of the development process. Although the Council approved the proposal in toto, it did not allocate any financial resources for its execution. So I put together the whole program with no funding from the UNDP or the UN. Nevertheless, I managed to organize more than twenty roundtable meetings, convened in various parts of the world, and several seminars, lectures, and discussion groups, in addition to publishing more than 16 books on current and future global issues.

Between 1983 and 1996, more than 1,500 renowned world thinkers, high-level national and international policy makers, senior officials of international organizations, leaders of private and public enterprises, and representatives of the media, academic, and nongovernmental organizations from more than 100 countries have participated in these meetings and contributed to my publications. This process has fostered a frank exchange of views, experiences, and knowledge on different policy aspects of economic, social, ecological, technological, and human development.

During this period, one of the most notable and long-lasting achievements is the formulation and advancement of the concept of "human development." Through extensive research and writings[4] and numerous multidisciplinary roundtable discussions, we succeeded in building the momentum that brought the concept of human development into the mainstream of the UNDP and the UN system's work and international policy dialogues. The idea of and argumentation for publishing the UNDP's annual Human Development Reports emanated from the Development Study Programme roundtable recommendations.[5] Through this process, the UNDP has gradually been transformed from a fund of multilateral technical cooperation to a sustainable human development organization.

During the early 1980s I also gave thought to the necessity of convening a UN conference on the role of human development in the process of development. This idea was first discussed at a brainstorming session among the senior staff of the UNDP in 1982. In 1984, the Administrator of UNDP informed high-level government officials that he intended to propose the convening of such a conference to the Governing Council of the UNDP at its June session. Subsequently, in his annual policy address to the Council, he made a strong plea to the governments in that respect:

> The time has come to recognize that human development has been a neglected dimension in the development process which has not only inhibited economic and social progress in developing countries, but has also meant that the maximum benefit has not been achieved from the funds that have been provided on the capital side. . . . No investment can be sustained, maintained, or maximized unless the developing country in which it is made has the indigenous human capacity to sustain, maintain, and maximize it.

Although the proposal to convene such a conference was well received and supported by most of the members of the Council, an unresolved political question related to a country program led to objections by one country. As a result, the Council was unable to take an action on this important proposal. Thus, a good idea that could have helped the promotion of human development, was shelved for ten years until the convening of the World Summit on Social Development in 1995, in Copenhagen, Denmark.

As we approach the new millennium, the world is increasingly confronted with issues that affect humanity as a whole; these range from the economic requirements of finance, trade, monetary exchanges and urbanization to the need for food, health services, education, employment, housing, from energy to the preservation of the ecology, from information to new discoveries in genetics and biotechnology. All of these issues have a strong human dimension, because people are at the core of all of them. Human development, therefore, will assume an even greater importance during the twenty-first century. In addition, many of the crucial problems affecting the well-being of a large segment of humanity can no longer be solved by strictly national and fragmented efforts. They need concerted multilateral action and the logical place for this action is the UN. Yet, paradoxically, there is widespread doubt about the capabilities of the UN. To succeed in meeting the major global challenges of the twenty-first century, these realities must first be recognized.

In the innovative and challenging undertakings of the Development Study Programme, I have been extremely fortunate to enjoy the company, cooperation, and intellectual support of a large, extraordinary group of people to whom I am greatly indebted.[6] Unfortunately some of them are no longer with us, including the late President of Turkey Turgut Özal; Prime Minster of Bulgaria Andre Lukanov; Nobel Laureate Abdus Salam; my coeditor Leonard Silk; Bradford Morse, James Grant, Arthur Brown, Professor Dankwart A. Rustow, Göran Ohlin. The others vigorously continue to contribute to the betterment of human lives. I would like to mention a few in particular: HRH Crown Prince Hassan Bin Talal, HRH Princess Basma Bint Talal, Ali Attiga, Y. Seyyid Abdulai, Abdul Rahman Al-Awaidi, Joan Anstee, Lourdes Arizpe, Philip Allott, Dragoslav Avramovic, Nicolos Ardito-Barletta, Alicia Barcena, Nancy Barry, Benjamin Bassin, Yves Berthelot, Keith Bezanson, John Brademas, Ingar Brüggerman, Francis Blanchard, Nicholea Malet de Carteret, Margaret Catley-Carson, Ella Cisneros, Mary Chinery-Hesse, Michael Cohen, Helle Degn, Nitin Desai, Louis Emmerij, Amal El-Ferhan, Olivier Giscard D'Estaing, Ingrid Eide, Neva Goodwin, Daram Ghai, Keith Griffin, Mahbub and Khadija Haq, Evelyn Herfkins, Hazel Henderson, Nolen Heyzer, Paul Marc Henry, Ryokachi Hirono, Enrique Iglesias, Shafiqul Islam, Richard Jolly, Lord Judd of Portsea, Inge Kaul, Lawrence Klein, Azizur Rahman Khan, John Langmore, Flora Lewis, Stephen Lewis, Maria Lourdes de Pintasilgo, Charles William Maynes, Wangari Maathai, Frederick Mayor, Valentine Moghadam, Robert McNamara, Gertrude Mongella, Solita Monsod, Cecilia Lopez Montano, Caroline Moser, Aziz Ali Mohammed, Wally N'Dow, G.O.P. Obasi, Mauren O'Neil, Olara Otunnu, Lisbet Palme, I.G. Patel, Barbara Pyle, Shirdarth Ramphal, Gustav Ranis, Leticia Ramos Shahani, Eric Rouleau, Jean Ripert, Nafis Sadik, John W. Sewell, Mihaly Simai, Juan Somavia, Heitor Gurgulino de Souza, Maurice Strong, Paul Streeten, Makoto Taniguchi, Carl Tham, Victor Tokman, David Turnham, Klaus Töpfer,

Ben Turok, John Williamson, Joseph Wheeler, Anders Wijkman, Y.C. Richard Wong, Layashi Yaker, Fernando Zumbado, my compatriots Ishak Alaton, Emre Gönensay, Orhan Güvenen, Talat Halman, my cousins Professor Ihsan Dogramaci and Nemir Kırdar. The list goes on and on, and so does my gratitude.

During the implementation of these undertakings, I have been helped tremendously by my able assistants—Teresita Dominguez, Behrooz Clubwala, Barbara Assa, and Maria Figueroa, and by Jessie Reyes, Edwina Zgutowicz, and Rachel Gogos. In publishing several books, I have been helped by Barbara A. Chernow and George A. Vallasi of Chernow Editorial Services, the personnel of the United Nations Publications, and New York University Press. During my long journey at the services of the UN, however, the greatest support came from my dear wife Berna Kırdar and my children Konca, Àsû, and Mehmet.

All of these wonderful people have contributed to and enriched my life in some way. Looking back, I feel that my cup is full, because of to their friendship, support, and collaboration. I am indebted and grateful to all of them. The torch has now been passed to my friend and colleague Inge Kaul and her young team. I wish them all the best and the same wonderful experiences.

Notes

1. Üner Kırdar, *Structure of United Nations Economic Aid,* The Hague, Martinus Nijhoff, 1966 and 1968.
2. These resolutions include "Measures to promote private investments to developing countries," which resulted in the establishment of the Multilateral Investment Insurance scheme that is currently under the auspices of the World Bank (1964); "A Charter and Global Plan for Economic Development," primarily focused on poverty alleviation (1968); "Better coordination at the national level for international policymaking" (1969), "Convocation of the first United Nations Conference on Environment" (1970); and establishment of the "World Tourism Organization" (1971).
3. To mention a few: Formulation and coordination of the study of the Secretary-General on the Review of the Relationship Agreements between the United Nations and the Specialized Agencies (1972–74); Secretary of the High Level Group of Experts on the Restructuring of the Economic and Social Sectors of the United Nations System (1975) (It is the far-reaching recommendations of this group that has guided and greatly influenced the reform process of the UN since that time); Secretary of the first United Nations Conference on Human Settlements (HABITAT I) (1976) and its prepatory committee (1974–1976); Formulation and negotiation of the *Programme of Assistance to the Palestinian People* (1979); Director of External Relations and the Secretariat of the

Governing Council of UNDP (1980–1991): Director of UNDP Development Study Programme (1981–1995); the organization of the first ever "World Hearings on Developmen" under the President of UN General Assembly (1994), the coordination of the organizational operations of the Second UN Conference on Human Settlement (HABITAT II) (1994–1996).

4. Our first roundtable on this subject took place in September 1983 in Istanbul, Turkey. The North–South Roundtable of the Society for International Development wanted to convene a roundtable on world monetary and financial issues. Its chairman, my friend Mahbub ul Haq, working at that time at the World Bank, approached me for assistance from the UNDP. After consulting the Administrator, Bradford Morse, I replied that we would gladly become a cosponsor of the roundtable and not only finance it, but also organize it, subject to the condition that the meeting would also consider the issues related to human resource development. After some hesitation, the North–South Roundtable accepted our proposal. It was difficult for the hard-core monetary economists at that time to understand the linkages between the debt issues and human development. As a matter of fact, one of them later told me that in his view this was a forced marriage. But after three sessions of the roundtable, he changed his mind and said that the marriage was a relevant and happy one!

Two years later, on a cold February day in 1985, I had a meeting in my office at the UNDP with Gustav Ranis of Yale University and Frances Stewart from Oxford. We prepared jointly a proposal for the consideration of Maurice Strong, then the Chairman of the North–South Roundtable, and Bradford Morse, then Administrator of the UNDP, for the launching of a new series of roundtables, specifically on the subject of "the human element in development." With their approval, we organized four very successful sessions of Human Development Roundtables: namely, Human Dimension of Development (2–4 September 1985, in Istanbul, Turkey); Adjustment with Human Development (7–9 September 1986, in Salzburg, Austria); Managing Human Development (6–9 September 1987, in Budapest, Hungary); Human Development and Strategies for the Year 2000 (3–5 September 1988, in Amman, Jordan).

5. See Üner Kırdar, "Human Resources Development: Challenge for the 80s," *Crisis of the 80s,* North–South Roundtable (SID) Publications, 1984; "Impact of IMF Conditionality on Human Conditions," *Adjustment with Growth,* North–South Roundtable (SID) Publications, 1985; "International Debt and Its Impact on Human Conditions," *The Lingering Debt Crisis,* North–South Roundtable (SID) Publications, 1985; "International Institutions and Human Development: A Critique," *Human Development: The Neglected Dimension,* ed. by Khadija Haq and Üner Kırdar, United Nations Publications, 1987; "Policies and Strategies for Human Devel-

opment: Recent Record," *Managing Human Development,* ed. by Khadija Haq and Üner Kırdar, United Nations Publications, 1988; "A Review of Past Strategies," *Development for People,* ed. by Khadija Haq and Üner Kırdar, United Nations Publications, 1989.

6. The proposal was first made during the Istanbul Roundtable on world monetary, financial, and human resource development issues (August 29-September 1, 1983). The meeting recognized the need for an annual report on the state of human development as a counterpart to the World Development Reports and the World Economic Outlooks. It recommended that such reports take stock of the year's setbacks and progress, review various countries' experiences, provide different paradigms of human development, and demonstrate the results of IMF conditionality and other policies in terms of human and social costs. See Üner Kırdar, "An Overview," *Crisis of the 80s,* North–South Roundtable (SID) Publications, 1984, p. 207.

Overview

Üner Kırdar

Two critical challenges facing the world community today are rapid urbanization and the so-called globalization process. The world is becoming predominantly urban, and its economy global.

In the eighteenth-century, only three percent of the world's population lived in cities. In contrast, by the year 2000, more than 50 percent (3.2 billion people) will be living in urban areas. And, it is estimated that by the year 2025, two-thirds of the world's 5.5 billion people will be city dwellers. In addition, the sizes of the cities themselves are reaching unprecedented dimensions. By the beginning of the twenty first century, there will be 23 megacities, each with a population of ten million or more; 18 will be in developing countries.

These cities will likely experience enormous critical social and environmental problems which will push their inhabitants to the limits of their ability to sustain reasonable human life. All of them will share certain common fundamental problems, such as polarization between rich and poor, fewer employment possibilities along with lower earnings, inadequate housing and infrastructure services, as well as severe environmental strains, such as air and water pollution, traffic congestion, and increasing social tensions and violence.

At the doorstep of a new millennium, these serious global problems affect all people and require imminent and coherent policy actions that go far beyond the short-term interests of each nation–state. Thus, there are compelling reasons for developing practical policy measures and options that make the world's cities more economically viable, politically participatory, ecologically sustainable, and humanely and socially just.

The Creation of *Cities Fit for People*

To assist the process, the United Nations Development Programme, in collaboration with the secretariat of the Habitat II Conference and with the support of the government of Turkey, organized a roundtable meeting on the subject of "The Next Millennium: Cities for People in a Globalizing World." The roundtable, which was held in Marmaris, Turkey, from 19 to 21 April 1996, discussed most of these issues. A major objective of the meeting was to provide an intellectual framework for the final global United Nations Conference of the 1990s—the Second United Nations Conference on Human Settlements (HABITAT II)—generally referred to as the "City Summit," that occurred two months later in Istanbul.

The roundtable brought together 130 development thinkers, including housing and environmental administrators, mayors, architects, representatives of community and civil-society organizations, investment bankers, and journalists. The meeting's deliberations were supported by more than 80 background papers submitted by the participants.

This book is based on edited and abbreviated versions of a select number of these papers and on the extremely rich and comprehensive debates that took place at the Marmaris Roundtable and later at the City Summit in Istanbul. The authors are expressing their personal views, which should not necessarily be attributed to the institutions with which they are affiliated. Final responsibility for the selection and editing of the papers rests with the editor.

I am deeply indebted to everyone who joined me in this collaborative international effort and who made possible the publishing of *Cities Fit for People*. My gratitude also goes to the Secretary-General of the United Nations, Kofi Annan, for writing the foreword, and to the Administrator of the United Nations Development Programme, James Gustave Speth, for his introduction, leadership, and unfailing encouragement.

I have chosen the title *Cities Fit for People* to maintain the same spirit of thought reflected in a previous book—*A World Fit for People*—which I edited with my late friend Leonard Silk several years ago. That book dealt with the issues of ongoing worldwide changes in a variety of governing systems, and their possible effects on the lives of people. It put forward global policy proposals to make the world fit for ordinary people and expressed hope for a better, safer, and more rewarding future. The present book is arguably more realistic than the previous one. After all, cities are a microcosm of today's world. To have a world fit for people, we must first have cities fit for people—cities that are safer, healthier, more humane, and sustainable.

Cities and Citizens

The word city has various meanings, depending on whether it is defined by demographers, politicians, economists, historians, or social scientists. To the student of Greek and Roman history, it means not only such walled towns as Athens, Rome, and Istanbul, but also the territory surrounding these towns, whose inhabitants enjoyed the privileges and responsibilities of citizenship. The word citizen also has different meanings. In modern usage, citizenship is the legal link that binds people to the *national* state. The individual receives guaranteed rights, privileges, and protections in return for allegiance and obligations.[1] At present, the terms citizen and national are frequently used interchangeably. However, the original English meaning of citizen is a person who is a member of a borough or local municipal corporation. Similarly, in continental Europe, a definition of citizenship (droit de cité, cittadinanza, ciudadania, Bürgerrecht) reflects the historical concept of a relationship to a city, imparting certain liberties.[2]

In this book, the term citizen is used in the European sense. In the ancient Greco-Roman world, the ideas of both the city, or "polis," and the citizen reached their peak. For citizens at least, the city and its laws constituted a moral order, symbolized in magnificent buildings and public assemblies. It was, in Aristotle's phrase, "a common life for a noble end."[3] Two thousand years ago, the citizens of Athens were obliged to take the following oath: "We will strive for the ideals and sacred things of the city, both alone and with many. . . . We will transmit this city not only not less, but greater, better and more beautiful than it was transmitted to us."

In a modern city, where civic life is both essential and difficult, the good citizen must first be a good person, who is also responsible, informed, and prepared to subordinate his or her individual advantages to common goods, to the respect for human dignity and rights of the others, and to the preservation of common values.

Our values are made more concrete in cities, for good and ill. Cities are expressions of the dynamism of the human spirit—the centers of culture, creativity, and the interchange of ideas. But cities also emphasize the extremes of wealth and poverty, and take a disproportionate toll on the life support systems of the planet. Standing on the threshold of the urban millennium, there is, therefore, an urgent need for radical changes in values and policies to reconcile the conflicts in cities—between the rich and poor and between humanity and the environment. Cities can only be made workable for the next millennium by such changes.

The task is urgent. The scale of urbanization and growing inequality has resulted in higher levels of poverty throughout the world. Cities, already near the breaking point, will have to accommodate an unprecedented growth in numbers. Meanwhile, cities also confront increasing violence, armed criminals, substance abuse and addiction, mental illness, and the disintegration of communities. Wally N'Dow, in his section, "An Urbanizing World," deals holistically with the different aspects of the present urbanization trends.

Globalization

As a result of the globalization process, the world's economy is experiencing revolutionary changes, especially in its financial, securities, trade, and production markets. New technological, information, and communication facilities permit 24-hour-a-day transactions, trading, and flow of information worldwide. The transnational movement of capital is becoming one of the most obvious forces of the world economy. Currently, worldwide financial exchanges are outwaiting trade in goods at a ratio of twenty to one. The powerful role of the corporate world in the globalization process and channeling of capital in the world economy becomes more apparent each day. With this process of globalization, which Mihaly Simai examines in "A Globalizing World," several cities are becoming global cities, as they host the main or a significant part of corporate activities in the world of finance, production, and trade. The efficiency of a city determines its role in this expanding and borderless economy.

The globalization process has both positive and negative implications for life in the cities. For example, globalization, which is closely linked to economic liberalization, has had some positive effects on growth and employment in much of Asia, but these are counterbalanced by negative effects elsewhere. It has also encouraged migration to urban areas, hastened the deterioration of urban infrastructures and social services, and increased the inequalities in most, although not all, countries.

Yet the message of this book is one of hope as well as of challenge: "More sustainable and humane cities are primarily a matter of choice: do-able policy options, as well as requisite resources, are available. How tomorrow's generation will live largely depends on 'us', how we choose to live today."

Urban administrations face enormous pressures in such areas as funding education and health services, law and order, and emergency services. Yet, human and financial resources are waiting to be tapped, if ways can be found to successfully direct and channel them. These resources will be all the more valuable if applied to new priorities that emphasize human development, the eradication of poverty, and environmental sustainability. Louis Emmerij, in his article, "An Urban Renaissance," examines how several cities that were on the decline have turned themselves around to become regional poles of development.

Building Positive Actions

Thus, our overall goal must be to develop cities for a humane society. A humane habitat creates a climate of hope and opportunity, in which all segments of society have access to sustainable incomes, basic services, and justice, and in which the human spirit can flourish with dignity.

As many residents as possible, no matter where they have come from, must be involved in the decisions that affect their lives. Cities are successful if they are hospitable, participatory, equitable, and in balance with the natural resource base they utilize. Some cities have already taken substantial steps along this path, but the journey is only beginning.

To encourage this process of practical action, "An Agenda for Making Cities Fit for People," offers do-able policy options. That essay is based on an analysis of the ideas expressed in these chapters, which deal mainly with the following nine points, as referred to by Richard Jolly, during his summing up of the findings of the Marmaris Roundtable.

New approaches to Governance and participation: Addressing the crises in cities and realizing their potential to create solutions requires the full participation of their peoples. This requires open, accountable governance, based on democratic elections and political pluralism, and the encouragement of freedom of expression. Governance is more than governments: governance requires less emphasis on formal structures.

What is needed is people-participatory decision-making, devolving decisions as far as possible to the community level, where people have the greatest knowledge of their needs and resources. This would give people who are currently marginalized or disenfranchised a chance to help shape their habitat, instead of having it effectively imposed on them. Special attention needs to be paid to ensuring the participation of women, who when given the chance, often take the most constructive, responsible, and innovative roles in their families and communities.

A new vision for cities—more humane and more sustainable with less poverty: Humane cities would achieve a balance across society, even between rural and urban areas. All residents would be fully incorporated into society through access to employment, a livable income, basic services, and the judicial system. The needs of different groups, such as children and elderly people, would be recognized. Hope, opportunity, and other needs and values would be emphasized over economic expansion. Above all, cities would be committed to an assault on absolute poverty. Each city should prepare its own plan of action, setting forth a vision of its own development, identifying priority actions, and setting clear goals and targets. These should embrace poverty reduction, human development and environmental sustainability.

New voices to help form the vision and set the targets: Establishing this vision and creating a development plan should be part of a process that includes participation by all sections of the community, including community groups and the private sector, not just government organizations and housing associations. The technical work of professional planners will be needed, but it should, wherever possible, incorporate the views of the people, rather than drive the process. For instance, children in cities desire and need more green space, clean air, and places to play that are free from violence, drugs, and speeding traffic. Most cities would gain fresh insights into these challenges—and their solutions—if more ways were found to hear directly from children and other groups such as people who are aged and disabled, commuters, and working people with children.

New responsibilities for implementing the vision: Participation implies responsibility; they are two sides of the same coin. Allowing people to participate means sharing responsibility with them; this both spreads the burden and taps new human resources. Responsibility should no longer be borne entirely by politicians and civil servants, but should be shared widely, with such groups as the poor, business and community groups, and nongovernmental organizations. Involving women is particularly important. Such shared responsibility in the private, public, and civic sectors is a prerequisite for healthy cities in the next millennium.

New sources of finance for cities: Present forms of local finance are costly and unlikely to be effective in mobilizing the resources needed to tackle urban problems worldwide. However, there is growing evidence in cities throughout the world that poor households and communities have both the capacity and the willingness to pay for the many services they require. Such "financing from below" has great untapped potential as a method of mobilizing financial resources. An enabling environment for household community finance needs to be created.

The mobilization and multiplication of household and community resources does not necessarily provide the resources for all urban financial needs; one example would be the infrastructure networks. National public financial resources are also limited. In these instances, private capital–both domestic and international–must be mobilized, Mayors need to develop a policy for seeking external private finance. The government has the responsibility to perform such key functions as channeling resources towards priority needs, regulating the process of investment, and ensuring that the public interest, including environmental impact and social consequences, is protected.

Cities in a more sustainable society: Today's urban impacts—their ecological footprints—may already exceed the carrying capacity of the earth. A quadrupling of the efficiency with which these resources are used is a necessary possible and first step in ensuring that they tread more lightly on the planet.

Specific measures to attain this include promoting cyclical instead of linear flows of resources, by, for example, systematically using organic wastes to regenerate soil fertility; pricing resources so that they reflect their true costs by reducing subsidies on energy, water, and fertilizer, while making special provisions for the needs of the urban poor; shifting tax burdens from labor to natural resource use by ecological tax reform and creating tax incentives for green investment, both of which would generate ecological efficiency and work opportunities; defining mandatory standards for resource use and pollution, for example, from cars, heating, and household goods; environment education in its broadest sense; and a crash program to design and implement indicators of environmental and social conditions. Supporting food production in and near towns and cities will reduce food scarcity, generate income, and improve the environment. Local Agenda 21s, now being formulated in 1,200 local authorities in 33 countries, provide one mechanism with great potential.

Cities in a more humane economy: Economic development is essential, particularly in developing countries, but its aim must be maximizing human development, rather than economic growth for its own sake. A selective approach to globalization and economic liberalization will ensure their positive effects and will improve their impact on employment and the informal sector. This would, for example, involve less reliance on direct foreign investment and more joint venture and local investment.

The dynamic elements of the informal sector should be encouraged, by enhancing links with the formal sector and providing the appropriate infrastructure for economic and social development and for generating employment. Infrastructure should be balanced between the cities and the countryside, and between the countryside and cities and towns of different regions and sizes. Training should be provided, including for owners of small-scale enterprises.

New partnerships for cities: Cities have always depended on their hinterland, but now their hinterland is the globe. They will need to form partnerships at all levels, between urban areas and the countryside, between national and local governments, between the local and the global, as they follow the recommendations of the Habitat II Conference.

International municipal cooperation—and active partnerships between cities, countries, and international agencies—can improve the transfer of knowledge on successful urban practices and promote technical cooperation. One useful mechanism may be international twinning that is designed to provide mutual help in achieving action plans rather than merely serve ceremonial or cultural purposes. Internally there is also a need for partnerships between the public and private sectors, and between the different groups within the cities.

Bold leadership for creative participation and partnerships: Implementing such a program will require imaginative and bold leadership, which will only be possible if it rests on a consensus of popular support. The roles of all levels of government will have to be rethought to cope with the coming urban crisis; new structures may be necessary. United Nations agencies and international financial institutions need to refocus and reorganize their activities to allow better integration of their programs and policies.

Cities for Human Society

In sum, cities are the meeting places at which all of the general systems of society interact, they affect human beings in their everyday life. Each city has its own problems, processes, and potentialities, but no city is an island unto itself. Each is part of the general social process, which extends beyond the cities and which determines the life of each city. This process is taking place at several levels: the rural setting of the city; the city itself; the subnational region; the nation; the supranational; the transnational; and the global. This process has competing economic, social, and ecological goals. All cities are also caught up in some aspects of the process of globalization, be they financial, trade, production, pollution, insecurity, drugs, or migration. Cities cannot opt out of this process of globalization. Soon, most of humanity will be living in the cities. Therefore, cities will be the objects as well as the subjects of global effects, both good and bad. Cities now share a range of common benefits and problems. As Philip Allott indicates in his section, "Price of Civilization and Dilemma of Urbanization," cities are wonderful sources of dynamic human energy and creativity, but they are also the centers of human suffering, poverty, alienation, crime, and drugs.

Each city needs an efficient social process, at all levels, for resolving its conflicting goals. Such a process needs to be holistic, integrative, and participatory, because the city is the focus of social phenomena at all levels and—above all—because a city is not merely buildings. A city is people—and the habitat of people. Cities, therefore, must be the source of positive visions of people—where all have a safe, healthy, and sustainable environment; basic and cultural services; democratic rights and duties; freely chosen employment possibilities; and participatory decision-making power. No rebuilding of a decayed infrastructure will be sufficient to ensure that the cities are safe, healthy, and livable, until its resident's thoughts, souls, and spirits flourish.

Notes

1. See *Encyclopedia Americana*, 1995 ed., Vol. 6, p. 7.
2. See *Encyclopedia Brittanica*, 1967 ed., Vol. 5, p. 806.
3. *Ibid.*, p. 809.

An Agenda for Making Cities Fit for People

Inge Kaul and
Üner Kırdar

This book takes a fresh look at the challenge of making cities fit for people and proposes a ten-step agenda with practical policy options. It suggests that this challenge is not a quantitative one; not a problem of urban growth rates or the size of cities. Rather, it is a qualitative problem, a question of reorienting our development strategies to achieve three major goals:

- Balance economic growth, social progress, and the environment;
- Partnership among all developmental players; and
- Full resource mobilization—public and private, as well as financial and nonfinancial.

The contributors to this book believe that attaining these objectives requires new and innovative, but also practical, policy approaches. After reviewing a wide range of available experiences, they suggest a range of possible do-able policy options that could provide new avenues for:

- reducing the damaging ecological footprint of cities;
- forging a social contract between rich and poor;
- allowing cities to "bank on the poor";
- attracting more private finance;
- mobilizing revenues and using public resources, including external assistance, more efficiently;
- making cities think more globally;
- making cities think more locally;
- promoting "learning" cities;
- creating and strengthening partnership fora; and
- listening to tomorrow's "citizens'—today's children

Most of the recommendations are addressed specifically to mayors and municipalities. But, all of us—all citizens of the world—must assume some responsibility for creating more humane and sustainable cities. Success will depend on the sustainable partnerships—between the state and the private sector, between rural and urban areas, between the employed and the unemployed, among the different levels of government, and between industrial and developing countries.

An agenda for the citizens of the twenty-first century should deal with, among other things, four main issues:

- making patterns of urban production and consumption more sustainable;
- improving the human-development record of cities;
- strengthening social and political governance; and
- mobilizing, and optimizing the use of, resources for urban development.

Such an agenda should first reconfirm the importance of many well-established policies and endorse the recommendations that emanated from the development conferences of the 1990s, notably the Earth Summit, the World Summit on Social Development, the Human Rights Conference, the Population and Development Conference, the Women's Conference, and the HABITAT II Conference. The list of "good" policy principles and measures should include, among others, the following:

- a political commitment at all levels of government toward moving development on to more environmentally sound and people-centered paths;
- the decentralization of both developmental responsibility and implementation to the local and community levels in an effort to foster the participation of people and to direct policy measures to city-specific conditions;
- the encouragement of voluntary initiatives, as well as small-scale enterprises, in both the formal and informal sectors;
- the creation at all levels of government of an enabling environment for private initiative as well as social equity and sustainability;
- the promotion of mutually reinforcing linkages among human rights, transparency, accountability, and development; and
- the setting of targets for achieving intended goals and objectives, such as the eradication of poverty, as called for by the World Summit on Social Development, and the establishment of indicators for measuring progress.

Moving beyond these principles, a number of additional options for urban policy innovation could be elaborated. Two main issues are (1) the definition of the "urban challenge"; and (2) policy measures for responding to this challenge. To fully understand present concerns about urbanization, the key facts and figures should be briefly reexamined.

The Scale and Nature of Urban Change

A number of the sections of this book specifically address the question of how to define the "urban issue." The data presented in these sections show that at the beginning of the twentieth century, a mere 14 percent of the world's population lived in urban areas. By the year 2000, this figure will increase to more than 50 percent. By 2025, it is estimated that two-thirds of humankind will live in cities.

Most of the urban growth is and will continue occur in developing countries. Two-thirds of the current urban population is in developing countries and two-thirds of the population growth in these countries will be in urban areas. Africa will experience the highest urban growth rates—more than four percent annually until the year 2010.

Although these figures are high, they are not unprecedented. In earlier decades, many cities grew even faster. In the United States, for example, Fort Lauderdale, Miami, Orlando, and Phoenix had growth rates of more than eight percent for at least two decades during the period 1900 to 1960. The problem is neither the rate of change nor the absolute size of a city's populations. "Mega-cities"—cities with more than 10 million inhabitants—attract a great deal of attention, even though they are home to only about three percent of the world's population. The real problem is that urban development has become increasingly unsustainable. This is true environmentally, socially, and, in the longer-term, also economically.

Today's Cities: Mirrors of Past Development Strategies

The concern about the sustainability of today's urban development does not mean "being against cities." Cities have both advantages and disadvantages. Among their advantages are the following: urban settlements—marked by high population density—destroy less of the natural habitat than more sprawling settlement patterns; they facilitate the provision of such public services as environment-friendly mass transportation, clean water, electricity, health services, and education; and as many observers argue, their diversity and complexity unleashes human ingenuity and innovation.

No, the problem of today's cities is not—at least, not exclusively—one of size. Rather, the problems are the result of the neglect of human and environmental concerns as reflected in our past development strategies. Put differently, it derives from our past overemphasis on economic growth.

Poverty afflicts approximately one-third of the urban population and it signals the existence of many other forms of human deprivation, including the lack of clean water and sanitation facilities for all; lack of adequate shelter; unemployment; social disintegration and its consequences, such as crime, violence, destruction of family life; "street children," and child prostitution. The result is expanding "ghettos" of the poor and shrinking, increasingly fortress-like, "citadels" of the rich.

But, in these respects, cities are not significantly different from suburban or rural areas. Human neglect has been a serious shortcoming in all of our past development strategies, but the effects are more pronounced and obvious on the residents of cities because of the higher population density.

Similarly, production and consumption patterns show that environmental neglect and its resultant problems of sustainability are not the "fault" of cities. They, too, are the consequences of the past overemphasis on economic growth. In fact, without cities and space-saving high-rise dwellings, our environmental situation could be worse.

Environmental degradation spread, in large measure, because present cost-benefit analyses do not take into account the environmental effects of our activities. Natural resources are treated as a free commodity. We do not "value" them. The same holds true of the human costs of our activities. Who has ever calculated the human costs of city noise, overcrowded living conditions, or the fear that results from street crime and violence? Who has calculated the benefits of "city life" in terms of social equality and mobility?

Because current decision-making is driven largely by considerations of economic efficiency, our policies, including subsidy and taxation policies, often send the "wrong signals." They encourage – instead of discourage – the production, use, and emission of pollutants and other environmentally harmful substances. They discourage – instead of encourage – the use of labor and investment in human and social capital.

Urban problems are the accumulated effects of decades of human and environmental neglect. But population growth and technological change, coupled with modifications of our production and consumption patterns, have exacerbated the situation. Urban problems have also been negatively affected by the debt crisis of the 1980s in developing countries; the fiscal crisis in both industrial and developing countries in the 1990s; structural adjustment programmes; the suddent transition from centrally planned to free market economies; and industrial restructuring.

Certainly, liberalization and market orientation have brought gains in economic efficiency. But, in many cases, these have not yet translated into economic and human developmental gains. Often, the new policies have, at least initially, entailed added social and environmental costs, including increased socioeconomic disparity, which results in increased social and political instability; higher unemployment; and declining health standards.

In these areas, experiences differ from country to country and from city to city, depending on their integration into the world economy. As the chapter on "Learning from Experiences" shows, new economic growth opportunities have in some cities—notably those in East Asia—led to enhanced human development and accelerated urbanization. In other areas, such as Africa, growing marginalization and lack of economic growth seem to be fueling urbanization. In the former group of cities, the challenge is "managing the urban consequences of fast economic growth." In the latter group, it is "managing the urban consequences of sluggish or stagnant economic growth, coupled in several instances, with civil strife, political unrest, and even war.

However different "the urban challenge" may be in different countries and different regions, the problems of city residents are in no way unique to developing countries. Urban poverty and other "inner-city" problems, such as unemployment, pollution, social disintegration, personal insecurity, abuse of drugs, homelessness, and inequitable rural–urban relationships, are also found in virtually all rich countries. A high income is no guarantee of successful urban development.

The ubiquity of the urban challenge shows that the overall approach to development matters much more than whether a city is rich or poor, fast or slow growing. Solving the urban crisis requires changing the way we "do" development, including urban development.

Today's Policy Choices: Tomorrow's Cities

Fortunately, humanity is facing not only daunting developmental challenges but also new, exciting opportunities to address and resolve them. The time is ripe for embarking on a new—more people-centred and environmentally sound—path of development.

The ground for such a reorientation of development has been well prepared by the political processes that have led to, and been unleashed by, the various global development conferences of the 1990s: the UN Conference on Environment and Development, the International Human Rights Conference, the International Population and Development Conference, the World Summit on Social Development, the Fourth World Conference on Women, and the HABITAT II Conference. As a result of the policy debates at these conferences, a new development consensus has emerged that development must pursue multiple objectives. It must be pro-growth, pro-poor, and pro-people.

The end of the cold war has provided another avenue for policy reorientation. It has led to a new partnership between the state and the private sector. It has also provided the economic and financial liberalization that allows freer movements of goods, services, capital, and increasingly also labor, across national borders. It has created room for a freer exchange of information and world-wide networking among people, civil society organizations, municipalities, and other governmental authorities, as well as business enterprises.

In addition, during the past five decades, world income has grown sevenfold in real terms and 2.5 times on a per capita basis. People today are richer than ever before and hence better equipped to exploit its vast stock of knowledge and experience to resolve existing problems, including making its cities more humane and environment friendly.

With these changes in mind, there is an urgent need for a renaissance in development thinking. Future development policy, including urban development policy, should have three characteristic elements:

- Balance – in the sense of greater consistency between economic growth targets and environmental and social goals. This means more than giving a little added attention to social and environmental issues. It means putting people at the center of all concerns and achieving a proper balance among investments in physical, natural-resource and human/social capital;
- Partnership – in the sense of cooperation among all developmental players: the private sector, civil society, the state, rich and poor, men and women, rural and urban areas, North and South, East and West. In today's interdependent world, cooperation rather than competitiveness will be the key to longer-term developmental sustainability and progress; and
- Full resource mobilization – in the sense that too many resources still remain untapped. There are nonfinancial resources, such as a moral and ethical commitment to people-centered and sustainable development. Then, there is the creative and productive potential of women and the energies of the poor, who are often compelled to engage in inefficient, low-productivity tasks because of a lack of better opportunities.

  Although a tremendous amount of available private capital is available, only a small amount of is currently being used to finance development. Examples include "growth plus" objectives, such as environmental regeneration, human-capital formation, and the empowerment of people.

From the analyses and viewpoints presented in this book on these three new development orientations, it becomes evident that many cities and countries are already experimenting with, or have firmly in place, policy measures that could bring about the desired changes for their residents. Interestingly, current policy recommendations emphasize policy management rather than specific policy outcomes or objectives. Although fully recognizing the need for city and country-specificity in policy design, the importance of "learning from available experience" should not be overlooked. It is with the same reservation and cautionary note, therefore, that the following section lists ten major ideas for the empowerment of people and urban policy innovation that emerged from the contributions to this book.

Ten Do-able Policy Options

Although the magnitude and complexity of today's urban problems call for a bold new policy vision, making this vision operational requires practical policy steps. The following ten major policy options shows that many changes are economically desirable and technically feasible. Disseminating this information as widely as possible could help make the changes also politically feasible.

1. The damaging footprint of cities on the environment could be dramatically reduced through environmental accounting.

Urban production and consumption are not just a function of a city's population; they also depend on such variables as income distribution, technology choices, import/export policies, incentive policies, social values, and democratic participation. For example, the life styles of the rich consume many more resources than those of the poor, who simply cannot afford such items as air-conditioning, refrigerators, cars, lavish dinners, or large sprinkler-fed lawns. Because cities tend to be richer than rural areas, they consume more. To meet these consumption requirements they "import" large volumes of food, water, building and production materials, and energy.

The input requirements of cities often exceed the production capacity of the surrounding areas; and the waste, which cities generate as a result of their production and consumption, by far exceeds the absorptive capacity of surrounding areas. As a result, cities have a degrading effect on surrounding ecosystems.

Cities must not be allowed to have this effect. Much would be gained in the future if cities pursued more cyclical production and consumption patterns rather than perpetuate the present linear flow of resources. For example, organic waste could be used to regenerate soil fertility. Coupled with other measures, such as refocused tax incentives, full environmental-cost accounting, promotion of urban agriculture, and more environmentally friendly technologies, this change in a city's metabolism could lead to a quadrupling in resource-use efficiency.

Maintaining human settlement accounts would be an effective way of keeping track of the natural-resource requirements (inputs) of cities and the burdens they place on their host environments (outputs). Such accounts could also form the basis for other policy measures, such as tradable pollution permits or user fees for scarce public space, a point that will be discussed further in policy option number four. What is important in the present context is that the introduction of policy measures, such as pollution permits, could facilitate a more equitable distribution of income between cities on the one hand, and rural and suburban areas, on the other hand. Today, the latter tend to "give" and cities tend to take—they take without full analyses of the costs and benefits involved, and hence, without fair compensation.

2. A new social contract between the rich and the poor could be a "win–win" situation for all.

It is often argued that countries or cities are too poor to fight poverty. Poverty, however, is itself a costly burden that most cities and countries can ill afford. For example, a lack of adequate water and sanitation translates into increased health costs and loss of productivity. The lack of adequate shelter and employment opportunities results in disrupted family life, "street children," social alienation, learning disabilities, crime and violence, larger police forces, the need for prison expansion, and increased spending on private security. So why not use the money that is now being spent to "fight the consequences of poverty" on "preventing poverty"—ensuring positive investments in people as well equal access to assets and economic opportunities?

If the costs of human deprivation and inequity were demonstrated more fully and more publicly, it would become evident that without a better life for all, no one is really better off. Thus, it is in everybody's interest to ensure that at least people's basic needs are met and all people are able to help themselves.

The World Summit on Social Development called on all countries to establish their own target dates for the eradication of poverty. The struggle against poverty must be waged in both rural and urban areas. In other words, the eradication of poverty must be a national goal. Cities alone cannot achieve it. Successful development requires a better ecological balance between rural and urban areas, as well as a better social balance—one that is broader based and equitable.

In today's world of open economies, one could even argue that, for two reasons, the eradication of poverty must be universal. The first is that socioeconomic disparities may set in motion extensive migration movements which, as experience has shown, cannot be stopped by no legal barriers, fences, or border controls. The second is that with current patterns of capital mobility and high unemployment, poverty anywhere in the world can have a negative impact on working and living conditions elsewhere in the world. The solution is not protectionism; it is global human development.

The eradication of poverty would often be cheaper than "fighting the consequences of poverty." If approached in a participatory way, such a policy would place a minimal burden on city coffers, while offering important pay-offs in terms of the overall development.

3. Cities can "bank on the poor" for their development.

Although world income in real terms has grown approximately sevenfold during the past five decades, the gains have been distributed unevenly. In 1960, the richest 20 percent of the world's population earned 30 times the income of the world's poorest 20 percent; today the rich earn more than 60 times the income of the poor; and they control, on average, more than 85 percent of most other economic activities, be they investment, commercial credit, or trade opportunities.

The world, and in particular, cities, are rich enough to afford the eradication of poverty. But while income transfers and public programs are necessary, they are not sufficient and often not desirable. The poor do not need handouts; they want to and can, if given the correct opportunities, make it on their own.

As the practices of the Grameen Bank in Bangladesh show, the poor are creditworthy and are a "good credit risk." They do not need subsidized interest rates. They will pay market rates, if granted a loan. The same holds true for small-scale entrepreneurs. In addition to the Grameen Bank, other successful "banking on the poor" initiatives include the Women's World Banking, the Kenyan Rural Enterprise Initiative, and the SEWA Bank in India. Experience demonstrates that this strategy works in the housing sector as well.

To give the poor access to credit on a broader and more sustainable basis, the focus needs to be on institution building. In this respect, the role of governments, including those of municipalities, is twofold. Public funds can be used to promote business NGOs, such as cooperatives, credit unions, and community groups. These NGOs can then act as savings mobilizers, lenders, and providers of business and other advice and services for the poor, including women. This strategy has been used in many industrial countries, as illustrated by savings and loan associations in France and Germany.

Available public finance could be well spent by providing start-up capital, refinancing opportunities, and other support to such financial intermediaries. If the intermediaries operate efficiently and apply strict repayment criteria, this could also be good business for private banks.

Governments could also help by establishing public financial intermediaries, such as housing development finance corporations. Such institutions would be critical in moving "credit for the poor" from the project level to a more sustained basis.

Needless to say, such savings and credit strategies will succeed only if the overall economic and financial situation of the city and the country are sound, property rights are guaranteed, and reliable standards of accountability and transparency are maintained.

Credit for the poor will be the starting point for more small-scale enterprise development, for employment growth, and for increased private spending on human development. Ultimately, this means better urban development.

As the experiences of several developing countries have shown, informal-sector development through such measures as credit program and other business-support services can contribute to formal-sector growth. Such linkages between the formal and the informal sectors of the economy will only develop if informal-sector enterprises are able to interact with formal-sector enterprises—if they have the capacity to function efficiently and to meet expected quality standards.

4. There are many ways of attracting private finance to meet the needs of people.

In recent years, many countries have undergone a process of decentralization: making local authorities more responsible for their own development. This devolution of responsibility happened just as many national governments began to reduce public spending and to increasingly rely on market forces for economic growth. Existing tax systems, as well as subsidy programs, have come under close scrutiny. Cities must, therefore, rely more and more on private capital to meet future investment requirements.

More important is the fact that more than three quarters of all investments are private. Development cannot succeed without private enterprise. Governments at all levels will have to "put their houses in order" and aim at meeting financial-market expectations, including those of the financial rating agencies.

But, by itself, attracting financial investment does not lead to sustainable, people-centred development. This can be seen in the "booming" cities of East Asia. It has also been the experience of many Latin American cities, as well as cities in industrialized countries. Much depends on how investment funds are used. Therefore, there is an urgent need for financial innovation. We need to explore new and innovative ways for private enterprise to make profitable investments out of projects that are directly relevant to creating more sustainable, people-centred development. For example, studies have shown that the environmental compliance market in Asia alone will offer profitable investment opportunities amounting to more than US $500 billion by the year 2000.

There is also a need for new financial instruments. For example, one ought to analyze experiences with municipal bonds so that we can explore the possiblity of issuing "human development" or "environment" bonds. Central governments could support such initiatives by helping municipalities to bundle their investment requirements in relevant fields, such as public transportation or water and sanitation facilities.

One can also mention the experiences gained with "green funds" and "social-responsibility funds." "Affinity cards," credit cards linked to certain "causes," such as environmental protection or support for children, could also be another innovative financial instrument. Ecolabeling could also be a way of putting more private money behind "good" developmental causes.

5. Urban development needs private finance, but it also needs adequate public finance, including external assistance, that is used more optimally.

Relying on private finance is certainly an increasingly important policy option for cities, but smaller cities may continue to be more dependent on public revenue. This is particularly true in cities where poverty, civil strife, and war are the driving forces behind urbanization.

To enable cities to meet their public-finance needs, the devolution of developmental responsibility to local levels would have to be coordinated with the changes in the distribution of the power to tax and the distribution of public revenue among the different levels of government.

But increased public finance, including more external assistance, would not necessarily yield the desired results. Resource allocations must be efficient, realizing the highest possible social returns on public investment. This requires more than professional management. It calls for bold, committed leadership, democratic governance, transparency, and accountability.

Both larger and smaller cities would also have to review their systems of taxation to determine if they encourage or discourage the production of "developmental goods," such as the reuse of waste, public rather than private transportation, and labor-intensive—rather than capital-intensive—production.

Central governments, together with local bodies, should establish task forces to explore possibilities for innovative mobilization of resources, including the introduction of new or additional tradable permits for pollution, the auctioning of scarce space, or the introduction of user fees for highways, especially the use of motorways during rush hours. Singapore's experiences, as well as those of cities in California, are especially interesting in this connection.

Growing urbanization may also warrant a reorientation of development assistance towards urban areas. Put put differently, it requires a more balanced approach to both rural and urban development. After all, the majority of the world's poor are in cities; but the rural emphasis of development programs to date has not been able to stem the tide of urban migration. A redistribution of funds in favor of the urban poor might, in the light of past and current development trends, be in order.

6. Cities need to think globally. They must develop expertise in international development, finance, and trade.

Much has been written about the hardships often imposed on companies by the need to be competitive. Recently, discussion has also focused on the competitiveness of states in offering private capital a hospitable and stable investment climate. Given today's open economies and decentralized development, cities will also have to increasingly compete for investors if they are to be economically successful and provide employment opportunities and attractive living conditions for their residents. The "Bombay First" initiative which is described in this book, is just one of many such initiatives taken by municipal authorities and their key partners to ensure that the city stays at, or reaches, the leading edge.

To adjust to constantly changing world market conditions and new technological opportunities, cities will, among other things, have to carefully analyze shifts in production to determine which are likely "sunset" sectors and enterprises and which are "sunrise" activities. Assisting companies and workers in foreseeing these trends and responding to new opportunities could considerably reduce the costs of industrial restructuring and and its impact on workers. The new trend in "downsizing" has prompted many companies to shed tens of thousands of workers in recent years.

Municipal authorities will also have to deal increasingly with stock and bond markets, private investment and pension funds. Thus, urban leaders must have the capacity to analyze financial markets and be familiar with investors' expectations. They will also have assist local enterprises in obtaining information and advice on international trade, either for the city's exports or its imports.

Cities cannot any longer think and act just locally. They must integrate themselves into the global system so that they can use it to their advantage and to satisfy their local needs.

7. Cities need to think more locally, too. There are many unexploited resources and opportunities within their boundaries.

A case in point is the largely untapped productive potential of the poor to which reference has already been made. Another example is the underexploited developmental potential of women. Empirical studies have shown that if women gain access to credit they invest their money wisely and tend to use their income prudently, often investing it in their children's education and health.

Many cities around the world, in both developing and industrial countries, have also realized the importance of the voluntary sector—neighborhood associations, community groups, and charities. These groups often play an important advocacy role as well as a financial role.

Cities in poor and rich countries have also experimented with local currencies: paying the salaries for certain public jobs in script that can only be used locally to ensure that wages are being spent on basic goods and services rather than on items, such as drugs, that might drive people into poverty and out of society.

Another area of as yet underexploited potential is urban agriculture. As pointed out before, cities have daily massive intake needs in terms of goods and services, including food. Cities, however, can be transformed from primarily consumers of food and other agricultural products, into important resource-conserving, health-improving, sustainable generators of these products.

The relationship between urban agriculture and resources is three-fold. Some urban by-products, such as waste water and organic solid waste, can be recycled and transformed into resources or opportunities for growing agricultural products within urban and periurban areas. Some city areas, such as idle lands and bodies of water, can be converted into intensive agricultural production. Third, some natural resources, such as energy for cooling or transportation, can be conserved through urban agriculture. Experts hold the view that neither sustainable agriculture nor sustainable, human habitats will be possible in the future without urban agriculture.

Urban agriculture is necessary to ensure adequate urban food supplies. In addition, urban agriculture creates jobs by stimulating new industries. The same holds true for the recycling—or, even better, reusing—plastic, paper, aluminium, and other waste to create local capacities and facilities that will generate additional employment and allow cities to embark on the new, circular production/consumption mode.

8. Successful cities will be "learning" cities, relying on city universities and information-exchange networks with other cities.

Development is proceeding at an ever faster pace. This is the result of, among other factors, modern means of communication and transportation, as well as the greater competitiveness that economic and financial liberalization have brought about.

In addition, past developmental strategies are increasingly clashing with environmental and social sustainability. Development theories and strategies have, therefore, to be rethought in a fundamental way. This is also because new—or, newly rediscovered—developmental players, such as women, the poor, and the private sector—have to be integrated into our developmental equations.

The fact that new policy commitments, such as sustainable human development, do not receive the desired speedy follow-up action is often not the result of a lack of political will. Rather, the problem frequently is simply that policy makers and experts do not yet know how to attain the established goals. To generate a comprehensive, empirically grounded, and reliable body of knowledge about the "how to" of sustainable human development, a lot of research has as yet to be undertaken.

One way of making faster progress in this direction would be for cities to encourage their universities to be true city universities: to undertake research focussed on the problems of their host city and research that is relevant to policy-making.

Another way in which cities could ensure continuous learning and stay abreast of new policy developments would be to strengthen networking arrangements with other cities nationally, regionally, and globally. There is no doubt that, for example, many cities around the world have benefited from hearing about the experiences of Curitiba in Brazil.

9. Cities and their residents need new and strengthened partnership fora and communication channels.

None of the previously mentioned policy measures can be implemented by government decrees alone. They will only succeed if all concerned players act in concert. This requires consultation, cooperation, and negotiation. In addition, policy implementation will often require the active involvement of several actors. Top-down decision-making and program delivery simply will not work.

Moreover, development is not necessarily an issue that involves government. NGOs often deal with business directly on issues of highest developmental importance, such as environmental and social responsibility.

It would therefore be useful for all major developmental players to ensure the existence of fora and mechanisms for communication, consultation, negotiation, and joint implementation. City governments, in particular, have a responsibility in this respect: they ought to ensure that they are in regular contact with their development partners and, in addition, they should encourage all other participants to create their own fora.

10. Children have their own views about tomorrow's cities – simple to do, hard to resist.

The world citizens of tomorrow are the children of today. Therefore, one should consider how children would like the cities of the future – their cities – to be.

One point is clear: tomorrow's cities will have to be significantly different from today's if they are to meet the expectations of today's children.

The transportation system in the cities of the future must be different: fewer cars; cleaner cars, because children in particular suffer from car fumes; some roads open only to bicyclists and people on rollerskates; amd safe and clean public transportation.

Another major change the children want is a better balance between developed and natural space in cities. Children want to live with nature: to be aware of seasons, to smell trees, grass, and flowers, to hear and see birds. They want to use the natural space in cities as playgrounds and for leisure time with their parents, relatives, and friends.

Children want violence-free cities. They do not want to be afraid when walking in the streets or going to parks.

The cities of tomorrow should, in the children's view, also be less stressful. Today's city life often makes adults feel aggressive and tense; family life—the children's life—would benefit from a more harmonious environment.

What children argue for, in brief, are "greener," more humane cities. Their suggestions, which are simple, include closing every second street in the city to car traffic; building more parks; and putting a swimming pool in the middle of the city. What is difficult about these suggestions is to reject them—not to do what they propose.

In summary, our overall message is one of hope. To make cities fit for people is primarily a matter of choise. How tomorrow's generation will live largely depends on "us"—on our policy choices. Do-able policy options, as well as requisite resources, are available to us, now.

Part 1

Globalization and Urbanization

Section 1 An Urbanizing World

Wally N'Dow

In the first section of this book, we will review the current state of the worldwide urbanization phenomenon and its likely conditions into the twenty-first century. The section also provides an assessment of major issues and trends accounting for the complex transition into a world dominated by cities.

While in 1975 only 37 percent of the world's population lived in towns and cities, this rate rose to 45 percent in 1995. At the start of the next millennium, half of all people are expected to live in an urban area, and this trend is likely to continue. This transition has enormous implications for the world economy, for social conditions, as well as for the state of the world environment. Urbanization may be seen as an essential part of most nations' development toward more stable and productive economies. If well managed, it has the potential to lead to improvements in the living standards of a considerable proportion of the concerned country's population.

As a matter of fact, most countries of the developing world with high rates of urbanization in the last decade experienced higher economic growth. In addition, an increasing number of cities have taken on significant roles in the globalization of the economy, particularly with regard to financial services, commerce, transport, and telecommunication. However, in many countries, the rates of urbanization exceed the capacity of national and local governments to plan and organize this transformation. As a result, new forms of urban poverty have emerged, manifested through poor housing conditions, insecure land tenure, and homelessness. Moreover, poorly managed cities lead to environmental deterioration. They contribute to unsustainable production and consumption patterns. Poorly managed cities also generate unmanageable wastes, which negatively impact on land and water resources, as well as on the atmosphere. Sustaining healthy environments in the urbanized world of the twenty-first century represents a major challenge for humanity.

With increased social, economic, and environmental impacts of urbanization; growing consumption levels; and renewed concerns for sustainable development since the adoption of Agenda 21 by the United Nations Conference on Environment and Development in 1992, the necessity for planning becomes more evident. Environmentally sound land-use planning is central to the achievement of healthy, productive, and socially accountable human settlements. The challenge is not only how to direct and contain urban growths, but also how to mobilize human, financial, and technical resources to ensure that social, economic, and environmental needs are adequately addressed. Considering the limited effectiveness of current methods and approaches to settlements planning, new procedures have to be devised that can be adapted to each society's present conditions and future goals, based on new forms of partnership and good governance.

Global Context

In recent decades, trends in urbanization have reflected economic and political changes, some long rooted, some of more recent origin. A major factor in the steady increase in the level of urbanization worldwide since 1950 is that the size of the world's economy has grown many times over and has also changed from one dominated by relatively closed national economies or trading blocs to one where most countries have more open economies and where production and the services it needs are increasingly integrated internationally. In 1950, most of the world's workforce was employed in agriculture; by 1990, most worked in services. The period since 1950 has brought not only enormous changes in the scale, scope, and nature of economic activity but also in the size and nature of households, in the scale and distribution of incomes within and between nations, and in the scale and nature of government.

Although in aggregate, the world economy has expanded considerably over the last two decades, it has experienced a fluctuating growth pattern. The 1980s began with the fear of a return to high inflation, following the 1979 to 1980 oil price increase. This, coupled with the structural problems facing the major economies, created a fear of recession. However, the leading economies were better prepared and were able to use firmer monetary and fiscal policies that not only contained inflation, but also improved economic performance. By 1984, the average inflation level within OECD stood at approximately 5 percent, compared with nearly 13 percent in 1980. However, the recovery remained weak.

In East and Central Europe and in the Republics of the former USSR, economic declines in the early 1990s were considerable. Political revolutions of 1989 brought abrupt changes in both governmental and economic organization.

For most countries in the South, from 1975 to 1995, there was little growth in per capital income. Between 1980 and 1991, annual average change in per capital income was negative for the regions of Sub-Saharan Africa, the Middle East and North Africa, Latin America, and the Caribbean. As a result of global recession and rising real interest rates, many countries could not repay their foreign debts. The main exceptions were the leading Asian economies, such as China and what have been termed the Dynamic Asian Economies, which sustained high economic growth rates for most or all of the 1980s and early 1990s.

For most countries in the South, the "lost decades" of the 1980s also brought very inadequate investment in infrastructure, housing, and services related to shelter, which were seriously deteriorating. Planned investments in expanding city infrastructure and services were often among the first to be cut during a recession. The lack of investment funds was further aggravated by the prevailing debt situation. For the transition economies, there was a lull in growth associated mainly with reforms and later transition to market-based production system. The elimination of subsidies and the state withdrawal from production sectors targeted for reforms, such as housing development, meant less investment in the build environment and in infrastructure and services.

Inflationary conditions also reduce business confidence so that short-term projects are preferred over long-term investments, which require long payback periods. Because most large infrastructure projects have high returns but long payback periods, the number of such projects declined. This was the case in rapidly growing cities with great need for significant expansion in roads, public transportation, water supply, sanitation, drainage, and power. Construction has been constrained further by limited foreign currency reserves, which have also partly been negatively affected by the tightening of global credit conditions.

Structural reforms have been very important in both the North and south since the 1970s, but become even more crucial in the 1980s. They have had the same primary aim of building capacity for sustained economic development. The difference in policies used has arisen out of the differences in the structures of the economies and the kinds and degree of marketing distortions and inflexibilities.

One of the principal policies in the structural reform programs in both North and south has been to cut public spending and to reduce budgetary deficits. The cuts made are usually in sectors not considered as priority or core productive sectors which, in many cases, include human settlements.

Structural adjustment policies have an impact on human settlements through several channels: the national economic growth rates; the size and allocation of government expenditure; and the impacts of government policies on different sectors. The immediate impact on the economy is deflationary, reducing domestic consumption and encouraging exports and, through reduced government expenditure, encouraging private sector expansion. The overall effects of reduced housing finance and demand was lower levels of lending and hence less construction, improvement, and renovation.

The structural change within the world economy have helped to reorder the relative importance of cities around the world and, for many cities, to reshape their physical form and the spatial distribution of enterprises and residents within them. Regions and cities have proved more flexible than nations in adapting to changing economic conditions—and certain key regions and cities have become successful locales of the new wave of innovation and investment. The large and increasing share of the world's economy controlled by transnational corporations has led to certain cities becoming what are often termed "global" or "world" cities.

Changes in Population and in Households

The world's total population in 1995 was estimated at 5.7 billion. The rate of growth was essentially constant between 1975 and 1990 (at approximately 1.7 percent a year) and is projected to drop an average of approximately 1.5 percent a year during the 1990s. Fertility rates have declined almost everywhere in recent years. In most societies, in recent decades, there have been rapid changes in the size of households and in their structure.

One of the most dramatic has been the increase in the proportion of households headed by women, now thought to comprise more than one fifth of the total worldwide—although with large variations among countries. In most societies, there is or has been an increase in the proportion of nuclear families and a fall in the average size of households.

Another important change, recorded in many countries in the North, is a rapid increase in the proportion of single-person households. These and other changes in the size and composition of households have important and often underrated influences on urban changes and housing markets. They bring major changes in the number of households that need accommodation; a rapid growth in the number of households can mean that housing demand rises, even as the overall population of a city falls. They also bring changes in the type of accommodation that is sought, in household income, and in geographical preferences.

International Migration

Great diversity in the scale and nature of migration reflects social, economic, and political changes within the region and nation. The scale of international migration has certainly increased over the last 10 to 15 years. Estimates suggest that by 1992 more than 100 million people lived outside their own country.

There has also been a considerable growth in international migration flows of highly qualified or skilled labor migrants, which include the professional and managerial staff transferred within the international labor markets of transnational corporations. A considerable part of the flows are also a consequence of an increasingly globalized economy. Between 25 and 30 million migrants are thought to be foreign workers, most of whom will return to their own countries. An estimate for 1991 suggested that the total value of their remittances back to their own countries was $71 billion and if this is accurate, then it means that total remittance flows are larger than total aid flows and makes remittance flows one of the largest items in international trade.

Impact on Cities and Their Inhabitants

All of these factors inevitably influence settlements and their patterns. At the start of the next millennium, it is projected that half the world's population will live in cities. This transition into an urbanized world has enormous implications for the world economy, for social conditions, as well as for the state of the world environment. Perhaps the most fundamental influences on the world's settlement system in recent decades have come from the unprecedented changes in economic and political conditions.

Rapid population growth in large cities, however, has often been considered problematic because government agencies fail to ensure that infrastructure and service provision keeps up with the growth in population and often fail to enforce pollution control and other regulations needed to protect the quality of life in urban areas. Although the debate about the role of cities in development and in environmental problems continues, their key role in dynamic and competitive economies has been increasingly acknowledged since the 1980s and 1990s. So too has the fact that major cities generally have a significantly higher concentration of the nation's economic output than its rural areas.

Urbanization has helped underpin improvements in living standards for a considerable proportion of the world's population. Cities and towns also have important roles in social transformation. They are centers of artistic, scientific, and technological innovation, of culture and education. The history of cities and towns therefore is inextricably linked to that of civilization in general. One reason is that rising levels of urbanization are strongly associated with growing and diversifying economies—and most of the nations in the developing world whose economic performance over the last two decades is so envied by other nations are also those with the most rapid growth in their levels of urbanization. The nature of this relationship between the scale of the economy and the scale of the urban population is also illustrated by the fact that most of the world's largest cities are in the world's largest economies.

The dramatic post-World War II increases in urbanization have impacted not only on economic but also on social, environmental and institutional conditions and trends and all these reflect on living and working conditions of the population and on the overall tone of human settlements. These ramifications pose serious challenges to human settlements management.

One of the great ironies of course is that the signs of urbanization and its problems are now so evident, so much a part of our daily lives, that we have almost come to take them for granted as part of the "normal" urban scene: the slums and ghettos, the homeless, the paralyzing traffic, the poisoning of our urban air and water, drugs, crime, the alienation of our youth, and the resurgence of old diseases, such as tuberculosis, and the spread of new ones, such as AIDS. But progress is being made against these urban ills.

Although rapid population growth is often given as the reason for urban problems, what is apparent is not so much the speed with which cities are growing but the scale of the housing and environmental problems in cities and the deficits in the provision for services such as piped water, sanitation, drains, roads, schools, health centers, and other forms of infrastructure and services provisions. The link between the scale of these problems and the speed with which the city grows are usually weak. As the Global Report on Human Settlements[1] describes, some of the largest and most rapidly growing cities also have some of the best records in improving infrastructure and service provision while some of the worst housing conditions are found in declining industrial centers and stagnant smaller towns.

Social–Economic Trends

During the last 30 to 40 years, virtually all countries have achieved considerable economic and social gains that can be seen in the improvements in housing and living conditions and in the increased proportion of the world's population with access to essential services such as piped water, sanitation, health care, and education. They are also evident in much increased life expectancy and the reduction in the proportion of the world's population facing hunger, life-threatening deprivation, and easily preventable or curable diseases. The world average for life expectancy increased from 53.2 to 65.6 years, between 1960 and 1992; the average for the developing countries alone increased by 17 years from a base of 46.2 years in 1960.

But there has been evidence of a slowing in social progress or even a halt and decline in some countries during the 1980s. In absolute terms, the proportion of the population living below the "poverty line" increased during the 1980s. In the South, much of this is associated with economic stagnation and/or debt crises and with structural adjustment. In several of the wealthiest countries, the slowing in social progress was associated with changes in the labor market, including a growth in long-term unemployment, and with political changes that reduced expenditures on social welfare and gave a low priority to addressing such issues as structural unemployment and rising homelessness.

Between a fifth and a quarter of the world's population still live in poverty, without adequate food, clothing, and shelter. More than 90 percent of these live in the developing countries. By 1990, at least 600 million people in the urban areas in Latin America, Asia, and Africa were living in housing of such poor quality and with such inadequate provision for water, sanitation, and drainage that their lives and health were under continuous threat. The same is true for more than 1 billion rural dwellers, largely because of inadequate provision for water and sanitation. In the developed countries, while millions of low-income people may live in poor quality housing, most live in housing with piped water, toilets connected to sewers, drains, and bathrooms. This greatly reduces the health burden of being poor in these regions. Recent estimates suggest that the urban population in the developing countries will grow by more than 600 million during the 1990s; without major improvements in housing markets and in the expansion and improved provision of infrastructure and services, the number of people living in such conditions will expand very rapidly.

Worldwide, the number of homeless people are estimated at anywhere from 100 million to one billion or more, depending on how homelessness is defined. The estimate of 100 million would apply to those who have no shelter at all. The estimate of one billion homeless people would also include those in accommodation that is very insecure or temporary, and often poor quality.

The number of people who live in accommodation that is both insecure and substandard is highest in Africa, Asia and Latin America. For instance, hundreds of millions live in illegal settlements under threat of eviction and in shelters lacking basic services such as piped water and provision for sanitation and drainage and services such as schools and health care centers. Indeed, we cannot get a true picture of today's shelter crisis without counting the number of people in the rural areas who also live in life and health-threatening situations. And when we do so, it adds another 600 million to the global total, even as millions more in the developing countries flee environmental disasters and wars, intensifying the problem all the more. In fact, unless a revolution in urban problem-solving takes place, it is estimated that these numbing statistics will triple by the first quarter of the next century.

Homelessness is certainly not concentrated in low-income countries. Several million people are homeless in Europe and North America. Using the most conservative definition of homelessness, nearly 2.5 million people were estimated to be homeless in 1993 within the 12 countries of the European Union. In the United States, official estimates for the mid-1980s suggest between 250,000 and 350,000; the National Coalition for the Homeless puts the figure much higher—at more than 3 million, with between 60,000 and 80,000 in New York City alone. In Canada, estimates for the number of homeless people based on the number using temporary night shelters and those living and sleeping outside suggest between 130,000 and 250,000.

During the 1960s and early 1970s most governments in the developing countries either launched large public housing programs or greatly enlarged existing ones. New public housing agencies were set up during the 1970s and new housing finance institutions were also set up. Certain public housing programs achieved a considerable scale. For instance, the National Housing Bank of Brazil set up in 1964 and closed down in 1986 had provided the core of a housing finance system that had produced around 4 million units. The scale of support for public housing programs diminished in most countries during the late 1980s or early 1990s; the reaffirmation of the importance of market forces influenced this. In many countries in the South, recession and the cuts in public expenditures linked to debt crises and structural adjustment also had a role. The privatization of the state housing stock may be the single most distinguishing feature of the transition in East and Central European countries. There is a clear pattern across this diverse group of countries in the form of decentralization of the ownership of state housing to local authorities and the cut in national funding for public housing construction.

The issue of how to ensure that urban land markets serve the economic and social needs of urban inhabitants and enterprises remains one of the most complex—perhaps the most complex—task for urban governments. In regard to the legal land market, most governments adopted policies that have contributed to land shortages rather than land availability. Government policies have largely emphasized the control and regulation of land use rather than supporting and facilitating the supply and development of land to ensure demand is met as quickly and cheaply as possible. Governments have also failed to act on the fact that one of the most effective ways to support a city's economy and to improve housing conditions is to ensure that land with sound infrastructure is available for a great range of activities at the lowest possible price. Few governments have used their powers and investment capacities to stimulate increased supplies, which would often help to meet economic, social, and environmental goals more effectively than controlling use.

However, a range of informal and illegal land markets have provided the means by which the cost of housing—for renting, self-building, or purchase—could be brought down sufficiently to become affordable by a much larger proportion of each city's population. Governments have tolerated informal land market to defuse what was potentially a huge political problem—the fact that a high and growing proportion of the population could not afford the cheapest legal house or site. But this tolerance was virtually always within strict limits, so most land for housing was not occupied illegally, and where it was, only rarely was it on valuable privately owned land. Most illegal land occupation took place on government land or land of very poor quality with limited commercial value. And over time, conventional land and housing markets developed in most illegal or informal settlements so what originally appeared to be a threat to the existing order ended up fully integrated into that order.

The extent to which governments develop a major program to provide secure tenure and basic infrastructure and services to those living in illegal settlements and the choice of settlements that get priority is likely to be influenced by the extent to which those living in illegal settlements are organized. There are many case studies of squatter or popular movements in Latin America negotiating successfully with the state.

Environmental Trends

A review of urban environmental conditions and trends indicates that many health problems affecting poorer groups are associated with overcrowding, including household accidents, acute respiratory infections, tuberculosis, and other airborne infections. In the predominantly low-income residential areas in cities of the developing countries, often an average of four or more persons occupy one room. Poor quality indoor environments bring high levels of environmental risk. Despite considerable progress in improving or extending water supplies in the developing countries during the International Drinking Water Supply and Sanitation Decade that began in 1980, by the end of the decade, 245 million urban dwellers and over one billion rural dwellers still had no alternative but to use water whose quality was not assured. For urban areas in the developing countries, an assessment in 1991 suggested that around half the population had water piped into their houses while around a quarter were supplied through less convenient means—public standpipes, yard taps, protected dug wells, and boreholes/handpumps. The remaining 350 million or so urban dwellers did not have a safe, protected water supply. The latest estimates (for 1994) suggest the number without suitable water services had increased to about 280 million for urban dwellers while the number of unserved rural dwellers had been reduced to 835 million. A lack of readily available drinking water, of sewage connections and of basic measures to prevent disease can result in many debilitating and easily preventable diseases becoming endemic among poorer households – including diarrheal diseases, typhoid, many intestinal parasites, and food poisoning. Waterborne diseases account for more than 4 million infant and child deaths per year and hold back the physical and mental development of tens of millions more.

These statistics, however, should not detract from the considerable achievements in improving water supplies. For instance, it is clear that major progress has been made in Brazil in improving the provision of water supply (and sanitation) during the late 1970s and the 1980s. In São Paulo, for instance, the public water supply network reaches some 95 percent of all households. Similarly, in Chile, the proportion of the urban population with piped water grew from 78 percent in 1976 to 98 percent in 1987.

Many cities around the world are facing serious shortages of fresh water, and this is even the case in cities where half the population are not adequately served with safe, sufficient supplies. Many cities have outgrown the capacity of their locality to provide adequate, sustainable water supplies. For instance, Mexico City has to supplement its groundwater supplies by bringing water from ever more distant river systems and pumping this water up several hundred meters to reach the Valley of Mexico where the city is located; the energy needed to pump this water represents a significant part of Mexico City's total energy consumption. Overexploitation of underground water has also made the city sink, producing serious damage in many buildings and sewage and drainage pipes.

Hundreds of urban centers in relatively arid areas have also grown beyond the point where adequate water supplies can be drawn from local or even regional sources. Examples include many of the coastal cities in Peru (including Lima), La Rioja and Catamarca in Argentina, and various cities in Northern Mexico. Bangkok and Jakarta are among the many major coastal cities with serious subsidence problems as a result of drawing too much water from underground aquifers; they also face problems from saline intrusion into such groundwaters.

Environmentally tied to water supply is sanitation. Official statistics for 1991 suggest that at least a third of the developing countries' urban population and more than half its rural population have no means to dispose of waste waters. The problems with sanitation are growing with the size and density of settlements. In high-density residential areas only sewers or toilets connected to septic tanks can ensure adequate provision for sanitation, but quite a number of places in the developing countries have no sewers at all. Most of their inhabitants also lack connection to septic tanks. Excrement and waste water ends up in rivers, streams, canals, gullies, and ditches, untreated.

Most cities are facing mounting problems with the collection and disposal of solid wastes. In high-income countries, the problems usually center on the difficulties and high costs of disposing of the large quantities of wastes generated by households and businesses. In lower income countries, the problems have more to do with collection. These problems are especially serious for the inhabitants of the larger and most densely populated informal or illegal settlements or tenement districts that have no regular garbage collection service.

Governance

Given the foregoing economic, social and environmental ramifications of urbanization, concomitant developments have taken place in the governance or administration and management of settlements. Realizing the potentials of an urbanizing world depends to a large extent on city authorities. Good urban governance also needs the appropriate legislative framework and support from national governments.

The governance of settlements has become a major issue over the last decade. Three factors have helped "local governance" emerge as a key issue in the discussion of policies and strategies for human settlements: the elaboration and implementation of decentralization policies; the introduction of or return to democratic principles of government in many countries during the 1980s and early 1990s, at both the national and local levels; and the increased importance of citizen and community pressure – including urban social movements – combined with the growth worldwide of environmental movements that have helped to place a greater emphasis on local control and involvement in decision making.

During the 1980s, concern grew about the inability of many governments to deliver development programs at the local level, so that a wide debate began in many countries about the balance of power and distribution of functions between national and local governments. Decentralization policies of different kind have since been or are still being implemented as follows:

- Deconcentration, or the transfer of functions, but not power, from a central unit to a local administrative office. This is one of the "weakest" forms of decentralization and has become a common response by higher levels of government to deflect the blame for inadequate service provision or delivery;
- Delegation, which involves, in most cases, the transfer of certain powers to parastatal agencies of the central state. While the parastatals have a certain autonomy in day-to-day management, they are usually controlled ultimately by the central government;

- Devolution, considered by some as "real decentralization," since power and functions are actually transferred to subnational political entities, who, in turn, have real autonomy in many important respects; and
- Privatization, which involves the transfer of power and responsibility for certain state functions to private groups or companies.

With so many cases of decentralization underway, and so many differences in the form that the decentralization takes, it is virtually impossible to generalize about either the reasons for any particular exercise or the success or failure of the decentralization effort as a whole. However, a number of cogent arguments can be put forward to explain why decentralization strategies have been adopted. First, demand for public services varies from place to place both in quantity and quality, so that only decentralization of the provision for these services can ensure an efficient response to this variation in demand. A second argument is based on efficiency, in that locally financed and provided services can be produced at a lower cost—and with local government also able to work more easily with local community-based or voluntary sector organizations in ways that allow significant cost reductions. While this may be counterbalanced by the argument for larger units of service provision that achieve greater efficiency than smaller units at the lower level, it is still prevalent. A third argument is based on accountability, that is, a decentralized institution should in principle be more accountable to its constituents, who are more likely to have easy access to service providers and a better understanding of whether services and institutions operate at a lower level than at a national or centralized level. Finally, there is the argument for coordination. Many local services are interdependent, so the cost savings from coordination can more easily be attained.

Although there are good, or at least locally persuasive, arguments for decentralization in the current economic climate—whether this decentralization involves privatization of services or localization of functions and responsibility—any shift of responsibility and financial power from one level of government to another level or agency brings both benefits and costs. Since arguments for central government provision of services include the presumption that they can be more equally distributed among the population as a whole, that they can be more effectively related to macroeconomic policy, and that they may benefit from higher levels of technology and information support, there can be costs when certain services are decentralized. One of these is the growth of disparities between local governments in terms of services provided, since some local governments have a greater ability to finance these services than others. In many large cities, there are large disparities between neighboring municipalities—for instance between the middle and upper income suburbs and the peripheral municipalities with high concentrations of illegal and informal settlements.

Another potential disadvantage of decentralization is central government's loss of control over fiscal policy, when some local and territorial governments spend or borrow disproportionately for their own needs and so contribute to inflation or increasing the debt service costs for the country as a whole. There are also the potential disadvantages related to privatization. One is the reduced transparency and accountability of infrastructure and service provision, when what was previously a government responsibility is privatized. Here, one particular concern is the privatization of those forms of infrastructure and services that are "natural monopolies"; once a piped-water system or electricity distribution network or sewage and storm drainage system is built and becomes the responsibility of one company, it is virtually impossible for another company to compete by building another such system. Customers cannot turn to another supplier for water, drains, or electricity, if the quality is poor and/or prices are too high. A second potential disadvantage of privatization is the loss of public assets if these are sold at below their real value. A third is the difficulty of ensuring that lower income households and areas receive basic infrastructure and services. Privatization actually reinforces the need for competent, effective, and accountable local government to act on behalf of the inhabitants in its jurisdiction to ensure that private companies maintain quality and coverage in infrastructure and service provision and do not abuse any natural monopoly position by raising prices.

As noted earlier, these various conditions and trends pose challenges to human settlements management and both governments and nongovernmental actors in the field have responded to these with varying degrees of effectiveness. It is now accepted that a predominantly urban world is not only an inevitable part of a wealthy economy, but also one that brings many advantages. The challenge therefore is how to manage cities and other scales of human settlements within an increasingly urbanizing world. Such management must encourage cities to remain innovative and adaptable but also capitalize on their potential to provide high quality living conditions with much reduced resources use and environmental impact.

Responses to Urbanization Challenges

To cope with the challenges posed by urbanization and its ramifications, countries, some assisted by international agencies and institutions, have developed, adopted, and implemented varying policies, strategies, programs, methods, and approaches to cope with the problems posed. These have ranged from evolving approaches to settlements planning, to supply of housing and basic services: innovative approaches to land development, management of environmental infrastructure and urban transportation; and the financing of these, among others.

One of the first and earliest responses to urbanization was to attempt to regulate and manage settlements development through planning. The planning response to urbanization and the urban settlement development process has itself evolved through several paradigms—from the comprehensive planning approaches of the 1960s, to the disjointed incrementalism of the 1970s, to the structure planning approaches of the 1980s. Between and along with these have been the planning scheme, the project and the more recently emerging action-planning approaches.

Traditional approaches to settlements planning typically set out to document a finite long-term plan that, once legally adopted, forms the basis for infrastructure and service investment and a detailed system of land use regulation and control. Traditional rationales for urban planning interventions, such as developing an appropriate "environmental protection" service, were already the concerns of early planning systems in many countries. In this context, settlements planning advances the process of controlling negative externalities or nuisances, and by varying the range of permitted activities from place to place, can ensure that there will be a place for every worthwhile activity while keeping any from constituting a nuisance. Control and management of negative externalities, and protection of public health, social, and economic welfare of the community are therefore the principal rationales for urban settlement planning. This form of settlements planning, however, tended to mirror the widespread development model of the postwar period, and state economic planning. It worked well in many OECD countries with urban conditions characterized by slow growth, high average incomes, effective land use regulations and enforcement procedures, and at first in the many developing countries to which it was exported.

However, since the 1960s, traditional approaches to settlements planning have been found wanting, although they continue to be used in many countries. The reasons for these inadequacies include:

- Their insufficient concern with financial implications of the plan proposals;
- Their lack of coordination with sectoral, socioeconomic, and financial strategies for urban development;
- Their a two-dimensional approach to urban development in which the plan is seen as an end in itself rather than one component in the management of urban areas;
- Uncertainty about the relationship between spatial and economic planning;

- Their being too static to cope with or permit rapid adjustment to the demands of increasingly rapid urbanization; and their being too complex, detailed, and time-consuming;
- An elitism in the sense that the people and their community organizations are seldom meaningfully involved in the process;
- Inappropriate land use regulations and development controls built into them which often generate more costs than benefits and do not reflect the actual ability to pay of city residents;
- Institutional shortcomings in the public sector resulting from over-centralization of planning powers in central government and antagonism between the public and private sectors.

The net effect of such inadequacies is that much of urban growth in developing countries where these approaches still predominate is now in informal settlement structures.

New approaches are however developing that recognize more decentralized planning. The powers of local government to prepare plans, regulate land use, and coordinate the actions of the public and private sector in land development have hitherto been restricted by central government. Such a situation may have been acceptable when the urban sector was rather small, but the increasing demands of rapid urban growth make such a centralized approach less and less relevant. The extent to which delegated or decentralized powers are needed depends of course on national and local political realities. Generally, the degree of local responsibility for tasks in plan formulation and land use regulation and the role of the private sector, community groups and organizations, and NGOs is growing.

As the level of governance closest to the people, local authorities play a vital role in educating, mobilizing, and responding to the public to promote sustainable development. Lack of resources and technical capacity within most local authorities in the developing countries and the fact that local governments are often restricted by central government both in respect to raising finance and in other activities will of course to some extent impede local implementation.

From Housing Supply to Enablement

Another response has been a change of strategy to improving urban housing supply and housing conditions, especially during the last 10 to 15 years. These were influenced by many factors but among the most important are changes in economic conditions (and in government responses to them), changes in the concept of what governments should do (and should not do) to improve housing conditions, and, in many developing countries democratic pressures. At the same time, there were changes in the concept of what governments should do to improve housing conditions, resulting in the crystallization of three distinct concepts of the role of government in housing programs: state provision; the "enabling" approach; and the "market provision" approach, although no government's position falls entirely within one of these approaches.

The enabling approach helped to develop what might be termed a new agenda for shelter as it relied on market forces for many aspects of shelter provision, but within a framework that addressed those areas where private, unregulated markets do not work well. The new approach gained strength throughout the 1980s, supported by two related, international initiatives. The first, promoted by UNCHS (Habitat), centered on the concept of the "enabling approach" that was elaborated, in 1988, in the Global Strategy for Shelter to the Year 2000. Here, the role of government was redefined to focus on managing the legal, regulatory, and economic framework so that people, NGOs, and the private-sector were more able to produce housing and related services more effectively. Scarce government resources could then be directed to areas such as capital-intensive infrastructure which the poor could not fund, and which commercial interests would not finance themselves. Thus, it used the advantages of private markets for land, building materials, finance, and finished housing in terms of cost reductions, rapid response to changing demands, and a diverse range of housing available for sale or rent. However, it is not only private sector firms, but also third sector institutions such as NGOs, voluntary agencies, and community organizations that are seen as more cost-effective producers and providers of shelter than government bureaucracies. This new approach accepts that the privatization of some services can bring major benefits but that privatization is no longer the standard response for all services. The "enabling" approach is also associated with political reforms, especially democratization. Popular participation and decentralization now receive more official support than they used to. Civil society is also given a much greater role through NGOs, community-based organizations and citizens' movements. There is a more explicit and informed attempt to ensure that housing provision better matches the needs and priorities of lower income groups.

The second international support for a new approach to shelter policy in the 1980s and early 1990s emerged from the World Bank. Although it shared and supported many of the characteristics of the "enabling approach" during the second half of the 1980s, its shelter policy developed more of a focus on economic issues, especially on "enabling housing markets to work," and paid less attention to social and political matters such as enabling poor people to gain access to housing and land. The most important elements in this new agenda included secure property rights, developing private mortgage finance, rationalizing subsidies, promoting cost recovery in infrastructure development, reducing shelter standards and regulatory complexity, and promoting private-sector activity in all areas. Thus, different interpretations of "enablement" mean different kinds and levels of government intervention.

It is however now widely accepted that all cities are the result of an enormous range of investments of capital, expertise, and time by individuals, households, communities, voluntary organizations, NGOs, private enterprises, investors, and government agencies. Many of the most effective and innovative initiatives to improve housing conditions among low-income groups have come from local NGOs or community organizations, including women's groups. Without the active involvement of these individuals in shelter provision, housing conditions would have been much worse than they are.

Management of the Environment

In most developing countries environmental infrastructure has not been managed in an integrated manner, even where the different forms of infrastructure provision were under the same government agency, local authority, or parastatal. However, integrated management is needed as inadequate water supply leads to poor sanitation while inadequate provision for sanitation can mean a contamination of surface and groundwater resources. Similarly, the absence of a well-managed solid waste collection and disposal system often leads to refuse blocking drains, causing flooding in low lying areas, and water pollution. An integrated approach is also needed to promote the conservation of water resources both in terms of quality and quantity, and the efficient and equitable allocation of scarce water resources among competing uses.

In the past and to a large extent in many countries today, investment in environmental infrastructure has been financed largely from tax revenues and government borrowing. Thus, governments bore all the associated risks. However, public funds fall far short of the required level of investment to cover the rapidly growing demand in many urban areas, especially in the developing countries, and the economic problems faced by most countries in Africa, Asia and Latin America has further reduced the availability of these funds.

Mobilizing private capital is another way to fill the funding gap. However, private capital is not unlimited and environmental infrastructure has to compete with sectors that yield a higher return on investment. To date, only limited amounts of private capital have been used to finance investment in the sector. A survey published in October 1993 by Public Works Financing showed that of 148 private infrastructure projects funded worldwide since the early 1980s at a total cost of over $60 billion, only 16% were for environmental infrastructure, and none were in low-income countries.

As a result of governments' inability to meet existing demands, communities, households, and NGOs are also becoming more involved in mobilizing funds to build their water and sanitation schemes or to operate and maintain existing ones. Women, in particular, play an important role in organizing their communities and mobilizing local resources. However, these activities often do not evolve into sustainable forms of settlements development and resource management since they are carried out in an informal manner, reacting to immediate needs, with varying degrees of success. In the past, the focus was on the design of more efficient, environmentally sound waste treatment and disposal facilities. But financial constraints and increasing waste production have brought about a change of focus to promoting waste minimization and a reduction of pollutant load at source, waste recycling, the use of water saving devices, metering of services, and new tariff structures.

Evolving Directions

During the last two and a half decades, the focus of human settlements policies has shifted from housing the urban poor through a combination of informal settlements upgrading and sites and services schemes, to the "enabling approach" and the related idea of "partnerships," both of which were at the core of the Global Strategy for Shelter to the Year 2000 adopted by the international community in 1988. A latter shift in policy focus has been towards the concept of "Sustainable Development," which was the central theme and message of the United Nations Conference on Environment and Development (UNCED) and Agenda 21 adopted in Rio de Janeiro in 1992. These shifts in policy focus have been against the background of continuing rapid urbanization. The main challenge now is how to manage the development of human settlements in a rapidly urbanizing world, in such a way as to satisfy the socioeconomic and environmental objectives of sustainable development, overcome the limitations of past human settlement policies, and satisfy the growing demand for democratic governance at all levels of society.

The Habitat Agenda—embodying the goals, the principles, commitments and Global Plan of Action of the just concluded United Nations Conference on Human Settlements (Habitat II) embodies and consolidates the foregoing policies and approaches and provides the blueprint and framework for addressing this urbanization challenge.

Sustainable Human Development

Sustainable human development brings together two strands of thought about managing human activity. The first concentrates on development, including a concern for equity, while the second looks to achieving development without damaging the planet's life support systems or jeopardizing the interests of future generations. Within the context of human settlements, a commitment to sustainable development means adding additional goals to those that are the traditional concerns of urban authorities. Meeting human needs has long been a central responsibility of city and municipal authorities. Their objectives generally include a desire for greater prosperity, better social conditions (and fewer social problems), and (more recently) better environmental standards within their jurisdiction. These have long been important concerns for urban residents. A concern for "sustainable development" retains these conventional concerns but with two more added. The first is for the impact of city-based production and consumption on the needs of all people, not just those within their jurisdiction. The second is an understanding of the finite nature of many resources (or ecosystems from which they are drawn) and of the capacities of ecosystems in the wider regional, national, and international context to absorb or break down wastes.

In the long term, no city can remain prosperous if the aggregate impact of all cities' production and their inhabitants' consumption draws on global resources at unsustainable rates and deposits wastes in global sinks at levels that undermine health and disrupt the functioning of ecosystems. Adding a concern for "ecological sustainability" to existing development concerns means setting limits on the rights of city enterprises or consumers to use scarce resources and to generate nonbiodegradable wastes. This has many implications for inhabitants, businesses, and city authorities. Perhaps the most important for cities in the developed countries and the wealthier countries in the developing countries is how to separate high standards of living/quality of life from high levels of resource use and waste generation.

Although the economic dimensions of "sustainable development" are increasingly well understood and strongly woven into the current literature on sustainability, the social dimension is less well formed, but just as crucial. Social equity, social justice, social integration, and social stability are of fundamental importance to a well-functioning urban society. Their absence leads not only to social tension and unrest, but also to civil wars, violent ethnic conflicts, and other human-made disasters.

Partnerships

One of the distinctive characteristic of the Habitat II Conference was that it was a Conference of "Partnerships" between governments and several groups of nongovernmental participants. The Conference, while endorsing the pivotal role of government, underlined that this is principally one of creating conditions and contexts that "enabled" the various participants to contribute optimally to development. The Istanbul Declaration (paragraph 12) by Heads of State and Government Strongly emphasized this approach.

The "enabling framework" encourages and supports the multiplicity of large and small initiatives, investments, and expenditures by individuals, households, communities, businesses, and voluntary organizations. This concept is based on the understanding that most human investments, activities, and choices, all of which influence the achievement of development goals and the extent of environmental impacts, take place outside "government." Most are beyond the control of governments, even where governments seek some regulation. The 1980s brought a growing realization that inappropriate government controls and regulations discourage and distort the scale and vitality of individual, family, and community investments and activities, all of which are essential for healthy and prosperous cities. But there is also recognition that, without controls and regulations that are scrupulously enforced, individuals, communities, and enterprises can impose their externalities on others. Preventing this is one of the main tasks of governance. One of the key issues and challenges for city governance is then what kind of "enabling" institution is needed that best complements the efforts of individuals, households, communities, and voluntary organizations and ensures more coherence between them all so they all contribute toward citywide improvements, and how funding and technical advice/assistance can be availed in ways that match the diverse needs and priorities of the different categories of settlements—with the accountability and transparency built into them.

Good Governance

Good governance means coping with conflicting goals and the competing claims of different interests. Furthermore, city authorities must encourage local innovation. In addition, the principle of subsidiarity remains important as responsibilities, tasks, and control over resources are decentralized to the lowest level where their implementation will be effective. Governance extends beyond governments. It includes the strengthening of institutions for collective decision-making and the resolution of conflicts. It implies new alliances and partnerships. Good governance develops a framework that succeeds in encouraging and supporting innovation and partnerships at household, community, city, and regional levels. The achievement of sustainable development goals within a city will need an enormous range of household or community projects whose individual impact may be small but whose collective effect is significant. Institutions and partnerships between the different participants—NGOs, community organizations, business and commercial enterprises, professional organizations or associations, national and local government—are needed to achieve sustainable development across all sectors and geographic scales and promote beneficial interproject linkages.

Given the diversity of cities both in terms of their size and population growth rates and in their economic, social, political, cultural, and ecological underpinnings, it is difficult to consider "sustainable development" and cities in general terms. Much of the action to achieve sustainable development has to be formulated and implemented locally by city governments, since centralized decision-making structures have great difficulty in developing and implementing plans that respond appropriately to such diversity. It is the city government that has to: (a) promote more sustainable patterns of resource use and waste minimization among consumers and producers; (b) ensure a good match between demand and supply for land for all the different land uses that are part of any city while using its planning and regulatory system and mechanisms to promote resource conserving buildings and settlement patterns; (c) invest in needed infrastructure and services (or plan and coordinate their provision by other agencies/enterprises), again within a resource conserving framework; (d) work with local businesses to enhance the locality's attraction for new productive investment; and (e) encourage and develop local partnerships to help achieve the above and other sustainable development goals within the city.

Governments at both national and local levels must develop the conditions to support and sustain economic prosperity but, in most instances, they are dependent on private sector commercial and industrial enterprises to respond to these opportunities. With the collapse of communist governments in Eastern Europe and the former Soviet Union and the privatization of many government agencies and responsibilities in most countries, investment opportunities are increasingly in the domain of the private sector. The private sector has a clear interest in the economic aspects of sustainable development and in the provision of infrastructure and services, but a more ambiguous position in regard to equity—both within contemporary society and intergenerationally.

It is difficult for any city or municipal authority to act in isolation. National governments have the key role in linking local and global ecological sustainability. Internationally, they have the responsibility for reaching agreements to limit each nation's call on the world's environmental capital. Nationally, they are responsible for providing the framework to ensure local actions can meet development goals without compromising local and global sustainability. It is also the task of national government to consider the social and environmental impacts of their macro-economic and sectoral policies which may contribute to the very problems their sustainable development policies are seeking to avoid. The achievement of urban development goals that also seek to promote ecological sustainability requires both incentives and regulations.

Conclusions

Cities have long been blamed for many human failings, among them the inadequacies of the government institutions located there, the inequalities in income that the contrasts between their richest and poorest districts make visible, environmental degradation, and the corrosion of the social fabric. Within the current concern for "sustainable development," cities are often cited as the main "problem." Studies preparatory to the Habitat II Conference had surveyed the evidence but found little substance to these criticisms, which forget the central role that cities and urban systems have in stronger and more stable economies, which in turn have underpinned great improvements in living standards for a considerable proportion of the world's population over the last few decades.

The tendency to consider "rapid urbanization" as a problem ignores the close association between urbanization and economic growth. While it is true that many cities have grown very rapidly, this is largely a reflection of the rate at which their economies grew. In general, the higher the level of urbanization in a country, the lower the level of absolute poverty. The most urbanized nations are also generally those with the highest life expectancies. Those who live in or move to cities generally have smaller families in the long run than those living elsewhere and the countries with the largest increase in their level of urbanization over the last 20 to 30 years are also generally those with the largest declines in population growth rates.

It is not cities per se therefore that are responsible for most resource use, waste, pollution, and greenhouse gas emissions, but particular industries and commercial and industrial enterprises (or corporations) and middle and upper income groups with high-consumption lifestyles. Cities have the potential to combine safe and healthy living conditions and culturally rich and enjoyable lifestyles with remarkably low levels of energy consumption, resource use, and wastes.

Perhaps the single most important—and difficult—aspect of urban development is developing the institutional structure to manage it in ways that ensure that the advantages noted above are utilized—and also done in ways that are accountable to urban populations. Making full use of the potential that cities have to offer requires "good governance." "Good governance" can be assessed in the extent to which city, regional, and national governments ensure that people within their boundaries have jobs; safe, sufficient water supplies; provision for sanitation, education and health care; among other services. A successful city is one where the many different goals of its inhabitants and enterprises are met, without passing on costs to other people (including future generations) or to their regions. But in the absence of "good governance," cities tend to be centers of pollution and waste, and can be unhealthy and dangerous places in which to live and work.

One of the key international issues for the next few decades will be how to resolve the pursuit of increased wealth by individual nations (most of whose members have strong preferences for minimal constraints on their consumption levels) within a global recognition of the material limits of the biosphere. There are also international factors far beyond the competence and capacity of national and municipal governments that influence the quality of city environments. The very poor environmental conditions evident in the cities of most developing countries are a reflection of the very difficult circumstances in which most developing countries find themselves. Stagnant economies and heavy debt burdens do not provide a suitable economic base from which to develop good governance. Many developing economies have no alternative but to increase the exploitation of their natural resources to earn the foreign exchange to meet debt repayments. In the discussions about new "enabling frameworks" that the City Summit promotes, what must not be forgotten is the "enabling framework" needed at international level that is far more supportive of economic stability and greater prosperity for the lower income nations.

In the words of the Istanbul Declaration on Human Settlements (paragraph 15), the Habitat II Conference "marks a new era of cooperation, an era of a culture of solidarity. As we move into the twenty-first century, we offer a positive vision of sustainable human settlements, a sense of hope for our common future and an exhortation to join a truly worthwhile and engaging challenge, that of building together a world where everyone can live in a safe home with a promise of a decent life of dignity, good health, safety, happiness and hope."

Even with the formidable challenge of its problems, it will be in the urban areas where we may be able to best provide services to people, alleviate poverty, improve life expectancy, and more effectively manage our planet's massive population growth. The challenge is to anticipate, plan, and manage them much better than hitherto.

Notes

1. UNCHS (Habitat), *An Urbanizing World: Global Report on Human Settlements*. London: Oxford University Press, 1996, p. 13.

Section 2 A Globalizing World

Mihály Simai

Globalization has become a catchword in the late twentieth century, used extensively by political and business leaders, academics, journalists, and above all by people working in international organizations. The opening up of many economies and the rise of global investment, trade, and migration offer many new opportunities. There is also increasing concern about other "external" problems relating to globalization.[1] To understand the role of globalization in the development process, it is necessary to analyze various aspects of this complex and multidimensional force for change.

The main area of globalization is the international economic system or world economy, which is the totality of global production, consumption, and exchange activities undertaken by individuals working within national economies and/or the world market. Economic growth has been made far more interdependent internationally by the growth of world trade and the increasing role and transformation of capital and money markets because of the global diffusion of new technology and the global consequences of environmental change.

In the 1990s, globalization developed at different rates in different directions, and at different sectoral intensities in technology, economics, trade, and culture. The process is rooted above all in the increasing role and transformation of the capital and money markets, the global diffusion of new technology, the global consequences of environmental change, and the development of global organizations, intergovernmental cooperation regimes, and transnational corporations. A multitude of relationships have developed in the global system, linking these different performers in a wide variety of fields. Some such relationships tend to integrate, whereas others can lead to disintegration and fragmentation.

Research has revealed three simultaneous, interrelated, and interacting processes. Alongside globalization, there is regionalization and fragmentation. All three are shaping events and changes in the lives of the people, states, and the international community. These processes are not necessarily developing in a contradictory, mutually exclusive, fashion. At the end of the twentieth century, globalization emerges as the strongest and most comprehensive of the three, representing the greatest challenge to all regions and countries.

Growth, Interdependence, and Development

The central component in the hierarchy of factors that shape the development process has always been economic growth, even though, as many experts have recognized, growth alone does not constitute development. The period since World War II has shown that a system of sustained and widespread growth in demand and output is fundamental for maintaining a high level of employment, satisfying social needs, alleviating poverty, and resolving the major problems facing the world economy. It has also been generally recognized that it is not just economic growth, but also an appropriate per capital growth rate that is needed to supply the basic needs of the population and ensure the sustainability of policies required for improving the quality of life in various societies.

Since the 1960s, there has been a deceleration of global economic growth, accompanied by growing regional differences in growth rates, both in general and per capital terms. The present growth rates are below those in a large number of countries that contributed to unprecedented economic and social improvement. In Japan, an annual GDP growth of 4 percent is needed to sustain the socioeconomic balance. In the United States, there is increasing concern that the "age of affluence" has come to an end. The recession in the former socialist, transition economies has been greater than those experienced during the Great Depression in the United States and Germany. The fast-growing countries are not large enough to stimulate an increase in global growth. Slow growth, stagnation, or recession encourage nationalism and protectionism. Slow economic growth, especially when it derives from slow productivity growth, undermines and weakens social cohesion. Besides having an impact on unemployment, it causes a deterioration in the quality of jobs and a decline in incomes, while highlighting inequalities of income distribution.

Reviving Economic Growth

Can the rates of global growth be increased under the present world economic conditions? Those who advocate the theory of long cycles insist that the growth path of the world is determined by strong historical "regulating forces." Others relate the higher growth rates of earlier decades, particularly the 1960s, to a "golden age" of capitalism.

Analysis of the main growth factors in past decades reveals a wide range of external and internal factors responsible for slowing down global growth. They include changing macroeconomic priorities, internal and external deficits, excessive regulation, structural changes in the economy, new relationships between the "paper" and the real economy, the 1970s oil price explosion and consequent debt crisis, changing economic geography, increasing global competition, and sluggishness in various demand factors.

The feasibility of faster economic growth – a major concern for much of the world's population, especially in the developing and former socialist countries – is not just a question of fiscal or monetary incentives. It has important structural constraints. For instance, the growth potentials of the service sector, which has become dominant in the economies of the industrial countries, and the spillover from such growth, differs from the potentials of material production. An important question relates to the increasing role of speculative capital movements. If a growing volume of savings is moving into this area, countries that depend on the availability of resources for productive investments will benefit less.

The future of the global trading regime will also be an important issue for the future patterns and rates of global growth. There are also important environmental implications of global growth rates. The recent experiences of the fast-growing countries in Asia, notably China, has also underlined the complex interaction and sometimes adverse results of growing too fast. It is important that the growth rates be optimal for the various types of countries, in terms of their economic and social needs, whose satisfaction depends on economic growth, or of the sustainability of the relatively liberal global trading regime. During the global recession of the early 1990s, the fast-growing Asian countries played an important role in sustaining a relatively high level of global trade. Their domestic markets have expanded rapidly, making them increasingly important markets to each other. This shows that the oft-mooted idea of intra-South trade cannot be divorced from the sectoral and spatial attributes of global economic growth.

A further important issue is the extent to which the rural economy, especially agriculture, can play a more significant role in growth and development. There are often disregarded potentials for growth, for example, in biomass processing, relocation of industry and service activities to rural areas, and modernization of small farms.

To identify the politically and economically feasible conditions for revitalizing economic growth in excess of the rates and patterns conditioned by the world market entails gauging countries political and economic preparedness and identifying what factors can serve as its "locomotives." Preliminary empirical findings suggest that the dominating economic philosophies and policies in most industrial countries have other priorities. Many have shifted from growth-oriented institutional and structural policies to ones aimed at macroeconomic stabilization. Although globally harmonized acceleration of growth seems to be a remote possibility, the issue, with its structural conditions and implications, will remain to many developing countries and the postsocialist economies.

Globalization, Trade, and Development

An important consequence of globalization is the growing dependence of economic growth and development on external factors, especially on global finance and world trade. Although most of the global product is consumed within the country of origin, national development has become more extensively embedded in a global framework. At the same time, it has become more complex, following several concurrent paths. Changes, such as growth and recession, sudden setbacks, and breakdowns are transmitted from country to country much faster than they were, particularly in developing countries. The example of Mexico in 1995 proved both the destabilizing potentials of globalization and the interest of the industrial world in helping to avert a collapse. Approximately one fifth of the income of the industrial countries and one third of the income of developing countries depends directly on exports. It is estimated that 40 to 45 percent of the world's jobs in manufacturing and 10 to 12 percent in the modern service sectors are directly or indirectly related to foreign trade. Trade, moreover, remains a major channel for the redistribution of global income, through, for example, changes in terms of trade (which lost Africa US $50 billion during the 1980s), or facilitation of special rents from monopolistic positions.

The shift in the development strategies of almost all countries shifted from import substitution to export orientation was a consequence of globalization and a factor behind it.[2] The change has made external sources of economic growth more important and had major implications in areas such as technological change, capital flows, and income distribution. The reciprocal relationship between trade and industrial development is also changing, as the South becomes more export oriented. It is becoming more important to raise global competitiveness through diversification and technical upgrading. The changes create a number of new social constraints as well.

Globalization of economic growth in recent decades has been promoted most directly by foreign direct investment (FDI). The globalization process accelerated as the diverse markets, particularly for capital, technology, and goods, and to some extent for labor, became increasingly linked and integrated into the multitier networks of transnational corporations. These are most important organizations in the globalization process, constantly creating new linkages in output, product development, design, product universalization, and marketing.

Of the total of more than 250,000 affiliates of transnationals, more than 101,000 are located in developing countries, which account for approximately 20 to 25 percent of the foreign direct investment stocks.

In a more recent trend, an increasing number of these transnationals (approximately 3,800 out of 38,000) originate from the developing countries themselves, which reflects the fact, that market forces create similar patterns and sustain strong structures.[3] These transnational economic centers of power press for constant expansion onto new markets, and for relatively liberal and uniform rules in the business environment. They also serve as important instruments for the globalization of markets, by spreading the information infrastructure, which increases the speed and reduces the costs of transactions. Although a number transnationals deal in the traditional commodity sector, many have assisted the industrial restructuring of developing countries, establishing new industries, notably car manufacturing, petrochemicals, machinery, electronics, and modernizing traditional industries, such as textiles and food processing.

Three especially important changes since the early 1970s have helped to alter radically the patterns of relationship among trade, growth, and development on a global level. The new technological revolution and its global spread has brought major structural and institutional shifts in the relationships between production and the services and in both the manufacturing and service sectors.

New Technologies

There has been an improvement in the innovative capabilities of countries in the broadest sense. Social and institutional innovations, which will increase flexibility and efficiency of an economy, and innovations, which promote technical change, have become crucially important sources of growth. New inventions and their efficient commercialization will play a central role in shaping the global market competitiveness of firms and the structural competitiveness of an economy. The crucial roles of science, technology, and innovation in promoting countries in the global hierarchy of political and economic power and transforming the global system are by the emerging global economic system and the advanced technologies being introduced. Science and technology are influencing the scope and intensity of global changes in the environment, the high degree of internationalization of economic growth, the globalization of markets, and multinational corporate development. The role of science in global changes is more widespread, pervasive, and multidimensional than ever before. In the 1990s, The current process of transition to a new technological era is taking place in a highly diverse and increasingly two-track global economy. During the past 15 to 20 years, the majority of industrial countries and a small group of developing countries have managed to implement policies that enabled and supported the technological transformation.

The vast majority of the developing countries, struggling with grave social and economic problems, have not developed such capabilities, which has left them increasingly marginalized in scientific and technological terms. The peculiar technical capabilities of the former socialist were distorted by a number of factors, including strategic considerations and the predominance of defense-related programs. This resulted in a closed and very costly scientific and technological bloc, with little or no spillover to other sectors. Their entry into the new technological era has been slow, uneven, and distorted by political, strategic, and economic systemic factors.[4] For them, it is crucial for the transition to a market system to be shaped so as to facilitate a radical improvement in their innovative capabilities and utilization of their present capacities in science and technology.

New Competitors

The second important factor is that the global technical and economic map has been redrawn. New competitors have been emerging, especially through the fast growth of manufacturing in the developing world. Between 1950 and 1990, world trade in industrial products expanded almost twice as fast as manufacturing output. Major shifts occurred that corresponded to the impact of industries on production and consumption patterns, cost and price relationships, comparative market positions, and the regional locations of industry.

Although dependence on exports of primary products is still strong, the share of commodities in the export of the developing countries has been falling. The share of primary commodities in East Asia's exports declined from 69 percent in 1970 to 26 percent in 1992. In South Asia, the fall was from 53 percent to 27 percent, in Latin America from 88 percent to 62 percent, in the Middle East and North Africa from 92 percent to 90 percent, and in the Sub-Saharan Africa from 88 percent to 76 percent. The traditional dominant patterns of the colonial division of labor (flows of natural resources from the agricultural or raw-material exporting countries to the industrial world) have been gradually replaced. The industrial division of labor with comparative advantages related by natural-resource endowments has gradually been giving was to "acquired" advantages, particularly in developing countries able to industrialize fast.

Much of the blame for rising unemployment in the North has been placed on the South (mainly on Asian countries) and their export successes, especially in textiles and garments. These have been associated in people's minds with supposedly unfair competitive advantages from extremely cheap labor (including child labor). Even in the growing field of teleworking, people can "price themselves into a job." For example, the wage of an Indian working at home is one tenth that of a European teleworker. The wide gap between the industrialized North and the industrializing South is usually explained in terms of the latter's lower productivity. However, if world-class technology is made available through foreign direct investments or licensing agreements, there are few reasons why productivity in the modern, exporting sectors of the South should be much lower than in industrial countries, which should mean higher wages in those sectors. There may, on the other hand, be a deliberate lowering of social standards by a government intent on attracting foreign capital. These problems raise the question of how to manage increased international competition.

It is important to note that although a number of high-technology products exported by developed countries are also produced in developing countries, most of the latter cannot produce such goods. There remain important technical and economic forces sustaining a pattern of North–South division of labor. The North imports textiles, garments, consumer electronics, toys, and so on, while the South imports aeronautics, precision instruments, construction equipment, engines, arms, vehicle components, and so on. Even disregarding the traditional colonial division of labor, North and South may be more complementary than some ideological debates have allowed.

New Liberalization Policies

The last important change has occurred in the goals of national policy and regulatory regimes for trade and capital flows (export orientation, deregulation, liberalization, privatization). Many developing countries face new challenges, but it becomes increasingly difficult for them to make the appropriate policy responses. The national institutions are often unprepared for the new tasks related to constant structural adjustment needs and other pressures, the liberalization process and deregulation, and the new forms of reciprocal connection with the increasingly competitive global markets. The institutional aspects of countries' competitive advantages have been receiving more emphasis as a crucial factor than they did in the past.[5] For a number of countries, the problem of how efforts to increase competitive advantages can be squared with the social goals in their development strategies becomes a crucial one. The experiences in Southeast Asia, China, and some Latin American countries indicate the complex nature of the task.[6]

The inequalities in the global economy and the asymmetries of interdependence influence the relationships among globalization, growth, and development in many ways. They are also the consequences of the patterns of global economic growth. The inequality in output, consumption, and investment appears in the following figures for the distribution of the global product. Countries have been placed in three groups according to whether they have high, medium, or low levels of development and income.

The global product in 1995 was approximately US $24,000 billion, with a world population of approximately 5.6 billion. Thus, global per capita income was approximately US $4,300. The global product per head of labor (GDP/labor force) was approximately US $9,700, per capital personal consumption US $2,714, and per capita gross investment US $1,470 Per capita global exports were approximately US $700, and the per capita stock of foreign direct investments US $450.

Some 80 percent of global GDP, approximately US $19.2 trillion, was accounted for by 24 high-income countries, with 14.5 percent of the world's population. Their per capita income was approximately US $23,200, product per head of labor US $51,318, per capita personal consumption was approximately US $14,800, and per capita gross investments US $3,650. Exports per capita were US $3,600 and per capita stock of foreign direct investments US $2,350.

Approximately 15 percent of the global product, approximately US $3,600 billion was produced by 63 middle-income countries, with approximately 31.5 percent of the world's population. Their per capita income was approximately US $2,000, product per head of labor US $5,471, per capita personal consumption US $1,440, and per capita gross investment US $520. Per capita export in this group was US $410 and per capita stock of foreign direct investment US $250.

The remaining 5 percent of the global GDP, approximately US $1,200 billion, was generated by 45 low-income countries, with approximately 55 percent of the world's population. Their per capita income was approximately US $324, product head per labor US $836, personal consumption per capita US $236, and per capita gross investment US $84. Per capita exports were US $50 and per capita stock of foreign direct investment US $32.

The gaps in income, output, consumption and savings also increased between and within the developing countries. By the end of the century, the developing world was becoming more complex and diverse than it had been 40 to 50 years ago. These changes also diversified the development process and its patterns, and the interests of the countries concerned. Although globalization and liberalization opened new opportunities for growth, trade, consumption, and investments, globalization also became a major source of marginalization and impoverishment.

The implications of the global asymmetries and inequalities influence the development process in a number of ways. One relates to the changing capabilities of the less-developed countries to catch up with the developed world. There are at least three important aspects of the "catching-up" problem: First, newcomers today can learn from a greater choice of models that succeeded or failed in the past. Moreover, the merits, weaknesses and sociopolitical applicability of these models is better understood. Debate on the effectiveness and the applicability intensified in the 1990s. Second, catching up is not just an issue of national pride; it is a matter of how countries share global income and how competitive they are. These are crucially important factors in succeeding in a global market system. Third, catching up does not require complete identity of production and consumption patterns. In a realistic way, it can take place in certain segments of the economy, which may grow faster, becoming more efficient and productive. The spillover effect of these segments or sectors, and their role in raising the level of the economy as a whole, is what matters in the long term. During recent decades, only a few newly industrialized countries (NICs) or territories, such as South Korea, Singapore, and Taiwan have managed to graduate to the upper middle-income category. Others, such as Malaysia, have reached the brink of this. Meanwhile, some countries have been downgraded. Since the 1970s, gaps in the levels of technology, productivity, and standard of living have grown significantly, especially in the former Soviet Union and several countries in Central and Eastern Europe. On the whole, many of these nations have remained outside the international technological–industrial and service revolutions (the chief exception being the military sector) and have not participated in the globalization process that adjusts products, production processes, and management practices. Similarly, most developing countries, especially those dependent on the production and export of raw materials, have been marginalized by world market forces.

One of the sources of the increasing asymmetries and inequalities has been the fact that the global development process has encompassed both growth and decline, as normally happens in a highly complex system. The decline may be confined to some elements in society or the economy (agriculture as a declining sector, a declining rural population), or affect the system as a whole.

With systemic decline, the question is when and how the process becomes predominant, influencing the fundamental components of the system. With socioeconomic systems, empires, or countries decline can be understood in relative terms (loss of international competitiveness, slower economic growth, diminishing military power, as compared to others) or in absolute terms (shrinking population, contraction of the economy, diminishing incomes, and so on). Decline in per capita income affected 1.2 billion people during the 1980s, or approximately 23 percent of the world's population. After stagnating in the 1980s, per capita income growth in the former Soviet Union and in Central and Eastern Europe has also declined, adding another 360 million people to this crisis-ridden group. At the same time, parts of Asia, especially East and Southeast Asia, have experienced a relatively large growth of per capita GDP. The inequalities among the main regions of the world in per capita income have increased. Parallel with a better understanding of the conditions and systemic difficulties in the efforts to catch up, there is a major challenge for many countries in how to live with decline.

Globalization and Urbanization

An important trend related to the globalization of the world economy and the development process is the continuing mass urbanization and the prospects it raises. Urbanization is transforming the way societies function in many ways and has a major influence on individuals, families, and other communities, for it is more than a change in settlement patterns. Tomorrow's world will be an urban world, and the urbanization process, in scale and consequences, presents a historical hiatus in human development.

Cities are becoming key actors in the national and global society, while themselves entering a new stage of development. They are becoming culturally more diverse, especially in multiethnic states. The economic development has been the cause and effect of complex social processes. In many parts of the world, the business city is emerging as a key interest group. The political city is already a crucial force in the struggle for shares of national political power. Conurbations are also centers of organized crime and targets of terrorism. Cities increasingly compete with each other for investments, budget resources, and foreign capital. In some countries, they are becoming competitors with the central government in income redistribution. So the management of the cities is becoming a highly sophisticated, multidimensional task.

Most socioeconomic problems related to urbanization have been researched. Academic and practical attention has been devoted to migration, employment, labor absorption, the informal sector, infrastructure, services, social stratification, urban–rural polarization, housing, slums, problems of megacities, management of conurbations, and environmental problems. Much less is known about other issues, such as the kind of interactions likely to develop in a predominantly urbanized world between the urban and rural communities, or the future role of provincial towns, and how economic growth and migration will influence them. Another important question whose implications must be better understood is the role of the cities in the process of globalization.

Urban areas act in many ways as the funnels directing the impact of globalization. First, the cities in many countries are dependent on imports of food and energy. This lengthens their supply lines and may also increase their costs. The cities are the main scene of global standardization of consumption and cultures. They are the places where most of the transnationals concentrate their activities. So, will urbanization hasten the process of globalization? Will inner-city political and institutional cooperation come to constitute a new field of international relations?

Also unknown is how the urbanization process will affect growth and development in the developing countries. A key Indian urban specialist stated recently that "the efficiency of the cities will determine the economic growth. What does the efficiency of a city mean? In a simplified or conventional term, the costs and benefits and the sustainability of urban development represent the key challenges, in the light of current congestion, pollution, and the extremes of wealth and poverty.

How can a rapidly growing urban population can access to sources of income? New strategic responses are needed. In this decade alone, more than 230 million new jobs are needed in the cities of the developing world. It is crucial to reinforce the abilities of cities to deal with this problem.

The management of the cities, especially the financing of the infrastructure and housing needs are important challenges facing the developing countries. The estimated requirements of these countries to meet these needs alone are approximately US $100 to 150 billion a year. How can these costs be covered?

A key task for international society is to anticipate and handle the new conflicts emerging as a result of urbanization and the characteristics of urban development. Cities have been traditionally been centers of social struggles. In the past, these were related to a large extent to the workplace, or to communal relationships, such as ethnic and religious conflicts and segregation. In the new era, the crucial sources of conflict become "residential" issues: large income gaps between rich and poor, and unequal access to urban services, including water, sanitation, health, and education. These are often related to communal problems and social exclusions.

There are sociopolitical conflicts of other natures. The political and economic transformation of the former socialist countries, for example, has affected the status of various cities and regions, as the hierarchy of the old system has given way to a more democratic structure. Both the national and international importance of cities other than the capital has increased. In many developing countries, however, the capital city plays a dominant role by concentrating power, opportunities, and wealth. This may arouse new regional conflicts. So, another important area for future research is the influence of the urbanization process on national and international institutions.

Globalization and Sustainability

The globalization of economic development has allowed economic, technical, and social changes to exert increasingly global influences on the global ecosystem. This has turned the environmental sustainability of development into a global issue. The world cannot afford to continue its present patterns of wasting resources and inflicting ecological damage.

A quarter of a century ago, the prime minister of a major developing country was still able to say without being challenged "pollute us, but give us industry." Such views have become untenable in the face of shrinking rain forests, encroaching deserts, depleting oil supplies, polluted water, deteriorating city environments, growing energy problems, and increasing environmental vulnerability of the developing world. The concept of sustainable development and the demand for it came to the forefront in the 1980s. It was defined concisely by the Bruntland Commission: "Sustainable development is development that meets the needs of the present without compromising the ability of the future generations to meet their own needs." The FAO definition calls it "management and conservation of the resource base and the orientation of technological and institutional changes in such a manner as to ensure the attainment and continued satisfaction of human needs for present and future generations. Such sustainable development is environmentally non-degrading, technically appropriate, economically viable and socially acceptable."

One difficult, but essential, task is to change sustainable development from a political catchword into a practical policy line, nationally and internationally. The developing countries, for instance, must pursue rational strategies, by using efficient sources of energy, alternative transport and production technologies, changing agricultural practices to prevent soil erosion, desertification, wastage of water, and so on. The developing countries are unable at present to make most of these changes. They also need to establish alternative consumption patterns. Sustainability needs to become a major component of international cooperation. The common interest in such cooperation is evident, when one looks at the effects of global warming, nuclear radiation, and water pollution.

Effects of Globalization on Human Development

The issue of sustainability relates directly to the human dimension of the global development process in several ways, through the influence of sheer numbers of people and through various forms of human interactions and their consequences. There are also several sides to the effect of globalization on the human dimension of the development process. The demographic aspects of globalization, much emphasized in past debates on development prospects, have taken on a new light in terms of sustainability and employment.

By the end of 1995, the world population reached approximately 5.7 billion. According to UN projections, it will surpass 6.2 billion by the year 2000 and 7.2 billion by 2010. The period 1975 to 2000 will bring the greatest absolute growth in world population of any quarter century in history: more than 2.2 billion people. According to UN estimates, the world labor force in 1995 was 2.4 billion. This labor force had become more educated and experienced in recent decades. Yet, the number of not productively employed was close to 800 million, just over 33 percent of the workforce, the number of registered unemployed was over 120 million (a quarter of these in the industrial world), and the number of underemployed was over 700 million. Job creation and unemployment may well be the main socioeconomic issue of the next 20 to 25 years.

More than 75 percent of the global labor force is found in developing countries. Although the rise in industrial employment has been quite rapid in the developing countries (from approximately 4 percent to 4.5 percent in the past 25 years, though with large regional differences), it was able to absorb only 22 to 24 percent of those of working age. However, there have been important differences in the population trends of the developed and developing countries, and between developing countries. The different rates of population growth have brought major changes in the territorial and age distributions of the population in many regions of the world, and the continuation of these will further accentuate the demographic shifts.

All these changes are related to the employment problems. The most direct measures of how many jobs are and will be required in the world are the number and proportion of people of working age (15 to 64 years of age). Not all those of working age intend to enter the labor force. The proportion of the world population of working age rose from 57 percent in 1970 to 62 percent in 1990, and was projected to reach 64 percent by the year 2000. In the developed industrial countries, it has stayed quite high (close to two thirds of the population). In developing countries, it will rise from 54.4 percent in 1970 to over 60 percent by the year 2000. The world increment between 1970 and 1990 was approximately 1.4 billion, of which more than 1 billion were added in developing countries. UN projections suggest a further increment of 1.36 billion in the years from 1990 to 2010 (620 million in the 1990s and 740 million in the first decade of the twenty-first century). Only 4.7 percent of this will be in the development world, and more than 95 percent in the developing countries (an extra 1.3 billion). The increase will be fastest in the Middle East, South and Central America, and some African countries. In absolute numbers, the largest increments will be in South Asia and China.

According to estimates for the rise in population of working age, levels of unemployment, and increasing participation by women, approximately 1 billion new jobs will be needed in the next decade. This unprecedented task calls for internationally coordinated policies to raise employment, lest the employment issue become a source of global instability. The waste of human resources is a major loss to the global community, especially in certain countries that have often invested heavily in education. The high unemployment level of the mid-1990s signals of major structural problems and policy deficiencies in the world economy. Exclusion from the labor force, unemployment, and underemployment cause poverty and lower living standards in much of the world. The politics and economics of employment are crucial issues for the future of global development.

Welfare and Poverty

Another effect of globalization on the human dimension concerns welfare, because it has important influences on the growth and the global distribution (and redistribution) of incomes and wealth. All the aggregate indicators used to measure welfare show that despite significant material progress, there is increasing cause for concern in most countries, particularly developing and postsocialist countries, over deteriorating living conditions caused by economic decline and worsening income distribution, both directly and indirectly. The social aspects of human development are tied most closely to the rate and nature of economic growth, but not exclusively related to it. It has been emphasized that the intention should be for growth to benefit all segments of society. Human welfare must be the ultimate yardstick for measuring the outcome of development efforts.

The factors and forces creating new inequalities (and sustaining or reproducing old ones) are more complex in the late twentieth century than in the past. The various kinds of welfare states in the industrial world and the improvements in mortality and literacy rates and in the overall health and educational conditions in most developing countries and former socialist countries reflected the impact of deliberate national commitments and income redistribution policies. In a number of developing countries, past development strategies reflected priorities based on such values as equity and fellow feeling.

The recent global summit on the world's social problems showed that these social achievements are in grave danger, with a social crisis evolving in many countries. Resources and opportunities are distributed according to profitability and economic power under the current liberalizing and globalizing market system. If global market forces alone are allowed to decide the global distribution of income (based on profit), the existing international inequalities will be increased and enhanced.

There is much debate on what degree of equity can be sustained by a world dominated only by market forces. Human-centered development can be defined as a process in which social goals control development, ecological factors are noted and accepted as constraints, and economic goals treated as instruments. The hierarchy of forces governing the development process today differ from such priorities. Liberalization and structural adjustment have increasingly subordinated the social dimension of the development to external economic forces and processes, especially in the developing countries and the transition economies. The decline of employment in the formal sector and the growth of the informal-sector employment, increasing income inequalities, cuts in per capita expenditure on education and health, falling school enrollments, and in the former socialist countries, rising mortality rates, are signs of an evolving global social crisis, aggravated by declining global social solidarity and cuts in assistance programs.

Except in a handful of countries, such as China, India, and the NICs, the patterns of development prevailing in the developing countries since the early 1980s have failed to improve significantly the complex linkages between economic growth and individual, family, and community welfare. The achievements of some Asian countries in reducing poverty are of not inconsiderable, but a high concentration of poverty remains there. Poverty continues to grow in Africa and remains a grave problem in Latin America. A number of industrial countries have mounting social problems, including poverty. The declining standard of living in the former socialist countries has added several million to the global total of the poor.

Thus, the extent of poverty is among the dominant problems in the current international system, for human security is becoming a serious source of problems and risks. The "search for security" must be understood in a comprehensive, multidimensional way, and become a central force in the human dimension of development. This is the one general conclusion to be drawn from the many changes taking place. A multidimensional framework would have to include the security of individuals, nations, regions, and the international community. The comprehensive search for human security must also include such fields as sustainability of the ecosystem, food security, security of oil and raw-material supplies, access to new technology, and institutional reliability of international cooperation under various frameworks. These and other factors imply a growing need to handle and manage efficiently changes at all levels, especially in those areas which most directly affecting people's present and future conditions.

Revival of Traditionalism

The human dimension of development includes its cultural aspects. Sociocultural factors—the complex of solutions a community inherits, adapts, or invents in response to the challenges of its natural and social environment—have been seen in some cases as an impediment, and in some regions of the world as an asset that shapes the development process. Discussion in recent decades often focused on the influence of cultural factors, such as Confucianism's on the East Asian development model, and on the constraints imposed by cultural differences on applying that model in other regions, such as Africa. By the end of the century, the role of the sociocultural factors, including education, has become better understood.

The most recent issues raised here relate to the revival of traditionalism or fundamentalism in a number of countries, particularly to the revival of Islam. Questions have been raised about Islam's compatibility with modern attitudes and feasibility of developing an Islamic model in a nonsecular state. Fundamentalism and revived traditionalism are mainly rooted in growing poverty and despair among ordinary people, whom the dominant patterns of modernization have left with feelings of personal inadequacy, alienation, helplessness, and mistrust of government and modern institutions that do not serve the poor. The conflicts between modernization and traditional values have been heightened by recent trends toward greater gender equality and social participation by women, and emphasis on human rights, such as the universality of human rights and the rights of the child. The issues are more complex than the universalistic, Western world outlook spread by the mass media would imply.

Modernization also needs defining in a multidimensional way. This is important for the former socialist countries, where state socialism and its practices were treated as the most advanced social formation, while the new ideology of modernization advocates a Western market system. The on modernization is often confined to technology, whereas modernization also relates closely to changing human values and attitudes, which are affected by the urbanization process.[7]

Institutional Reforms and Globalization

In the debates of the 1990s, the roles of the state and market have appeared as two key contrasting factors and forces behind the development process. The conflict between these two approaches was present from the beginnings of the modern debates on development. However, there is another angle from which the interrelations between the state and the market must be viewed, and that is the historical one. The functions and the instruments of the state are changing, and the market is likewise going through major transformations, as are people's attitudes. The debate about the roles of the state and the market has certainly been influenced by the collapse of the state socialist regimes in Central and Eastern Europe and the former Soviet Union. The outcome of the changes has also an interesting influence. The dominant view is that better, and not necessarily less state, is the solution. Of course, it is necessary to define what better state would be. Democracy, accountability, transparency, absence of corruption are often mentioned.

The quality of governance, and the characteristics of "good governance" are regarded as crucial postulates of the development process. According to the IMF Managing Director's definition of good governance, "Governments must be accountable and participatory; laws must be transparent; nonessential regulations eliminated and the competence and impartiality ensured."

The debates on national institutional changes in recent decades have been influenced by two rival utopias. At one extreme was Soviet model, suggesting a development process managed by the state, completely subordinated to the collective will and allegedly expressed by the "visible hand," central government. it is interesting, though, that Marx in his writings never denied the historical role of the market in the development process. He saw the market as a solvent that would break down the traditional rigidities of society and allow development. At the other extreme was liberal utopia, in which the master is the "invisible hand" of the market, and the state's role in development had best be limited to safeguarding property rights and removing obstacles to market efficiency. Advocates of this ideology suggested that the inefficiency of allocation in the developing countries was the result of by market failures induced by excessive state intervention. Both extreme views have been ideological overcharged and counterproductive. A third approach, suggesting full decentralization based on cooperatives, voluntary associations, nonprofit structures, and NGOs, which could be called the populist utopia, has had an increasing influence on the global debates in many countries.

Looking at the development process in relation to national institutions, the Japanese, East Asian, and Chinese experiences have shown that greater success comes from hybrid solutions, or mixed economics, as they used to be called. Such approaches assume that the roles of the state and the market reinforce rather than exclude each other. It is also recognized that the three most important postulates of the development process – economic growth, macroeconomic stability, and distributive justice – cannot be achieved without an appropriate balance between the state and the market forces. Hybrid solutions mean at this stage applying market-oriented regulations wherever feasible, so as to fulfill the traditional government functions more cheaply and efficiently. It implies decentralizing and downsizing government in a number of areas, such as social services, education, and environmental measures, where the costs and benefits become more transparent at the community level.

The debate about the role of the state and the market has several dimensions: ideological, political, social, economic, administrative, and technical. The sources of important lessons about the positive and negative roles of the state and the cost–benefit analysis of the market are not confined to the developing and former socialist countries. The dominant problems of the 1990s show that the debate on the role of the state and the market cannot and should not be confined to the traditional "market failure" or "government failure" or to the issue of "externalities." The entire set of issues must be viewed in comprehensively, in terms of the development process in its broadest sense, going far beyond economic growth.

Conclusions

A number of important conclusions can be drawn from the past and present. First, there is no such thing as a purely neutral or autonomous state. Every state is embedded in the society it governs and is closely linked to and penetrated by social forces. The state is dependent on the economy, whose resources allow it to function. It does not exist in a political or power vacuum. It is a reflection of the balance of power within the society. All these circumstances influence the state in defining and fulfilling its functions. A number of the factors that created a "strong" state are now fading away in the new era of global development. In the past, the entrepreneurs of weaker countries used the state as a source of capital, or an instrument for protecting their markets from foreign competition. This kind of state involvement may disappear all too fast.

Second, the role of the state and the market cannot be examined in isolation from the achieved level of development. Less developed countries have built more invasive states because of their weaker position in the global economy. The intention was to reconstruct their economies and create better trade positions for themselves with the help of the state. A development-oriented state can be defined in different ways: as a government for which the goals of economic development have top priority, as a state that is simultaneously redistributive and repressive, or as one that adopts a policy of development with human face, combating poverty and emphasizing social objectives.

Third, a high level of state involvement does not preclude a future predominance of market relations. A number of industrial countries (including France and Japan) having successfully industrialized, then turned to more open policies, while depending on a state role in helping active industrial adjustment. As economic development is the sum total of economic activity by economic agents—government, business, and individuals—the quality of the economic agent is an important issue. The role of governments in this may be indispensable. For the main economic players, the state is a market instrument.

Fourth, the role of the state must also be seen in terms of external challenges presented by new sources of interconnection, such as internationally integrated global production of transnational corporations, various types of capital movement, greater dependence on trade in goods and services, and the international flows of information. In principle, the state has every power to disrupt these processes, but the domestic cost of doing so would be very high. The state may have less power than it had to deal with the unpredictable, and often adverse, influence of these factors on the domestic economy and society in general. Most of the states in the world economy have far less power than the key industrial countries to deal with the domestic consequences of exchange-rate fluctuations and speculative capital movements. They are the "price takers" in the global economy and may also lack experience and policy instruments, as is the case with new market economies.

Another important institutional change relates to global democratization, which has resulted in a highly diverse system of governance. This has opened up new opportunities for hundreds of millions of people to govern their own lives, but also stimulated political struggles within countries, along ethnic, tribal, or socioeconomic lines. These will increasingly occur around such issues as poverty, exclusion, and income distribution.

One of the central issues is to decide whether democratic or dictatorial regimes are better at serving the purposes of development. In looking at the historical evidence, some important qualifications must be made. Democracy cannot be reduced simply to elections and political parties, least of all in the context of development. It must include respect for human rights, including economic and social rights.

Finally, the microprocesses of development in the world cannot be controlled and managed from global centers or by regional and national bureaucracies. The importance of grassroots institutions, organizations, and activities is growing. Some ideologists of globalization, such as John Naisbitt,[8] suggest that globalization increases the chances for small groups or firms, because they have greater flexibility than larger units. According to Naisbitt, the essence of the global paradox is that the more global or universal humankind becomes, the more "tribal" people act. This reduces the traditional role of the state and changes its functions. "Now, with the electronics revolution, both representative democracy and economies of scale are obsolete. Now everyone can have efficient direct democracy." The fragmentation process, however, is not just the consequence of a "new tribalism," but of the fact that globalization constantly causes marginalization and exclusion, due to its highly unequal character.

Notes

1. We define globalization as the entirety of such universal processes as technological transformation; interdependence caused by mass communications; trade and capital flows; homogenization and standardization of production and consumption; the predominance of the world market in trade, investment, and other corporate transactions; special and institutional integration of markets; and growing identity or similarity of economic regulations, institutions, and policies. Mihály Simai, *The Future of Global Governance.* Washington, DC: USIP, 1994, p. 283.

2. Import substitution strategies, which were seen as the counterpoint to export orientation, had many different origins. They derived from beliefs that the independent nationhood and economic decolonization required protectionism and autocracy. They were also encouraged by the example of some successful development patterns based on inward-looking, import-substituting strategies in the past, such as Germany's or the former Soviet Union's. The rise of an export orientation also has origins other than globalization. They include the failures of import substitution, the pressure of the international financial institutions, and the examples of Japan and Southeast Asia.
3. UNCTAD, *World Investment Report,* 1995.
4. We use the concept of a "technological era" in a meaning similar to the one developed in the theories of long cycles. A technological era is defined first of all by the dominant technologies on which the social production system rests. These are of primary importance in shaping the structure of output and consumption and determining the increase in total factor productivity. Their "logic" and postulates influence skill and employment patterns, investment needs, and so on. They influence the style and quality of life, and transform the systems of organization, infrastructure, information, and entrepreneurship, and the choices available to the society. They radically alter the patterns of the international division of labor and the functioning of the global markets, and may have major consequences for national security and military doctrine.
5. See Michael E. Porter, *The Competitive Advantage of Nations.* New York: Free Press, 990, pp. 1-33.
6. An interesting definition of national competitiveness appeared in the U.S. *Report of the President's Commission on Industrial Competitiveness* in the 1980s: "A nation's competitiveness is that degree to which it can under free and fair market conditions produce goods and services that meet the test of international markets while simultaneously expanding the real incomes of its citizens. Competitiveness at the national level is based on superior productivity performance and the economy's ability to shift output to high productivity areas, which in turn can generate high levels of real wages. Competitiveness is associated with rising living standards, expanding employment opportunities, and the abilities of a nation to maintain its international obligations. It is not just a measure of the nation's ability to sell abroad and to maintain a trade equilibrium."
7. In this context, the modernity syndrome of individuals as understood in the West is defined as follows:
   a. Openness to new experiences, with people and procedures, such as birth control;
   b. Greater independence from traditional authority figures like parents and priests, in favor of leaders of government, public affairs, unions, cooperatives, and so on;

c. Belief in the efficacy of science and medicine, and a general abandonment of passiveness and fatalism in facing life's difficulties;
d. Occupational and educational ambitions for oneself and one's children;
e. A preference for punctuality and interest in careful advance planning;
f. Strong interest and involvement in civic and community affairs and local politics; and
g. Energetic efforts to follow current affairs, with a preference for news of national and international, rather than local, importance

8. Quotations in this paragraph are from John Naisbitt, *Global Paradox.* New York: Avon, 1995, pp. 25, 47.

Section 3 The Urban Challenge

Reino Hjerppe and
Pii Elina Berghäll

The first Habitat Conference was held in Vancouver, Canada, in June 1976, to improve the global human settlements situation of the world's citizens. Adequate shelter is one of the core human needs because so many of the other basic needs satisfied within the household are grouped under the same roof and the agglomerations they constitute. Most factors constituting the quality of life are clustered around human settlements. Habitat I centered around human settlements and its legacy points to the need for further action:

> Rising urbanization and urban poverty, coupled with declining government resources, have rendered implementation of the Vancouver Action Plan extremely problematic. There has also been a lack of commitment to implementation among some donors and governments. Although it is difficult to generalize about trends in the shelter options of the urban poor, it seems on the surface to be a depressing story worldwide. The shelter options of the urban poor are closely linked to trends in urban poverty, which is on the rise (United Nations, 1995).

Over the years, it has been recognized that broader "trends in urban shelter are intimately related to trends in the wider economy. Indeed, one of the clearest lessons of the last twenty years is that significant shelter improvements cannot be achieved in a declining macroeconomic climate."

Although the focus in Habitat I was on shelter and poverty, which certainly are still central issues, twenty years later the Habitat II Conference in Istanbul, in June 1996, has included the urban and urbanization related issues as a whole. For social scientists today, it is increasingly evident that the core of all socioeconomic and political processes related to cities are of fundamental importance to better understand how contemporary society functions and changes. Historical experiences have proved that while cities may not always be healthy places for human beings to live, they are both the natural and necessary consequence of economic and cultural development. A disproportionately large number of achievements in economics, science, literature, music, and other fields, have been accomplished in cities. For economists in particular, the central role played by cities in the process of economic growth has now been widely recognized.

Tomorrow's world will be an urban world. The ongoing urbanization process represents, both in scale and consequence, an unprecedented phenomenon in the history of humanity. Not only will the majority of the world's population live in an urban environment, but megacities will continue to grow. In the political arena, cities are becoming key actors in the national and global societies. Indeed,

> urbanization is an inevitable trend which forces countries to face mounting problems of homelessness, crime, unemployment, deterioration of the living environment, etc. Habitat II provides a chance for countries rich and poor to exchange ideas and experiences on how the enormous challenges can best be responded to. Awareness of the trends and developments make them better prepared to address the problems and enable them to adopt efficient effective strategies well in advance. This could ease pressure and contribute to global security and stability. The clear establishment of development priorities will help direct resources into the most rewarding areas. Both developed and developing countries stand to gain, since problems such as massive international migration, pollution, crime, political and economic instability do not respect frontiers.[1]

There is a serious gap in understanding urban issues. During the 1980s, there was a decline in interest toward urban research and, consequently, only few countries have a sound basis for urban policy. This conforms with what Krugman says,

> while neoclassical urban systems theory may suggest that competition among city developers yield optimal results, the more recent literature does not contain any such suggestion . . . (however) . . . . The definite conclusion is that whatever the changes made in economic policies (including trade liberalization, decentralization and improvement in transport infrastructure), their implications for urban and regional development within countries are an important, neglected issue.[2]

Impact of Economic and Political Globalization

This section of *Cities Fit for People* attempts to evaluate the implications of the ongoing global economic and political processes of urbanization on people – the citizens. These processes include, for example, globalization, regionalization, liberalization, decentralization and democratization. It is not always easy to make a distinction between economic and political processes. For instance, liberalization of the economy is often related to political developments. Many new political phenomena, like the tendency toward democratization, have emerged as a result of the end of the cold war. Also, rapid and extensive technological changes are introducing many new economic issues. Economic forces, like the development of productivity, natural resources, and relative prices, shape the comparative advantages of different locations. Also the increasing mobility of capital and transnational corporations are some of the dominant tendencies. Structural adjustment policies, implemented since the early 1980s, are of specific relevance to developing countries as an almost all-encompassing trend. It is quite commonly believed that many of the current tendencies weaken the role of the nation–state. Although economic comparative advantages do not always conform to national boundaries, borders are important in shaping the economic and political landscape by creating global barriers to international trade.

What is clear is that as a result of these trends, the role and management of cities will be different and perhaps more complex in the future. The trends have to be taken into account in urban policy-making. In contrast to the laissez-faire policy attitudes of the 1980s, we believe that the quality and type of city management can make a difference. There is ample evidence to prove that good policy at the national level can make significant contributions to economic development. This principle should apply at the local level also. However, this is a rather undisputed fact. The controversy becomes more apparent when one considers what kind of policy, or intervention should be applied and how it should be implemented.

Although important, this section does not review congestion and quality of environment, two of the major negative urban externalities. It concentrates on the economic and political processes of urbanization and their implications.

Urbanization, by concentrating huge numbers of people in a relatively short period to the same location, is a highly visible process. Rapid population growth looms behind urbanization and ever since the early days of industrialization, people have moved to the cities in the hope of improving their odds at gaining a livelihood. According to UN estimates, the majority of the world's population will live in urban areas by 2005.

The UN forecasts that world population will reach approximately 10 billion in 2050. The pace of world population growth is, however, declining. At its peak during the 1960s, annual population growth reached 2.4 percent; it is now 1.6 percent. The most recent data on the decline in fertility rates imply that the figure of 10 billion may actually be a slight overestimation. The UN center for Human Settlements forecasts that 3.7 billion people will be added to the current 5.8 billion by 2030. This is a huge increase, of which 90 percent is projected to flow to urban areas, and particularly to developing world settlements.

There are large regional differences both in degree of urbanization and in urban growth rates. The most rapid urbanization phases seem to have already been passed in many parts of the world. However, only 30 percent of China is urbanized and rapid urbanization resulting from economic restructuring is likely to have an effect on global averages. The most recent UN projections, however, indicate that the pace of Chinese urbanization is also leveling off and will further slow down in the future.

> All countries in all regions have experienced sustained urbanization as annual growth rates of approximately 4 percent have added 45 to 50 million new residents to the cities every year. Yet, the global picture shows considerable differences in rates of urbanization. Rapid population growth and rural-urban migration in developing countries had shifted already by 1975 the balance of urban population in their favor. By 1990, the share of developing countries had increased to 61 percent, and by 2025 they are estimated to have four times as many urban dwellers as the developed countries, i.e., 77 percent of urban dwellers will be living in developing countries. Excluding the Arab countries, the rate of urbanization is the highest in Africa and Asia, the two least urbanized continents.[3]

The cities of the world are entering into a new stage of development. It is not just the size of the city populations that is growing everywhere—and especially in multiethnic states—but also their cultural diversity. They are also becoming more diverse both socially and economically, reflecting partly the different pace of industrialization in the different countries of the world. As in the past, many become will be industrial centers, but there will be also "service cities" based on traditional, modern, technological, commercial, administrative, and other activities. The diversity will be apparent for many decades in the cohabitation of ultramodern districts and slums. Cities are also characterized by the two poles of society: poverty and wealth.

Urbanization and Economic Development

The central role played by urban areas in international trade, economic growth and development has been increasingly recognized. Consequently, there has recently been a revival of interest in the spatial aspects of economic growth and of those related to urbanization. The need to integrate "location" more consistently to economic theory has been proposed. It has been argued that economic theory has proceeded in the past without paying attention to the location of economic activity:

> the analysis of international trade makes virtually no use of insights from economic geography or location theory. . . . the tendency of international economists to turn a blind eye to the fact that countries both occupy and exist in space . . . had some serious costs. These lie not so much in the lack of realism—all economic analysis is more or less unrealistic—as in the exclusion of important issues and, above all, of important sources of evidence[4]

Furthermore, researchers of urban issues have recently started to more widely recognize the strong relationship between urbanization and economic growth. From the 1950s, or perhaps even much earlier during the first industrial revolution, a negative perspective of the development of cities—the so-called "urban bias" view—dominated thinking. Accordingly, policies were directed to slowing down the growth of big cities to reach more balanced regional growth. Although many people still regard urbanization as detrimental,[5] it is now argued that this has been a misconception, and indeed, to slow city growth may also retard national economic growth. Furthermore, in spite of past efforts to limit city growth with regional policies, the growth of cities seems to persist.[6] However, neither mainstream economists nor other researchers currently advocate a return to the so-called urban biased policies which were common especially in the developing countries until the structural adjustment policies of the 1980s.

The correlation between urban and economic growth is more than 70 percent.[7] The World Bank estimates that 60 percent of the value of developing countries' output and 80 percent of the growth in its value are generated in urban areas. Indeed, the productivity gap between urban and rural areas seems to be widening. In general, the poorer the country, the more central a city is to its economic development.

There are various factors that generate economic growth in cities. The economic benefits of urbanization are called agglomeration economies. They are created by a combination of factors present in cities that reduce distances and transport costs and enable increasing returns to be utilized. They also facilitate specialization and the division of labor. Cities provide entrepreneurs with a pool of skilled labor, and offer, in general, a greater variety of specialized inputs and services. An additional factor contributing to agglomeration economies is knowledge spillovers between companies which are more frequent in cities than in less populated areas. These spillovers may consist of technological factors as well as marketing and management ideas. In sum, the benefits of urbanization can be said to arise from expanded market size and the more fruitful environment for the emergence and employment of ideas. Economies of scale, specialization, and competition benefit from the increased market size. Ideas emerge because knowledge, even in the information age, is still location specific and diversity contributes to economic growth. All these result in the multiplier accelerator phenomenon being much stronger in the big cities than in the economy in general.

Primary production, such as agriculture, hunting, and fishing is mostly land or territory intensive. Industrialization, however, is capital intensive and leads to village formation and the growth of urban agglomerations. In general, industrialization and urbanization are positively correlated.

To a large extent, the location of cities appears to depend on historical coincidences. This is especially true for industries that are based on some specific new product idea. Not only is high tech spatially concentrated, often it is the low-tech enterprises that can benefit the most from agglomeration economies of scale.

It has to be noted, however, that national economic growth and city growth do not always coincide. Especially in economic downturns and structural adjustments, some cities fare worse than others. There are examples of cities that during past decades lost entire manufacturing industries that once were their prime engines of urban growth. It is also an open question whether the volatility of structural changes has recently increased and whether the world has subsequently become more "uncertain" as some people tend to think. Increasing capital mobility could be a reason for the more rapid structural changes.

The causes of urbanization – whether they have been push or pull factors – have varied, although it has been argued in the past that economic pull factors of cities were the primary causes for urban migration. Economic benefits and the cultural variety of cities, together with increasing productivity in agriculture releasing surplus rural labor, are still major factors creating rural to urban migration flows. In spite of various restrictions on city migration, the agricultural productivity growth in China has pushed out a large share of rural population who now float between the cities and rural areas. In the economies in transition some reversal of these flows has happened.

Taking the considerable multiplier effects into account, perhaps the growth of cities should not be hindered at all, or national economic development, as a consequence, could suffer. Indeed, as will be discussed in the section on urban management, economic growth priorities have prevailed over regional policy objectives, which in many countries have been secondary to industrial goals. Recently, for example, in Korea, however, the emphasis shifted to favor regional industrial policy, as it has been recognized that unbalanced spatial development implies an undeveloped domestic market, which could be a major obstacle to the country's long-term economic growth.[9]. Furthermore, urban growth has negative externalities which needs to be taken into account.

Issues Affecting World Citizens

Despite all the benefits of urbanization, are not cities ultimately becoming too large to be governed? Such underlying fears have upheld the negative attitudes on urbanization in favor of idyllic views of a harmoniously developing countryside where people lead happy lives. Especially the so-called megacities with populations exceeding eight million inhabitants are on the increase. However, at the moment nobody seems to know how big a megacity can grow. If people prefer to live in megacities and if it cannot be proved that their growth is the result of a gross misallocation of resources, then why should urbanization be slowed down? The growing world population has to live somewhere and if the choice is the big city, there basically should be no objections.

To some extent, the fears are certainly very well founded. The negative aspects of urbanization include poverty, slums, crime, traffic congestion, pollution, unemployment, and street children. Urban congestion and alienation, having socioeconomic and psychological consequences, are increasing also in the developing countries. With unemployment the only likely future for the growing youth, resignation is replacing optimism of the future. Crime in the urban environment has been linked to democracy and the urban way life.

Under the mounting pressure of problems, many urban governments may fear that their cities will grow too large to be governed. The poorest of the poor in cities live in appalling, undignified conditions of destitution that verge on the brink of survival. Undernourishment often prevents the poor from utilizing their full potential in earning their livelihood. Their living environments are often congested and dangerously polluted, and they lack access to clean water and sanitation. Despite such common deplorable conditions in urban, especially periurban areas, cities continue to attract migrants from rural areas and to grow.

Although at first glance the situation may resemble that of the early industrialization period in Europe, when cities had high mortality rates because of their unhealthy conditions, it is actually much worse. During the early days of industrialization, cities attracted labor from rural areas because there was demand. If the push factors are more important than pull factors in bringing migrants to urban areas, claims of "overurbanization" are more justified in the context of many developing countries today. Even though migrants cannot be blamed for moving into urban areas if they consider themselves better off as a result, this exodus may not necessarily lead to a corresponding economic growth in a city large enough to mitigate the adverse effects of urban growth.

Like the benefits of urbanization, negative externalities have multiplying accelerators.

In principle, an optimal city size is achieved when an equilibrium has been reached between the positive and negative externalities of the city. Externalities continually change, making them difficult to estimate. Therefore the concept of optimal size has so far had relatively little use in practice.

Urban Poverty

Poverty represents a waste – the failure to capture the potential output from existing resources. Coupled with crime and corruption, the negative impacts of urban poverty and ill health on the productivity of people further reduce the efficiency of third world economies.

Recently, poverty has increased in Latin America and Eastern Europe but decreased in China and India.[10] In Sub-Saharan Africa, urban poverty is growing in relation to rural poverty, and it is likely that income gaps will further widen at even faster rates. Poverty in the cities increases as the transformation of rural poverty, and solutions are needed to attack the problem at both urban and rural levels.

For the urban poor, there are few ways to escape poverty. The options available are usually migration to another urban area in the home country or in a foreign one, community participation, or employment in the informal sector which may function as a safety net.

It is often argued that cities increase poverty but, as mentioned above, in reality we are witnessing the urbanization of rural poverty. However, there appears to be somewhat conflicting views on the causality of linkages. Some argue that it is not the poorest population who migrate to the cities, but rather the young and the educated from all income echelons.[11] Others claim that migrants mainly come from the high- and low-income brackets of the rural areas. Although some claim that urban poverty is increasing because the rural poor are moving to cities and that the real problem is thus rural poverty, others argue that the newcomers mostly gain employment. Thus they are not overrepresented in the informal sectors of the cities and end up better off than the poorest urban citizens. In any case, the poor may still be better off in the urban areas. Indeed, it has been pointed out that poverty does not increase proportionately to urbanization, but less and the proportion of the poor tends to decline as the city's population increases. Fourteen percent of the world's urban population are classified as poor, while a third of rural inhabitants are considered as such. These two aspects imply that poverty has not increased as a result of urbanization; a view that has been advocated in the urban bias literature. On the contrary, poverty – in the absence of urbanization – be might much worse.

Often, urban poverty results from the vicious circle in which the urban people are trapped. Thus, the main problem is not the attempt to integrate newcomers into the urban economy as they are not over-represented in the informal sector. In the cities, the poor are affected more severely than the urban averages with regard to education, health, nutrition, family planning, and other social services. The adverse conditions compound poverty where a combination of various factors results in low productivity and therefore lower incomes.

Consequently, productivity growth and improved technology alone are not sufficient to alleviate poverty or break the vicious circle; capacity or human capital building of the poor is needed. The Indian government, for instance, has found that improving human capital is a much better form of helping the poor than outright handouts. The best safety nets lie in capacity building and human development, which the poor can employ also within the informal sector. Given the opportunity, the poor are good at providing housing and building cities, but these efforts may be frustrated by obstacles put in their way by their own governments. Mechanisms should be developed to assist the poor, not to harass them.[12] Unfortunately, since periurban centers consist of mostly illegally occupied areas, they are not included in urban plans, and thus are often simply ignored in connection with improvement efforts. Reinforced local planning, which might be facilitated by decentralization, is needed, although it is unlikely to materialize without political will and the means to tackle poverty.

Street Children

One of the most heartbreaking phenomena giving specificity to the conspicuous nature of urban poverty is the increasing number of street children. This phenomenon is not only detrimental to balanced urban growth, but is a major source of prostitution, drug abuse, and criminal activities in the cities.

The issue of street children is at the heart of urbanization and human settlements, although it is not always the result of poverty and lack of adequate shelter that they leave home. Leaving home for them is often a way of escaping from abuse within the household. The role of men in the family and the worldwide erosion of family ties should also be in focus. Although street children in Latin America have been in the limelight, their numbers are on the rise, especially in the transitory economies where it is a new phenomenon, and they can be found in any large city in the developing world. There are four different categories of street children. The first two groups, although they may have left school, still live at home. The two other groups live on the street or sometimes in shelters for homeless children provided by various aid agencies. Although street kids are often blamed for crime, it is interesting to note that the most violent street children are those who still have a home to go to and who thus should be relatively secure, unlike the children living on the street with no security against exploitation and abuse. The fourth group consists of the children of street children unable to look after their own offspring, thus creating a vicious circle. The insecurity and lack of stability that rule their lives is directly related to the lack of adequate shelter and sustainable urban development.

Most countries are not equipped to deal with the street child problem in a humane and future oriented way. As fertility rates climb, the higher becomes the risk of children being affected by poverty. Housing policies have failed to provide adequate titles, incentives, investment or planning and the educational systems have failed to keep children in school. Poverty alleviation is not enough to tackle the various problems. What is needed is family planning policies, education, and, ultimately, urban land reform. Furthermore, institutional assistance should endeavor to protect the street orphans, not discriminate against this vulnerable group.

Employment Policies

Although most people employed in the informal sector work long hours every day of the week, the common drawback of informal employment, because of its low productivity and value added, is the low income levels which are barely enough for subsistence. Still one of the main causes of rising urban poverty is unemployment. Increasing opportunities for higher education may not always be the remedy to persistent unemployment as is indicated by the fact that urban unemployment among the highly educated is on the raise, causing frustration and depression. Governments should be more aware of the high costs of unemployment, which amount to much more than just direct allowances. Safety nets as such are not sufficient. Improved incomes, more forceful employment, and the provision of basic infrastructure and services could do much to alleviate poverty. In this context, the following recommendations are offered.

Often, urbanization is seen to increase the growth of the informal sector. Recent experiences show that the unskilled labor force is increasing faster than the absorption capacities of the cities. In spite of the fact that urbanization opens up new opportunities for increasing skills faster than the rural environment, the urbanization process also adds to the growth of the informal sector. But the capacities of the cities to adjust are not sufficient.

It is a common belief that the informal sector greases the wheels of economic activity in the urban economy and helps to maintain its growth momentum. In this regard, it has been argued that the functioning of the informal sector should be facilitated, because urban productivity cannot be increased without increasing the productivity of the urban informal sector. Types of infrastructure and services that can increase productivity of the informal sector and which are employment generating include water supply, drainage, and flood control, transport systems and accessibility, waste management, and electrification.

Despite frequent references to the "informal sector" in the literature on development, the concept itself has been criticized as too broad, often misleading, and perhaps even totally useless. Because of the scarcity of data, the size and other relevant figures of the informal sector usually have to be estimated. Sometimes, activities tend to remain informal because incomes are higher, although income levels on the average are below the official taxation level. In contrast, the black or parallel economy (in India, for instance) consists largely of individuals and corporations operating in the formal economy, not the informal sector. Large organized industry and trade may pay taxes, but questions are invariably raised as to what extent the total liability is met.

Moreover, the apparent efficiency of the informal sector is often a consequence of the fact that regulations have been used to extract bribes instead of improving economic development. In India, organized industry and trade have access to subsidized finance, development inputs and land. In sharp contrast, the market cost inputs, finance, and services are mobilized by the informal sector. Although the informal sector may be accused of misappropriating collective goods such as street pavements, they often pay much higher prices for inputs and services than formal sector actors, although not officially to public authorities.[13]

The specific role of the urban informal sector is to be the source of jobs and income for the working poor. Between a third and one half of the jobs in many major cities of the developing world are in this sector. However, the informal sector should not be considered as a viable option to the employment question because it combines poverty and misery with illegal actions.

Global Economic Factors

Both economic and political forces are shaping the global urbanization process. Economic forces are often placed under the label of liberalization of trade and capital flows, which have been coupled with deregulation and efforts to reduce the relative size of the public sector in the economy. Political developments have been mainly shaped by the end of the cold war. In reality, both economic and political forces interact with each other.

Globalization has been defined as a compression of the world, not only as far as new patterns of production are concerned, financial markets are integrated, and cultures are becoming more homogeneous, but also in regard to the subjective perception of the world by individuals.[14]

Complex forms of cross-border activities increasingly characterize the international system. Globalization includes changes in:

- markets; that is, a rise in the role played by technology-intensive products and services, capital movements, transnational corporations, and changing patterns of trade;
- culture; that is, ethical, legal, and political values, as well as occupational subcultures and cosmopolitan people; and
- security; that is, new global weapons, growing military interdependence, recognized sovereignty, and new threats on the global environment.

One important reason for new globalism is that large parts of the world have become industrialized during the past decades. Global production and competition have increased. Firms increasingly design global corporate strategies and obviously, international trade and capital flows are affected. On the other hand, a large part of the developing world still remains "not so global" and therefore globalization is more a phenomenon of the developed world.

At the same time, there are "new regional" tendencies, which have emerged in a multipolar world, while the "old regionalism" developed in the bipolar cold war context. Old regionalism was created from above (i.e., top-down by the superpowers), whereas "new regionalism" is a more spontaneous process, originating from "below," where constituent states are the main actors. As demonstrated in European integration, the objectives in the new regional tendencies have also been more comprehensive than those within the old regionalism. The new regional coalitions aim for more than the establishment of pure trading blocs. New regionalism can also be "open." For instance, Southeast Asian integration is open to all members of World Trade Organization – and not merely to the countries in the region.

The diminishing role of the nation–state, the increasing importance of regions, individual cities, and localities are believed to be the implications of globalism and regionalism. In the new world, nation–states no longer have the means to pursue certain policies even if they wished to do so, because technological innovations and capital flows, for instance, spill over national boundaries more easily than before. Lowering trade barriers presumably also reduces the importance of the nation as an economic entity and enhances the opportunities of more "natural" economic regions such as cities.

As the role of nation–states declines, cities become increasingly important elements in world economic development, global organization, the global economic and social system, and in production for global markets. The system is a dynamic process susceptible to changes in communication and the economy, and so on. The acceleration and the spread of the global process that has made cities into centers of human activity, is both the cause and the effect of highly complex socioeconomic changes in the functioning of societies. As centers of innovation, production, and services, cities and their subsequent roles are affected by information, capital, and labor flows on an international and national level. Increasingly, cities also compete with each other for investments, budgetary resources, foreign capital, and for specific functions in the global market such as financial or trade centers.

As one important causal factor, the development of communication links has brought about a new interconnectedness of the world community. The information revolution may have strengthened the attractiveness of urban centers and further hastened the pace of urbanization, although the opposite could also result as communication technologies reduce distances and the relative advantage of proximity in cities. New communication techniques allow cities to combine networks; some are capable of forming global networks, but others may not be able to compete and are excluded. In principle, even small urban agglomerations can be "world cities," as more developed communication facilities and progressively rapid transportation networks release cities from the locational constraints of the past.

The patterns of savings and investments are also changing. Savings are becoming increasingly institutionalized through the development of banks and pension funds. At the same time, there is an added risk that more mobile capital threatens local markets with abrupt changes. The cities require greater investment because building infrastructure in cities is capital intensive. Consumption patterns are influenced by urbanization. New urban consumer markets—characterized by greater stratification and standardized consumption patterns requiring new marketing and distribution patterns—are developing. Thus the institutional characteristics and conditions of economic growth are experiencing rapid change due to the renewed role of the main actors.

The political map of the world has been transformed rapidly, which has been considered as one factor of the strong global forces favoring democratization, which also plays a role in urban development by strengthening the opportunities for decentralization.

The new type of interplay between economic and political forces present decision makers with extra challenges and constraints. For instance, in the economic sphere, capital is mobile while labor is relatively immobile, thus tilting the balance of political power and distribution of income in favor of capital. In particular, in the context of urbanization, large cities are becoming increasingly independent of their surroundings and more tied to a global city network. Consequently, it has become necessary to reconsider the distribution of power between central and local levels of government. Urban governments should have the means and power to be able to respond not only to global challenges, but also to implement the necessary policies to combat the mounting local problems, such as organized crime and terrorist activities, that may have international origins.

In these contexts, the management of cities is becoming a more complex, highly specialized, and multidimensional task of governance. New policy paradigms push for decentralization. In certain countries, cities are competing with the central governments in the field of economic distribution. In many parts of the world, the entrepreneurial city is emerging as a key national—and in certain cases international—interest group, and the political city may already be the dominant force in the struggle for national political power.

In the new global environment, multinationals, already globalized to a large extent, may play a central role. However, multinationals are also becoming decentralized to be able to respond more readily to the variations in local demand. The diversity of experiences and patterns of development of the cities create confusion, and it is difficult to predict future changes. But global functions should not be overemphasized; the majority of production is still directed to domestic markets and local transactions will always remain important.

The welfare effects of the growth process are also changing, although this is an area where researchers have not been able to give full account. Although urban poverty is rising, it is important to add that a new urban middle class is emerging and growing in some developing world cities. This middle class represents a major factor in the domestic market, with its special needs of consumption, education, transport, culture, and in other areas related to the quality of life and participation in politics.

Liberalization

In the developed countries, central governments still have considerable leverage with regard to economic policies. Ever since the debt crisis of 1982, developing countries have, however, been more or less involuntarily saddled with economic stabilization and structural adjustment policies as a condition for the renegotiation and rescheduling of their debts, new lending and debt cancellation. These policies influence urbanization. It is well documented how overvalued exchange rates; public expenditure favoring capital cities; and credit allocation to urban areas contributed to an urban bias in numerous countries. Some case studies of developing countries have pointed out the consequences on urban development of the austerity measures that include a reduction in financial resources and jobs in the public sector, and in investment opportunities. Structural adjustment has been an influential factor tending to reduce the share of production of goods that cannot be traded in the economy in favor of goods that can be traded. It reduces the urban bias of import substituting economies if it succeeds in shifting the terms of trade to favor agricultural and export production. Thus structural adjustment should, in principle, reduce at least the size of central cities in favor of secondary municipalities. In certain parts of the world, medium-sized cities may therefore be experiencing the most rapid growth as population expansion in megacities eventually slows down. Current trends of urbanization point to the increasing importance of secondary and minor cities, with implications for rural development. Whether this is an overall trend still needs to be confirmed by empirical studies.

The sources of finance for local governments vary substantially from country to country. In addition, the financing of city activities is an increasingly complex problem that results from the speed and scope of the urbanization process and increasing capital mobility. It influences the national financial system as the whole, and it must be dealt with in this national framework. It connects the urban process with national fiscal policies, on the one hand, and with capital markets, on the other hand. The development of capital markets and decentralization should therefore be harmonized. In most cases, local governments need borrowing. Economic liberalization has broadened the scope of financing available for urbanization. It has often been suggested that capital circulating in international markets should be tapped to finance good causes. However, for individual developing countries, the recently available financing has increasingly been short-term private capital, "hot money," which, because of the high risks involved, should be employed only to a limited extent to finance urban growth.

External capital is mainly available to local governments only when there are sufficient guarantees of repayment, such as a central government bailout. Even in the presence of an implicit bailout, decentralization may increase macroeconomic instability through overborrowing by local governments and thus create conditions for a new developing country debt crisis, especially when sovereign capital is employed. In the absence of decentralization, on the other hand, central governments may restrain local government borrowing, and to reduce local public demand and expenditure to prevent overheating in the face of large capital inflows. In other words, even though external capital might be in abundant supply, it may not be available to local urban development because the central government may wish to control the money supply. Thus the very abundance of capital on the country level may reduce its availability for urban development. To minimize financial risks, domestic resources and savings have to provide the bulk of funds to finance urban growth.

Consequently, central governments should develop measures to reduce reliance on short-term external capital for infrastructure finance, and to control the flows of short-term finance. In the absence of an implicit or explicit bailout promise, local governments should have sufficient ability to raise fiscal revenues. To enhance this on the supply side, domestic capital markets, especially pension funds, can be used to raise the availability of long-term capital on the local market. Financial liberalization is risky for countries in their early stages of financial market development. Financial restraint and controls on the cost of capital by surveillance authorities may be necessary for the development of reputational capital on financial markets in order to develop institutions that supply local long-term credits for urban economic activity. Central governments can also develop incentives for foreign direct investment into urban development, while preventing the formation of private monopolies and ensuring sufficient competition. On the demand side, the scope for borrowing from domestic markets can be expanded by improving legal rights to raise local tax revenue, and by reducing central government borrowing and crowding out. Finally, local governments can reduce their borrowing costs through cooperation with other localities and urban governments.

Decentralization Trends

Cities are emerging as important political centers. Therefore, urbanization is changing the character of the political process and cities may gain importance at the expense of the state to the extent that some researchers even predict a return to city–states in the future. Many countries are still, however, predominantly centralized, reflecting a high concentration of power. With decentralization on the agenda, the political balance is changing. In the economic field, cities are becoming management and service centers for societies, while manufacturing activities decline in urban areas. Overall, hierarchies are changing at a rapid speed, although implementation of decentralization may have been retarded by the lack of political will to delegate power and responsibilities, particularly in financial matters, and to increase revenue sharing.

The advantages of decentralization for government can be similar to those that competition introduced in the private sector. Decentralization can help identify the preferences for public goods of the different population groups, improve local governments' supply of these goods, enabling taxation or pricing to be set according to the benefit they enjoy. Because taxpayers are mobile and may move to the municipality that best reflects their preferences, the final outcome will resemble that of the market mechanism. Furthermore, decentralization has been seen as a means to improve efficiency and urban service delivery, allowing for experimentation and improving incentives for better performance.[15]

In the developing world, the responsibilities of local governments vary greatly. For example, local governments in South Korea have mainly executed orders from higher authorities, while locally elected authorities in India have had considerable independence on financial matters. The global trend seems to point toward an increase in the share of responsibilities. If decentralization is used to define some form of transfer of political and fiscal power and responsibilities to local government, only 16 percent of 75 developing and transitional countries with populations over 5 million have refrained from venturing into any form of decentralization. In principle, there are four different types of decentralization.[16]

Thus privatization is seen as a natural part of the decentralization process. In spite of all efforts to decontrol, centralization is still the predominant pattern of governance and the developing countries tend to be more pronounced in this form of governance than the developed ones.

Privatization

An important issue is the role of the state and the market within the economic factors influencing urbanization. The forces affecting the development of cities are too complex to be applied to either a set formula or to top-down control. To justify privatization, it is often argued that urban policy makers should recognize the superior ability of free markets to handle complexity and generate information. The free market entails competition among localities for firms and citizens. It facilitates individual choice without top-down control. It has also been suggested that higher utility levels may be reached by setting prices according to efficiency criteria instead of equity and by using privatization and localization.

However, the very presence of cities suggests that there are important positive externalities involved. On the other hand, there are also negative externalities, such as the higher rates of crime, pollution, and congestion in urban areas, and therefore government intervention is regarded as necessary for balanced urban development.

In most of the developing countries neither the state nor the market may function properly. Markets are embedded in the characteristics of society, and they function in the framework given by society. In other words, privatization can rarely change anything if public entities are already functioning as private businesses. Therefore, parallel to privatization, it is necessary to ensure that competition and adequate regulation for the efficient functioning of private and public companies are present. A privatized monopoly may be worse than a public monopoly. Competition would at least reduce monopoly rents. Deregulation would not necessarily change anything either, if regulations do not command respect. Deregulation is needed to abolish ineffective regulations which only undermine the authority of public institutions, or worse, are used to extract bribes and benefits.

Therefore privatization and deregulation as such do not necessarily eliminate problems. On the contrary, there is the danger that the resulting severe budget constraints may force governments to privatize in situations where adequate competition and enforcement of appropriate regulations cannot be ensured. Thus the risk of creating private monopolies exists, with adverse consequences for the efficiency of infrastructure service provision and functioning of urban areas.

It has been argued that the global privatization trend has not reached housing yet, although it can be regarded as an alternative solution with considerable potential to solve housing problems in the developing countries.[17]

Gender Dimension

Perhaps it has not been adequately recognized so far that urbanization and its outcomes are highly gender oriented. From a purely formal point of view, analyzing urbanization with a gender variable can be considered to convey important and relevant information for policy makers. This is because gender is an influential factor in the decision to migrate. This gendering of urbanization varies a great deal between places; in South Asia, North Africa, the Middle East, and many parts of Sub-Saharan Africa, migration is male dominated, while the opposite is true in East and Southeast Asia, Latin America, and the Caribbean. The extent of female participation in agriculture, the demand for female workers in urban areas, and the gender ideology specific to the area, determine migration and headship patterns. Although income is an important motive for female migration, it is critical to recognize that women perhaps may not move to towns of their own volition but, especially in the case of young unmarried women, at the behest of, or through pressure from their rural families. Furthermore, male migration, in an increasing number of cases, is a polite word for desertion, which is a male rather than a female survival strategy. Male migration mostly reduces the household resources more than its expenses.

It is difficult to consider the various gender aspects of urban growth and development without reference to such household circumstances as transformations in household employment. These are very much interconnected because transformations in household structure, for instance, have implications on the supply of labor which is dictated by social customs and traditional roles of female workers.

In designing policies for human settlements, it should be recognized that the number of households headed by women is increasing to a noticeable extent, both in the developing and the developed countries. This is often the result of gender selective urbanization or migration patterns. Although the "feminization" of household headship during urbanization may bring about changes in gender roles and relations, it can by no means be regarded as signaling unilateral improvement in the status of women. Nor is poverty necessarily a cause or characteristic of female headship, although increased poverty and unemployment have been seen as giving rise to female headship which, in turn, is seen to intensify poverty. However, households headed by women are not necessarily the poorest of the poor. Women use their wages more for the benefit of the household, spending more on education and nutrition than male breadwinners, who sometimes contribute only 50 percent of their earnings to domestic needs.

Management of Urban Change

In the 1960s, market failures were strongly emphasized, and interventionist government policies were common and popular. In the first Habitat Conference in 1976, planning and the public sector were considered the essential tools for urban policy making. However, during the 1970s, the concept of government failure came to the forefront, paving the way for the privatization counterrevolution. At the height of the liberal counterrevolution, numerous policy analysts demanded for radical reductions in the size of government. At the end of the 1980s, a more balanced view gradually emerged. The examples of the rapidly growing newly industrialized countries of Southeast Asia have provided support to the view that success may require determinant policy action on the part of the government.

Some general theoretical views on the appropriate roles of the government have emerged. To enable private economic agents to rely on policies, they should be credible, stable, and predictable, without being too rigid to prevent necessary change. Moreover, to release the suppressed capacities of individuals and enterprises, enabling, and more recently, empowerment strategies have gained ground. The major task now is to find the appropriate government policies, but their identification is not a straightforward task. The controversies involved have been—and still are—considerable. But certainly the search for appropriate policies and their implementation appear to be very relevant challenges.

Because political instability may discourage investment and economic growth, governments tend to respond to political influence. Consequently, interest groups can extract benefits from the central government by destabilizing or by threatening to destabilize. In the attempt to maintain political stability, urban areas in many political regimes have been given priority over the hinterlands. This is what the urban bias view advocates. Urbanization in itself may cause the concentration of political tensions and has therefore distinct correlation to rioting, for example. At the extreme, the expansion of massive cities with little economic function can accelerate despite the fact that their existence is mostly based on the extraction of governmental handouts. This type of urban bias is most evident in unstable regimes or dictatorships where the major cities seem to be on the average 50 percent larger than cities in stable democracies. The process is self-reinforcing because, the stronger the neglect of hinterlands, the more unstable the regimes tend to be. Thus political centralization can be both the cause and the consequence of urbanization.

Decentralization presents both opportunities and risks. Opportunities include the potential gains from a more efficient assignment of responsibilities and revenues between the national and subnational governments and greater accountability of local officials. Among the potential risks are the possibility that the central government will have difficulty in implementing important welfare improving and economy strengthening reforms effectively; the possibility that subnational governments will not be technically and institutionally able to carry out their new responsibilities efficiently; and that there will be reduced fiscal discipline because of political pressure from the newly elected subnational government officials on the central government to increase transfers. Decentralization should normally be accompanied by increased revenue generating powers for local authorities.

The establishment of the right incentives for efficiency and fiscal discipline in the national and/or subnational transfer system is particularly important. Care should thus be taken that decentralization and the transfer of revenue generating powers to local governments do not pose a threat to national economic stability and development. The development of capital markets and decentralization should also be synchronized. Local governments should develop their borrowing by, for instance, centralizing it to reduce costs. In the absence of an implicit or explicit bailout promise, local governments should have sufficient ability to raise fiscal revenues as guarantee for borrowing.

Ideally, a nation is composed of municipalities and regional governments able to create the resources necessary to keep up with international competition and service provision. Local service production should be financed by local taxation and user charges. While local authorities may be responsible for welfare services, such as health care, education, and social services, it is the responsibility of the national government to provide equal opportunities for people to develop their abilities and basic social security. But regional transfers from the central government to local governments should be reduced in order to counteract the resource drain from internationally competitive clusters and industries. Municipalities and regional governments could be more self-sufficient.

As a general rule, local authorities should have responsibility for all functions that include incentives to work effectively toward the local common good. These incentives can also be created with the help of central transfers which should always be structured to reward good fiscal performance. The objective of decentralization should ensure that citizens are able to deal with all administrative matters within their own municipality.

In the former socialist countries, urbanization was caused by forced migration into industrial urban areas. In these budget-oriented economies, heavy industry was prioritized over housing and service industries. Not many resources were available for urban development, as the building of infrastructure was at the bottom of the priority list. At the time of transformation, urbanization levels were much lower than in the West, and rural–urban migration can be expected to increase in the future. Now, these countries face a challenge to build up decentralized structures of governance.

The trend to decentralize has various implications for urban management at the local city level. Economic liberalization and globalization have reduced the dependence of cities on their surrounding areas and the national government. Cities have become players on the international and national scenes, competing for foreign and domestic capital, budgetary resources, investments, employment and income creating ventures, as well as for specific functions in the global market, such as their relative importance as financial or trade centers. In many countries, cities offer a number of incentives for transnational corporations and other entrepreneurs to attract investment. In order to respond more quickly to the rapid pace of development, cities are increasingly operating as private agencies and a growing role has been given to markets in development.

In practice, the weakness of local democracy can be an obstacle to the effective application of the principle of subsidiarity. The coexistence of several independent local government units with their own economic responsibilities, planning competencies, combined with competition for taxpayers, create coordination problems at the top city management. Separate tasks may also create opportunities for local government units as well as privileged groups to adopt free-rider strategies. The weaknesses of land use planning may aggravate these free-rider problems. For instance, because of segregated housing, small communities within an urban region may become tax havens for the rich people, thus free-riding on educational, housing, and infrastructure services of the larger metropolitan urban area.

Although migration to urban areas can provide an escape from rigid traditional rural hierarchies, it also erodes social ties and thus contributes to the weakening of community solidarity. It is a widespread belief that local cooperation in small traditional societies has been more effective than in large urban areas.

In circumstances where the problems caused by the lack of collective responsibility are especially pronounced, there is a necessity to enhance the desire of the people to work for the interest of the public and to preserve collective goods. The present trend toward decentralization, localization, and civic engagement may well serve this purpose. Civic engagement offers an opportunity to restore the pursuit of collective goods and reduce free-riding at the local level. The active involvement of communities in the process of decentralization could provide at least a partial and gradual solution to the problem of misappropriation of collective goods. This necessitates the strengthening of actors and institutions from both within the civil society and the public sector who have a better understanding of collective rationality and a strong commitment to these interests. Communities should be looking for methods of increasing popular participation at the grassroots level in order to improve the quality of life. Improved involvement of people in decision-making would probably also lead to better and more rational regulations which would also command more respect.

Housing Polices

Broadly defined, housing consists not only of shelter, but also the plot on which the dwelling stands, water and sewage facilities, access to off-site services (e.g., education and health services), and employment and other amenities offered by the local community to the household.

In developing countries, slums constitute a large share of housing. In many cities, more than half of the population live in slums with poor access to water and sanitary facilities. Unfortunately, the trend seems to point toward an aggravating situation in some countries.

Although there are major differences in the housing markets in the developing and developed countries between different types of cities and groups of people living in them, there are also clear similarities. Although it is very difficult to generalize or draw any universally applicable conclusions, issues that typify housing markets in some countries where government intervention is excessive are (1) housing shortages, (2) exaggerated rationing of land for housing, (3) exorbitant construction costs, (4) rigidity as to locations and types of housing, (5) extreme quality requirements, (6) rent controls, (7) excessive price fluctuations, and (8) housing finance deficiencies.

Appropriate government roles vary according to the actual conditions prevailing in the market. The governments should at least be engaged in the provision of property rights, company law for housing and ownership, land use controls, isolation of noxious facilities, financial institutions, and infrastructure. The very poor can only afford subsidized housing. In some countries, subsidy programs impair housing market performance, while it is very difficult to target subsidized housing to low-income residents in general without large leakages of benefits to middle-income residents.

Similarly, appropriate government roles regarding the housing sector vary from country to country, as well as within the country. Special attention should be given to market failures, such as the lack of long-term finance, for instance. There appear to be alternating cycles of regulation and deregulation. Despite the adverse effects of excessive government intervention, it has been argued that housing, like agriculture, is a special sector requiring regulation because of the cyclical overshooting of housing and rental prices, which have repercussions on the national economy. However, government policy and regulation have not always been responsive to demand.

Enabling Paradigm

It has been extensively documented that reliance on the direct provision of housing by the public sector has usually been a mistake. Housing provided by the government tends to be expensive and insensitive to the needs of future inhabitants. The resources tied up in public construction projects could be employed more effectively elsewhere. The success of Hong Kong and Singapore in public housing provision are widely regarded as exceptions, with credit for their achievement being generally accorded to the determination and commitment as well as the financial means of the governments.

The internationally advocated enabling approach to deal with housing shortages evolved from the lessons learned from past failures in government policies to deliver shelter for all. It emphasizes that governments should not be directly involved with constructing houses, but that their resources should be directed to removing the constraints in the supply of resources and institutional arrangements. Enabling policy was thus not considered to be laissez-faire policy, but active, consistent, and concerted public sector support, promotion and even advocacy of regulation to mobilize, facilitate and guide the efforts of the nongovernmental sectors. Accordingly, the public and the private sector have to share roles in the most efficient ways possible.

Some problems arise when the enabling concept is linked to the normative concept of adequate housing. Strengthening the position of the weakest and ensuring a reasonable outcome to all groups are key issues of the "enabling" concept, and the redistribution of resources becomes the very core of the political economy of housing. However, the concept of adequacy may limit actors' autonomy in decision making. Indeed, when the poor cannot afford the level of adequacy in terms of all basic needs and the public sector cannot afford to subsidize them to the scale required, increasing well-being in one sector by imposing a minimum level of housing.

In spite of all rhetoric, many signals seem to indicate that the enabling approach has not been fully introduced into the praxis of housing policy. This may be related to the incapability of making such a policy change. There are usually strong vested interests working against measures aimed at improving the land delivery system and making it more equitable, or at simplifying permit procedures, for instance. The issue of power being at the heart of all politics, talks about empowerment are hardly credible without strong political commitment.

Land Policy

Land policy, and land distribution in particular, is an important question related to urbanization in the context of urban–rural interactions. Rapid migration places heavy pressures on land markets. For example, in Istanbul there are half a million new migrants every year, and to manage such a huge flow of people places heavy demands on the housing markets. Because of these pressures, the spread of slums to public land and its "legalization" caused considerable land speculation in many countries. Governments should have a clear role in land policy. They should assist in land development, be responsible for zoning, and try to guarantee a flexible supply of land for construction. Property ownership in land is a crucial precondition for an efficient housing market. Clear property rights to land and land use by planning are especially important.

Construction

Construction is more a sector than an industry comprising a flexible agglomeration of agents and activities that produce buildings and infrastructure. It generally accounts for approximately 50 percent of gross fixed capital formation, the other half consisting of investment in machinery and equipment. The percentage of construction (value-added) in GDP has been found to increase with increasing per capita GDP from an average of 4 percent per capita to 8 percent per capita at US $1,000 per capita GDP. Thus the availability of income is the determinant rather than the rate of economic activity or industrialization. The share of construction in GDP increases with GDP because of the capital requirements. While relatively poor countries invest 3 to 4 percent of GDP, developed countries on the average invest 8 percent of GDP in construction.

When talking about multiplier effects, one should keep in mind that it is not the infrastructure itself, but rather the service generated by the infrastructure investment that enhances economic growth as well as the quality of life in the longer term. Another important point is that construction can also have negative multiplier effects. These can be caused to the crowding out of other more productive investments, or inflationary pressures created by the construction investment. An all too common occurrence in developing countries is that political pressures push politicians to start projects that cannot be completed and which consequently tie up scarce resources. In sum, investment in construction can have negative as well as positive effects on macroeconomic stability and economic growth, in both the short and the longer term. Investment in construction is a necessary condition for economic growth, but it alone is not sufficient, and not all construction promotes growth.

Provision of Infrastructure

During the next 30 years, the need for new, additional infrastructure will surpass the existing infrastructure systems of the developed world. Having adequate infrastructure is a major element in successful structural adjustment of developing country economies. Infrastructure cannot be separated from economic development. In developing countries, returns on infrastructure investments can be even more attractive, because serious deficiencies already exist in infrastructure, causing bottlenecks on economic growth. Demand for infrastructure investment is especially high and likely to increase in countries that are experiencing rapid growth in economic and population. In another group of countries, macroeconomic adjustment has forced prolonged underinvestment in infrastructure, causing overutilization and deterioration of existing structures. Unfortunately, the need for improvements and the lack of financing frequently coincide, as urbanization often aggravates the macroeconomic crisis in poor countries by increasing the need for food imports and adding to budget and balance of payments deficits. The most common problems with infrastructure provision are undefined goals, lack of managerial autonomy, and accountability, financial difficulties, as well as wage and labor problems.

Once again, human and institutional capacity building are needed. If the government is not able to provide adequate infrastructure, it should try to form partnerships with local communities and enable the people needing infrastructure to pool their resources for this purpose. Also appropriate pricing of infrastructure is important for its efficient use and development. Data indicates that in developing countries cost recovery of telecommunications is more than 100 percent, while it is approximately 80 percent for gas production and approximately 60 percent for power generation.

Conclusions

Although increasing urbanization is a global trend and there are many similarities between its favorable and adverse consequences, there is also great diversity in the problems and in the capabilities to solve them. Some of the main sources of the diversities, such as historical traditions, demographic patterns, and ethnic characteristics, must be taken into account in dealing with the problems of urbanization in human settlements.

Cities will be larger in the future. This is mainly the result of natural push and pull factors in the economy and should therefore not cause alarm as such. However, at least theoretically, unless congestion and environmental effects are internalized as economic costs, cities may grow "too large." On the other hand, cities generate positive externalities in the form of agglomeration economies and cultural diversity.

Urban centers are also centers of economic growth. Their success is fundamental for the national economy, and there is some evidence that the productivity gap between cities and rural areas is increasing. Most of global economic value added—and even larger share of its expansion—is created in cities. In general, the role of the city in the economic development of a country is positive.

The growth factors in an economy change because of demographic developments, urbanization, structural adjustment policies, globalization, and decentralization. These affect the economic base and local tax base, as well as physical and spatial configuration of urban centers.

Cities in developing countries face enormous challenges of extreme poverty, an expanding informal sector, increasing crime, street children, miserable shelter for some of their inhabitants, with little or no access to essential infrastructure services, such as safe water and sanitation services. These remain serious challenges for future action. It is often argued that cities increase poverty, but it has also been pointed out that the poverty does not increase proportionately to urbanization, but less. The proportion of the poor tends to decline as the city's population increases. Persistent problems of urban poverty call for revitalized efforts of city management requiring participatory and cooperative solutions together with the communities and inhabitants. Human capacity building is needed, since improving human capital has been found to be a more reliable form of helping the poor than outright handouts. The problems of street children are also connected with poverty. However, alleviating poverty is not enough to tackle this problem. What is needed is general urban reform, family planning policies, and reforms in education, as school systems have failed to keep children in school.

The current job-creating effects of cities in the developing world are well below the historical role of cities in the industrialized world. Consequently labor is pushed more and more to the informal sector—currently at a historically unprecedented rate. Poverty can best be alleviated by gainful employment. In this context, new labor-intensive approaches are recommended. Urban productivity cannot be increased without increasing the productivity of the large urban informal sector.

Urbanization raises a number of important challenges for nation-states. One of the key issues is the sharing of political power between the central government and the cities in a number of areas, such as political autonomy and tax revenue. There is still too much centralization, especially in developing countries. National governments should recognize the importance of cities for the national economy and allow for the sustained decentralization of cities. City management is becoming more complex and challenging. Cities have to develop new management tools to respond to new challenges. One possibility is to design a strategic economic plan for the city, in which the roles and objectives of different actors and sectors are specified.

The role of markets in urban management is growing. Markets are embedded into the characteristics of society, and they function according to the instructions given to them by society. Competition is central in ensuring the functioning of the market, and not just the form of ownership. Ineffective regulations should also be abolished because they only end up undermining the authority of public institutions, or worse, may be used to extract bribes and benefits. Instead it is necessary to ensure competition and adequate regulation for the efficient functioning of private and public companies.

The financing of cities is an increasingly complex problem due to the speed and scope of urbanization. The development of capital markets and decentralization should therefore be harmonized. Domestic savings need to remain the primary source of financing. To enhance this, domestic capital markets, especially regarding pension funds, need to be developed to raise the supply of long-term capital on the local market. Local governments can reduce their borrowing costs through cooperation with other localities and urban governments. Central governments can also develop incentives for foreign direct investment into urban development while preventing the creation of private monopolies and ensuring sufficient competition.

Gender relations and inequalities shape the urbanization process and determine many of the outcomes, such as alternatives in the urban labor market. Households headed by women are increasing in both developing and developed countries and are no longer a minority. This is often the result of gender selective urbanization or migration patterns.

There is a need to enhance people's desire to work for the public interest and preserve collective goods. Civic engagement may be a way to improve community solidarity. This necessitates the gathering of actors and institutions from both the civil society and the public sector, who have a better understanding of collective rationality and a strong commitment to collective interests. The present trend toward decentralization, localization, and civic engagement may well serve this purpose.

It is important to consider the appropriate roles of private and public housing activities. Appropriate government roles vary according to the situation. Governments should at least be engaged in the provision of property rights, company law for housing and ownership, land use controls, segregation of noxious facilities, financial institutions, and infrastructure. In general, the public sector should leave the construction of housing to the private sector, while improving infrastructures in cooperation with inhabitants.

According to the enablement approach in housing and urban development, governments are to take full responsibility for the indirect actions required to facilitate the efforts of other actors. Enabling policy is thus not laissez-faire policy, but active, consistent, and concerted public sector support, promotion and even advocacy of regulation to mobilize, facilitate and guide the efforts of the nongovernmental sector.

Because a large part of housing construction is taking place in the informal sector, measures should be targeted in such a way that they improve the efficiency of the informal sector. All this requires strong political commitment.

The construction industry is playing a key role in economic development in general. Its efficiency and character is of importance for the solution of urban housing issues. High priority should be given to the following to improve productivity and performance in the construction industry: improvement of management and administration of construction work, simplification and standardization of design and specification of projects, and adoption of a pragmatic approach to the implementation of the work.

There are no simple answers to be offered to individual cities. Rather, cities should be active and try to approach their problems from their specific circumstances and initial conditions.

The process of urbanization has become irreversible. Whether urbanization is increasing or diminishing the vulnerability of humankind; whether it is increasing or endangering global security, are essential issues to be explored further. Urbanization may open new opportunities for human life to deal with some of the major problems of misery, backwardness, and ignorance, which have been haunting past and recent history. Although the scope and pace of developments are at an unprecedented scale, time has not run out yet from determined action to tackle the roots of the problems. Policy makers and all other relevant actors should seize this opportunity to make a difference and guide the future developments to come.

Notes

1. E. Berghäll, *Habitat II and the Urban Economy: A Review of Recent Developments and Literature.* Helsinki: UNU/WIDER Research for Action series, 1995.
2. P. Krugman, "Urban Concentration: The Role of Increasing Returns and Transport Costs." In *Proceedings of the World Bank Annual Conference on Development Economics.* The World Bank, 1995, pp. 241–278.

3. Statistics available from the UN.
4. Krugman, 1995, p. 23.
5. P. Bairoch, *Cities and Economic Development: From the Dawn of History to the Present.* University of Chicago Press, 1988.
6. N. Harris (with assistance from Araceli Damian Gonzales, Development Planning Unit), "Urbanization in Developing Countries: A World Overview." University College London, June, 1994 (mimeograph).
7. E. L. Glaeser, "Cities and Economic Development." Paper presented at the UNU/WIDER conference on Human Settlements in the Changing Global Political and Economic Processes, Helsinki, 25–27 August 1995.
8. P. Krugman, *Geography and Trade.* Cambridge, MA: MIT Press, 1991.
9. J. H. Kim, "Urbanization and Regional Development in Korea: Policies for Balanced Regional Development." Paper presented at the UNU/WIDER conference on Human Settlements in the Changing Global Political and Economic Processes, Helsinki, 25–27 August 1995.
10. G. A. Cornia, "Government Interventions to Counter Poverty in the Light of Changes in Economic Conditions of the Last 20 Years." Paper presented at the Queen Elizabeth House 40th Anniversary Conference, Oxford 5–8 July 1995.
11. A. M. Hamer and J. F. Linn, "Urbanization in the Developing World: Patterns, Issues and Policies." In Edwin S. Mills, ed., *Handbook of Regional and Urban Economics,* vol. 2. New York: Elsevier–North Holland, 1987.
12. V. Lall, "Economic Liberalization and the Informal Sector." Paper presented at the UNU/WIDER conference on Human Settlements in the Changing Global Political and Economic Processes, Helsinki, 25–27 August 1995.
13. *Ibid.*
14. R. Robertson, *Globalization: Social Theory and Global Culture.* London: Sage, 1992.
15. W. Dillinger, *Decentralization and Its Implications for Service Delivery.* Washington, DC: UNDP/UNCHS/World Bank Urban Management Programme, 1994.
17. E. S. Mills, "Housing: The Step-Child of the Privatization and Deregulation Movement." Paper presented at the UNU/WIDER conference on Human Settlements in the Changing Global Political and Economic Processes, Helsinki, 25–27 August 1995.

Section 1 In the Midst of Paradoxes: An Urban Renaissance?

Louis Emmerij

In recent years, globalization has justifiably received a great deal of international attention. Under the process of globalization the nation-state is responsible for solving most social problems. As a result, it exacerbates, particularly in urban settings, the trend toward global wealth and individual poverty. For example, in my native city of Rotterdam, the biggest port in the world and one of the richest, 25 percent of the population is unemployed; even more are marginalized. If this is true in Rotterdam, one can only imagine the situation elsewhere in the world.

The paradox of urbanization is best described by paraphrasing the opening lines of Charles Dickens's *A Tale of Two Cities*. The city offers the best of times and the worst of times. It is both hell and miracle. The question then becomes: Why do people, particularly in developing countries, continue to flock to the cities. The short answer is because of the "bright lights" and the possibility of better and higher remunerated employment. That this is a lottery with many losers becomes obvious only later.

Thus, while the advent of globalization and global enterprises tends to bypass national governments, it has paradoxically stimulated local initiatives, as reflected in the rise of growth poles in and around the European cities of Lyons, Barcelona, and Milan. Thus, in addition to the urban paradox, there are paradoxes of globalization.

The Paradox of Globalization: Global Wealth and National Poverty

Because globalization is a phenomenon driven by the private sector, it sharpens competitiveness. This, in turn, requires both businesses and individuals to be more efficient and cost-effective. As a result, global enterprises undertake their multifarious activities in those locations that provide a cost-effective environment, including favorable tax policies. If appropriate, parts of the final product may be produced in different locations. As a result of these changes, national governments are becoming relatively impoverished.

In addition, other problems related to globalization are mounting and intensifying, such as unemployment and underemployment, traffic in narcotics, drug use, crime, and the number of political and economic refugees. What may have once been national problems have taken on global proportions.

In this context, the following questions require urgent examination:

1. What are the exact relationships between the rise of globalization and the growing problems of unemployment, drug use, and crime? These relationships are real, and a growing body of literature is beginning to analyze them.[1]
2. What are the costs and benefits of globalization in the economic and financial sectors? How can the benefits be maximized and the costs minimized? If the relationship between economic and financial globalization on the one hand and increased social problems on the other is real, should special taxes be imposed on global economic and financial activities to better arm the nation—state with the resources needed to tackle social issues? One example is the so-called Tobin tax, named after the Nobel prize-winning economist James Tobin.[2]

These considerations raise questions about the relationships among all of the factors of globalization—state and market; free trade and protection; economic and social needs; international, regional, and national activities and policies. In addition, the paradox of globalization illustrates how much an internationally active private sector has put the passive and impoverished nation-state on the defensive.

The Paradox of Technological Progress: A Curse and a Blessing

Technological progress has created its own paradox—one that significantly affects the issue of unemployment. The blessing of technological progress is, of course, that it enables people to produce more with less effort. It is amazing to observe how—once again—a blessing has been turned into a curse because people lacked insight and organizational skills.

In industrial countries, the core problem is that economic and technological changes have not been accompanied by societal changes. For example, the organization and structure of labor markets, educational systems, and pension schemes, have not kept pace with the new economy. In fact, they have not changed in decades.

The result is high levels of open and hidden unemployment in industrial countries generally, but particularly in Europe. We are indeed producing more with less effort and in fewer hours, but the benefits are distributed so unevenly that in some countries 25 to 30 percent of the population is being socially and economically marginalized.

The old-fashioned goal of full employment is no longer attainable. In fact, it is not even desirable. We must move toward a new style of full employment, which is based on a societal structure that allows people to move in and out of school, of work, and of creative leave in a recurrent, rather than a sequential, order. The resulting qualitative changes in the economy and society will lead to a different form of full employment—one that can be combined with a more creative life.[3]

As long as the employment problem is not solved in industrial countries, these nations will remain on the defensive with respect to countries in the East and South. Solving the employment problem in the West is therefore crucially important for developing countries and for countries in transition.

The problem in developing countries is not different in essence from the problems in the West, but it needs a different policy treatment because of the manner in which the problem presents itself. The emphasis in developing countries must be on identifying the correct balance between high-tech production processes in the export sectors and the equally high-tech, but more labor intensive technologies, in the domestic sectors. The main issue is not (yet) to redistribute the available work in a more intelligent and creative fashion, but to create additional employment opportunities and to increase the productivity of those employed people who have low levels of income.[4]

Global Markets and Global Governance

Unlike globalization, which is driven by the private sector, regionalization is driven by the state. As usual, the public sector is one lap behind the private sector!

Just as there must be a balance between the state and the private sector at the regional and national levels, so must there be a balance at the global level. Unfortunately, just when we need an equivalent of the state at the global level, none exists. This lack is made more serious because the institutions we do have—such as the United Nations and the Bretton Woods Institutions—are coming under increasingly severe attack.

The solution needs a sensitive and subtle approach; it would be easy to go overboard and present utterly unrealistic proposals. Basically, we need to bring new flesh and blood into existing institutions at the global and regional levels, so they will become more relevant and can effectively deal with the new reality of global markets and global enterprises—in short, the reality of global private power.

The Paradox of Competition

Another consequence of globalization is that it pushes competition to a worldwide extreme. Nobody will deny that competition up to an extent is positive. A healthy competition—at school, at work, in research, as well as in the economy—helps a society or an individual progress and remain innovative. The origin of the verb "to compete" is "cum petere" which means searching together. This definition is a far cry from the current meaning of competition. It is now an arm with which to wipe out the adversary. It has become an ideology and an imperative; some even speak of the gospel of competition.[5]

Competition has become the answer to everything. Is there an increasing unemployment problem? You must become more competitive. Is there a growing poverty problem in certain countries? You must become more competitive. Education and training must be geared more and more to the gospel of competition. The discussion is reminiscent of the proposals concerning a "flat tax" in the United States during the presidential campaign of 1996. This is also a case in which a proposal is supposed to remedy every ill in society.

Competition is thus in the process of becoming the only solution to the problem of globalization. The result is that our societies are ever more engaged in an economic battle without mercy. Reports abound with such titles as *Winning in a World Economy,* and the cult of competition even has its own "scientific" instrument, namely the World Competitiveness Index, published every year by the World Economic Forum. This index plays the same role as the ATP in classifying professional tennis players.

Competitiveness pushed to such an extreme has undesirable effects. It creates distortions in national economies, as well as such negative social repercussions as increasing unemployment. This results in lower salaries and, as a result of this reduced income, growing inequalities. For instance, in the United States, 50 percent of the labor force has seen its real income reduced between 1973 and 1993.

Such an extreme system is bound to flounder. Indeed, extreme competition diminishes the degree of diversity in a society and contributes to social exclusion. Individuals, enterprises, cities, and nations that are not competitive are being marginalized and eliminated from the economic race. This is unacceptable morally and inefficient economically. The more a system loses its variety, the more it will lose its capacity to renew itself. But above all, the ideology of competition devalues cooperation—searching together. It wipes out solidarity and it is, therefore, not surprising that this era is also witnessing serious attacks on the welfare state.

The question could reasonably be asked: What will the final winner in this competition rat race do all alone? But, the most important weakness in this philosophy of competitive fundamentalism is its inability to reconcile social justice, economic efficiency, environmental sustainability, political democracy, and cultural diversity.

Thus, current trends in globalization and competitiveness are intensifying social and economic problems, such as unemployment and increasing pressure to decrease the real income of parts of the population. This results in skewed income distributions. These problems are becoming themselves globalized, as are the growing issues of narcotics trafficking, crime, and the urban problems in general.

These social problems are intensified by the private sector, which drives the global financial and goods markets, and are left on the plate of nation to solve. Unfortunately, these states are experiencing problems with public finance and are cutting back their welfare systems at the very moment when they are needed most. A growing imbalance exists between the power of the free market and the influence and weight of the state. Nowhere is this more visible than in the social arena and in the lack of a state equivalent at the global level.

As a result, the gains made in social and welfare policy that the industrial countries experienced during the decades after World War II are now being reversed—and an end to this reversal, which began 15 years ago, is not in sight. If this reversal continues, we will slip back into nineteenth-century circumstances. We will witness increased global wealth in the midst of growing national and individual poverty. In other words, we will observe a growing dualism. This recurrence and intensification of dualism is also very visible at the urban level.

The Urban Paradox Today

The facts are well known. One half of the world's population lives in urban conglomerates; 75 percent of the population of industrial countries and of Latin America live in cities. The increase in the urban population since 1965 has been 1.5 billion; during the next 10 years, another 1 billion more people will be living in cities, most of them in the developing countries. Out of 21 megacities, 17 are in the South.

Behind these cold figures are mounting problems that are common to industrial and developing countries and that have given rise to the "Urban Question." The growing inequality between and within nations that has been observed during the past 15 to 20 years is most starkly reflected in cities. The growing urban dualism and informalization have created cities that are divided against themselves.[6]

The urban problem is essentially social in character; poverty and marginalization have become structural. Along with globalization of world's economy and financial system, we have observed the growth of global social problems. Older citizens, single parent families, the unemployed, the disabled, certain ethnic groups seem to be excluded from participating in this new economy. In addition, many urban centers have seen an increase in street children, child prostitution, child labor, and drug addiction. This lack of social cohesion is leading to the phenomenon of divided cities. Most cities are losing the battle against poverty, and different urban groups are rapidly growing apart.

Obviously, the urban explosion has both a sunny and a dark side. The sunny side is best captured in Lewis Mumford's phrase: "The city is the most precious collective invention of civilization. . . second only to language itself in the transmission of culture." Indeed, the city offers better quality and more choice in education, material comforts, medical care, employment opportunities, and self-expression. It provides a wide variety of skills, services, cultures, delivery systems, and so on. People are not fools because they are attracted by the bright city lights; they will eventually find their universe within this mass of steel and glass.

Or, at least, that is what they wish to believe. And here comes the dark side. The megacities of the South, and increasingly of the North, are "Romes without empires." They have been boosted artificially. As a result, they cannot, for example, afford to invest in expanding or repairing the infrastructure or addressing the issues of growing unemployment, squatting, crime, and wasting of resources. Drinking water is pumped to the cities from further and further away.

The urban question has many dimensions, including poverty, housing, unemployment and underemployment, slums, crime, drugs, and street children. But the urban question amounts to more than the sum total of its different problem areas. It is difficult to express what this "value added" is, but it certainly has a lot to do with the quality of life, or the lack of it, in the urban setting. The quality of life affects both poor and rich, as the urban situation deteriorates.

In the industrial countries, cities have started to grow again. A cycle—from the center to the suburbs to "developments" even further away back to the center—is coming full circle. One of the paradoxes is that, in many instances, the downtown areas have started growing again, but so have the suburbs. The slums, in comparison, are becoming worse.

On the whole, we can observe common problems in the urban conglomerates. These are:

1. Growing inequalities, dualism, and informalization leading up to the phenomenon of "cities divided against themselves."
2. The social character of the urban problem: poverty and marginalization have become structural.

This is reflected not only in the growing number of people who have nothing to offer to these globalizing and liberalized economies, but also in the growing problems of street children, child prostitution, child labor, and drug addition. Bangkok, with an economic growth rate of 10 percent, is a spectacular illustration of global wealth and individual misery at the urban level.

Thus, we observe a growing lack of social cohesion; a losing battle against urban poverty; and a rapidly growing division among urban groups, with a "new apartheid" looming on the horizon.

What can be done? What policies can be put in motion to realize an urban renaissance not only quantitatively, but also qualitatively?

The Way Ahead

We have already discussed the sunny and dark sides of cities. The positive aspects of urbanization stimulate economic and cultural activities that make the urban setting more attractive to many people than the rural countryside.

Another paradox, however, is the movement of many enterprises outside of the cities in an effort to escape the darker side of urban life. As a result, they create "cities in disguise." This is the case, for instance, of Silicon Valley, Route 128 North of Boston, or the Po Valley. The creation of a great many new enterprises in these regions has resulted in "clusters" that have become cities in a more pleasant disguise, at least for the time being.

The darker side of urban life is partly the result of the speed with which cities have grown. Many overestimated the capacities of the sunny side. As a result, the urban informal sector has ballooned. This informal sector consists of people who moved to the cities and found themselves on the losing end of the employment opportunity lottery. They exist on the margin of the formal economy and of the city itself. This sector has many positive characteristics, but also explains the artificial boosting of the cities in the South.

To "get cities right," we need to support three clusters of policy initiative. First, the regions and cities must receive decision-making power and financial resources. There is a lot of talk these days about the desirability of decentralization, "municipalization," and so on. And indeed, in many countries, there is a trend towards this kind of "vertical" decentralization. However the problem too often is that this type of decentralization and "municipalization" consists in delegating responsibilities down the line, while the financial resources remain centralized in the national government. This results in further deterioration of the urban environment. Decentralization must include giving local authorities the financial means to meet their new decision-making responsibilities.

Second, within the cities more initiatives must be given to neighborhoods, districts, "arondissements," and whatever the municipal components of cities are called. Such decentralization within the urban conglomerates must, of course, meet the same conditions as those mentioned above.

Third, we must obviously make sure that the macrocontext is correct for the productivity of the urban population and the demand for labor to increase. Access to basic infrastructure and social services, including decent housing, must be expanded.

These three clusters create a circle. Each feeds positively off the others, resulting in a continuous and self-propelled process. One can provide concrete examples of changes that have been taking place in two cities, one in an industrial and the other in a developing country.

In Indianapolis, the mayor and the municipal council decided to privatize 60 municipal services, from street sweeping to managing the airport. These services are now implemented in a more efficient manner that is saving the municipality 300 million dollars per year. This is an illustration of decentralizing and delegating responsibilities within a city, maintaining supervisory control, and leaving the implementation and direct responsibility to a set of decentralized private service agencies.

The Brazilian city of Curitiba has recently attracted attention because of its imaginative urban policies. The mayor and his council have recycled nineteenth-century industrial buildings, turning them into office space and apartments. They have also improved conditions in the slums by exchanging bags of garbage exchanged for bags of food. The introduction of express bus lanes, which they call the "surface subway," has made collective transportation a much more attractive means of locomotion. The creation of bicycle lanes has diminished the need for private cars. City leaders have also installed pedestrian malls. These initiatives were based on surveys conducted among the population of Curitiba, in which the people expressed their priorities for improving their city.

In both instances – in Indianapolis as well as in Curitiba – the impulse for these daring innovations was given by strong mayors, who were surrounded by imaginative advisers in close contact with the people of the cities.

Conclusion

In industrial countries, and mainly in Europe, one can speak of an Urban Renaissance in the sense that city centers once on the decline are growing again and that many of the "intermediate" cities are turning into regional poles of development. Certainly, there are still problems, as reflected in the discussion of Rotterdam at the beginning of this section, but a change for the better is occurring in more and more locations.

This cannot be said for most of the cities in the developing countries. There, the situation is much more serious. The cities are growing too fast and there are not enough cities of "intermediate" size to attract people away from the metropolises.[7] The phenomenon of "value added" is reflected in a declining quality of life the great majority of city dwellers. Obviously, there are also positive aspects to big cities in the South, but they are outnumbered by negative factors.

For the Urban Renaissance to occur in the urban conglomerates of the South, exceptional individual leaders are needed, who are sure enough of themselves to give more power to the citizens and their representative bodies.

Notes

1. For an excellent summary, see UNRISD, *States of Disarray: The Social Effects of Globalisation.* Geneva, 1995.
2. See UNDP, *Human Development Report 1995.* New York and Oxford: Oxford University Press, 1995. For more details, see Haq, Kaul, Grunberg, eds., *The Tobin Tax: Coping with Financial Volatility.* Oxford and New York: Oxford University Press, 1996.
3. I have written extensively on the necessity of changing the concept of full employment. There are indications that European may finally be coming around to such a concept, which would bring the societal structure in line with the economic and technological changes that have taken place. See, for example, Louis Emmerij, "Education and Training in the Face of Rapid Technological Change." In Khadija Haq and Üner Kırdar, eds., *Managing Human Development.* New York: North–South and United Nations Publication, 1988.
4. See UNDP, *Human Development Report 1996/* New York and Oxford: Oxford University Press, 1996, Chapter 4.
5. See the Group of Lisbon, *The Limits to Competition.* Cambridge, MA: MIT Press, 1996.
6. "Every city or household divided against itself will not stand" (Matthew 12:25).
7. For an interesting discussion concerning intermediate city development, see J. G. M. Hilhorst, *Regional Studies and Regional Development.* London: Gower, 1990, Chapter 9.

Section 2 Two Worlds in One Place

Michael A. Cohen

In the last four years, the world's annual urban growth rate has increased from 50 million to 80 million, which is the equivalent to adding a Rabat, Pittsburgh, Ibadan, or Hanoi each week. The world's GDP grows by about US $1 billion each day, or about US $400 billion annually. This is roughly equal to the annual GDP growth of all of South Asia.[1]

In 1984, 1,025 computers were directly connected to the Internet; ten years later there were 3.8 million. A billion e-mail messages pass among 35 million users, and the volume of traffic on the Internet is doubling every 10 months. [2]

The scale and accelerating pace of this transformation has created new global political, economic, and social realities, fundamentally changing the role of cities in the world. Thinking globally leads to the indisputable need for local authorities to take into account global pressures and consequences. The policy concerns of the First United Nations Conference on Human Settlements, at Vancouver in 1976, focused on housing, land, and the needs of growing numbers of urban poor. During the last decade, these issues have been bypassed and transformed.

Changing Forces

As globalization spreads, cities must come to terms with many changes, including:

- new perceptions of the dynamics and power of global economic and financial forces,
- new technological opportunities for information and communication,
- continued high urban demographic growth far outstripping earlier projections,
- new urban spatial patterns that have extended from central cities and suburbs to edge cities, network cities, urban corridors, and urban regions,

- new emerging labor forces and shifting patterns of employment and livelihoods,
- mobilization of neighborhoods and communities, new political forces, nongovernmental organizations, and parts of civil society,
- growing social conflicts over the access to opportunities.

These changes have led to:

- a new realization that the negotiated solutions to those city problems will have important impacts on global patterns, and
- awareness that environmental impacts of cities have the power to alter the Earth's ecological balance itself.

The policies of the 1970s and 1980s, which were designed to protect the comparative advantage of countries, have been challenged to evolve toward enabling national and local economies to both benefit from and protect themselves against the risks of what might be called "competitive interdependence." The Rio Summit was above all a global acknowledgment of mutual interdependence. It was followed by global and regional trade agreements and the rapid expansion of trade in all directions. Competition over markets, monopolistic pressures, and the natural resources to supply markets have, in some cases, begun to threaten the natural resource base required for continued livelihoods. This has led to renewed calls for responsible management of the natural world to reduce the risks of unfettered market-driven behavior.

These processes are also being increasingly influenced by the new role of information and technology, of networks among individuals and group who have found common interests. There is a growing awareness of what Rosabeth Kanter describes as "collaborative advantage," when she observes the new modes of production and services of the global economy of the late 1990s.[3]

Social Dimensions

Yet within this celebration of new connectivity and access to global processes and opportunities, there is also the reality of social Darwinist inequalities between and within countries and cities. There is an explosion of foreign direct investment at the global level. Yet a March 1996 World Bank report shows that although 20 developing countries have access to private markets for bonds, commercial bank loans, and portfolio equity, more than 100 countries are shut out by so-called "creditworthiness constraints."[4] In many cases, these constraints are policy related, demonstrating that countries that do not "perform" do not deserve access to credit. But blaming the victim ignores many historical reasons for their predicaments, not the least of which are global patterns of production and ownership. The unsustainability of this situation is being recognized in recent discussions of debt relief, but debt and access to the resources and opportunities of an exploding global financial market stand as important dividing lines in the so-called "integrated global economy."

The rush for national economic growth and private returns to capital underlies the concern of many for the need to redefine, and thus reaffirm, the common good, whether at the level of the global commons or the local community. What is the public interest in a market economy? And how can we protect social and environmental justice in contexts of growing and dizzying inequities? The challenges to the environmental movement in North America reflect similar debates elsewhere, in which private interests argue that market-driven economic growth that provides jobs is threatened by romantic, green views of the need to protect the environment.

For some, particularly in East Asia, it is a heady time, filled with opportunities for those who have access to resources and capacities to enjoy them. But the 1990s has also been a decade of despair for many people of our generation: a decade of hopes unfulfilled and a growing realization for most people that our children and certainly our grandchildren will not have the same quality of life and opportunity that we have enjoyed. Some of this worry is reflected in legitimate concerns about fiscal deficits and public debt, but it is a remarkable situation when the hard-won health benefits of people in their 60s and 70s are now perceived as a debt burden on the future financial stability of their children. Reducing deficits appear to justify reducing investments in education and training for future productivity, as well as in the quality of life.

In many countries a contradiction exists between the social model of the last fifty years of providing social services and health care to increase the length and quality of life and the fiscal debates that describe that agenda as no longer sustainable. Budgetary debates and strikes in the United States, Canada, Sweden, and France in 1995 have all reflected that tension. Thinking about the massive urbanization of China and Japan, one may ask which models of the twentieth century are in fact sustainable?

These questions are indicative of profound contradictions that challenge the premises of our view of an expanding global economy and information society. And they also serve as a provocative backdrop to the discussion of the challenges of the next millennium.

Turning to the City

The embodiment of these problems is the city in the next millennium. If the global patterns are increasingly understood, even as transitional paths, their ultimate destinations and consequences are far from clear.

Yet there is little doubt, and history supports this assertion, that the path to the future runs through the town square and the municipal market. But, these places, themselves, are no longer isolated from the world of global forces. Indeed, they may be individual places in a physical and locational sense, but they are part of at least two different worlds: the "virtual world" of global economic forces and information and the "terrestrial world" of human settlements, with their social, institutional, and environmental components.

At present, one may argue that there is a growing "urban convergence" around the world; that cities in both North and South are experiencing a set of common problems, including growing unemployment, deteriorating infrastructure, a degraded environment with severe health consequences, increasing social conflict, and a growing local fiscal crisis. Although the origins, severity, and indeed the meaning of these phenomena differ from city to city, they present a set of interrelated policy problems that cities face.[5] Visitors to the World Cup in Los Angeles from São Paulo remarked, "We've been here before. It looks like home."

This hypothesis has been strongly challenged by analysts who correctly argue that the subjective perceptions of those problems are profoundly different. I agree and argue that, at the same time that these problems are found in most urban areas, these same communities are asserting that they are "special" and "different" from one another. Localism is resurgent in all countries, regardless of level of development.[6] There is "Beautiful Melbourne" and "Washington, A Capital City." The fact they all assert that they are different is yet further evidence of convergence.

Indeed, part of the reason to assert these differences is in response to what is perceived as the homogenizing forces of globalization. If we all have access to the same information on the Internet, replacing the perhaps less pernicious influences of Coca Cola and McDonalds, will we all become the same? Or phrased differently, how can we remain ourselves? I am walking in a shopping center, but am I in Manila, Munich, or Minneapolis? Do these patterns mean that our range of choices will narrow and that we will lose control over critical decisions that affect our lives?

Facing the challenge of homogeneity, we must certainly worry about protecting our identities, but also diversity more generally. Protection of diversity within and between communities is a subset of the broader issue of biodiversity, and some of the same principles apply. We know, for example, that biodiversity is one source of protection against risks. If a group is homogenized, all of its members may be susceptible to the same risks. If we are different, the sustainability of our species (of communities?) may be greater. We know too that diversity creates new, often unexpected opportunities for interaction and creativity. Indeed, diversity is the critical component of the "city air," which medieval thinkers celebrated as they watched the transformation of Europe.

These are not simply historical or philosophical perspectives; they have immediate implications for how to place cities within the broader debates on patterns of sustainable human development, and what we consider to be proper areas of concern for urban policy in the future. If participants in the first Conference on Human Settlements in Vancouver worried about building codes and zoning regulations, the combatants in Istanbul at the second HABITAT Conference debated the most difficult and compelling issues of our time: the future of employment, legal and economic discrimination against women in the city, health and environmental pollution, growing social and ethnic conflict and crime, rising taxes and declining expenditures, and even the definition of the city itself. Housing and the built environment was part of the debate, but many argued that they were residuals of more profound economic and social questions. Others argued that the answers to many questions could be found not in official pronouncements, but in behavior in the streets and in community spaces. In fact, those officials who claim to "make urban policy," whether at the national or local levels, are now at pains to prove that their actions are truly relevant to the majority of people living in cities and towns.

It is frequently said that old age is not for the fainthearted. However, the same applies to urban policy. It is not that we are seeking complexity, but rather, understanding these myriad dimensions is what gives us the simultaneous feeling of frustration and exhilaration, what Charles Correa has referred to as "terrible place, wonderful city."[7]

So within patterns of convergence, we see profound differences in perception and meaning. And these are accentuated by global forces that are leading to unknown destinations. If this is true for the globe, for nations, and even communities, what does this mean for individuals? How are we to understand what is happening around us? Places such as Goma, Sarajevo, or Bhopal become realities that take on great symbolic value when we consider future urban disasters. Only a fraction of those who recognize these places have heard of Curitiba. In a world of thousands of cities and towns around the world, only a handful are ever celebrated for their accomplishments. Does this reflect what we know or simply what we communicate? In a competitive but also interdependent world, what do we need to know?

Ethical Values and Professional Choices

Before proposing a way to answer that question, it is necessary to raise the stakes for this discussion. We are all involved in the world of policy and action to some degree. How can we link our understanding of these issues to the values that must inform our decisions and our actions? Put differently, what values are relevant to sensible ethical and professional choices in cities for the next century? In our eagerness to discover and analyze urban realities, this normative dimension must not be lost. Indeed, regardless of the multiple worlds in which cities exist, it is precisely those values that permit us to maintain our bearings in an atmosphere of buffeting change.

We need to consider several different, but interrelated, aspccts of this issue. First, we need to identify and specify the current impacts of global forces as they affect cities. What interactions occur through patterns of production and consumption, and how do those patterns affect the use of natural resources and the quality of the environment?

Second, how do those patterns affect the livelihoods of people, their employment and income-earning opportunities? Do they increase or reduce inequality? How do cities respond? Can we identify implicit or explicit urban social policies?

Third, what is the role of governance in these economic, social, and environmental processes? Has growing decentralization increased the effectiveness of public institutions or weakened the sense of order and public authority needed for implementation of policy? What is the interaction between governance and culture? How have new patterns of culture and the roles of women, youth, work, life style, household composition, and material changes influenced patterns of participation and governance?

Fourth, with many new participants, how will resources be mobilized in the future? What are reasonable expectations about the private sector? about communities? How can we reasonably reconcile the Grameen Bank with global capital flows?

Finally, can these multiple dimensions be integrated into a set of actionable policies with predictable consequences toward sustainable futures?

Global Forces Affecting the Cities

The growing number of recent conferences and items in the literature that address this question demonstrate the growing perception that cities are affected by some highly significant global patterns.[8] These patterns include the following:

1. the change in the global composition of transactions among countries from trade toward international financial flows, with the monetary value of the latter now significantly larger than trade as a result of foreign direct investment having grown three times faster than trade during the 1980s;[9]

2. the share of foreign direct investment in GDP in many countries has also grown dramatically, at 22 percent annually between 1985 and 1994 in contrast to 3 percent in the previous five years, contributing to economic growth but also shifting patterns of ownership of capital and assets, including units of production, services, and infrastructure;[10]
3. the management of these flows, with the necessary telecommunications and services, have been concentrated in already dynamic urban centers and transnational marketplaces which Saskia Sassen has called "global cities";[11]
4. these processes have resulted in two specific new features of urban economies themselves: first, a sharp increase in the share of economic activity, which is itself part of a globalized process, as production of components of machinery, but also as services within commercial transactions, a process which Savitch terms "delocalization,"[12] and secondly, the growing service intensity in the organization of industries;
5. these economic patterns create what Sassen calls "a new geography of centers and margins," in which the territorial dispersal of activities requires at the same time the growth of centralized specialized functions and operations.[13]
6. if the information distance between center and periphery has been reduced, the disparities in economic and financial power between center and periphery have grown, as with the emergence of new concentrations of economic and financial power with global reaches;[14]
7. the transnational migration of capital has also been accompanied by the international migration of labor, with dramatic changes in the nationality composition of individual city populations on every continent;
8. four processes, according to Rosabeth Kanter, characterize this globalization: mobility, simultaneity, bypass, and pluralism. Together they allow more choices by increasing numbers of actors which in turn act as multipliers at the global and local levels;[15]

Although these processes have multiplied economic activities across the globe and between places which heretofore had been unconnected, they have also resulted in a new set of external incentives and pressures arising from intensified competition, which have called into question local judgments about the sustainable pressures on the use of local natural resources, wage levels, and local interests. It is not surprising that workers in Surabaya or Monterey are prepared to work for lower wages than their counterparts in Delft or Detroit; they can ill afford to lose their low-paying jobs to some distant community halfway around the world, or perhaps down the road. It is similarly not surprising that poor communities are prepared to ignore industrial pollution and health hazards in this process of holding on to economic security, at least for the short term.

Finally, it is not sufficient for cities to have cheap labor to attract transnational investment; these cities must be connected to the world, with infrastructure, with skills, and even, as many mayors practice, a foreign policy! These are all essential if the global economy is, as Kanter suggests, is to work locally.[16]

The Globalized Local Economy

A major set of consequences of these economic patterns concerns the protection of natural resources. If local economic and business judgments are so heavily affected by factors outside local areas, it is not surprising that local preferences for clean air or safely disposed industrial waste will receive less weight than if only local economic forces affected local decisions. The combination of intense pressure for jobs, reflected in a 1994 UNDP-sponsored survey finding that 150 mayors agreed that unemployment was the major problem faced by their cities, and fear of distant competitors sharply tilts the local calculus, and local opinion, about whether new infrastructure for production is more important than investment in environmental protection.

These economic judgments compound the realities that urban environmental infrastructure is sadly lacking in most cities in developing countries. It is striking that even in Latin America, a relatively advanced region, only 2 percent of urban human waste is treated before disposal. The statistics on provision of potable water, sanitation services, solid waste collection, and the very existence of local environmental authorities who might enforce environmental regulations if they exist, are all testimony to a significantly deteriorating situation, as most recently presented in the 1996/1997 issue of the *World Resources Report,* which focuses on the urban environment.

The authors of that report conclude that conditions will worsen in developing country cities before they improve—a version of the Kuznets curve—with the expected calamitous consequences for the urban poor, for local environments, for surrounding national environments, and even for the impacts of urban environmental hazards on global ecological balances. This underlines the importance of giving particularly loud voice to urban environmental and social concerns.

Global Economic Processes, Jobs, and Opportunities

A third set of issues is how do global economic processes affect the availability of employment and the degree of inequality within cities?

With increasing shares of jobs in the service sector—both formal and informal—it is critical to evaluate how these sectors can benefit from increased economic activities. In the section, "The Urban Informal Sector," Professors Gustav Ranis and Frances Stewart clarified the impact on the urban informal sector of the global economy.[17] The 1995 *World Development Report* presents data that show that the informal sector shrinks as GDP per capita increases, with levels as high as 75 percent in Burkina Faso or Sierra Leone to about 25 percent in Argentina. [18] Even when levels of development are held constant, however, wage levels and earnings for similar occupations differ tremendously from city to city. [19]

One aspect of this experience has been the low wage experience of workers in the maquiladora factories in northern Mexico, where literally hundreds of foreign-owned enterprises employ Mexican labor at wage levels that keep people alive but allow surprisingly little to be repatriated to home towns and households. Low investments in local infrastructure, shelter, and services increase the costs of living in these company towns—workers in Ciudad Juarez paid 29 percent of their income for urban transportation each week in 1992.

Unable to invest in urban assets, including housing, this growing low-wage labor force must live from disposable income and, not surprisingly, lives an economically very risky existence. Many of these households in Mexico, Manila, Bangkok, and Bangalore are unable to benefit from holding assets over time, an economic fact that is critical to building wealth rather than just consuming income. These urban working classes not surprisingly are also unable to invest in the education of their children and future improved income-earning capacities. The result are stagnant, if not downward-spiraling socioeconomic conditions.

These situations are further exacerbated by macroeconomic instability and shocks. Recent studies by Caroline Moser in Guayaquil, Lusaka, Manila, and Budapest demonstrate that these macroeconomic changes—with their impacts on prices, contracting labor markets, and reduced public expenditures for education and health—all have particularly dangerous and heavy impacts on women and young girls.[20]

Together, this situation raises the question of urban social policy. What is the implicit social policy being followed by national and local governments in cities? What are their components? Will short-run neglect of these issues have heavy consequences later? Will that neglect prove not be so benign?

Governance and Culture

Looking for social policy leads to the question of governance. Who is governing in 1996? Does the proliferation of local governments in Latin America and Asia imply a larger, more effective role of the public sector in managing the difficult processes described above? If the devolution of national responsibility to local levels is to be welcomed in the name of accountability and autonomy, is this true without the financial and technical resources to go with nominal authority? Does devolution actually imply a democratization of local political systems or does it simply allow local elites to extend informal power into effective local control?

Questions about the framework of governance also provoke inquiries about civic leadership and culture. How does governance mirror changes in status, power, and the number of relevant actors within the population? Does the weakness of "government" result in new forms of lifestyle and association, for example gangs or the prevalence of drugs? Does the timidity of government and decline of effective power lead to an increase urban violence and a loss of legitimacy of public authorities? When citizens take control of areas of policy or service provision back from government, such as neighborhood policing, garbage collection, or snow removal, do these actions diminish governmental capacity to perform other functions?

If the relationships between government and the people are changing, what is happening to culture itself? Indian cinema has long celebrated the drama (and melodrama) of nonpublic lives, in what might be called pulp fiction in other contexts. When urban youth see that the violence on television and in the movies is now reflected on the streets, how do they adjust their understanding of the differences between fact and fiction? Studies of young children in some cities reveal that children no longer believe in "the future." Today is too scary to believe in tomorrow. It is also reflected in an American industrial worker's comment about the future: "I no longer buy green bananas."

And yet, many communities organize, prosper, and fend off external threats. They find many ways to enhance their daily life, through recreation, the arts, music, sports, and shared community improvement projects. They find ingenious ways to outsmart local authorities to stop proposed public actions and insist on their own priorities.[21] City maps, which start from the doorsteps of individual residents instead of from City Hall, reflect how citizens really perceive the urban terrain, with its opportunities and its dangers.

Mobilizing Resources

It is intriguing, but perhaps not surprising, that the greatest energy and potential for mobilizing resources in cities is no longer from the local public sector. Local taxation is too expensive and inefficient to mobilize the resources required to solve urban problems. In contrast, that energy and potential can now be found at two other levels: from global financial markets and transactions and from community banks and organizations. Major infrastructure, commercial and industrial development, and large-scale residential investments are now more likely to come from nonlocal, private financial flows than from local public or private investment. Whether privatized infrastructure in Bangkok, commercial malls in Singapore or Mexico City, or industrial plants outside of Jakarta, these projects are more likely to be financed by sources outside those cities.

At the same time, there has been a proliferation of community banks such as the Grameen Bank, which have proven that the poor are sound credit risks and effective users of small amounts of capital. The spread of these institutions, as well as their accessibility and responsiveness to potential citizen-consumers, is reflected in the dynamism of community projects, which contrast sharply to the public sector investments of national and local public institutions. It is not only that the small institutions work faster and more efficiently, but they deliver "just-in-time" resources when they are needed for high-priority projects of an appropriate scale. Community banks represent a new form of civic leadership in an operational mode.

These parallel developments raise interesting questions about the future of local taxation and the balance among investment, operations, and maintenance. Will there be a role for the public sector? If the "public" is diminished, who will safeguard the "public interest"? Does this new pattern of resource mobilization imply a new pattern of governance and accountability within the city?

Conclusions

After identifying the new forces and trends already shaping cities and towns, how can these forces be brought together in time and space to build an integrated action agenda for the future? Setting the parameters of time and space will help us to understand how sectoral processes and concerns might be integrated.

The notions of "delocalized" and simultaneous economic activity were cited earlier in this section. They suggest that the very essence of "urban": place and time, are being altered by economic and technological change. If "local" refers to place, it is clear that place itself is being redefined to include what might be called "cyberplace." I have an address and mailbox, but they are no longer stationary, they can move and be accessed in infinite locations. If I have become "delocalized," what are the roots which bind me to "place." J. B. Jackson writes about changes in time and movement, with place and permanence becoming less important.[22] And yet, I do live in a place, but in two worlds, one "virtual" and the other "terrestrial."

Although these discussions can become quite esoteric very quickly, they suggest important changes about the economic and social roots of individuals and communities. Richard Sennett reminded us that the

Greeks believed in "the conscience of the eye," that our social conscience is awakened by what we see.[23] But if we are in "cyberplace," what will we see? Will our roots and social responsibility be diffused and weakened as social and physical realities become more distant? These are perhaps only initial consequences of much more profound changes we can anticipate.

Issues such as urban cultural heritage take on much greater significance than they were given in the post-World War II period. As we run faster towards the future, the past may become more important in helping to clarify our identities and enduring values. New tensions will appear between the permanent and the transient.

But how does this debate relate to sustainability—the aspiration of the 1990s? What is to be sustained if even the temporal, physical, and spatial dimensions of the city are changing? Here we can return to the earlier writings of Sir Ralf Dahrendorf who, in his book on *Life Chances*[24] argues that people and societies need both roots, which he terms "ligatures," to their social order, and opportunities for economic and social mobility. The fast-moving technological world of the global economy may be expanding opportunities and even displacing parameters of time and place which previously seemed immutable. But the social meaning and value of that mobility and "progress" will depend on subjective perceptions not performance indicators.

It is here where, regardless of the dynamics of the economy, more attention will have to be devoted to the social meaning of the natural world, how people depend on natural resources, because the water and the land does not move. That immobility is the immutable root around which urban settlements were established in the first place, in proximity to rivers, ports, and other bodies of water.

Perhaps landscape is more than physical infrastructure but in fact social infrastructure as well. The natural world may be the social, if no longer the economic anchor in the sea change we are experiencing. In policy terms, this suggests that reinforcing the "environmental" dimension of communities may be the critical "entry point" or "policy lever" to determine other behaviors, give them meaning, and help to demonstrate principles of integration, of compatibility, and mutual reinforcement. Some observers have asserted that the next millennium will be one of integration and of coming together. The challenge is to discover these mutually reinforcing policies, actions, and behaviors which offer the promise of longer term sustainability.

Notes

1. World Bank, *World Tables, 1995.*
2. Rob Pegoraro, "Nothing But Net," *Washington Post: Fast Forward,* March 1995.

3. Rosabeth Moss Kanter, *World Class,* 1995.
4. World Bank, *Global Economic Prospects and the Developing Countries,* March 1996.
5. Michael Cohen, "The Hypothesis of Urban Convergence." In Michael Cohen, Blair A. Ruble, Joseph S. Tulchin, and Allison Garland, eds., Preparing the Urban Future: Global Pressures and Local Forces. Baltimore: Johns Hopkins University Press, 1996.
6. Edward Goetz and Susan Clarke, eds., *The New Localism.* London: Sage, 1993.
7. Quoted in Ismail Serageldin, Michael Cohen, and K. C. Sivaramakrishnan, eds., *The Human Face of the Urban Environment.* World Bank, 1994.
8. See, for example, OECD and the Government of Australia, *Cities and the New Global Economy,* 1995; Saskia Sassen, *Cities in a World Economy.* Pine Forge Press, 1994.
9. Sassen, 1994.
10. World Bank, 1996.
11. Sassen, 1994.
12. H. V. Savitch, "Cities in a Global Era," in Cohen et al., 1996.
13. Sassen, 1996.
14. *Ibid.*
15. Kanter, 1995.
16. *Ibid.*
17. See Part 2, Chapter 2, Section 3 of this book.
18. World Bank, *World Development Report,* p. 35.
19. *Ibid.,* p. 11.
20. Caroline O. N. Moser, *Confronting Crisis: A Summary of Household Responses to Poverty and Vulnerability in Four Poor Urban Communities.* World Bank, 1996.
21. Rip Rapson and Gretchen Nicholls, *Defining Community: A Neighborhood Perspective.* University of Minnesota Design Center for the American Urban Landscape, 1996.
22. J. B. Jackson, *A Sense of Place, a Sense of Time.* New Haven: Yale University Press, 1994.
23. Richard Sennett, *The Conscience of the Eye.* New York: Alfred Knopf, 1990.
24. Ralf Dahrendorf, *Life Chances.* University of Chicago Press, 1979.

Section 3 The Transition Period to the Next Millennium

Jorge Wilheim

Many of us are already preparing for the twenty-first century and the next millennium; a rare occasion for happy festivities. But, the new century really started some years ago – in 1991.

Centuries are usually historically known by their main characteristics, and these are rarely born coinciding with the first year of a calendar century. We have studied the century of enlightenment and that of mercantilism; the one of the industrial revolution and imperialism; and the one of the renaissance. In this historical and non-Gregorian context, we had long and sometimes short centuries. The so-called nineteenth century was certainly long, starting shortly after the French Revolution and ending in 1914, with the outbreak of World War I. The war started a new century, a short one that probably ended with the demise of the Soviet Union, of political and ideological bipolarity, and the rapid expansion of the global economy.

The Twentieth Century

The so-called twentieth century will probably be known as a murderous one: 187 million people are estimated to have been killed or abandoned to death, ten percent of the global population in 1990. But, in spite of this, the population increased threefold, reaching approximately 6 billion in the 1990s. The twentieth century will also be known as the era of the decay of nineteenth-century liberalism, of the failure of a state-controlled economy, and of the first worldwide economic depression, which was followed by fascism and war. It is the century in which Europocentrism and colonialism ended and in which the number of nation–states increased from 65 to 185, as colonies became independent. This is the era when space was penetrated, computers invented, and satellites integrated into the world's information flow. It is the era of cinema and television. A short century that began with the fear that institutions would be changed by the revolution of workers and ends with the need to change the very institutions that caused the fear.

These concepts, which are inspired by Hobsbawm and other historians, have only one meaning. If something is ending, something else is beginning. The characteristics of the new century, which will probably be a long one, might be found in the form of seeds, of tentative movements, of shreds of incubating ideologies in the middle of the debris of the era that is coming to an end.

It is certainly not "history" that is coming to and end; only a cycle, a certain "world" is coming to and end, and with it, the whole system of governance and institutions to which we have grown accustomed is being severely challenged. In other words, humanity has entered into a transition period. We are now observing some symptoms of change and some examples of the gradual birth of a new era—some seeds of the future.

The Symptoms of Change

Industrial production is more and more the assemblage of components from remote places as a result of improving transportation links and strict global rules of standardization. Robotics and informatics are changing everything: the design of products, the management of plants, the skills required of workers, the structure of employment, the size and the sites of industrial units, and the structure of investment.

Since the invention of the electronic chip, the rapid advancements in informational technology have created the electronic flux of information, the new dimension of cyberspace, a new sense of global connectedness, an extraordinary acceleration of all processes served by telematics (i.e., telecommunication plus computers).

Money is not where it used to be. As Michael Hirsch points out in *Newsweek*, October 3, 1994, capital "has become phenomenally mobile and much harder for economies to hold on to and to control." In 1993, the enormous amount of US $3 trillion in 1993, almost triple the amount available three years before, circulated rapidly through the telematic network, coming from giant mutual, pension, and insurance funds, as well a from stock exchange operations. Roy Smith, a New York expert in global finance, said in the *Newsweek* article, "This private money totals three quarters the amount of the annual government budgets of the seven largest industrial nations. But more significant is the changing mix. As recently as 1990, $468 billion was in syndicated bank loans against $756 billion raised through the stock and bond markets now sprouting around the world. Three years later, in 1993, the proportion had changed radically: $555 billion in bank money to a staggering $42.3 trillion coming from the capital markets. This is clearly money that is outside the reach of governments." Still, we should add another innovation— that of electronic cash, money that moves along several channels all widely outside the established channels of banks, checks, and government regulation. As has been said, banking is essential to the modern economy, but banks are not.

Financial resources have left the public sector. Governments are being challenged, as never before in recent times, as they fail to perform up to previous standards in providing welfare, security, and direction. They are failing not only because of the lack of financial resources, but also because, as the result of the disappearance of state planning, as represented by the former Soviet Union. All planning is now discredited; some authors even think that public policies should be limited to guaranteeing the functioning of the markets. Civil society is increasingly organized and active. Thus, government itself is at stake if it does not adapt to new times.

Governance is also challenged by the exposure of corruption, especially because the scandal often affects the government more than the private businessperson also involved in the activities.

To complete this picture of change, we need to point out some specific seeds of innovation that are worthy of examination. In many cities and countries, the governance crisis is being bypassed by partnerships promoted by local authorities or by several interested groups and nongovernmental organizations. They usually intend to focus on solving just one problem, but in fact this is a learning process—an enabling process. As a result, these partnerships are gradually creating a new social contract, a new distribution of tasks and responsibilities, a new social distribution of power.

In several countries, the economy is active and includes not only the informal sector, but also adequate systems of credit for poor families. In these more "popular" economies, we can also include new collective economies that are rapidly increasing in number and are represented by several forms of savings.

Even new institutions are being created. We tend to believe that everything that is public involves the state, and that the only other kind of organization is private. But this dichotomy does not provide a place for museums, research institutions, and universities that are clearly public, but not state owned or managed. They are real examples of new forms of public organizations born from partnerships.

The New Frontiers

In this period of change, what can we expect of the future, of the first years of the new millennium? When the values, systems, mechanisms, and institutions that we know are disappearing, anxiety toward the future occupies our daily lives. Uncertainty is our common playing field worldwide. We cannot know what the future will bring, although we are, willingly or not, constructing that future right now.

Periods of uncertainty in human history are well known. They are difficult times when people tend to selfishly exclude others in order to diminish competition. Policies of exclusion are reenacted or new ones invented as a short-sighted self-preservation strategy for the survival of individuals, groups, classes, corporations, institutions, and states. They are the periods of intolerance and, often, of sadism and violence. They are the tragic periods in which conviviality and cultural diversity—both crucial to the progress of humanity—are replaced by nationalism, ethnic "cleansing," and cultural uniformity. In the long run, this is a self-defeating illusion of security.

But periods of transition are also times of opportunity. They are a time of technological breakthroughs, a time when visionary and daring people receive social and financial acceptance. In the middle the destruction of the existing structure of employment, as brought about by globalization of the world economy and the information revolution, new windows of opportunity, mainly for new independent service, are being created.

From policies of exclusion and intolerance to new opportunities, the present period of transition offers challenges related to three related factors: the globalization of the economy, the technological information revolution, and accelerated urbanization.

The Challenges of Globalization

Globalization is not just an expansion of international trade that has been made possible by improved communications. Rather, it is a change in the very nature of international trade as a result of the formation of transnational corporations. This change became at the same time as the development of the silicone chip inaugurated a new era of information. The more than 50,000 transnational companies are not always large; they have their own growth strategies that do not always follow the production and trade policies of the country in which they are based. These strategies include the vision of a production network, instead of hierarchical corporate management, that will shape companies that decide, act, and change as needed on the local level. The need for speed in decision making has been a byproduct of the information revolution.

Thus, the entire structure of production and employment has changed. The immediate challenge is the exclusion of the un-informed and the recycling of the unemployment. Another challenge is the establishment of a new world geography, one that follows the global network of businesses. In place of a North–South cleavage, we can imagine isolated islands of poor, both in the North and South, surrounded by oceans of excluded people. This beginnings of this new "map" can already be seen.

Another challenge is that the global system is vulnerable. Failure in one area instantaneously affects the entire system. This effect, which was seen in the depression years of the 1920s and 1930s, was one of the reasons for the rise of fascism. Ultimately, it resulted in World War II. The coupling of two phenomena – globalization of the economy and the predominance of capitalism – makes the global system very vulnerable and the planning of national development very difficult.

To this vulnerability, we should add another challenge – the poverty that increases even when a nation's GNP and average income are statistically on the rise. As James Gustave Speth, the Administrator of the United Nations Development Programme, pointed out: "the gap between the rich and the poor has not narrowed over the past 30 years, but has in fact widened greatly. In 1962, the richest 20 percent of the world's population had 30 times the income of the poorest 20 percent. Today the gap has doubled to 60 fold."

The Challenges of Informational Technology

The vast amount of data that is now available electronically at great speed and at a low cost is another challenge. We should understand that data are not information, that information is just one element of knowledge, and that knowledge is not the same thing as wisdom. People have to reinvent education and develop a new philosophy that will cope with the convenience of the technological revolution in information to put people on the gradual road to knowledge and wisdom. As stated by P. Rucker, technology is just "man at work." Civilization needs more than that.

The Challenges of Urbanization

Trends are significant, and the trend of urbanization clearly indicates that increasing numbers of people are concentrating in very large cities. Of these, 13 of the 21 largest megacities are located in the South. What is surprising is not the size of the cities, but the speed of their growth. This speed has resulted in difficulties in housing, infrastructure, waste disposal, and unemployment.

More than twenty nations with populations of at least one million in 1990 tripled that figure by 1996. Most of these countries are in Eastern Africa, Western Asia, and Central American. Even in North America, settlement patterns that had been dominated since the 1940s by industrialization and shipping, are being reordered into new metropolitan areas. The new large cities are service, not industrial, centers. In Europe, mass migration, urban reorganization, unemployment, homelessness, as well as the localized destruction of homes and cities, are also changing the urban landscape.

Urban growth, states the Global Report prepared for HABITAT II, has not occurred in an "uncontrolled" or random way. Unplanned urban growth is not necessarily illogical or unreasonable. This growth is linked to definite economic changes. Still, two thirds of the world's "million cities" have been important cities for at least 800 years. There is always some logical basis for urban sprawl, but we can only identify it by understanding that a city is built by many actors with conflicting interests in the distribution of power.

Although there is plenty of room to create policies that will enable cities to become safer, healthier, and more equitable, we must understand that promoting urban change and progress is, above all, a political—not just a technical—issue. We can achieve sustainable results only with the support of a significant part of the stakeholders. It is in this arena that we find the main challenges of urbanization.

The political challenges can be seen if we make a list of well-known demands: (1)to stop aggravating traffic congestion by establishing rules that create a balance between the number of cars and road capacity; (2) to abate lethal air pollution by setting a date for the replacement of gasoline by alternative fuels or a breakthrough in combustion technology; (3) to make international financing available to local authorities by adapting the policies of multilateral institutions and nations; (4) to extend credit to women and small businesses by changing banking rules and policies; (5) to enable local authorities and their partners to take over local initiatives and development by sharing with them national legislative and political power as well as financial resources; (6) to moderate the growth rate of megacities by establishing national urban policies that strengthen the diversified urban network and stimulate job creation in rural areas; and (7) to learn how to properly change the "illegal" city into a legal one.

Conclusion

Each of these demands requires a strong political commitment to negotiate conflicting interests and establish a new public policy. Although many of these issues have financial, technological, and managerial dimensions, on the whole they necessitate a political commitment: to make the international, national, and local communities aware that at the local level, humanity itself is at stake; that peacekeeping and development are at stake; that human solidarity and the partnership of a new "social contract" are at stake. And that in this dramatic transitional period, when the role of the state and government must change and must be reinforced, the challenges and strategies of sustainable development for all, are to be found mainly in human settlements. That is where we have to change; that is where change is already occurring. From there, we can learn.

The time has come to think locally in order to learn how to act globally. This is as true as the reverse.

Section 1 Sustainable Development and Cities[1]

Diana Mitlin and
David Satterthwaite

The term "sustainable development" has become widely used to stress the need for the simultaneous achievement of development and environmental goals. As long as its meaning is kept this unspecific, few people disagree with it. But as governments or international agencies develop projects or programs to implement it, the disagreements surface. There are many interpretations of what "development" is and how it should be achieved, what constitutes adequate attention to environmental aspects, and what is to be "sustained" by sustainable development. Among the proponents of sustainable development, there is a large gulf between those whose primary concern is conservation and those whose primary concern is meeting human needs.[2] At present, the bias in most discussions on sustainable development is towards conservation. Even among "environmentalists," there is the gulf between those whose primary concern is protecting the natural environment from destruction or degradation and those whose concerns include reducing environmental hazards for human populations and promoting environmental justice for those people lacking a healthy environment and adequate natural resource base for their livelihoods.

What Is to Be Sustained?

One of the main sources of disagreement within the debate about sustainable development is what is to be "sustained." Some consider that it is natural or environmental capital that has to be sustained and that this commitment to sustaining environmental capital has to be combined with a commitment to ensuring that people's needs are met; this is how it is understood in the rest of this section. But for many people writing on sustainable development, it is different aspects of development or of human activities that have to be sustained—for instance, sustaining economic growth or "human" development or achieving social or political sustainability. Thus, a discussion of sustainable development might focus on how to sustain a person's livelihood, a development project, a policy, an institution, a business, a society or some subset of a society (e.g., a "community"), culture, or economic growth (in general or for some specific country). It may also focus on sustaining a nation, a city, or a region.

In contrast to this work on how to sustain some aspect of "development," a large literature exists on sustainable development that contains no "development" component in the sense of better meeting human needs.[3] In such literature, the terms "sustainable development" and "sustainability" are commonly used interchangeably, with no recognition that the two mean or imply different things. A review of the literature on sustainable development published in 1992 commented that

> Much of the writing, and many discussions, in the North concentrate primarily on "sustainability" rather than sustainable development. These authors' main focus is how present environmental constraints might be overcome and the standard of living maintained. The need for development, of ensuring that all people in the world might obtain the resources they need for survival and development is ignored or given little attention.[4]

This is also true for much of the literature on sustainable development published since then. The exclusive concentration of many authors on "ecological sustainability" as the only goal of sustainable development is one reason why it has often proved difficult to engage the interest of development practitioners in environmental issues. There is much discussion under the heading of "sustainable development" about the actions needed to sustain the global resource base (soils, biodiversity, mineral resources, forests) and about limiting the disruption to global cycles as a result of human activities—especially greenhouse gas emissions and the depletion of the stratospheric ozone layer. Such discussion tends to forget three other critical environmental issues or to downplay their importance. The first is the hundreds of millions of people in both rural and urban areas who lack access to safe and convenient supply of water for drinking and domestic use.[5] The second is the hundreds of millions of households that depend for part or all of their livelihood on raising crops or livestock. Their poverty (and the malnutrition and ill-health that generally accompanies it) are the result of inadequate access to water and fertile land. This lack of access to land and water for crop cultivation or livestock underlies the poverty of around one fifth of the world's population.[6] Yet many discussions about "sustainability" in regard to soil erosion and deforestation give little or no consideration to the needs of these people and may indeed portray these people as "the problem."

The third environmental issue whose importance is often downplayed (or not even mentioned) is the ill health and premature death caused by pathogens in the human environment—in water, food, air, and soil. Each year, these contribute to the premature death of millions of people (mostly infants and children) and to the ill health or disability of hundreds of millions more. As the World Health Organization points out,[7] this includes:

- the three million infants or children who die each year from diarrheal diseases and the hundreds of millions whose physical and mental development is impaired by repeated attacks of diarrhea— largely as a result of contaminated food or water.
- the two million people who die from malaria each year, three quarters of whom are children under five years of age; in Africa alone, an estimated 800,000 children died from malaria in 1991.[8] Tens of millions of people suffer prolonged or repeated bouts of malaria each year.
- the hundreds of millions of people of all ages who suffer from debilitating intestinal parasitic infestations caused by pathogens in the soil, water, or food, and from respiratory and other diseases caused or exacerbated by pathogens in the air, both indoors and outdoors.

The proportion of infants who die from infectious and parasitic diseases among households living in the poorest quality housing in Africa, Asia, and Latin America is several hundred times higher than for households in Western Europe or North America; all such diseases are transmitted by airborne, waterborne, or foodborne pathogens or by disease vectors such as insects or snails. Of the 12.2 million deaths of children under five years of age every year in the South, 97 percent would not have occurred if the children had been born and lived in countries with the best health and social conditions.[9] One estimate suggested that in cities in the South, at least 600 million people live in homes and neighborhoods in which the shelters are of such poor quality, are so overcrowded, and have such inadequate provision for piped water, sanitation, drainage, and health care that their health and, indeed, their lives are constantly threatened.[10] This number is more than the total urban population of the South just 30 years ago. Thus, much of the literature on sustainable development tends to "marginalize the primary environmental concerns of the poor, even as they claim to incorporate them."[11]

When "sustainable development" includes a concern for meeting human needs, it must consider why so many people's needs are not currently met—and this means considering the underlying economic, social, and political causes of poverty and deprivation. Most of the literature on sustainable development does not do this. It does not question the current distribution of power and the ownership of resources, except when these become factors in "unsustainable practices." The literature assumes that national conservation plans or national sustainable development plans can be implemented within existing social and political structures. Much of the literature assumes that the integration of conservation and development will meet people's needs which, as Adams points out, is disastrously naive.[12]

However, those people whose primary concern within sustainable development is conservation or environmental protection can point to the fact that the most powerful government agencies or ministries concerned with "development" and the largest and most powerful international development agencies also failed to consider the environmental implications of their projects or the sum of the environmental impacts of their projects on global problems. Development projects have often been a cause of environmental degradation rather than a solution to environmental problems.[13] Although the debate about sustainable development has helped make such agencies more aware of environmental issues, this certainly does not mean that most international agencies and most governments in the South are taking these aspects seriously. For example, many development assistance agencies have never funded a public transportation project and many may still have not considered the long-term implications for greenhouse gas emissions of the support they give to transport and energy.

While wanting to encourage greater attention within discussions about sustainable development to the needs, rights, and priorities of low-income groups, or of other groups whose needs and priorities are ignored, it is not appropriate to discuss this under "sustainability." Instead, we suggest that the concept of sustainability should be used only in terms of natural capital, both because of the lack of consensus as to what sustainability might mean when applied to human activities and institutions and the ambiguity as to what is to be sustained. Ensuring that human rights are respected and that people have the right to express their own needs and to influence the ways in which they are fulfilled fall more clearly within the "development" component of sustainable development.

This means that for governments and international "development" agencies that wish to move from a concern with development to a concern with sustainable development, they have to add onto existing development goals the requirement that their achievement minimizes the depletion of natural capital—for instance, the degradation of such renewable resources as soil and the depletion of scarce nonrenewable resources and/or the degradation of ecosystems. This allows one to avoid the confusions inherent in such concepts as social sustainability or cultural sustainability. Thus, desirable social, economic, or political goals at community, city, regional, or national level are best understood as being within the "development" part of sustainable development, while the "sustainable" component is part of ecological sustainability. It also required a consideration of the environmental implications of development initiatives that are not only concerned with environmental impacts on surrounding areas, but also on their contribution to global environmental problems.

A Framework for Considering Sustainable Development and Cities

Most of the literature on sustainable development does not mention cities. This reluctance to discuss sustainable development and cities has occurred because many who write on environmental issues have long regarded cities with disdain,[14] even if they choose to live in them. Among those who write about sustainable development, many probably consider cities as a key part of "the problem." This has meant a rather poorly developed literature on sustainable development and cities, even though urban centers now include within their boundaries close to one half of the world's population and a higher proportion of the world's consumption of nonrenewable resources and generation of wastes.

However, it is important to clarify that it is not the cities that are not directly responsible for most resource use, waste, pollution, and greenhouse gas emissions. Rather, the responsibility falls on particular commercial and industrial enterprises (or corporations), and on middle- and upper-income groups with high-consumption lifestyles. A high proportion of such enterprises and consumers may be concentrated in cities, but a considerable (and probably growing) proportion are not. In the North and in the wealthier cities or regions of the South, it is the middle- or upper-income household living in a rural area, small town, or low-density outer suburb, with two or three cars, that has the highest rate of resource consumption—generally much more than households with similar incomes living in cities.

In developing a framework for "sustainable development and cities," we will start with a key defining statement from *Our Common Future*, the Report of the World Commission on Environment and Development (also known as the Brundtland Commission), published in 1987.[15] Although a concern for combining environmental and development goals go back several decades and were much discussed throughout the 1970s,[16] this concern was made more explicit, and the use of the term "sustainable development" promoted by this report. It states that we must meet "the needs of the present generation without compromising the ability of future generations to meet their own needs."[17] This has become the most widely quoted summary of the goals of sustainable development.

Meeting the needs of the present can be interpreted as the "development" component of sustainable development. As a result, a discussion of this component encompasses all the discussions and debates about needs—whose needs are to be met, what needs are to be met, who defines these needs, and who is given the power and resources to ensure that they are met. These obviously include economic, social, cultural, health, and political needs.

Many city authorities are officially responsible for fulfilling many of these needs and rights. These responsibilities are also specified in the United Nations Universal Declaration of Human Rights—that is, the need to meet each person's right to a standard of living adequate for health and well-being, including food, clothing, housing and medical care, and necessary social services.[18] This Declaration, subsequent UN documents, and *Our Common Future* all stress that development goals should include the right to vote within representative government structures. Perhaps the most relevant debate is the long-established discussion as to whether existing structures and institutions will ever improve their performances in ensuring that human needs are met. For instance, much discussion now centers on "governance" at the city and municipal level. These discussions are not only among community organizations, NGOs, and other parts of "civil society," but also among governments and international agencies.[19] The concern is not only to give city and municipal authorities sufficient power and resources to better meet their responsibilities, but also to make them more accountable, transparent, and democratic, and to give more responsibility and resources to community-based or neighborhood-based organizations, NGOs, and other voluntary sector groups.[20] Discussions about changes in social structure that are needed to achieve sustainable development goals are also becoming more explicit. As an official UN report states, "strategies for achieving social equity, social integration and social stability are essential underpinnings of sustainable development."[21]

The "sustainable" component of sustainable development translates into ensuring these needs are met within a level of resource use and waste generation that does not threaten local, regional, and global ecological sustainability. The "sustainable" component requires that there be no depletion or degradation of four kinds of "natural capital." The first is the finite stock of nonrenewable resources—for instance, fossil fuels, metals, and other mineral resources. Most of these resources (especially the fossil fuels that are burned for heat and power) are consumed when used (i.e., they are not renewable), so finite stocks are depleted with use. Other resources are not totally "consumed," because the resource remains in the waste—for instance, metals used in capital and consumer goods. But even for these nonrenewable resources, energy and cost constraints limit the ability to recover a high proportion of the total amount of the resource consumed from the resulting waste streams. These resources may be considered partially "renewable"; the amount is defined by the proportion of materials in discarded goods that can be reclaimed and recycled. Biological diversity, a key part of environmental capital, might also be considered a nonrenewable resource.

The second component of environmental capital is what might be termed the nonrenewable natural sink capacity, that is, the finite capacity of local and global ecosystems to absorb or dilute nonbiodegradable wastes without adverse effects. One area of concern is the increasing concentration of persistent biocides. Another is the large volume of nonbiodegradable wastes arising from human activities that have to be stored and kept completely isolated because of the potential damage they pose to the ecosystem and human health. For instance, many industrial processes generate large volumes of hazardous wastes. The wastes from nuclear power stations are also a particular concern; these include wastes that will maintain dangerously high levels of radioactivity for tens of thousands of years. Throughout the world, one of the most pressing problems is the finite capacity of global systems to absorb greenhouse gases without climatic changes that pose serious direct and indirect threats to the health of individuals and to the ecosystem.

The third is the finite capacity of ecosystems to provide sustainable levels of renewable resources. Human use of some renewable resources (e.g., the direct and indirect use of solar power) does not deplete the resource, but many of these resources (especially pasture land, crops, and trees) are renewable only within finite limits set by the ecosystems within which they grow. Fresh water resources are also finite; in the case of aquifers, for example, human use often exceeds their natural rate of recharge. Under these conditions, such levels of use are unsustainable.

The fourth component of environmental capital is the renewable sink capacity—the finite capacity of ecosystems to break down biodegradable wastes. Although most wastes arising from production and consumption are biodegradable, each ecozone or water body has a finite capacity to break down such wastes without itself being degraded.

When considering whether some development initiative is appropriate within a commitment to sustainable development, a further distinction is needed between particular projects/activities and larger systems (sometimes citywide, nationwide, or worldwide). It is useful to differentiate between the two applications of the term because both are important to sustainable development. Simple interrelationships between specific development activities (for instance, expanding a piped water supply or developing an irrigation system) and environmental capital can be assessed and evaluated according to whether there is a decrease in any of the four kinds of environmental capital outlined above. Alternatively, the focus can be much broader; it can be concerned with large aggregates and systems of activities. The first approach makes a single part of the system compatible with ecological sustainability. The second approach recognizes that it is difficult to require that all activities contribute towards ecological sustainability; that what is important is that the sum (or net effect) of the activities within a specific area be ecologically sustainable. To successfully achieve sustainable development, society must create institutions that ensure the sum effect of individual projects is acceptable without imposing conditions so stringent that they inhibit the achievement of development goals.

Sustainable Development and Cities, Not Sustainable Cities

The territorial boundaries for sustainable development is a particularly important part of the debate about cities. A concentration on "sustainable cities," rather than on "sustainable development" focuses too much on achieving ecological sustainability within increasingly isolated "ecoregions" or "bioregions." The concept of "sustainable cities" implies that each city must meet the resource needs of its population and local enterprises from its immediate surroundings. But, the goals of sustainable development are to meet human needs within all cities (and rural areas) while maintaining a local, national, and international level of resource use and waste generation that is compatible with ecological sustainability. It is unrealistic to demand that major cities support themselves using only the resources produced in their immediate surroundings, but entirely appropriate to require that consumers and producers in high-consumption, high-waste cities reduce their level of resource use and waste and reduce or halt the damaging ecological impacts of their demands for fresh water and other resources on their surroundings.

Although the discussions and recommendations about "sustainable cities" are relevant to reducing the depletion of environmental capital caused by production and consumption in cities in the North, they concentrate too much on individual city performance. What is more important for sustainable development is the local, national, and international frameworks needed to ensure the achievement of sustainable development goals worldwide, including the appropriate frameworks for cities.

What Sustainable Development Implies for City Authorities

A commitment to sustainable development by city authorities means adding additional goals beyond those that are the traditional concerns of local authorities. Meeting development goals have long been a central responsibility of city and municipal authorities. Their objectives generally include a desire for greater prosperity, better social conditions (and fewer social problems), basic services, adequate housing, and (more recently) better environmental standards within their jurisdiction. This does not imply that city and municipal authorities need be major providers of basic services; they can also act as supervisors and/or supporters of private or community service providers.

In addition to these traditional concerns, an interest in "sustainable development" adds two more. The first is a concern for the environmental impact of city-based production and consumption on the needs of all people, not just those within their jurisdiction. The second is an understanding of the finite nature of many natural resources (or the ecosystems from which they are drawn) and of the capacities of ecosystems in the wider regional, national, and international contexts to absorb or break down wastes.

Historically, these have not been considered within the remit of city authorities. Indeed, many cities in the North have only made considerable progress in achieving sustainable development goals within their own boundaries (i.e., reducing poverty, ensuring high quality living environments, protecting local ecosystems, and developing more representative and accountable government) by drawing heavily on the environmental capital of other regions or nations and on the waste absorption capacity of "the global commons."[22] But in the long term, no city can remain prosperous if the aggregate impact of all cities' production and their inhabitants' consumption draws on global resources at unsustainable rates and deposits wastes in global sinks at levels that undermine health and disrupt the functioning of ecosystems.

Adding a concern for "ecological sustainability" to existing development concerns means setting limits on the rights of city enterprises or consumers to use scarce resources and to generate nonbiodegradable wastes. This has many implications for citizens, businesses, and city authorities. Perhaps the most important for cities in the North and the wealthier countries in the South is the role of city and municipal authorities in promoting the delinking of high standards of living/quality of life from high levels of resource use and waste generation.

What Is Currently Unsustainable?

There is growing evidence that many current global trends in the use of resources or sinks for wastes are not sustainable—and this is something unique to the late twentieth century.[23] Although there are many examples of human activities destroying or seriously damaging natural resources and systems throughout history, only relatively recently has the sum of all human resource consumption and waste generation reached the point where it can adversely affect the present and future state of the global environment, seriously diminish biodiversity and reduce the availability of certain natural resources. This obviously alters the parameters of the environmental debate, as the scale and scope of global environmental problems are recognized.[24]

Although much uncertainty remains about the current level of risk and how much the risk (and its ecological consequences) will increase in the future, the costs are already apparent (as in the health effects of stratospheric ozone depletion) or likely to become apparent soon. In the South, the problems are largely the worrying trends of unsustainable levels of use for some renewable resources (e.g., deforestation, soil degradation, and the use of groundwater resources much faster than their natural rate of recharge). In the North, the problem centers on the scale of renewable and nonrenewable resource use, waste, pollution, and greenhouse gas emissions.

The link between what is unsustainable in terms of environmental capital and the resources needed to achieve "development" goals does not appear to be problematic in the short term. The resources needed to meet the needs of poorer people of all ages in both the North and South do not imply an unsustainable level of resource use. However, extending the levels of resource consumption and waste generation currently enjoyed by the rich minority to an increasing proportion of the world's population almost certainly does.[25] Thus, how development meets human needs will determine the extent to which it is compatible with or contrary to ecological sustainability. If "development" is "high economic growth with very limited or no redistribution of assets and pass on environmental costs to other regions or the future," i.e., the pattern of development that has been followed by the world's wealthiest countries, it is not ecologically sustainable.

Cities and the Use of Renewable Resources and Sinks

Consideration of the sustainability of any city must take into account the ecological impacts of the demand for renewable resources the city concentrates drawn from forests, rangelands, farmlands, watersheds, or aquatic ecosystems from outside its boundaries.

Certain natural resources are essential to the existence of any city—fresh water, food, and fuel supplies. Many of the economic activities on which a city's prosperity depends require regular supplies of renewable resources; without a continuing supply of fresh water, agricultural goods and forest products, the economy of many cities would rapidly diminish. Many other formal and informal economic activities, although not directly linked to resource exploitation, depend on such exploitation to generate the income to support their own activities.

In the past, the size and economic base of any city was constrained by the size and quality of the resource endowments of its surrounding region. The relatively high cost of transporting food, raw materials, and fresh water always limited the extent to which a city could survive by drawing resources from outside its region. The high costs of transporting city-generated wastes away from the surrounding region promoted local solutions, and there was a need to ensure that such wastes did not damage the soils and water on which local agricultural production (and often fishing) depended. If local ecosystems were degraded, the prosperity of the city suffered—or in extreme cases, its viability as a city was threatened.[26]

Motorized transportation systems enormously cheapened the possibility of disassociating the scale of renewable resource use in cities from the productivity of its region. The more developed the transportation system, the larger this disassociation. This has now reached a scale where the progress achieved in and around wealthy cities in terms of much improved protection of the region's forests, soils, and areas of ecological importance is achieved by appropriating the soils and water resources of distant ecosystems.[27] Wealthy nations now import many of the land-intensive and water-intensive goods their consumers or producers need, so the depletion of soil and the overexploitation of fresh water resources these cause are not environmental costs borne within their boundaries. Wealthy nations can also import goods whose production has high environmental and health costs—for instance, the high use of pesticides that are applied without adequate protection for the workforce involved in the production—but with none of these health or environmental costs affecting their own inhabitants or ecosystems. Thus, the wealthiest nations can maintain the highest environmental standards within their own countries, even though the ecological and health costs of producing the goods they import are very high. Prosperous cities in the North now draw from the entire planet as their "ecological hinterland" for food and raw materials. If consumers in (say) London or New York are drawing their fruit, vegetables, cereals, meat, and fish from an enormous variety of countries, how can a link be established between this consumption and its ecological consequences in the areas where this food is produced?

Fresh water can also be drawn from distant watersheds and even pumped hundreds of meters up hills, as long as little consideration is given to the high energy costs that this entails (usually coming from thermal power stations, which also means not only high levels of fossil fuel use but also high levels of greenhouse gas emissions). Such technology and its high energy requirements obscure the link between a city's renewable resource use and the impact of this use on the ecosystem where the resource is produced. Prosperous cities can also transport their wastes and dispose of them beyond their own region—in extreme cases, even shipping them abroad. Or they can "export" their air pollution to surrounding regions through acid precipitation and urban pollution plumes that can damage vegetation in large areas downwind of the city.[28] Perhaps only when the cost of oil-based transport comes to reflect its true ecological cost in terms both of a depleting nonrenewable resource and its contribution to greenhouse gas emissions will a stronger connection be reestablished between resource use within cities and the productive capacity of the regions in which they are located.

One example of a scarce "renewable resource" is fresh water. Many cities around the world are facing serious shortages of fresh water, and this is even the case in cities in which one half the population is not adequately served with safe, sufficient supplies. Many cities have outgrown the capacity of their locality to provide adequate, sustainable water supplies. For instance, in Dakar (Senegal), local groundwater supplies are fully used (and polluted) and local aquifers overpumped, resulting in saltwater intrusion; a substantial proportion of the city's water now has to be brought in from the Lac de Guiers, 200 kilometers away.[29] Mexico City also has to supplement its very large ground water supplies by bringing water from ever more distant river systems and pumping this water up several hundred meters to reach the Valley of Mexico where the city is located. Overexploitation of its own underground water has also made the city sink—in some areas by up to nine meters—with serious subsidence damage for many buildings and sewage and drainage pipes.[30]

Hundreds of urban centers in relatively arid areas have also grown beyond the point where adequate water supplies can be drawn from local sources. Examples include many of the coastal cities in Peru (including Lima), La Rioja and Catamarca in Argentina, and various cities in Northern Mexico. Many urban centers in Africa's dryland areas face particularly serious problems because of a combination of rapid growth in demand for water and unusually low rainfall in recent years, with the consequent dwindling of local fresh water resources.

For most urban centers worldwide, an examination of the use of renewable resources by consumers and enterprises within their boundaries reveals a scale and complexity of linkages with rural producers and ecosystems within their own region or nation. This implies that "sustainable urban development" and "sustainable rural development" cannot be separated. The rural–urban linkages can be positive in both developmental and environmental terms. For instance, demand for rural produce from city-based enterprises and households can support prosperous farmers and prosperous rural settlements, where environmental capital is not being depleted. Few governments in the South appreciate the extent to which productive, intensive agriculture can support development goals in both rural and urban areas.[31] Increasing agricultural production can support rising prosperity for rural populations and rapid urban development within or close to the main farming areas—the two supporting each other. There are also many examples of organic solid and liquid wastes, that originate from city-based consumers or industries, being returned to soils. These rural–urban links can also have negative aspects. For instance, agricultural land can be lost as cities' built-up areas expand without control and land speculation on urban fringes drives out cultivators; this appears more common in most nations

In regard to the use of local sinks for city wastes, some progress has been achieved. In most countries, environmental legislation has limited the right of industries and utilities to use local sinks for wastes – for instance, disposing of untreated wastes in rivers, lakes, or other local water bodies or generating high levels of air pollution. However, the extent to which the environmental legislation is enforced varies widely. In many countries in the South, there is little enforcement. Rivers, lakes, and estuaries in or close to major cities or industrial complexes in the South are usually heavily polluted, and this has often led to a drastic reduction in fish production and the loss of livelihoods for those who formerly made their living from fishing.[32] In addition, most countries have been less successful in controlling air pollution arising from motor vehicles, except for the reduction in lead emissions that has been achieved in many countries by the increasing proportion of vehicles that use lead-free petrol.

But cities also have some important potential advantages in regard to the use of renewable resources. For instance, the close proximity of so many water consumers gives greater scope for recycling or directly reusing waste waters – and the techniques for greatly reducing the use of fresh water in city homes and enterprises are well known, where fresh water resources are scarce[33] – although it is agriculture, not cities, that dominate the use of fresh water in most nations.[34] Cities also concentrate populations in ways that usually reduce the demand for land relative to population. In most countries, the area taken up by cities and towns is less than one percent of the total surface area of the nation. The world's current urban population of around 2.6 billion people would fit into an area of 200,000 square kilometers – roughly the size of Senegal or Oman – at densities similar to those of high-class, much valued inner-city residential areas in European cities (for instance Chelsea in London).[35] This is a reminder of how some of the most expensive and desired residential areas in the world also have densities that suburban developers and municipal authorities regard as "too high," even though these are often areas that also have good provision for parks, a diverse employment structure, and good cultural facilities. There are also examples of increasing populations in the central districts of certain cities, as governments controlled private automobiles, improved public transportation, and encouraged a rich and diverse street life.[36] The fact that cities also concentrate demand for fresh fruit, vegetables, fish, and dairy products also means considerable potential for their production in the area around a city—especially if their promotion is integrated with a citywide and regionwide plan to protect watersheds, control urban sprawl, encourage urban or periurban agriculture, and ensure adequate provision for open space.[37] In many cities in Africa and Asia, this would support existing practices as a significant proportion of the food consumed by city inhabitants is grown within city boundaries or in areas immediately adjacent to the built-up areas—often with city wastes also used to fertilize or condition the soil.[38]

Cities and Nonrenewable Resources and Sinks

It was a concern about possible global shortages of key nonrenewable resources (oil, natural gas, and certain minerals) that provided a strong stimulus to the environmental movement in the early 1970s—as in, for instance, the Club of Rome report, *The Limits to Growth.*[39] If the concerns about environment and development in the early 1990s are compared to those in the mid 1970s, this concern now receives less prominence. Two other concerns have grown in prominence. The first is the much increased concern about damage from human activities to global natural systems; the depletion of the stratospheric ozone layer and atmospheric warming are now perceived as far more serious threats to sustainability than was the case in the early 1970s. The second is the much increased concern about the finite nature of many renewable resources (especially fertile soil and fresh water). As noted above, they are only renewable within particular limits.

Levels of resource use per person for nonrenewable resources vary by a factor of between ten and 100 or more, when comparing per capita averages between wealthy and poor nations. The same is also true for levels of waste generation.[40] The disparities become even greater when considering the total consumption to date of nonrenewable resource use and the total contribution over time to existing concentrations of persistent chemicals or of greenhouse gases in the atmosphere. Even if prices for most nonrenewable resources have not risen to reflect their overall scarcity, many would be likely to do so if all countries in the South came to have consumption levels similar to those in the North.

But in one sense, comparisons of averages for resource use or waste (including greenhouse gas emissions) per person between nations is misleading, in that it is essentially the middle- and upper-income groups that account for most resource use and most waste generation; this only becomes a North–South issue because most of the world's middle- and upper-income people with high consumption life styles live in Europe, North America, Japan, and Australasia. High-income households in Africa, Asia, and Latin America may have levels of nonrenewable resource use comparable to high-income households in the richest nations; it is the fact that there are so many fewer of them that keeps national averages much lower.

Levels of household wealth alone are insufficient to explain the disparities in terms of averages for resource use per person. Other factors must be considered. For instance, figures for the use of gasoline per person in different cities are particularly interesting, because this represents both a draw on a finite nonrenewable resource (oil) and a major contributor to greenhouse gases. In 1980, gasoline use per capita in cities such as Houston, Detroit, and Los Angeles was five to seven times that of three of Europe's most prosperous and attractive cities: Amsterdam, Vienna, and Copenhagen.[41] Averages for resource use per person are not only linked to incomes and prices, but also to the incentive and regulatory framework provided by governments to encourage resource conservation or penalize high levels of resource use and waste.

Although cities are generally considered locations that concentrate high levels of nonrenewable resource use, they can also be viewed as places with tremendous potential to cut down the use of nonrenewable resources. By concentrating production and consumption, cities also make possible a greater range and possibility for the efficient use of non-renewable resources—through the reclamation of materials from waste streams and its reuse or recycling—and for the specialist enterprises that ensure this can happen safely. Cities make possible material or waste exchanges among industries. The collection of recyclable or reusable wastes from homes and businesses is generally cheaper per person served. Cities have cheaper unit costs for many measures to promote the use of reusable containers (and cut down on disposable containers). In many cities in the South, there are also long-established traditions that ensure high levels of recycling or reuse of wastes on which government's solid waste management can build.[42]

The fact that cities concentrate production and residential areas also means a considerable potential for reducing fossil fuel use in heating and/or cooling and in transportation. For heating, this can be achieved through the use of waste process heat from industry or thermal power stations to provide space heating for homes and commercial buildings. Certain forms of high-density housing, such as terraces and apartment blocks, also considerably reduce heat loss from each housing unit when compared to detached housing. There are also many measures that can be taken to reduce heat gain in buildings to eliminate or greatly reduce the demand for electricity for air conditioning. In regard to transportation, cities represent a much greater potential for limiting the use of motor vehicles—including greatly reducing the fossil fuels they need and the air pollution and high levels of resource consumption that their use implies. This might sound contradictory, because most of the world's largest cities have serious problems with congestion and motor-vehicle generated air pollution. But cities ensure that many more trips can be made through walking or bicycling. They also make possible a much greater use of public transportation and make high-quality service economically feasible. Thus, although cities tend to be associated with a high level of private automobile use, cities and urban systems also represent the greatest potential for allowing their inhabitants quick and cheap access to a great range of locations, without the need to use private automobiles.

Two points in regard to nonrenewable sources need to be emphasized. The first is that the finite nature of the resource base is not in doubt, even if the predictions as to when resource shortages (or price rises associated with shortages) will begin have receded. The second is that high consumption levels for nonrenewable resources are also associated with high levels of waste generation and greenhouse gas emissions. Reducing greenhouse gas emissions certainly implies lower levels of use and waste in nonrenewable resources. There may be sufficient nonrenewable resources to ensure that 9 to 10 billion people on earth, late in the next century, have their needs met. But it is unlikely that the world's resources and ecosystems could sustain a world population of 9 or 10 billion with a per capita consumption of nonrenewable resources similar to those enjoyed by the richest households today or even the average figure for the world's high-consumption cities, such as Houston and Los Angeles.

While there has been some progress in many countries in protecting renewable resources (especially soils and forests) and in limiting the ecological damage from city-generated wastes on their surrounding regions, there is much less progress on achieving more sustainable patterns of resource use and waste generation in the use of nonrenewable resources and sinks for nonbiodegradable wastes. This includes the "global sink," as the reduction in the stratospheric ozone layer brings new environmental and health costs and as global warming appears likely to continue and to bring increasingly serious health and environmental costs. Progress on addressing environmental problems is easier where those creating or exacerbating the problem (for instance the polluters) and those affected by the problem are within the same locality or nation. Even if those whose livelihoods and health have been adversely affected by the environmental consequences of other people's or businesses' activities have often found it difficult to get these activities halted or their environmental impacts reduced, at least within most societies there are laws and institutions which allow such problems to be addressed.

Where environmental problems are caused or exacerbated by activities in other countries, it is much more difficult for those affected to stop it. For instance, how can those people who are adversely affected by floods or extreme weather conditions that are probably linked to global warming get redress from past and current middle- and upper-income households with high consumption levels that have been a major cause of global warming?

The problem becomes even more complex when considered across generations – how can those who are likely to lose their livelihoods (and possibly their lives) from storms and floods and changes in rainfall patterns that are linked to global warming in the future get redress from the people whose high consumption and waste levels were the main underlying cause of their losses? It has proved possible to halt or modify investment decisions that imply serious social and environmental costs either in the immediate locality or at least within that nation's boundaries (although much more needs to be done), but it is very difficult to halt or modify investment decisions that imply serious social and environmental costs in distant (foreign) ecosystems or for future generations.

In addition, if governments and international agencies give such inadequate attention to the needs and priorities of people who lack the income or assets to adequately meet their own needs, are they likely to act to safeguard the needs and priorities of future generations? The lack of a commitment to intragenerational equity (i.e., to lessening unequal access to natural resources and to safe and healthy living environments within the contemporary world) does not auger well for obtaining a real commitment to intergenerational equity. Achieving the intergenerational equity aspect of sustainable development is, in effect, a commitment by middle- and upper-income groups all round the world to change life styles and consumption patterns to safeguard the needs of future generations. Although the extent of the needed changes is strongly debated, the need for changes has become evident.

Global Warming and Cities

Although there is still much uncertainty about the possible scale of global warming in the future, the scale of possible disruption to cities (and other settlements and ecosystems) and of increases in extreme weather events if there is a sustained trend towards atmospheric warming make curbs on greenhouse gas emissions particularly important. The most direct effects of global warming are higher global mean temperatures, sea level rises, and changes in weather patterns (including those of rainfall and other forms of precipitation) and in the frequency and severity of extreme weather conditions (storms, sea surges). These can lead to major changes in the function and structure of ecosystems. They will also pose direct threats to human health and life, especially through increased incidence and severity of floods and storms and through decreased potential for crop production in particular areas.

Sea level rises will obviously be most disruptive to settlements on coastal and estuarine areas, and this is where a considerable proportion of the world's population lives. Sea level rises will flood low-lying areas unless flood protection is built (and such protection may be prohibitively expensive for many settlements and societies). They will also bring rising ground-water levels in coastal areas that will threaten existing sewerage and drainage systems and may undermine buildings. Most coastal cities will need extensive and expensive modifications to their water supply and sanitation and drainage systems. Many of the world's most densely populated areas are river deltas and low-lying coastal areas. Many of the world's largest cities are ports that also developed as major industrial, commercial, and financial centers; these will be particularly vulnerable to sea level rises. So too will the many industries and thermal power stations that are concentrated on coasts because of their need for cooling water or because the sea was a convenient dumping ground for their waste.[43]

Global warming will also mean increased human exposure to exceptional heat waves. This is likely to cause discomfort for many and premature death for some. The elderly, the very young, and those with incapacitating diseases are likely to suffer most.[44] Those living in cities that are already heat islands where temperatures remain significantly above those of the surrounding regions will also be particularly at risk. High relative humidity will considerably amplify heat stress.[45] Increased temperatures in cities can also increase the concentrations of ground-level ozone, as it increases the reaction rates among the pollutants that form ozone.

Global warming will also bring changes in the distribution of infectious diseases. Warmer average temperatures permit an expansion in the area in which "tropical diseases" can occur. This is likely to be the case for many diseases spread by insect vectors—for instance global warming is likely to permit an expansion of the area in which mosquitoes that are the vectors for malaria, dengue fever, and filariasis can survive and breed.[46] The areas in which the aquatic snail that is the vector for schistosomiasis may expand considerably. Increasing temperatures and changes in weather patterns will lead to changes in ecosystems that in turn impact on the livelihoods of those who exploit or rely on natural resources for their livelihoods. Both traditional and modern agricultural practices may be vulnerable to the relatively rapid changes in temperature, rainfall, flooding, and storms that global warming can bring. In many regions, the additional stress placed on farmers and pastoralists by changing temperatures and weather patterns will be added to what are already serious stresses on ecosystems' carrying capacities.

However, a long-term program initiated now can, over time, greatly reduce the emission of "greenhouse gases" that underlie global warming without high social and economic costs. Many of the actions needed to reduce the emissions of these gases have other social, economic, or environmental benefits. The main difficulty in the more wealthy, urbanized societies where most greenhouse gas emissions currently take place is initiating a process that steadily reduces these emissions. The main difficulty in less wealthy societies is ensuring that the prioritization of economic growth and improved standards of living take place within resource efficient, waste-minimizing settlements. Both require ways to ensure that individuals and enterprises revise the basis on which investment and consumption decisions are made so these take sufficient account of dangers that are most acute several decades into the future.

Poverty and the Loss of Environmental Capital

Much of the writing about sustainable development has not only ignored the needs and priorities of low-income groups, but also cast low-income groups as major causes of environmental degradation.[47] But low-income groups contribute very little to the depletion of at least three of the four kinds of environmental capital discussed earlier. Their consumption per person of nonrenewable resources is very low—which is not surprising given the fact that they lack the income to own private automobiles and to own or use other resource-intensive capital goods. They generally use the least resource-intensive forms of transport—walking, bicycling and public transport. The levels of waste they generate per person are much lower than those of richer groups—and low-income households in rural and urban areas often reuse or recycle much of what wealthier households would thrown away.[48] Their contribution per person to greenhouse gases and to stratospheric ozone depleting chemicals both directly through their actions and indirectly through the goods they own or use is very low in comparison to wealthier groups. The same is true for other nonbiodegradable wastes.

The only components of natural capital to whose depletion low-income groups may contribute is in certain renewable resources—for instance, to soil degradation or the degradation of forests or the overuse of freshwater. But a large proportion of low-income households contribute little or nothing to this—for instance, those living in urban areas or those who are landless in rural areas and who make a living through wage labor. The only basis for accusing "the poor" of contributing to unsustainable resource use is for that portion of "the poor" that make their living as farmers (usually on smallholdings), pastoralists, and forest users. But even for these, they cannot be a major force for the degradation of soils or forests worldwide since their poverty is a result of them having so little land and such inadequate access to forests. Most deforestation and soil erosion takes place on land that the poor do not own and to which they do not have access. Wealthy farmers, landowners, commercial companies, and governments own most of the worlds farmland and forests so it is difficult to see how the poor can be blamed for their overuse. Thus, the discussion of the contribution of poverty to unsustainable resource use is only in regard to the very small proportion of the world's soils, forests, pastures, and fisheries to which poor farmers, pastoralists, hunter gatherers, and those who fish have access to.

The fact that these people are poor will also mean that they generally have the most marginal or fragile renewable resources on which to draw their livelihoods. The more intense the competition for access to resources, the more the lowest income groups or indigenous peoples are pushed to the least valuable margins. As such, they have the greatest difficulties in sustaining production levels and are most likely to forsake long term sustainability because of short term survival. It is common for many low-income households to be involved in deforestation on the agricultural frontier and to be expanding cultivation on land ill suited to agriculture. But this does not mean that they are major contributors to unsustainable resource use on a global scale. And even if low-income households have to sustain themselves on inadequate land holdings and poor quality soil, there is not necessarily evidence of environmental degradation and many examples of low income groups involved in environmental protection and careful resource management.[49] There are also many examples of "low-income" communities whose indigenous knowledge and practices are far more oriented to long-term ecological sustainability than most modern farming and forestry practices.[50]

There is certainly a link between poverty and serious problems of environmental health as low-income groups lack access to safe and sufficient water supplies, provision for sanitation, safe and adequate housing and access to health care. But this should not be confused with the depletion of environmental capital. The environment-related diseases and injuries that low-income households suffer are not depleting soils or forests or using nonrenewable resources or seriously disrupting ecosystems.

Development Advantages of Cities

We have already discussed the current or potential advantages of cities in reducing a society's call on natural capital and thus contributing to a more "ecologically sustainable" pattern of development. But it should also be recalled that cities present advantages in development terms. For instance, the higher densities in cities also mean much lower costs per household and per enterprise for the provision of piped, treated water supplies, the collection and disposal of household and human wastes, advanced telecommunications, and most forms of health care and education. Higher densities also make much cheaper the provision of emergency services – for instance firefighting and the emergency response to acute illness or injury that can greatly reduce the health burden for the people affected.

However, in the absence of effective governance in cities, including the institutional means to ensure the provision of infrastructure and services, the control of pollution, and the encouragement of efficient resource use, environmental problems are greatly exacerbated. The concentration of human, household, commercial, and industrial wastes causes major environmental health problems for city inhabitants and overwhelm local sinks' capacity to break them down or dilute them. In the absence of an adequate drainage system, flooding and waterlogging usually cause serious problems. Thus, cities' potential advantages for high-quality infrastructure and service provision and efficient use of resources is not utilized. Meanwhile, in the absence of a planning framework, city expansion takes place haphazardly and often with urban sprawl over the best quality farmland. Meanwhile, poorer groups usually live in illegal or informal settlements which develop on land ill suited to housing – for instance, on floodplains or steep slopes with a high risk of landslides or mudslides – because these are the only land sites that they can afford. It is much more this failure of effective governance within cities that explains the poor environmental performance of so many cities rather than an inherent characteristic of cities in general.

The achievement of sustainable development goals in cities should also be viewed more positively in terms of employment creation. There is a considerable employment potential in moving towards more resource conserving and waste-minimizing patterns of production and consumption in the North and in the wealthier cities in the South. The main reason is that levels of resource use, waste generation, and pollution are so high that there are many possibilities for substituting labor and knowledge for resource use and waste. There is great potential for combining employment generation with the transition to a more resource-efficient, minimum waste production and consumption pattern in:

- improving insulation levels in residential, commercial, and industrial buildings and in adopting other innovations that limit electricity or fossil fuel consumption;
- the manufacture, installation, and maintenance of machinery and equipment that is more resource efficient and less polluting; and
- the industrial and service enterprises associated with waste minimization, recycling, reuse, and resource reclamation.

However, there are employment losses arising from the greater cost of certain goods or services, especially those whose production or use requires major changes to reduce unacceptable levels of resource use or waste generation. But there are many examples of industrial processes where resource use and pollution levels have been cut with no overall increase in costs and, in some cases, with significant cost savings.[51] In addition, even if costs do rise, they only do so to compensate for environmental costs that previously had been ignored.

A move to patterns of production within cities that are more compatible with sustainable development (because they are more resource conserving with minimal wastes) implies a series of shifts in the relative importance of employment in different sectors.[52] For instance, declining employment in the manufacture of automobiles and the material inputs into this process is compensated through expanding employment in public transportation equipment and systems, traffic management, air pollution control equipment for motor vehicles, and reclamation and recycling of materials used in road vehicles. Similarly, declining employment in the coal, oil, natural gas, and electricity industries is balanced by increasing employment in energy conservation in all sectors and in the manufacture and installation of energy-efficient appliances. Employment also grows within the renewable energy sector as higher prices for nonrenewable fuels, technological advances, and public support for renewable resource use expand the potential to tap renewable energy sources. It is quite feasible in the North for living standards and the number of households to continue growing, but with a steady decline in the level of fossil fuel use.[53] Investments in energy conservation are generally more labor intensive than investments in increasing the energy supply—especially when comparing the cost of increasing the electricity supply with the cost of reducing demand through conservation or the use of more efficient appliances, so that supplies no longer need to increase.

Another employment shift within this move to more sustainable production patterns is declining employment in mining and primary metals industries and paper and glass industries (and other industries associated with packaging production) and expanding employment in urban management systems that maximize recycling, reuse, and reclamation, and promote waste minimization. Another employment shift is declining employment in producing and selling the fertilizers and biocides now widely used in industrial agriculture and horticulture, but increasing employment in lower input farming, ecologically-based farming and land management, and resource efficient, high-intensity crop production systems, such as those based on hydroponics and permaculture. This includes much increased scope for urban agriculture and horticulture that can also brings considerable ecological advantages, as well as employment opportunities and incomes.[54]

There are also likely to be increased employment opportunities in the water supply and sewage treatment industries, as higher standards are met and water conservation programs implemented, and in the managerial and technical staff within municipalities and companies or corporations, whose task is environmental management.

Although there are employment benefits in moving towards more ecologically sustainable patterns of production and consumption, the employment losses fall heavily on certain employees and on urban centers or regions that have the traditional logging, "smokestack," and mining industries. Most of the job losses in these industries in Europe and North America during the last two decades have little to do with environmental regulation and much more to do with the gradual shift in production to cheaper areas or to new technologies that greatly reduce the need for labor. But it is little comfort to the miners and steelworkers and their families when jobs disappear, to know that policies promoting resource conservation and waste minimization are creating more employment elsewhere. Thus, one of the most important roles for government in promoting this transition is addressing the needs of the workforce in the resource- and waste-intensive industries that lose their employment. There are some interesting cases on this—for instance, the case of Hamilton–Wentworth in Canada, which lost a large part of its employment base as the steel mills closed down, moved away, or cut down their workforce. Its response was to try to promote the city as a good location for industries concerned with environmental protection and resource conservation and to develop its environmental quality as a key part of attracting new investment.[55]

Linking Global and Local Sustainability

The possible contradictions between ecological sustainability at global and at local level have already been noted. So too has the fact that most of the world's wealthiest nations have been relatively successful at meeting some sustainable development goals within their own nation or region by drawing heavily on the environmental capital of other regions or nations and on the global sink. In effect, they have imported environmental capital and depleted the world's stock of such capital; it is often their production and consumption patterns which underlie (or contribute significantly to) unsustainable forest, soil or freshwater exploitation in poorer nations.

This implies the need for international agreements that set limits for each national society's consumption of resources and use of the global sink for their wastes. But it is also clear that most action to achieve sustainable development has to be formulated and implemented locally. The fact that each village, province, or city and its insertion within local and regional ecosystems is unique implies the need for optimal use of local resources, knowledge, and skills for the achievement of development goals within a detailed knowledge of the local and regional ecological carrying capacity. This demands a considerable degree of local self-determination, because centralized decision-making structures have great difficulty in implementing decisions that respond appropriately to such diversity. Nevertheless, some new international institutions are required to ensure that individual cities or countries do not take advantage of others' restraint.

National governments inevitably have the key role in linking local and global sustainability. Internationally, they have the responsibility for reaching agreements to limit the call that consumers and businesses within their country make on the world's environmental capital. Nationally, they are responsible for providing the framework to ensure local actions can meet development goals without compromising local and global sustainability. But there is little evidence of national governments setting up the regulatory and incentive structure to ensure that the aggregate impact of their economic activities and citizens' consumption is in accordance with global sustainability—although a few in Europe have taken some tentative steps towards some aspects.[56] Such an incentive and regulatory structure is relatively easy to conceive, as an abstract exercise. Certainly, poverty can be greatly reduced without an expansion in resource use and waste generation that threatens ecological sustainability. It is also possible to envisage a considerable reduction in resource use and waste generation by middle- and upper-income households, without diminishing their quality of life (and in some aspects actually enhancing it). The prosperity and economic stability that the poorer nations need to underpin secure livelihoods for their populations and the needed enhancement in the competence and accountability of their government can be achieved without a much-increased call on environmental capital. However, the prospects for actually translating what is possible into reality both within nations and globally remains much less certain. Powerful vested interests oppose most if not all the needed policies and priorities. Richer groups are unlikely to willingly forsake the comfort and mobility that they currently enjoy. Technological change can help to a limited extent—for instance, moderating the impact of rising gasoline prices through the relatively rapid introduction of increasingly fuel-efficient automobiles and the introduction of alternative fuels derived from renewable energy sources. But if combating atmospheric warming does demand a rapid reduction in greenhouse gas emissions, this will imply changes in people's right to use private automobiles that cannot be met by new technologies and alternative ("renewable") fuels—at least at costs which will prove politically acceptable. So many existing commercial, industrial, and residential buildings and urban forms (for instance low-density suburban developments and out-of-town shopping malls) have high levels of energy use built into them and these are not easily or rapidly changed.[57]

At the same time, in the South, the achievement of development goals that minimize the call on local and global environmental capital demands a competence and capacity by local governments that is currently very rarely present. The achievement of key development goals is also unlikely without strong democratic pressures and processes influencing decisions about the use of public resources.

Governance

Achieving three of the main principles that underlie sustainable development[58] – more intergenerational equity, more intragenerational equity, and greater transfrontier responsibility by resource users and waste generators – implies substantial political changes. It implies major changes in ownership rights for land and natural resources.[59] It also implies changes in the configuration of the political systems at local and global levels that had previously allowed or even encouraged undesirable environmental impacts.[60]

This helps explain why the discussion of urban problems has been moving away from discussing "what should be done" to discussing what kind of "governance" structure is needed to allow effective decisions to be made about what has to be done. The discussion of governance is much broader than the roles and responsibilities of governments as "governance" includes the contribution of community and voluntary organizations and other social groups and their relations with "government."[61] One of the most important aspects of this change is the move from discussing "what poor people need" to "what decision-making powers, access to resources, and political influence should low-income people have to allow them to ensure that their needs are met, their rights respected, and their priorities addressed." City inhabitants and their community organizations not only require more influence on their "future city," but they also require governments, corporations, and international agencies to be more accountable for the actions and investments they make.[62]

The debate about city and municipal authorities in the South has also moved in this direction. The concern in the late 1970s and early 1980s was largely that they lacked the power, authority, and resources to meet their responsibilities. More recently, the concern has come to include how democratic, accountable, and transparent they are and their capacity to work with, encourage, and support a great range of community organizations, voluntary associations, and social groups.

An important part of this move from "government" to "governance" has been the greater appreciation of the role of individuals and households and of community and voluntary organizations in building and managing each city. All cities are the result of an enormous range of investments of capital, expertise, and time by individuals, households, communities, voluntary organizations, and NGOs, as well as by private enterprises, investors, and government agencies. During the last 20 years, many of the most effective initiatives to improve housing conditions among low-income groups have come from local NGOs or community organizations. These include new models for housing finance which provide loans to households whose incomes are too low or uncertain to get finance from the private sector, but which nonetheless achieve lower levels of loan default than banks obtain from loans to higher-income groups.[63] They include new ways for governments to work with low-income groups and their community organizations in improving housing conditions and health.[64] They include municipal authorities that make their whole budgeting process more open and more subject to the demands of citizens.[65] Many more governments and a few donor agencies are learning how to support these processes that build and develop cities. What can be achieved by supporting the efforts of several hundred community organizations in a single city can vastly outweigh what any single government agency can do by itself.

Another important change is the innovation showed in many local Agenda 21 plans developed by cities in both the North and the South.[66] These seek to address environment and development issues that are of direct relevance to the citizens. Many have pioneered new ways of fully involving the inhabitants in their formulation and implementation. But many have also sought to address environment and development problems of relevance to people outside their boundaries and to the depletion of environmental capital elsewhere.[67] These are showing a new commitment to intergenerational equity and transfrontier responsibility. Although these provide encouraging examples, what is so lacking in most countries and within international negotiations is any sign of the national and international framework that is needed to support such initiatives and to ensure they become the norm rather than the exceptions.[68]

National governments in both North and South are unlikely to set the incentives and regulations needed to promote sustainable development outside their national boundaries without international agreements. One of the key international issues in the next few decades will be how to resolve the pursuit of increased wealth by national societies (most of whose members have strong preferences for minimal constraints on their consumption levels) within a global recognition of the ecological and material limits of the biosphere. There is little doubt that the world's natural resource endowments and natural systems can sustain the world's population both now and in the near future with absolute poverty eliminated, human needs met, and all nations having life expectancies comparable to those in the richer nations. In the richest nations, it is also possible to envisage much more resource-conserving societies without a fall in living standards. Indeed, as outlined earlier, in many respects, far more resource- conserving societies will have higher living standards and broader and more fulfilling employment structures. What is far more in question is whether the political processes within and among nations can put in place both the agreements and the regulatory and incentive structures to ensure that this is achieved. The power and profitability of many major corporations and the authority of national governments will be reduced by such a move. Many jobs may also be threatened although, as noted earlier, more attention to resource conservation is likely to create more jobs than it removes. Some necessary measures are likely to prove politically unpopular. Even when international agreement is reached, the world has little experience of the institutions needed to ensure compliance.

Achieving this is made all the more difficult by incomplete knowledge about the scale and nature of the environmental costs that current production and consumption patterns are passing onto current and future generations.[69] The precautionary principle may be well understood and widely quoted but it is not being integrated into economic decisions. One of the most difficult issues to resolve is on what basis to value the different kinds of environmental assets widely used in production and consumption[70] and how to ensure that this valuation contributes to greater intergenerational and intragenerational equity. Another is the extent to which other forms of capital are substitutable for natural capital.[71]

Another is how to ensure that social capital (including social institutions that have great importance to ensuring human needs are met) and human capital (including people's knowledge and level of education and their health) are also not also depleted.[72] There is an increasing recognition of the importance of what it often termed the "social economy," not only for the benefits it brings to each street or neighborhood, but also for the economic and social costs it saves the wider society.[73] The social economy is a term given to a great variety of initiatives and actions that are organized and controlled locally and that are not profit oriented. It includes many activities that are unwaged and unmonetized – including the work of citizen groups, residents' associations, street or neighborhood (barrio) clubs, youth clubs, and volunteers who help support local schools and prevention-oriented health care and provide services for the elderly, the physically disabled, or other individuals in need of special support. It includes many initiatives that make cities safer and more fun – helping provide supervised play space and sport and recreational opportunities for children and youth.[74]

There are also international factors far beyond the competence and capacity of national and municipal governments that influence the quality of city environments. The very poor environmental conditions evident in most Southern cities are an expression of the very difficult circumstances in which most Southern countries find themselves. Stagnant economies and heavy debt burdens do not provide a suitable base from which to develop good governance. Governments from the North and international agencies may promote environmental policies, but there is little progress on changing the international economic system to permit more economic stability and prosperity among the poorest nations. Many Southern economies have no alternative but to increase the exploitation of their natural resources to earn the foreign exchange to meet debt repayments. In the end, despite the possibility of pointing to innovative programs and practices in both the North and the South that move cities towards a more successful combining of environmental and development goals, the present economic and political structures within which they operate and the great lack of progress in introducing even modest changes to these do not auger well for their spread and further development.

Conclusion

This section of *Cities Fit for People* examined how the unmet needs of city inhabitants, especially in the South, can be articulated and addressed, without imposing environmental costs on other people (including those living in the areas around cities) or depleting environmental capital to the point where it imposes high environmental costs on future generations). We concluded that this requires considerable change for most city and municipal authorities, as the citizens within their jurisdiction acquire more power to define their needs and influence how they are addressed. It also means an expansion of the responsibilities of city and municipal authorities, because the use of resources and the generation of wastes within city boundaries have to take account of the needs and rights of others living elsewhere and of future generations. Finally, we offered a framework for considering the multiple goals that are embedded within the term "sustainable development" for cities and considered the potential advantages that cities have for meeting the priorities of their citizens while also reducing the degradation or depletion of environmental capital. In very few cities is it environmental constraints that prevent the achievement of sustainable development goals. It is much more institutional constraints within government structures and the vested interests within nations and within the increasingly globalized economy who do not want the redistribution of power, the greater accountability and the control of environmental degradation that the achievement of sustainable development goals requires.

Notes

1. This is a condensed version of a chapter with this title in Cedric Pugh, ed., Sustainability, the Environment and Urbanization, London: Earthscan Publications, 1996. This in turn developed themes that the

authors first wrote about with Jorge Hardoy in Chapter 6 of J. E. Hardoy, Diana Mitlin, and David Satterthwaite, *Environmental Problems in Third World Cities.* London: Earthscan Publications, 1992

2. See W. M. Adams, *Green Development: Environment and Sustainability in the Third World.* London and New York: Routledge, 1990.

3. D. Mitlin, "Sustainable Development: A Guide to the Literature," *Environment and Urbanization* 1992, 4(1): 111–124.

4. *Ibid.*, p. 111.

5. Official statistics on water supply provision greatly overstate the proportion of the world's population with safe and convenient supplies. See D. Satterthwaite, "The Underestimation of Poverty and Its Health Consequences," *Third World Planning Review* 1995, 17(4): iii-xii.

6. See, for example, Idriss Jazairy, Mohiuddin Alamgir, and Theresa Panuccio, *The State of World Rural Poverty: An Inquiry into Its Causes and Consequences.* London: IT Publications, 1992.

7. World Health Organization, *Our Planet, Our Health.* Geneva: Commission on Health and Environment, 1992.

8. Division of Control of Tropical Diseases, World Health Organization, "World Malaria Situation, 1990," *World Health Statistics Quarterly* 1992, 45(2/3): 257–266.

9. World Health Organization, *The World Health Report 1995: Bridging the Gaps.* Geneva: World Health Organization,1995.

10. Sandy Cairncross, Jorge E. Hardoy, and David Satterthwaite "The Urban Context." In Jorge E. Hardoy, Sandy Cairncross, and David Satterthwaite, eds., *The Poor Die Young: Housing and Health in Third World Cities.* London: Earthscan Publications, 1990. This estimate was subsequently endorsed by the World Health Organization, 1992, and by UNCHS (Habitat) *An Urbanizing World: Global Report on Human Settlements, 1996,* Oxford and New York: Oxford University Press, 1996.

11. Gordon McGranahan, Jacob Songsore, Marianne Kjellén, Pedro Jacobi, and Charles Surjadi "Sustainability, Poverty and Urban Environmental transitions," in Pugh, 1996.

12. Adams, 1990.

13. Adams, 1990.

14. Graham Haughton and Colin Hunter, *Sustainable Cities.* Regional Policy and Development Series. London: Jessica Kingsley, 1994.

15. As noted in C. J. Barrow, "Sustainable Development: Concept, Value and Practice," *Third World Planning Review* 1995, 17(4): 369–386, the importance of the Brundtland Commission was not so much in its innovative ideas, but in rekindling environmental interests within development. The economic crises of the early 1980s and the political realignments in the North had hindered action on what might be termed "Brundtland-like" demands made during the 1970s.

16. There is also an assumption that the concern for sustainable development is new when the key conceptual underpinnings of sustainable development were widely discussed and described in the early 1970s and possibly earlier. The term sustainable development arose primarily to acknowledge the development needs of low-income groups and low-income countries within the growing interest in local, national, and global environmental issues in the North and the understanding of the international dimensions of environmentalism. The need to reconcile these two aspects was widely discussed before, during, and after the UN Conference on the Human Environment at Stockholm in 1972, even if this was not called "sustainable development" at that time. The Brundtland Commission's stress on "meeting the needs of the present without compromising the ability of future generations to meet their own needs" had been a central theme in the writings of Barbara Ward throughout the 1970s – although this was usually phrased as meeting the "inner limits" of human needs and rights without exceeding the "outer limits" of the planet's ability to sustain life, now and in the future. See for instance The Cocoyoc Declaration adopted by the participants of the UNEP/UNCTAD symposium on Pattern of Resource Use, Environment and Development Strategies in 1974 that was drafted by Barbara Ward and republished in *World Development* 1975, 3(2–3). See also Barbara Ward and René Dubos, *Only One Earth: The Care and Maintenance of a Small Planet.* London: Andre Deutsch, 1972; Barbara Ward, "The Inner and the Outer Limits," Clifford Clark Memorial Lectures, *Canadian Public Administration* 1976, 19(3): 385–416; and Barbara Ward, *Progress for a Small Planet.* London: Penguin, 1979 and London: Earthscan Publications, 1989.
17. World Commission on Environment and Development, *Our Common Future.* Oxford and New York: Oxford University Press, 1987.
18. See the Universal Declaration of Human Rights, Article 25 (1), United Nations.
19. See for instance UNCHS (Habitat), *An Urbanizing World: Global Report on Human Settlements, 1996.* Oxford and New York: Oxford University Press, 1996.
20. *Ibid.*
21. *Ibid.*
22. William E. Rees, "Ecological Footprints and Appropriated Carrying Capacity," *Environment and Urbanization* 1992, 4(2): 121–130.
23. Haughton and Hunter, 1994.
24. Haughton and Hunter, 1994.
25. WHO, 1992.
26. There are many historic examples of wealthy and powerful cities that drew resources from a much wider region, but these were exceptions. See Herbert Giradet, *The Gaia Atlas of Cities.* London: Gaia, 1992.
27. Rees, 1992.

28. Gordon R. Conway and Jules N. Pretty, *Unwelcome Harvest.* London: Earthscan Publications, 1991.
29. Rodney R. White, "The International Transfer of Urban Technology: Does the North Have Anything to Offer for the Global Environmental Crisis?" *Environment and Urbanization* 1992, 4(2): 109–120.
30. Araceli Damián, "Ciudad de México: servicios urbanos en los noventas" *Vivienda* 1992, 3(1): 29–40; and Sandra Postel, *The Last Oasis; Facing Water Scarcity, Worldwatch Environmental Alert Series.* London: Earthscan Publications, 1992.
31. See for instance Mabel Manzanal and Cesar Vapnarsky, "The Development of the Upper Valley of Rio Negro and Its Periphery Within the Comahue Region, Argentina." In Jorge E. Hardoy and David Satterthwaite, eds., *Small and Intermediate Urban Centres: Their Role in Regional and National Development in the Third World.* London: Hodder and Stoughton, 1986; and Mary Tiffen and Michael Mortimore, "Environment, Population Growth and Productivity in Kenya: A Case Study of Machakos District," *Development Policy Review* 1992, 10: 359–387.
32. Hardoy, Mitlin, and Satterthwaite, 1992.
33. See, for example, The Water Program, *Water Efficiency: A Resource for Utility Managers, Community Planners and other Decision Makers.* Rocky Mountain Institute, 1991.
34. See World Resources Institute, *World Resources 1990–91: A Guide to the Global Environment.* Oxford and New York: Oxford University Press, 1990, Table 22.1, pp. 330–331..
35. The example of Chelsea was chosen because it combines very high-quality housing, very little of which is in high rises (and most of which is pre-twentieth century) with a diverse economic base, large amounts of open space, and among the best educational and cultural facilities in London. With a population density of approximately 120 persons per hectare, it is an example of how relatively high density need not imply overcrowding or poor quality living environments. The world's urban population of around 2.6 billion in 1995 would fit into an area of land similar to that of Senegal (197,000 square kilometers) or Oman (212,000 square kilometers) at a density comparable to that of Chelsea.
36. UNCHS, 1996.
37. See, for example, Jac Smit and others, *Urban Agriculture: Food, Jobs And Sustainable Cities.* UNDP, 1996.
38. Smit and others, 1996.
39. Donella H. Meadows, Dennis L. Meadows, Jorgen Randers and William W. Behrens III, *The Limits to Growth.* London: Pan, 1974.
40. UNCHS, 1996.
41. Peter W. G. Newman and Jeffrey R. Kenworthy, *Cities and Automobile Dependence: An International Sourcebook.* Aldershot, England: Gower, 1989.

42. See, for example, Christine Furedy, "Social Aspects of Solid Waste Recovery in Asian Cities," *Environmental Sanitation Reviews*, vol. 30. Bangkok: ENSIC, Asian Institute of Technology, 1990, pp. 2–52; Christine Furedy, "Garbage: Exploring Non-conventional Options in Asian Cities," *Environment and Urbanization* 1992, 4(2): 42–61.
43. Martin Parry, "The Urban Economy." Paper presented at Cities and Climate Change, a conference at the Royal Geographical Society, 31 March 1992
44. WHO, 1992.
45. *Ibid.*
46. *Ibid.*
47. See, for example, UNDP, *Human Development Report 1991.* Oxford and New York: Oxford University Press, 1991, which claims that "significant environmental degradation is usually caused by poverty in the South" (p. 28). Poverty is also considered as a major factor in environmental degradation in Johan Holmberg, *Poverty, Environment and Development: Proposals for Action.* Stockholm: Swedish International Development Authority, 1992; H. Jeffrey Leonard, "Environment and the Poor: Development Strategies for a Common Agenda." In H. Jeffrey Leonard and contributors, *Environment and the Poor: Development Strategies for a Common Agenda.* New Brunswick, NJ: 1989.
48. Some enterprises owned by low-income groups do create or contribute to serious problems of air pollution and liquid and solid wastes within their locality, but this does not change the fact that low-income groups in general generate far less wastes than middle- and upper-income groups.
49. See, for example, J. N. Pretty and Irene Guijt, "Primary Environmental Care: An Alternative Paradigm for Development Assistance." *Environment and Urbanization* 1992, 4(1): 22–36; also David Satterthwaite, Roger Hart, Caren Levy, Diana Mitlin, David Ross, Jac Smit, and Carolyn Stephens, *The Environment for Children.*, London and New York: Earthscan Publications and UNICEF, 1996, Chapter 6.
50. Ecologist, The, *Whose Common Future: Reclaiming the Commons.* London: Earthscan Publications, 1992.
51. Stephen Schmidheiny (with the Business Council for Sustainable Development), *Changing Course: A Global Business Perspective on Development and the Environment.* Cambridge, MA: MIT Press, 1992.
52. This point is developed in more detail in UNCHS, 1996.
53. Several studies in the late 1970s and early 1980s demonstrated this. See Gerald Leach, et al., *A Low Energy Strategy for the United Kingdom.* London: Science Reviews, 1979, for details of how increasing prosperity need not imply increased fossil fuel use in the United Kingdom.
54. See Smit and others, 1996.
55. Charles Wilkins, "Steeltown Charts a New Course," *Canadian Geographic* 1993, 113(4): 42–55; Regional Municipality of Hamilton-

Wentworth, *Implementing Vision 2020: Directions for Creating a Sustainable Region.* Regional Chairman's Taskforce on Sustainable Development, 1993; and Regional Municipality of Hamilton-Wentworth, *Towards a Sustainable Region: Hamilton-Wentworth Region, Official Plan (Draft).* Regional Planning and Development Department, 1993; Staff Working Group on Sustainable Development, *Hamilton-Wentworth's Sustainable Community Decision-Making Guide.* Regional Municipality of Hamilton-Went worth, 1993.

56. See, for example, UNCHS, 1996.

57. Charles Gore, "Policies and Mechanisms for Sustainable Development: The Transport Sector," 1991 (mimeograph).

58. Haughton and Hunter, 1994.

59. Joachim von Amsberg, *Project Evaluation and the Depletion of Natural Capital: An Application of the Sustainability Principle.* Environment Working Paper No. 56. Washington, DC: Environment Department, World Bank, 1993.

60. Haughton and Hunter, 1994.

61. UNCHS, 1996.

62. See, for example, Enrique Ortiz, "Towards a City of Solidarity and Citizenship," David Korten, "Civic Engagement in Creating Future Cities," and Doris Balvin Diaz, Jose Luiz Lopez Follegatti, and Micky Hordijk, "Innovative Environmental Management in Ilo, Peru," *Environment and Urbanization* 1996, 8(1) (special issue).

63. Diana Mitlin, Building with Credit: Housing Finance for Low-Income Households. *Third World Planning Review* 1997, 19(1): 21–50.

64. UNCHS, 1996.

65. Paulo Roberto Paixão Bretas, "Participative Budgeting in Belo Horizonte: Democratisation and Citizenship," *Environment and Urbanization* 1996, 8(1): 213–222.

66. UNCHS, 1996; Voula Mega, "Our City, Our Future: Towards Sustainable Development in European Cities," *Environment and Urbanization* 1996, 8(1): 133–154.

67. *Ibid.*

68. For instance, initial steps have been taken at the national level in Sweden and the Netherlands to encourage a move towards sustainable development goals among urban authorities. See *Expert Group on the Urban Environment.* European Sustainable Cities, Part 1. Brussels: European Commission, 1994.

69. Ismail Serageldin, "Making Development Sustainable," *Finance and Development* 1993, 30(4): 6–10.

70. Serageldin, 1993; J. T. Winpenny, *Values for the Environment: A Guide to Economic Appraisal.* London: HMSO, 1991.

71. See, for example, Ismail Serageldin, "Sustainability and the Wealth of Nations: First Steps in an Ongoing Journey." Paper presented at the

Third Annual World Bank Conference on Environmentally Sustainable Development, 1995.
72. Serageldin, 1995.
73. This material on the social economy is drawn largely from David C. Korten, "Civic Engagement to Create Just and Sustainable Societies for the 21st Century." Paper Prepared for Habitat II, 1995; and Graham Boyd, *The Urban Social Economy: Urban Examples.* New York: UNICEF, 1995.
74. Korten, 1995; Boyd, 1994; UNCHS, 1996.

Section 2 Cities and Citizens: Their Sustainability

Herbert Girardet

To make the present urban growth globally sustainable, we have to take a close look at how our cities function. As dense centers of human habitation, the cities have the potential for making efficient use of resources. But, how can they fulfill this potential? How can cities become a viable home for humanity? There are several key issues at stake.

Cities, and particularly large modern cities, are astonishingly complex systems. They are predominantly centers of human coexistence, although as structures superimposed on living landscapes, they also harbor vast assemblies of other species. For their sustenance, cities rely on the supply of resources from beyond their boundaries. The critical issue for a sustainable future is: can cities, despite their dependent status, be sustainable, self-regulating systems, both in terms of their internal functioning, as well as in their relationship to the outside world? With urbanization becoming the dominant feature of the human presence on earth, an answer to this question may be critical to the future well-being.

In their internal functioning, cities are certainly superorganisms, following James Lovelock's definition of these as "an ensemble of living and non-living matter which acts as a single, self-regulating system."[1] They are self-regulating systems created for the benefit of humans and their sustained livelihood. Their inhabitants collectively attempt to keep their "constant comfortable state when faced with internal or external change."[2]

Unlike other feedback systems, cities, as natural, physical as well as cultural systems, exhibit additional layers of complexity. Cities as centers of human social activity are characterized by their highly developed division of labor, way beyond the fulfillment of human needs. They are not homogeneous systems in which each of its component parts acts identically. Processes of deliberate and varied social interaction feature much more strongly in cities than in purely natural systems.

External Linkages

The regulation of interactions within cities, then, tends towards the maintenance of conditions favorable to human existence. But while cities also, ultimately depend on maintaining a stable relationship with the ecological system,, their very character as centers of intense economic activity makes them agents for modifying the preexisting assembly of life on earth. Cities ultimately cannot be self-regulating superorganisms, unless they maintain stable linkages with the hinterland from which they draw their resources and into which they currently release their wastes. Cities depend on a multitude of supplies from elsewhere, and this includes land-based resources, such as foodstuffs and timber, as well as of subterranean resources, such as metals and fossil fuels. The way these resources are used, through processing, combustion, and disposal, has profound effects on the biosphere.

Urban systems with several million human inhabitants are unique to the current age, and they are the most complex products of collective human creativity. They are multidimensional in that they reach underground and can rise several hundred feet into the air; they also stretch out horizontally over large territories. They are both organisms and mechanisms in that they utilize biological reproduction, as well as mechanical production processes. The physiology of modern cities is characterized by their routine use of fossil fuels to power production, commerce, transport, water and supplies, as well as domestic comforts. Without the routine use of fossil fuels, the growth of megacities of ten million people and more would have been impossible. A major issue for urban sustainability is whether renewable energy technologies may reduce this dependence in the future.

The physiology of traditional towns and cities was defined by transportation systems and production systems based on muscle power. A major effect of fossil-fuel based private and transportation technologies has been that the high density of traditional cities has given way to urban sprawl. Fossil-fuel powered transportation has also caused many cities to stop relying on resources from their local regions and to become dependent on an increasingly global hinterland.

Urbanization is becoming the dominant feature of the human presence on earth, with city dwellers consuming the bulk of the earth's resources and producing unprecedented amounts of waste. As humanity urbanizes, it also changes its relationship to its host planet. Global urbanization has increased human living standards and the use of resources. This can be witnessed today in developing countries, where urban people, typically, have much higher levels of consumption than rural dwellers, depending on massively increased through-put of fossil fuels, metals, meat, and manufactured products.

As cities draw resources from further and further afield, they also accumulate large amounts of materials within them. Vienna, with 1.6 million inhabitants, increases its actual weight every day by some 35.000 tons.[3] Much of this is relatively inert materials, such as concrete and tarmac. Other materials, such as heavy metals, gradually leach from the roofs of buildings and from water pipes. Nitrates, phosphates, heavy metals, and a host of manufactured materials, such as chlorinated hydrocarbons, accumulate in the urban environment and build up in water courses and soils, with as yet uncertain consequences for future inhabitants. Beyond the immediate urban environment, waste gases, such as nitrogen dioxide and sulfur dioxide, discharged by chimneys and exhaust pipes, affect forests and farmland downwind of our cities. A large proportion of the increase of carbon dioxide in the atmosphere is attributable to combustion in the world's cities. In addition, most rail, road, and airplane traffic occurs between cities. Concern about climate change, resulting mainly from fossil fuel burning, is now shared by virtually all the world's climatologists.

Evolution of the Urban Systems

At the end of the twentieth century, humanity is involved in an unprecedented experiment: we are turning ourselves into an urban species. Large cities, not rural villages and towns, are becoming our habitat. In one century, global urban populations will have expanded from 15 to 50 percent and this figure will increase further in the coming decades. By 2000, half of humanity will live and work in cities, while the other half will depend increasingly on cities and towns for their economic survival.

The size of modern cities, too, in terms of numbers as well physical scale, is unprecedented: in 1800 there was only one city with a million people, London. At that time, the largest 100 cities in the world had 20 million inhabitants, with each city usually extending to just a few thousand hectares.

In 1990 the world's 100 largest cities accommodated 540 million people and 220 million people lived in the 20 largest cities, megacities of more than 10 million people, each extending to hundreds of thousands of hectares. In addition, there were 35 cities with more than 5 million and hundreds with more than one million people.[4] In the nineteenth and early twentieth centuries, urban growth occurred mainly in the North, as a result of the spread of industrialization and the associated rapid increase in the use of fossil fuels. Today, the world's largest and fastest growing cities are emerging in the South, because of urban–industrial development, and as a consequence of rural decline.

City growth is changing the face the earth and the condition of humanity. Can the planet accommodate an urbanized humanity, drawing its resources from an increasingly global hinterland? And, can humanity learn to cope with urban density and complexity while maintaining a stable relationship with the biosphere?

To answer such questions we, first of all, need a better understanding of how the current position arose. Cities have long acted as engines of human cultural, technological, and economic development. The evolution of humanity into our current status of "amplified human beings," people amplified by their technology, occurred in cities. Their historical development is also the story of the emergence of complex forms of human organization, with the appearance of formalized political and spiritual hierarchies, administrations, writing, and military power. Urban systems in their early form also depended on new levels in the human control of nature through the use of technology, and particularly, through farming. The development of sedentary living of thousands of people in one space was only possible through the concentration of food production on limited, defined areas, a dramatic departure from millions of years of nomadic hunting-gathering.

Sedentary living certainly requires a clear understanding of sustainable urban interactions with nature that was not required before urbanization got underway. Above all else, it requires the management of soil fertility and crops for the assured supply of foodstuffs to urban populations over sustained periods of time. Early cities, such as Ur in Mesopotamia some 3,500 years ago were themselves centers of food production. One author conjures up an image of Ur: "Most of the people we pass in the streets would be farmers, market gardeners, herdsmen and fishermen and correspondingly many of the goods transported in carts would be food products. However, some of the farmers could have had other roles as well: carpenters, smiths, potters, stone-cutters, basket-makers, leatherworkers, wool-spinners, baker and brewers are all recorded, as are merchants and what we might call the 'civil service' of the temple community—the priests and the scribes."[5]

But early towns such as Ur did not acquire their prosperity purely on the basis of urban agriculture. They also drew in resources from outside, most importantly forest products. Deforestation certainly occurred on a dramatic scale on the hills around Sumerian cities, both, for acquisition of timber and firewood as well as for the expansion of farmland. In the case of Ur this eventually had dramatic consequences. When Sir Leonard Woolley excavated Ur in the 1880s, he found a three-foot layer of mud that had inundated the city around 2,500 B.C.[6] and other cities in Mesopotamia suffered similar fates. The eventual decline of that civilization is linked to a further environmental factor: the salinization of farmland as a consequence of the injudicious use of irrigation water, with catastrophic consequences for the productivity of farmland feeding these cities. First the yields of wheat, then barley, declined, and eventually the only food plants that would still grow were date palms. When Europeans first traveled extensively in Mesopotamia in the nineteenth century, they found few traces of the ancient cities, only mounds of sand and rubble in a salt-encrusted desert landscape.

Cities are complex systems both in the way they organize themselves, by division of labor and purposeful interaction of different professions, as well as the way they organize their supply lines. The adaptation of cities to their hinterland ultimately defines their sustainability, or the lack of it. This is strikingly illustrated in the case of ancient Rome. As it grew into a city of hundreds of thousands of people, its supplies of timber and food also came from ever more distant territories. It was Julius Caesar who decided that North Africa would be a suitable region for supplying Rome with grain, having exhausted the fertility of farmland in Italy itself, as well as that of territories elsewhere in the Mediterranean basin. Caesar's armies conquered much of the African territory north of the Sahara. It was a largely wooded landscape and one Roman writer, Pliny, marveled at the abundance of fruits in the forests on the slopes of the Atlas mountains and the great variety of animals. The night, Pliny wrote, was filled with the sounds of drums, cymbals, flutes – the sounds of dancing.[7]

Roman veterans who were settled in North Africa, got on with the job of land conquest from nomadic tribes, with deforestation, and of the conversion of forests into farmland. Forest timber was converted into ships or exported to Rome itself. Many animals – lions, elephants, zebras, and gorillas – were captured and shipped to Rome to be put up against gladiators in the Coliseum. For some 200 years, North Africa supplied some 500,000 tons of grain to 300,000 Romans who were eligible for free grain, some two thirds of its total grain supply.[8] Some 500 towns were constructed that acted as epicenters of Rome's economy. Their construction and food and fuel supply took their own toll on the landscape. But over 200 years climate change from deforestation, salinization from irrigation, and loss of soil fertility took their toll. Around 250 A.D. St Cyprian, bishop of Carthage, wrote that the "world has grown old and does not remain in its former vigor. It bears witness to its own decline. The rainfall and the sun's warmth are both diminishing; the metals are nearly exhausted; the husbandman is failing in his fields. Springs which once gushed forth liberally . . . now barely give a trickle of water."[9]

The German scientist, Justus Liebig, one of the pioneers of modern chemistry, working in the mid-nineteenth century, was a student of Roman history, and tried to understand urban environmental impacts. In his work on agriculture he was concerned about the way Rome had removed plants nutrients contained in North African soil as grain was exported from there. The minerals contained in the grain – nitrogen, potash, phosphate, magnesium, and calcium – were removed from the farmland and, through Rome's Cloaca Magna flushed into the Mediterranean, never to be returned to the land. Liebig was observing the unprecedented growth of cities in the nineteenth century and was concerned about the impact of this process on Europe's farmland. Would urban growth in Europe permanently deplete the fertility of its farmland the way Rome had done 1800 years before?[10]

A major difference between nineteenth century Europe and ancient Rome was the scale of urban growth. Rome, before its collapse, had grown to approximately one million people and only a few cities in history (Constantinople, Tokyo, Beijing) approximated that size. London's growth was of a new order of magnitude: in 1800 it had 865,000 people, by 1850 it had reached an unprecedented population of some 4 million people. (By 1940 it finally reached its maximum size of 8,65 million people.)

Large cities are complex systems in terms of their internal organization, as well as that of their supply routes, and London's supply routes did not just stretch across the Mediterranean, but right across the globe. The larger a city, the more complex the system, the city's division of labor, the social and cultural complexity. But what about self-regulation and sustainability? Rome's final collapse occurred for a variety of reasons. Internal dissension was certainly a major factor. Lack of sustainable relationships to the environments from which it drew its resources was certainly another critical feature.

The major difference between Rome and much larger modern cities such as London is their vast use of energy, which makes their sustained existence highly precarious. There has never been a city of more than a million people not running on fossil fuels. Contemporary London, with 7 million people, uses approximately 20 million tons of oil equivalent per year, or two supertankers a week. The critical issue is whether, and how, this figure can be reduced in the process of assuring greater sustainability. Can modern cities reduce their impact on the "vital organs" of Gaia by processes of self-regulation?

Cities and the Ecological System

A few years ago, while producing a television documentary on deforestation in the Amazon basin and the resulting loss of biodiversity, we noticed at the port of Belem a huge stack of mahogany timber with "London" stamped on it being loaded into a freighter. This provoked us to take an interest in the connection between urban consumption patterns and human impact on the biosphere. Certainly, logging of virgin forests, or their conversion into cattle ranches and into fields of Soya beans for cattle fodder (in Brazil's Mato Grosso region) or of manioc for pig feed (in the former rainforest regions of Thailand), was not the most rational way of supplying urban markets. Can the vast appetites of cities for biological resources be curtailed? How can cities, the main habitat of the one now dominant species, learn to live at peace with Gaia?

In one century, urban populations have increased tenfold to some 2.5 billion people. Cities today are center stage in the global environmental drama of pollution, land degradation, and loss of species diversity. Concentration of intense economic processes and high levels of consumption in cities increase their resource demands. Beyond their boundaries, cities also profoundly affect traditional rural economies and their cultural adaptation to biological diversity. As better roads are built and access to urban products is assured, rural people acquire urban standards of living and the mind set to go with this. The world's major environmental problems will only be solved through new cultural approaches to the way we conceptualize cities.

Recently the Canadian economist William Rees[11] started a debate about the footprint of cities, which he defines as the land required to supply them with food and timber products and to absorb their CO2 output through areas of growing vegetation. I have examined the footprint of the city where I live, London, which also happens to be the "mother of megacities." Today London's total footprint, following Rees's definition, extends to around 125 times its surface area of 159,000 hectares, or nearly 20 million hectares. With 12 percent of Britain's population, London requires the equivalent of Britain's entire productive land.[12] This land, of course, stretches to far-flung places, such as the wheat prairies of Kansas, the tea gardens of Assam, and the copper mines of Zambia.

The critical question today, as humanity moves to full urbanization, is whether living standards in our cities can be maintained while curbing their environmental impacts. To answer this question it helps to draw up balance sheets comparing urban resource flows. It is becoming apparent that similar-sized cities supply their needs with a greatly varying throughput of resources. Most large cities have been studied in considerable detail and in many cases it is not very difficult to compare their use of resources. Resource use depends on the way cities function, as well as their standards of living. The metabolism of most "modern" cities is essentially linear, with resources flowing through the urban system without much concern about their origin and about the destination of wastes.

Demand for energy defines modern cities more than any other single factor. All their key activities—transportation, electricity, heating, services provision and manufacturing—depend on the routine use of fossil fuels. London uses 20 million tons of oil equivalent per year and discharges some 60 million tons of carbon dioxide. Its per capita energy consumption is among the highest in Europe, yet the know-how exists to bring down these figures by between 30 and 50 percent without affecting living standards and while creating up to 100,000 jobs in the process over 20 years.[10]

To make them more sustainable and to reduce their footprint and their impact on the biosphere, cities today require a whole range of new resource efficient technologies. These include combined heat-and-power systems, heat pumps, fuel cells, and photovoltaic modules. Enormous reductions in fossil fuel use can be achieved the use of photovoltaics. London could supply most of its current summer electricity consumption by installing photovoltaic modules on the roofs and walls of its buildings.[14] Large-scale production of these modules would massively reduce unit costs.

In the field of waste management, major steps can be taken toward urban sustainability. London every day disposes of 6,600 tons of household waste of which only some 4 percent is recycled. Meanwhile most cities in western Europe are developing and adopting ambitious technologies for recycling and composting waste.

In conventionally run cities, metabolic processes are usually linear—inputs and outputs are considered as largely unrelated. Trees are felled for timber or pulp and forests are not replenished. Raw materials are extracted, combined and processed into consumer goods that end up as rubbish that cannot be beneficially reabsorbed into living nature. Fossil fuels are extracted from rock strata, refined and burned; their fumes are discharged into the atmosphere.

Nutrients are taken from the land as food is grown, and not returned. All too often urban sewage systems are linear, collecting human wastes and discharging them into rivers and coastal waters downstream from population centers. Today coastal waters are enriched both with human sewage and toxic effluents as well as the runoff of mineral fertilizer applied to farmland feeding cities all over the world.

The linear metabolic system of most cities is profoundly different from nature's circular metabolism, in which every output by an organism is also an input that renews and sustains the living environment. Cities which develop a self-regulating, sustainable relationship with Gaia will adopt circular metabolic systems that are concerned with the continuing viability of the environments on which they depend. Outputs are also inputs into the production system, with routine recycling of paper, metals, plastic and glass, and the conversion of organic materials into compost, returning plant nutrients to keep farmland productive.

Some cities in history adopted sustainable relationships with their hinterland as the only assured way to guarantee their continuity. This applies to medieval cities, with their concentric rings of market gardens, forests, orchards, farm and grazing land. Chinese cities have long practiced the return of nightsoil onto local farmland as a way of assuring sustained yields of foodstuffs.[15] Today most Chinese cities administer their own, adjacent areas of farmland and, until the recent rapid urban–industrial growth, were largely self-sufficient in food.[16]

Some cities have made circularity and resource efficiency a top priority, installing sophisticated equipment for resource recovery. Cities right across Europe are installing waste recycling and composting systems. Austrian, Swiss, and French cities have taken the lead. In German towns and cities, 27 composting plants are now under construction with a combined annual capacity of 600,000 tons. Throughout the developing world, cities have made it their business to encourage recycling and composting of wastes.[17] Brazil's Curitiba is often cited for its energetic efforts toward urban sustainability, not only in waste management but also in creating a system of fast, convenient bus routes and persuading drivers to leave their cars at home.

Cities worthy of a new millennium will be energy and resource efficient, and culturally rich, with active democracies assuring the best uses of human energies. In northern megacities, such as London and New York, prudent inward investment in resource efficiency will contribute significantly to achieving higher levels of employment. In cities in the South, significant investment in infrastructure will make a vast difference to health and living conditions. Cities, particularly those in the North, have yet to prove that they can be a home for humanity that is compatible with a healthy biosphere. This is an unaccustomed challenge for business people, planners, architects, politicians, and citizens.

Some writers have argued that cities can actually be better for the global environment than adjacent rural areas.[18] They emphasize that often impressive range of plant and animal species present in cities. They suggest that the very density of human life in cities makes for energy efficiency in home heating as well as in transportation. Systems for waste recycling are more easily organized in densely inhabited areas. And urban agriculture, too, if well developed, could make a significant contribution to feeding cities.

Urban food growing is certainly no unusual activity in the late twentieth century—a new book published by UNDP proves the point: Singapore is fully self-reliant in meat and produces 25 percent of its vegetable needs. Bamako, Mali, is self-sufficient in vegetables and produces half or more of the chickens it consumes. Dar-es-Salaam, one of the world's the fastest growing large cities, now has 67 percent of families engaged in farming, compared with 18 percent in 1967. In Moscow, 65 percent of families are involved in food production, compared with 20 percent in 1970. There are 80,000 community gardeners on municipal land in Berlin, with a waiting list of 16,000. The 1980 U.S. census found that urban metropolitan areas produced 30 percent of the dollar value of U.S. agricultural production. By 1990, this figure had increased to 40 percent.[19]

Central and local governments are increasingly aware that efforts to improve the living environment must focus on cities. Ecofriendly urban development could well become the greatest challenge of the twenty-first century, not only for human self-interest, but also for the sake of a sustainable relationship between cities and the biosphere on which humanity ultimately depends.

Conclusion

Cities today are highly dependent systems with their tentacles stretching across the planet. Modern cities have a global hinterland, partly as a result of abundant supplies of energy. Modern communications have dramatically improved the nervous system of cities, as the production centers, the nerve centers, and the brains of the global human effort. The complexity of urban systems is thus defined by the development and uses of technologies that underpin them.

Their relationship to the ecological system is certainly highly problematic. Many of our global environmental problems center on the resource use of our cities. The critical issue today is how to initiate a cultural process of urban self-regulation in which cities take on the role of monitoring, comprehending, and ameliorating their impact on the ecology. Ultimately that cannot be done without changing the value systems underpinning our cities, as well as taking concrete measures to improving their resource efficiency. They will only be sustainable if they are prepared to reorganize the way they relate to the global environment.

Cities today certainly dominate global resource consumption. With nearly half the world's population, they take up only 2 percent of the world's land surface, yet they use more than 75 percent of the world's resources.

Cities all over the world are beginning to reorganize themselves under the auspices of Agenda 21.[20], From this trend, one can postulate that modern cities could develop daisyworld-type feedback systems, responding actively to the challenge of achieving sustainability. Taming urban systems and limiting their resource consumption and waste output through technological and organizational measures will certainly be critically important for an urbanizing humanity. To make cities more sustainable, they may need to reintroduce both greater density and a greater reliance on local and renewable resources. They need to take a close look at how they could make more efficient use of resources while fulfilling the needs of city people.

As we have seen, the metabolism of cities is characterized by linear throughput of resources. Adopting circular resource flows will help cities reduce their footprint, and thus their impact on the ecology. Initiatives to that effect are now in evidence all over the world. One can have a cautious sense of optimism that cities, and their people, are becoming aware that the urban superorganism can be a sustainable, self-regulating system through the introduction of appropriate cultural processes. The realization is growing, the implementation has just begun.

Notes

1. James Lovelock, *Gaia: The Practical Science of Planetary Medicine.* London: Gaia, 1991.
2. *Ibid.*
3. Paul Brunner, TU, Vienna, personal communication.
4. Extracted from David Satterthwaite, *An Urbanising World: The Second Global Report on Human Settlements.* Oxford and New York: Oxford University Press, 1996.
5. Ruth Whitehouse, *The First Cities.* Oxford: Phaidon, 1977.
6. Leonard Woolley, *Ur of the Chaldees.* London: Herbert Press, 1982.
7. Quoted in Susan Raven, *Rome in Africa.* London: Longman, 1984.
8. *Ibid.*
9. V. D. Carter and T. Dale, *Topsoil and Civilization.* Norman: University of Oklahoma Press, 1974.
10. Justus Liebig, *Agrikulturchemie, neunte Auflage.* Branschweig, German: Vieweg Verlag, 1876.
11. Mathis Wackernagel and William Rees, *Our Ecological Footprint.* New Society, 1996.
12. Herbert Girardet, *Getting London in Shape for 2000.* London: London First, 1996.
13. *Ibid.*
14. Rod Scott, BP Solar, personal communication.
15. F. H. King, *Farmers of Forty Centuries.* Emmaus, PA: Rodale Press, 1911.
16. Victor Sit, ed., *Chinese Cities: The Growth of the Metropolis since 1949.* Oxford and New York; Oxford University Press, 1988.
17. *Warmer Bulletin,* Summer 1995.
18. Richard Gilbert, in Richard Gilbert, Don Stevenson, and Herbert Girardet, eds., *Making Cities Work: The Role of Local Authorities in the Urban Environment.* London: Earthscan Publications, 1996;
19. UNDP, *Urban Agriculture.* New York: UNDP, 1996.
20. *Ibid.*

Section 3 Sustainable Financing

Sixto K. Roxas

In view of the cutbacks in the foreign aid budgets of major donor countries, there is at present in developing countries an intensified search for mechanisms, incentives, and instruments to channel mainstream capital flows into environmental and sustainable development programs and projects.

This has focused attention on the international flow of private savings, both philanthropic and commercial. There are increasing discussions on how even international portfolio funds might be channeled to social and environmental projects. What would it take to bring the programs and projects of sustainable human development into the mainstream of capital market financing?

There are problems both on the supply and demand sides of these savings flows. From the supply side, the first question is the risk involved. For conventional capital that seeks a repayment of capital, there are business, investment, and political risks. For philanthropic funds, there is the risk of misapplied funds. For different sources, these will vary and will be correlated with the risk. Some people are quite cold-blooded about maximizing returns in relation to risks. Others are prepared to trade off returns for different nonbusiness or noncommercial considerations: ethical funds, green funds, environmental funds, and so on. Finally, the cost of the transactions and administering the investment over its life is an additional problem.

From the demand side, the questions are first how to match the terms on which the funds are made available to the needs and inherent requirements of the uses to which they must be put. Obviously, the uses that provide no financial returns require grants; those that can generate financial returns in various degrees need sources that seek returns in relation to risks. Also, fending off cooptation of local initiatives, sense of priorities, and reconciling the conditions of finance with the local perceptions of need and prerequisites are additional problems. One can also add the difficulties of matching local styles of operations, local modes of documentation and articulation, and local methods of management with those that give funders an adequate level of comfort.

The current preoccupation with sustainable financing raises a twofold challenge: (1) to induce funding sources to become more flexible about accepting less stringent terms, and (2) to assist the users of fund with the required creative and competent technical assistance to make their projects increasingly attractive to funders.

Sustainable Development Organizations

In the world of corporate finance, creative design and promotion has been the traditional domain of the investment or merchant banker. In short, the need is for sustainable development investment or merchant banking; we need the professional skills of SDIBs ("Sustainable Development Investment Bankers"). The cost of manageable transactions hinges around an effective and efficient delivery system. Thus, the question of wholesale versus retail delivery mechanisms and the entire question of intermediation design enter into the picture.

The problem of sustainable development must be resolved before we can really talk about financing gaps and delivery systems. Resources are generated by the prevailing economic organization. Out of these flows, savings provide the wherewithal to meet local, national, and global society's needs. if the prevailing modes of production and resource generation are themselves unsustainable, then the system is at cross-purposes. Savings are used merely to undo the damage caused by the very methods of resource generation that provide the savings. If the savings are used to discourage unsustainable modes that account for the larger portion of resource generation, then the very success of the effort will cause the sources of savings to dry up, unless there are clearly defined alternative modes of production and resource generation that are sustainable.

But this is what we mean by an alternative sustainable development organization—a mode that encompasses in the very character of its operation all three specifications of sustainability: ecological soundness, social equity, and economic efficiency. The neoliberal system simply assumes that freedom of enterprise and markets will automatically achieve both economic efficiency and social equity. The Bretton Woods Institutions themselves, which embody these principles, recognize that more direct interventions are required to address the problems both of social equity and environmental destruction. The Copenhagen Summit is the dramatic evidence that the system has exacerbated social exclusion.

The search for alternative intermediation systems to bring financing to microenterprises and the poorer majority, addresses the social equity problem directly. It provides no answer, however, to the problem of an adequate economic organization with the scale and efficiency to be economically sustainable. The ruling strategy assumes that if financing supports viable individual enterprises and their capital projects, and government projects that provide the necessary infrastructure and climate to enable these enterprises to thrive in relatively free and competitive markets, then the goals of economic efficiency and social equity will be met. The only problem is to correct the markets for externalized environmental costs.

The specifications for viability are rigorously defined and are identical with the conditions for bankability. Viability applies as well to the financial intermediation business—as long as the institutions in that industry are themselves viable, which means that their operations cover transaction costs and the competitive cost of capital, then the whole system is sound and sustainable. This reduces the whole sustainability problem to one of correcting market failures and inappropriate and distorting government policies and regulations to reflect full environmental costs.

On the other hand, the advocates of special financial services for the poor and marginalized sectors, argue precisely that the ruling order results in social exclusion and marginalization of large segments of the population. They propose special measures to divert savings to target populations and microenterprises, where the average transactions raise transaction costs to levels that make them uneconomic for the formal financial service industry. They address the question of how resources are made accessible to the poor and the self-employed microentrepreneurs of the informal sector.

They do not address the question of an alternative economic order in which the unit organization encompasses in its normal operations the objectives of ecological integrity and social equity, along with economic efficiency. One that defines in the same rigorous fashion the tests of viability and sustainability for the unit organization and its projects, and offers in its systemic linkages the mutual enhancement of overall efficiencies in resource usage and preservation that are prerequisites of local global sustainability.

The strategy then becomes clear: financing of these sustainable unit organizations that bring them to full self-sustaining stages will generate the savings to meet their own and the system's needs for expanding sustainable operations.

Principles of a Viable Financial Sector

The financial viability of the finance industry itself is based on certain assumptions with respect to the life cycle of the projects it finances. At the level of the micro-unit, an enterprise or a project, a soundly conceived and efficiently operated venture, requires capital investments to establish its asset and organizational base to operate. Over an appropriate gestation period, it then starts up successfully, achieves normal operations, generates its expected surpluses out of which it provides earnings and pays back its capital. Financial intermediaries rely on that cycle for their own viability. The portfolios of venture capitalists, investors, and private banks derive their quality from the expectation that a reasonable proportion of the ventures they finance successfully achieve the payback stage.

International financial institutions—both private and state—make a further assumption. They assume that a critical mass of successful individual projects launches the nation–state as a whole into an analogous cycle of viability that includes startup, takeoff into self-sustaining growth, and a period of payment and will generate balance of payments surpluses to pay off its international debts. The only proviso is that governments pursue sound fiscal and monetary policies and not cause a diversion of resources generated by growth into extravagant public investments or social welfare expenditures the nation "cannot afford."

The history of projects, enterprises, institutions, and nation–states during the past two hundred years has established the apparent validity of these assumptions. Projects have been conceived and executed with success. Enterprises have gone from birth to growth in diversification and expansion in scope and size within and beyond national boundaries. Nation–states have broken away from traditional rural, agricultural modes to become gigantic industrial, metropolitan powers. The finance industry has grown in scope and diversity in tandem. Deriving its own dynamism from that of the projects, enterprises, and governments it has financed.

But at this juncture, the costs of that dynamic growth strategy, heretofore hidden, have burst out with a vengeance in environmental, social, and political upheavals. Humanity has realized the world cannot go on much further on the same path. Growth in the economy, like cancer in the body, can kill. We must change paths, find a sustainable course.

On the surface, the old modality seemed to have proven its economic and financial sustainability, at the micro level. it has become evident that, added up, the totality it created was not sustainable at the macro level. We must find macrosustainability. For this to be operational in terms of viable individual units, its imperatives must be translated into the same life cycle at project, enterprise, government, and community levels. This is the problem.

The Role of the Markets in Meeting Sustainability

What is the appropriate unit whose performance criteria could subsume ecological, social, as well as economic and financial sustainability? The total planetary system is unsustainable precisely because the individual units that constitute it are able to achieve economic and financial viability at the expense of ecological and social sustainability. The operating criteria of the financial institutions that cater to them do not need to encompass the imperatives of social equity and ecological wholeness for their own viability.

Over the long run, continued viability of these institutions and their clients are threatened by the nonsustainability of the growth paths. But by the time that threat becomes manifest at the micro level, it may be too late for humanity and the planet. But what of the market mechanism? Do not markets precisely meet this problem? If they are kept free, then do not the signals they send to individual enterprises and the valuations they reflect on project feasibility studies ensure ecological, social, economic, and financial sustainability as well?

The market is an age-old mechanism through which people and institutions have exchanged products, services, and assets to maximize the utilities and satisfactions they derive from material goods and services. Economists have used the maximization and perfect market logic to establish norms of production and distribution efficiency. But in real life, allocations through markets and the priorities established by the prices they set have not reflected the optimum welfare that economists's models predict. They fail in two major areas: (1) in establishing appropriate priorities among human needs and (2) in reflecting the imperatives of economic sustainability.

The first was recognized earlier even by economists and project evaluators in multilateral development banks. The practice of calculating economic rates of returns through shadow pricing of costs and benefits, recognize the divergence, particularly in developing countries, between private and social returns. The second has been catapulted into global attention in more recent times. Work is in progress to reflect environmental costs as in national income accounting, and although at somewhat earlier stages, in project evaluation as well. The wider requirement of Environmental Impact Assessments and Social Impact Assessments,[1] as well as the even more recent introduction of "Social Acceptability" criteria for development projects reflect the rising level of awareness. Project economies and project appraisal methods are grounded in an economic theory in which enterprise-centered, profit-maximizing logic in a free competitive market has become the norm for efficiency.

The logic underlying the calculation of economic or social as opposed to merely private rates of return was addressed in 1951 by Alfred Kahn, when he proposed the use of the Social Marginal Productivity test as the basis for establishing investment criteria in developing countries. It recognized in the allocation of capital resources that private rates of return were not a sufficient guide for efficiency. The benefit from an investment project was to be measured from the viewpoint of the economy, meaning the nation–state. So the first approximation was the contribution to national income. The total reflected products and factors at market prices. Adjustments needed to be made in the benefits to reflect premiums on certain results not reflected in the market price, such as the employment of labor where the opportunity cost was zero, balance of payments effects, and external economies. In an article written two years after Kahn's, Hollis Chenery formulated a more "operational" application of the Social Marginal Productivity criterion to include adjustments for effects as well as on income distribution, employment, and balance of payments equilibrium. This approach was admittedly based on a partial equilibrium method with heavy *ceteris paribus* assumptions.

More refined application of shadow pricing techniques then began to be introduced, with the use of general equilibrium models, and optimization programs using linear or nonlinear programming techniques. Economic Rates of Return (ERR) calculations are based on measurements of social productivity of projects and are calculated as adjustments in private rates of returns. These adjustments, however, are to numbers derived from an accounting system that is informed by the same postulates as provide the theoretical underpinning of the present System of National Accounts (SNA).

The System of National Accounts continues to be basically neoclassical in its theoretical basis. The hard core propositions of this theory are:

1. The ultimate unit of economic activity is the enterprise, and the enterprise Chart of Accounts is the framework within which transactors and transactions are classified.
2. The basis of valuation is market price in product and factor markets.
3. Adjustments for nonmarketed products and services are appended at the margin through imputations. Over time, revisions have attempted to encompass more of these nonmarket activities.

The present paradigm leaves economic optimization on first glance at the individual and enterprise levels, and there is no intervention to effect intermediate trade-offs until the nation–state level. What would be the effect if a unit of management were defined in which a balance sheet and income statement manager would intervene to optimize community welfare long before state intervention at the national level and in-between the enterprise and the nation–state. National accounts would then be a consolidation primarily of community accounts reflecting effective social optimization at that level, instead of, primarily as at present, enterprise accounts reflecting their profit-maximizing decisions.

What, for example, would be the impact of such a perspective on the comparative economics of energy projects, to take an area where shadow pricing is often applied?[2]

The assumption of perfect knowledge and equal bargaining power such that communities effectively register their valuations and the resulting orders of priority in a virtual market would provide a set of derived demand prices for energy. The change-path of demand configuration for electric power would reflect a difference from the "colonization" mode of development. Maximum capacity, average per unit usage small and scattered, and load factors would be low. But the demand price would be relatively high because the priority of the needs from which the demand is derived will have a high marginal valuation. These valuations would be reflected in the shadow pricing of natural resources, capital, and manpower, which would show higher opportunity costs for alternative usage. The alternative usage would then show lower rates of economic returns.

Over a longer horizon, a community-demand-centered development and industrialization trajectory would create its own modes of urban concentration to avail of scale economies in processing, exchange, services, and administration. Scientific research and technology development, now following the dictates of community-based and ecologically sustainable imperative, would move in the direction of consumption and production systems involving lower energy usage and generating less material throughput.

Economists have long recognized that market failures are more or less normal in developing countries. It is taken for granted then that private rates of return will deviate from economic rates of return. In project feasibility studies, the practice is fairly established of adjusting private rates to reflect economic rates of return. This is accomplished through a process of setting "shadow prices"[3] for specific cost items and for measurement of product benefits.

These calculations recognize the concept of what we might call in more contemporary terms "virtual market prices." Such prices are no longer the result of real but calculated market prices. The market remains the standard. But the adjustments are made on a notational basis for imputing virtual markets. The process is then deeply dependent on the theory that forms the basis for constructing the virtual markets and the prices derived from them.

It is from this consensus that there has emerged quite a literature on the formulation and application of "investment criteria" in investment programs of developing countries.[4] One of the earliest formulations was Alfred Kahn in 1951 and then Hollis Chenery in 1953. The World Bank has incorporated shadow pricing in its manuals on project evaluation, in which financial values are adjusted to reflect "economic" values. Thus, in Gittinger's *Economic Analysis of Agricultural Products,* Chapter 7, "Determining Economic Values" prescribes the process of going from "financial prices" to the "value to the society as a whole of both the inputs and outputs of the project," the "opportunity cost to the society" that is the "shadow price" or "accounting price."[5]

Chenery's article states the theoretical premise that underlies the practice:

> In developed countries, perfect competition provides a standard for judging such a distribution of resources without the necessity of measuring he marginal productivity save in exceptional cases. . . . In underdeveloped areas, it is generally recognized that both private value and private cost may deviate from social value and social cost. In such cases, perfect competition cannot even be used as a standard for many sectors of the economy; rather, it is necessary to measure social productivity and to provide for some form of government intervention to achieve more or less efficient distribution of investment resources.[6]

The practice is standard specifically in the evaluation of power projects. Dr. Mohan Munasinghe of the World Bank devotes a chapter to "Shadow Pricing" in his study of *The Economics of Power System Reliability and Planning*, published by the World Bank in 1979. Munasinghe is somewhat more specific in stating the theoretical justification for shadow pricing: "In the idealized world of perfect competition, the interaction of atomistic profit-maximizing producers and atomistic utility-maximizing consumers yields a situation called pareto-optimal. In this state, prices reflect the true marginal costs, scarce resources are efficiently allocated, and for a given income distribution, no one person can be made better off without someone else worse off."[7]

Going from this generally accepted assumption that the perfect competition criterion needs to be modified to reflect some concept and measurement of social opportunity costs and benefits, a community—rather than an enterprise-centered—analysis would point to a different tack from that of the conventional, neoclassical economics. Shadow pricing clearly takes the valuation exercise out of the realm of actual markets and real world valuation into the realm of theory. The late Professor Tinbergen used a most felicitous term for the exercise. These "accounting prices" are those derived not from the real plan, but from the "shadow plan."[8]

In undertaking the "correction," it is essential to understand where precisely the market breakdown occurs and to visualize the process of remedying what Tinbergen called "fundamental disequilibria."[9] The failure would be at two points in the system:

1. Perfect knowledge on the part of the market players—knowledge of the full range of alternative options and the cost–benefit relationship of each option. The shadow pricing process fills this knowledge gap

by making the options explicit and assuming that the values will settle on those established by the options that are optimal from the viewpoint of the transactors.

2. Equality of bargaining power. The players have equal bargaining power, so that the choice of options is backed by sufficient bargaining power so that no one party is able to impose an option that is unduly advantageous to it and override the choice of others.

The practice of shadow pricing fills the imperfect knowledge gap with a neoclassical model of efficiency—calculating the optimal shadow prices from an approximation of an equilibrium condition under perfect competition among atomized individual consumers maximizing utility and atomized enterprises maximizing profits. This is done either through partial or general equilibrium methods, rigorously optimized through linear programming or roughly approximated by sectoral criteria (shadow exchange rate or shadow wages, etc.). This is the exercise that Tinbergen would call "shadow programming."

The theory takes no account of either equity or ecological and sustainability criteria. It is a problem to introduce these criteria precisely because of the choice of decision units in the model; atomized individuals and profit-maximizing enterprises. In terms of responsibility, these units exclude from their responsibility either communal welfare or ecological integrity, which are externalities, falling outside the mainstream concern of the players.

Modern economic policy in fact attempts to remedy this failing, but only at the level of the nation–state. The practice may be interpreted in the following manner. It makes an omniscient and omnipotent state a market player. The calculated shadow prices represent the valuations given by its omniscience to the relevant items in costs and benefits. The state's omnipotence then gives it the bargaining power to reflect its valuations on the project costs and benefits.

This interpretation raises the question: upon what sort of theoretical framework does this omniscient state make its valuation judgment? It is here that alternative methodologies represent options from which practice selects one. But why should the option selected be the "right" one? And what is so sacred about a system that assumes atomized individuals and enterprises and their maximizing logic to be the proper base on which then the adjustments are introduced at the level of the nation–state? Why should not the notional reconfiguration take place much earlier than the nation–state, at some level between atomized individuals and the country?

Both from the viewpoint of appropriate theory and effective organization and management, intervention at the country level is too late. It is interesting that John Maynard Keynes in his 1926 essay, entitled

"The End of Laissez-Faire," advances the notion that there should be a level of decision making somewhere between the individual and the state. but he thought this might be the large public corporation then coming into prominence (public here meaning really endowed with a public purpose, such as "public utilities," rather than publicly listed on the stock exchange).

The notion that we are advancing is the community as a unit of integration and decision making. The concept of community must include both the human settlement and its territory as habitat. The community is posited as a transactor in the market, reflecting then its valuations, which are the results, on first glance, of the optimization of its objective function, which is defined as the "highest and best sustainable use" of its resources. The two primary indicators of community welfare would be the concepts of "net community income" and "community net worth."

In February 1992, Lewis Preston, the former President of the World Bank, organized a "Portfolio Management Task Force" to examine the problems affecting the quality of the Bank's active portfolio of loans and credits. The resulting report, known as Wapenhams report, examined examining the financial portfolio and assessed its developmental impact. One of its key recommendations was to "introduce the concept of country portfolio performance management linked to the bank's core business process."[10]

The formalization of valuation exercises of the sort proposed would fit in with the thrust of the Wapenhams report's suggestion that the World Bank view the management of its programs in terms of country portfolios instead of single projects, to get a more integrated and systemic view of development impact. This perspective would bring the view down to subcountry territories and look at community portfolios to evaluate development impact. This suggests that the nation–state is not a meaningful unit for evaluating system impact of integrated project clusters.

The requisite scale for purposes of portfolio administration economics in a financial institution would be achieved by precisely looking at ecologically engineered production networks. In other words, portfolios would not only depart from single-project, but also from single-sector, approaches.

A serious rethinking in International Financial Institutions of Operating Department approaches to project design would, in fact, provide empowerment finance to communities, move their participatory planning processes from shadow to reality, and give needed support to the project engineering of the future: "industrial ecology."

Conclusion

The passage of communities from start-up on a sustainable development path to a self-reliant payback stage describes a new viability cycle that can form the basis for viable financial intermediation as well. The evolution of the asset patterns of such communities as they traverse this path [illegible] on the capital and liability side particular configurations that mirror the balance sheets of the intermediaries that supply the financing.

That evolution could be simulated for entire urban communities. The asset build-up would be related to the financial flows over a gestation period during which net cash flow deficits need to be financed by savings from outside to a normalization and maturation period when assets generate net surpluses that payback the financing.

Notes

1. For example, the World Bank guidelines proposed earlier this year set forth the rationale for a "Social Assessment and Participation Strategy" to guide operational departments. "Social assessment is needed to:

a. "Ensure the appropriateness and acceptability of project objectives and activities to the range of people who are intended to benefit (including women and vulnerable groups;

b. "Enhance the involvement of beneficiaries in project design d implementation;

c. "Ensure that institutional mechanisms (for the delivery of services, participation, etc.) are sustainable and appropriate to project beneficiaries;

d. "Anticipate, minimize and mitigate any negative social effects of projects."

(Internal World Bank, February 14, 1994, memorandum addressed to the Social Policy Thematic Team on the subject "Guidelines for Incorporating Social Assessment and Participation into Bank Projects.")

2. The paragraphs following are taken from Sixto K. Roxas, "A Comparison of Energy Economics in Two Alternative Systems: Conventional Enclave Development and Community-Based Sustainable Settings." In Paul Kleindorfer et al., eds., *Energy, Environment, and the Economy: Asian Perspectives.* United States and United Kingdom: Edward Elger, 1996, pp. 107-121.

3. Shadow price is "the opportunity cost to a society of engaging in some economic activity. . . . In a perfectly functioning economy, market prices will be equal to marginal cost, which itself represents the true costs to society of producing one extra unit of a community; it is equivalent to the value of the items that could have been made as alternatives to the last unit of the community produced, with the same resources. In the competitive economy, therefore, the market price of an item is equal to the opportunity cost of producing that item. In an economy which does not function perfectly, however, this is not so. . . . More generally, shadow prices are used in valuing any item which is implicitly

rationed or constrained in some way. Shadow prices can be derived using linear programming techniques, and can be used in social cost–benefit analysis, which attempts to achieve an optimal resource allocation in the absence of an effective price system. (Graham Bannock, et al. *Dictionary of Economics,* 4th ed., 1987, pp. 372-373.

4. For an excellent survey of the literature, see UN, ECAFE, "Criteria for Allocating Investment Resources Among Various Fields of Development in Underdeveloped Countries," *Economic Bulletin for Asia and the Far East,* 1961 (June).

5. J. Price Gittinger, *Economic analysis of Agricultural Projects,* 2nd ed. Baltimore: Johns Hopkins University Press, 1982, pp. 243-284.

6. "The Application of Investment Criteria." *Quarterly Journal of Economics,* 1953 (Feb.): 76.

7. Munasinghe cites Francis J. Bator's simplified geometry on welfare maximization in the March 1957 issue of the *American Economic Review,* pp. 22-59.

8. He describes the calculation as "the application to all physical elements of net income (i.e., output of products and input of factors) of accounting prices representing the 'true value' of these products and factors. . . . In principle, this calculation requires a 'shadow development program,' differing from the 'real' program in that equilibria would be obtained by flexible pricing instead of, as may be the case in reality, by quantitative restrictions and rigid pricing." *the Design of Development.* The Economic Development Institute, International Bank for Reconstruction and Development, 1958, p. 82). His 1958 development manual, "The Design of Development" prepared for the Economic Development Institute of the World Bank, still bears reading. In this work, Professor Tinbergen still advocates the contribution to national income as a first approximation of benefits from a project. But to compensate for market failures, the values need to be adjusted through estimated "accounting prices."

9. It is interesting to read his 1958 manual in light of articles Professor Tinbergen wrote just before his death. I refer particularly to the piece written jointly with Roefie Hueting on the distorted signals given by the markets to relative scarcities and values. "Market prices and economic indicators based on them, such as national income and cost–benefit analyses, misleadingly signal to society and therefore must be corrected. The factor for which correction is most urgently needed is the environment."

10. World Bank, "Effective Implementation: Key to Development Impact," *Report of the Portfolio Management Task Force,* 1992 (internal document).

Part 2

Citizens

Section 1 The Price of Civilization and the Dilemma of Urbanization

Philip Allott

This section is written entirely from the point of view of European culture and experience. It is a great merit of the United Nations system in general, and the UNDP in particular, that they enable all forms of human culture and experience to be brought into fruitful contact. This essay is offered as a contribution to that process.

> After roaming the streets of the capital a day or two, making headway with difficulty through the human turmoil and the endless lines of vehicles, after visiting the slums of the metropolis, one realizes for the first time that these Londoners have been forced to sacrifice the best qualities of their human nature, to bring to pass all the marvels of civilization which crowd their city; that a hundred powers which slumbered within them have remained inactive, have been suppressed in order that a few might be developed more fully multiply through union with those of others. The very turmoil of the streets has something repulsive, something against which human nature rebels. . . . The brutal indifference, the unfeeling isolation of each in his private interest becomes the more repellent and offensive, the more these individuals are crowded together, within a limited space. . . . The dissolution of mankind into monads, of which each has a separate principle, the world of atoms, is here carried out to its utmost extreme.[1]

Thus, Friedrich Engels described the London of 1844. London was not the first hypertrophic city in the history of the world, and it would become one among many. But Engels had already identified in Victorian London what would become a familiar fact of life all over the world—*the price of civilization, the dilemma of urbanization.*[2] All the great dynamic gains from the aggregation of human energy—all at the price of great human suffering. All the great material and mental benefits of extreme socialization—all at the price of great burdens at the level of human individuality and human autonomy. It is right, at the end of the twentieth century, to reconsider the price of civilization and the dilemma of urbanization, to consider whether it would be possible to imagine a form of urbanization that would cost less in terms of human alienation.

In European social history, the city has performed three kinds of functions: (1) It has been a political center, an urban polis in which the citizens could pursue the good life materially and spiritually, sustained by and sustaining the life of the neighboring countryside; (2) It has been a commercial center, a marketplace in which products could be traded, and which gives rise, through the division of labor, to all the trades and services ancillary to commerce; and (3) It has been an industrial center, in which the extreme aggregation of labor on a large scale is used to generate extreme wealth.

It is worth distinguishing among these three functions because different cities have performed the different functions to significantly differing degrees and because over the course of European social history, these different functions have had different consequences for the structure and functioning of the national society at different times.

The centralizing of British and French political society on London and Paris respectively contributed substantially to the forming of the British and French nations in the late Middle Ages, and to the essentially unitary political structure that those two countries have retained to the present day. In Spain, the purposeful establishment of Madrid as the center of royal power and administration had a similar effect – and it is tempting to see it as a major contributory factor in the making of Spain's Golden Century.

In Germany, no city established its political dominance until at least the nineteenth century. Even in the time of the early Holy Roman Empire, from the tenth century onward, there was no clearly fixed and dominant imperial capital. Even when Berlin became the capital of the new German Reich in 1871, it did not (or did not have time to) establish a dominance over Germany's other major cities, to an extent comparable with the dominance of London, Paris, or Madrid. Germany's unification in the form of federation is, perhaps, one of the side effects of these facts.

In Italy, which resembled Germany in its long centuries of vigorous multiplicity, Rome, perhaps because of its domination by the Papacy for at least a thousand years after the end of the Roman Empire in the West, did not acquire a political dominance over the other strongly self-identifying cities and city–republics. For the European mind, ancient Athens and ancient Rome had been the cities *par excellence*, and, after Italian reunification in 1866, Rome became the capital of the new Italy once again – an Italy that would, like Britain and France and Spain, be organized as a unitary, rather than a federal, state. In each of these supposedly unitary states, there are deep currents of federalism, of multiplicity in unity.

Social Development and the City

But the role played by the city in the social development of Europe had another crucially important aspect. The city played a major part in the profound transformation of society, which began in the High Middle Ages (from the eleventh century onwards). The city was essential to the transformation of agricultural society to postfeudal/preindustrial society. And that transformation played a major part in the transformation of monarchical to democratic society.

The story is significantly different in each European country, both in its details and its chronology. In what is an intensely controversial area of social history, one might suggest the following as common threads.

1. *The city as fortress.* In the period before public order (national and international) could be assured by monarchs (and other holders of widespread political power), cities were created or re-formed to act as havens of security, self-regulating microrepublics.
2. *The city as marketplace.* Trade, national and international, played a significant part in the rapid economic development of some of the European countries toward the end of the Middle Ages. The city, with its relatively settled laws and customs and institutions, lent itself perfectly to the task.
3. *The city as realm of freedom.* Perhaps most interestingly of all, the city provided a place of counterculture, an alternative society, to the social forms (especially the forms of what came to be called feudalism), which had survived from previous centuries. In the free cities of northern Europe, the language and the ideals of political autonomy were spoken first from the mouths of those who had a self-interest, especially an economic interest, in personal autonomy.
4. *The city as social engine of innovation.* The city became a place for the development of new crafts and new systems of manufacture, new financial services, new legal forms (guilds, corporations, new forms of intangible property, contracts, legal procedures).
5. *The city as the focus of social aspiration.* Putting all the above together, a city became a place of competition and emulation (intracity and, especially, intercity). If you could make it in a big city, you could make it anywhere. The city could support cultural institutions, including cathedrals and universities and libraries, theaters, book publishing, newspapers, learned societies, political parties.. . . . The city could be fertile ground for rebellion and revolution.
6. *The city as a fountain of national wealth.* The city became able to generate levels of wealth which were in principle infinite, at

least as compared with the presumably finite wealth produced from land. The characteristic urban belief in the possibility of multiplying wealth indefinitely—through manufacture, commerce, education, innovation—changed the potentiality of those nations that urbanized themselves. Competition and emulation between national urbanized wealth-machines became an integral part of national self-creating and self-identifying—and hence the basis of intense international rivalries that would alter the history of a world far beyond Europe.

New forms of warfare, new forms of diplomacy, new forms of colonialism, and a new form of international law were generated as by-products of urbanized nationalism. It is not possible to say—and probably meaningless to ask—which caused which: urbanization and the dramatic development of most European countries after, say, the year 1400? But it seems right to conclude that the latter would not have occurred without the former.

Industrial Development and the City

The city was called upon to play another essential role—in the transition to industrialism. The city became a concentration camp for the new army of industrial workers. We, who have had two centuries in which to learn of the greed, the cynicism, and the hypocrisy of those whose highest value is the maximization of profit, may still feel anger and disgust at the oppression of countless millions of human beings in the name of industrialism.

It was not simply that the peasantry were driven by need, after centuries of oppression, like animals into the towns. The new urban peasantry were, for the most part, generated biologically—the multiplication of human beings, born to tend the machines. Instead of the hovels of the countryside, the new peasantry were given urban hovels, with the minimum conditions of human existence, on marginal wages sufficient only to allow them to remain fit for work and to reproduce. The city became a place of slavery.

It was not all cities that became industrial cities. The industrial cities arose, either newly implanted or as a development of some existing city, where and when economic factors dictated—the supply of raw materials (especially coal and water), convenience of transportation (rivers, canals, the sea). But the nonindustrial cities shared in the dramatically increasing aggregate "wealth of the nation." And some cities developed powerfully as ancillaries to the new process of industrialism, generating vast quantities of new forms of commercial and financial services.

To this day, most European countries are characterized by the coexistence of the three kinds of city—political or administrative centers (national capital cities, provincial and regional and county capital cities—

often cathedral towns, where bishops had taken up residence in the Middle Ages); commercial centers (still referred to as "market-towns" in England); and industrial centers. London and Paris, for example, did not become industrial cities, although they continued to account for a very great proportion of the economic output of their respective countries. Their populations increased rapidly to service relatively light industry and the services ancillary to industrialism. And they generated their own kind of slums.

Economic and Sociopolitical Revolution

The new industrial economy was an exponential development of the economy that had preceded it. What came to be called the Industrial Revolution was revolutionary in more ways than one. It was discovered that the wealth-generating potentiality of aggregated labor could be raised to much higher levels of energy by the combination of machines and masses of people. But the economic revolution called for a sociopolitical revolution. High levels of social energy call for high levels of legislation and public administration. It was necessary to re-create systems for manufacturing law and administration commensurate with the manufacturing of goods and services.

Parliaments and/or bureaucracies were fundamentally reformed in the nineteenth century to provide the mass of law and administration necessary for the rationalization of the immense density and dynamism of industrialism. The European mind was also busy generating the appropriate explanations and justifications of the new form of society. The freedom to make money for oneself and thereby for the nation was rationalized in a set of ideas which came to be known as capitalism. The mobilizing of social consent to the necessary law and administration was rationalized through a set of ideas which came to be known as democracy.

For those called upon to pay the price of industrialism in their daily lives, it might seem that what was called capitalism was better rationalized as the enforcement of economic inequality through the unequal distribution of money power, and what was called democracy might better be rationalized as the enforcement of social inequality through the unequal distribution of legal power.

But the system justified itself by deeds, not merely by words. Eventually the living standards of the mass of the people began to rise. Apparently democracy–capitalism has become a system for generating ever-increasing national wealth at levels unimaginable to previous generations.

The public realms of the urbanized industrialized nations came to be conceived as states – rationalistic machines for managing the business of the nation – and those states externalized themselves as states, in the external sense, generating new levels in the intensity of international competition and emulation—and, in particular, new levels of warfare. The so-called world wars of the twentieth century were a struggle to the death among the new state–wealth machines, obeying instincts carried over from earlier centuries, but instincts that have now been harnessed to the needs of an urbanized world. A particularly effective spiral of wealth creation had been created: competitive wealth creation leads to competitive nationalism, which leads to technologically based warfare, which leads to the competitive manufacture and marketing of weapons of war, which leads to more wealth creation and so on and on.

Three Contradictions of Urban Alienation

The alienation caused by urbanization reaches into the deepest structures of our consciousness. The price and the burden of urbanization that Engels saw so vividly displayed in the streets of Victorian London are the practical manifestation of a philosophy of alienated human existence. Urban alienation means, in the first place, that we live in a place that is located somewhere between a Lost Paradise and a Promised Land. For a very long time (at least since Hesiod and the Book of Genesis, written some twenty-six centuries ago), we have thought of ourselves as the unworthy successors of those who lived in a Golden Age, unworthy exiles from a Garden of Eden. But, by an equal and opposite movement of thought, we have seen ourselves as masters of our destiny, as capable of self-redemption.

In the city, we seem to have lost the naturalness and the innocence of pre-urban, presumably rural life, the idyll of Arcadia. But we seem also to have freed ourselves from what Marx and Engels called "rural idiocy," to have given ourselves the possibility to achieve, by our own efforts, all that we might want, to become what we might want to become, capable of self-perfecting, of regaining paradise, of remaking the golden age. Urban life contains a self-denying nostalgia, for all we have lost and for all that we have gained by losing so much. In the city we live between two illusions—an illusory past and an illusory future.

The first symptom of the contradiction of urban alienation is thus a devaluing of the present moment. In an agricultural society, the natural framework of time is the endless recurring of the seasons, a time for sowing and a time for reaping, life and death and new life. In a city we are exiles from time present. The present is a wasteland between the past and the future. Today is merely the place where yesterday and tomorrow meet. Today is the surpassing of yesterday with a view to the making of tomorrow. In a city, human time is the separate chronologies of an infinity of human activities.

The second contradiction of urban alienation is the need to destroy in order to create. Constructing the future demands that anything that needs to be destroyed will be destroyed – buildings, institutions, loyalties, beliefs, values. It is the alienation of instrumentalism, an alienation from personal attachment. The city is the place of the organized transformation of things and people, the unceasing surpassing of all that is, in favor of all that might be. Everything and everyone has value only as potentiality, never as actuality.

In the city, value is not value for itself, but rather value for something else. Money is the archetypal medium of urban value, the value shared by the seller and the buyer, whatever may be the incompatibility of their other values. Human beings themselves acquire an exchange value, measurable in terms of money. Human life is something that is used rather than enjoyed. As workers we exhaust ourselves in order to enrich society. As citizens, we profit, unequally, from our own exhaustion.

The third contradiction of urban alienation is that the citizen is required to live the belief that personal subjection to society is the source of personal freedom. In a classic formulation of Rousseau and Hegel, the individual is forced to be free. It is an alienation of human autonomy, an alienation of human selfhood, an alienation from human intimacy.

In the city the citizen is, to use Engels' expressions, atom and monad, self-contained but other possessed. The city is a place of mutual dependence, of total mutuality – a mutuality that is as great as the concentration of many human beings into a small place imposes. In a city, human space is the intersection of an infinity of human lives.

By participating in the life of the city, we participate in the dynamic effects of collectivism, of the aggregation of human effort. The wealth of the city is the wealth of the citizens. Urban wealth is wealth of the citizen, by the citizen, for the citizen. Inequalities and inefficiencies in the distribution of urban wealth are contingent, the product of circumstances which can always change.

The contradictions of urbanization may thus be expressed briefly, and Orwellianly, as follows: The promised land is a paradise lost; to destroy is to create; and collectivism is individualism.

Expressed in this raw form they reveal a wider significance. And that wider significance is of ever-increasing importance as the essential characteristics of European urbanization spread across the face of the whole human world.

The modern city is the physical manifestation of a form of civilization, in the wider sense of that word. The modern city is the physical manifestation of a particular form of consciousness. It is a consciousness that is founded on the ideas of rationality and progress.

European culture separated itself from many, if not all, other ancient cultures by its incorporation of rationality and progress as primary concepts and as primary values of its collective consciousness. Rationality meant that humanity could be regarded as self-producing. Progress meant that humanity could be regarded as self-evolving. This profound humanism obviously had a very great potentiality for human empowerment, human striving, organized human effort. And this extraordinary and distinctive potentiality was proudly, if prematurely, proclaimed in the Periclean Athens of the fifth century BC—the city that imagined itself for a moment as an earthly reflection of an ideal polis.

The ideas of rationality and progress were not incompatible with religion. Christianity—a mixture of Hellenism and Judaism—could paradoxically lead either to the life of the hermit in the desert or to the life of the busy merchant in the town. Christianity could even be used to inspire and justify the acquisition of personal wealth. It could even, especially during the eras of European colonialism, be used to justify the inclusion of other peoples in the process of rational progress socially organized. A writer of the fifth century AD considered the right relationship between the City of Man and the City of God, a new formulation of what has been, from Plato to the present day, a central question and challenge for rationality.

The ideas of rationality and progress have caused the unceasing restlessness which is so striking a feature of western culture—and which is strikingly apparent in the modern city. They have caused the endless striving which is another striking feature of that culture and of the modern city. They have caused the overwhelming sociality which is yet another striking feature of that culture and of the modern city. Aristotle called the human being a political animal, a natural polis dweller, a natural citizen. Twenty-three centuries later, we may say that, whatever the species characteristics which we have inherited from evolution, humanity is rapidly making itself into the city-dwelling species.

There is no prospect of halting the progress of urban civilization all over the world. There is no present possibility of regaining a lost rural paradise, of finding another kind of promised land. The challenge, therefore, is to find a way to redeem the city, to save it from itself.

It has been the purpose of this section of *Cities Fit for People* to suggest that (a) the problems of urbanization have their roots in the long history of human social organization (the dynamic effect of human concentration); (b) these problems are inextricably connected with the problems of a particular form of social organization (democracy–capitalism); and (c) they are intimately connected with a particularly successful form of general social consciousness (articulated in terms of rationality and progress). It has also been suggested that the overwhelming pyschic effect of the city can be expressed in terms of a single phenomenon—alienation—a sense of being an outsider in one's only home.

Human and Spiritual Aspects of the City

The problems of city life can and will continue to be dealt with by the usual processes of piecemeal social engineering, the methods of rationalistic reform. But they might also be addressed at another level—the level of social philosophy. And they might even be addressed at the ultimate level—the level of human self-consciousness as a whole, including its spiritual aspects.

Would it be possible to reimagine human life in the city in such a way that there was a reversal of focus—so that the ideal of the city came to be a place for human self-perfecting rather than the arena for competitive wealth producing? It would mean reconceiving the city as a chosen instrument of human self-evolving rather than as merely an inevitable and comprehensible by-product of a certain stage of human social organization.

It would mean substituting an idea of the rational city for the idea of the random city. It would mean changing the orientation of the city's force field, so that it would not be irresistibly centripetal, concentrating all life into itself, but would be open structured, including countryside within it, including subordinate entities (villages) within it, and flowing more freely into its surrounding neighborhood. One might say that in Europe landowners have for centuries vigorously resisted the trespassing of cities on to agricultural land. The compromises that have been reached (e.g., zoning, planning, "green-belts") have been based on the hidden assumption that urbanization is a plague to be controlled, rather than a form of living to be perfected.

Conclusion

In short, the change of mind in question would be a psychic taking of power over the idea and the fact of the city, including a recognition of the great benefits it has brought and the terrible price that it has exacted, with a view to treating it as a natural home of the good life for human beings.

Given the processes that now exist for bringing into fruitful contact, at the global level, forms of human consciousness that express an indefinite number of forms of philosophy and culture and experience, and an indefinite number of patterns of historical development, it may be that we have the opportunity, at the end of the twentieth century, to reconsider the city at the two higher levels—of philosophy and spirituality. It may be that it will be our last chance to do so, before inhuman and instrumental urbanization takes absolute power over the whole of humanity.

Notes

1. F. Engels, *The Condition of the Working Class in England in 1844,* F. K. Wischnewetzky, trans. London: Allen & Unwin, 1891, pp. 23–24.

Section 2 The Culture of Cities and Citizens[1]

Paul Streeten

The twentieth century is the century of urbanization and city life. For thousands of years, rural existence was the dominant way of life of humanity. But, the turn of the century will find us in an urban world, with only small rural pockets. The passage from a predominantly rural to an urban existence is a complex phenomenon, involving technological, economic, social, political, and cultural forces. It may well be regarded by future generations as the most important change in this century.

In 1950, 29.3 percent of the world's population lived in urban areas; in 1995 it reached 44 percent, and the estimate for the year 2025 is that at least 65 percent of the world's population (an estimated 8 billion people) will be living in urban areas.[2] Between 1960 and 1992, the number of city dwellers worldwide rose by 1.4 billion. During the next 15 years, it will rise by approximately 1 billion more. These changes imply a massive movement of people from the countryside to towns and cities. To this has to be added the natural population growth.

There are great variations among countries: the highest income countries became urbanized earlier and now three fourths of their populations live in urban areas. This is expected to grow to 84 percent in the next thirty years. The least developed countries have 21.9 percent of their population in urban areas, which will grow to 43.5 percent in 2025.

Megacities of more than 8 million people are growing rapidly, particularly in Asia. In 1950, only New York and London fitted into this category. In 1994, there were 22 cities of this size and 16 of them were in the developing countries (12 in Asia). The Asian share of these cities is growing and will continue to brow (21 of the 33 megacities expected by the year 2015; 55 percent of the megacities' population in 1995; 64 percent in 2015). The proportion of the world's population living in the largest cities (more than 10 million), which increased from 1.7 to 7.1 percent between 1950 and 1990, is expected to reach 10.9 percent in 1015.

The megacities in the less-developed regions are growing faster than those in the more advanced regions and are expected to continue to do so until 2015. A double process is underway: urbanization, implying the move from the countryside to the towns and cities, and "metropolization," faster growth in the largest conurbations. In some parts of the high-income world, a countertrend has been setting in; the deconcentration of population from some megacities into suburban areas and smaller cities. This was first experienced in the United States and later in some European countries and Japan. This process is still underway, with declines in some large cities. On the other hand, the populations of some of the North's larger cities have stopped falling in the 1980s. The populations of both London and Paris, for example, both dropped by nearly 20 percent during the 1970s. Yet in the 1980s that of Paris leveled off and that of London recovered from 6.7 million in 1981 to approximately 7 million in 1991. Even in America, where large companies and middle-income earners flee from urban blight, drugs, crime, environmental degradation, and violence, by 1990 two more cities had joined the ranks of those with more than 5 million inhabitants (New York, Chicago, and Los Angeles)—namely San Francisco and Philadelphia. In the future, some counterurbanization may occur in the less-developed areas of the world. In fact, the rate of growth of megacities in Latin America slowed down in the 1980s.

Now 56 percent of the world's urban population still lives in smaller cities of less than 500,000, and their share is expected to decrease somewhat in the future. Nevertheless, more than half of the world's urban population is expected to live in such cities by 2015. This pattern of urbanization, characterized by a majority of the urban population living in cities of fewer than 500,000, is common to both the less and the more advanced regions of the world.

Capital and information are highly mobile, whereas cities rely on immobile factors: housing, public services, infrastructure, and, above all, distinctive political and cultural traditions. Because the mobile factors have advanced much more rapidly than the immobile ones, some have concluded that cities are finished. Although it may seem that modern communication technology and the fall in the share of manufacturing in national income has reduced the advantage of physical proximity, and the need for the static factors, cities are in the fact flourishing. They have increased not only in size, but also in economic importance. In developing countries cities generate national income on the average twice their share in the population. Some of this consists, however, not of extra goods, or net additions to welfare, but of "anti-bads," needed to combat the "bads" created by city life, such as longer and more expensive journeys to work, more expensive housing, or the need to be more expensively dressed than in a rural setting. The secret of the success of cities lies in economies of large scale. Financial services (dominated by New York, Tokyo, and London, although increasing globalized), design, marketing, advertising, film, and television will all tend to cluster in one place. Clustering can occur in places other than cities: computer firms in Silicon Valley (near Stanford University) and on Route 128 outside Boston (near the Massachusetts Institute of Technology), fashion design in the Po Valley in North Italy. But these locations have a lot in common with what we would recognize as an urban environment.[3]

The City and Culture

If we define culture as a way of life, there can be no doubt that urbanization and the growth of cities are the most significant cultural shifts in this century. Living in a city or in the country makes a big difference to the way in which we organize our lives. Only recently have technical developments in computers, communications, and transport made the "hooked-up" rural inhabitant part of the vanguard of the new way of life.

Rural societies have incorporated nature's concerns in their world-view, while urban societies forget or neglect environmental problems. Urban populations have often lost touch with the natural environment. It is a challenge to the people in towns and cities to reconstruct the links between nature and nurture; this is part of the new global ethics.

Cities create and nurture their own culture. Urban culture brings with it dynamic, creative tensions arising from population density and spatial proximity. Many of the landmarks of the cultural heritage of humanity are in the great cities of the world. It is also manifested in the cultural creativity of everyday life, in the variety, diversity, and heterogeneity of institutions, patterns of interaction, and activities catering for minority interests, in the shared meanings and in their expression in the so-called "popular culture."

Very early in the history of urban agglomerations, the fact of urban life gave way to the concept of the city as the locus of power, as an entity that is more than the sum of its inhabitants. At the turn of the century, the classical thinkers of modernity have treated the city as a cultural creation and as the engine of development (e.g., Max Weber and Georg Simmel). They saw cities as the places for diversity and heterogeneity, the places for the encounter with the "stranger," with the variety of "others" that allow for self-reflection, for the recognitions of the uniqueness of ourselves and of the enrichment that emerges from dialogue and interaction.

The Dark Side

The optimism that linked urbanization with creativity, innovation, and modernity later turned into the pessimism as the ills of city life became visible: the urban underclass, panhandling, drugs, crime, violence, hatred, and low mass culture were seen not as frictional phenomena linked to the rapid pace of change, but as permanent and enduring features of urban life. Urban air and water pollution and the dumping of rubbish in residential areas have made urban life miserable for its residents. In the United States, cutbacks in the contributions of central revenue to city governments have led to delayed garbage pickups, closed libraries, dirty streets, the shutting down of parks and playgrounds, and a rise in crime. Jobless people dominate inner-city communities, partly as the result of the decline of mass production manufacturing. Persistent unemployment leads to different habits, styles of living and orientation, and a different culture from that of those with regular jobs. In a vicious circle, these cultural factors marginalize people and make them unemployable. Children growing up in this environment acquire the habits of their parents.

In the developing world there was the charge of "urban bias," that towns were favored at the expense of rural areas by subsidized food, education and health services, and expensive infrastructure. The better-off urban elites, consisting of the urban middle class (including the industrial workers employed in modern sector firms), civil servants, politicians, and the military, were seen to be exploiting the much poorer farmers. "Urban bias" was also reinforced by the belief that urban industrialization, assisted by protection of trade, is essential for development and that an "investable surplus" must be squeezed out of agriculture. The prosperity of the urban workers with jobs is accompanied by a large army of unemployed or underemployed immigrants from the countryside. They have come to the towns in the hope of getting a well-paid job, but most of them have to eke out an existence by low- or zero-productivity activities.

The time has come to strike a balance: to recognize the rich texture of urban life and, at the same time, to face the challenges and problems that cities offer. Policies of urban bias have been greatly reduced or abandoned in the 1980s. Protectionism that has favored urban industry has become unfashionable. The costs of urban housing have been reduced by site and service schemes and by showing that good houses can be constructed at a fraction of the costs that had previously been thought necessary. Cities have continued to grow.

It should, however, be clear that not all of the problems often attributed to urban existence are intrinsic to city life. Some are the consequences of the wrong policies, the lack of resources, of poverty, great inequality, and polarization. Often the anonymity of city life and the uprooting of migration are referred to in this context. It has to be stressed that the urban problems are not necessary or inherent traits of urban life. There is much evidence that change can result in solidarity and mutual support, and that disruptions of normal life are accepted as opportunities for enrichment and innovations.

Urban Infrastructure: New Technologies, New Problems, New Solutions

Since the emergence of the first human settlements, technological innovations have been a key determinant of social and spatial organization; they, in turn, have been conditioned by diverse needs and features of social and territorial structures. The very idea of a city and its shapes can be seen, through history, as the spatial translation of technical changes in the ways of doing and organizing, conveying at the same time cultural, ideological, and even philosophical mutations.

Nowadays, cities—and particularly megacities—are the privileged scenarios for the development and application of new technologies, especially in communications and information. Yet, these new technologies have not been incorporated in thinking about and in planning the cities in spite of the fact that there is a double link between technology and social space. Undoubtedly, technological changes have a significant social, cultural, ideological, and spatial impact on the societies into which they are introduced. These technologies, in turn, will be transformed and adapted by the social forces that exert their own demands and pressures on the techniques.

It is not easy for a city or country to introduce modern technology. Recent experience shows that it can be done in an integrated way when the state has a strong presence in the production, provision, management, and financing of public services and collective equipment, when the development of science and technology are policy priorities, when there are high-quality statistical information services for the design and evaluation of urban policies, when there are subsidies to collective services and equipment for the poor. Obviously, they also depend on relatively high levels of income per head and not so obviously on sustained political stability. Democratic regimes where local-level political institutions are based on representative government that allow freedom in the flow of information, transparency in the functioning of public institutions, and formal and informal participation by citizens in urban management may also be helpful.

Of course, few countries meet these conditions. The trend of economic adjustment policies in many countries goes in the opposite direction. In these cases, modern technological innovations will be introduced according to narrow financial considerations, in a fragmented manner, in services that benefit high-income earners.

Cultural Creativity in City Life

Modern urban life is sometimes associated with mass society, uniformity of consumption, the tyranny of the marketplace, and the ubiquity of power and dominance. If this were true, the result would be the uniformity of the shopping mall, repeated everywhere. It would mean the successful creation, through advertising and emulation, of uniform demands, to be satisfied with uniform products.

Yet, in spite of the concentration of resources and power in the hands of global firms and of the impact of mass production of cars, televisions, and blue jeans, those who are ready to look carefully will find hat ordinary men and women can escape the dictates of mass consumption and shape their everyday lives. Be it through practices of resistance, diverse tricks or shrewdness, new uses of language, movement, humor, or more practical shortcuts, people appropriate for themselves whatever is offered to them, creating their own way of life. Mass society is not a disciplined, obedient, and passive crowd following leaders and consuming imposed products. People open their own roads, with their art of using and doing, finding ways to free themselves in order to live, in the best possible way, from the violence of power.

this explains why, in spite of the trend toward globalization, we observe a great variety of life styles and practices in the cities of the world. In urban infrastructure and technology, or in urban landscapes and layouts, rhythms and peoples, diversity and heterogeneity are to be found. Claiming the recognition of the creativity and ingenuity of people is a good antidote to pessimistic and fatalistic views of the world, and especially of the evils of the city. There are, however, dangers in simply celebrating this pluralism and diversity. One danger lies in going to the extremes of radical cultural relativism in an era of globalization and tendencies toward mass culture: the belief that whatever people do is good. This means, ultimately, that anything goes and there are no universal criteria to compare and evaluate social practices.

A further danger implied in this perspective is to accept and even applaud the status quo. Because what we stressed is the inventiveness and apparent freedom of ordinary people, rather than the ubiquity of power and domination and the social dimensions of inequality and polarization, complacency with its ensuing apparent diversity would follow.[4] They key issue here is that the diversity and pluralism to be fostered have to be founded on the satisfaction of basic needs, a requirement that precludes exclusion and marginalization; a minimum of resources and capacities (from freedom from hunger to adequate heath, education, and shelter) have to be guaranteed to be able to claim "the right to have rights" (in Hannah Arendt's words) and the right to express one's own unique identity.

Conclusion

Not all cultural creations and patterns of behavior found in urban life are equally desirable or permissible. Not all of them can be interpreted as creative responses of subjects who appropriate for themselves what modern mass culture has to offer and creatively to "invent" their everyday life. On the contrary, they often are the recurrent results of deprivation and cumulative social harm, and require political and social intervention to attack these problems at their root.

A first challenge facing policy is how to assure individual and collective access to resources for urban life, resources that become prerequisites for the full enjoyment of choice. A second challenge that would lead to a reassurance of cultural diversity of the citizens is to find ways to open the world to more voices and products, again with the intention of widening choices, with the multiplying effects of all the creative interactions that this would entail.

to make life more agreeable, the expansion of green and open spaces is essential. Urban pollution has become a serious problem in many cities of the developing world. Pollution and emission rates of pollutants should be monitored and reduced. Spaces should be created for cultural expressions, such as music, amateur theater, and the arts.

Notes

1. This paper builds on some sections of *Our Creative Diversity,* a Report of the World Commission on Culture and Development, to which I was editorial consultant. It incorporates ideas contributed by Dr. Lourdes Arizpe and Dr. Elizabeth Jelin.
2. These and the following data are taken from *The World Urbanization Prospects,* 1994 rev. ed. United Nations, 1995.
3. "A Survey of Cities," *The Economist,* 29 July 1995.
4. Such a view leads to reduced emphasis on the services of the welfare state. It claims that the ingenuity and creativity of the poor allow them to cope with and solve their problems. This leads to the conclusion that the informal sector should be left unattended and the allegation that the ingenuity will nurture a new breed of entrepreneur. The linguistic shift from informal workers to microentrepreneurs is characteristic of this danger.

Section 3 From Vernacularism to Globalism

Nezar AlSayyad

The purpose of this section is to bring the issues of history, culture, and identity to the discourse on urbanism in the era of globalization. Michael Cohen, in his contribution to this book, citing several socioeconomic convergence areas argued that cities in the North and South are becoming more alike in their most important characteristics.[1] Although this may indeed be the case, in terms of urbanism, the similarities in built environments of those cities are only apparent, not real. By tracing the historical relationship between cities of the North and South, three distinct phases can be identified: (1) colonization, (2) independence/nationalism, and (3) globalization. Many of the physical development of the cities in the last phase may be properly interpreted only when grounded in their true cultural and historical contexts. From this perspective, urbanism, defined as the form and culture of cities, may encounter little change under the new world order. In the era of globalization, when culture is becoming increasingly placeless, urbanism will maintain some relevance because of its ability to explain the specificity of local cultures. Urbanism will continue to be a vibrant arena in which one can observe how the forms of global domination are mediated by local struggles.

As we approach the twenty-first century and as we start to deal with the problems of our cities today, we cannot ignore the revolutionary developments that occurred in the world during the last two or three decades. Trends, such as the transnationalization of capital, the internationalization of labor, the steady increase in global trading and communication, and the ensuing competition among cities have all lead individuals, businesses, industries, and governments to attempt to position themselves globally.[2] It follows that in a globally compressed world, composed of national societies that are becoming increasingly aware of their ethnic and racial roots, the conditions for the identification of individual and collective selves become very complex.[3] It is important to take into account that any theory of globalization must recognize the distinctive cultural and unequal conditions under which the notion of the "global" was constructed. It also becomes difficult to comprehend globalization without recognizing the historical specificity of traditional cultures, their colonization, and their later emergence as nation–states. There are indeed many conceptions of globalization that were developed in the social sciences or are rooted in economic theories. This section mainly builds on the discourse in the field of cultural studies.

Problems of Artificial Identity Creation

At the heart of all these issues is the question of identity. Of course, the connection between the identity of a people and the form and culture of the cities they produce has been the subject of much research. Family, ethnicity, religion, language, and history have all been identified as identity-constituting elements that are handed down in a process normally referred to as "tradition."[4]

Tradition is based on valuing constraint and in a technological world of limitless choices, the conflicts between the traditional and the modern in the urbanism of cities become unavoidable. But as much research has demonstrated, the traditional/modern dialectic is very problematic. Dichotomies, such as East vs. West, North vs. South, first world vs. third world, core vs. periphery, and developed vs. underdeveloped nations may be considered artificial categories. An approach that takes into account the discursive constitution of "cultures" would recognize that those societies are constructed in relation to one another, produced, represented, and perceived through the ideologies and narratives of situated discourse.[5] The dominant factor in each of these dualities (West, North, core, etc.) is mainly defined as difference, constructed in opposition to the other, although it is not a monolithic preexisting real subject itself.[6]

The subordinate term (East, South, periphery, etc.) is equally an invention produced in a variety of postcolonial and anticolonial discourses. The only purpose of these dualities then lies in that they force us, as scholars, to articulate our theoretical positions beyond the realm of binary opposition and in the process reveal the complex dimensions of what is being categorized—and in this case, it is the underlying political bases of urbanization.

In studying the relationship between these two realms, and its effect on the identity of citizens and their cities, as stated above, three historic phases can be identified: the colonial period, the era of independence and nation–state building, and globalization. These phases seem to have been accompanied also by three respective urban forms: the hybrid; the modern and pseudomodern; and the postmodern.

Before the era of colonialism and in most of what is today the "developing world," we had traditional communities living in preindustrial and often insular conditions. Although some form of economic exchange occurred between the two worlds, the curiosity about the "other" was limited. The vernacular form of settlements in this time appear to be shaped more by their sociocultural realm and the surrounding natural environment. It also reflects, possibly at a subconscious level, the identity of their inhabitants.

Colonialism and the Hybridization of Settlements

Around the middle of the nineteenth century, the world witnessed the rise of modern industrial capitalism and the emergence of organized political dominance represented by colonialism. Under this colonial paradigm, the world became divided into two kinds of people and two types of societies: (1)powerful, administratively advanced, racially Caucasoid, nominally Christian, and principally European dominant nations and (2) powerless, organizationally backward, traditionally rooted, and mainly non-white dominated societies.

The paradigm shift from the traditional to the colonial created a relationship of unequal cultural and socioeconomic exchange. And if we are to analyze the issues of identity in the cities of the developing world, we must take this into account and understand the processes by which this identity was violated, ignored, distorted, or stereotyped throughout history. Artistically, Jean Leon Gerome's *Reception of the Siamese Ambassador at Fontainebleau* was one of the clearest expressions of this unequal relationship between the newly dominant and the newly dominated. In 1850, the Siamese were forced to open their ports to European trade and to exchange ambassadors with France. When Gerome was commissioned to document the ceremony, he chose to paint the single moment in which the Siamese envoys kneeled down to the representatives of Western Imperial might. Here the problem of representation becomes central, because much of these artistic creations contributed to the making of the "other" and to enlarging the gulf between the dominant and the dominated. Several art historians tell us that Gerome was the most accurate and scientific painter of his generation in representing the oriental environment. It was also Gerome who gave us the *Snake Charmer,* a beautiful painting depicting a scene with a nude boy entertaining a bunch of Arab tramps in the portico of the blue mosque in Cairo. Clearly, the political intentions behind this artistic reading cannot be ignored, an understanding that led Edward Said (1978) to use this image on the cover of his seminal book, *Orientalism.* Now that the backwardness of this traditional population had been established, at least to the rest of the masses of the colonial motherland, it became legitimate to go about reforming it. the colonial regimes proceeded to sniff out the ethnicity of the colonized cultures. When it failed to do so by force, it resorted to the psychological techniques of hypnotizing the middle class as demonstrated by the Gao House sculpture in New Delhi, which shows the white settler subjugating the Buddha. Obviously, all of this had an effect on the physical fabric of cities. Everywhere they went, the colonists introduced their own brand of settlements.

What is referred to here is the overall planning model that determined the pattern of urban developments in both the cores and the peripheries. This was the era, as Le Corbusier's sketches would indicate, when ideas would flow from Paris down to Algiers and further south to French Black Africa. Ironically, in the 1950s, when the Algerians launched their liberation war against France, the latter resorted to the age0old urban strategy. Thousands of traditional villages were destroyed in order to regroup the population in checkerboard resettlement towns under the banner of modernization. This uprooting operation was obviously meant to break the subversive influence of the rebels and not to improve conditions for the local population.

The colonial era gave us a hybrid urban condition. At that time, we started to see a certain architecture and urban language that, at least on a visual level, unifies the lands of colonial empires. For example, variations of the bungalow, a hybrid dwelling type introduced by the British in India, started to appear all over the empire, making it at times difficult to identify its origins.

Independence, Nationalism, and Modernity

When the people of the dominated societies started to rebel against this colonial world order, they had little to cling to in their drive to establish their own sovereignty other than using the terms of the existing order, with its baggage of physical realities and ideological constructs, such as the nation–state. Groups of people living in one region under a colonial power, possibly only having a common colonial history but belonging to different religions, languages, ethnicities, and traditions had to band together to achieve this new, supposedly more advanced stage of independence. The few commonalities were highlighted by the political bodies, while the differences suppressed in pursuit of the noble goal of freedom. a national identity based on short-term political interest and the ideology of struggle emerged as the driving force behind most nationalistic movements. Once independence was achieved, the league that bound together the various groups was no longer as pervasive. Indeed, the events of the late 1980s and early 1990s, in places such as the former Soviet Union and Yugoslavia, are a testament to the true associations of these people, where ethnic origin, race, and religion are emerging as the prime definers of their collective identity.

In terms of urbanism, this second phase of independence and nationalism did not necessarily improve the quality of cities in the developing world, nor did it resolve the conflicts that plagued the traditional settlements of those societies. During the ear of colonialism, important and irreversible decisions that affect the production of the built environment had been taken. In the Arab Middle East, for example, new building codes based on Western norms requiring setbacks forced the traditional courtyard house out of existence. Instead we saw it replaced with banal single-family dwelling units that were not suitable from a climatic point of view, to say the least. Because of a host of cultural complexities, these traditional people did indeed prefer the modern type, even if it required some bizarre adaptations, such as building into the street to protect their possessions. And, in a society that cherished privacy very much, some had to build freestanding walls as high as forty feet to shield them from their neighbors. In some countries, we even witnessed the abandonment of entire efficient systems of construction because they were no longer appropriate in the modern era. At some level, the urban system was now grossly out of balance and the urban environment of many developing societies was being rapidly pseudomarginalized.

The obsession with modernity, which accompanied the early years of nationalism and independence, was a major characteristic of most new governments in the developing world. The Western pattern of urban development continued to serve as the reference point for the indigenous populations, particularly in the urban middle classes, which were now running the bureaucracies in these countries.

During this time, the construction of public housing was in many parts of the Western world an instrument of achieving social justice, a social justice that had become a myth with the demise of such projects as Pruitt–Igoe. But the influences of modernism were very strong and, in the developing world, the public housing model was often copied verbatim. Governments, this time, used it as an instrument of nation building in an attempt to buy the allegiances of their citizenry. At the same time that Pruitt–Igoe was being torn down, a project in the desert outside of Teheran was being completed. For whom, one may ask? The answer may be for a traditional population whose government yearned for joining the so-called "modern" world—obviously this population had other plans. In a touch of irony, in other parts of the developing world, this public housing was being reappropriated by the people. Here, Egypt serves as a good example. Under the socialist and nationalist regime of Nasser, thousands of public housing blocks were built all over the country. Suffering from such traditional problems as lack of maintenance, empty and unused spaces, and the need to accommodate expanding families, many residents took matters into their own hands. One person decided to add a room to his apartment on the ground floor. Once build, the next person above had a balcony; what would prevent that person from making it into a room? Of course, the traditional government response in most of the world is to send a bulldozer to remove these infringements on public property. But the residents were quite belligerent. They go the only place from which the bulldozer could dome and they erect a mosque. The government would not hesitate to demolish residential infringements on public property, but a mosque, they would not dare! The information additions continue and the original blocks are totally absorbed by them. This example demonstrates that to achieve their objectives, the residents resorted to the power of religion, which, with ethnicity and race, are the new emerging forms of community identifications, in both the developed and the developing worlds.

Globalization and the Postmodern Urban Form

This brings us to "globalization," or the third phase in the relationship between the dominant and the dominated. This is an era in which the search for and the reconstruction of identity become paramount. Once independence was achieved and once the dust from the struggle had settled, the problem of creating harmony between the nation and the community surfaced. Where it was not resolved, religious and political fundamentalism flourished. To understand the impact on urbanism, we have to pay closer attention to the difficulties associated with defining national identity. The primary elements of national identity – race, language, religion, history, territory, and tradition – have always been essential but unequal components in its formation. The political units that formed nations following both world wars were expected to be homogeneous entities with common cultures. The reality was otherwise because these nation–states were mainly created by international deals that displayed little concern with or knowledge of the will of the people who inhabited them.

Of course, national identity, as perceived by governments, is inherently tied to the image the government wishes to project in the international arena. The state, through its monopoly of policies and resources, can, over time, create a national culture, even if it lacked one in the first place.[7] Can one design a national identity? Can this national identity be designed by a foreign power? These questions were often faced by the politicians who governed newly independent states. Architecturally speaking, it was also faced by architects and planners who worked for them. Because cities are mainly forms that convey specific meanings, it becomes important to look at this physical dimension.

The Danish architect Jørn Utzon has claimed that his national assembly building for Kuwait, made with concrete, evokes the traditional Bedouin tent in its roof, while its plan is based on an Islamic bazaar. Louis Khan's famous Assembly in Dacca, a work of high drama, engages in a similar exercise. Some have argued that its form may have been more appropriate for another country, one with closer links to the Roman classicist architecture that inspired it. Yet, it has fast become a symbol of Bangladesh, even though much of its inspiration was not derived from Bangladesh. Lawrence Vale remarks, "At what point, one may ask, did the pyramid become an Egyptian form? Like the pyramids of Giza or the Eiffel Tower, the Citadel of Assembly may someday be seen as being quintessentially of its country as well."[8] Of course, identity cannot be based on some myth from precolonial times. Many nations and their planners have often resorted to a past around which identity may coalesce, as a solace against the perceived dominator. Respect for the past in the developing world must include accepting and coming to terms with the colonial urban legacy.

If we accept that national identity is a social construct tied to temporal events, then it follows that the urbanism that accompanies it can only symbolize national identity as observed by a single individual or groups of individuals at a specific point in time. We also have to recognize that there comes a point in the lives of all formally colonized people when they must cease to perceive their colonial history as colonial and start absorbing this heritage as their own. When is this point reached? When did the forms of the British colonizers become the vernacular heritage of the eastern United States? When did the Spanish colonial settlement forms in many parts of Latin America emerge as the traditional architecture that today attracts tourists to these societies.

The problem of national identity is further complicated by extensive global economic exchange. Not only do nations have to mediate between precolonial and colonial legacies, between the traditional and the modern, but they also must deal with the effects of globalization and the new world order. Globalization, as referred to here, is the process by which the world is becoming one economic entity, characterized by its informational, interconnected modes of production and exchange, and its transnational flows of labor and capital, under a predominantly capitalist world system. It would be convenient here to adopt Giddens' view that globalization introduced new forms of world interdependence "in which once again there were no others."[9] However, because capitalism thrives on the construction of difference, such an economic universalism, under the confines of a world composed of national units, can only lead to further cultural division. Culture then becomes the globally authoritative paradigm for explaining difference as a means of locating the "other."

Indeed, the considerable migration from the former colonies to the lands of the former colonizers and the infiltration of ethnic subcultures into mainstream first world Western societies cannot be dismissed. In fact, this phenomena has often been the cause of many social conflicts, as these local subcultures often resort to ethnic, racial, or religious allegiances to defend their identity from being swallowed by the dominant majority culture. The current struggles of multiculturalism and gender politics in the United States may be a good example of an ideology that attempts to embrace difference as a fundamental constituent of national identity.

It is ironic that the national identity of the former colonizers is undergoing major change, often becoming more exclusive and more directly linked to national origin or religious association. Indeed, the twentieth century has witnessed the return of states where belonging to a particular religion or ethnic identity is a prerequisite for nationality.[10] We have to remember that national identity is always in a state of transition and flux. The often contradictory forces of globalization are playing havoc with traditional loyalties and values and are challenging the older ideologies and practices.

Indeed some of the cultural conflicts, whose meanings are lost in cyberspace, require a very careful dissection if we are to understand the effects of a one-world system on our cities. All of us have two conflicting sentiments toward culture and tradition. In the first, one resorts to culture and tradition out of fear of change, a change that in and of itself may be inevitable. Protection against the unknown does, however, turn into fundamentalism. The second sentiment, characterized by interest in the culture of the mysterious "other," emerges from a totally different feeling: the desire to have the choice to merge with the "other" and share in a wider or a different collective consciousness. The tremendous movement of citizens across borders and the rise of protected ethnic minorities demonstrate that the two sentiments, both legitimate, are not necessarily contradictory. In fact, they may indeed happen simultaneously or alternatively, based on time and place.

Culture and Urbanism in a Global Era

For those of us interested in the study of culture and urbanism in a global era, there are a few lessons to be learned. First, one may argue that even if there is a "world culture," it is a culture marked by the management of diversity rather than the replication of uniformity. It is also essentially a culture of dominant groups, in which the persistent diversity of the constituent local cultures is often a product of globalization itself. In terms of urbanism, this may imply that any convergence indicators only reflect the self-representation of the dominant particular and not a true integration of the cities of the South into a world system.

The second lesson involves the connection between this "world culture" and space, for this latter is a placeless culture created through the increasing interconnectedness of local and national communities without a clear base in one place. The impact on urbanism is that cultural experience may likely become less place rooted and more informationally based. Some will argue that identity cannot be placeless and that culture cannot be swallowed up by informational flows. Indeed, some of the identities we carry on us will remain place based. However, in the technologically crazed communication era in which we live, experience is being increasingly shaped by "virtual reality" environments,[11] rather than actual places. We must come to terms with the effect of this change on the form of cities in the twenty-first century.

Conclusion

For all of this talk about globalization, the history of the world demonstrates a movement toward cultural differentiation and not homogenization, in which each individual increasingly belongs to many cultures and in which people have multiple cultural identities. In this sense, identity is always under construction and in constant evolution. For if we accept hybridization as an inherent constituent of national identity, then we must accept the ensuing urbanism as only a reflection of a specific transitional stage in the life of this society. Indeed, globalization has made the issues of identity and representation in urbanism very cumbersome, and it has cast a doubt on urbanism's ability to fully represent the peoples, nations, and cultures within which it exists. But, since culture has become increasingly placeless, urbanism will be an arena in which one can observe the specificity of local cultures and their attempts to mediate global domination.

As the nations of the new globalized world order become more conscious of their religious, ethnic, and racial roots, they are likely to seek forms and norms that represent these subidentities, even if these send confused messages to global audience that will ultimately experience it through the space of flows. Only time can tell what this will mean to the study of urbanism in the next century. For it is only in context that we can understand our own reality.

Notes

1. Michael Cohen, Part 1, Chapter 2, Section 2 of this book.
2. Anthony King, ed. *Culture, Globalization and the World-System.* London: Macmillan, 1991.
3. Roland Robertson, "Social Theory, Cultural Relativity and the Problem of Globality," in King, 1991.
4. Nezar AlSayyad and Jean Paul Bourdier, *Dwellings, Settlements and Tradition.* New York: University Press of America, 1989.
5. Janet Wolff, "The Global and the Specific: Reconsidering Conflicting Theories of Culture," in King, 1991.
6. Stuart Hall, "Old and New Identities, Old and New Ethnicities," in King, 1991.
7. Immanuel Wallerstein, "The National and the Universal: Can There Be Such a Thing as World Culture," in King, 1991.
8. Lawrence Vale, *Architecture, Power and National Identity.* New Haven: Yale University Press, 1992.

9. Anthony Giddens, *The Consequences of Modernity.* Stanford University Press, 1990.
10. Nezar AlSayyad, "Urbanism and the Dominance Equation." In Nezar AlSayyad, ed., *Forms of Dominance: On the Architecture and Urbanism of the Colonial Experience.* London: Avebury, 1992.
11. The term "virtual reality" was introduced in computer science in the last decade to designate nearly exact simulations of audiovisual experience. The field is now growing to include simulations of holistic environments.

Section 4 Global Common Values

Deborah Moldow

Today, city residents already live in a global community. It is not unusual for a woman in Los Angeles to wear a blouse from Mexico and a skirt from India, to drive a Japanese car filled with oil from Saudi Arabia to a Greek restaurant while listening to African music. But the changes leading to globalization have occurred so rapidly that human consciousness has not yet expanded sufficiently to accept this reality.

We are caught in an outmoded world view of separate identities competing for power and resources on a national as well as an individual basis. As the vision of global community becomes more and more apparent, there is a backlash of clinging to regional, ethnic, and religious identities.

These may be the birth pains heralding the shift in consciousness that will be necessary for the flowering of the coming millennium. As a species, our ability to love outside our families is a faculty that is capable of growing and expanding, much like the way in which a child learns to recognize first its own needs, then its role as a family member, then the function of friendship, and later pride in various communities, from school to work to civic responsibility. When this expansion happens too rapidly, or when one is called upon for economic or political reasons to be part of a larger community with which one does not identify, there will be strife until a feeling of belonging has been established. This identification occurs through commitment to common goals and a mutual support system, sustained by an agreed-on set of values.

We are living in a unique time in the history of the human race. For the first time, we are able to see a picture of the earth from space and to conceive of a community that spans the globe. A sense is dawning of the fragility of the blue ball glowing in the black void and the interconnectedness of all the life forms that share it. The challenge is to move from fear of scarcity and domination into a new era of love, trust, cooperation, and sharing. The question now is whether, as a species, we are able to make the leap toward living as global neighbors in our shared community.

Common Values

The identification and recognition of common values will eventually help in this transition. As a matter of fact, the report of the Commission on Global Governance, states: "The broad acceptance of a global civic ethic to guide action is vital to the quality of life in the global neighborhood. From a practical point of view, we therefore need a set of common, core values around which we can unite people, irrespective of their cultural, political, religious or philosophical backgrounds—values which are appropriate to the growing needs of our crowded and diverse planet."[1]

The journey of the human being from hunter–gatherer to planetary steward has been one of continuous unfolding and outreaching of the creative spirit. Although it is our nature to be constantly growing and changing, we are resistant to this unsettled state and experience it as a source of stress. In the early stages of our development as a species, major breakthroughs, such as the use of fire or the invention of the wheel, were slow in coming and were followed by long periods of gradual adaptation. Some of the most significant breakthroughs were those that led to an increasing complexity of social organization. When loose family groupings began to grow into tribes, much suspicion had to be worked through before the families could cooperate as necessary for hunting expeditions and for the mutual protection of homesites.

The rise of agriculture led to more permanent settlements, requiring greater cooperation to achieve a measure of security from climate, predators, and rival tribal groups. The same force that was used to provide meat proved effective in subduing competitors for desirable territory or for settling disputes arising from the volatility of human emotions. The use of force could only increase suspicion and mistrust among groups. Learning to mine metals led to the fashioning of powerful weapons as well as agricultural and domestic tools. Warrior tribes consolidated their conquests and maintained cohesiveness, exacting tributes in return for security. The spirit of cooperation was enforced by might, but human consciousness was expanding to include larger domains.

As farther-reaching communities arose, trade began to develop among them so they could share different resources. This led to the emergence of trading centers, which grew into towns and later cities. Great empires reached across immense territories, exploring and incorporating new cultures. Expansion was generally accompanied by violent conquest, as people rarely accept domination by another group without a struggle. But, over time, these mighty empires achieved periods of peace characterized by political stability, including the establishment of a body of laws, economic cohesiveness, and a cultural renaissance, all of which bound members of society together in a feeling of community.

Major religions grew and developed, codifying ethics rooted deeply in the human conscience by which people could live together with greater solidarity and mutual purpose than by civil law alone. Settlements in some parts of the world became larger and more permanent, allowing language groupings to stabilize and giving rise, through power struggles and warfare, to the nation–state. Subjects were expected to develop loyalty to these agglomerations, usually personified by a king, that transcended their more immediate identification with any ethnic or religious group.

The human spirit reached outward, creating new inventions that enhanced the comfort of travel and the efficiency of communications, as our species began to cover more of the globe. The more technically sophisticated cultures sent explorers, then warriors, and then tradesmen to conquer distant lands, where the weaponry was less developed, creating colonies that provided natural resources for the growing industries at home. The Industrial Revolution heralded the greatest era of change in history, as people from rural areas flocked to the swelling cities in search of jobs in the new factories and expanding businesses. The pace of change quickened, accompanied by its stress, as urban centers began to redefine our notion of community.

Democracy: A Major Step Toward Shared Values

The beginnings of the Industrial Age were also marked by perhaps the most significant movement in human settlements: the popularization of democracy, which was earlier experienced in the ancient cities of Athens and Rome. The loyalty demanded by nation–states was difficult to achieve throughout a diverse population unless all members of the society had a voice in governance. Democracy is a revolutionary concept in many societies, and, in fact, required revolutions in many countries before it took hold. But the core principle of democracy, the use of the popular vote rather than coercion to make governing decisions, allowed a whole new realm of participation. This was a fundamental stepping stone in the growth of human consciousness, enabling people to form large communities grounded in the idea of citizenship, with its attendant rights and responsibilities.

The idea is so powerful that it led to a growing worldwide acceptance of the principle of self-determination, which gradually ended the colonial era. Allowing free expression of opinion and the participation of a diversity of voices representing all elements of society is a key basis for an expanding world community.

The human creative spirit has continued to burst forth, bringing about the revolution in science and technology that is the hallmark of the twentieth 20th century, with change occurring at a dizzying rate. As the sophistication of production increased, so did the efficiency of the weapons of war, so that this new century has been characterized by human destruction of unparalleled scope, leading to the previously inconceivable power to actually obliterate all of life on the planet through nuclear weaponry. At the same time, the success of the species in harnessing natural resources for our survival and enjoyment has produced yet another power to destroy life—through the degradation of the environment—a threat undreamed of in the history of the human race.

The development of the human species has completed its phase of childhood innocence and exploration. We have entered a troubled yet exhilarating adolescence, possessing powerful tools and just beginning to awaken to our adult responsibilities. It is not surprising that we have made mistakes in our restless "youth," but we must now mature quickly as a civilization if we are to manage our tools and ourselves wisely.

A Search for Global Values

We are now entering a new, very powerful Age of Information, but in truth our ancestors have hungered for information for as long as we have had the gift of rational thought. Before the invention of writing and printing made information more readily available and easier to preserve, designated members of every human community were charged with keeping the wisdom that had been accumulated thus far. These wisdom keepers were the shamans and priests of the earliest religions, teaching behaviors that would allow the community to feel a sense of protection from the harshness of the natural world. Some of these behaviors were rituals that also served to create a group identity. This group identity was a positive, cohesive force, enhancing cooperation and a feeling of security, but it also aggravated the sense of separateness from other groups with different beliefs and rituals, sometimes increased by different skin pigments or other contrasting physical characteristics. Conquering warriors frequently imposed their belief systems on their subjects, although tribal traditions were often woven into the new religions as well. The vast spread of Judaism, Buddhism, Christianity, and Islam all contributed to unifying people across the globe around strong values-related positions.

Of course, the search for truth has had its dark side as well. All religions teach peace, yet it is an often-observed irony that so many wars have been fought over differences of religion. Although religions provided the social frameworks for societies, the sovereign power was usually held by the warrior leaders, and religious beliefs often reflected a warrior spirit.

The patriarchal traditions of some of these power alliances have sometimes been responsible for inequality of opportunity between the genders. And, while indigenous practices have traditionally stressed living in harmony with the natural world, it is widely believed that the material growth of the Western world has been directly influenced by the relatively recent development of the monotheistic world view, in which people are held to be in a position of dominion over the rest of creation.

When most of the human race lived in tribal cultures, it was understandable for each culture to feel very different from the others. But in our current age of global travel and communication, it has become apparent to all thinking people that the differences among us lie only in our appearances and our beliefs, and that the essence of what makes us human is the same in all men and women. This egalitarian notion, however, has come to us slowly over the course of human development, and only began to achieve a foothold about 200 years ago, during the American and French Revolutions. It is out of this idea also that the once common practice of slavery has been all but abolished in our modern world, and that the concept of human rights has taken hold.

Yet, in spite of our growing sense of the human race as one global family, we continue to live separated by national boundaries and ethnic and religious identities. One of the results of this is a richness of cultural heritage that is a treasure of humanity and encourages us to champion our diversity. Another result is the natural inclination to want our own group to have its share of the land, the resources, the power. We have not yet expanded our feelings of family to match our thoughts. This is natural, given how new the concept of global family actually is. And even in closely knit families, there is a struggle for dominance that demands patience and maturity from all members. But the challenge of the next millennium will be to achieve this transformation of consciousness that is the only road to lasting peace.

The Search for a New Universalism

At the beginning of World War II, a group called The International Consultative Group of Geneva met to study why peace had failed. Its report stated:

> As it becomes increasingly evident that the crisis of Western civilization is in the last resort a spiritual crisis which due to the absence of great common and compelling convictions, and that none of the ideologies which are at present in control can pretend to bring about a true integration, men everywhere are searching for a new universalism. It is rightly believed that international society has become so interdependent that it will only be able to live in a harmonious and orderly fashion if some fundamental common convictions concerning man and society are held by all nations, however different they may remain in other respects. . . . [2]

This vision called out for a body capable of moral leadership in an increasingly global civilization.

The United Nations arose out of the ashes of two world wars and the detonation of the first atomic bomb as a weapon of war. Although the UN was founded on a clear image of a globe divided into nation–states, the view of the Earth taken from space has given us a picture with no such divisions.

The UN holds an awesome responsibility as the only forum where independent and all too often hostile states may resolve their differences and work together for the betterment of all life on Earth. Most of its operation were during the Cold War era, when battling ideologies were used to keep the world divided into two outrageously overarmed camps. Political decisions were simplified for both sides by the existence of a clear enemy, and so a certain stasis was maintained—one that did not encourage a vision of global community. With the recent collapse of the Soviet Union and the resulting dissolution of the Cold War, the UN has been expected to take on a stronger role, but this transition has been marked by painful conflicts around the world. Human consciousness has not quite evolved to the stage where we can motivate our passions without the existence of an enemy. If there is someone to blame, then we need not take full responsibility for the circumstances ourselves, and we can vent our anger to a chorus of strong agreement from our side. If there is no one to blame, it is easy to manufacture an enemy from an old resentment. Many recent conflicts have been based on resurgent ethnic and religious identities at odds with the nation–states that contain them, expressing historical grudges in bloody vengeance within national borders, out of the UN's intended jurisdiction.

A Voice for Human Values

The only forum currently in place to serve as a clearinghouse for transnational, transethnic, and transreligious thinking is the UN. Many societies are feeling an erosion of traditional values because of the globalization of the capitalist economy, with its emphasis on the accumulation of wealth and its cult of individual performance. There is a strong sense of the loss of the spirit of caring for fellow members of the community, which is encouraged by all religious traditions. The UN is the only institution that can take a stand for universal human values to guide our world in its struggle to be a community.

And, although many would say that it would be an insurmountable task to codify and proclaim which values are in fact universal, the UN has actually took its first steps toward such an impressive achievement with its founding. The preamble to the Charter of the United Nations begins with a brief outline of its mission:

> to save succeeding generations from the scourge of war. . . to reaffirm faith in fundamental human rights, in the dignity and worth of the human person, in the equal rights of men and women and of nations large and small, and to establish conditions under which justice and respect for the obligations arising from. . . international law can be maintained, and to promote social progress and better standards of life in larger freedom, . . . to practice tolerance and live together in peace with one another as good neighbors, and to unite our strength to maintain international peace and security, and to ensure. . . that armed forces shall not be used, save in the common interest, and to employ international machinery for the promotion of the economic and social advancement of all peoples. . . .

This Charter spells out an international code of ethics to which each nation gave its tacit approval by joining the organization.

The first resolution of the General Assembly addressed the elimination of atomic and other weapons of mass destruction, stressing peace as its most fundamental commitment. And on December 10, 1948, the General Assembly adopted the Universal Declaration of Human Rights, reaffirming the principles of the Charter and offering to widely disseminate them through the member states. Unfortunately, the UN did not and still does not have the moral authority to ensure these rights within the borders of its member states. Yet it has been creating a blueprint for a global culture of ethics based on the values of peace and of human rights, especially in the areas of political and economic opportunity.

The Global Conferences

Another important way in which the UN has expressed and promoted the values needed for achieving global community is through the series of international conferences that began with the First UN Environment Conference in Stockholm in 1972. These have created a framework for a shift in consciousness at the global level through a three-fold process. First, each conference has focused world attention on a particular critical issue. Then, each conference has produced a multinational document addressing the issue, sometimes in bold and innovative ways. Even the word "environment" was not widely used before the Stockholm Conference in the sense it is today. Another important concept that was shaped into specific language was "sustainable development." Such terms are vital in articulating the values we need to bring us into the twenty-first century. The third step in the conference process is effecting about the action plans formulated in the document, creating values in action.

The pace of these conferences picked up again during the 1990s, beginning with the World Summit for Children convened by UNICEF in 1990, followed by the historic UN Conference on Environment and Development, known as the "Earth Summit," in Rio de Janeiro in 1992. UNCED resulted in Agenda 21, a plan of action for environmentally sustainable development. While many have been frustrated that tangible differences have been slow to arise from commitments to Agenda 21, there is certainly a global awareness that simply did not exist before the conference concerning the deterioration of the environment caused by careless human consumption of natural resources and disposal of waste. UNCED proved the ability of a United Nations initiative to make a powerful difference in shifting human consciousness.

The UN conferences of this decade can be credited with formulating some of humanity's most important values, including protection of the environment, the right to human dignity, the rights of children, respect for women, and the social development of humankind. And none of these can be attained, of course, without the primary vision of the UN to create peace on earth. Viewed in this context, the UN has a moral obligation, in addition to its admirable achievements as a planetary social service administrator, to provide visionary leadership to our world.

The Habitat II Conference, held in Istanbul in June 1996, nicknamed "The City Summit," because it addressed the growing urbanization of the planet, was the culminating event of the entire series multinational conferences. In the Goals and Principles section of the HABITAT Agenda adopted by the Istanbul Conference, the language is rather more inspiring, beginning with the states committing to "a political, economic, environmental, ethical and spiritual vision of human settlements based on the principles of equality, solidarity, partnership, human dignity, respect and cooperation." Adherence to the principles of the Charter is reaffirmed, as well as commitment to the Universal Declaration of Human Rights, the International Covenant on Economic, Social and Cultural Rights, the International Convention on the Elimination of all Forms of Racial Discrimination, the Convention on the Elimination of all Forms of Discrimination against Women and the Convention on the Rights of the Child. It then lists what may be seen as the values that the Conference will promote: equal opportunity, the eradication of poverty, sustainable development, physical and spatial quality of life, protection of the family, good citizenship, partnerships on all levels, solidarity with the less fortunate, and financial aid to developing countries. What we are seeing is a growing agreement among nations on a code of behavior. Language hotly disputed at an earlier conference may show up as a given in the Habitat Agenda, as the countries of the world begin to accept the terms of a global community.

The Need for Moral Leadership

The UN is capable of providing moral leadership, but it would require using resources that are currently underutilized. One of these is the faith communities. The world's religions have been promoting transcendent values of love and compassion for thousands of years. Naturally, they have arisen in different parts of the world and therefore speak through different cultures and languages, but they represent a rich and scarcely tapped resource for building community. The UN could build successful alliances with religious organizations around the world, as long as these relationships remained inclusive and democratic in nature. An example is the Environmental Sabbath initiated by the UN Environment Programme in North America in 1986, where the faith communities pooled their efforts to celebrate World Environment Day in churches, synagogues, and mosques all over the United States and Canada. Many religious leaders would no doubt welcome any invitation to support the UN in its mission of peace. In fact, the International Day of Peace provides a perfect opportunity to enlist the support of spiritual communities in celebrating the vision of the United Nations for a world of harmony.

The UN could also provide a forum for interfaith dialogue, so that the keepers of the world's wisdom would have a greater opportunity to get to know one another and to voice their suggestions for promoting peace. This could be done through interfaith centers in major cities around the world, where the UN has a presence, to promote understanding and increase trust. The leaders of faith traditions would then be accessible to consult in times of armed conflicts, which have often used religion as a weapon instead of a tool of peace, and perhaps be able to influence their followers to settle their grievances in a peaceful manner.

There is a great fear of religious fundamentalist movements in various parts of the world, often linked with terrorism carried out in the name of deep religious convictions. This belligerent behavior must be understood in the context of the threat to traditional values by the materialist culture that has been expanding its greedy reach into the smallest villages of every continent. Leaders of fundamentalist sects must have their voices heard along with those of more tolerant religions, so that their followers may be assured that they are entitled to practice according to their beliefs, wherever the people so choose. It is important to work from a framework of recognition that all religions sincerely seek the well-being of their followers, so that even points of view containing great conflicts can one day live side by side in peace assured by mutual respect and understanding.

The UN must also take bold steps to encourage respect for acknowledged spiritual leaders in spite of the political considerations of the member states. The promotion of open dialogue must never be squelched for political expediency. The world cannot afford to miss out on a source of wisdom to accommodate a narrow interest group.

Boutros Boutros-Ghali, the former Secretary-General of the United Nations, has demonstrated his vision in many ways. Early in his tenure, he published *An Agenda for Peace* and later *An Agenda for Development*, addressing the issues of greatest concern to today's world. Yet few people outside of UN circles even know of the existence of these documents, which have not been discussed on popular radio and television programs. The UN must develop a face and a voice, so that the public can better understand its positions, its achievements and its challenges.

Partnerships for Human Values

The UN has come to recognize that it cannot do the job alone. Since the end of the Cold War, the expectations of the world have come to rest on the shoulders of the UN, and it is a burden that must be shared. Although governments are reluctant to take on increased responsibilities because of the implied financial burden, nongovernmental organizations (NGOs) are anxious to be included as willing partners. The NGOs often have a particular mission to advance a specific human value, such as human rights, women's issues, the plight of refugees, or spirituality. Many of these organizations have proven useful to UN staff by providing humanitarian aid quickly and efficiently in times of disaster. Also, international NGOs represent interest groups that transcend national boundaries, offering yet another global perspective. The NGO voice has been significant during the international conferences of this decade, championing and publicizing the work of the UN. NGOs were particularly effective in building global awareness in support of the Earth Summit in 1992 and the Fourth International Conference on Women in Beijing in 1995, as well as highlighting the controversial issues of the 1994 International Conference on Population and Development in Cairo. NGO participation was welcomed, encouraged, and ensured during the entire process of Habitat II. The Conference made an unprecedented outreach to community-based organizations and local political leadership to work together on issues of building community and recognizing "best practices" around the world.

The inclusion of civil society in international governance has also provided some balance for the other partner that must be included: the corporate sector. Private enterprise must be encouraged to contribute to finding solutions to the world's problems with its resources and communications. There is a growing fear that transnational corporations, with budgets larger than some of the nation–states, will become increasing difficult to regulate without international controls. Corporations large and small must be involved in the process of building a better world and help share the responsibility of promoting global values. Certain business communities have already begun to move in this direction, encouraging socially responsible practices as a source of pride.

This has been beautifully demonstrated by the Caux Roundtable, an initiative of business leaders from different parts of the world promoting "the importance of global corporate responsibility in reducing social and economic threats to world peace and stability. . . based on a common respect for the highest moral values. . . . "[3] The "Principles for Business" advanced by this forward-thinking group offer a model for global corporate consciousness based on a meaningful context of citizenship and contribution that need not negate the profit-making incentive.

Yet another source of partnership explored in innovative ways by the Habitat II Conference is on-line communications through the worldwide Internet. Not only were the Habitat Agenda and other related documents available on-line, but there were also new opportunities for computer conferencing during the event itself. The technology is now in place for remote participation by individuals in all corners of the world, bringing the principle of democratic participation to new heights of expression.

Conclusion

In 1995, the United Nations Educational, Scientific and Cultural Organization (UNESCO), launched what it called "A Culture of Peace." This idea was born at the International Congress on Peace in the Minds of Men in Yamoussoukro, Côte d'Ivoire in 1989. The Congress urged UNESCO to "construct a new vision of peace by developing a peace culture based on the universal values of respect for life, liberty, justice, solidarity, tolerance, human rights and equality between men and women."[4] It is indeed "a new vision of peace" that is urgently needed.

It is not easy to envisage a culture of peace on a planet where heroes have traditionally come from battlegrounds, not negotiating tables. Yet as our consciousness expands, on a firm grounding of democracy and human rights, it becomes less and less imaginable to make war.

Our pooled energies are desperately needed to create sustainable living conditions for everyone on our planet. We must do whatever it takes to let go of old hostilities and move forward together.

We need a new understanding of security, not as safety in a world that will always be dangerous, but in the trust that neighbors have for one another. Some neighborhoods may be richer and some poorer, but all must feel safe enough to leave their doors open. Only the security of worldwide community will lead us into a peaceful twenty-first century. The UN cannot survive as an army, but it is vital as an instrument of education, putting forth a vision of a new world order not to be feared but embraced by all of humankind.

Global community can be based on nothing less than mutual respect and understanding, cooperation, and sharing, the foundations and basic rules of traditional citizenship. These rules teach us that our greatest fulfillment will come in service to others, in honoring our elders, in caring for the needy, in refraining from violence, and in loving our neighbor as ourselves. In a world inspired by common goals and values, we may finally have the freedom to practice these lofty precepts and to reach a state unknown to humankind: peace on earth.

Notes

1. *Our Global Neighbourhood.* Geneva: The Commission on Global Governance, 1995, p. 9.
2. Carnegie Endowment for International Peace, "International Conciliation," No. 363, October 1940.
3. "Principles for Business," Caux Roundtable, 1994, p. 1.
4. UNESCO, "Towards a Global Culture of Peace," November 1995, p. 5 (working paper).

Section 1 The Poor in Town and Country

Flora Lewis

Leaving Bombay a few years ago, I got into a conversation with the Indian businessman sitting next to me on the plan. He asked me what I thought of his city, and I could not hide how depressing I had found it. In the daytime, bustle and rush, color, activity, the noise of people struggling eagerly, determinedly with life. But as soon as the dark came, every sidewalk, every bridge parapet, every space by the streets was covered with huddled bundles. The street people were settling down for the night in the only place they had, and they used up all the place there was. Yet, the streets were clean, much cleaner than New York, because there was not a bit of rubbish or garbage or paper, because someone had had a use for it and had scooped it up. Why did they stay in such demeaning conditions? The poorest village offers better than that.

The Connection to Jobs

They did not really stay sleeping on the streets indefinitely, my seatmate said. Many of them found some kind of work, traded, offered services, and earned enough to move to some kind of shelter. But their numbers never diminished, because there were always more people pouring in from the countryside to tempt their luck, to put their foot on the very lowest rung of a ladder that did not exist in the homes they had left. The flourishing city, its shops and traffic jams, proved that here there was a ladder that some had already climbed.

The explosive growth of cities, particularly in the developing world, is not only the result of rapid population increases. As Eugene Linden pointed out in a lucid article in *Foreign Affairs Quarterly* (January/February 1996), at the turn of the century, some 50 percent of the world's people lived in cities with a population of more than 100,000 (when the world's population was under 2 billion). Now, an estimated 45 percent live in urban centers. Between 1950 and 1995, the number of cities with populations of more than 1 million people grew more than sixfold, from 34 to 213, in the developing world, while they slightly more than doubled, from 49 to 112, in developed countries during the same period. He cites UN estimates that by the year 2025, the rural population will remain steady, but more than 5 billion, 61 percent of humanity, will live in cities.

Further, there is reason to believe that no one really knows how many live in the flagrantly cramped megalopolises of Cairo, Mexico City, Rio, São Paolo, New Delhi, Beijing, and such, because census figures are probably unreliable, and these cities have large floating populations from the countryside. But the fastest growing are not the well-known capitals, but the little noticed secondary cities of which there are tens of thousands, usually with no planning and little infrastructure. Linden used Kanpur, India, as an example. Kanpur has a population of more than a million people and four times the infant mortality rate of Delhi. Similarly, El Alto in Bolivia has a population of 500,000 people that is increasing at the rate of 9 percent each year.

The causes are manifold. Development itself is one, with the expectation of jobs, however modest a lure, the encroachment on agricultural land, the improvements in transportation and communications, and increased mobility. In a number of countries, government policies have worked to swell the flood to the cities, keeping farm prices low for the benefit of urban workers who, it has been pointed out, are thereby receiving a huge subsidy. In theory, although often not in fact, cities offer services that are scarce or unavailable in the countryside, such as access to water, energy, education, and health care. The cities are gleaming sirens of hope, not only for the most destitute, but for any who aspire to an easier, more exciting, more rewarding life.

Temptation Makes Poverty Harder

Because cities do display, even flaunt, what is possible for the fortunate, they intensify the awareness and indignity of utter poverty and heighten the sense of injustice. To the statistician, it can hardly be said that the poor in America's cities, for example, who throw broken refrigerators and worn mattresses in the streets, are in the same category as the 1 billion people in other parts of the world who cannot afford enough food to perform normal work. But these people feel terribly poor when they walk along streets crowded with cars and lined with fine shops and see the luxury items displayed in advertisements. Rich neighbors make poverty harder to bear.

The city tends to stratify people and, in a paradox of human social relations, deprive them of social cohesion, even as their numbers multiply. The focus is on the individual. Reliable inclusion in a well-defined family, however extended, breaks down and the need is to fend for oneself. The dilution of attachment and support is one reason for the proliferation of youth gangs in developed societies; they are self-selected groups that offer recognition and bonds.

The lack of space and natural resource renewal makes it harder to fight filth in cities, or anyway, it becomes a good deal more expensive. They also tend to be polluted. Disease spreads more rapidly.

In villages and small towns, where people all know each other, it is more obvious that needs are common, and there is a basis, as well as a tradition, for communal action when possible. These are people who belong to a group by the sheer fact of their existence. Their surroundings are familiar.

Poor People on the Doorsteps of the Rich

Linden also points out that it took 1,800 years, from the decline of Rome to nineteenth-century London, before a city reached a population of 1 million. Clearly, it was the result of the Industrial Revolution, which drove people off the farms and into the concentrated centers of manufacturing. In between, there were great migrations, but they tended to spread people out over newly acquired lands that offered better conditions for family sustenance. Now, the techniques of agriculture drastically reduce the numbers of arms needed for production, so that rural people feel the pressure of surplus population and competition, and go to seek their chance in the cities.

The pernicious results of this rising trend are evident and have been well described. There has already been some reversal in the developed countries, with the flight from the cities to the suburbs to the exurbs, as people seek more space, gardens, better air, more quiet, and often lower costs. The newest technologies make deconcentration possible. Mammoth factories with tens of thousands of workers are no longer an economic necessity, as materials, parts, and products can be delivered and distributed relatively inexpensively. With computers and instant communications, big companies can and do organize their clerical staffs in a dozen different places thousands of miles apart and actually gain efficiency. But this development tends to leave the poor behind in the big cities, reducing the tax base for the services they need and increasing the neglect of the infrastructure.

For the future, one does not see that this reversal offers prospects of relief for the developing countries, which are following the same patterns as the industrialized countries did in the nineteenth century. Their assets and hopes are to follow in the footsteps and take the place of the workers being discarded in economically advanced states. For them, concentration remains an incentive despite the pain and the misery it involves.

Microenterprise: A New Service

One approach to countering the negative effects of urbanization in both developing and developed countries is to encourage what has been called "microenterprise." This means very small businesses, with an emphasis on enterprise rather than on jobs. Hal Kane points out in an article for *World Watch* (March/April 1996) that "the job" is a relatively modern concept, also a consequcnce of the Industrial Revolution. People always did work, but they did not always have a job. The point is to enable them to work and earn a living without being organized into giant firms that dictate where they live and how to go about it. "Micro-enterprise" means recognizing and providing microcapital for the many things people already included in the notion of "business." As it is, Kane says, "the world's 500 largest corporations control 25 percent of the world's economic output. Yet they employ only one-twentieth of one percent of the world's population." Even in the United States, he notes, more than a quarter of all employees work in establishments of less than 20 people, which comprise 87 percent of all U.S. enterprises.

The key to expanding this opportunity is finance, the provision of credit in circumstances that established banks would not consider. The Grameen Bank in Bangladesh established the remarkably successful model with minuscule loans on no collateral, except agreement among a small group of five or six individuals to share responsibility for each other's debt. Repayment reached nearly 100 percent, and people were launched on self-reliant work that changed their lives. The formula has been tried successfully in some American inner cities. It is especially adaptable to the countryside and can provide an incentive to stay at home instead of risking the fright and distress of migration.

Making Cities a Livable Place

Perhaps the first and most important defense against urban blight is just that, to make staying in villages and small towns more appealing. Where living standards are acceptable, television and modern communications go far toward breaking the isolation and sense of being left behind that rural life used to mean. In fact, in the most technologically advanced societies, there is a fear that the new communications will lead to fragmentation and estrangement, as people do their work, their shopping, their socializing, and their searching for entertainment electronically. Whatever the trend, there is always some excessive behavior to worry about.

Nonetheless, increasingly larger cities are probably inevitable and the problem is to keep them from becoming unlivable. Linden gives an example of sound development in the city of Curitiba, the capital of the southern Brazilian state of Parana, that has a population of 2.2 million.

The region is agricultural, and the city ha achieved a "healthy mix" of manufacturing, services, and commerce, which provide its residents with an average annual income of only $2,000, but amenities that many first world cities do not deliver. Its Speedy Line bus service provides transportation approaching subway efficiency at one three hundredth the cost and can be installed in six months. It has many parks and good public housing and keeps poor neighborhoods beyond the reach of sanitation trucks clean by a program that trades fresh vegetables for the deliver of garbage. Its former mayor, Jaime Lerner, says that "if people feel respected, they will assume responsibility to solve other problems." And Linden concludes that the secret of Curitiba's notable success is above all "quality leadership." That is not a surplus commodity, but it is possible to learn from good examples as well as from bad ones.

In other, much more prosperous cities, experiments to fight pollution with tax measures have shown some good results. Vancouver cut its waste disposal problem dramatically in that way. A new movement is growing to promote an "environmental tax base," which reduces income tax by increasing taxes that penalize pollution and waste, thus at the same time reducing the cost of cleaning up.

Conclusion

Clearly, there is no single answer to the question of how to maintain urban amenities and keep cities—where most people will soon live—functioning and tolerable. It will take a combination of a great many measures that inspire individual responsibility, social will, and economic innovation. No doubt "quality leadership" is a key factor, and people must be able to find where to look for it.

Section 2 Putting the Poor at the Center of Urban Strategies

Nancy Barry and
Celina Kawas

Nearly half of the developing world's people already live in cities, and the rate of migration is swelling many urban areas. In developing countries, nearly 2 billion people lived in cities in 1990, up from about 1.5 billion in 1980. Most of the world's urban poor live in Asia, but the fastest urban growth has been in Africa. The number of poor people in urban areas of the developing world will continue to grow rapidly. By the year 2000, over half of the people living in absolute poverty will be in cities. Most people living in cities are poor, and most poor people in urban areas live in informal settlements and work in the informal sector. The most rapidly growing segment of the world's urban population is in informal settlements. Slums and shanties already house 30 to 60 percent of the urban populations of most developing countries. The growth and the proliferation of informal settlements has far outpaced the capacity of existing systems to integrate them. Hundreds of millions of people live outside the system, in substandard conditions and in poverty. Most economically active people in cities, particularly the poor, earn their livelihoods in the informal sector, and this is not likely to change. The economically active population in urban areas will be about 825 million people by the year 2000, and roughly 1.7 billion by 2025. For these people to be employed, more than 200 million new jobs will be needed by 2000, and nearly 900 million by 2025. This will be in a period in which government and large corporations continue to downsize, with most new employment continuing to come from smaller firms. Most poor families in urban areas will need to make a living combining incomes from a number of informal sector sources.

Traditional systems of service delivery and employment cannot cope. Government budgets and agencies cannot and will not be able to provide these people with the shelter, services, or income sources that they need. Government roles, revenues and ranks are being reduced. Private corporate structures are becoming leaner and will not be employing many urban slum dwellers. If the problems of urban poverty and degradation are to be addressed, it will be by poor people helping themselves, with others backing their local initiatives.

Poor People Fighting Poverty

Fortunately for the future of the world's cities, the urban poor in developing countries are perhaps the most resourceful people on earth. Poor people come to cities to make a better life. What they find does not make it easy. The stories of poor families in urban slums are the stories of household members and informal communities working together in highly ingenious ways. Their strategies to build livelihoods and shelter enable poor people to survive, create some security, and struggle out of poverty slowly, incrementally. It is by learning from, building on, and investing in the economic strategies, systems, and structures that the poor have built for themselves that outsiders can help reduce urban poverty. Priority needs to be placed on understanding and supporting those economic activities of poor people that enable them to improve their living standards.

Poor people work first to survive, and then to build sustainable sources of income. Given their lack of traditional employment and income generating opportunities, poor families normally juggle a number of informal sector economic activities. This juggling involves continuous decisions and trade-offs in expenditures and in the use of resources, including family labor, capital, and land.

Poor people seek to extend basic economic security through time and across generations. The capacity of poor people to move beyond survival to build more acceptable income and living standards depends on their abilities to build income and assets, and to reduce the risk of losing the economic security they have already achieved.

Women as Managers

If policy makers and service deliverers are to help solve the problems of poverty in the world's cities, they need to begin seeing women and their roles differently. Poor women are still lumped into the disadvantaged category among the poor. Arguments are made that women are poorer, more vulnerable, more marginalized. Women's lack of access is decried on equity and social grounds.

Although women are in fact poorer and do lack equitable access, what these arguments miss is that poor women hold the keys to solving poverty. If households are the basic enterprises or economic units of the urban poor, women are the managers.

In the act of managing small household incomes from a variety of sources, women are often the jugglers. And when the woman manages the purse strings, a higher portion of family income remains in the household. In India, if a low-income woman earns and manages the end use of 100 rupees, more than 90 are spent on food, medicine, schoolbooks, and housing for her children. If her husband earns and manages the 100 rupees, only 40 gets into the household economy.

Almost all poor urban women work, often contributing the most stable source of the family's income. Often women earn small amounts from a variety of low-paying economic activities, including petty trading, services, animal-raising, and crafts. These earnings act as a substantial, stable, and risk-minimizing component of household income. In urban households, women increasingly are major, primary, or sole sources of family income. With the large and growing number of female-headed households, the capacity of women to increase income and assets becomes more central to the family's livelihood. With increasing unemployment in the formal sector, even when the male is in the household, women's economic contributions to household incomes are increasing.

Because women need to juggle their productive and reproductive responsibilities, most women use their home as either their place or base of work. This facilitates the woman's role in organizing the various economic and support functions of different family members. It also makes her shelter a needed and valuable productive asset. The dramatically successful record of poor women in repaying small loans and taking advantage of user-friendly savings systems is a major demonstration of the key role that women play as responsible economic agents. Women's higher proclivity to save and build the economic security of their household is probably a function of women's more central concern about their children, and their children's children. If poor women are making such an important contribution to tackling urban poverty now, it becomes critically important that policy makers understand the role of poor women as entrepreneurs, producers, savers, investors, and managers of complex and diversified family enterprises. The arguments that the poor hold the solutions to their own problems can be made forcefully for poor women. Therefore, policy makers should support women by:

- encouraging savings, lending, and other programs that give poor women more control over resource generation and allocation, asset building, and economic security measures within the household.
- addressing the legal, administrative, and social factors that constrain women's access to land, other assets, and credit.
- helping women improve the productivity and value added of their economic activities.
- utilizing the commitment and energy of poor women in economic and community development efforts.
- recognizing shelter as a key productive resource for poor families, particularly women.

- giving priority to solving infrastructure problems—water supply, transportation—that take time from a woman's day and ability to perform her central role in her household's economy.

Putting the Poor First

If poor people are going to solve their own problems of employment, housing, and urban services, they need to have the means to increase their incomes and assets. Strategies that help poor people increase their economic strength and security need to be put at the center of urban planning. Once poor people have economic security, they will send their children to school, but if they are struggling to survive, their children will be mobilized for this struggle. Poor people will use increased incomes to build their shelters; with some economic security, poor people are able to organize to build access to basic infrastructure. Poor people are much more efficient resource allocators and managers than are municipal authorities.

Structural adjustment programs and macroeconomic reforms, while necessary, are clearly grossly inadequate in providing the means by which the bottom 50 to 70 percent of the economically active population can participate in economic growth and social development. Most poor people are self-employed or work in microbusinesses and small business. Growth in formal sector employment is unlikely to change this pattern over the next ten years. If poverty is to be reduced and if the economic potential of the majority is to be realized, the economic activities of poor people need to be financed. Macroreforms in financial systems need to be complemented by measures that encourage the institutions, instruments, relationships, and financing arrangements that provide sound, responsive financial services to the majority of enterprises that have not previously had access.

Over the last ten years, the successful experience providing finance to millions of low income entrepreneurs and producers demonstrates that poor people—when given access to responsive financial services at market rates—repay their loans and use the proceeds to increase their income and assets. Low-income entrepreneurs use savings to build reliable social safety nets for their firms and families.

The economic activities of the poor usually do not yield high income. Most poor people would like to have a stable job, with adequate pay and benefits—rather than combining petty trading, slum-based informal enterprises, and small rent returns to pull together a livelihood. Strategies to build the modern economy and related employment opportunities need to be pursued; this requires economic liberalization, export promotion, incentives, and investments in human capital. Poor people benefit from overall economic growth, mainly through the increased demand for their goods and services, rather than as direct employees in the modern sector. However, the pace of employment growth will depend largely on decisions by private companies, acting in the competitive global market place. Measures to increase formal sector employment will be too little, too late for the hundreds of millions of poor people in cities.

Poor people need opportunities to improve the productivity of their ventures. Financial services alone will not be sufficient to help most poor people move out of poverty. Poor entrepreneurs need access to markets, input sourcing arrangements, and technology. Unfortunately, many approaches to training and technical services have been ineffective, with limited benefits, to few people, at unsustainably high costs. Although financial services are being built to serve the poor majority, innovation and more promotional approaches need to be adopted in enabling the poor to expand their productivity, incomes, and assets.

Municipal authorities, therefore, need to encourage rather than discourage the economic activities of the poor by liberalizing zoning regulations to facilitate petty trade; incorporating home-based enterprises in the way urban shelter is treated; and recognizing that poor people need to use multifamily and commercial rentals as a significant source of income. Policy makers, service providers, and funders also need to encourage local subsector-specific organizations that enable poor people to improve their market power, purchase in bulk, organize joint economic activities, and expand sales. Private commercial concerns, NGOs, and government purchasing agents need to build enterprise networks, commercial linkages, and subcontracting to connect low-income entrepreneurs and producers to know-how and more promising economic opportunities.

The Role of Shelter

For poor people, as for all people, owning a home is a major source of economic and psychological security. It is an asset, often more secure than cash or financial assets as a hedge against inflation and other economic uncertainties. As an investment, it is a result of and a vehicle for household savings. As an asset, it can be used as security in gaining access to additional financial resources. And homes give families a secure place to live and a social position in society. For these reasons, housing is normally considered a consumer good, not a productive asset.

Most poor families in urban areas cannot afford to think of their homes as a consumer good. Shelter forms an integral part of poor people's economic strategies. Dwellings serve as productive assets and resources for poor families, in several ways. Poor people's dwellings are the factories for home-based production and service operations. Homes are where poor people store raw materials, inventories, and finished products for their small trading operations and for their informal sector microenterprises. This capacity to store goods means that poor entrepreneurs can purchase in bulk, buy when the prices are low, and sell when the prices are high. Having a dwelling enables poor people to diversify beyond petty trading to build a home-based enterprise.

Poor people use their land and dwellings as rental property, renting to families and members of their community for shelter and commercial uses. This rental income produces an average of 10 percent of poor urban dwellers' household incomes. Joint ownership agreements among family members and tenancy arrangements enable poorer families to access land or shelter or start income generating activities. Having a dwelling enables poor people to juggle different economic activities, adjusting to changing family situations and economic conditions. Families can adapt economic strategies to fit current and anticipated resources, opportunities, and benefits. Building materials are a major means of savings for low-income urban households. Dwellings are built incrementally and building materials can be used or sold depending on the household's needs.

Recent migrants soon learn to invest most of their savings in real estate, to secure their own future. Shelter and related land account for over 60 percent of total assets owned by low-income households in urban areas. When economic adversity strikes, poor families will do whatever it takes—drawing down savings, cutting expenditures, enduring hardships—to hold onto their dwelling, demonstrating the economic value they attach to their dwelling.

When informal settlements are regularized, property values appreciate sharply, commercial areas emerge, public transportation becomes available, and infrastructure is progressively introduced. Solidarity associations devise and help secure water lines and electricity connections that further increase the productive value of dwellings. With land values rising rapidly in relation to real earnings in most poor urban areas, investment in land and dwellings may be the most attractive income generating activity available to many poor households. Even when poor households do not have land tenure, investments in dwelling improvements normally have positive financial returns.

The Role of Microfinance

Most poor people manage to mobilize enough resources to develop their enterprises and their dwellings slowly, over time. Financial services enable poor people to leverage this local initiative, accelerating the process of building incomes, assets, and economic security. Poor entrepreneurs have taken small market-based loans to make significant gains.

Poverty banks, NGOs, and grassroots savings and credit groups around the world have shown that these microenterprise loans can be profitable for the borrower and for the lender, making microfinance one of the most effective poverty-reducing strategies. To the extent that the financial institutions providing these services become financially viable, self-sustaining, and integral to the communities in which they operate, these microfinance institutions have the potential to attract more resources and expand services to clients.

Despite the success of microfinance institutions, only approximately 2 percent of the world's roughly 500 million low-income entrepreneurs have access to financial services. It is critically important that these financial services are increased dramatically over the next ten years, using the principles, standards, and support modalities that have proven to be effective.

Based upon the experience of leading practitioners and funders, the keys to building successful financial services for low-income entrepreneurs are a range of financial intermediaries—including commercial banks, NGOs, cooperatives, credit unions, and grass-roots groups—that provide client-responsive services and generate domestic resources. These financial intermediaries must have the capacity to meet high incremental and absolute performance standards. They must achieve excellent repayments and provide access, not subsidies, to clients. And they must be building toward operating and financial self-sufficiency. If the microfinancing institutions meet high standards of financial performance and client reach, they need access to capitalization, loan funds, and effective institutional development support.

All successful microfinance practitioners have used a broad-based approach. They have not attempted to gear financial services to specific sectors. They have built savings and lending services to support income generating activities. Successful microfinance practitioners recognize that the actual end use of microloans often differs somewhat or substantially from the purpose outlined in the loan application. A loan application may describe a fairly narrow economic activity, such as sewing or trading, when in fact the loan is used for a combination of working capital, home improvements, and even school fees. Microlenders use small initial amounts and maturities, rigorous repayment requirements, and successive repeat loans as the means to build financial discipline. Successful microfinance institutions recognize that the household is the basic enterprise unit, and that the purpose is to generate increased income adequate to repay the loan, build businesses, and family livelihoods.

Housing finance has not been an explicit focus of most microfinance operations. However, there are strong indications that many microentrepreneurs use a small portion of loan amounts and a significant portion of increased incomes on shelter improvements. And several leading microfinance organizations have begun to build specific housing finance products, as part of the microfinance continuum.

Several microcredit organizations lend directly to clients for housing loans. Grameen Bank began to make housing improvement loans in 1984, and by 1994, 10.5 percent of its loans were for housing.

Typically, housing in Bangladesh is made of jute sticks for walling, and thatch for roofing, which needs renewal every year. Because many of its clients lived in these poor conditions, the bank began to see the value of housing improvement loans for client's who worked in their homes. The bank developed architecture, materials, and technology especially suitable to the conditions in Bangladesh—subject as the area is to flooding and other disasters. The construction elements of such new housing arc durable, houses are placed on pillars, and houses can be shifted during hazardous conditions.

The housing improvement loans started small, with an average loan size in 1984 of US $75 reaching a maximum loan of US $180. Loans for new houses now range from US $300 to US $625. The repayment recovery rate is more than 98 percent

Given the increasing recognition of shelter as a productive asset for the poor, these developments should be encouraged.

Incremental Approaches

The way-low income people in cities approach housing is similar to their approach to economic activities, juggling and making progress in increments. In most countries, land may be purchased or inherited first, with construction taking place in stages over many years. Poor people in informal settlements often hold their savings in the form of building materials, constructing a room when an adequate quantity of bricks is accumulated.

The difficulty with this slow self improvement approach is that the productive use of the housing asset can only be realized once the storage room is built, once the roof is on, once the floor level has been raised to prevent flood damage. Experience by some microlenders indicates that this incremental, shelter improvement approach can be accelerated with very small, short-term loans, treated in the same way as loans for microenterprise. SEWA Bank's "new house" loans range from US $285 to US $714, with repayment terms of the equivalent of US $1.50 a month. Grameen Bank's 20-square-meter home structure loans range from US $300 to US $625. In both cases, these small housing loans are made to repeat clients. The clients are eligible for the housing loan once a repayment record has been established through prior loans directed at more conventional microenterprise activities.

Microfinance Principles Applied to Housing Finance

If most housing improvement needs that poor people are able to afford can be met with small, relatively short-term loans provided without subsidies, then the principles of microfinance can be applied to housing finance, and housing finance can be considered as a product for microenterprise borrowers. There are several arguments for treating housing finance for the poor as part of the microfinance continuum.

The clients are the same people. Most microenterprise clients are poor, working in informal enterprises in informal settlements, with home and enterprise intertwined. These clients already have shown that they can successfully use credit and savings to improve their businesses and livelihoods. Both income generating and shelter provision are informal, incremental activities. Both activities lend themselves to savings mobilization and lending services that can help accelerate, but not fundamentally alter, local custom, practice, and organizing modes.

Sustainable institutions not projects need to be built. In both enterprise development and housing finance, subsidized, project approaches have failed to survive or grow to serve significant numbers of poor people. The focus needs to be in building institutions that become integral to the community by providing market-based services on a sustainable basis.

To finance in amounts that poor people can afford, services need to be responsive to client's needs, using approaches that reflect local practices and ways of organizing. Clients also need to have a stake in the success of the financial services, with strong built-in incentives to repay, and with savings normally used as a means to build commitment and financial discipline.

Microenterprise for Shelter Provision

Most shelter is built by the informal sector. More than 60 percent of the shelter constructed in developing countries is built by the informal sector. Many of these activities can be financed with normal microloans. As government and private agencies increase their support for shelter upgrading and infrastructure improvements, it is important that means are sought to use and enhance the local capacity of small and microentrepreneurs in the manufacture of building materials, construction, and civil works.

Small enterprises can provide urban services. The quality and quantity of urban services need to be increased. Governments are generally held accountable for the provision of these services, but are not in the position to provide these services. Microenterprises are increasingly recognized as effective providers of urban services in the developing world. Microenterprises already offer many services ordinarily considered to require capital investments beyond the scope of very small firms, including garbage collection, small-scale energy production, and water supply. Even if governments continue to encourage and support the expansion and development of conventional approaches to housing and urban services, their efforts normally will not get to the poor.

To date, public sector housing has not worked successfully. In most cases, private sector housing does not reach the poor. Formal sector housing loans are almost always inaccessible to poor households. Costs of traditional service delivery and financing approaches are high. As a result, resources are scarce, reducing the capacity and interest in building new approaches to reach low- income clients. Some public and private housing finance institutions are beginning to build financial services for poor people, and this should be encouraged. However, these measures will not meet the financing requirements of the hundreds of millions of poor people, because costs are prohibitive.

Investment should focus on poor people's self-help activities. Poor people, and the people-based organizations that serve them, have taken the initiative to build shelter, infrastructure, and urban services in their own communities. Rather than expecting public services and traditional financial institutions to fill the large and growing gap, the focus should be on capitalizing the people's organizations that have demonstrated the commitment and competence to provide these services. Women-owned credit organizations have proven their creditworthiness and self-sufficiency.

People's economic organizations deserve support. As with micro-finance, a range of institutions, large and small, in the public, private, and people's sectors should be encouraged to provide shelter finance for the poor. Recognizing the difficulty of having traditional institutions crossing into the informal sector, greater emphasis should be placed on building up people's organizations. This will require increasing the visibility, capitalization, credit-related infrastructure, and entry of people's organizations in the housing and urban service market. People's organizations can include cooperatives, credit unions, NGOs, and grass-roots savings and credit groups that meet performance and reach standards.

Community organizations can deliver basic services. Informal and formal neighborhood, community, and sectoral associations have emerged in many urban settlements, organized around joint savings and credit activities, infrastructure improvements, and organizing access to service delivery. These associations have potential in expanding community participation in service provision, increasing local mobilization of human and financial contributions to civil works, and being the vehicles for channeling urban services, financial services, and human capital inputs. These community-based organizations and the NGOs that work with them can also be the vehicles for linking communities to government services, formal financial systems, and commercial and social networks that cut across dual structures and provide the channels for upward mobility.

The Roles of the Public, Private, and People's Sectors

Central governments and municipal authorities have major roles to play in enacting positive legislation that helps ensure that poor people's access to financial resources, infrastructure, and urban services gets the priority it deserves. They can ensure that policies, legislation, and regulations are enacted and enforced that encourage slum dwelling self-improvements and other activities that the poor undertake to better their own economic and human conditions. They can also liberalize policies, legislation, and regulations that restrict the businesses of home-based workers and street vendors, and can ensure that policies and legislation are enacted and enforced that give poor women their rights in land ownership, contractual arrangements on their own behalf, and access to credit and savings services in their own names.

Central governments and municipal authorities also have the responsibility to see that infrastructure, urban services, and economic opportunities are available to all city dwellers, including the poor. Financial and management constraints in the public sector will preclude governments from being the primary providers of credit, infrastructure, and housing for the poor majority. Governments do have a responsibility to allocate more resources to these activities, and to use scarce resources more effectively.

Central governments and municipal authorities in cities around the world are finding that one of the most cost-effective means of using scarce public resources to provide urban services is by entering into contractual, concession, and franchising arrangements with private sector organizations and community groups that are in the position to provide these services more effectively and at lower cost. During the last ten years, international funders and governments have moved from a focus on housing to building urban systems, with government providing ancillary support and encouraging private sector provision of infrastructure, housing, and basic urban services. Increasingly the focus needs to be on private provision of public services in electricity, telecommunications, urban transportation, housing, as well as in health and education. The private sector incorporates for-profit firms, NGOs, and community organizations or the people's sector. Governments have key roles as policy makers, catalysts, and funders. The leveraging ratios on public investment and expenditures with this catalytic approach can be impressive, with substantial in-cash and in-kind resources mobilized from the private sector and from the community served.

This change in focus creates many opportunities for microenterprises as contractors and subcontractors. It creates opportunities for community associations to function as primary service providers. Innovative municipal authorities and funders are breaking down large public works into small contracts, and building certification processes and technical services to encourage the development of small contractors that can engage in public works, maintain urban services, and provide building materials.

If delivery systems involving community organizations and microenterprises are to be expanded to reach the millions of unserved slum dwellers with infrastructure, housing, and other urban services, collaborations among public finance, formal financial institutions, and municipal authorities on the one hand and the informal delivery system on the other, will need to be expanded dramatically. Rather than expecting those formal sector institutions to begin reaching the population they have not been able to serve over the last twenty years, energy and resources should be focused on building the financial institutions, community organizations, and informal-sector enterprises that have the commitment and core competencies to serve the urban poor.

NGOs have a critically important role to play in the delivery processes, and should be incorporated in policy formulation and program design for systems that seek to improve economic opportunities and living standards of the urban poor. NGOs with grounding in marginalized urban communities have important roles to play in delivering services to lower-income households, in the coordination of community initiatives, and in accessing public and private agencies that can provide services and resources.

The most important agents for change and development of urban slums will be the poor people in these areas. They have the strongest vested interests in seeing these improvements made. Most improvements made to date have been by poor people helping themselves, using income from a whole host of economic activities, mainly in the informal sector. The focus in cities must be on investing in the poor majority, by encouraging the economic activities of the poor and by building the capacities and capital of the financial and community organizations providing services to this most enterprising majority.

Conclusions

Central governments and municipal authorities should give increased priority to poor people's access to financial resources, infrastructure, housing, and urban services. They can play a major role in addressing the legal, administrative, and social factors that constrain women's access to shelter, other assets, and credit. Governments should enact and enforce policies, legislation, and regulations to:

- Encourage slum dwelling self-improvements and other activities that the poor undertake to better their own economic and human conditions;

- Liberalize zoning restrictions on the businesses of home-based workers and street vendors; and
- Give poor women land ownership rights, contractual arrangements on their own behalf, and access to credit and savings services in their own names.

Governments have key roles as policy makers, catalysts, and funders. The leveraging ratios on public investment and expenditures with this catalytic approach can be impressive. Governments should allocate and leverage more resources to:

- Provide housing, infrastructure, urban services, and economic opportunities to city-dwellers, including the poor;
- Mobilize substantial in-cash and in-kind resources from the private sector and from the community served; and
- Use scarce resources more effectively.

Government agencies should not attempt to provide housing loans directly, instead they should design and implement a regulatory and incentive structure that encourages the entry and growth of a range of private intermediaries, including peoples' organizations and informal sector enterprises that have the commitment and competence to provide broad-based financial services to the poor majority. They should help national development banks become second-tier institutions that operate as autonomous, nonbureaucratic catalysts. Second-tier development finance institutions should make available market-based refinance to those specialized financial intermediaries, NGOs, and commercial banks that provide credit for shelter to large numbers of the urban poor.

They should also should encourage successful and innovative institutions that reach large numbers of the urban poor with credit for microenterprise and shelter, by helping ensure that those institutions that meet performance standards are capitalized, eligible for refinance, and receive institutional development support.

They should promote strong, long-term relationships between formal financial institutions and nongovernmental organizations through leveraged bank–NGO–client credit lines, joint training and technology development, and other mutually advantageous collaborations that mobilize banks' resources for improving access to shelter by the urban poor.

Governments should include NGOs and people's organizations in policy formulation and program design for systems that seek to improve economic opportunities, living standards, and shelter needs of the urban poor. They should advocate, showcase, and disseminate successful models of financial services geared at providing shelter to the urban poor.

Financial institutions need not and should not subsidize interest rates for shelter loans. Financial intermediaries should be free to set interest rates that cover the financial and operating costs, and risk provisions of an efficient intermediary. Microfinance institutions need to build efficient lending operations and volumes to reduce costs and interest rates. Financial institutions that serve the urban poor should build organizations, housing loan delivery systems, and performance that enable significant reach and sustainable operations. Standards of excellence should be adopted, whether the financial intermediary is a commercial bank, a credit union, an NGO, or another specialized financial intermediary.

Business NGOs should provide commercial banks with linkage mechanisms designed to facilitate reaching low-income urban dwellers with shelter loans. NGOs need to demonstrate the advantage of these linkage mechanisms to the banks in banker's terms. As their volumes expand, business NGOs should seek funding on commercial terms and develop innovative means to mobilize funding from financial markets. Banks should be encouraged to reduce minimum deposit and other requirements for opening bank accounts, to help the urban poor build relationships with the formal banking system.

International funders need to see their primary target population as the bottom 50 percent of the world's economically active people. They should allocate a significant percentage of their resources to measures that give the urban poor access to finance, business development, and self-empowerment services. These measures will increase the income and assets, including shelter, of the urban poor. They should provide flexible funding—including funds for institutional development, loan funds, capitalization and equity—to a wide range of qualified financial intermediaries of all sizes that meet high standards of performance, and that are positioned to expand their scale.

International funders should also develop and support well-designed guarantee funds, as instruments for mobilizing funding from local sources by specialized retail institutions. They should innovate in the development of new financial instruments and approaches to this market, such as equity funds, leasing, and accounts receivable. They should encourage, assist, and fund institutional development, with a focus on lateral learning among practitioners, and dissemination of success stories, best practice, and successful forms of intermediation in service delivery.

Finally, policy makers, service providers, and funders need to encourage local subsector-specific organizations that enable poor people to improve their market power, purchase in bulk, organize joint economic activities, and expand sales. Private commercial concerns, NGOs, and government purchasing agents need to build enterprise networks, commercial linkages, and subcontracting to connect low-income entrepreneurs and producers to know-how and more promising business opportunities.

Section 3 The Urban Informal Sector Within a Global Economy

Gustav Ranis and
Frances Stewart

The urban informal sector of the developing world is of enormous importance to the living standards of a large proportion of the urban population, accounting for one half or more of the urban labor force in many countries. To date, analysis of this sector has almost completely neglected global influences on its size and composition, focusing exclusively on the domestic context. It is rarely appreciated that global forces have a pervasive, albeit indirect, impact, in addition to their direct influence through foreign direct investment and technology transfer. Both the size and character of the urban informal sector and the incomes and poverty levels of the people working in it are directly affected by these global forces. In this section of *Cities Fit for People*, we explore some of these relationships.

Linkages of Formal Urban Actors

The formal urban sector in a developing country has linkages in three directions: (1) with the global economy; (2) with its own rural economy, both agricultural and nonagricultural; and (3) with the urban informal sector.

Its linkages with the rest of the world are of two kinds: (1) the global economy supplies some of the technology, capital inputs, and management for the formal sector's urban enterprises and (2) it exercises substantial influence on the consumption patterns of those working in the sector. The linkages of the urban formal sector with the rural economy consist of the provision of food, of labor no longer required in agriculture, and often of net savings, moving in one direction. In exchange, the formal sector provides industrial goods, both of the consumer and producer variety, for the rural economy.

The urban formal sector, directly linked into the global economy through trade, technology, and capital movements, is inhabited by entrepreneurs, managers, and workers who tend to be relatively well paid;

they consume imported products or products produced domestically using predominantly foreign technology. In general, only a minority of the population is employed in this sector, and in most economies the consequent slow growth of labor absorption – partly the result of the increasingly capital- and import-intensive nature of the output mix and the methods of production – means that employment growth barely keeps pace with population growth.[1]

The rural economy may be dynamic, permitting ample agricultural savings to be generated for transfer to the urban areas along with unskilled labor, or it may be stagnant. In either case, the relatively higher incomes in the urban formal sector are likely to attract people from the countryside into the cities, but they cannot all find employment in this sector, especially if agricultural savings are unable to make a sufficient contribution to urban capital formation. Consequently, some workers seek alternatives, leading to the creation of an urban informal sector.

Urban Informal Sector

The informal sector typically accounts for a high proportion of the urban workforce in developing countries. It is often described[2] as a low-productivity backwater "sponge" that absorbs those who cannot find productive employment in the rural areas or in formal urban activities. In contrast, others suggest that the sector can make an important and indeed increasing contribution to production and income generation.[3]

There is much discussion about how to define the urban informal sector. Some define it with reference to its legal status (i.e., comprising all activities which fall outside the reach of government regulations).[4] Others define it mainly in terms of the size of establishments, broadly covering microenterprises of less than 10 workers. Still others emphasize the use of simple, traditional technology.

In our section we shall spend little energy on definitions. Our main focus will be on establishments of 10 (mainly family) workers or less, even if, in some contexts, some of these establishments might well be classified as "formal" by some of the above criteria. The pursuit of precise definitions is not critical to the argument.

In contrast to most of the literature on the informal sector, which treats it as an undifferentiated whole, we think it important to distinguish between a more productive and dynamic component and a traditional, relatively stagnant component, which more closely fits the customary image of the sector.[5] We thus differentiate between two major types of activity: those we describe as "traditional," informal sector, with very low levels of capitalization, low labor productivity, low per capita incomes, very small size (three or less workers) and static technology, often organized within the home. The second component of urban informal sector, consists of "modernizing" activities. These typically are more capital-intensive, usually larger in size (up to ten workers), and more dynamic in technology. This subsector tends to use more skilled labor, some coming from urban formal sector and some generated through learning and training activities within urban informal sector itself; its labor productivity is higher and its entrepreneurial incomes can be substantial.

The dividing line between this subsector of informal sector and the component of formal sector that is often called the S&M (small and medium enterprise) is difficult to draw precisely.

The major differences are the access to formal sector credit and the extent of being subject to government tax and other regulations, including minimum wage legislation. We arbitrarily include all enterprises between three and ten workers as belonging to the modernizing urban informal sector.

This sector has few direct links to the global economy, but it has important links to the urban formal sector. The informal sector can produce both consumer goods and producer goods, including some simple machines and intermediate products. As far as consumer products are concerned (which form the majority of its activities), the links consist of the sale of products produced by consumer goods to workers employed in the formal sector. Producer goods provide intermediate products for formal sector, often through a subcontracting relationship. Consequently, the dynamism of the markets for the modernizing informal sector is highly dependent on developments in the formal sector. We shall return to this issue below.

In contrast, the traditional informal sector, which only produces consumer products, has very few links with the formal sector. Its customers tend to be very low-income urban people, those working in the traditional informal sector itself, and also some working in the modernizing informal sector.

The relative size of these three components of the urban productive system, namely formal, modernizing, and traditional informal sectors, is of critical importance in determining both the level and distribution of urban income. In general, employment in the formal sector tends to be that of the urban elite – even the wage earners are usually earning salaries well above what they can get elsewhere. The traditional informal sector usually offers appallingly low incomes, even below those obtainable in the rural areas. It is this subsector that is associated with the palpable urban poverty observed in so many cities of the third world. The modernizing urban informal sector is an intermediate case: its entrepreneurs often receive incomes comparable to or above those of the formal sector wage earners (indeed they typically are exworkers from the formal sector); its employees have lower wages, but usually above those obtainable in the traditional informal sector. It is also intermediate in terms of its contribution to development. While the traditional informal sector provides some minimal safety net income support to the near destitute, it otherwise has little positive contribution to make. But the modernizing subsector can be a growing and increasingly significant source of incomes, output, and savings. Hence a key issue for analyzing urban incomes and urban poverty is the relative size of the two components of the urban informal sector.

Overall Size of the Urban Informal Sector

In our view determinants of the size of the two urban subinformal sectors depends, first, on what makes people migrate to cities looking for work, because these forces determine the total size of the urban work force. Depending on the size and rate of growth of the formal sector some of these people get work there; the remainder are distributed between the two subsectors of informal sectors. Opportunities for earning a decent income are generally significantly better in the modernizing informal sector than the traditional informal sector. But these opportunities are limited both by the extent of market demand for the products of this subsector and by the availability of physical and human capital. The traditional urban informal sector is a residual sector which is forced to accept everyone who cannot find employment in formal sector or the modernizing informal sectors. Hence the relative size of the two subsectors depends on the determinants of the size of the modernizing informal sector, with the traditional informal sector as a residual parking lot for those waiting to move into either the modernizing informal sector or, possibly, the formal sector. There are two levels of analysis to be considered in determining the outcome.

The size of the total urban informal sector labor force is the cumulative outcome of a number of interactions within the developing economy as a whole. These include the dynamism of the agricultural sector determining both the extent to which the rural sector is able to absorb the growing labor force and rural wage levels; the rural–urban wage gaps; and the employment opportunities offered by the growth of the urban formal sector.

Although the Harris–Todaro model[6] ignores the urban informal sector, it provides powerful insights into the determinants of its size. As they put it, relative employment opportunities and wage gaps between the rural economy and the urban formal sector explain the rate of rural–urban migration. Although in their model, open urban unemployment is the outcome of this process, rural–urban migration also feeds the urban informal sector. Indeed, for very poor people, joining the urban informal sector is nearly always preferable to open unemployment, because it provides some income without preventing the continued search for a formal sector job.

If we modify the Harris–Todaro model of migration to include the urban informal sector, the equilibrium employment of the urban informal sector at any point in time will depend on: (1) labor absorption in the rural sector relative to population pressure, a function of productivity growth and incomes in agriculture and rural nonagriculture; (2) the rate of growth of formal sector employment; and (3) wages in the two urban sectors relative to the rural alternatives.

It follows that the urban informal sector employment can grow rapidly in a number of different circumstances: for example, where rural growth is low and fails to absorb significant additions to its labor force, even a small rise in urban formal sector employment can lead to rapid rural–urban migration, as for example in Mexico. Alternatively, even where rural productivity growth is high and employment in the urban formal sector is consequently growing faster, rural migrants may still be attracted in excess of formal sector employment opportunities, as in China today. In contrast, where urban formal sector employment is actually contracting, or real wages in the formal sector are falling, as in some African countries, we could expect, *ceteris paribus,* a reverse flow of migration to rural areas and/or an increase in the size of the urban informal sector labor force.

The overall size of the urban informal sector thus depends on population pressures, wages, and employment opportunities elsewhere in the economy. The nature and extent of the links of the formal sector with the global economy become important in this context, because when they are strong and increasing (i.e., with rapid growth of capital and technology imports, as well as manufactured exports by the formal sector) the growth of employment opportunities is likely to attract higher levels of migration to the city. The same is true for consumer goods imports (i.e., the "global life-style" effect), because as patterns of consumption become more visible (e.g., with the spread of television) and attainable (with higher formal sector incomes), this may further add to the apparent attractions of city life.

The Modernizing Urban Informal Sector

The size of modernizing urban informal sector, which lies at the heart of our analysis, depends mainly on the strength and vitality of its links with the formal sector. As noted above, the modernizing urban informal sector has important supply links to the formal sector, selling its consumer products to workers in that sector and also selling intermediate products to its producers. Consequently, for any given strength of these links, the growth rate of the formal sector itself is important. When the formal sector is growing rapidly—usually associated with growing exports to the world economy, growing imports of technology and capital (i.e. with strong global links) – the demand for the products of the modernizing urban informal sector will also grow. But an additional factor determining the strength of the links to the modernizing urban informal sector is the nature of the formal sector. For example, if the income distribution in the formal sector is more unequal, demand will be directed more toward globally specified luxury goods and less toward the products of the modernizing urban informal sector or even of the formal sector itself.

Another crucial issue is the strength of the demand from formal sector enterprises for the intermediate and capital goods of the modernizing urban informal sector (i.e., producer goods). We define the linkage ratio as the level of demand for producer goods generated by a given level of the formal sector. The strength of this demand again depends on both the size and the character of the formal sector. The larger and faster growing the the formal sector, *ceteris paribus,* the more extensive its subcontracting relationships with the modernizing urban informal; the more competitive the formal sector, the more likely it is to seek such relationships in search of cost-cutting opportunities.

Some formal sector firms organize themselves largely through vertical integration, while others subcontract extensively in the Japanese style, including to households through the putting out system. Moreover, some industries are technologically more suitable for subcontracting than others. Government interventions, such as health and safety standards, can also affect the strength of these linkages (i.e., unduly precise standards tend to diminish the procurement of intermediate products from the informal sector). In contrast, when taxes are levied and minimum wages enforced only in the formal sector, this provides an additional encouragement for subcontracting to the informal sector.

Again, incomes generated in the formal sector are partly spent on consumer goods produced by the modernizing informal subsector, on its own output, as well as on imports. The strength of consumption linkages between the two sectors depends on the character of the formal sector, including its distribution of income. Given that, for the most part, producer goods have low-income characteristics, a more egalitarian distribution of income within the formal sector will generate larger demand for these goods.

In essence there, indeed, exists a continuum of consumer goods of varying characteristics, ranging from those produced by the urban traditional informal, modernizing informal, or formal sectors, to imported or global varieties. The characteristics of these products tend to be increasingly suitable for people with higher incomes as one moves through the continuum, so that elite households mainly consume imported and formal sector produced goods; middle-income households choose mainly between formal-sector and informal sector consumer goods; and low-income households mainly between the informal sector consumer goods and the traditional informal sector.

The extent and character of the demands for informal sector consumer goods and producer goods depend also, of course, on the characteristics of the modernizing urban informal sector, in both its qualitative and quantitative dimensions. The potential output of informal sector producer goods, for example, depends on the resources available to the modernizing informal subsector, including the education, training, and skills incorporated in its labor force, its technological and entrepreneurial capacities, as well as its access to appropriate institutions, information, infrastructure, and informal sources of finance. At any point in time, the accumulation of capital and skills in the subsector are, of course, the product of historical developments. Where structures and policies have favored the sector over a fairly long period, a strong supply potential will have developed, facilitating its response to new demands.

The Effects of Global Links

How will global links affect these relationships? There are likely to be relatively few direct global links with the modernizing urban informal sector. But, global links with the help of the formal sector determine that sector's growth and quality and, hence, the strength of its linkages with the modernizing subsector. Here we are moving into more speculative territory and need to differentiate among various categories of global links.

The first are very strong global links, in the form of large-scale direct foreign capital and technology imports, in the presence of weak domestic links because of stagnant agriculture. These may exist in the presence of either outward (exports) or inward (import substitution) oriented policies. The precise composition of a given volume of foreign investment (e.g., wholly owned subsidiaries versus joint ventures) will also affect the character of the formal sector and, in turn, its linkage ratio to the modernizing informal sector.

The second are moderate global links that may be defined in terms of a lower volume of technology imports and direct foreign investment; the greater extent of local ownership of medium-scale industry; more balanced growth domestically, given a relatively dynamic rural economy, and the avoidance of excessive foreign debt.

The third is a completely autarchic policy toward foreign capital and technology where almost all global links are severed.

A strongly "global-oriented" economy (Category A) is likely to have weaker links with the modernizing informal sector than one that is more oriented toward balanced growth domestically and local entrepeneurship (Category B) for the following reasons.

On the production side, when foreign direct investment dominates production in the formal sector and there is little domestic adaptation of technology, there may be little scope for subcontracting to the modernizing informal sector. However, a large foreign presence can be consistent with strong linkages between these two sectors, if the foreign presence is, for example, represented by joint ventures and trading companies dealing with medium- and small-scale domestic formal sector firms.

On the consumption side, strong global influences seem to be associated with worsening income distribution[7] in some (e.g., Latin American) countries with cultural influences tending to push consumption patterns toward imported or formal sector products. However, this tendency has not been pronounced in East Asia or historical Japan where, however, global links have been in some important respects closer to the moderate model.

In Category C, the formal sector might have strong links with the modernizing informal sector, but it may also show low aggregate growth and consequently low growth opportunities for both sectors.

Hence the modernizing informal sector is likely to be strongest in absolute size in the intermediate Category B-type economies. Moreover, the modernizing informal sector is likely to be larger relative to the traditional informal sector because migration to the cities is likely to be smaller when the rural economy is dynamic, balanced growth is in effect, and global cultural influences are relatively weaker.

It is useful to illustrate various alternative patterns of urban informal sector development with some country cases. Looking at urban developments across developing countries, we can differentiate among types and stages of development.

NICs of East Asia

Among the more developed countries or the NICs of East Asia, the initial rural labor surplus was exhausted two decades ago, given the rapid labor absorption by the formal sector, largely resulting from a sustained growth in exports. This is the case of Taiwan, South Korea, and Singapore today. In each instance, spectacular economic performance over a prolonged period ultimately led to a shortage of labor and rising wages.

In Taiwan especially, given a dynamic agriculture and rapidly expanding rural nonagricultural sector, the modernizing informal sector played an important role. Competitive structures and a predominance of the S&M component of the formal sector industry helped establish strong linkages with the modernizing informal sector. The traditional informal sector was historically rather insignificant, as buoyant agricultural and rural nonagricultural performance helped avoid mass migration to the cities, which has virtually disappeared, along with urban poverty. Global links helped to sustain the rapid growth of the formal sector, but domestic policies towards agriculture, infrastructure, and support for small-scale industry were essential for the success of both the formal and modernizing informal sectors.

Rapidly Growing Developing Countries

Some countries that are at an earlier stage of development and have not yet exhausted their labor surplus have a dynamic formal sector, with strong linkages to the modernizing informal, which is contributing to reduced urban poverty. Thailand is a good example. There has been rapid growth in the formal sector, associated with the growth of manufactured exports, along with high rates of savings and investment. There are strong links with the modernizing informal sector, which has grown rapidly. Despite high rates of rural–urban migration, it appears that the traditional informal sector is diminishing relatively, and poverty is falling. Rapid and relatively well-balanced economic growth over the past decade is transforming the country into the category of a "newly industrializing country." In addition to the expansion of large-scale formal sector firms using imported capital, there is a significant informal sector in evidence, which has a large modernizing component. It is the successful interaction between agriculture and the formal sector and between the formal and the informal sectors, together with the rapid growth of output and demand in the economy as a whole, that has made the modernizing informal sector flourish.

Since 1971, paid employment in small enterprises has been rising as a proportion of total employment and that of the self-employed and unpaid family workers has been declining as a proportion of total employment, indicating a rise in the modernizing component. This is also indicated by the high and rising proportion of total registered enterprises accounted for by small-scale firms (below 10 employees), which, of course, excludes the many unregistered activities. It is estimated that the informal sector as a whole accounted for about one half of the total urban labor force in the mid-1980s.

Recent surveys have drawn attention to dynamic elements in Thailand's informal sector. While these were mostly purposively designed to focus on modernizing elements and, hence, do not indicate how prevalent such activity really is, they do testify to the existence of strong, modernizing informal sector elements. The elements include metalworking and electronics, wood and metal furniture manufacture, garments, umbrella manufacturing, and food processing. Many firms had modified their techniques during the previous five years and introduced new products. The average size of enterprises grew during the 1980s in response to the growth in demand.[8] Moreover, many of the enterprises surveyed had subcontracting relationships with the formal sector. The average size of the enterprises was relatively high (5.9 workers).[9] A random survey of microenterprises (employment below 20) found that more than half of the enterprises had added to their investments between 1989 and 1992, and 9 percent had increased their number of employees.[10]

The total size of the informal sector as a proportion of the total urban labor force appears to have begun to decline, while the share of the modernizing informal sector has risen and that of the traditional informal sector has fallen. Urban poverty has been estimated at only 7 percent in 1990, a sharp reduction from the 19 percent level at the beginning of the 1980s.

China

China has shown a somewhat similar performance, with both output and exports growing by more than 11 percent annually during the 1980s. Employment grew rapidly in both the formal and modernizing informal sectors. Relatively egalitarian income distribution and controlled exposure to Western products generated good consumption linkages between formal and the modernizing informal sector. Rural–urban migration speeded up in the 1980s as compared with the 1970s. Yet, at least until recently, this labor was largely successfully absorbed by formal and modernizing informal sectors. Urban and rural poverty rates declined.

Two elements of China's performance require emphasis: first, much industrial activity took place initially in small and medium-sized towns, in response to demands arising from growing incomes in agriculture, with a strong supply response facilitated by government support of infrastructure. Global links have been controlled (i.e. while they have had an impact through capital and technology imports into the formal sector and the rapid growth in manufacturing exports, their relative role has not been dominant). However, in the 1990s there has been a tendency toward accelerating rural–urban migration in excess of formal sector employment opportunities. Income distribution seems to have worsened and the initial dynamics of the modernizing informal sector has recently slowed relative to traditional modernizing informal sector.

Latin American Countries

A third case occurs when there is reasonably high-income growth of the formal sector, but of a type that generates a highly unequal income distribution, with consequently low consumption linkages, while a noncompetitive formal sector also leads to low production linkages. The growth pattern of many Latin American countries in the 1960s and 1970s was of this type. Failed "trickle down" occurred partly because the modernizing informal sector was not of significant size and the rapid migration induced by the success in the formal sector had to be absorbed by the traditional informal sector. Consequently, urban poverty rates remained high. The pattern of development in Mexico or Brazil before the debt crisis exemplifies this case. In general, this pattern of growth seems to be associated with second stage import-substituting industrialization, sometimes in the presence of strong global links through direct foreign investment and technology transfer.

Stagnating Economies

A fourth case is represented by economies whose formal sector is stagnating, offering few opportunities for modernizing informal sector expansion. Where the rural sector is also doing poorly, migration continues to be high, the traditional informal sector tends to grow, and urban poverty escalates. We illustrate this case by the performance of the Philippines and Zambia in the 1980s.

At the time of independence, the Philippine Government inherited an economy biased toward cash crop primary products, to the neglect of overall rural development. A long period of heavy emphasis on urban import-substituting industrialization followed, relying on capital goods imports and the selective promotion of large-scale firms. In the 1970s, population growth outstripped labor absorption within agriculture and the urban formal sector. The result was falling real wages, with mass migration into urban areas and the expansion of the urban informal sector. The share of urban employment in total employment rose from 30% in the early 1970s to 47% in 1991.[11] This was associated with a growing urban informal sector, which accounted for 62% of total urban employment in 1976.[12] The informal sector grew further during the 1980s and was estimated to account for 82 percent of nonagricultural employment by the end of the 1980s.[13]

There is some evidence of a proportionate growth in the modernizing informal sector (although less than in Thailand), with a rise in small-scale industrial activities relative to household enterprises during the 1960s, including growth in metalworking, electrical machinery, and chemical products. But from the mid 1970s to the end of the 1980s, a rise in the share of own account workers, from 24 to 30 percent of total urban employment, is an indication of the relatively faster growth of the traditional informal sector.[14] There was also a shift away from manufacturing towards the service sector and away from wages and salary work towards self-employment in the 1970s and 1980s.[15]

During the early 1970s when the modernizing informal sector was rising, the rate of poverty fell. But in the 1980s, relative increases in traditional informal sector were associated with sharply rising urban poverty, from an estimated 38.4 percent in 1971 to 56.1 percent in 1985.[16]

In Zambia there has been prolonged economic decline, largely owing to the collapse of copper prices. Average per capita incomes have been falling over the last quarter of a century. Rural poverty rates have been substantially and persistently above urban poverty rates, although there has been some narrowing in rural–urban differentials in the 1980s. Although the rapid rate of urban migration slowed in the 1980s, as employment opportunities and real urban wages declined, urban population growth continued at nearly 4 percent annually, far outpacing formal sector employment opportunities. The proportion of the labor force in the formal sector fell from 24 percent in 1980 to less than 10 percent ten years later.[17] Consequently the informal sector grew rapidly. The formal sector performance did not encourage the modernizing informal sector, partly because total output in the formal had been stagnating and partly because the import substituting and oligopolistic character of the formal did not encourage strong links with the modernizing informal sector. Hence the growing informal sector has been mainly of the traditional informal sector variety. Urban poverty has grown, from an estimated 4 percent in 1975 to 50 percent in 1989.[18]

Global influences have been significant in Zambia: exports account for more than one third of GDP; import restrictions were drastically reduced; and the economy was opened to foreign investment during this period. But the linkage between the domestic formal sector and the global economy has not been successful in recent years, with deteriorating commodity prices, no diversification of exports, and very limited foreign investment.

Conclusion

It is apparent that the size and quality of the formal sector are of overriding importance for the development of the modernizing informal sector. Global influences are certainly relevant, even if not unit directional in their effect. For Zambia, dependent on copper and with an inflexible economy, opening up to the global economy has not brought success in the formal or the informal sectors. In contrast, Taiwan has been selective in the global influences admitted and has achieved success in terms of both formal and the modernizing informal sector growth. A dynamic formal sector seems to be a necessary condition for success in the modernizing informal sector, but other conditions are also needed to reinforce this, including a relatively egalitarian income distribution and strong production linkages between the formal and modernizing informal sectors. In the absence of these, the formal sector's growth may be accompanied by a growing traditional informal sector and only limited development of the modernizing informal sector—as in many Latin American countries and the Philippines during the 1970s.

It should thus be clear that the impact of global forces, on the one hand, and of rural mobilization efforts, on the other, help determine the role of the urban informal sector during the transition process. Given the explosive rise in population of many cities of the developing world and the growing concern with urban poverty, the analysis above permits a better understanding of both the potential of and the constraints on the development of a dynamic informal sector and its linkages to the rest of the world, as well as the appropriate direction for policy change.

Notes

1. We should note that formal sectors differ according to the degree of their openness to foreign trade; the degree of foreign direct investment; the type of ownership; the extent of competition; and the extent of technological adaptation.
2. Most influential was the ILO's 1972 report on Kenya.
3. See, for example, D. Turnham, B. Salome, and A. Schwarz, eds., *Dynamism in the Informal Sector in a Fast Growing Economy: The Case of Bangkok.* New Delhi: ILO, 1990. For a most useful recent survey of this literature see H. Lubell, *The Informal Sector in the 1980's and 1990's.* Paris: OECD Development Centre, 1991.
4. See, for example, Hernando de Soto, "Constraints on People: The Origin of Underground Economies and Limits to their Growth." In J. Jenkins, ed., *Beyond the Informal Sector: Including the Excluded in Developing Countries.* San Francisco: Institute for Contemporary Studies, 1988.
5. A somewhat similar distinction has been made by G. Nihan, E. Denal and J. Comlan, "The Modern Informal Sector in Lome." *International Labour Review,* 1979, 118: 5; and G. Fields, "Labor Market Modelling and the Urban Informal Sector: Theory and Evidence," in Turnham, et al., 1990, who differentiates between "easy entry" and "upper tier" components.
6. J. Harris and M. Todaro, "Migration, Unemployment and Development: A Two-Sector Analysis," *American Economic Review* 1970.
7. See A. Berry and F. Stewart, "Market Liberalization and Income Distribution: The Experience of the 1980's." In A. Berry, R. Culpepper, and F. Stewart, eds., *Essays in Honour of G. K. Helleiner.* Macmillan (forthcoming).
8. Romijn divides his sample into 0–4 and 5–20 and finds that the latter grew much more than the former.
9. Data from A. Amin, *Macro-perspectives on the growth of the informal sector in selected Asian countries.* New Delhi: ILO, 1989.
10. C. Morrisson, H.-B. Solignac Lecomte, and X. Oudin, *Microenterprises and the Institutional Framework in Developing Countries.* Paris: OECD, 1994.

11. A. M. Balisacan, "Urban Poverty in the Philippines: Nature, Causes and Policy Measures," *Asian Development Review* 1989, 12: 1. Part of the rise is the result of differences in definitions.
12. World Bank, *Philippines: Industrial Development Strategy and Policies.* Washington, DC, 1980.
13. This includes rural as well as urban informal sectors. See Balisacan, 1994. Part of the rise is the result of differences in definitions.
14. See Balisacan, 1994.
15. See Alonzo, 1988.
16. See UNICEF, "Redirecting Adjustment Programmes Towards Growth and the Protection of the Poor: The Philippine Case." In G. A. Bornia, R. Jolly, and F. Stewart, eds., *Adjustment with a Human Face,* vol. 2. Oxford: Oxford University Press, 1987.
17. Prices and Incomes Commission, 1991.
20. H. White, *Zambia in the 1990s as a Case of Adjustment in Africa.* The Hague: ISS (processed), 1995.

Section 1 The Role of Women Citizens[1]

Sylvia Chant

This section of the book highlights key aspects of how gender and housing affect low-income women in urban areas in developing countries. Its main aims are to demonstrate the interacting dynamics between gender and urbanization processes, to review the main problems associated with gender-differentiated experiences of shelter, and to identify the importance of mainstreaming gender in urban planning and policy making.

The notion of "gendered" urban development encompasses not only the idea that urbanization impacts on gender roles and relations, but that gender itself is a vital component of urbanization processes. Gendered urbanization clearly also interrelates with sociocultural factors. Because households usually correspond with housing units and are also a crucial arena of women's lives, it is effectively impossible to disentangle aspects of household form and organization from the analysis of gender and shelter. The urban women's experiences, livelihoods, and welfare may be heavily mediated by the households to which they belong, although this varies from place to place. The household and individual well-being cannot necessarily be treated as one and the same thing. The female household members are often disadvantaged relative to their male counterparts in regard to disparities between their inputs to and benefits from household survival strategies. The links between labor and shelter are also particularly pertinent in contemporary cities for two reasons. First, because economic crisis and restructuring have placed greater pressure on households to generate additional sources of income; and second, because many informal economic activities are based in the home.

Low-income groups face extreme disadvantages in housing and are using ill cared for by shelter programs. In many countries, levels of urban poverty have risen over the last 15 years, both in absolute terms and relative to rural areas. Increased urban poverty has been strongly linked with neoliberal structural adjustment and stabilization programs that have been implemented in at least 70 countries in Eastern Europe and the developing world since the 1980s. In turn, the combined effects of economic restructuring, such as rising prices, falling wages, declining formal sector employment, cutbacks in social and welfare programs, and the marketization of basic services, seem to have impacted heavily on women. Yet, the gender-differentiated consequences of urban poverty and crisis vary from place to place, and, in regard to housing in particular, are mediated, among other things, by the character of national and local development, pre- and/or postadjustment, by state approaches to the provision of shelter and services for the urban poor, by norms of family and household organization, and by gendered access to such resources as land, labor, and income.

Gender Urban Development

Gender is intrinsic to the analysis of urbanization in developing countries. Not only does urban economic growth and development often provoke changes in gender roles, relationships, and inequalities, but the urbanization process itself is frequently shaped by prevailing constructions of gender. In other words, the causes, nature, and outcomes of urbanization may be highly gendered. Recognition of this phenomenon is vital both for understanding urban evolution and its consequences, and for shaping policy interventions. As observed by Caroline Moser,

> Although more marked in the 1906s and 1970s than it is today, gender-blindness still prevents many researchers from appreciating the pivotal nature of gender relations in determining women's participation in urban life, their roles in resolving urban problems and planning for urban futures.[2]

Gender-Selective Migration to Urban Areas

One basic, and seemingly ubiquitous, factor contributing to gendered urbanization in developing regions is the differential movement of men and women from rural to urban areas. On one hand, gender-selective migration reflects a range of social and economic imperatives and constraints surrounding men's and women's activities, power and status in rural communities; on the other, it may induce new patterns of behavior, access to resources, and social organization. In this way, gender-differentiated rural–urban mobility is not only a barometer of existing gender roles and relations, but can act as a catalyst for change.

Broadly speaking, rural–urban migration in Latin America and Southeast Asia is female-dominated, whereas in sub-Saharan Africa, North Africa, the Middle East, and South Asia men have been the majority of migrants. These interregional variations are attributable to a number of interacting factors, one important one is the nature of women's roles in rural economies. In Latin America, for example, women's preponderance in rural–urban migration flows has been linked to their limited access to rural employment. This is reflected in low rates of labor force participation, with women being fewer than 20 percent of agricultural workers in most parts of the continent. This contrasts markedly with the situation in sub-Saharan Africa, where female participation in the agricultural labor force is more than 40 percent and in some western, central, and southern areas, where it is more than 50 percent. In addition, women in sub-Saharan Africa are more likely to have access to land in their own right than in Latin America. Greater possibilities for African women to generate a livelihood in rural areas may well contribute to the fact that urban migration in the region has long been male dominated. By the same token, African women's migration to towns is also likely to have been discouraged by limited employment opportunities in services and industry. In contrast, cities in Latin America (and Southeast Asia) have traditionally offered more jobs to low-income women than rural areas. In Latin America, for instance, domestic service has absorbed large numbers of female migrants, and the growth of urban-based export-manufacturing in countries such as Mexico, Costa Rica, Puerto Rico, and the Dominican Republic is playing an increasingly important role in providing employment for female entrants to the job market. The demand for female labor in Southeast Asian cities has also been associated with the expansion of multinational export manufacturing and the growth of unskilled or semiskilled occupations in such tertiary activities as domestic service, commerce, and prostitution. Women's shares of urban employment both in Latin America and Southeast Asia are usually at least 30 percent and generally far in excess of those in rural areas.

Having illustrated a broad correlation between patterns of gender-selective migration and women's relative access to a livelihood in rural and urban areas, it is critical to recognize that female migration cannot be reduced to simple differentials in labor opportunities and/or wage rates between countryside and town. Although women may well be more likely to move to towns when they have limited involvement in agriculture, the latter itself is socially determined by such factors as gender and generational divisions of labor in rural households, gendered access to land and machinery, differing demand for male and female labor in large or multinational farming enterprises, and by levels of unemployment and underemployment. Beyond this, ideologies of family, kinship, and gender have an important part to play in shaping motives for migration and the relative autonomy of migrant decision-making. Having intimated that income is an important motive for female migration, it must be recognized that women may not move to towns of their own volition, but at the behest of, or through pressure from, their rural families. This is especially the case with young unmarried women. In Southeast Asia, for instance, there is often considerable pressure on single teenage and adult daughters to repay their parents for bringing them up. Although similar notions of duty and filial piety may be instilled in sons, in countries such as the Philippines, Taiwan, and Indonesia, parents usually prefer their daughters to become labor migrants because they are more likely to send money back home. In other contexts, such as South Asia, prevailing gender ideologies may inhibit any independent mobility among women at all. While recent work on Bangladesh suggests that expansion in female factory jobs in urban areas is encouraging city-bound streams of lone female migrants, in most of the region, social and cultural constraints have usually confined female movement to migration for marriage or to join husbands already established in towns or cities. Whatever the case in specific places, it is clear that gender plays an important part in structuring mobility patterns, whether by means of gender ideologies governing personal conduct, divisions of labor in rural homes, or gender differences in employment and/or production in countryside and town. Indeed gender may also play a part in influencing the nature of urban economic activities themselves, insofar as multinational factories are likely to be attracted to areas where they are able to capitalize on low wage costs associated with the recruitment of female workers.

An important outcome of gender-selective migration for urban environments is the impact on sex ratios. Where migration to cities is female-led, this usually leads to a "surplus" female population. This, in turn, may have a range of consequences, not least of which is a rise in female household headship. In areas where women outnumber men, women are less likely to have coresident partners or fathers. This was borne out at an interregional level by a broad three-way correspondence between rural–urban variations in female headship, sex ratios, and migrant selectivity. In South Asia, North Africa, the Middle East, and much of sub-Saharan Africa, for instance, urban sex ratios tend to be masculine and women-headed households are more common in rural than urban areas. In the towns and cities of East and Southeast Asia, Latin America, and the Caribbean, on the other hand, rural-outmigration is female-selective, urban sex ratios are usually feminine, and levels of female household headship are higher in towns and cities. In Latin America, for example, female-headed households are rarely more than 10 percent of the population in rural communities, but up to 25 percent in many urban areas.

Although in countries such as the Philippines the relative proportions of women in urban areas do not seem to display any consistent relationship with levels of female household headship, in others there would appear to be positive correlations. For example, data from the 1984 census of Costa Rica indicate a strongly feminine urban sex ratio, with an average of only 91 men per 100 women in urban localities at a national level, compared with a sex ratio of 107 men per 100 women in rural areas. In the same year, women-headed households were 22.7 percent of urban households but only 12.0 percent in the countryside. In Zimbabwe, on the other hand, where women-headed households are approximately one third of households nationally, only half of this level are found in the capital Harare, which undoubtedly is partly the result of strongly masculine urban sex ratios (averaging 114 men per 100 women in 1982).

Despite some association between sex ratios and female household headship, it is clear that demographic factors are not the only influence on women-headed units, nor do they operate independently of other variables. As noted earlier, for example, greater access to employment and incomes in urban areas is likely to attract rural women to towns and cities, particularly female heads of households, who have sole financial responsibility for children. At the same time, the formation of female-headed households may be more common within urban areas because women have a greater economic capacity to survive alone. In other words, higher rates of economic activity among urban women might just as easily be a cause as an effect of greater female household headship in towns and cities. Although other reasons for increases in female household headship will be considered later in this section, three factors of critical importance to gender, housing, and urban development are in need of emphasis here. One is that even if urbanization itself may be predicated in part on gender differences and inequalities, the feminization of household headship may have important implications for gender at the domestic level. Second, an increased number and concentration of women-headed households in urban areas tends to increase the visibility of a traditionally marginalized group and brings to the fore the fact that women are in need of equal rights as citizens. Third, and related to this, women-headed households may form a major client group for housing in certain areas, with different needs from other households in regard to land, dwellings, and urban services. All of these issues should become clearer as gender is examined in its household context.

Gender and Households

Although there are several debates in the gender and development literature on the criteria that constitute a "household" and on the desirability of generating definitions that might be universally applicable,[3] the most common for developing countries is that a household comprising individuals who live in the same dwelling and who share basic domestic and/or reproductive activities, such as cooking and eating.[4] This effective definition of household as a "housekeeping unit," tends to be favored in international data sources and to make sense to people at the grassroots.[4] Nonetheless, numerous problems have been identified with it, one being the difficulties of pinpointing what "domestic functions" actually are.

It is also important to acknowledge that household reproduction may not depend entirely, or even predominantly, on the efforts of household members, but on wider networks of kin, friends, and neighbors with whom there may be fundamental and enduring links. In many African countries, for example, the boundaries between households are often so fluid that a large share of domestic functions are performed outside the residential unit. A greater problem still, however, and one that requires brief consideration of theoretical models of household economics, is the notion of defining households on the basis of shared and/or collective participation in daily life. This has been viewed as obscuring important intrahousehold inequalities on such grounds as gender, age, civil status, and/or individual members' positions relative to other members. In short, empirical studies have progressively brought to light the fact that households may well be an "uneasy aggregate of individual survival strategies."

In addition to gender divisions of labor, power, and interests within household units, there may also be considerable inequalities in material resources. Although men may be the sole or major breadwinners in male-headed households, it is not always the case that their earnings benefit other household members. In fact, evidence from a wide range of places indicates that instead of contributing all (or even the bulk) of their wage to household needs, men retain varying proportions for discretionary personal expenditure. Men's expenditure is also widely observed to end up being channeled to "nonmerit" items and/or recreational activities, such as drinking, gambling, smoking, drug use, and extramarital affairs.

Although such patterns may represent a sole (and socially legitimate) outlet for male escapism in the context of precarious employment and/or low and irregular earnings, their role in causing serious secondary poverty among other household members should not be ignored. In the short term, secondary poverty makes wives and children live on less than an adult male's full earnings, and in the longer term can lead to lower levels of human capital among younger household members (through diverting resources away from nutrition, education, and so on), as well as forcing others to bear the costs of health consequences incurred by personal indulgence. Suboptimal use of the labor supply combined with lack of access to personal income can clearly make women very vulnerable, further highlighting the need to disaggregate and/or deconstruct household units when analyzing individual well-being.

A further aspect of gender inequality in intrahousehold resource distribution is that men and boys may be systematically given greater amounts of food and medical care than women. Such factors in turn have macrolevel gender impacts, as evidenced in South Asia's greater rates of female mortality and rising masculine sex ratio.[6]

Gender differentials in resource distribution are also reflected in housing insofar as investments in shelter improvements may not be given much priority by men who spend considerable amounts of time out of the house. In turn, the consequences can fall heavily on women, whose ties to the domestic environment are enforced through housework and childcare. Poorly consolidated housing not only affects women's comfort and well-being, but makes their reproductive chores more difficult and time consuming, as well as influencing their abilities to generate income, as discussed later in the context of gendered experiences of shelter. Another factor is that housing itself is a material resource over which women's legal and social rights may be extremely weak, with major implications for their capacity to determine their own lives.

Although gender inequalities are often fomented within households, it is important to recognize that various types of gender inequality can be mediated by the particular type of household to which people belong. For example, when households lack a male "head," adult women may be in a very different position to those with partners in terms of having greater personal freedom and autonomy. Similarly, when households consist of a mixed range of kin, rather than just parents and children, patterns of work, resource allocation, decision-making, and so on may be less rigidly gender differentiated. In brief, the particular identities and experiences of individual men and women are likely to be strongly influenced by the nature of their household organization and membership, notwithstanding that households may metamorphose several times in the course of the life cycle, and even within a matter of months.

Urban Development and Household Structure

Household structure embraces two main elements: sex of the household head and household composition. The latter refers to membership and describes the types of persons households consist of, whether kin or unrelated individuals, parents and children with or without additional relatives, people of the same sex and so on. A wide variety of household forms comprising varying combinations of headship and composition have been identified for developing countries.[7] Broadly speaking, however, mainstream debates on household change during urbanization have concentrated on size and composition, and more specifically, the shifting proportions of nuclear and extended households (nuclear households being those consisting of parents and children, and extended households usually being based around a parent-child unit and including other relatives as well, such as aunts, uncles, cousins and/or grandchildren).

Until relatively recently, the dominant assumption about household change was that extended households predominated in rural areas, but lost ground to nuclear units as societies urbanized. One of the main reasons given for the extended-to-nuclear transition in both historical and contemporary settings was that the spread of capitalist economic development, urban settlement, and the rise of individualized wage employment eroded production-related imperatives for large extended households (coresidence among kin had been a useful strategy to maximize resources such as land, tools, and labor for collective subsistence production). Reduced needs for households to provide the means of reproduction (education, health care, and so on) as the state and larger private entities took on these functions were also seen to fuel the process of family nuclearization.[8] Additional factors, largely emanating from Marxist discussions, were that nuclear households were more able to respond to the labor migrations required by spatially uneven capitalist development, that they provided a more secure market for mass-produced goods, and that they both reflected and reinforced the individualist ideologies underpinning capitalist production.[9]

The reasons put forward to explain the existence of extended units among the urban poor include migration (urban households often take in migrant relatives from rural areas who come to towns and cities to study, to work, or to reunite with kin who have established themselves in urban environments), housing shortages, the need to pool labor for childcare, or for greater economic security or mobility, and/or social and kinship obligations.[10] Although some evidence suggests that extended households in urban areas may be smaller in size and contain a more limited range of kin than in the countryside, again this is highly dependent on context. While recession in Mexico, for example, seems to have resulted in a greater incidence of household extension and an increase in average household size among the urban poor during the last decade or so, in cities in the Philippines, there appears to have been some shedding of relatives from extended structures. Such variations relate, among other things, to different types of household extension, to different rationales underpinning the incorporation of relatives at different points in time, to the levels and longevity of urbanization in different countries, to economic and infrastructural disparities between rural and urban areas, and to the macroeconomic context in which policy reforms have occurred. In Mexico, for example, approximately three quarters of the population are now urbanized, rural–urban differences in the provision of schools and health facilities are less marked than in the past, and the tide of rural–urban migration has slowed substantially in recent years.

Although reciprocity among kin is clearly observed and valued, urban households in the last decade have often extended for what might be termed positive pragmatic and strategic reasons (for example, relatives have joined forces in the interests of active collaboration in productive or reproductive work and have often benefited economically in the process). In the Philippines, on the other hand, large-scale urbanization is a more recent phenomenon (a little under half the population live in towns or cities), and significant rural–urban differences in social service provision, welfare, and employment remain. Coupled with the fact that people adhere strongly to customary practices of familial obligation, extension of households in urban areas has often taken the form of young dependent relatives moving in with urban kin to take advantage of the opportunity to study. Unfortunately, greater poverty has meant that for some households this is becoming a luxury they cannot afford. In short, although there is little doubt that household composition usually undergoes some change in the course of urban development, these changes take different forms at different times in different places, and make it very difficult to derive general patterns, to draw cross-cultural comparisons, or even to discern country-specific trends. Similarly, although the effects on gender relations of differing types of household membership might be marked in specific areas, neither can (nor should) these be decontextualized and/or generalized.

The Effects of Urbanization on Household Headship

One significant outcome of gendered urbanization is a rise in women-headed households. Even if it is difficult to ascertain long-term trends in female headship with any degree of precision, households headed by women seem to be a growing proportion of households in many parts of the developing world. Although they are by no means a new phenomenon, nor are they unique to urban areas, a number of factors responsible for female-headed household formation seem to arise with urbanization. Aside from female-selective migration, one of the factors most commonly linked with the growth of towns and cities is that the individualized nature of urban employment gives women greater scope to determine their own actions. Even if women do not exercise this prerogative, potential access to a personal source of income seems to afford women more freedom to act independently than in situations where land and the means of livelihood are held by corporate patriarchal entities (whether households or kin groups), as is often the case in rural areas.[11] To some extent, this argument is borne out by the fact that in localities where urbanization is associated with increased female labor force participation (especially in Latin America and the Caribbean), female headship has also risen.

Other reasons offered for the rising incidence of women-headed units relate to economic crisis and restructuring. For example, where men's declining employment opportunities prompt them to migrate elsewhere to find work, whether on a short- or long-term basis, the fragmentation of family units can cause discord and increase propensity for marital breakdown.[12] Another factor conceivably exacerbating the prospects of marital dissolution is stress, or loss of self-esteem among men who become unable to fulfill their socially expected role of breadwinner. This may be especially marked where wives are working. Indeed, some young men may avoid marriage altogether when they know they have limited prospects of getting regular employment and/or occupying a position of responsibility within their families.

Another factor that also accounts for increases in female household headship is the effects of poverty on kinship obligations. Whereas it has been customary in many parts of South Asia and North Africa for abandoned or widowed women to be taken back into the homes of male natal family members (for example, fathers or brothers), increasing numbers of women who fall into this position are now having to fend for themselves. Yet although the rise in women-headed households has frequently, and perhaps preponderantly, been viewed as a negative outcome of economic crisis with women being the victims of abandonment either by men or their kinfolk, this is by no means universal. For example, where men make little contribution to household survival, women too may opt to set up their own homes. Although women rarely choose to become female heads, an increasing number of studies indicate that women are either eschewing marriage or taking the decision to separate or divorce.

Observations of this nature are increasingly acting to challenge popular conventional wisdoms about female-headed households being the poorest of the poor and/or representing an archetypal outcome of the late twentieth-century feminization of poverty in developing countries.[13] On the one hand, as examined later, intrahousehold poverty levels may be scaled down (rather than exacerbated) by female headship. On the other hand, women-headed households are not always found in the greatest number at the bottom rungs of the socioeconomic hierarchy. For example, World Bank data show that while female-headed households are likely to be overrepresented among the poor in Asia and Latin America, this is less so in Africa.[14] A closer look at intraregional patterns qualifies even this observation. For example, within Central America, only Nicaragua and El Salvador have higher levels of female headship among the poor than the national average, notwithstanding that two thirds to three quarters of the population of all six nations in the region are deemed as falling below the poverty line. Beyond this, a variety of nationally based or city-based studies have indicated that women-headed households are found at all levels of the socioeconomic spectrum and are by no means disproportionately represented among low-income groups.

Whatever the origins or socioeconomic position of female-headed households, on a world scale they are estimated to constitute approximately one fifth of all households, being 19.1 percent of households in Africa, 18.2% in Latin America and the Caribbean and 13 percen

Asia and the Pacific. Although in some countries, such as India and the Philippines, female household headship does not seem to have risen much or at all since the 1960s, in others (especially in Latin America and the Caribbean) it has grown quite substantially. In Brazil, for example, women-headed households moved from 5.2 to 20.6 percent of the household population between 1960 and 1987, in Mexico from 13.6 to 17.3 percent between 1960 and 1990, in Puerto Rico from 16 to 23.2 percent between 1970 and 1990, and in Guyana, from 22.4 to 35 percent between 1970 and 1987. Even if female headship has often been high in sub-Saharan Africa and rises may not be so marked (for example, in Botswana, female-headship grew only marginally between 1980 and 1990 – from 45.2 to 45.9 percent – in Ghana, women-headed households increased from 22 to 29 percent between 1960 and 1987. This is strongly linked to the effects of structural adjustment on Ghanaian society.[15]

Gender Implications of Female Household Headship

Although the feminization of household headship may remove the immediacy or directness of male control over women's lives, it by no means leads to unilateral gains. In fact, in rural areas in which women are left behind by male migrants as de facto female heads, material and psychological well-being may well deteriorate. In many parts of South Asia, for example, women's ability to farm family plots may be limited by lack of access to finance for inputs, access to machinery, and by social taboos surrounding their freedom of movement and activity. On top of this, men may still exert control over their households from a distance. When women remain heavily reliant on their husbands for remittances to ensure household subsistence, and these are small or irregular, women's vulnerability obviously increases.

Beyond this, de facto female heads have to undergo the stress associated with separation from their menfolk, and/or the possibility that their relationships may culminate in abandonment or divorce. They may also find that as long as they are attached to men that they do not achieve the status or entitlements normally linked with household headship in their communities.

As for de jure female heads, who are more likely to be found in urban areas (especially in Latin America and the Caribbean), the situation may be somewhat more positive. Although these women may come up against various forms of discrimination from neighbors, employers, public officials and so on, at least they are likely to be free of patriarchy at the domestic level, especially where they are not subject to the control of male relatives in wider kin groups and/or to the authority of adult sons. In this way, female heads of household are not usually in the position of having to defer to anyone when making decisions about their lives, and evidence from a range of contexts indicates that other potential benefits of female headship include greater self-esteem, more personal freedom, higher degrees of flexibility in terms of taking paid work and choosing from a wider range of occupations, a sense of achievement in parenting under difficult circumstances (in the case of lone mothers), a reduction or absence of physical and/or emotional abuse, and the chance to move beyond the confines of the gendered divisions of labor common to heterosexual partnerships.

Moreover, although women-headed households are widely noted as exacerbating poverty on account of having fewer wage earners than male-headed households, or because they are confined to part-time, informal jobs with low earnings and few or nonexistent fringe benefits because of discrimination by employers and/or the difficulties of reconciling employment with childcare,[16] a large number of factors act to qualify this. For example, even if women have an inferior position in the labor market and are clearly vulnerable to poverty, this is not an automatic indicator of household welfare if female-headed households have multiple earners, drawn either from their own offspring or from coresident kin.[17] Notwithstanding that women-headed households may need more workers because women's earnings are lower than men's, this combined with the generally smaller size of female-headed households means that dependency burdens (i.e., numbers of nonearners per worker) are often lower and per capita incomes higher than in male-headed units.

Beyond this, another intrahousehold factor that acts to temper poverty among the members of female-headed units is that expenditure is usually directed toward nutrition and education as opposed to "nonmerit" goods.[18] There may also be fewer inequalities between sons and daughters in terms of access to food, schooling, and other social and economic resources. This can contrast quite markedly with patterns in some male-headed units and highlights the need not only to acknowledge that "being a member of a male-headed household does not guarantee high levels of well-being for women and children,[19] but that poverty cannot be meaningfully assessed without reference to such intrahousehold factors as per capita earnings, resource allocation, and expenditure. In summary, blanket assumptions about the poverty of female-headed households may not only be inaccurate, but run the danger of obscuring the fact that women may suffer to an even greater degree as members of male-headed structures. All these factors, in turn, reinforce the importance of exercising caution in abstracting gender from its household context, and in recognizing the mediating effects of household structure.

Extrahousehold and Community Relations

Notwithstanding the primacy of households in the analysis of gender roles, relations, and inequalities, it is important to recall that households are not isolated entities. In the case of de facto female-headed households, for example, remittances from migrant spouses may well be accompanied by considerable retention of male control over household matters, even where men are absent for long periods. As for de jure female-headed households, contact with expartners may be unavoidable if men desire an ongoing relationship with children. Although male departures from conjugal unions in Guanacaste, Costa Rica, are usually marked by abandonment of all marital and parental obligations, some men pay maintenance in order to ensure rights of access to their offspring. This also applies to Mexico and is sometimes used as a means of bribing women into a continued sexual relationship. In this light it is not surprising that some women eschew maintenance, viewing their economic independence as a means of marking their wider social and sexual autonomy.

Yet, even where women have no communication with former partners, it is important to recognize that social pressures emanating from their wider kin groups and communities may force them into adopting certain kinds of behavior to fend off advances from other men or so as not to contravene prevailing codes of female propriety. This may involve women living in the homes of parents or others as embedded female heads, or having limited social lives or friendship networks, notwithstanding that kin and neighbor networks can also be a vital source of support for female heads as well as women in other types of households. Yet in some contexts, such as among the Bajou of Sabah, East Malaysia, swift remarriage may be the only option for widows and divorcees widely regarded both as "vulnerable" and "dangerous," not least in respect of threatening other people's marriages.

Gender Importance in Shelter

As the social and infrastructural context in which households are embedded, people's homes and communities clearly play a vital role in underpinning their efforts to secure the basic means of subsistence for themselves and other household members. All too often, however, housing acts to reinforce disadvantage and inequality, not least on grounds of gender. Not only do inadequate dwellings and deficient services affect people's labor, but some individuals and households may find they have very limited access to any form of shelter (and the security that normally accompanies this) in their own right.

Housing markets for the urban poor vary greatly from country to country, but generally speaking three main alternatives can be identified. One is self-help housing, whereby people settle land and organize the building of their own dwellings. Self-help housing is usually constructed on plots to which inhabitants have no legal claim (at least in the first instance). The term "irregular settlement" is commonly given to such areas, where land acquisition is through squatting or unauthorized purchase from subdividers who lack planning permission and/or who fail to provide the services or infrastructure legally stipulated for residential development. Self-help settlements are likely to be situated on the margins of cities, and often emerge in greatest number during the early stages of urban development, when land is in less demand and peripheral locations are still relatively near the economic core of cities. House building within these settlements is usually incremental, and, providing inhabitants escape eviction, they eventually benefit from the introduction of services, infrastructure, and the legalization of tenure. As such, residence in self-help housing may well lead to full home ownership over time. Owner-occupied self-help housing is found in cities in all developing regions, although probably to a greater extent in Latin America than in Asia or Africa. Having said this, nonowned housing is also widespread and in many places seems to be on the increase.

The most important type of nonowned housing option is rental housing. This commonly takes two forms, the first and more traditional type being inner-city tenement accommodation, either purpose built, or converted from workers dormitories, from dilapidated former mansions or from old colonial properties. In many parts of Latin America, inner city tenement accommodation is high density and takes the form of individual rooms positioned around a central courtyard with communal services.[20] The other rental alternative is within self-help settlements, usually older-established neighborhoods, where owner–occupiers rent out rooms or dwellings on their land plots. An increase in rental accommodation in such areas often stems from a drying up of land supply for new self-help settlements. It can also arise because of government improvement schemes that impose costs on owner–occupiers who are then forced to let rooms to cover their additional outgoings. Although renting may not be as prestigious or desirable as home ownership, this does not negate the fact that in many parts of Africa and Asia, urban dwellers have often preferred to rent because they eventually intend to move back or rejoin their families in rural areas.

The final major housing option is sharing or rent-free accommodation, which involves the temporary habitation of a dwelling without charge. In La Paz, Bolivia, for example, this arrangement is referred to as *cedida,* and is the second most common form of tenure among low-income groups after ownership. The most usual arrangement is where owner–occupiers lend out part of their plot of land (or house) to a relative (often a married son or daughter). This has huge advantages for recipients in that it saves them money by not having to pay high rents in central areas, and allows them to be close to work opportunities. It also permits them to save money to acquire their own piece of land or house and or to invest in a business. Sharing may also afford greater privacy than renting, yet since *cedida* is effectively a moral contract people rarely tend to abuse it by overstaying their welcome. At the same time, longer-term sharing can also have immense benefits for hosts in that it provides parents with access to support from their offspring in later life, thus acting as a form of intergenerational family survival strategy.[21]

All the above housing alternatives are, significantly, of a private and informal nature. In many respects this reflects failure on the part of governments to provide housing for low-income groups. Where governments have built conventional owner-occupied or rental housing units for the urban poor, these have often ended up in the hands of middle-income groups. Nonetheless, certain types of state intervention have arguably conferred some benefits to the urban poor. Rent controls, for example, that have normally been introduced in inner-city areas have often protected long-term tenants from financial pressure and from evictions, although all too often it has also led to disinvestment by landlords and the running down of housing stock.

Squatter upgrading programs, which involve the introduction of services, improvements in community infrastructure, and/or the regularization of tenure in existing self-help settlements, can also be positive for low-income groups. Indeed, although upgrading measures can cause inconvenience, not to mention unwelcome demands on residents' time and money, they have been generally more than site-and-service schemes. Site-and-service projects involve creating new settlements and granting households land plots, access to credit, technical advice on building, and so on. One variant is "core housing" projects where people are given a basic shell (usually the "wet core" of a kitchen and bathroom, plus a small living area), which they add to in their own time. Although these "progressive housing projects" are an attempt to formalize a process originating from the bottom up, state site-and-service schemes have not only failed in most countries to meet demand, but have tended to raise the entry costs to low-income home ownership, and as with conventional housing programs, have also excluded the poorest of the poor.[22]

Gendered Access to Housing

Having noted that government or agency-sponsored housing programs may exclude the poorest of the poor, one group particularly prone to exclusion, and often regardless of their intrahousehold poverty levels, are female household heads. Female heads of household are frequently denied access to formal housing schemes. Small and/or fluctuating incomes also play a part in barring women from sponsored self-build shelter projects. Additional barriers to eligibility for this type of housing stem from assumptions about women's lack of time, resources, and/or skills to construct dwellings as rapidly or to the same standards as their male counterparts, not to mention the fact that beneficiaries are often specified as family units which are implicitly equated with male-headed nuclear households.

Stereotypical notions of this nature are dangerous, first, because, as we have seen, households in urban areas are diverse and women-headed households are a growing rather than a declining phenomenon; second, because women in self-help settlements often do build homes of an equal or better quality than men by investing larger proportions of their earnings; third, because women with young children may need such housing (which generally offers the prospect of owner occupancy) as a basis for income-generating activities; and fourth, because lack of independent access to shelter restricts women's freedom to dictate the forms that their households might take. Housing is essential in the strategy of household formation and a dwelling of one's own is important not only for unmarried women's survival in town, but also for supporting their identity as independent women and when fulfilling their roles as mothers.

As for informal housing, women are more likely to rent or share than own self-help dwellings. This is often because women do not have the money to gain entry to informal settlements (which generally involves some payment to community leaders), because they lack sufficient access to savings, have less recourse to loans than male household heads because of their smaller kin networks, and/or are unable to obtain credit through formal banking channels. Women may also be less confident about their ability to build houses without the help of hired labor which clearly raises costs. Access to home ownership may also be curtailed if men are given preference by parents in sharing arrangements. In Mexico, for example, single daughters with children are more often in the position of either having to rent or live within their parents' households, whereas married sons are usually given their own piece of land on plots big enough to accommodate two or more dwellings.[23] This can disadvantage women when sharing is often a first step on the ladder to home ownership in allowing people to save money and/or ensuring de facto land inheritance. Economic constraints on home ownership have also been observed to push lone mothers into embedded subfamily arrangements in places such as Ecuador, Zambia, and the Philippines.

Over and above access to housing, the type of housing in which people live also influences their ability to manipulate household organization and membership. To manage increased burdens of reproductive or productive tasks, for example, women may need to call upon the help of other people and expand household membership. Household extension can be a positive survival strategy for women, not only because the inclusion of additional members may boost household incomes, but because the incorporation of kin often spares daughters the onus of assuming the tasks left by working mothers, and/or increases women's labor market flexibility and enhances their decision-making capacity.[23] Clearly, people's scope to extend their households may be constrained by small sized land plots, dwellings of rudimentary or makeshift material or with shallow foundations that can only be extended horizontally rather than vertically, and/or restrictions on multifamily occupancy in rented or shared accommodation.

Although possibilities for household expansion are important, the power to contract household membership is equally significant and relates not so much to space as to issues of control and rights over land and property. For example, although some women may require spouses who make little contribution to collective well-being to leave home, this is frequently held in check by their limited access to land ownership in developing cities. Generally speaking, land titles are registered in men's names leaving women (and usually children) very unprotected. For example, in Nigeria, although women can technically buy land on the open market, traditionally land is allocated through a husband or male member of the natal family, and in the event of divorce, separation, or conflict, women have to move out. Although legislative initiatives might attempt to eradicate this bias, the force of customary pressures may be strong. Legislation may also be weakened by lack of enforcement by the appropriate authorities. For example, the Law Promoting Social Equality for Women passed in Costa Rica in 1990 stipulated that property acquired during marriage should be registered in the joint names of husband and wife, and in common-law or consensual unions, in the woman's name.

Yet whether women are likely to exercise their rights in the face of male violence is doubtful. In fact, although the Social Equality Law also attempted to increase protection for women against domestic violence, male abuse of wives continues, not uncommonly resulting in disabling or even fatal injuries. As such, when women who ask their husbands to leave home are subject to menacing behavior or to break-ins, their only option may be to forfeit their assets and set up home elsewhere. The same applies in Mexico, where women may move considerable distances—sometimes to another city—to protect their anonymity and independence, and, in the process, slip down the housing ladder from owning to renting or sharing. As Caroline Moser sums up

> Without rights to land, women are often unable to protect themselves and their children from unstable or violent domestic situations; property rights tend to reinforce the control that the man, as primary income earner, already has over the household and its dependents; without land rights women are often unable to provide collateral to gain access to credit; finally, ownership of land represents a form of saving, as it appreciates in value.

Thus where women have no title to land they may end up without capital in the event of marital separation.[25]

At the other end of the spectrum, resistance to relinquish a home in which they have invested considerable amounts of time, labor, and money may act to dissuade women from acting in their best personal, emotional or psychological interests. In fact, given that security of tenure is widely seen to be a sine qua non of housing consolidation in general, it could also be surmised that women in fragile sexual partnerships might be reluctant to commit any effort or resources to dwelling improvements, despite the practical consequences for their daily life and labor.

Gender, Shelter, and Labor

Inadequacies in dwellings, community amenities, and infrastructure play a major role in intensifying reproductive work, which, given gender divisions of household labor, rebound disproportionately on women. For example, small and overcrowded houses mean that rooms frequently have multiple functions, with the same area sometimes being used not only for sleeping, studying and the rest, and recreation of family members, but for cooking as well. This involves women reorganizing space for different activities at different times of day and extra cleaning and washing attached to the constant use of multipurpose items, such as bedspreads and tables.

In placing greater pressure on the unpaid sector to absorb rising prices of basic goods and services and cutbacks in social expenditure, structural adjustment programs have aggravated the problems posed by shelter for women's contributions to household survival. Women have to devise strategies to minimize expenditure on food and essential consumer items by spending more time shopping around or finding ways to increase capacity for household self-provisioning. Mounting costs of healthcare place an even greater onus on women to prevent disease through ensuring the attainment of basic nutritional and hygiene requirements for households, as well as to treat and care for household members afflicted by short or long-term illness. These additional responsibilities clearly exact a price not only in terms of women's own health and well-being, but that of other household members, especially where the time women spend in domestic work constrains their possibilities of generating additional income for household needs.

Productive Labor

Shelter deficiencies exert pressure on women's productive or income-generating work. Economic activity among poor urban women is predominantly of an informal, and frequently home- or community-based, nature because of discrimination in formal employment, women's lack of human capital (skills, education, job experience), social restrictions on female mobility, and the problems of reconciling childcare and domestic work with income-generating ventures. The crucial importance of shelter in women's income-generating endeavors is underlined by the fact that rates of female labor force participation in many countries have risen in the last 10 to 15 years. This has often entailed an increase in women taking jobs during the years when they are most likely to be bearing and rearing children.

Women's increased involvement in income-generating activities is the result, in large part, to the financial pressures on households incurred by economic restructuring such as rising prices, falling real wages, and increased rates of male unemployment. Aside from some openings in a limited range of formal sector establishments, most women are forced to resort to their own devices to make cash, and for the reasons identified above, these are usually based in or from the home. Such activities commonly involve renting out rooms or revolve around domestic skills, such as the preparation and sale of foodstuffs, taking in laundry, sewing or dressmaking, giving cosmetic treatments or hairdressing, establishing petty retail outlets, and engaging in small-scale handicraft production. The latter may be linked into the production regimes of larger manufacturing firms, where the drive to cut labor costs has meant increased levels of subcontracting to home-based piece-rate workers.[26]

Although in many societies dwellings have historically been the basis of subsistence production and cottage industry, the current decline in waged employment seems to be forcing greater amounts of economic activity back into the domestic domain. This renewed importance of home and community as a locus of paid as well as unpaid work raises important issues for various aspects of shelter policy. Where zoning laws prohibit economic activity in residential areas, for example, women may be forced into flouting regulations and to operate under a more precarious set of conditions than usual. Similarly, restrictions on subletting may be inappropriate when the ability to construct and rent out rooms in low-income settlements provides an important source of income for women, at the same time as offering shelter opportunities for recently arrived migrants or temporary workers in urban areas. Beyond this, women in shared or rented accommodation might not have the same options for residentially based economic activity. Nonetheless, home ownership may not be an easy state either, given the circumstances in which people usually have to undertake building operations.

Given the fact that women are commonly involved in secondary jobs of housing construction, especially fetching and carrying for male laborers, the impacts of these difficulties are gender-differentiated. Despite the fact that in some parts of the world, such as in rural areas of sub-Saharan Africa, women do considerable amounts of house building, there is still a tendency for men to erect the basic structure of the dwelling, while women dedicate themselves to supplying the materials for construction, and to the finishing and upkeep of the property. This is partly the result of the fact that specialized construction is seen as male work, and even if women are employed in the construction industry (where they may be able to learn useful tasks), this is usually in unskilled jobs.

Gendered Needs in Housing and Shelter

One of the crucial elements in gender-aware planning is recognizing that women have different and special needs from men. In turn, it is equally crucial to acknowledge that needs are not inscribed by biological difference, but are socially constructed.

Practical gender needs in housing refer to the immediate material and infrastructural needs of men and women in the context of their existing and/or normative gender roles. Notwithstanding variations between places and that people's definition of needs is "culturally specific, historically contingent and subject to symbolic processes of identification," women generally have a greater range of practical gender needs in housing than men. Although men may be unemployed or organize their breadwinning activities from home, women's roles as mothers and housewives (and increasingly as self-employed domestic-based workers), means that a larger part of their time is spent in their homes and communities. Women's practical gender needs in the arena of housing and shelter may include the construction of better housing and the provision of basic urban services, such as clean and accessible water supplies that enable women to perform their reproductive tasks more efficiently and/or to use the time they save on household chores to generate more income for their families. Indeed, since women's traditional gender-assigned roles, whether paid or unpaid, often revolve around the care and nurture of husbands and children, the satisfaction of women's practical gender needs is likely not only to benefit women, but all members of their households.

Women's strategic gender needs, alternatively, extend beyond the function of housing in fulfilling reproductive and/or secondary income-generating roles, to embrace improvements in female status and the challenging of gender inequalities. As Moser describes the concept in general:

> Strategic gender needs are the needs women identify because of their subordinate position to men in their society. . . . They relate to gender divisions of labor, power and control and may include such issues as legal rights, domestic violence, equal wages and women's control over their bodies. Meeting strategic gender needs helps women to achieve greater equality.

It also changes existing roles and therefore challenges women's subordinate position.[27]

Given that housing is not only a basis for household organization, but is also highly symbolic in respect of identity and psychological security, measures to meet strategic gender needs might include improved land and property rights for women, greater access to credit, and greater female participation in decision-making over housing and in community life, all of which are likely to give women greater autonomy or control over their own lives.

Conclusion

Although there are huge variations in urbanization and its gender corollaries in different places, it is important to consider the links among gender, housing, and urban development as a basis for a deeper understanding of low-income women's lives and experiences in towns and cities of developing countries. Gender awareness has also become critical in the context of economic restructuring, where women are bearing the brunt of housing disadvantage and mounting urban poverty. Indeed, gender-sensitive housing investment may be one of the few means by which individuals and households can cushion themselves against further deterioration in living standards, if not to forge an escape route out of poverty. How these findings might translate into specific urban or shelter policies is complex, although one thing is clear: gender must be brought up-front.

To explore how gender might be given greater priority, this discussion looks first at issues of mainstreaming gender in policy and operational procedures, and then at more specific and substantive aspects of potential shelter interventions.

Mainstreaming gender in urban planning entails a number of measures, one important one being training in gender-awareness among policy-makers and housing professionals. Another critical move is arguably the framing of strategies for housing and shelter within a Gender and Development (GAD) as opposed to Women in Development (WID) perspective. Whereas WID argues that women should be integrated into development structures and processes, it has traditionally tended to look at women in isolation and to neglect the fact that existing development institutions and policies are male dominated. WID conceives of women's development "as a logistical problem, rather than something requiring a fundamental reassessment of gender relations and ideology." GAD, on the other hand, shifts the focus from women to gender. This means that instead of viewing women as a homogeneous group on account of their biological differences with men, the emphasis is on the social construction of gender and its variability across space and through time, and/or in accordance with people's insertion into other social categories on grounds of class, race, and age. Although this makes baseline research and analysis more difficult, it also signifies that men's and women's roles and relations are amenable to change.

A second major difference between WID and GAD is that GAD explicitly acknowledges that planning for change in women's situations entails changes for men, and ipso facto means that the relationships between women and men need to problematized and renegotiated. Although women's position as the subordinate gender justifies a continued emphasis on women in GAD, given that responsibility for change lies with men and women at all levels of the development process, women's issues stand less risk of being marginalized and change is likely both to be more profound and more sustainable. GAD views structural changes in the power relations between men and women as "a necessary pre-condition for any development process with long-term sustainability." Commitment to sustainability is reinforced by GAD calls for both short- and long-term approaches to women's development. The short-term goals of GAD are much along the same lines as WID (for example, improved education, access to credit, legal rights for women, and so on), its long-term goals include "ways to empower women through collective action, to encourage women to challenge gender ideologies and institutions that subordinate women."

Despite the clear advantages of GAD in respect of tackling gender inequality at the grassroots, it is also, unsurprisingly, a "confrontational" alternative. For this reason, WID-type policies have held sway among major development agencies, especially the "efficiency" approach which, in the context of structural adjustment, has attempted to harness women's labor in the interests of poverty alleviation and wider development objectives and tended to get women working for development than development working for women.

These kinds of assumptions translate into policies and programs that do little to benefit women and, if anything, merely serve to reinforce and exacerbate the already onerous gamut of activities for which women are responsible. For this reason, notions of empowering women through increasing control over their own lives, strengthening their capacity, and enlarging their choices are more appropriate, with due regard being given to the formulation of priorities by women in developing countries over and above those of governments and/or international agencies. Empowerment is about recognizing that grassroots inputs to plans and projects are vital and that gender-aware planning principles should be open to 'sympathetic and imaginative interpretation' in different contexts. The process of empowering women involves exposing the oppressive power of the existing gender relations, critically challenging them and creatively trying to shape different social relations.

Given that the essence of the empowerment approach to gender and development, an appropriate starting point for shelter policies might be extensive consultation with women on their short- and long-term needs for housing, income-generating opportunities, neighborhood infrastructure, and urban services. In conjunction with acknowledging women's voices, it is also important to create channels by which these might work up the various tiers of the development planning hierarchy (perhaps through NGOs which are increasingly regarded as an important entity in development), and efforts made to ensure that women's contributions to the economic and social life of cities are recognized, assisted and duly rewarded.

It is clear that there can be no hard-and-fast prescriptions for housing policy when gender divisions of labor and shelter conditions vary from place to place, and when programs and projects need to be responsive to women's needs in local contexts. Nonetheless, bearing in mind the general importance of minimizing gender inequalities in access to housing tenure, formal housing programs and credit for house purchase, and introducing gender awareness into the design of dwellings and urban services.

One critical issue for policy is recognizing diversity, not only in terms of patterns of urban growth in different societies, but in terms of different groups of women and men. While the discussion has concentrated primarily on household-based diversity in urban areas, other axes of differentiation such as ethnicity, stage in the life course, class, and so on, are also vitally important. Because women and men are not only different from each other, but in themselves form highly heterogeneous groups, this means that policies geared to alleviating disadvantage must be free of a priori and/or generalized assumptions, and explore more rigorously which particular groups (e.g., female household heads, ethnic minority women, elderly men, and/or women) are in greatest need in different spheres of shelter provision. Such initiatives will require flexibility in targeting beneficiaries. In respect to housing, for example, policy makers need to understand that nuclear families are by no means the only type of household unit in urban areas, and care must be taken to ensure that alternative domestic arrangements are catered for in shelter programs. Accepting that policy approaches to housing need to take on board the need for flexibility in household headship as well as composition, provision also needs to be made for women's access to land and property in their own right through removing discriminatory laws, institutional obstacles, and, where relevant, making moves to lessen male bias in customary inheritance practices.

Another vital factor in gender-aware shelter policy and planning is recognizing that housing is increasingly resuming its former role as an arena of production, as well as reproduction. In light of the limited likelihood of economic restructuring being accompanied by major expansion in extradomestic employment opportunities (and what this means for future poverty), steps should be taken to follow the lead of institutions, such as the United Nations Centre for Human Settlements, the International Labour Office, and the World Bank, in their recommendations for maximizing the economic utility of dwellings.

Given that women have limited assets to start business ventures and that female neighbors are often in competition with one another through the manufacture or sale of similar products, programs to promote collective community enterprises may be appropriate. These could include the provision of space, machinery, credit, skills training, and so on. Enhancing women's economic capacity in the above kinds of ways may also give them greater power to determine their household arrangements, and, in turn, further enhance individual and household survival opportunities. Indeed, although, on the one hand, the encouragement of home- or neighborhood-based economic ventures may reinforce women's identification with the domestic sphere and primarily fulfill a practical gender need, under given conditions there is scope to broach strategic gender needs through providing women with resources that enable them to exert greater control over their own lives. Moreover, given the squeeze on formal sector employment and job losses among men, investment in economic projects at the community level might encourage men to set up home- or neighborhood-based enterprises. By the same token, provision would have to be made to prevent men from taking over women's economic activities and/or pushing them out of production.

Finally, if housing is to become a greater recipient of development resources, then it is vital that decision-making over the allocation of these resources is shared in a gender-fair manner. Women in most parts of the world have long been the principal users of housing, whatever their household status. As such, they must not only be consulted but fully integrated into decision-making and, preferably, play a primary role in setting agendas. To galvanize and sustain such a process, it is not only necessary for housing professionals to be gender sensitive, but to be committed to working toward the kinds of gender transformations desired by women at the grassroots and to be responsive to changing needs and interests over time.

Whether gender-aware formulas will lead to gender-fair outcomes is, of course, another issue, and there is certainly growing acknowledgment that a shift from a "rights-based formal equality" to a "results-based substantive form" is vital to ensure that women gain their due share of development benefits. In line with the GAD approach to gender-aware policy and planning, this would require a major restructuring of gender relations and ideologies at all levels of the development process. It would also entail a diminution in the traditionally hierarchical divisions between "professional" and "popular" groups, between donors and beneficaries, and between North and South. All this is eminently desirable, but may prove to be a distant, if not unattainable, goal in a heterogeneous and unequal world. Although equal partnerships and joint visions are likely to be elusive, however, they should undoubtedly be worked at if they mean improvements and empowerment among people at the grassroots. Within this process, directing resources to women's shelter needs and priorities is essential, and could well be the means by which the dismantling of gender inequalities in urban environments is most readily assured.

Notes

1. This section of *Cities Fit for People* is based on Sylvia Chant's book, *Gender, Urban Development and Housing.* New York: UNDP, April 1996, which was published for the HABITAT II Conference. It has been edited and abbreviated by Üner Kırdar for this book.
2. Caroline Moser, "Women, Gender and Urban Development Policy: Challenges for Current and Future Research," *Third World Planning Review* 1995, 17(2): 223-235.
3. Jane Guyer and Pauline Peters. "Conceptualising the Household: Issues of Theory and Policy in Africa," *Development and Change* 1987, 18: 197-214.
4. Maureen Mackintosh, "Domestic Labour and the Household." In Sandra Burman, ed., *Fit Work for Women.* London: Croom Helm, 1979, pp. 173-191.
5. U. Kalpagam. "Women and the Household: What the Indian Data Sources Have to Offer." In K. Saradamoni, ed., *Finding the Household: Methodological and Empirical Issues.* New Delhi: Sage, 1992, pp. 75-131.
6. Barbara Harriss and Elizabeth Watson, "The Sex Ratio in South Asia." In Janet Momsen and Janet Townsend, eds., *Geography of Gender in the Third World.* London: Hutchinson, 1987, pp. 85-115.
7. Lynne Brydon and Sylvia Chant. *Women in the Third World: Gender Issues in Rural and Urban Areas.* Aldershot, England: Edward Elgar, 1989.
8. E. Wilbur Bock, Sugiyama Iutaka, and Felix Berardo, "Urbanisation and the Extended Family in Brazil." In Man Singh Das and Clinton Jesser, eds., *The Family in Latin America.* New Delhi: Vikas, 1980, pp. 161-184.
9. Michèle Barrett, *Women's Oppression Today: Problems in Marxist Feminist Analysis,* 5th ed. London: Verso, 1986.
10. Maila Stivens, "Family and State in Malaysian Industrialisation: The Case of Rembau, Negeri Sembilan, Malaysia." In Haleh Afshar, ed., *Women, State and Ideology: Studies from Africa and Asia.* Basingstoke, England: Macmillan, 1987, pp. 89-110.

11. Sarah Bradshaw, "Female-Headed Households in Honduras: Perspectives on Rural–Urban Differences," *Third World Planning Review* 1995, 17(2): 117-131.
12. Julia Cleves Mosse, *Half the World, Half a Chance: An Introduction to Gender and Development.* Oxford: Oxfam, 1993.
13. Janine Brodie, "Shifting the Boundaries: Gender and the Politics of Restructuring." In Isabella Bakker, ed., *The Strategic Silence: Gender and Economic Policy.* London: Zed, 1994.
14. Eileen Kennedy, "Development Policy, Gender of Head of Household, and Nutrition." In Eileen Kennedy and Mercedes González de la Rocha, eds., *Poverty and Well-Being in the Household: Case Studies of the Developing World.* San Diego: UCLA Center for Iberian and Latin American Studies, 1994, pp. 25-42.
15. Lynne Brydon and Karen Legge, *Adjusting Society: The IMF, the World Bank and Ghana.* London: Tauris, 1996.
16. C. H. Browner, "Women, Household and Health in Latin America," *Social Science and Medicine* 1989, 28(5): 461-473.
17. Sylvia Chant. "Family Formation and Female Roles in Querétaro, Mexico," *Bulletin of Latin American Research* 1985, 4(1): 17-32; and Sylvia Chant, "Single-Parent Families: Choice or Constraint? The Formation of Female-Headed Households in Mexican Shanty Towns," *Development and Change* 1985, 16(4): 635-656.
18. Simon Appleton, "Gender Dimensions of Structural Adjustment: The Role of Economic Theory and Quantitative Analysis," *IDS Bulletin* (Sussex) 1991, 22(1): 17-22.
20. Frans Beijard, "Rental and Rent-Free Housing as Coping Mechanisms in La Paz, Bolivia," *Environment and Urbanisation* 1995, 7(2): 167-182.
21. Carolina Moser. "The Responses of Poor Urban Households to Economic Stress: Results of a Comparative Study of Four Communities." Washington, DC: World Bank Transportation, Water and Urban Development Division (mimeograph).
22. Alan Gilbert and Josef Gugler, *Cities, Poverty and Development: Urbanisation in the Third World,* 2nd ed. Oxford: Oxford University Press, 1992.
23. Ann Valey, "Gender and Housing: The Provision of Accommodation for Young Adults in three Mexican Cities." *Habitat International* 1993, 17(4): 13-30.
24. Sylvia Chant, *Women and Survival in Mexican Cities: Perspectives on Gender, Labour Markets and Low-Income Households.* Manchester University Press, 1991.
25. Caroline Moser, "Women, Human Settlements and Housing: A Conceptual Framework for Analysis and Policy-Making." In Caroline Moser and Linda Peake, eds., *Women, Human Settlements and Housing.* London: Tavistock, 1987, pp. 12-32.

26. Valentine Moghadam, "Gender Aspects of Employment and Unemployment in a Global Perspective." In Mihály Simai (with Valentine Moghadam and Arvo Kuddo), eds., *Global Employment: An International Investigation into the Future of Work.* London: Zed, 1995, pp. 111-134, and Valentine Moghadam, "Gender Dynamics of Restructuring in the Semiperiphery." In Rae Lesser Blumberg, Cathy Rakowski, Irene Tinker, and Michael Monteón, eds., *Engendering Wealth and Well-Being: Empowerment for Global Change.* Boulder, CO: Westvicw, 1995, pp. 17-37.
27. Caroline Moser, *Gender Planning and Development: Theory, Practice and Training.* London: Routledge, 1993.

Section 2 From Women's Perspective: Globalization, Economic Growth, and Social Policies

Noeleen Heyzer

The world is undergoing a massive process of globalization. Capital, labor, and goods are moving much more rapidly across national boundaries, unleashing much fiercer international competition. In addition to the speed of technological change, there is the computerization of production and communications systems. This has brought about changes in employment patterns, destroying many jobs and creating others. The international mass media have gained new importance: their news programs are not merely reporting events, but also helping determine their course. Societies are becoming more and more knowledge based. All this has dramatic consequences for the shape of human society as we move toward the twenty-first century. The process of globalization has opened up new opportunities but also exposed us to new risks. There are increasingly complex problems that criss-cross national boundaries. These global economic and political trends have a specific impact on women's lives and work.

Women and Six Areas of Concern

International Migration

The global extension of market forces, especially in indebted societies, has been deeply disruptive for many people and communities. Many have been forced to migrate in search of a better life. At the end of 1993, 100 million people were living outside their country of citizenship. The issue here is that many developing countries are losing some of their most talented and educated people. At the same time, US $70 billion are earned each year through remittances. Added to these are millions of refugees who have been driven across national frontiers by famine, drought, war, or environmental problems. Today, in addition to men, millions of women are on the move, migrating across borders. The most important categories are women refugees and women migrating in search of livelihoods. In many war-torn areas, ecologically fragile zones, and communities undergoing economic and social disintegration, women and children comprise 75 percent of the some 16 million affected and displaced people.

Criminality

Globalization is making crime much more transnational. And criminals are the first to take advantage of any relaxation of national controls and advances in transportation and communication. Drug trafficking, money laundering, and trafficking in women and children are three of the most widespread activities. More than US $100 billion of drug money have been laundered annually in Europe and North America during the past decade. The illegal drug business is now a huge transnational industry worth US $500 billion a year.

Rebuilding Wartorn Nations

In 1993, there were 52 major conflicts in 42 countries, mainly in Eastern Europe, Central Asia, and Africa, involving large numbers of civilians and high levels of brutality and collective violence. As many as 90 percent of war casualties in recent years are not soldiers, but noncombatants, mostly women and children.

Ecological Destruction

The world is facing an ecological crisis as never before. There has been an extensive loss of natural resources on which our livelihoods depend, including the loss of forests, flora and fauna, topsoil, water quality, and air quality. The current rate of resource extraction is 10,000 times the rate of renewal. The worldwide consumption of energy resources has grown even faster than the population, with an estimated 20 to 25 percent increase in energy use versus an 8 percent increase in population since 1985. This unsustainable rate of resource use is threatening the livelihood base of future generations. On top of this, there are problems of toxic waste management that have severe consequences for our health and the health of all living species.

Growth of Unregulated Markets

Although many national institutions are being weakened and communities and families are forced to take on added burdens, other institutions are enjoying much greater freedom without any increase in responsibility. Everyday US $1 trillion change hands in the capital markets, creating billionaires overnight, but also impoverishing many. Transnational company sales in 1992 were US $5.5 trillion, untouched by any form of international regulations or code of conduct. In the shift to unregulated markets, social safety nets and other support systems have eroded or stretched to breaking points. Policies come to be made by people and institutions that are more and more remote from the suffering. Deregulation of the current scale have allowed too many economic actors to free themselves from social, ethical, and political constraints. This will continue to threaten sustainable human development by dismantling the social fabric on which even economic efficiency depends.

Family Fragmentation

Many governments want families to take over responsibility for meeting social needs in the era of globalization. Yet the process of economic globalization itself is dispersing family members further apart and creating more heterogeneous types of family. Many people blame recent changes in family structures for all social ills—from rising crime to teenage pregnancies to increased drug abuse. The recommendation is to promote "family values." In reality, changes in personal relationships and family relationships are less a major cause of social and economic changes, than a response to them.

Women's Lives in the Era of Globalization

We are entering the twenty-first century with a rather uncertain situation for women. The "feminization of poverty" has become a global phenomenon. The number of rural women living in poverty has nearly doubled in the last 20 years. Women constitute at least 70 percent of the world's 1.3 billion absolute poor. Women within poor countries and communities are more impoverished than men are. In African countries, for example, women account for more than 60 percent of the agricultural labor force, contribute up to 80 percent of the total food production, and receive less than 10 percent of the credit available to small farmers and less than 1 percent of the total credit available to agriculture. The impoverishment of women is also the impoverishment of children. In developing countries, over 95 million children are working.

We need to understand the underlying causes for the feminization of poverty. One is women's reduced access to increasingly scarce resources. In the context of competitive unregulated markets, women are particularly affected by the fierce competition over scarce resources—in particular, land and the means of livelihood. A consequence of this competitive resource use and allocation is the dislocation and dispossession of many communities. This has led to an increase of female-headed families struggling to survive, with very little capacity to take advantage of any new economic opportunities.

Women earn one tenth of the world's income and own less than 1 percent of the world's property, but work two thirds of the world's working hours. Globally, women's labor force participation has increased by only 3 percent in 20 years, from 37 percent in 1970 to 40 percent in 1990. Women's wages are generally only three quarters of men's wages in the nonagricultural sector in 56 countries. Although women's work is already seriously undervalued, their work burden increases when support systems break down.

These existing inequalities may be further deepened and new inequalities may emerge in the context of the two global trends, namely (1) the economic shift to competitive, unregulated markets; and (2) the changing political nature of nation–states. The gains made over the last twenty years in terms of reducing the gender gap in education and health may be lost. The effort to close the remaining gender gaps in basic needs over the next decade through an accelerated investment in sustainable human development at country level may be derailed unless key interventions are urgently made. Without these, gender gaps may even widen.

Otherwise, the picture we will have is women working longer hours, taking care of the sick, the young, and the old, and women maintaining households on reduced resources. We will also see the increased transmission of intergenerational poverty along gender lines as girls are deprived of scarce household resources, held back from school, and expected to be the family's secondary nurturer. Women currently form 60 percent of the 1 billion adults who have no access to basic education. Girls constitute the majority of the 130 million children who have no access to primary schooling. These numbers may even increase if no positive action is taken. In other words, the feminization of poverty will worsen and there will be more societal breakdowns. This could be a life-and-death situation for girls. As it is, there are already 100 million missing girls as a result of infanticide.

Competitive Unregulated Markets

In the shift to unregulated markets, social safety nets and other support systems have been seriously eroded or stretched. The people and institutions that create policy are increasingly remote from those who suffer. Deregulation on the current scale has allowed too many economic actors to free themselves of any social, ethical, or political constraints. This will threaten sustainable human development by eroding the social cohesion on which efficiency depends.

The current economic situation has been described as a "champagne glass civilization," in which 20 percent of humanity controls 85 percent of the world's income and the bottom 15 percent survives on only 1.4 percent. We have a world where 358 individuals have accumulated personal capital worth approximately US$762 billion. This is concurrent with the fact that in many countries, there is a diminishing middle class. In short, the gap between rich and poor is widening.

We tend to forget that the most successful economic miracles in East Asia occurred in countries that pursued coherent national development strategies. They invested in social development, including women's education. They built strong national industrial and technological foundations. They intervened heavily in the market to channel investments toward strategic sectors, thereby containing income inequality.

Women have a particular interest in regulating markets. They have suffered disproportionately as deregulation has undermined that ability of society to protect the social quality of everyday life. There have been cuts in social security and revenue for human development. Of particular concern is the impact on women's work:

- Women continue to be the last to benefit from job expansion and the first to suffer from job contraction. This imbalance frequently forces women to create their own jobs and enterprises, usually with few resources and little support.
- The casualization of women's work has occurred because many of the jobs created in the recent industrial expansion represent a shift to flexible labor relations, in which labor-intensive, lower-paid informal activities are subcontracted to women.
- The deregulation of labor markets affects women by undermining whatever protective regulation had existed on wages, benefits, and working hours.

The clear message is that the unregulated market has simultaneously created the new rich and the new poor. Women have become steadily poorer in the struggle for scarce resources, and a denser concentration of wealth has taken place at the top of a steep pyramid. When resources are scarce, gender hierarchies tend to be more rigid in the allocation of resources. Women often end up having no land, fewer livelihood resources, less food, less health care, less education, and lower economic returns for their labor.

Markets and States

The relationship among women, markets, and states is complex. The market does not always act against women, nor does the state act always on women's behalf. The interplay of market forces, state policies, and women's lives must be evaluated through the lens of concrete experience, particularly the experience of daily life. Poor women's lives are structured not just by markets and states, but through the interaction of class, gender, and ethnicity, as well by their roles as producers and reproducers within distinct household, community, and kinship systems. The concept of gender, here defined as the power relationship that allows both men and women equal access to the scarce and valued resources of their society, provides a useful yardstick of evaluation. Most women do not have an interest in "reducing the role of the state and increasing the role of the market" or vice versa. Rather, they want decent wages, employment, leisure, health-care, education, personal autonomy, and the ability to make decisions about their own lives. Therefore, the important question is not the simplistic market versus state opposition, but more complex considerations, such as what kind of market growth and which types of state-led development improve specific aspects of gender equity, and how both markets and states can be restructured to improve the life chances of women.

Markets and Women

The Asian development experience provides useful data about the effects of different types of market growth and state interventions on women's lives. It can be classified into four categories: high growth with social development (Japan and Korea); fluctuating growth with social development (Malaysia, Thailand, and Indonesia); low growth with social development (Vietnam, Sri Lanka, and China in the late 1970s); and low growth with low investment in social development (a substantial number of South Asian countries).

With high growth with social development policies, on the whole, women have profited from investment in education, health care, and new employment opportunities. However, the degree to which individual women enjoy the benefits of social development varies greatly according to their class, ethnicity, age, and geographic origin. For example, high growth based on the promotion of labor-intensive export industries greatly expanded the manufacturing-sector employment of young, single women with some secondary-level education. These women earn independent incomes and have access to urban facilities, contacts, and services. Despite these advantages, however, they are paid relatively low wages, have few prospects of upward mobility, and face numerous occupational hazards. Growth in the commercial, financial, and service sectors, together with rising educational levels, have resulted in the formation of a large middle class. Middle-class, educated women have entered the labor market, but the ensuing problems of social reproduction remain unresolved. In the Korean and Japanese cases, women leave the formal market after marriage and work part-time, enter the informal sector, or become unpaid workers at home. In Singapore, the burden of social reproduction and household work is transferred to migrant domestics from low-growth countries.

Growth in the fluctuating economies of the Asian countries was initially natural resource and commodity-based. The drop in commodity prices worldwide in the 1980s and issues of trade created pressure for a restructuring of the agricultural sector and greater involvement in the industrial and service sectors. These changes have had varied impacts on women. In Malaysia, for example, the plantation sector's shift from rubber to palm oil precipitated an outmigration of male rubber tappers. The ensuing labor shortage gave incentive to plantation owners to regularize the status of previously part-time female workers, increase their salaries, and provide maternity allowances, housing, child care, and nearby schooling. By the late 1980s, however, commodity price fluctuations led to the replacement of women workers with illegal male migrants from low-growth, war-torn, and poverty-stricken neighboring countries.

Rural–urban migration has been another result of the shift from agriculture to service-oriented economies. In Malaysia, the New Economic Policy and the establishment of employment quotas for various ethnic groups has encouraged young Malay women to migrate to the cities. In Thailand, rural–urban inequities generated by the growth process have led to indebted parents bonding and selling their young daughters into domestic service or prostitution in the cities. Other rural families rely on the remittances of daughters employed in urban centers. Despite the urban boom, however, female outmigration outstrips the expansion in labor demand in the manufacturing and informal sectors, pushing many young migrants into risky and demeaning work in the so-called entertainment industry.

Finally, some growth processes have in fact created new patterns of poverty and deprivation, as livelihood systems of the poor are destroyed to further the interests of the powerful. For example, in many Asian countries, timber logging is carried out by "rent-seeking" outsiders, who exploit an area's natural resources as quickly as possible without, as with entrepreneurs, a stake in investing in the region, creating jobs for the local population, and ensuring sustainability. Logging causes deforestation, amendments to native land tenure, soil erosion, water quality degradation, and the loss of forest products, fisheries, and animals. These changes are devastating to livelihoods dependent on gathering, hunting, and swidden agriculture, as are those of many indigenous groups. The effect on women is particularly adverse: shortages and contamination of essential natural resources mean longer hours of work, heavier workloads, a drop in nutritional status and income, an increase in environment-related illness, and a breakdown in traditional resource management systems that gave significant control to women. Furthermore, the outmigration of men whose livelihoods have been destroyed means a greater burden for women.

Countries dominated by the low-growth agricultural sector and characterized by high rates of poverty and landlessness are found primarily in South Asia. Profound rural poverty creates pressures for people to move to urban squatter settlements and pavement living; however, life for the poor in the urban centers is little better, with employment primarily concentrated in the informal sector and access to water, sewage, and other public services severely limited.

Technological changes introduced in the agricultural sector have not necessarily benefited women living in poverty. In India, the Green Revolution, with its package of improved seeds and technology, better irrigation, and chemical fertilizers, has increased employment of casual laborers not only because of increased yields, but also because modernization has been accompanied by the resumption of land and the eviction of tenants by landowners. Increased demand for labor has not increased wages or standards of living, particularly for women, who are commonly paid 40 percent to 60 percent of male wages for the more arduous tasks of weeding, transplanting, and harvesting. In land programs like the Mahaweli Scheme of Sri Lanka, ownership of land is bestowed on the male heads of household regardless of traditional inheritance rights of women.

Structural adjustment policies adopted by these countries at the behest of the IMF and World Bank, which seek to improve private-sector incentives through changes in prices, taxes, subsidies, and interest rates, and to release resource for the private sector by reducing public-sector expenditure, have taken a serious toll on poor women. A key component of adjustment programs is an increase in food prices and the removal of food subsidies. When higher prices force poor households to reduce food consumption in areas with rigid gender hierarchies, women and girls end up eating less than men and boys. When charges are introduced for previously free health care or schooling, it is women and girls who go without. What is then regarded at the macrolevel as "increased efficiency" is actually the transfer of cost from the paid economy to the unpaid, "elastic" work of women, who take the government's place in caring for the sick, the elderly, and the young, who go without food, school, or medical care, and who work longer hours.

Countries with low growth with social development, which are commonly called "command economies," were initially successful in generating growth, meeting basic needs, and addressing equity and social development. Deliberate steps were taken to give women equal rights and to provide education, health care, independent incomes, low-cost child-care, and housing. Because of too much bureaucracy and a lack of incentives, innovation, and technological change, however, these states could not compete in the global economic system and therefore moved to decentralize decision-making, cut social security, and open up to international markets. In the former Soviet Republics of Central Asia, the change from command to market economy has been sudden (the "big bang" approach), whereas in China, Vietnam, and Laos, the transition has been more gradual. The opening to investments from high-growth Asian neighbors has introduced profit as a dominant force, thus intensifying problems related to overextraction of resources, bad business practices, segmented labor markets, and cuts in social services.

Women's experience in transitional economies in many ways mirrors their encounter with structural adjustment, although it varies according to the type of transition. The "big bang" transition has precipitated sky-rocketing food and housing prices, medicine shortages, increased male alcoholism, and decreased subsidies, child care, and other social security services.

In the gradualist approach, represented by China, the reorganization of the commune and the adoption of the household responsibility system created incentives and rewarded production at the family level. The expansion of "sideline occupations," crop diversification, rural industrialization, and the formation of special agricultural zones contributed to an overall decline in rural–urban inequity, although inequity increased within and between rural areas. Men are moving away from farms in search of more lucrative work and women are assuming the major responsibility for the household agricultural system, increasing their burden. There is a return to high rates of female illiteracy as daughters leave school to help their mothers. The formation of village and private enterprises has provided new employment, particularly for educated women, but those without skills suffer doubly: from exclusion from new opportunities and cutbacks in the protective systems of social security. New patterns of impoverishment have been created, leaving some women and their children to work as beggars.

States and Women

State structures are changing throughout the world. Some types may not continue to exist; many are not held accountable. The global process of political restructuring that is underway has created the following types of states:

1. The command states have either collapsed economically or become transitional.
2. Many welfare states that have tried to be responsible to their people have declined economically and have become debtor states.
3. The more affluent states have become major players in and facilitators of the global market. They are becoming increasingly responsive to the market and to the corporate sector. The welfare of people is seen primarily in terms of economic efficiency.
4. There are also corrupt states where power cliques have captured governmental positions, but have not allocated resources to their people. Instead, they have appropriated the resources of the state as a private estate for themselves.
5. There are states that have totally collapsed in wartorn situations.
6. There are also emerging state formations based on ethnic and religious fundamentalism.

Although weak states have sometimes been accompanied by the rise of ethnicity, the spread of gangsterism, the growth of violence, and an unraveling of the fabric of society, strong states, too, have created problems, chief among them authoritarianism, bureaucratic rigidity, the promotion of class interests, and the enforcement of patriarchal values. As with the market, the question is not whether women are for or against the state, but rather what kind of state-led development is good for women.

States that invest in social development will benefit women. Such investment is found in states with high economic growth—such as Singapore and Malaysia, as well as in those with lower economic growth—such as China and Vietnam during the heyday of the command economy. This is borne out by UNDP's 1995 *Human Development Report* that focuses on the measurement of gender equality as an important index of human development. An important finding of this report is that gender equity does not correlate with the income level of a society. This has important policy implications, since it debunks the argument that gender equity is a "luxury" that poor countries cannot afford.

The existence today of state planning and antipoverty programs in Asia stems from the evolution of development theory from the "trickle-down" approach of the 1950s and 1960s to the "basic needs" thrust of the 1970s. Although in the 1980s structural adjustment began to push aside both of these approaches, macroplanning and antipoverty programs are still an important feature of state-led development efforts. A typical state-led development plan involves a definition of objectives and an allocation/mobilization of resources across sectors. A plan generally has hard and soft sections, the former being the core productive sectors of the economy, while the latter includes poverty alleviation and programs with so-called social objectives. In general, the soft sections receive fewer resources, their accountability is weak, and they are viewed by planners as unproductive. Women are commonly dealt with as a special group within the poverty program or through bureaus or departments within ministries. As structural adjustment squeezes the soft sections of development plans, women's concerns get crowded out.

Two key assumptions shape planners' attitudes: first, they see a trade-off between the productive and soft sectors; and second, they believe that the sectoral approach is the only possible way to plan. The trade-off paradigm sees resource allocation as a zero-sum game; what goes to the soft sector is then lost to the productive sector. What planners fail to recognize is that for the large section of the population below the poverty line, the trade-off is meaningless. Women are generally by-passed by macrolevel increases in production or productivity, but tend to bear the brunt of cuts in the soft-sections of the plan. If there is a trade-off, it is not between production and poverty alleviation in the abstract, but between those who benefit when the former is stressed versus those whose interests lie in the latter. The second axiom relates to sectoral planning. Insufficient attention has been paid to the possibility of combining area planning with sectoral planning. The former has greater potential for a holistic approach to an area's problems, allows more room for local-level problem definition, and does not generate situations in which sectoral plans work at cross purposes.

In addition to these key axiomatic assumptions, numerous other untested stereotypes also color the vision of the world that informs state planners' policy recommendations. Chief among them is the notion that men support households, when, in fact, men and women do so together (or, increasingly, women do so alone). The use of the household rather than household members as the unit of analysis also creates policy risk, for it ignores economic and social behaviors that occur within and without the household. Households do not think with one mind; their members can have competing as well as complementary needs. There are gender differences in intrahousehold allocation of production and consumption and these differences affect the quality of family life, the nutritional status and educational level of children, and household stability itself. Other misleading assumptions are the artificial distinction drawn between domestic and nondomestic work and the identification of the nuclear family as the basic social unit. Policies misinformed by a vision of women as dependent housewives and secondary workers in nuclear households not only plant the seeds of their own eventual failure, they also validate and reinforce the patriarchal gender ideology that keeps women in a subordinate position both socially and economically.

The state is not a coherent, monolithic, and easily defined entity any more than the household is. The state has multidimensional aspects, some of which contradict and even oppose one another. Policies of some state agencies may help women, while others unintentionally hinder them. Ultimately, it is important for women to know more about the political, economic, and social conditions of different types of states, as well as the multidimensional aspects of state policy and the contradictions within it.

Development Alternatives

The development experience of many Asian countries is marked by a reliance upon both the market and the state to address problems of economic growth and social equity. The combinations of markets and state-led development, the nature and degree of market orientation, the character of the policy environment with regard to popular participation, and the involvement of nongovernmental actors in policy formulation have varied widely in the region. State, market, and policy environment have played both distinct and interdependent roles in confronting poverty;

their interaction with questions of gender equity, however, is more complex.

Women's access to both formal and informal markets has afforded them new employment and income-generating opportunities, allowing them to earn independent incomes and to increase their bargaining power within the household. Despite these gains, however, women are unable to compete with men on equal terms because of the gender differentials in levels of education, skill, information, burden of work, and capital. Government support to the private sector goes to large foreign and local enterprises owned mainly by men, and competition from these large firms puts severe limitations on the market opportunities open to poor women. Women are thus marginalized and forced into the nooks and crevices of the economy. Not only are the number of opportunities seriously curtailed, but the quality of market openings for women is also second rate. Women work disproportionately in the informal sector where their jobs are not stable, their benefits are few to none, they are subject to harassment by police and exploitation by middlemen, and their bargaining power and freedom to organize are virtually nonexistent. At the same time, the commercialization of common property and cutbacks in and privatization of health-care, education, and social security have deprived women in poverty of ways to improve their lot.

Although governments can intervene to bring about social equity, often they do not, for states themselves reflect the interests of powerful, organized groups and are subject to pressures by donor agencies. Because women in poverty are many societies' most powerless and marginalized citizens, they have the greatest difficulty in holding states accountable in meeting their needs. By and large, cuts in public expenditures, ways of promoting productivity and growth, and patterns of resource allocation have been designed and implemented without incorporating the experiences of poor women.

The types of state-led development efforts that can have positive effects on gender equity are those that invest in social development by increasing women's access to education and training; introduce and uphold health and safety regulations; provide services such as sanitation, transportation, and child care; establish a legal framework for the regulation of the market so that the entitlements of the poor can be strengthened through better access and protection; acknowledge poor women's productive and reproductive roles; and recognize women as citizens in their own right and not as "dependents," "target groups," or "instruments of development."

For women to hold both market and state accountable, poor women's rights to their own person and labor, to land, capital, and opportunities, and to active participation in the public sphere must first be strengthened. To further this end, the potential role of education, nongovernmental organizations, and women's groups in developing the capacity of poor women to define, defend, and exercise their rights through the empowerment process cannot be understated. However, many women's groups and NGOs must themselves face and resolve issues of fragmentation, tensions, institutional capacity, and lack of accountability that stem from different visions, approaches, strategies, and personality styles, as well as competition for scarce resources, within various social movements. Increasingly, NGOs are called upon to take the place of the state in service delivery, with complex results. While increased partnership has improved the relationship between NGOs and the state in some cases, in others it has curbed the ability of NGOs to act as advocates for poor women and inhibited their ability to make women's voices heard and create pressure for the development of market and state alternatives.

Market and state alternatives that would benefit poor women include four components: economic growth with social equity; sustainable livelihoods (defined as how people survive, produce, consume, and reproduce in conditions of social inequality); social justice (people's basic needs and their right to political participation); and ecological sustainability and renewability in the context of finite natural resources.

To bring these alternatives into practice, women's networks and their strategic allies have worked to make market and state-led development more responsive to gender and poverty and to promote true gender equity by moving women's needs and interests out of the "soft," social realm and into the such productive sectors as agriculture and industry. They have also worked to expand women's opportunities in the labor market, to increase women's bargaining power, and to reform laws, regulations, and programs that directly impinge on the working lives and economic well being of women. Women have reexamined and sought to improve development models in the areas of women, work, and poverty and have stepped outside the dominant paradigms to question development models themselves.

Key to the vision of those who hope to promote an alternative conception of development is women's empowerment. Women's empowerment has four components: women's sense of internal strength and confidence to face life; the right to determine choices; the power to control their own lives within and outside the home; and the ability to influence the direction of social change toward the creation of a more just social and economic order nationally and internationally.

The concept of empowerment emphasizes women's freedom of choice and power to control their own lives at both the personal level within the home and at the public level of socioeconomic change. The challenge now is to direct these strategies of empowerment to the creation of markets and states responsive to women's needs and contributions as both producers and reproducers.

Sustainable Human Development

The concept of "sustainable human development" promoted by the United Nations is a major step forward in the promotion of an ethic of equity. As stated by James Gustave Speth, the Administrator of the United Nations Development Programme, "Sustainable human development is development that is pro-poor, pro-nature, pro-jobs, and pro-women. It gives priority to the poor, enlarging their choices and opportunities and providing for their participation in decisions affecting them.

Development, to be truly sustainable, must have three key dimensions, namely, (1) ecological sustainability, (2) economic sustainability, and (3) social sustainability.

The global environmental crisis cannot be addressed nor can there be sustainable development if the livelihoods of local communities are at risk. Yet there is a seeming contradiction between shorter-term economic needs and longer-term ecological imperatives. On the one hand, shorter-term economic needs have to be met without destroying long-term concerns for sustainability. On the other hand, longer-term ecological imperatives have to be addressed without neglecting the immediate livelihood needs of local communities. There is thus an urgent need to balance economic viability with ecological sustainability in an increasingly globalized world economy, where the social crisis of poverty converges with environmental crisis.

Women in many societies mediate between these dualities. Women's reproductive labor, both biological and social, underwrites the entire process of human development. Not only do women bear and rear children, they are usually the managers of local resources on which everyday life depends. They attend to the long-term ecological imperatives of sustainability and renewability, while also attending to the short-term livelihood needs of families and communities. In conditions of rapid change – including environmental degradation, the outmigration of men, changing economic activities and aspirations, and government interventions – women play an even more crucial role in the maintenance of livelihoods, cultural continuity, and community cohesiveness.

At the Fourth World Conference of Women, 40,000 women gathered to affirm the kind of world they want to live in. This world is one where development processes will empower people and women in particular. It has to be one where we can create sustainable livelihoods, build stable lives in healthy communities, where we can build peace and resolve conflict on a long-term basis. For this to happen, we need a new development ethics and morality to be placed at the core of development thinking and practice. This has to include the perspectives and realities of women's lives.

Women: A Global Force for Change

Women are a global force in the shaping of international development debates and in providing directions for sustainable human development. This has been most evident at the recent series of UN Conferences,

These conferences marked a turning point for the international women's movement. Women were highly visible as leaders of civil society, who were able to introduce a gender perspective into all development issues. The advocacy of the women's movement at these international conferences was spearheaded by a strategic coalition that spanned international, national, and nongovernment organizations. As a result, a consensus achieved at these conferences is the recognition that none of these global developmental issues can be adequately addressed without focussing on women's realities and perspectives.

The 1992 UN Conference on Environment and Development, popularly known as the Earth Summit, is important as the first conference on an issue that is not conventionally identified as a women's issue, but that nevertheless highlighted women's key role in the management of natural resources. This was largely the result of the active role played by the international women's movement in placing women's concerns on the environmental agenda. In preparation for the Earth Summit, women's NGOs organized regional meetings that culminated in a Global Assembly in Miami, Florida, in November 1991. This led to a World Women's Congress for a Healthy Planet that a statement called the Women's Action Agenda 21, demanding that women's concerns on environmental issues be addressed by the UN Conference on Environment and Development (UNCED). Consequently, governments did indeed recognize women's vital role in achieving ecological sustainability.

At the World Conference on Human Rights held in Vienna in 1993, the Women's Movement played a key role in putting forward the issue of women's rights as human rights in both private and public domains. The issue of violence against women was taken up as a human rights issue. This expanded the scope of human rights beyond conventional civil liberties. Women made clear, in solidarity with the international community, that there must be respect for the human rights and dignity of all persons in all domains, if development is to be effective. This transformed the human rights movement, allowing it to see private rights as a necessary precondition of public civil rights, to draw lessons from violence against women to war, and to bring on board economic and political rights as simultaneously necessary—not one before the other.

The International Conference on Population and Development (ICPD) in Cairo held in 1994 was a watershed for its visible demonstration that women must be central to any population policy and development goal. Women again took center stage at this conference. Their participation substantially changed the outcome of the debate on population. Because of women's concerted lobbying, the population debate was widened beyond its prior concerns, which centered on family planning and sometimes coercive birth control, without regard to women's health. Women's empowerment, health, and reproductive rights are now recognized as the cornerstone of effective population policies. The radical shift at Cairo was that, for the first time, the population issue was discussed not just as a technical, demographic problem to be handled only by experts, but as a choice that women should be empowered to make, within the context of their reproductive health and rights.

At the World Summit on Social Development in Copenhagen, women put forward the issue that poverty eradication cannot be achieved without addressing women's economic needs and priorities. Governments and international organizations at this Conference recognized that poverty has a female face.

The Fourth World Conference of Women in Beijing built on the consensus reached at these previous UN Conferences that women's realities and perspectives are central to all issues of global development. The Women's Movement has thus participated actively in setting the agenda of the development debate across a whole range of issues. As a result, the Women's Movement is now a broad yet coherent movement that takes on all issues related to human society, yet remains unified by a gender perspective that views gender equity as a core ethic of development.

Finally, the Second Conference on Human Settlements (HABITAT II) in Istanbul clearly recognized that sustainable human settlements cannot be achieved unless gender equality is realized in human settlements development. Therefore, governments committed themselves to promote the full and equal participation of women in developing related legislation policy, programs, and projects.

These UN Conferences are not just one-off events. All of them were preceded by preparatory processes that involved all sectors of society and all of them are followed by long-term implementation processes at global, regional, and national levels. The Women's Movement has played a very key role both in setting the agenda, as well as in ensuring that the recommendations and gains achieved at the regional and international level would make a difference to the lives of women in local communities and at the national level. In this process, new partnerships are being forged between governments and civil society, between women and men, between local communities and international organizations.

Conclusion

The UN is currently the only international forum with near-universal membership. In a world where all issues are increasingly global issues, the UN is needed more than ever. At this time of global need, if we did not have the UN, we would have had to invent it from scratch.

The UN was founded in the aftermath of World War II, with the nations of the world envisioning a global institution that would promote international peace, security and cooperation. This great founding vision was partly frozen during the forty years of the Cold War. But now with the ending of the Cold War and with the celebration of its first fifty years, the UN is going through a process of reform to revitalize its founding vision and to increase its effectiveness and credibility in dealing with an increasingly complex world where so many problems cut across national boundaries. This process of reform can be achieved only if the realities and concerns of women as half the world are placed squarely on the development agenda of the UN. Women's voices coming up from all levels of society must thus be heard loud and clear at the highest levels of decision-making within the UN system to bring about the economic and political empowerment of women all around the world.

Section 3 Women's Participation in Urban Employment

Valentine M. Moghadam

As more and more women have entered the labor force in countries throughout the world, development specialists and women's advocates have called for increased attention to the problems and prospects of women's employment, particularly in large urban settings. The supply of job-seeking women has grown in tandem with the demand for female labor in the services and industrial sectors, and this pool of women includes urban dwellers, recent rural migrants, immigrants, and foreign contract workers. These female workers may be young, single women, married women, or women maintaining households alone. Nevertheless, social policies, labor legislation, and the urban infrastructure have not kept up with the large-scale entry of women in urban labor markets, with the differentiation of the female labor force, or with the vicissitudes of women's labor-force entry and exit. Education and training programs for women are not extensive, leaving women workers vulnerable to recession, increasing labor-market competition, and redundancies. Existing legislation providing social protection for women workers tends to be limited in scope and coverage, with benefits reaching a relatively small proportion of the total urban female labor force. At the same time, such legislation, including maternity leave provisions, childcare facilities, and affirmative-action-type programs to encourage the employment of women, have come under attack in the context of the expansion of neoliberal economic policies. As a result, many countries have streamlined the entitlements and programs geared to women in the work force. Apart from the harm done to children and families, these cutbacks limit women's ability to participate fully in market activities and to compete fairly with men in the labor market. Unemployment or deteriorating real incomes have forced women in some countries to enter into prostitution.

It is therefore necessary to reconsider some of the recent policy reforms and to reorient current thinking in the direction of promoting habitats of sustainable human development. This would include attention to the ways and means of enlarging the choices available to women in urban labor markets—enabling the formation of women's human capabilities (such as improved health, knowledge, and skills) partly by improving the social and physical infrastructure. In this way, women may contribute to economic growth and national development while also themselves reaping the economic, social, and political benefits of the development process. This section addresses the issue of promoting the participation of women with appropriate urban social policies, through a focus on women's urban employment in developing countries.

Production, Reproduction, and Gender

During the past 20 years women-in-development (WID) specialists have successfully demonstrated how women across different types of societies, cultures, and stages of development are situated in the spheres of production and reproduction, through their market- and nonmarket-oriented roles as workers and producers, as consumers, as care providers, and as household and community managers.[1] More recently, gender-and-development (GAD) research and sociological studies have sought to show the links among gender (as distinct from the individual, as in neoclassical economics, or class, as in Marxist theory), labor market processes, and social policies.[2] The concept of gender—defined as the asymmetrical relationship between men and women (its structural dimension) and as the social meanings given to biological sex differences (its cultural dimension)—is a key analytical category for understanding the differential access of men and women to resources, the differential allocation of rewards to men and women, and the assumptions and biases inherent in the framework of policies and legislation. The literature on labor markets shows that gender is one of the "fault lines" in segmented labor markets and a good predictor of the distribution of rewards and costs among different categories of women and men.[3] The literature on structural adjustment shows how the interaction of gender with market processes and neoliberal economic thought results in greater burdens for women, particularly in their unpaid reproductive roles.[4] Women's access to productive activities, including employment, and the amount of time spent on unpaid reproductive activities, are shaped largely by social class (including education and family income), but they are also greatly influenced by public policies. That is, although gender is itself a predictor of access to resources and location in the spheres of production and reproduction, the state can intervene to provide an enabling environment for women's participation. This it can do through appropriate social policies, labor legislation, and infrastructural development.

During the 1970s and 1980s female labor-force participation grew significantly throughout the world. This was caused by an increase in the supply of job-seeking women and the demand for female labor in white-collar and blue-collar occupations alike. East and Southeast Asia saw the most spectacular increases in levels of female employment (around 40 percent of the labor force in 1990); in Eastern Europe and the former Soviet Union half the labor force consisted of women in full-time employment; and Western Europe and North America saw a trend in the labor-force attachment of women, including that of married women with children. Even regions where cultural restrictions and economic structures inhibited female employment—specifically, the Middle East, North Africa, and South Asia—saw increases in women's labor-force participation and in their share of the urban labor force. On a global basis, some 37 percent of women over the age of 15 are engaged in productive activities, comprising more than one third of the labor force. In postindustrial countries, women's participation is nearly equal to that of men, and is concentrated in public and private services. In developing and industrializing countries, women are similarly largely found in the professional/technical, clerical/service, and sales occupations, followed by manufacturing/transportation and administration/ management.[5] In some manufacturing sectors, however, such as in export-oriented enterprises producing textiles, garments, toys, or electronics in Mexico, South Korea, China, and Tunisia, women may predominate. The manufacturing sector claims more than 25 percent of the female labor force only in the East Asian NICs, the former socialist countries, Tunisia, and Morocco. Throughout the world, the largest concentrations of women workers are in public and private services ("community, social, and personal services"), and especially in the areas of health, education, and social welfare—which is an example of the way that gender influences occupational distribution.

Another example of the way that gender influences labor-market processes is the well-known fact of the earnings gap. Women are paid less than men, especially in the manufacturing sector. In countries such as South Korea and Japan women workers' wages are only half of those of male workers. In other sectors, the gender gap in wages is narrowing, but women still lack access to high-paying jobs and to managerial and supervisory positions. Globally, women earn on average 74.9 percent of men's wages, and countries where women's earnings are even lower include the U.K., Hong Kong, Ireland, Thailand, Argentina, Canada, Philippines, Cyprus, Chile, Syria, China, South Korea, and Bangladesh. Moreover, women everywhere perform a balancing act between the market and the household, and public policy generally overlooks this gender difference. For women in the formal labor market—that is, the public sector and large private enterprises—employment-related social insurance is available, and labor legislation usually provides for such gender-specific entitlements as paid maternity leave with job-back guarantees, and, in industrial enterprises, creches and nursing breaks for new mothers. However, these entitlements are not enjoyed by women in the informal sector, in domestic service, or in home-working arrangements.

The burden of social reproduction is carried mainly by women, but much of this work is unacknowledged, unremunerated, or underenumerated. In developing countries, women's participation and contribution to the national product is insufficiently covered by national statistical systems because of the inadequate coverage of the informal sector and of women's unpaid family labor. This has resulted in a neglect of policies for women, or inattention to the gender-specific effects of economic policies. In recent years, however, the growing awareness of the importance of unpaid labor by women in developing countries has resulted in studies that attempt to quantify this economic contribution. These studies measure the activity either by the number of hours women spend at work (and the intensity of work), the economic value of this time, the volume of their production, or the value of what they produce.

Unpaid reproductive activities and intense time use are especially great among the urban poor, including low-income working-class women with family responsibilities. These are the women for whom changes in social services—such as the introduction of "user fees" for healthcare and schooling, and higher costs for childcare—result in greater care-giving, as well as financial, burdens. Similarly, higher costs for public transportation, if combined with low wages and family responsibilities, could act as a disincentive to labor-force participation, although this issue is underresearched. It should be noted that the same market forces that compel poor urban women to drop out of the labor force because of low wages, high costs, and family responsibilities, penalize them with even lower wages when they reenter.

Globalization, Urban Employment, and Social Policies for Working Women

A number of factors have converged to increase the proportion of women in the urban labor force. The supply of job-seeking women has been influenced by such demographic factors as the expansion of literacy and educational attainment among women, delayed marriage, declining fertility, increased divorce, and household headship. Improvements in home technology easing the burden of domestic labor is another factor. Declining wages received by male household members could also induce women to seek jobs to supplement the household budget. Thus economic need as well as personal aspiration have increased the supply of job-seeking women in cities throughout the world. At the same time, the supply of women has been responding to demand, or the availability of opportunities. The demand for women workers has been influenced by such factors as new technologies, the deskilling of some occupations, investment patterns, managerial preferences, economic policies, and social policies. On the part of the government, policies such as family law, labor law, social insurance, and social assistance have allowed women options outside the sphere of the family. Similarly, investments in infrastructure—the provision of plumbing, electricity, paved roads, and public transport—have also alleviated the burden of housework on women, reducing their time constraints and enhancing their choices in the labor market.

The relationship between the demand for women and the supply of job-seeking women is an interactive one; if demographic trends have increased the availability of women for jobs, it is also the case that women have been responding to the availability of opportunities. Thus it is plausible to argue that public policies providing for increased female access to education, training, family planning, good jobs, and a more "woman-friendly" social and physical infrastructure have resulted in higher female educational attainment, lower fertility, delayed marriage, and labor-force attachment. Causal links aside, the rapid growth of female employment and women's entry into occupations previously dominated by men led one analyst to designate this trend "the feminization of labor" and another to call it "the globalization of female employment." One aspect of this expansion is the flow of female migrant labor. As the Platform for Action of the Fourth World Conference on Women states, "Women migrant workers, including domestic workers, contribute to the economy of the sending country through their remittances and also to the economy of the receiving country through their participation in the labor force. Migrant women do, however, in many receiving countries, experience higher levels of unemployment compared with both nonmigrant workers and male migrant workers."[6] What should be added is that in many countries women migrant workers lack social and legal protection.

The globalization of markets and production has had a significant impact—both negative and positive—on the opportunity structure for women in urban labor markets. On the one hand, globalization—and its concomitants such as export manufacturing, increased trade and investment, the growth of tourism, and information technologies—is associated with increased job opportunities for women. On the other hand, globalization is also associated with high unemployment, deteriorating real wages, structural adjustment, the rolling back of the State, and cutbacks in social spending. For many, the term "flexible labor market" is a euphemism for increased labor-market competition, segmentation, and inequality, a decline in labor standards, employment insecurity, increased joblessness through industrial and other forms of restructuring, and a rise in atypical or precarious forms of employment that are casual, part-time, and temporary in nature, including home working. The trend toward the "withering away" of the redistributive, welfare state has major implications for women. Throughout the world, women have sought employment in the public sector for its affirmative action policies, generous benefits, and implementation of labor codes.

These have made the public sector – both public services and state-owned enterprises – a more woman-friendly employer than the private sector.[7] Increasingly, however, the public sector is shrinking [8] and women (and men) are expected to seek jobs in the private sector or to initiate self-employment.

The nonregular forms of employment, which are growing, are unstable and insecure, and often do not offer nonwage benefits to the women workers who are outside the coverage of standard labor legislation. The downscaling of the size of the public sector has also adversely affected women, not only because the government has been a major employer of women in many countries, but also because wages and employment conditions are on average better in the public sector. At a time when some have been calling for an expansion of social protection in developing countries – including social policies that would enable women with family responsibilities to compete more equally with men – social security systems, the welfare state and generous social benefits have come under attack in the postindustrial world, including the former socialist countries.

Among those aspects of social protection for working women that have been criticized and streamlined in recent years are labor laws that require maternity leaves and/or workplace nurseries, especially if the costs are imposed on individual employers. This is criticized for imposing an additional tax on employers and for acting as a disincentive to hiring women. Legislation on maternity usually exempts firms below a certain size (such as those with fewer than 50 employees) and requires that employees must have worked with the specific employer for some period of time (such as at least 12 months). Legislation on maternity can impose costs on employers if it requires that benefits be paid by them, and if the benefits are generous. The International Labor Organisation (ILO) recommends a minimum of 12 weeks' maternity leave at two thirds or 66 percent of salary, but in practice the level of maternity benefits varies significantly by country. In Vietnam, women workers were entitled, until recently, to six months' maternity leave at full pay; since the new labor law of June 1994, maternity leave has been set at four months – still above the ILO minimum. In Jordan, however, maternity leave is for six weeks at 50 percent of pay. A recent ILO survey shows that Eastern and Western Europe are the regions with the most generous maternity protection, followed by the countries of North America, those of Asia and the Pacific, Latin America, and Africa. Many countries allow paid maternity leave to be supplemented by unpaid or partially paid leave of up to one and in some cases two years. But as we shall see below in the case of Egypt, such generous maternity leaves could result in widespread stereotyping of women workers as unreliable and uncommitted.[9]

As with the level of maternity benefits, financing also varies considerably across countries. In some countries the maternity grant is paid by the national health insurance or by the social security system. In many Asian countries the costs are carried mainly by employers. It is interesting that this has not deterred Asian employers from hiring women—although there is anecdotal evidence of employer discrimination against married women and preference for young, single women. In China and Vietnam, antidiscrimination legislation has been enacted, and Vietnam's labor code further provides for tax cuts for enterprises that employ large numbers of women (as well as disabled persons). Recently it has been suggested that maternity benefits should be financed from general revenue or social insurance funds rather than through the employer.[10] This can reduce the direct costs of employing women and could pave the way for an expansion of coverage to women workers in the informal sector.

The availability of affordable childcare facilities has also been affected by recent economic developments and debates regarding cost effectiveness. In Eastern Europe and the former Soviet Union, an extensive network of creches and kindergartens enabled full-time employment by mothers in addition to caring for children, and was motivated by both ideological imperatives regarding women's equality and developmental concerns for a larger labor force and full productive labor participation by women. Since the dismantling of communism, however, the transition to a market economy has undermined both the previous ideology and the economic need for more labor. As a result also of enterprise privatization, childcare centers have lost their previous funding and the new costs have proven to be prohibitive to many working-class and lower-middle class families. This seems to have resulted in a decline in the rate of female labor-force participation, although female shares remain roughly the same. In Vietnam, enterprise restructuring—as well as reforms to the rural commune system—has resulted in the closure of many creches and kindergartens.

Government policy can successfully encourage women to enter the labor force and raise the level of women's urban employment, but not necessarily in a way that promotes gender equality. For example, in the early 1980s the Cyprus government faced a labor shortage; it wanted to attract more women into the formal workforce and to encourage part-time workers to become full-time, while also maintaining or increasing the population growth rate.

Policies to promote women's participation in urban employment include education and training programs that enhance women's employability, upgrade their skills, or retrain them in periods of restructuring. "Active labor market policies" are currently in vogue, but the extent to which they reach women is unclear. A 1993 study of Eastern Germany found that women workers were underrepresented in the labor market programs. In Middle Eastern countries currently undergoing structural adjustment, it is not clear that labor adjustment programs are addressing themselves to the needs and interests of women. In general, policies and programs to promote women's urban employment include those that provide training, credits, and loans for productive self-employment and earned income.[11]

For women, the physical infrastructure is as important as social policies in creating an enabling environment to promote their participation in urban employment. Poor women in particular suffer onerous burdens, time constraints, and prohibitive costs as a result of poor housing, shortage of water or electricity, lack of sanitation services, inadequate or expensive public transportation, and inadequate or expensive educational and childcare facilities. In some countries and cultural contexts, working women may require special means of transportation to and from work. For example, in Egypt, the horrendous condition of the urban transportation system, and the difficulties for women of traveling to and from work in frightfully crowded buses filled with men, has been identified as a constraint on women's labor-force participation. For poor women, the private minibuses that are available are too expensive. Housing is especially important to self-employed women and home workers. Adequate housing is of course a major concern; it is also critical to the successful realization of some of the current development objectives with respect to employment promotion and poverty alleviation.

Problems and Prospects of Women's Urban Employment in the Middle East

In Turkey, Egypt, Tunisia, Morocco, and Iran, a common trend is an increase in the supply of job-seeking women, which is partly a function of household survival strategies in response to declining real wages of male household heads, rising prices, unemployment of males, and availability of low-income jobs to women. (It is also a result of increased female educational attainment.) Indeed, in Turkey, household consumption data reveal an increasingly high female contribution to working-class household budgets. At the same time, exceedingly high unemployment rates exist among women, suggesting barriers to their participation in the urban labor market. Another trend is towards the "feminization" of government employment, as wages are eroded and men gravitate towards more lucrative businesses in the expanding private sector.

There is clearly a demand for cheap female labor in the export manufacturing sector, especially in Tunisia and Morocco, to a lesser degree in Egypt and Turkey (although in the latter is believed that much "disguised employment" takes place in the form of unenumerated home working, especially for the textiles and garments sector). Morocco and Tunisia depart from the general regional pattern of low female involvement in industry, and as such are more similar to Mexico, South Korea, and Malaysia. The recruitment of cheap female labor in the export sector has probably contributed to the competitiveness of Morocco's and Tunisia's garments industry. However, it appears that about half of the female manufacturing work force in those countries is nonregular, that is, self-employed women, or home workers receiving pay per piece produced. It also appears that these women are not beneficiaries of social or labor protection. Indeed, the private sector in the Middle East—largely undeveloped and characterized by small enterprises—is notoriously unfriendly to women.

Despite the increase in female employment, women's labor-force participation remains low by international standards in the Middle East and North Africa, and women's share of the salaried labor force is low when compared with other regions. This raises the question of whether women's availability for gainful employment is constrained by the costs of employment: commute time, quality and appropriateness of transportation, and expenditures on clothing, childcare, and meals. Working-class women have been entering the labor force without benefit of social policies and labor legislation that would facilitate their balancing act between employment and family responsibilities, thereby overstretching their labor time (as in the case of home-based garment workers). In many countries, the poor state of the social and physical infrastructure (e.g., schools, health facilities, childcare centers, the quality of housing, public transportation) overburdens working-class and middle-class women alike.

In the Middle East and North Africa, as in many other developing countries, tourism is being promoted as a way of employment generating and accumulation of foreign exchange. Historically, women have been underrepresented in hotel, retail, restaurant and similar types of occupations, but the official emphasis on tourism should change this. Still,the fact that in Tunisia and Turkey, the female labor force is still underrepresented in tourism-related services, despite the importance of tourism in both countries, suggests the need for affirmative-action-type policies. These could be directed towards encouraging women to become owners and managers of tourism-related establishments, as well as wage workers. Recruitment practices of employers will need to be monitored. And again, work conditions and employment status of women in hotels, restaurants, shops, and so on, need to be monitored. Vocational training and any employment programs geared to the tourism sector should include women.

In Egypt, women-owned businesses are growing, but many potential owners are blocked by the reluctance of banks to lend to women. If self-employment among women is to be encouraged, the modernization of Family Law, particularly with respect to inheritance and the right to travel without permission of a male family member, could assist women's ability to start up and manage a business. Training programs and credits for women should not be limited to traditional types of self-employment (e.g., garment making, carpet weaving). Some types of women-run businesses that could be especially socially useful as well as culturally appropriate are daycare centers, nursery schools, and kindergartens for the children. (These could be government-subsidized to benefit poor and working-class women.) Also very useful would be women-owned and managed cafes and restaurants and transport services.

As mentioned earlier, unemployment is a serious problem in the region, especially among urban women, with rates as high as 25 percent (compared with about 10 percent for men). Unemployed women appear to be both new entrants (with secondary school education, as well as poorer women with only primary school education) and previously employed women who have lost jobs with enterprise restructuring or privatization, especially in Tunisia and Turkey. It appears that the most vulnerable persons in the labor market are women with partial education, suggesting the need for vocational training, skills upgrading, and retraining programs geared to women.

Throughout the Middle East, as in other regions, there has been an ongoing debate on social policies for working women. Although the vast majority of economically active women are not beneficiaries of employment-related social insurance programs or labor legislation, the small numbers of women who are employed in the formal sector and are entitled to maternity leaves and childcare benefits have to confront widespread perceptions of them as less reliable than men and uncommitted to their work, as well as "expensive labor." This is especially the case in Egypt, where women public-sector employees have taken full advantage of the generous and lengthy maternity benefits available to them (three months' paid maternity leave and up to two years unpaid maternity leave, available up to three times, with no loss of seniority). Interviews conducted during fieldwork in Egypt in January 1995 confirmed that employers are very much opposed to lengthy maternity leaves. Moreover, a government study states: ". . . there seems to be implicit discrimination against female employment, especially in the private sector, mainly because of women's work discontinuity due to childbearing and rearing." Moreover, private-sector employers circumvent the labor law requiring creches and nursing breaks in enterprises with 100 or more women workers by deliberately hiring fewer than 100 women. Although Egypt has an antidiscrimination law, it is apparently not enforced, and compliance not monitored.

There is a view among Egyptian women professionals that the perception of the family attachment of women and their presumed unreliability is a pretext to reserve jobs for men, and that in recent years and as a result of the economic crisis, women workers are not taking lengthy unpaid maternity leaves because they cannot afford to do so. It may very well be that women are being unfairly singled out as "expensive labor"; benefits such as the one-month pilgrimage leave for all employees (invariably taken by male employees, once in their lifetime and at full salary) and rights to lengthy leaves with job-back guarantees are rarely articulated as problematical in labor-market or human-capital terms.

At present, the labor law is being revised and unified to bring the public-sector benefits in line with private-sector benefits. For women this will entail the reduction of the unpaid maternity leave to one year rather than two, taken twice instead of three times, and available to a woman employee after 10 months of service. Although there is some criticism of this by Egyptian women activists, it is possible that the streamlining of the maternity leave benefits would help to accomplish the following: (1) create a more equitable entitlements package for public-sector and private-sector women employees alike, and (2) gradually eliminate the perception of working mothers as uncommitted participants in the labor force, while also retaining the rights of mothers to, and the social need for, maternity leave and childcare.

In Iran, women represent a very small part of the salaried work force, with most employed in the government sector. Labor legislation on maternity leave follows the ILO recommendation. Currently, only employed women in urban areas and government employees are covered, which means that the majority of working women have no coverage. Another problem is that a maternity leave of three months is insufficient and is in the interest of neither the baby's health nor the mother's labor-force attachment. A better solution might be to extend maternity leave to six months and entitle women to take it at full pay twice in their career. This may encourage more women to enter the labor force.

In the Middle East, there are very good reasons why the package of social benefits, including labor laws and protective legislation for women, should be extended to private-sector and informal-sector workers through new forms of financing. If maternity leaves were regularized, this could contribute to women's labor-force attachment (as well as to the health of mother and child). And if social security programs were extended outside the relatively small formal sector, this would contribute to stabilization of population and labor-force growth, as well as old-age security of women. In addition, promoting women's participation in the urban labor market will require appropriate curriculum development in schools, vocational training programs, credit and loan programs for women entrepreneurs, attention to infrastructural needs, and possibly affirmative action programs to facilitate and accelerate the hiring of women, especially in the private sector. Perhaps an appropriate model may be the clauses in Vietnam's labor law that provide for tax breaks for enterprises hiring large numbers of women.

Conclusion

Promoting the participation of women in urban employment and sustainable urban living requires attention to, and public and private financing of, social policies and a conducive physical infrastructure that will serve women wage and salary workers, homeworkers, and entrepreneurs of various types. Because women's economic activities span the spheres of production and reproduction, measures are required to ease the burden of both kinds of activities and to enable women to balance work and family responsibilities. This is needed in order to allow women to compete fairly with men in urban labor markets.

Although this section has not addressed itself to the issue of participatory planning and policy-making, it should suffice to state that a top-down approach is insufficient and frequently wrong headed. Rather, social policies, infrastructural development, and indeed, economic policies themselves, should be debated publicly, and they should be designed or revised with the participation of government, financial institutions, and nongovernmental organizations, including women's groups.

It is frequently argued that in a globalized world, national states and national-based organizations are severely circumscribed in their capacity to control their own resources, determine distribution, and influence the direction of change. It is also argued that economic efficiency and productivity increase when labor legislation is substantially revised, social costs reduced, and "flexibility" made optimal. The first argument is partially true; but it is truer of some countries than of others. The second argument is debatable, for it is advanced from a certain point of view with its own, inherent bias. An alternative argument is that social security insurance brings order to the labor market and helps to price human resources efficiently.[12] Perhaps for these reasons, international conventions, laws, and instruments continue to hold governments accountable, while also calling on a combination of governmental, nongovernmental, private-sector, and international action towards the realization of certain objectives. For women, these objectives include policies to promote their participation, equality, empowerment, and well-being, through long-term public investments in education, health, infrastructure, and market access.

The Fourth World Conference on Women's Platform for Action recommends that "women's priorities [be] included in public investment programs for economic infrastructure, such as water and transportation, electrification and energy conservation, transport and road construction." It further calls for the promotion of "greater involvement of women beneficiaries at the project planning and implementation stages to ensure access to jobs and contracts." The Platform recommends that services be structured to reach rural and urban women involved in micro, small and medium-scale enterprises, "with special attention to young women, low income women, those belonging to ethnic and racial minorities, and indigenous women who lack access to capital and assets." For wage workers, it calls on governments, employers, employees, trade unions, and women's organizations to "eliminate discriminatory practices by employers on the basis of women's reproductive roles and functions, including refusal of employment and dismissal due to pregnancy and breast-feeding responsibilities," and to "develop and promote employment programs and services for women entering and/or re-entering the labor market, especially poor urban, rural, and young women, the self-employed and those negatively affected by structural adjustment." The Platform for Action has also addressed itself to the need for public policies to harmonize the work and family responsibilities of women (and men) in different types of occupations: "Adopt policies to ensure the appropriate protection of labor laws and social security benefits for part-time, temporary, seasonal and home-based workers; promote career development based on work conditions that harmonize work and family responsibilities; Ensure that full and part-time work can be freely chosen by women and men on an equal basis, and consider appropriate protection for atypical workers in terms of access to employment, working conditions, and social security."

The Platform for Action's recommendations on public policies to promote women's labor-force participation follow from earlier legal instruments, such as the Convention on the Elimination of All Forms of Discrimination Against Women. Worth mentioning is Article 11 (b) and (c), which calls on States Parties to "introduce maternity leave with pay or with comparable social benefits without loss of former employment, seniority or social allowances," and "to encourage the provision of the necessary supporting social services to enable parents to combine family obligations with work responsibilities and participation in public life, in particular through promoting the establishment and development of a network of child-care facilities."

Attention to social protection, training and credit programs, and appropriate physical infrastructure for working women, enforcement of existing national legislation, and implementation of international conventions are necessary in order that women's role in social reproduction be properly compensated, in order that women be allowed a wider array of choices in the urban labor market, and in order to achieve the objective of promoting habitats of sustainable human development in the twenty-first century.

Notes

1. Caroline O. N. Moser, *Gender Planning and Development: Theory, Practice, and Training*. London: Routledge, 1993.

2. Rae Lesser Blumberg, ed., *Gender, Family, and Economy: The Triple Overlap.* Newbury Park, CA: Sage, 1991.

3. Barbara F. Reskin and Heidi Hartmann, eds., *Women's Work, Men's Work, Sex Segregation on the Job.* Washington, DC: National Academy of Sciences, 1986.

4. Ingrid Palmer, *Gender and Population in the Adjustment of African Economies: Planning for Change.* Geneva: ILO, 1991; Diane Elson, "Male Bias in the Development Process: The Case of Structural Adjustjment." In Diane Elson, ed., *Male Bias in the Development Process.* Manchester University Press, 1991; and Haleh Afshar and Carolyne Dennis, eds., *Women and Adjustment Policies in the Third World.* London: Macmillan, 1992.

5. Valentine M. Moghadam, "Gender Aspects of Employment and Unemployment in a Global Perspective." In Mihály Simai (with Valentine Moghadam and Arvo Kuddo), eds., *Global Employment: An International Investigation into the Future of Work.* London: Zed, 1995.

6. United Nations, "Fourth World Conference on Women: Beijing Declaration and Platform for Action." New York: Advance Unedited Draft, Sept. 1995 (advanced unedited draft).

7. Valentine Moghadam, "Introduction and Overview." In Valentine M. Moghadam, ed., *Economic Reforms, Women's Employment, and Social Policies: Case Studies of China, Viet Nam, Egypt, and Cuba.* World Development Series, vol. 4. Helsinki: UNU/WIDER, 1995.

8. Wouter van Ginniken, "Labor Adjustment in the Public Sector: Policy Issues for Developing Countries. *International Labor Review* 1990, 129(4): 441–457.

9. ILO, *World Labor Report 1993.* Geneva: ILO, 1993.

10. Zafiris Tzannatos, "Economic Growth and Gender Equity in the Labor Market." World Bank, Education and Social Policy Department, Jan. 1995 (mimeograph).

11. Marguerite Berger and Mayra Buvinic, eds., *Women's Ventures: Assistance to the Informal Sector in Latin America.* West Hartford, CT: Kumarian Press, 1989.

12. Ingrid Palmer, "Public Finance from a Gender Perspective." *World Development* 1995, 23(11): 1981-1986.

Section 1 The Future of Urban Employment

Samir Radwan

The most serious problems confronting cities worldwide include lack of employment opportunities, spreading homelessness and expansion of squatter settlements, increased poverty and a widening gap between the rich and the poor, growing insecurity, deterioration of building stock, services and infrastructure, improper land use, rising traffic congestions and pollution, lack of green spaces, and an increased vulnerability to disaster.

The lack of employment opportunities comes first in this long, and by no means exhaustive, list of problems confronting our cities. Creating and protecting employment provides the key to alleviating, if not solving, all of the other problems on the list. This section of *Cities Fit for People* describes the so-called urban crisis, examine how the crisis came about—or in other words, where we have gone wrong—and finally raise the question of how to ensure the creation of employment opportunities and, thus, a sustainable reduction of poverty.

The Urban Crisis

The urban crisis is first of all a crisis of people, a crisis of urban populations. An unprecedented shift is taking place in the world. We are rapidly moving toward an urban world. Soon, half of humanity will be living and working in urban areas. Virtually all of this shift will be taking place in the developing countries. As it is, developing countries already account for the major share of the world's urban population.

Within the framework of world urbanization, the growth of megacities is a specific phenomenon. In 1950, there were only two cities, London and New York, with populations of more than 10 million. By 1994, there were 15, 11 of which were in developing countries. Two decades from now there will be 28. The "megacity," once remote from most of the world's population, is now an urban reality in many developing countries.

A Growing Urban Labor Force

A growing urban population means a growing urban labor force. More than 228 million new jobs will be needed in the urban areas of developing countries during the 1990s alone. An additional 875 million jobs will be needed during the following 25 years. Creating these jobs is the greatest challenge that we face today.

Poverty is now an urban problem. The rise in urban unemployment has been paralleled by the urbanization of poverty. A third of the world's urban population is presently living in a state of absolute poverty. In 1990 this would have meant approximately 400 million people, and the number is expected to grow to 1 billion by the end of the century. By the year 2000 more than half the developing countries' poor will be in cities and towns: 90 percent of poor households in Latin America, 45 percent in Asia, and 40 percent Africa.

The most vulnerable groups are the hardest hit by the urban crisis. The lack of employment opportunities is linked to other forms of social exclusion. Women, for example, continue to be marginalized and discriminated against. It is no coincidence that they are the poorest of the poor and are employed, if at all, in the most vulnerable jobs. The urban poor often have no land tenure, have no access to basic infrastructure, and receive no services. The poor often pay more than the relatively well off for such basic services as water supply, sanitation, and, when available, waste collection. The mushrooming of informal squatter and slum settlements is one of the tragic characteristics of both of developing country megacities and, all too often, of certain of the industrialized world's cities. Urban poverty is then both a local and global issue. Every first world city today has a third world city within it (immigrant shelters and slums), and every third world city has a first world city (the modern skyscrapers, banks, the fashion houses) within it.

Growing poverty and social exclusion, with its a widening gap between the rich and the poor, if left unchecked, will undermine the social fabric and sustainability of this world's cities. But there is a choice. We can continue with misguided policies and watch our cities crumble under the weight of these problems. Or we can take control, arrest the decline, and move forward on the path of development.

The Informal Sector

Formal sector jobs in many parts of the world have simply vanished or never materialized. As a result, the informal sector has become a major employer. In sub-Saharan Africa alone, the urban informal sector is estimated to employ more than 60 percent of the urban labor force. Unfortunately, most of this "employment" is in fact disguised "unemployment" in low-paying, unproductive, and unprotected jobs.

The problems of urban unemployment are not limited to just the developing countries. In the industrialized countries, unemployment is by and large an urban problem. With it has come the growth of a new informal sector that is represented by street vendors, unlicensed cab operators, and people trying to eke out a living on the streets. In the transitional countries, the closure and rationalization of large state enterprises have introduced the scourge of unemployment to a population that had previously been used to government subsidized policies of full employment. Small towns whose economic base was wholly dependent on a single state enterprise have been devastated. As a consequence, the urban informal sector, which was previously thought of as a developing country phenomenon, is now – although on a smaller scale – increasingly a feature of urban labor markets in some industrialized and transitional countries.

Urbanization and Economic Growth

Cities are engines of growth. Our cities are the backbone of our economies. In many countries, urban centers account for a disproportionately large share of national income. It is the very basis upon which economic development proceeds. For these reasons alone, cities should be valued as engines of economic growth.

However, if cities are engines of growth, why is there an urban crisis? What was gone wrong? We cannot afford to leave the urban agenda on the back burner on the basis of a so-called "urban bias." We have reached a critical threshold that calls for a strategic shift in our orientation and approach to finding solutions, not just outside the city but within the city itself.

Three questions need to be asked about the thrust of the policies toward urban development, which have particular significance for urban employment.

First, can urban crisis be solved solely by slowing down rural–urban migration? For many years, conventional wisdom regarded urban growth as a problem of rural–urban migration. Certain governments tried to solve the urban crisis by building walls and setting up elaborate controls to keep potential migrants out. Others periodically tried to round them up and ship them back to rural areas. However, such policies have proven to be unsuccessful.

Of course, in Africa and parts of Asia, where the rural population is still large, there is still a great potential for further rural–urban migration. Despite many efforts to improve rural living standards, migration to the cities continues unabated. Does rural development work to stop this migration? Improvements in education, infrastructure, and basic services in rural areas all result in the introduction of new skills, ambitions, values, and standards that can in fact help fuel migration. Although rural industrialization, as shown in China, can be successful in its own right, it is doubtful that this will solve the urban crisis.

Overall, however, natural population increase within cities is now the major factor in urban growth, particularly in megacities. Although policies to slow migration may be adopted, they will certainly have little impact on those who are already in town.

The second question is, will outlawing the urban informal sector solve the urban crisis? Despite good intentions of integrating the urban informal sector into mainstream development, this sector keeps growing. In fact national and world economies are undergoing a process of informalization. Informal sector operators are often tied into the web of globalization, with both opportunities for new sources of employment and danger of abuses, such as child labor. In a situation where there seems to be little hope of providing socially protected employment in the formal sector, outlawing or bulldozing the informal sector out of existence will have little positive impact on developing productive alternatives.

Finally, the third question is, has globalization, which has moved many of the levers of economic policy from the national to the international level, made our cities even more powerless to create employment? As the protective walls of national regulation disappear, cities will increasingly be operating within the same environment, facing a similar set of constraints and opportunities. The creation of a global marketplace will mean more competition—not just among countries but also among cities. Whether globalization is a positive or negative trend, one thing is clear. Both the national and the urban economies will display greater instability and be subjected to greater external economic shocks and competition than before. Cities and towns will have to learn to live with these conditions. If the proponents of globalization are right, there should be compensation in the form of faster growth and more jobs. But at this point, the possibility of such favorable outcomes remains an open question. One thing however is clear—if cities are to survive in a global marketplace, they must ensure that their resources—and this includes their human resources—are not left to stagnate and decline.

A growing urban labor force cannot be gainfully employed without sufficient demand, and increasingly, this demand is determined at the global level. In the face of unfavorable world economic conditions, can local policies actually work? Or are we merely "shifting deck chairs on the Titanic?" While local investment policies can work and do have an impact, at the same time they are greatly helped by favorable world market conditions (i.e., by periods of growing global demand). Mayors must learn how to take advantage of periods of growth and to cope with periods of economic stagnation.

The Strengths of Local Authorities for Creating Employment

Surprisingly, in some areas, local authorities have a growing comparative advantage over international and national organizations in solving the urban crisis, and in creating urban employment. What can workers, employers, and local governments do to create new employment opportunities and better protect existing employment in a globalizing world? How can a strategy to create employment build on the comparative strengths of participants at the municipal and local levels?

There is a strong move towards decentralization of finance and responsibilities to the municipal level. Municipal authorities are the ones that have to deal directly with the problems caused by urban unemployment and poverty. Yet all too often they act as a fire brigade that does not have the resources to prevent the fire in the first place. If city governments are to be involved in employment generation activities, they must be given a clear mandate and the necessary financial support from the central government. Under decentralization, more and more resources are being raised at the local level, and this gives municipal governments a new ability to shift priorities in favor of employment creation. Because they are the ones that pay the price of unemployment, they are also best motivated, if given the resources, to do something about it. We should not, however, paint a rosy picture of decentralization as a panacea. The technical capacity of many municipal authorities remains weak and the principles of transparency, accountability, consultation, collective participation, and local democracy are not always well established. If municipal authorities are to convince others of their ability to handle more responsibility, they must demonstrate their capacity to handle it.

Decentralization does not stop here. Given the heavy burden of urban poverty and unemployment, mechanisms should be established so poor and slum communities can have a say in urban management. Only by including, rather than excluding, the majority in the decision-making process and by harnessing its talents, aspirations, and commitments can local authorities use decentralization to their best advantage in creating employment.

Urban authorities have the ability to influence the regulatory framework, which includes labor standards, bylaws and regulations governing land and informal sector development, and finally contracting procedures. Whereas city officials cannot control international market forces, they can restructure, abolish, influence, and even design regulations that are friendly to employment creation and that protect workers in the face of globalization. One should emphasize the value of International Labor Standards as a tool at the disposal of local officials to ensure that globalization does not erode social protection. However, the regulatory framework can also be used to increase productivity of the urban informal sector, rather than to repress it. Contracting procedures can also be revised at the local level to facilitate market access to small contractors using labor-based methods.

By working at the local level, mayors and municipal officials are better able to develop new alliances through an "enabling approach" than is the case for those working at the national level. Municipalities have to directly forge new alliances, create synergies, and act as both leaders and facilitators. Municipalities can no longer be expected to provide public services, infrastructure, housing, and employment to urban populations singlehandedly.

There is a lot that municipal authorities can do, particularly in the following three key areas.

First, local authorities can influence investment policies, particularly in infrastructure and housing, to have a greater impact on employment creation and poverty alleviation. Infrastructure can provide cities with a competitive edge and create jobs, but cities need to reorient the way they approach infrastructure development. All too often, infrastructure investments provide services at the wrong standard, are badly maintained, and fail to generate employment. Infrastructure does not just mean factories, power plants, and airports, but also basic services required by all urban dwellers. The investments that are of greatest benefit to the urban poor are all conducive to labor-intensive technologies—and hence job creation—and provide direct improvements to the urban environment.

Cities also need to change the way they approach housing policy. Investing in shelter is not wasteful social consumption, but a direct means for creating jobs and generating demand. Shelter is much more than housing. And the employment effects of housing go well beyond construction and maintenance. If there is one lesson for planners in the massive literature on slums and squatter community life, it is that housing in these areas is not for home life alone.

Public housing provision has in many parts of the world been a dismal failure. More often than not it has been hijacked by middle- and high-income groups. The poor with limited resources are then often left to provide for themselves—often quite successfully. Yet they face severe discrimination and harassment, as seen, for example, in the number of evictions and the fact that they pay a higher price for basic services. To harness the potential of the housing sector, cities must begin by enhancing and upgrading the unassisted contribution that ordinary people are already making to improving their lives.

Second, local authorities can enable, rather than persecute, the urban informal sector. For better or worse, the informal sector is and will continue to be an urban reality. Improving basic urban services and infrastructure provides one "win–win" scenario that can improve incomes, productivity, and working conditions in the urban informal sector. Although it would be an illusion to expect formal sector mechanisms (labor inspectors, for example) to provide social protection to the informal sector, informal sectors can be given a greater voice in improving their own working conditions if they are encouraged and assisted in organizing themselves. Therefore, new alliances between labor unions and informal sector associations should be investigated. Local governments have the power to either use or abuse regulations. The case for removing and reappraising out-of-date or wholly inappropriate business and planning regulations cannot be overstressed. We have to carefully consider whether complicated procedures for registering enterprises, rigid zoning laws banning businesses from operating in residential areas, and a multiplicity of permits and reporting requirements are really necessary? What are the countereffects? Some enterprises remain illegal, simply because they cannot afford the cost that is imposed by prolonged bureaucratic processes and multiple legal requirements. Regulatory reforms are not beyond the competence of municipal authorities.

However, together with the establishing legal rights, we need programs that are required to provide basic social security, health care, and urban services, upgrade the physical working and living environment of the informal sector, improve productivity and incomes, help the self-employed to organize and strengthen their bargaining power and be aware of their rights.

Third, develop new alliances at the local level for employment creation. Local governments cannot do it alone. During the last 15 years there has been an almost universal policy shift from the State as a provider to the State as an enabler. Whatever opinions we may hold on this, it is clear that in the future local governments will have to increasingly forge partnerships with the private sector, with employers and workers organizations, with different levels of government, and with nongovernmental and community-based organizations. Partnerships can occur in different forms. It can be in the form of principal–agent, buyer–seller, or equal stakeholders in local economic development. The permutations are endless.

Conclusion

In view of the above, what is need is local action plans to create new sources of employment. These plans should, *inter alia* take the following issues into account.

- New alliances for employment creation and institutions for social dialog should be created at the local level and include municipal and local governments and employers' and workers' organizations, as well as other concerned parties. Workers' and employers' organizations should play a direct role in providing training and organization to this sector as the best means for increasing incomes and social protection;

- The regulatory framework, including contract procurement procedures, zoning laws and bylaws, and regulations and incentives affecting microenterprises and small-scale enterprises should be reexamined and modified to facilitate employment creation and improved working conditions;
- The productive capacity of urban informal sector enterprises should be harnessed, with a view to raising incomes and increasing social protection. Organized labor's experience should be called on to help the informal sector form representative associations as the best means to increase social protection;
- Appropriate training and retraining programs should be targeted to increase the capacity of the poor and to provide new opportunities for stable employment benefiting from the advances made in science and technology;
- International labor standards should be applied to protect fundamental human rights, ensure equality of access between women and men, and improve the quality of employment;
- Public and private investment policies and programs should be evaluated with a view to maximizing their impact on employment, as well as to respond to economic, social, and cultural needs; and
- Investment policy should include the upgrading and renewal of low-income neighborhoods in cities and towns to achieve a positive impact on the living and working environment. Improvements to drainage, sanitation, erosion control, urban forestry, and waste management should be used to create employment and to protect the urban environment.

In the final analysis, we are left with two questions. What capacity do municipal authorities have for formulating and implementing urban employment policies and what resources can they mobilize? Developing the capacity to implement new policies requires resources. To a certain extent, employment creation will pay for itself—and help pay for other badly needed municipal investments and services—by creating the necessary tax base. National governments and the international development community have a vital role to play in ensuring that these resources are allocated. We have to realize that we are at the start of a new development paradigm—a paradigm in which urban employment problems will hold center stage. The time for action is now.

Section 2 Globalization and Urban Employment

Azizur Rahman Khan

The phenomenon that has come to be known as the globalization of the world economy is very much the result of the actions taken by the less developed countries (LDCs). The increasing globalization of the world economy since the early 1980s consists of the reduction in the barriers to trade and capital flows among nations. Before the beginning of the ongoing phase of globalization, the two principal obstacles to free movement of goods, services, and capital were: (1) the import-substituting industrialization strategy of an overwhelming majority of less developed countries; and (2) the isolation of the socialist countries, officially classified as middle-income less developed countries, from the world economy and indeed from one another. During the decade of the 1980s both these obstacles broke down as a result of actions taken by the less developed countries. The increased globalization of the world economy since the early 1980s owes very little to the actions of the advanced industrial countries. The latter became somewhat more free trading among their respective trading blocs, but on balance more protectionist vis-à-vis the less developed countries, especially the labor-intensive exports from the latter.[1] It is therefore quite inappropriate to think of globalization as a phenomenon that has hit the less developed countries from the outside. It is very much a consequence of their collective action.

Impacts on Developing Countries

This does not mean that the less developed countries have generally done well during the era of globalization. Indeed Asia is the only part of the developing world that experienced reasonable, even accelerated, growth during the period of globalization. The rest of the developing world experienced a sharp reduction in growth. In sub-Saharan Africa, for example, per capita income steadily declined during the 1980s and the early 1990s. In the Middle Eastern and North African region, there has been only a very weak recovery from the decline in per capita income in the 1980s. Latin America experienced a sharp reduction in growth in per capita income in the 1980s which has only partly been reversed in the 1990s. The economies of former Soviet Union and Eastern Europe are, with only a few exceptions, continuing to crawl along a downward path. In contrast both South Asia and East and Southeast Asia (ESEA) accelerated their growth rates during the period of globalization.[2]

For the world as a whole the rate of urbanization during the period of globalization has been the same as that during the preceding decade. But it has varied quite a lot among different country groups. The advanced industrial economies, already highly urbanized, experienced a reduction in the rate of urbanization. The less developed countries as a whole continued to urbanize at about the same rate as before. According to World Bank estimates, the less developed countries with per capita incomes of less than US$695 in 1993 experienced an acceleration in the rate of urbanization.

The only regional group among the less developed countries that experienced an acceleration in the rate of urbanization during the period of globalization is ESEA. The other regional groups witnessed a reduction in the rate of urbanization (with the exception of sub-Saharan African, which had no change). The absolute rate of increase in urban population is, however, not an appropriate index of urbanization, because most of the developing world witnessed a reduction in the rate of population growth in the period of globalization (sub-Saharan Africa, the Middle East, and North Africa being exceptions). A better index is the elasticity of the urban population with respect to overall population, the ratio of the growth in the urban population to the growth of the total population. ESEA was the only country group for which this elasticity increased during the period of globalization, and the increase was dramatic! For all the other country groups, the elasticity fell. The one exception is the region of the former Soviet Union and Eastern Europe, where it remained virtually unchanged.

As is well documented, the ESEA countries achieved the best economic and social performance during the period of globalization. They grew faster, overcame the problem of macroeconomic imbalance more successfully, achieved greater equality in the distribution of income, and reduced the incidence of poverty more rapidly than any other country group.[3] One must therefore recognize that successful exploitation of the opportunities of globalization has coincided with rapid urbanization. This is brought out even more clearly by the experience of individual countries within ESEA: those with the greatest success have experienced extraordinarily high elasticity of urban growth (3.27 for the Republic of Korea, 3.07 for China, and 2.88 for Indonesia). *Prima facie,* it does not appear that putting a brake on urbanization is the way to grow successfully during the period of globalization.

Urban Employment During Globalization

The expectation that successful adjustment to the globalizing world economy should help increase employment in the less developed countries assumes that such adjustment means abandoning the strategy of import-substituting industrialization, which is notorious for its negative impact on employment, and a change in the structure of production in favor of exports. Given the relative abundance of labor in the less developed countries, exports are likely to consist of labor intensive goods, because integration with the world economy dictates a structure of incentives that promotes specialization in goods intensive in the use of abundant factors. An inflow of foreign capital, especially foreign direct investment (FDI) pursuing low real cost of labor, provides an additional impetus to employment expansion.

Yet, the experience of even the most successful cases of adjustment to globalization have mixed results when it comes to the expansion of urban employment. This is illustrated by the very different experiences of two remarkable ESEA countries, the Republic of Korea and China.

In Korea, the continuation of rapid urbanization during the period of globalization coincided with the continuation of a rapid reduction in agriculture's share of employment, from 34 percent in 1980 to 16 percent in 1992. Urban employment grew rapidly to absorb the increased supply of labor. During the early 1980s the output elasticity of employment in manufacturing industries was high. The share of employment in manufacturing peaked at about 28 percent of total employment at the end of the 1980s. Thereafter services became the principal source of labor absorption in the urban economy. Even so the output elasticity of employment in manufacturing averaged at 0.45 for the decade of the 1980s.[4] The overall effect was that the growth of employment in the nonagricultural economy was rapid enough to reduce the rate of unemployment in Korea from 5.2 percent in 1980 to 2.4 percent in 1992.[5]

The Chinese experience was very different. China's introduction to the global economy started shortly after it embarked on economic reform. The relevant period of globalization in China's case seems to be the decade from 1984 to 1994. During this period China's economy grew as rapidly as the economy of any other ESEA country over a comparable time period. Its GDP grew at an annual rate of 9 percent, its industrial sector grew at an annual rate of 12 percent, and its exports in dollar value grew at an annual rate of 14 percent. And yet unemployment, particularly urban unemployment, has become a major problem in China.

During this decade the proportion of total workers employed fell by less than 10 percentage points (from 64.0 percent to 54.3 percent) in agriculture, increased by a mere 2.7 percentage points (from 20 percent to 22.7 percent) in industries, and rose by 7 percentage points (from

16 percent to 23 percent) in services. Output elasticity of employment was 0.3 for agriculture, 0.27 for industries, and 0.58 for services. The reduction is agriculture's share of employment was modest by the standard of the other rapidly growing ESEA countries. The growth in employment in services has also been reasonably rapid. It is the industrial sector that had an apparently dismal employment performance. Employment elasticity for the sector was only 60 percent of what it was for Korea in the same period, an economy with a much higher level of real wages and technology. This low absorption of labor characterized the Chinese industries in a period of extremely rapid industrial growth and growth of manufactured exports which, according to the findings of a World Bank study, were labor intensive.[6]

The Case of China

How might one explain the paradox that industrialization based on the expansion of labor-intensive exports during the era of globalization resulted in such a slow growth in employment? The explanation seems to lie in the initial condition of Chinese industries. These industries, almost exclusively state and collectively owned until the beginning of globalization, had been based on an absorption of labor far in excess of requirement.

This is because of the past "iron-rice-bowl" principle of guaranteed employment to all members of the labor force. Even after the beginning of reforms, state and collective enterprises continued to avoid shedding surplus labor. In effect this meant a concealed system of unemployment insurance in a society that lacked formal institutions for the protection of the unemployed. Economic reform and globalization made it impossible for the state and collective enterprises to continue to implement this concealed system of social protection. Reforms brought into existence industrial enterprises under private—and a variety of alternative forms of–ownership. These enterprises were not subject to restrictions on hiring and dismissing workers. Compared to state and collective enterprises, these private and other kinds of enterprises thus had a great competitive advantage.

Furthermore China's integration in the globalizing world economy concentrated the attention of the enterprises on keeping down the unit labor cost, which was the critical determinant of external competitiveness and the principal instrument to attract foreign direct investment. Thus it became imperative to find a way to liberate state and collective enterprises from the burden of carrying the system of concealed unemployment insurance.

A 1986 regulation seriously dented the "iron-rice-bowl" system of guaranteed employment for one's lifetime by requiring that all new employment in state enterprises be based on fixed-term contracts for three to five years without an obligation of renewal on the part of the enterprises. State enterprises were simultaneously granted power to dismiss workers for inefficiency.

In 1988 State Bankruptcy Law was introduced to make it possible to liquidate or drastically restructure state enterprises, with a consequent reduction in employment. Armed with these changes in the legal and institutional framework, state and collective enterprises have started shedding some of the surplus labor. The decline in employment was sharpest in collective enterprises, 13.3 percent between the peak year of 1991 and 1994. In state enterprises, the decline was much more modest, 3.4 percent between the peak year of 1992 and 1994. In private and other enterprises employment grew rapidly, but not by as much as would be necessary to offset the fall in employment in state and collective enterprises. During the 1990s urban industrial employment increased very little and actually declined absolutely after 1993 in spite of an explosively rapid growth of output.

Indeed the process is likely to accelerate in the future. So far state enterprises have used, or have been allowed to use, the opportunity to reduce employment to a far lesser extent than is warranted by economic efficiency. It is common for the redundant workers to be kept on the payroll and temporarily sent home for a fraction, approximately one half, of the wage that is paid the working employees. The urban unemployment rate, which had declined to 1.9 percent in 1984, went up to 2.8 percent in 1994. But this estimate, excluding all but the officially unemployed among the those holding official resident permits *(hukou)*, is just the tip of the iceberg. At least two other groups should be included in this category: those who have been sent home on partial pay (concealed "unemployment benefit") and those who are among the estimated 50 million floating migrants from rural areas who remain unemployed.[7] Rudimentary estimates, based on local data on the incidence of these categories, suggest that the rate of urban unemployment, adjusted for these two factors, might be well above 10 percent.[8]

It is possible to argue that globalization should not be blamed for the problem of China's urban unemployment. Industrial employment, measured at constant intensity of employment per worker, has increased quite rapidly, but is hidden because of the effect of the reduction in concealed unemployment in state and collective enterprises on the head-count rate of employment. The validity of the argument is undeniable. It is however important to recognize that the dismantling of the concealed system of unemployment insurance needed to be offset by the institution of alternative systems of protection, either in the form of formal unemployment insurance schemes or in the form of transitional public works programs, if the social cost of the employment consequence of globalization were to be avoided. Globalization forced a pace of adjustment that has proved much faster than the capacity of the society to set up these alternative institutions and programs.

The incidence of urban poverty in China was estimated, both by the government and the international agencies, to have declined steadily since the beginning of reforms in 1978 until the mid 1980s, when it fluctuated around the negligible rate of 0.2 to 0.4 percent till 1990.[9] According to more recent official estimates for 1994, 15 million urban dwellers (about 5 percent of the urban population) are estimated to be in absolute poverty.[10] These estimates exclude the poor among the floating migrants, among whom the incidence of poverty must be greater. Clearly the number of the urban poor in China has increased during the period of globalization. The increased numbers of the unemployed members of the labor force, including those who have been sent home from state enterprises on partial pay and the unemployed and low-paid among the migrants, are the principal categories of the new urban poor.

Globalization has aggravated the problem of poverty in China in other ways as well. During the entire history of prereform development, China had little inflow of external resources. By 1993 China had become by far the largest recipient of external resources among all less developed countries. It accounted for a fifth of all net resource flows into less developed countries: a tenth of all official development assistance, nearly a fifth of all borrowing from private sources, five percent of portfolio equity and, most remarkably, two-fifths of all foreign direct investment. The growth in foreign direct investment continued to reach US$38 billion in 1995, 42 percent of the total for all less developed countries and approximately 4.5 percent of China's GDP. Foreign direct investment is almost exclusively attracted to the urban centers of the twelve rich provinces in the east—the eleven coastal provinces and Beijing—which have the best infrastructure and easiest access to export and lucrative domestic markets. The eleven coastal provinces, inhabited by 40 percent of China's population, account for 80 percent of China's exports. Eight of these twelve rich eastern provinces are ranked as the eight top provinces in terms of both per capita GDP and manufacturing wage. These provinces also achieved the highest growth in manufacturing wage rate and in per capita GDP in recent years (between 1989 and 1994). Most of the remaining provinces four provinces in this category also achieved faster rates of growth in per capita GDP than did China as a whole. According to a recent official report, the rate of growth of GDP in these twelve eastern provinces was 78 percent higher than the rate of growth of the central and western provinces during the period from 1991 to 1995. Available estimates show that today the poor in China mainly inhabit the central and western provinces. The failure to reduce poverty during a period of unprecedented growth was largely the result of the concentration of benefits of growth in the coastal areas. Globalization, based on the leading role of foreign direct investment provided a major impetus for this concentration. Public investment was not directed to offset the effect of concentration because of globalization. Had it done so, by investment in the improvement of infrastructure in the backward provinces to improve their attractiveness to investors and their linkage with the coastal growth poles, China might have succeeded in avoiding poverty-inducing growth during the period of globalization. But the cost of dispersed public investment for the decentralization of infrastructural development might have been to reduce the attraction of the industries under foreign direct investment for China.

Differences Between China and Korea

The difference in the outcome in urban employment between China and Korea is perhaps the result of many factors that have been left out of the scope of the present discussion. Two factors, however, stand out. The first relates to the initial industrial structure. In Korea, industries were not burdened with the kind of concealed unemployment insurance that characterized China's industries. Thus the gain in employment as a result of the expansion of labor-intensive exports was immediately reflected in the headcount of employment in Korea and was largely hidden in China in the form of reduced incidence of concealed unemployment. Once state and collective enterprises in China started terminating some of the concealed unemployed, urban unemployment and poverty increased. Orderly integration of China's industries with the globalizing world economy would have required new institutions and programs for the protection of the redundant employees of state and collective enterprises. The creation of these institutions and programs lagged far behind the warranted levels.

The second outstanding difference between China and Korea was the very different degree of dependence on foreign direct investment. In 1993, foreign direct investment amounted to 4.5 percent of GDP in China and a mere 0.15 percent of GDP in Korea. The price of attracting the massive volume of these investments was to let its flow decide the pattern of location of investment not only for itself but also for much of domestic investment which flocked around foreign direct investment enterprises. This led to a degree of concentration of investment in rich provinces that severely constrained China's ability to reduce poverty. Korea faced no such problem and, in any case, it did not face a problem of regional imbalance in development that was anywhere as serious as it is in much bigger and more varied China.

The Case of the Philippines

China is by no means the only Asian less developed country that has encountered serious problems of urban unemployment during the period of globalization. In the Philippines, the manufacturing sector failed to increase its share of employment in three decades. Indeed, in the Philippines the share of manufacturing in total employment declined a little during the period of globalization from 1980 to 1993. In the Philippines the problem was greatly exacerbated by the reduction in the rate of growth of the economy during the period of globalization. With agriculture gradually shedding labor and the manufacturing industries failing to increase its share of employment, the result was a tertiarization of employment that represents more a rise in the proportion of labor force in rudimentary and informal services than a healthy growth of demand for tertiary sectors.[11]

The Case of India

Outside of the ESEA, India is another example of an Asian country that experienced a decline in the growth of manufacturing employment during the period of globalization. Employment in Indian manufacturing increased at an annual rate of 3.9 percent during the 1970s. From 1980 to 1991, despite a significant acceleration in the rate of growth of the economy, the trend rate of growth in employment in manufacturing was not significantly different from zero.[12] Once again, the explanation seems to be somewhat similar to that for China. Industries were initially characterized by significant overemployment, either because they were public sector enterprises subject to the pressure of absorbing labor in excess of requirement or because of the strict regulation of conditions of termination in private industries. As globalization increased the pressure to reduce the unit labor cost, enterprises took all available opportunity to avoid hiring by trying to reduce concealed unemployment. In many cases the difficulty of terminating redundant workers increased the perceived cost of employment and encouraged a degree of "employment aversion" through resort to inappropriate technology.

Conclusion

The less developed countries that succeed in achieving high growth by exploiting the opportunities provided by the globalizing world economy should be aware of the strongly positive effect that such growth is likely to have on the rate of urbanization. This is because success in the context of globalization means an expansion of manufactured exports, an acceleration of industrialization, and an increased inflow of foreign direct investment. All these activities tend to increase the concentration of investment in and an increased flow of population and resources to urban areas. What the less developed countries should avoid, however, is an artificial incentive for excessive urbanization through the concentration of public investment in urban areas in advanced regions and the creation of bias in favor of the location of private investment in same locations. Same considerations dictate that labor market interventions leading to an increase in the difference between earnings in urban and rural economies be avoided.

A large majority of less developed countries making an adjustment to globalization would initially be burdened with inefficient industries developed in a regime of import-substituting industrialization. Paradoxically, successful globalization may exacerbate the problem of urban unemployment in these cases. Industries developed behind the protection of an import-substituting industrialization strategy, especially those that are in the public sector, usually have a good deal of concealed redundancy.

Globalization, with a powerful pressure for a reduction in unit labor cost, creates a strong incentive to shed redundant labor. Although the expansion of urban employment, at given intensity of employment per worker, is substantial, the increase in the headcount rate of employment may be low or even negative because the rise in employment takes the form of an increased intensity of employment per worker. This increases industrial efficiency and, in the long run, this is highly beneficial for the economy.

The problem is that this creates a transitional problem, often rather severe, of increased urban unemployment and poverty. The right policy is not to continue with inefficient labor market interventions (e.g., legal barriers to restructuring employment). These measures are self-defeating. They could obstruct an efficient exploitation of opportunities of globalization and create an aversion to employment expansion among the entrepreneurs. The right way to reduce the social cost of transition to globalization is to create institutions and programs (e.g., unemployment insurance, public works and training) to offset the adverse transitional effects of globalization.

Globalization has created a strong competition among the less developed countries for foreign direct investment. There is no harm in a healthy competition in keeping the real unit labor cost in foreign exchange low through such measures as the promotion of labor productivity through investment in human capital, maintaining macroeconomic stability, and adjusting the exchange rate to realistic levels. But it would not be appropriate to artificially inflate the profitability of foreign direct investment. Much has been said about the possible problems of capital surge in less developed countries by way of an appreciation of the real exchange rate and its adverse effect on export promotion, so graphically brought out by the Mexican crisis of December 1994.[13] What is often not realized is that foreign direct investment tends to increase urban concentration by being directed to centers that are best served with infrastructure, broadly defined. It is easy for the less developed countries, in their single-minded pursuit of foreign direct investment to keep distorting incentives in favor of urban concentration, rather than adopting policies and systems of incentives for a desirable decentralization of investment and wide geographic distribution of benefits of economic growth.

Notes

1. This may change with the implementation of the Uruguay Round agreements, which visualize an all-round reduction of protection, including a reduction of protection on the part of the advanced industrial countries.

2. South Asia consists of the countries lying between Afghanistan and Myanmar. East and Southeast Asia consist of the countries and areas to the east and north of Thailand. For detailed facts A. R. Khan, *Overcoming Unemployment.* Geneva: ILO and UNDP, 1994.

3. There are exceptions within ESEA to this general pattern. The Philippines performed far worse than the average ESEA country on all counts and Thailand's performance, impressive on all other counts, suffered from the blemish that it did not succeed in significantly reducing poverty. As discussed, China's remarkable growth performance led to a dramatic reduction in the incidence of poverty in early reform years and to more ambiguous distributional and poverty consequences in later years. For details, see Khan, 1994, as well as A. R. Khan, *Employment in a Globalizing and Liberalizing World: The Case of the Philippines.* Manila: ILO South-East Asia and the Pacific Multidisciplinary Advisory Team, 1995, and A. R. Khan, *Employment, Growth and liberalization: China's Growth in a Globalizing World Economy.* Bangkok: ILO East Asia Multidisciplinary Advisory Team, 1996. Admittedly these conclusions do not apply to the former Indo-China, Mongolia, and the Democratic Republic of Korea.

4. One of the notable features of the development experience of Korea—as of several other ESEA countries—is the very rapid growth of employment in services. This was especially prominent during the period of globalization. In this respect the pattern of ESEA development has been different from the earlier cases of development. In earlier cases, the share of employment in the tertiary sector reached such high levels only at a later stage of development. The share of employment in manufacturing industries also peaked at a higher level and at a later stage of development. The explanation of this phenomenon probably lies in the fact that the difference between technological advance in manufacturing industries today and what it was during the earlier industrialization experience is far greater than the corresponding advance in tertiary technology.

5. These conclusions for Korea and ESEA are based on the data in Khan, 1994; Khan, 1996; and the Korea Labor Institute, *Foreign Labor Statistics*. Seoul, 1994.
6. Andrew Boltho, *China's Emergence – Prospects, Opportunities and Challenges*. International Economics Department, World Bank, 1994.
7. Of these migrants, 30 million are estimated to have crossed provincial boundaries. Most of these migrants have found employment in informal activities and in less attractive formal jobs for which nearly half of the migrants are estimated to have been granted temporary resident permits.
8. The sources of data on which all the above and the following estimates and statements on China have been made are to be found in Khan, 1996.
9. World Bank, *China: Strategies for Reducing Poverty in the 1990s*. Washington, DC, June 1992.
10. This information, from the State Statistical Bureau (SSB) source, was quoted by the Ministry of Civil Affairs to the author in March 1996. The poverty income threshold used by the SSB was reported to be 1,440 yuan per person per year. Although it is not clear that this threshold corresponds to the one that was used in the earlier estimates, the magnitude of the new estimate suggests a sharp rise in the incidence of urban poverty. The All-China Federation of Trade Unions estimates that the number of urban poor was higher, 20 million.
11. See Khan, 1995, for an analysis of employment in the Philippines during the period of globalization.
12. These estimates are based on the data shown in World Bank, *World Tables 1995*. Baltimore: Johns Hopkins University Press, 1995, and World Bank, *The World Development Report 1995*. New York: Oxford University Press, 1995.
13. For an account of these problem, see Ricardo Ffrench-Davis and Stephanie Griffith-Jones, eds., *Coping with Capital Surges: The Return of Finance to Latin America*. Boulder, CO: Lunne Riemer, 1995.

Section 3 The Challenge of the Informal City

Mariken Vaa

Rapid urban growth in the developing world has been accompanied by severe environmental problems in the cities, partly linked to production and transportation, but primarily the result of inadequate shelter conditions and service provision. In more recent years, it has also become evident that both relative and absolute poverty are increasing in the cities. Even in cases where the economy as a whole has flourished, there is a dramatic, unmet demand for housing, services, and jobs. Inequities are deepening as large numbers of people are not participants in the growing prosperity.

A large proportion of the urban population is housed in unauthorized settlements, and considerable numbers find their livelihoods in what is often labeled the informal economy. Illegal housing and unregistered economic activity are the two main elements of the informal city, as understood here. They are often taken to be overlapping, and linked to poverty. The point, however, is that poverty, expressed *inter alia* in low incomes and substandard shelter, and the informal sources of income generation and unauthorized settlements are two distinct phenomena, even if they are empirically correlated.

Characteristics of the Informal Economy

The division of economic activities into a formal and an informal sector is not new. It is, for instance, related to such older dichotomies as modern/traditional, and capitalist/peasant. Informal economic activities have many names, such as black, hidden, irregular, underground or parallel. The labels formal/informal gained wide usage in the early 1970s, as the International Labour Office adopted this terminology in its various city case studies under the World Employment Programme. According to this definition, the formal sector consists of enumerated, large-scale, capital intensive firms, while the informal sector is seen as composed of the unenumerated self-employed, mainly providing a livelihood for new entrants into the cities.

One of the most widely used classifications is from the ILO report on Kenya. The informal sector is here characterized by its ease of entry, reliance on indigenous resources, family ownership of enterprises, small scale of operations, labor-intensive and adapted technology, skill acquired outside the formal school system, and unregulated and competitive markets. In a later summary of the various studies undertaken under the ILO Urbanisation and Employment Research Project, this definition is offered:

> The informal sector consists of small-scale units engaged in the production and distribution of goods and services with the primary objective of generating employment and incomes to their participants, notwithstanding the constraints on capital, both physical and human, and know-how.[1]

Here, the significance of urban population growth to the emergence of the informal sector is emphasized, and the definition provides a justification for focusing employment policies and development efforts on this sector.

The two-sector terminology of economic activities and employment has been much discussed and criticized, and many revisions and refinements have been suggested. To review all the arguments presented is outside the scope of this discussion. Let us only note that one of the most frequently voiced criticisms is that the division of all economic activities into two categories is not only a gross oversimplification, but tends to ignore the connections among various types of activities. Empirical studies also reveal that a wide range of activities have some of the characteristics of the formal sector and some of the informal one. Entrance into some activities may be far from easy, but dependent on means to acquire modern, imported and capital-intensive technology. Not all incomes generated in the informal sector are necessarily low or the result of extralegal activities. Some may be organized on a rather large scale and their markets may be monopolistic. Activities labeled informal seem to have only negative attributes in common. Not only is the work performed unenumerated in official statistics, but the "firms" or "enterprises" are not registered, and written contracts are rare. When people are hired, labor legislation is ignored and health and safety standards are not upheld. If taxes are paid at all, taxable income is not assessed on the basis of written accounts.

An alternative approach to that of ILO stress the heterogeneity of informal activities, and their unauthorized character:

> The informal economy . . . is a process of income-generation characterized by one central feature; it is unregulated by the institutions of society, in a legal and social environment in which similar activities are regulated.[2]

According to this definition, the informal economy is not a set of survival activities performed by destitute people on the margins of society, but a near universal phenomenon, present in countries and regions at very different levels of economic development. The forms of unregulated production and distribution, the incomes they yield, and their relationship to legal codes and law enforcement may vary widely, both among countries and also within the same city.

The informal economy is probably on the increase in many rich countries, but it is in the developing world that its links to urban poverty is the most striking. Large numbers find their livelihood in informal activities. A summary of the ILO studies states that the share of the urban labor force in the developing countries engaged in the informal sector ranged from 20 to 70 percent, the average being over 50 percent. At that time, income levels in informal activities compared favorably with wages in formal employment in many cases. Later studies from Latin America indicate a general decrease in urban wages during the 1980s, but the income of persons employed in the informal urban sector fell far lower than formal incomes.[3]

Both national governments and donor agencies have come to look for ways and means to promote the informal sector as part of their overall development efforts. But given its diversity, it is doubtful that any general policy measures can bring this about. Already in 1978, one observer noted that:

> It is often mistakenly believed that a single policy prescription can be applied to the whole informal sector, so that governments should adopt similar programs towards artisans making furniture, towards artisans illegally manufacturing fire-works, towards sellers of basic foodstuffs, and towards prostitutes or drug-peddlers. The informal sector is large enough to permit and diverse enough to necessitate a wide range of different policy measures, allowing governments to mix incentives, assistance, neglect, rehabilitation and persecution within the total range of policies.[4]

What policy measures are appropriate, or at all feasible for raising the productive capacities of informal activities, depends partly on the specific nature of the activities themselves, on the demand for them, and the constraints facing the producers. But the values held and the goals pursued by the workers in the informal sector themselves, the values that are predominant in the surrounding society, and the general and specific goals pursued by governments must also be considered. The possibility that these sometimes may be in direct opposition to each other should be recognized in any effort to formulate recommendations for reforms to improve the productivity of informal activities. Policies that may work well in one country, or in one segment of its economy, may be totally irrelevant or even counterproductive in another context.

Unauthorized Settlements

Unauthorized settlements have many names. In the descriptive as well as more analytical literature, terms such as the self-help city, the informal city, the spontaneous city, squatter areas, irregular settlements, and pirate urbanization are used. In less specialized accounts, the illegal settlements may be referred to by more general terms, such as low-income settlements, shanty towns, or simply slums. Some of these terms refer to different dimensions of how the settlements have emerged, others to type of housing and level of services, and yet others again to characteristics of their inhabitants, such as their poverty. In the present discussion, where the focus is their extralegality, the preferred terms will be unauthorized, informal, or irregular settlements.

Three principal forms, or ideal types, of illegality can be delineated in the creation of unauthorized settlements. The first is illegal occupation of land, which is an infringement of property rights. The second is illegal or clandestine subdivision of land in conflict with planning regulations, and the third is construction of houses without permission and in contravention of building codes. Both the first and the second usually overlap with the third, but not necessarily.

In a number of case studies, it has been documented that the population of unauthorized settlements are in many respects as heterogeneous as the rest of the city. Income levels are varied, but lower than city averages, indicating an overrepresentation of the poor and the very poor. However, residents of the irregular settlements are active in a large number of occupations, and people find their livelihoods both in the formal and informal sectors of the economy. Far from all residents are recent migrants to the city. Women-headed households are overrepresented and usually among the poorest. Both because of poverty and because they may face legal or other constraints in the formal housing market, de facto and de jure women-headed households tend to seek shelter as tenants in the cheapest sections of the unauthorized settlements. Some are able to secure a house there, and make a living from letting rooms.[5]

However, one major difference between living conditions in these settlements and the rest of the city is the lack of social and physical infrastructure, which is directly linked to their legal status. Unless some legalization process or upgrading project is envisaged, city authorities feel no obligation to provide water, sanitation and drainage, pave roads, collect garbage, and build schools and clinics. Air pollution and untreated toxic waste from industries exacerbate the situation.[6] Homes and neighborhoods come to represent daily health hazards, particularly for women and children, the primary users of local space.

Unauthorized settlements do not consist solely of self-help, owner-occupied housing. One finding from recent years is that housing in the informal settlements have become commercialized, and that these settlements have an increasing proportion of renters and of absentee owners. Both small-scale and large-scale landlordism may be important components; in some settlements, rental accommodation is the major form of tenancy. A variety of housing submarkets have emerged. These submarkets are changing over time, depending on political, social, and economic factors at neighborhood, city, and national levels.

There are enormous variations in the legal status of unauthorized settelements among countries. Some countries, particularly in Latin America, already faced the existence of the illegal city in the 1940s. Because of the populist character of many Latin American regimes, semirecognition of invasions and other unauthorized settlements became a more frequent response than in other parts of the world. In most Asian and African countries, up to the end of the 1960s, the prevailing policies ranged from laissez-faire or neglect to repression through forceful evictions and half-hearted attempts at resettlement in government-sponsored housing schemes.

The inefficiency of demolition and relocation in meeting the housing shortage became obvious, as official housing statistics documented mounting shelter deficits. Since the 1960s, the official negative view of slum and squatter settlements began to be questioned. Surveys and case studies from all parts of the developing world documented that squatters were people much like others, who were well integrated in the urban economy and who had by their own effort developed settlements fitting their incomes and housing preferences. Based on empirical work by social scientists, architects and other professionals, an alternative housing strategy was being formulated, where self-help housing was seen as the solution to the housing shortage, rather than a problem to be eradicated. The role of governments would not be to build houses, but to provide inexpensive land, basic services, and security of tenure.

At HABITAT I, the United Nations Conference on Human Settlements held in 1976, aided self-help was the frame of reference for the recommendations to national governments. The overwhelming majority of attending countries endorsed these recommendations, officially recognizing the necessity of taking appropriate measures to improve uncontrolled settlements and to integrate their inhabitants into the national development process. However, endorsing a policy does not necessarily mean that a government has the will or capacity to implement it. Most countries have undertaken individual projects based on Habitat recommendations, often attracted by the possibility of acquiring soft loans from international agencies. Few, if any, have radically changed the way in which land, capital, materials, and labor are allocated for urban housing and infrastructure.[7] It is a seeming paradox that governments that at international fora commit themselves to assisted self-help and upgrading, pursue their established policies of clearing settlements that they deem substandard and building subsidized apartments for the not so poor.[8]

Both the World Bank and the UNDP produced in 1991 new strategy papers for urban development. The UNDP defines the new urban agenda as consisting of the following four points: poverty alleviation, infrastructure and services provision for the poor, improvement of the environment, and promotion of the private sector and NGOs. While similarly stressing the need for poverty alleviation and improvement of the environment, the World Bank also advocates improving overall urban productivity and a reassessment of the linkages between the urban economy and macroeconomic performance. Both the UNDP and World Bank strategy formulations stress how past program and project approaches, be it financing site and services and upgrading of unauthorized settlements, or building urban infrastructure more generally, rarely had city wide impacts and largely bypassed the poorest. Cities were divided into projects, improving specific neighborhoods without affecting the prevailing urban policies and institutional framework.

In the meantime, new unauthorized settlements are appearing and the older ones continue to grow. The proportion of urban populations residing in such settlements range from 30 to well over 70 percent in some cities. The gap between the number of housing units produced by the formal sector and the growth of urban populations is considerable. It has been estimated that in recent years, between 70 and 95 percent of all new housing in the cities of the developing world has been built illegally .[9] What is new, is that a large proportion of these dwellings consist of substandard rental units, making established approaches of upgrading based on self-help less applicable.

Problems of Governance

Both unauthorized settlements and informal income generation pose at least three problem areas and dilemmas of governance. First is the difficulty of formulating and implementing sound policies when basic data are unknown. The second is the problem of resource mobilization, from the viewpoint of both the authorities and the individual or group, and the third is the question of the legitimacy of law-enforcement agencies, or of the political system itself.

During the last 25 years, a large number of studies of the informal sector have been produced, by international organizations and independent researchers, both expatriates, as well as nationals of the countries concerned. Yet, most studies consist of small-scale surveys, and even the more comprehensive ones do not give any precise knowledge of the sector's size, composition, organization, competitiveness, and links the formal economy. In most countries, the governmental planning process fails to recognize the contribution of the informal economy. Most development plans are weighted in favor of the formal economy, so are social accounting systems. A sector that on average engages 20 to 70 percent of the urban labor force and produces 20 to 35 percent of urban incomes remain outside development management processes.[10] One consequence of this neglect of attention is that it is simply not known how a given economy functions in its totality, possibly rendering the policy instruments in use inadequate or even irrelevant. Another is that measures geared to the formal economy may have a series of unintended and largely unknown effects on how the informal economy functions. A third implication of the current lack of information is that it is difficult to develop policy instruments for dealing with the informal economy in relation to policy goals that have been developed. Whether these goals are suppression, promotion, or regularization of the informal economy, to reach them is extremely difficult if its central features are unknown.

On the whole, more is probably known about the scope and forms of unauthorized shelter provision than about informal income generation. Houses are more tangible than transactions. But there is a dearth of knowledge from most cities on how the poorest actually find shelter, on how land and housing markets operate, and the links between formal and informal housing markets. The recent awareness of the importance of absentee ownership and rental housing in unauthorized settlements indicate that, although these settlements provide shelter primarily for the poor, they increasingly constitute opportunities for investment and incomes for better-off segments.

The question of resource mobilization has many facets. To provide better services for homes and economic enterprises, both local and national governments need money. However, in many cases, the authorities do not collect taxes on property and revenue from rents in irregular settlements, simply because their existence is not recognized. At the same time, it is well documented that the residents of unauthorized settlements often pay more for the minimal services they do receive, such as water from private vendors. Thus, there is both a willingness and an ability to pay for services. When it comes to value created in the informal economy, it is difficult to see how an adequate or equitable taxation system can be introduced without some form of recognition.

However, it is not only a question of increasing the resource base of governments and local authorities, but of allowing the workers and the dwellers of the informal city to use their resources more productively than they may be able to do at present. Bulldozing shacks does not add to the housing stock, nor does chasing hawkers off the streets add to their productivity. When government dealings with the informal city oscillate between ambiguity, accommodation and harassment, it is hard to see how individual and collective action can take on constructive rather than purely defensive forms.

A third problem area concerns the legitimacy of the government itself. Most countries in the developing world have inherited a legal framework and a planning tradition that were not formulated to cope with rapid urban growth, but are aimed at controlling the poor and assuring high standards for a tiny elite. Building and zoning laws and standards formulated within this framework represent wishful thinking rather than enforceable rules. When rules are visibly flouted by the rich and the poor alike, it is more than likely that many people cease to have much faith in laws. This may become a dangerous inheritance even if governments should undertake to revise their legal systems to be more equitable and suited to local realities.

Conclusion

There is a growing concern with urban management, reflected in seminars and conferences, books, and articles and also in some donor-financed projects, notably the Urban Management Programme, initiated in 1986 by the UNDP, the World Bank, and Habitat. The program started by focusing on three topics, namely, land management, municipal finance and administration, and infrastructure management. In 1990, improving the urban environment and in 1991, urban poverty alleviation were added to the agenda.[11] One of the insights gained so far, is that apart from some technical issues, there are few, if any, general solutions to the five points above. Urban problems are contextually based and solutions have to be worked out locally. One might add that the solutions are not technical, administrative or even economic, but primarily political.

The main conclusion of the UNDP's *Human Development Report 1991* was that the real cause of deprivation and poor human conditions in developing countries is not lack of resources, but lack of political commitment. The report focused on health and education, but the conclusion is validated by comparative data in all sectors, including housing, service provision and employment. Even if the political will is there, it does not equate with political capacity. To pursue redistributive policies is inevitably going to hurt powerful interests, some of which are entrenched in central bureaucracies and local administrations. For these reasons, most governments in developing countries have problems in coming to terms with the cities as they are (i.e., acknowledging the importance of the informal city, and the hardships of the poor).

Earlier in this discussion, it was stated that although poverty and informal income generation and settlements may be empirically correlated, they are two distinct phenomena. This may seem fairly self-evident, but it has important implications for the political feasibility of raising living and shelter standards and coming to grips with environmental deterioration. The informal city is not exclusively the domain of the poor. Better off segments of the urban population, including politicians and highly placed bureaucrats, may have strong interests in informal housing and informal production of goods and services. The problem is not that the informal city is cut off, but rather the ways in which it is integrated with the formal city.

Notes

1. S. W. Sethuraman, ed., *The Urban Informal Sector in Developing Countries*. Geneva: ILO, 1981.
2. Manuel Castells and Alejandro Portes, "World Underneath: The Origins, Dynamics and Effects of the Informal Economy." In Alejandro Portes, Manuel Castells, and Lauren A. Benton, eds., *The Informal Economy*. Baltimore: Johns Hopkins University Press, 1989, pp. 11–40.
3. Alfredo Rodríguez and Lucy Winchester, "Cities, Democracy and Governance in Latin America," *International Social Science Journal* 1996, 147: 73–84.
4. Ray Bromley, "The Urban Informal Sector: Why is it Worth Discussing?" *World Development* 1978, 6 (9/10), 1978.
5. Caroline Moser, "Women, Human Settlements and Housing: A Conceptual Framework for Analysis and Policy-Making." In Caroline Moser and Linda Peake, eds., *Women, Human Settlements and Housing*. London: Tavistock, 1987.
6. Jorge E. Hardoy and David Satterthwaite, "The Legal and the Illegal City." In Lloyd Rodwin, ed., *Shelter, Settlement and Development*. Boston: Allen & Unwin, 1987, pp. 304–338.
7. Gregory K. Payne, *Low-Income Housing in the Developing World*. New York: Wiley, 1984.
8. Lisa Peattie, "Housing Policy in Developing Countries: Two Puzzles," *World Development* 1979, 7: 1017–1022.
9. Jorge E. Hardoy and David Satterthwaite, "The Future City." In Jorge E. Hardoy, Sandy Cairncross, and David Sattherthwaite, eds., *The Poor Die Young: Housing and Health in Third World Cities*. London: Earthscan Publications, 1990.
10. Om Prakash Mathur, "Managing the Urban Informal Sector." In G. Shabbir Cheema, ed., *Urban Management: Policies and Innovations in Developing Countries*. Westport, CT: Prager, 1993, pp. 161–173.
11. Patrick McAuslan, "Issues of Urban Management." In Nigel Harris, ed., *Cities in the 1990s*. London: UCL Press, 1992, p. 103.

Part 3

Cities and Citizens

Section 1 The State, the Society, and Individuals

Hazem El-Beblawi

Good governance is needed equally at all levels—international, national, and local because they are mutually reinforcing. Local governance is but a microcosm of all governance problems. It can even be argued that solutions for governance problems, in general, should start at the local level, the grass roots.

This issue has received renewed attention in the aftermath of the cold war and the collapse of the socialist economics. The role of the State, in particular, has been reexamined and the old debate on the role of the State, which was revived in the 1980s, has become a topic of current interest. The need to rethink the role of the State in the economy has been reinforced by the demise of the Socialist bloc as well as the crisis in the developing countries. However, the new debate has a different perspective. In the old debate the role of the State was generally examined within the context of public and constitutional liberties, the present debate has evolved around such economic concepts as performance, productivity, and growth. Thus, economists are called upon to contribute to a field that was previously outside their domain. Certainly, the objective of these contributions should not be to do away with all the philosophical and political knowledge compiled on the subject. Quite the contrary, the analysis of the way the market economy works, and of its prerequisites, actually helps to determine the role of the State and the limits of its action.

Before discussing on this subject, let us first examine a few basic ideas on social organization.

Two Triads

During the eighteenth and nineteenth centuries, the Individual was often opposed to the State, or Society. All totalitarian regimes have deliberately fostered the implicit identification of the State with Society to provide a cloak of legitimacy for their actions. If the State is Society, then it represents the public interest. Therefore, whoever opposes the State automatically opposes the public interest. However, to analyze the behavior of public institutions, it is necessary to differentiate the State from Society. The Public Choice school of thought demonstrated that the State, rather than being an infallible, ideal construction that reflects Society, is only a set of human organizations in which decisions are taken by politicians, bureaucrats, technocrats, and others, who are only as rational as other people in pursuit of their own interests, financial or otherwise. The State, as with any other organization, is not a homogeneous entity. On the contrary, it is a combination of different groups and interests characterized by divergence and even hostility. Therefore, the Individual/State (or Society) duality must be replaced by the triad: the Individual, the State, and Society.

It is relatively easy to define the Individual. Society, however, seems more difficult to comprehend. Although Society encompasses all the individuals who comprise it, Society is more than the sum of its parts. Society is not only the present, it is the future generations as well as the common memory of the past. Certainly, Society cannot exist without political power and a concept of law. In short, Society is a complex reality, a historical fact and a sociopolitical entity. The State, for its part, is made up of all the juridical institutions and systems that enjoy a monopoly of legitimate coercion. Even though political power is a necessary element for any human society, a distinction must be made between the State and Society. It is true that the State is the political and judicial instrument of Society, but as a set of concrete institutions, the State has a certain logic, an independent behavior and specific values that make it different from Society. The State, a product of Society, has carved out its own autonomous existence. With this first triad, we learn about the main social actors or agents. the Individual, Society, and the State.

The distinction among the various actors in turn brings into play three instruments or fields of activity: Economics, Ethics, and Politics. This is our second triad.

As discussed, the Political is power; it is about the right to command on the one side and the duty to obey on the other. The subject matter of the Political is coercion and discipline. In contrast, the Economic involves self-interest, the search for profit or benefit, and its main field of activity is free exchange (i.e., the market). Finally, the Ethical covers all religious or other moral values that define behavioral norms, because all societies need to have a value system by which they distinguish good from evil.

There exists a correspondence in the relations between these two triads, that is, an actors-instruments paradigm: State/the political, Individual/the economic, and Society/the ethical. Although legitimate coercion is the exclusive monopoly of the State and the Individual excels at looking after his own interests, which makes him the principal actor in the market, Society is the custodian of values and mores. If the political is thus defined by its exclusive control of legitimate coercion by the State, the economy can only prosper with competition and values are based on solidarity and cohesion. Monopoly, competition, and solidarity are the underlying principles of the political, the economic, and the ethical, respectively.

It would be wrong, however, to view the political, the economic, and the ethical as being in opposition to one another. Rather, these elements must be integrated into an institutional dynamic leading to a dialectic of reciprocal interaction. It is important here to stress the need for a friendly institutional framework that lends itself to successful interaction among the political, the economic, and the ethical. The market economy, in particular, cannot function, let alone prosper, without a framework in which the political and the ethical strengthen, rather than hinder, the market logic. Historically, the rapid expansion of Western capitalism, and therefore of the market economy, coincided with the emergence of the modern State concept on the one hand and emancipation from the power of the church on the other hand. The political, the economic, and the ethical develop together, although each follows its own logic, which then defines the interrelation between them.

There is, therefore, a certain correspondence between the political, the economic, and the ethical in any Society, meaning a role for the State, another for the Individual, and a third for Society. Just as Montesquieu advocated a balance of power (executive, legislative, and judicial), we believe there is a need for checks and balances among the political, the economic, and the ethical, as distributed in the respective roles of the State, the Individual, and Society.

The legacy of our modern world is two features: hegemony or dominance of the political to the detriment of the economic and the ethical on the one hand, and the globalization of the economy on the other hand. Both have led to the emergence of a new order: the resurrection of the market economy and privatization. The role of the State cannot be defined without taking into account these two characteristics, especially where developing countries are concerned.

Hegemony of the Political: The State as Usurper

The twentieth century has witnessed the expansion of the modern State. The role of the State in the economy is no longer limited to acting as the guardian of law and order, regulating or promoting economic activity: the State has become the principal agent of this activity. Through central planning and the public sector, the political has invaded the economic sphere. Similarly, in countries with official ideologies – religious or secular—the State apparatus, together with its ideologues and apostles, has taken over morality. Not content to maintain order and social peace and secure the necessary conditions for economic and moral progress, the State imposes itself as the only omnipotent actor on the scene. Thus, the State becomes the only active player while the Individual and Society are reduced to passive spectators. The political game, the exclusive domain of coercion and command, ignores the rules of competition in economic activity, as well as voluntary solidarity and cohesion in societal activities. Imperialism, or the hegemony of the political, has stifled the Individual as well as civil Society. As a consequence, economy and morality have suffered, if not suffocated. The failure has been proportional to the degree of usurpation by the political. The experience has been an almost total failure in totalitarian countries, with a combination of economic bankruptcy and public deception. The situation has been better when the market and civil society have been able to maintain a role for themselves.

The failure of political hegemony is not so much a reason to condemn the political, as it is a failure to keep the political within its natural limits. Certainly, the State has an indispensable role to play, but not at the expense of the role of the Individual or that of civil Society.

The same twentieth century that gave the State its impetus and excesses is ending on a completely different note: the return of the State to its rightful place and the reinstatement of the market economy and civil society. This is the situation in a number of countries that went too far in asserting the role of the State and must now reverse the process and revive the market economy and civil society. It is a difficult task: the period of transition to a market economy will be even more difficult.

Globalization of the Economy

Without oversimplifying, it can be said that we are now witnessing a globalization of the economy. It is true that the national State remains the foundation of international politics, that national interests still define strategies and alliances, and that even a certain ethnic specificity, linguistic and religious, is being manifested more and more in the least likely places.

It remains true, however, that the underlying economy is becoming ever more global, while political boundaries are becoming less and less important. The Industrial Revolution and capitalism, both by their very nature universal in scope, continue their work of globalization. Indeed, since the World War II, the growth of international trade has been almost twice that of national economies. The world economy is becoming more interdependent. More and more, the most dynamic industrial actors are the multinationals and transnationals, and in the meantime industrial strategies in the most advanced sectors are being defined on a global scale.

This trend has been further strengthened by the revolution in information and communications, which is transforming the world into a kind of global village. A no less dramatic financial revolution is making political boundaries ever more obsolete. The integration of financial markets, as well as the movement of capital and foreign exchange fluctuations, has resulted in phenomenal worldwide surges in investment and savings.

The international institutional framework sanctions the globalization trend. The World Bank and especially the International Monetary Fund act as tsars of the world economy. With the new World Trade Organization, the circle is complete.

Notwithstanding the above, the trend for the globalization of the economy should not be exaggerated. National interests are still dominant; the result is tension between an ever more global economic reality and a political reality that nonetheless remains national, if not nationalistic. The burden of the globalization of the economy is felt more in the developing countries. That is why the role of the State in the economy of developing countries cannot be defined without taking into account the requirements of this globalization. The role of the State in these economies has to include these external considerations.

The Rule of Law

Recognizing the reality of the paradigm – State/political, Individual/economic, and Society/ethical – linking the above two triads requires the establishment of a legal framework to facilitate the proper functioning of this reality. Although it is true that no social life is conceivable without a legal system to regulate relations between rulers and ruled, not all legal systems respect the notion of a Rule of Law.

To understand the concept of the Rule of Law, one has to distinguish between rules and commands. Although rules are commands, they are characterized more by generalities and abstractions. A command is an order: the issue of this order tells a person to do or not to do a particular thing; it is almost a personal relationship. A rule, in contrast, is a general statement that specifies that in certain circumstances actions must satisfy certain conditions. In observing general rules, the Individual does not serve another person's ends, nor can we say that he is subject to his will. Like laws of nature, Hayek asserts, "the laws of the state provide fixed features in the environment in which he has to move; though they eliminate certain choices open to him, they do not, as a rule, limit the choice to some specific action that somebody else wants him to take." In other words, the law is not arbitrary.

The concept of a Rule of Law usually implies certain attributes for the legal system. First and foremost is the nonretroactive effect of the law. People are supposed to conform to existing rules known to them in advance and not to be subject to unknown rules not yet adopted. This not only satisfies judicial precepts, but also helps Individuals to plan their activities within a well-defined frame. Legal predictability is no less important than economic predictability. Equally important is the fact that the Rule of Law must ensure the equality of all before the law, as well as the respect of human rights without discrimination on the basis of sex, creed, or color.

The concept of the Rule of Law, thus defined, can safeguard the rights of the State, Society, and Individuals within their respective domains. The importance of this institutional aspect—in the form of an appropriate legal system—an hardly be overemphasized.

The State and the Economy

Every historical moment has its exigencies. It is evident that we are living through the moment of the market economy.

If we limit ourselves to the role of the State in the market economy, we have, first of all, to recognize the market reality. The time has passed when market and planning were mutually exclusive. Our experience in the twentieth century has shown that the market is superior to any other form of economic organization. The market, for its part, cannot be conceived of without a strong State that establishes the limits of economic activity.

Economists and public finance experts long ago defined the economic role of the State. In his already classic book, Musgrave distinguishes three branches of State activity in the economy: resource allocation or provision of public goods, income distribution, and stability or macroeconomics.

The concept of public goods highlights the limitations and shortcomings of the market in satisfying public and social needs. The market functions properly only when the "principle of exclusion" prevails, when profits and costs can be attributed solely to the concerned agent. In contrast, when profits or costs are spread on a wider scale, the functioning of the market seems most inadequate. Any rational being would refuse to shoulder the cost of a good that he can get for free. Everyone wants to be a "free rider." In such cases only public authorities, through their power of coercion, can manage to provide these goods.

The concept of public goods covers a wide range of State activities, from the provision of public goods and services to institutional organization. Most of the physical and institutional infrastructure is simply the result of the application of the concept of public goods. This holds true for activities in the fields of justice, defense, transport, communications, education, public health, and scientific research. One should remember that the concept of public goods is a dynamic one. However, it has to be borne in mind that the fact that a certain good or service is public does not necessarily mean that it should be produced by a public enterprise.

The role of the State is not limited to the provision of public goods. It also extends to securing a minimum level of living conditions for the most disadvantaged segments of the population and to eliminating or reducing blatant inequalities in society. Every society has a certain concept of social justice, and the State is the guarantor of social peace. In this field, opinions may differ, and there may be a conflict between the exigencies of efficiency and those of justice, which could lead to serious controversies. The advocates of social justice have been in favor of a greater intervention of the State in the redistribution of income and wealth, whereas the more liberal circles prefer a more moderate intervention, arguing that growth is the best guarantee of justice. It will be difficult to resolve this thorny question once and for all, A democratic regime is better suited to find solutions for such problems.

The State must define and implement a macroeconomic policy conducive to monetary stability and capable of creating the necessary conditions for growth and employment. It is a multifaceted policy involving monetary, fiscal, commercial, and employment issues. The State has at its disposal an ample stock of tools of persuasion and dissuasion, and it must use them wisely.

After this general overview of the functions of the State in the economy, it is perhaps necessary to emphasize the need for the State to maintain some sort of symbiosis between its interventions and the requirements of the market economy. The actions undertaken by the State must be integrated into the logic of the market. Because the market is the meetingplace of the actors, with their calculating, rational behavior, the State must promote such rationality. No economic calculation can be made in the absence of a solid monetary base or without adequate data. Maintaining monetary stability has always been considered as the sign of good government, and the availability of information and statistics (transparency) is also important for economic rationality. No less important is the judicial system and its transparency and efficiency. Last, but not least, a certain degree of predictability is necessary for the proper functioning of the market, for although risk is an inherent element in any economic activity, uncertainty is, on the contrary, its worst enemy.

The market economy needs the State, but only a certain type of State: a State that adheres to the Rule of Law. A planned economy and a police state can coexist. The market economy, however, suffocates under arbitrariness and uncertainty. The rules of the game in a market economy have to be established in advance and, more important still, they have to be adhered to strictly. Only a liberal State can support the market, and the shift from a planned economy to a market economy requires major institutional transformations, in particular an appropriate legal system: the Rule of Law.

Economic and Political Reform

The transformation of State economies into market economies poses serious problems, particularly regarding the relationship between economic reform and political reform. Does the transition to a market economy require political reform? Is democracy a prerequisite of or a complement to the market economy?

History is ambiguous in this regard, to say the least. Although in most Western countries democracy and capitalism went hand in hand, other examples prove the contrary. For example, Germany and Japan in the nineteenth century—and South-East Asian countries in the twentieth century—enjoyed prosperous market economies without any relaxation of the grip of politically authoritarian States. Today's China provides yet another example of such a paradox.

Without dwelling on this thorny issue, we should like to note one condition that seems to us indispensable. The market economy can only function in places where the concept of the Rule of Law prevails. With the Rule of Law, people do not obey other people. Everyone—governed and governor—is subject to the rule of law, free from arbitrariness and whim. The law defines the scope and limits of activity and guarantees respect for commitments. The Rule of Law constitutes, therefore, the minimal conditions necessary for a market economy.

Democracy is unquestionably based on the concept of the Rule of Law, but its brightest promise lies in the areas of political libel—ties, participation, changeover of powers, and respect for human rights. In a democratic regime, responsibility, accountability, and transparency are more or less guaranteed. Thus although democracy is not absolutely necessary for a market economy, it certainly is its most reliable ally.

Conclusion

Though the main argument of this sections raises issues of a general nature, we need to emphasize the relevance of its conclusions to local governance. However, it would be rather difficult to harmonize the Political, the Economic, and the Ethical at the local level if such harmony is lacking at the national level. In particular, the concept of the Rule of Law, if not adhered to at the national level, can hardly be conceived of at the local level. It seems thus imperative for good local governance to ensure the proper institutional framework at the national level.

Section 2 The Need for Effective Local Governance

William Gorham and
G. Thomas Kingley

Other sections of *Cities Fit for People* have documented the extraordinary growth now occurring in the world's cities and the tremendous pressure this is placing on the public sector to provide adequate services and address the other fundamental economic, social, and physical challenges that rapid urbanization implies. One response, implemented with surprising consistency in developing countries over the past decade, has been to decentralize government responsibility for urban management. But it is clear that the steps taken so far have not been adequate. In the world's burgeoning cities, service deficits remain enormous and millions still live in squalor.

This does not mean that decentralization was the wrong path. To the contrary, an important part of the problem in many countries is that decentralization has not been adequately implemented. But although decentralization is probably a necessary condition, it is not a sufficient one. Reforms in the basic character of governance at the local level are also required.

Promising avenues for change include (1) a series of internal reforms to make local governments more entrepreneurial, efficient, and performance driven, now often grouped under the term "reinventing government;" (2) the building of a stronger local civil society; and (3) taking advantage of impressive recent advances in the application of information in addressing urban problems.

The Role of Decentralization

It was once commonly thought that the primary barrier to the provision of adequate urban infrastructure in developing countries was that such infrastructure was too costly to be affordable. Recent research has shown, however, that this perception was faulty.[1] Urbanization is an impressive wealth-generating process. In the world's rapidly growing cities, it ought to be possible to tap into that wealth to pay for basic public infrastructure and services at modest but decent standards. The riches are being created, but governments have typically been unable or unwilling to access them sufficiently to address public needs.

In the early 1980s, there was growing acceptance of the view that a major reason why governments were unresponsive in this regard was that they were overcentralized. Infrastructure provision was then largely the responsibility of central governments, and they were characteristically rigid—too distant from local realities and without the incentives to respond to local needs efficiently. At the core of the argument in favor of decentralization is the conviction that because local governments are closer to the people, they should be more responsive to them. They should be better informed about real needs and opportunities and have stronger incentives for efficiency. They should also be better able to mobilize resources because, if the local citizens are getting services they want at reasonable prices, they should be more willing to pay for them.

The period since then has seen a wave of decentralization in all of the world's major regions.[2] The idea has been powerful and virtually pervasive. It is of interest that, although the privatization of the economies of the former Soviet block countries has received more attention, the creation of freely elected local governments and the devolution of substantial responsibility and property to those governments, were among the earliest reforms implemented by most nations in that region soon after 1989.[3]

Decentralization has led to improvements in performance, but it is clear that significant problems remain—for example, in the cities of most developing nations the provision of decent land and infrastructure seriously lag behind growth. To be sure, a part of the problem is that the decentralization process is not yet complete. In many countries, central governments that have officially delegated new functions to local governments have been slow to grant local officials enough flexibility to operate them efficiently or enough authority to raise the revenues needed to pay for them.

The World Bank suggests three directions for furthering decentralization and making it function more effectively:

1. Providing clearer definitions of functional responsibilities for all levels of government and giving local governments more managerial and fiscal discretion over the functions that have been assigned to them. "A clear linkage between a particular unit of government and a specific service is crucial if constituents are to hold that unit of government accountable for providing that service well."
2. Reforming revenues. "Typically, local revenue sources are limited and heavily regulated by central government. Generally speaking,

local governments need more financial autonomy to perform the responsibilities they have been assigned."

3. Balancing central regulation and local autonomy. "Some degree of national accountability through a national regulatory framework is appropriate," but emphasis is also needed on mechanisms to enhance the accountability of local officials to their constituents.[4]

Although there is general agreement that decentralization initiatives need to be implemented more fully by the mid-1990s, there has also been recognition that decentralization is no panacea. Unconstrained decentralization to localities could hinder macroeconomic stabilization and redistribution goals; enhanced efficiency is by no means assured. The choices are not so much whether one should decentralize in general, but rather what functions of what sectors for what areas can be most fruitfully decentralized.[5]

This line of thinking recognizes that further and more definitive decentralization will be needed for many functions, but that higher levels of government will still retain legitimate interests in outcomes for a large number of them. New and more productive mechanisms for collaboration between levels of government, rather than simply a "hands-off" or "fend for yourself" attitude on the part of central governments would seem appropriate.

It is also clear, however, that even when fully implemented, decentralization is no guarantee of effective performance by local agencies. It is well understood that public officials at all levels try to insulate themselves from penalties related to their performance. If they are allowed to do so, serious public service failures may result.

The free election of local leaders is a vital ingredient—the prospect of what will happen at the next election is a powerful motivator—but there is growing recognition that this alone is not enough. There are many opportunities even for elected leaders to insulate themselves between elections. We cannot expect public officials to perform effectively unless they are placed in a context that provides strong day-to-day incentives for them to give their best effort. This is where an element of the World Bank's third recommendation—accountability—deserves prominence. In most cases, decentralization will have to be accompanied by substantial reform in the basic character of governance at the local level—reform that makes public officials truly accountable for effective performance.

The process of making public servants more accountable requires doing a better job of educating the public on real cost/performance tradeoffs in service delivery. The same process, therefore, should also enhance the public's willingness to pay for services and thereby enhance financing options.

Reinventing Government

Substantial thinking about how local governments could be reformed along these lines has taken place throughout the world of late. Many of the key ideas have been summarized and put in context by Osborne and Graebler in their book Reinventing Government.[6]

Most important, they recognize that the goal should be good governancc, not large governments. They argue that the primary role of mayors and local councils should be leadership—reaching out beyond simply "administering" programs and functions handed down to them to exert creativity and entrepreneurship in doing what ever needs to be done to address the problems and opportunities of their citizens. This includes efforts to mobilize the private and NGO sectors in the public interest. In this way local officials are (and should feel) more personally responsible for the full range of local outcomes than would be the expected if they saw themselves only as administrators.

As leaders, mayors and councils should set goals and visions, establish and enforce the rules of the game, and organize and motivate resources to assure that basic public functions are provided. But this does not require that all local public functions be performed by government agencies. On the contrary, when it comes to the actual delivery of services, government agencies in the traditional position of monopoly providers, do not have strong incentives to perform efficiently. Performance is likely to be enhanced if competition is introduced. This can mean subcontracting specific functions to competing private firms, but it also can be accomplished by assigning activities to NGOs on a short-term contract basis and by introducing competition among units within government or having government units compete with firms and NGOs.

Although privatization most often means subcontracting functions to firms, it can of course imply broader arrangements (concessions, Build-Operate-Transfer [BOT] schemes, and so on. Important here is the retention of a public body to set and monitor policy and standards and to use a variety to mechanisms to stimulate and control the performance of the private entities involved.

A technique that has received much prominence recently is the performance contract: contracts that link the compensation (and continued employment) of suppliers to contractually specified performance targets. This heightens the sense that performance is what counts. Such contracts may be between higher levels of government and the supplying agency and/or between that agency and those responsible for subfunctions (internal departments or external private contractors). This approach exemplifies the theme of decentralization of responsibility within government—giving lower-level officials clear performance targets, but allowing them a great deal of latitude in deciding how those targets can best be met.

Whoever the responsible actors may be, reinventing government also highlights the need for performance measurement. Accountability requires some quantitative benchmarking – keeping clear records of the output of all agencies and relative measures of efficiency (e.g., cost per unit of service provided). In the United States, advances in performance measurement schemes have been substantial in the past few years. The first step is defining and monitoring the indicators, but equally essential steps include independent and objective audits of the measurement process and regular publication of the results so that they become familiar to the public. Another important theme is introducing customer orientation and access as an operating principle in government. A wide range of techniques are relevant here, including a publishing agency's operating plans and performance reports, establishing consumer "hotlines," establishing "one-stop shops" (e.g., to make it simpler to obtain licenses), performing regular surveys of consumer satisfaction and attitudes (and publicizing the results and using them as the basis for redesigning program delivery systems). Another technique is user participation by placing service beneficiaries on agency boards and management committees (to offset the strong producer interests that typically dominate them).

Together, these techniques can help make local governments accountable to their citizenry. Accountability is the key to better performance and resource mobilization.

Building Civil Society

Consistent with the theme of reinventing government, but moving beyond it, is the idea that sound governance and effective performance of public functions requires public-interest oriented organizations outside of government, such as community-based organizations, special interest NGOs, and broader nongovernmental leadership coalitions. Where this sort of civic infrastructure exists, accountability is likely to be enhanced. In addition, the "social capital" that is created supports and facilities the performance of all public functions. This is particularly valuable when such institutions and networks work collaboratively with government, and with each other.[7]

A basis for this is encouragement of direct public participation in setting expectations for government programs, monitoring them, and evaluating their results. A step in this direction is illustrated by experiments in several countries that permit the public to participate directly in reviewing options for local capital investment and setting priorities in the municipal capital budget.[8]

The next step beyond is developing new nongovernmental institutions to play a continuing role in governance. The most talked about examples here are the many grass-roots, community-based organizations that are emerging around the world. Sometimes they provide their own public services directly and/or make significant contributions to their financing. However, their *raison d'être* has often been to make governments more accountable. They have done this by articulating community needs, applying pressure to see that they are addressed, and watching over the performance of the agencies that deal with them.

A step up from the neighborhood level, a number of nongovernmental institutions exist primarily to address accountability at the municipal level. An advocacy NGO in Bangalore, India, for example, is now preparing a "City Report Card" with a number of indicators on local government performance. A voluntary organization in Ecuador helps municipalities accept and improve on their accountability. However, this category also includes a host of single-issue interest groups, such as environmental NGOs.

A more recent innovation is the development of broad-based metropolitan leadership coalitions, particularly in the United States. Some of these focus on single issues, again, for example, such metropolitan environmental issues as air quality. But others are more broad based in terms of substance. These often include representatives of a variety of civic groups and interests that see themselves as "long-term stakeholders" in the metropolis. Examples include major businesses, philanthropic community foundations, neighborhood development organizations, large universities and churches.

These coalitions most often operate as "active networks" rather than as defined organizations – individuals maintain an awareness of important trends and events and stay in contact with each other (among other ways, through overlapping membership on the boards of a number of individual institutions). They deal with a broad range of issues (e.g., economic development, problems of inner-city poverty and childhood development, fiscal inequity between the central cities and their suburbs), and they sometimes form special task forces to help address important problems as they emerge. They try to work in collaboration with local mayors and other political leaders, but they also bring independent views to those collaborations. A large part of what they do is to press in a variety of ways to improve government performance, but they may also participate in visioning exercises to clarify long-term community goals; take on some public service delivery functions directly; and promote the interests of their metropolis, both nationally and internationally.

Examples in Developing Countries

The themes of reinventing government and building civic society have been used to enhance government accountability in a number of cities around the world. Several examples were reviewed at a World Bank-sponsored Municipal Finance Conference held in September 1995. Two types of cases stand out as relevant.

The first relates accountability at the municipal level, to functions that are, by definition, citywide. Examples are the provision of trunk infrastructure (e.g., major highways, water mains), economic development, and education). Here, the most impressive stories were told by entrepreneurial mayors who had recognized that their constituents had lost faith that traditional government agencies would deliver results in the face of enormous demands for new infrastructure. Thus, although they recognized the need for such improvements, citizens were unwilling to pay more in taxes and user charges.

These mayors recognized that their first priority was to rebuild credibility. They formulated a clear plan of action for citywide infrastructure improvements (gaining ideas and suggestions from citizens along the way) and estimated the costs. They then publicized their plans, telling the people exactly how much and in what way they would have to pay to obtain the proposed improvements. Finally, they put the issue to a referendum (i.e., the government was making the commitment to produce clearly specified results, and a positive vote from the citizens' indicated their commitment to pay the price required to obtain them).

The success of these approaches reflected general public recognition of a new style of governance, which was exemplified by this approach exemplified. The new style was participative, transparent, and accountable. Its themes included setting clear targets for performance, encouraging public participation in the planning process, being explicit about costs and financing providing mechanisms for fulfillment, proactively communicating all proposals to the public at large (encouraging meaningful opportunities to respond), and monitoring and publishing data on actual results.

The second type relates to initiatives at the community level. Such partnerships directly involve community groups in planning and helping to pay for infrastructure improvements in their own neighborhoods.

In these instances, the mayors restructured and internally decentralized both resources and responsibility. Agreements were reached in which community groups planned and set priorities for their own internal infrastructure service improvements; the municipality and the community each provided part of the resources; the municipality provided technical assistance and in other ways facilitated the process; and the community groups played a sizable (if not primary) role in implementation. In at least one of these cases, the community groups were able to produce improvements at costs well below those of traditional government agencies.

These techniques seem to work because they represent a sensible application of the subsidiarity principle. Appropriate functions are delegated to the lowest level – the level at which the stakeholders are best able and most motivated to assure efficient performance. This, in turn motivates them to pay. The people make their own choices about priorities and see it as their own responsibility to monitor the work (with respect to both quality and cost). When the people have choice and more control, there is an obvious and direct link between expenditures and results.

The Potential Role of Information

A final theme is the role of information in this new environment. Many of the elements of "reinventing government" (incentives for performance coupled with flexibility, streamlining, and so on) and the building of civil society aim to remove constraints from human creativity in addressing the substantial opportunities and problems implied by urbanization. But it goes without saying that creative human beings are much more likely to achieve their objectives if they are well informed – if they have reliable information on current circumstances and trends to use in assessing the likely outcomes of different courses of actions – than if they are not.

In the United States, the 1960s saw great interest in developing systems of social indicators and the application of them to the social, economic, and urban problems of the time. Many relevant methodologies for urban policy analysis and program evaluation were developed in anticipation of what computer technology would ultimately make possible. The period since then had largely been one of disappointment, as assembling and manipulating the necessary data remained prohibitively expensive. In the past few years, however, technological improvements have been particularly dramatic.

These trends may finally make it possible to bring many of the long-promised benefits of the "information age" to bear on the problems of our cities. Capacity is growing at an astonishing pace. It will take some time before the same level of possibilities exist in the cities of the developing world, but it is not too early to start thinking about them.

What has changed in the U.S. experience? First, most administrative records of U.S. local agencies are now automated, and these contain data on shifting social and economic conditions as well as on government program activities. Second, computer capacity has expanded substantially, as its costs have plummeted. Desktop computers can now manipulate large databases with remarkable speed. They can also operate systems that geocode a sizable share of the relevant and available data. In conjunction with low-cost mapping-software, they can analyze trends in spatial patterns within cities, as well as aggregate trends for cities as a whole. They can also operate mathematical models capable of testing the implications of trends and policies that would have been costly on even the world's largest mainframes a decade ago.

One of our strongest interests is meeting the need for competent local performance measurement. The Urban Institute is now working with the International City/County Management Association to use these new capabilities to improve performance monitoring in 42 U.S. cities and counties. We have also done a considerable amount of work on the use of performance data in developing countries, particularly with respect to options for improving the efficiency of infrastructure provision.

But our interests in advancing the use of information are broader, including applications in strategic planning and facilitating program implementation, as well as in monitoring and evaluation—applications by the emerging institutions of civil society as well as by government agencies.

A recent survey of 40 major U.S. cities showed that most were increasingly frustrated by the lack of adequate information to guide their decisions and were working to develop data systems that will meet those needs. Representatives of some of the new leadership coalitions emphasized their inability to set priorities effectively because they simply had no reliable data to show which problems were getting better or worse, where, and to what extent.

In some cities, however, local nonprofit institutions have developed quite sophisticated information systems for these purposes. During the past year, we have been working in partnership with seven of these in The National Neighborhood Indicators Project to assess our partners' capabilities, to consider how their innovations can best be disseminated to spur similar developments in other cities, and to assemble comparable elements of their systems into a central database for use in national level policy analysis regarding neighborhood change.

All of our partners have computerized a considerable amount of data from administrative systems (e.g., crime rates, health data, property and land use conditions, vital statistics, economic indicators), as well from national census and other surveys, and all have advanced computer capacity for mapping and other forms of analysis.

More impressive, however, is the way they have used their data. Unlike typical research and planning institutions of the past, they see their job as facilitating the direct use of data by local stakeholders (citywide leadership coalitions, neighborhood groups, and other NGOs, as well as government bodies) rather than doing the analysis themselves. This gives the stakeholders a much greater sense of "ownership" of the findings and the conclusions of the analysis, and, as a result, considerably greater motivation to act on them. There are many examples of cases where such stakeholders have used their data to shatter conventional views about local problems, avoid (or overcome) mistaken courses of action that seemed appealing on the surface, and take advantage of new opportunities that had previously been unrecognized.

Perhaps most impressive has been their ability to use information as a bridge to build coalitions among local factions that had long been at odds. With a new information base and a "learning environment," the parties have often come out of the process with totally new points of view, recognizing that their past differences were more the result of incorrect perceptions about local circumstances than of differences in underlying values and objectives.

Conclusion

The approaches outlined above—a more complete implementation of decentralization coupled with reforms of the character of local governance that make it more accountable to local citizens, the strengthening of civil society, and the application of reliable information—are winning wider recognition. As evidenced by the examples cited above, along with many others, they can make a substantial difference in the performance of public functions.

More than anything else, they rest on the recognition that incentives matter. Existing governmental systems vary in the degree to which they provide incentives for good performance—features that make all of the participants in the implementation of the public agenda feel that they must provide their best effort, day by day, because they—and their families and communities—will reap either significant penalties or significant rewards depending on how well they perform.

This view stimulates self-reliance and empowerment and averts the inaction that accompanies perceptions of dependency. Local government officials must come to feel that the success of their cities rests on their shoulders. They have a legitimate claim on assistance from higher level governments, but they should feel that the basic thrust of policy—devising and successfully implementing creative and efficient new solutions—is their responsibility.

Similarly, the residents of neighborhoods must feel that they cannot sit by idly and wait for local government to solve all of their problems. They also have a legitimate claim on help from their city's treasury, but they are likely to achieve their objectives more effectively if they view such assistance only as one among a number of required inputs. They need to organize, assess, mobilize, and build on their own internal assets and to proactively seek to control their own destinies.

Notes

1. George E. Peterson, G. Thomas Kingsley, and Jeffrey P. Telgarsky, *Urban Economies and National Development.* Washington, DC: U.S. Agency for International Development, 1991.

2. Dennis A. Rondinelli, James S. McCullough, and Ronald Johnson, "Analyzing Decentralization Policies in Developing Countries: A Political-Economy Framework," *Development and Change,* 20(1): 57–87.
3. James F. Hicks and Bartlomeij Kaminski, "Local Government Reform and the Transition from Communism: The Case of Poland," *Journal of Developing Societies,* 1995, 11(1): 1–20.
4. World Bank, *Urban Service Delivery: Finding the Right Incentives.* Washington, DC: World Bank, 1995.
5. Remy Prud'homme, *On the Dangers of Decentralization: Transportation, Water, and Urban Development Department Policy Research Working Paper 1252.* Washington, DC: World Bank, Feb. 1994.
6. David Osborne and Ted Gaebler, *Reinventing Government.* New York: Plume, 1992.
7. James Coleman, "Social Capital in the Creation of Human Capital," *American Journal of Sociology,* 1988, 94(suppl.): S95–S210.
8. G. Thomas Kingsley, "Design Choices for Reducing Urban Infrastructure Costs." In George E. Peterson, G. Thomas Kingsley, and Jeffrey P. Telgarsky, *Infrastructure Finance.* Vol. 2: *Institutional and Macroeconomic Issues.* Washington, DC: Office of Housing and Urban Programs, U.S. Agency for International Development, 1992.

Section 3 Globalization and Decentralization

Isabelle Hentic

Globalization and decentralization may appear to be diametrically opposed, and yet today these two general trends closely complement each other. To participate fully in international trade, every country needs competitive and adequately equipped cities. No matter what economic and social development strategies they may formulate, governments must consider the fact that mechanisms for generating and distributing wealth are located and operate in cities and the urban systems to which they belong. Data on the sectoral composition of global economic growth show that the urban sector is its main engine. In 1990, 80 percent of the GNP in low- and middle-income countries came from the manufacturing and service sectors.

Yet the contribution that cities make to economic development thinly veils their inability to share this well-being, especially with the rest of the country. There is a fairly direct link between globalization and urbanization. The reasons for this are obvious and are dealt with in depth in earlier sections of *Cities Fit for People*. Inputs conducive to promising sectors in international trade are found in cities.

The link between urbanization and development remains unclear. Globalizing trade certainly does not mean globalizing prosperity. This is far from being the case. Globalization is accompanied by exclusion and marginalization, parallel or informal economies that are nevertheless the salvation of entire segments of societies in the midst of urbanization.

There is thus a missing link, and it is clearly found in cities, towns, and villages. They are genuine links between central governments and civil society in its broadest sense, true testing grounds for democracy. The ability of countries to benefit from global trade flows (goods, services, and information) and to redistribute their benefits equitably throughout society presupposes full and equal participation by all segments of society. This participation requires an intermediary.

Until societies in all their diverse forms are represented and served by local governments that they have freely chosen and given a mandate based on their priorities, sustainable development will remain an empty phrase with no real prospects for the future. Until local governments possess the legitimacy, credibility, and ability to perform their functions effectively, administrative reform will remain theoretical and cannot have any significantly positive impact on the living conditions of citizens. Thus, beneath the somewhat overworked term of decentralization lies the very foundations of local participatory democracy.

Practical experience in urban development shows that decentralizing decision making to the local level provides significant opportunities for popular participation. Municipal programs, plans, and service provision are more likely to reflect local needs if they are delivered through strong local administrations than through centralized systems.

To improve services and urban management at a time when cities have become vital links in economic, cultural and social progress, we must promote more decentralized and participatory systems, encourage civil society to engage in dialogue with responsible local governments.

Central governments are losing some of their purpose and legitimacy. Borders are actually or virtually being eliminated. Cities and local authorities must assume their rightful place on the national and international scene. These changes cannot be brought about unilaterally, either centrally or locally. They will have a better chance of succeeding in an environment of clear and reciprocal intergovernmental relations and through an iterative system of implementation.

The Right Choice: Globalizing While Localizing

At the turn of the twentieth century, human activity related mainly to agriculture and was based on trade with neighboring communities. Today, the majority of people live in cities, and global interaction is growing. The dynamics of regional economic alliances throughout this century and the rise of international trade–commercial and cultural goods, services, capital, technology, labor, information–have strengthened the role of cities on the international scene, both economically and politically.

At the same time, it is increasingly recognized that, to be sustainable, solutions to global problems (e.g., poverty and the environment) must mobilize and include all local stakeholders. This should tend to restore municipal and metropolitan-area governments to their rightful role as promoters of sustainable development and catalysts of local capabilities.

It is no accident that in 1992 the Earth Summit in Rio (Chapter 28) called upon all local governments and their associations to work closely with citizens to create and implement Agenda 21 at the local level. This was the starting point in recognizing that local governments and civil society are key stakeholders in addressing global issues.

Under both internal and external pressure, fed by information about events in Eastern Europe and elsewhere, the governments of most of the world's countries have initiated a process aimed at making political life more democratic, adopting varying forms and procedures despite difficult economic conditions. It is too early to assess this process, which has resulted in fairly successful experiments in some cases and some that have gone awry. Nevertheless, we must realize that the tide has begun and will continue, even though its progress will probably be marked by major crises. We must remember that making the political framework more democratic is a prerequisite for the rule of law to truly emerge, an essential condition for the long-term investment required for stable funding of sustainable development.

The almost spontaneous emergence of a multitude of initiatives, stemming from direct action at the grass-roots level, is part of this democratization process. Civil society and democratization go hand in hand. The creation of microenterprises, independent newspapers and associations of all kinds, as well as the growth of a host of local organizations, eloquently reflect this vitalization of civil society in developing countries.

The corollary of democratization is decentralization. The concept of decentralization has made headway as a result of government inability to deal with the recession of recent years. The decentralization occurring in many countries is thus related to the democratic process, the strong growth of urbanization in the past 30 years, and awareness that development can more easily be initiated at the local level than by central governments. Central governments must nevertheless provide the legislative and regulatory framework conducive to development activities.

Population increases cannot be channeled and new investments in urban networks in developing countries cannot be made through authoritarianism or through financial leadership by central governments that lack the necessary resources. The dynamic seems to be rooted at the local level, where the urban solution is needed as an attractive alternative for migrant populations and for investment. Civil society in developing countries must face challenges and must pick up the slack when governments fail. Organizations emerging from civil society, including the decentralized mechanisms that it has chosen, will have an increasingly important role to play in identifying issues and priorities, training managers, and alerting politicians before situations become sources of conflict or difficult to correct.

Because of the capabilities offered by new communications technologies, we are now seeing the formation of national and regional networks of civil-society organizations and associations of local authorities. These networks are generally designed to adapt local initiatives and expertise and make them sustainable, while ensuring that they are more widely and solidly disseminated. Networks represent a mode of operational organization in the current crisis of government and the inadequacy of the market. When government hierarchies fail, networks of municipalities, nongovernmental organizations (NGOs), and professionals offer an intermediate form of organization, based on flexibility, trust, and, above all, shared mutual interests in dialogue with government.

Decentralization Is Not a Cure-All

Decentralization is often seen as a cure-all for the excesses of the strong, centralized systems that prevail in many countries. It is increasingly seen as a possible response to what might be called the crisis of government in several developing countries or countries in transition. To avoid suggesting that this is a new "all-purpose" solution to complex problems of urban development, we must remember that decentralization is not the universal answer to the challenges of the current situation. This means that devolution, deconcentration, delegation or privatization efforts must periodically be put back in perspective. Also, decentralization can only be the institutional component of a broader policy of reforming the sharing of responsibilities between central and local governments. It must be defined in light of the characteristics of the various societies, particularly the kind of relations maintained between the different levels of government.

In several countries, the issue of decentralization and its corollary–setting up a system of subregional or municipal governments–develop in the following context:

- Persistent government financial crises, with the risk of seeing decentralization turned into a way for the government to offload its responsibilities to local communities without adequate funds.
- Continuing deterioration of urban living conditions, resulting in a crisis of the confidence that people have in local communities, and thus a crisis in local funding.
- Sustained high rates of urban growth with environmental and social risks that are hard to control.
- Insufficient knowledge of the dynamics at work in shaping the new urban reality, leading to ineffective decision making by urban managers. In particular, it is difficult to organize the assumption of responsibility for urban management by municipal authorities without considering standard and spontaneous practices in managing urban development. This is especially true in land use, as well as in the emergence and strengthening of NGOs and informal and community organizations in providing urban services. This tends to raise questions about the very legitimacy of local public authorities.
- Women are important vehicles of civic mindedness almost everywhere. An explanation must, however, be found for the gap between the vitality of women in all areas of economic and social life, and their poor representation in local governance.

- Several countries lack a vision of the future of cities. This causes stakeholders to adopt a wait-and-see attitude and to doubt the prospects that decentralization offers for development, democracy, and citizenship (civil society).

Recent studies of decentralization highlight certain benefits and constraints. Benefits include access to information about real needs, accountability to voters, the creation of new markets, the effectiveness of mechanisms for delivering services, and flexibility and variety in choosing solutions to problems. Reservations are usually voiced about the dangers of catering to local clienteles, the inadequacy of human resources, difficulty in raising taxes locally, and local protectionism and its distorting effects on regional markets. The increasing trend toward the decentralization and devolution of decision-making powers from the senior levels of government to local authorities raises the demand for knowledge and expertise from countries and cities with longer traditions of local participatory democracy.

In a recent publication, *Better Urban Services: Finding the Right incentives*, the World Bank recognizes how important it is for each country to find the right balance between two tendencies. Central regulation is needed to ensure the smooth functioning of local governments in areas of national interest, such as economic stabilization measures. Responsibilities are assigned to the local level based on the principle of subsidiarity. This means giving the mandate to provide a specific public service to the level of administration closest to those who will benefit from the service. In implementing reform, clearly and credibly defining operational responsibilities is an essential prerequisite to ensuring effective delivery of services and intergovernmental accountability.

In many cases, reforms in allocating revenue are also needed. Otherwise, limited sources of local funding (property and land taxes) may restrict the financial autonomy of local authorities. They are then unable to perform the functions legitimately assigned to them. Ultimately, they cannot provide basic services to the communities to which they are accountable. The credibility of local governments in the eyes of the governed is thus called into question, and minimum conditions for development are not met. Synchronizing the various parts of the intergovernmental relations and functions is thus a critical element of success of decentralization initiatives.

This is, indeed, a delicate equation. On the one hand, economic globalization dangles the prospect of prosperity for countries that are able to get on board. On the other hand, entire towns and villages do not even know the meaning of globalization. Local challenges to global changes are thus considerable.

Conclusion

Decentralization seems to be a necessary condition to make up for the withdrawal of central governments from many services and functions needed for sustainable urban development. However, it is certainly not a sufficient condition to initiate the spiral of development at the local level. In many cases, moreover, responsibilities cannot be decentralized because they do not even exist at the central level. They must be created. Communities have not waited for such reforms to be implemented. One has only to see the vitality and contribution of the informal sector and community initiatives for urban development to be persuaded otherwise.

Thus, one has to find new avenues to better contribute to local good governance, and to reduce the poverty and exclusion that affect human settlements in the developing world. To be sustainable, development must be shared and built on broad-based partnerships. Three levels of action strategies are needed to achieve sustainability:

1. Central government level: Support to the democratization and decentralization processes, integrated management of their territories (links between cities and rural areas), and the development of intermediate cities, necessary for building inclusive and more balanced urban systems.
2. Municipal or subregional government level: Strengthening of local institutions/admistrations, support to municipal/metropolitan management capacity building (particularly through intermunicipal cooperation), support to the implementation of local Agenda 21, as well as to dialogue and consultation with civil society in planning and decision-making exercises.
3. Community level: Integration of women in urban development, facilitated access to affordable housing, development of the formal and informal private sector, in partnership with the public sector, to provide basic infrastructures and services, support to dialogue and partnership with local governments.

In the current environment of globalization and decentralization, action by international associations of municipalities and local authorities is providing significant leverage in supporting urban development. Decentralized cooperation between cities (small and large) allows the sharing and exchange of technical knowledge, expertise, and resources based on mutual interests. It is a noteworthy example of international partnership based on exchanges of local experience and expertise to meet local needs more effectively.

For a long time, international cooperation was the private preserve of central governments and international aid agencies. Now it is becoming decentralized and filtering down to the grass-roots level. Adapting to accelerating change in our world is a challenge that local governments struggle with on a daily basis. This is why the exchange of information and collaboration on urban innovative and successful practices among local governments and players should help all of us find the ways and means of building positive change in our communities.

If we want to consolidate the benefits of building a global village, we must continue to support this new type of relationship based on seeking mutual benefits. The world's towns and villages will then have a better chance to find their rightful place in the system of global governanceœ.

Section 4 Local Governance: The South Asian Scene

K.C. Siva Rama Krishnan

Cities are not new to Asia. Beijing, Kyoto, Jogjakarta, Patna, and Delhi are names that evoke memories of great cities that flourished over the centuries. Yet, urbanization, as presently defined and understood, is a relatively new phenomenon in most Asian countries. Until twenty years ago Asian urban population of 482 million was just 23 percent of the total population of 2,102 million. By 1990, this had doubled to 974 million. Still the level of urbanization was 31 percent, less than a third. It is therefore understandable that most Asian countries have continued to perceive themselves as predominantly rural. "India lives in its villages" has been not merely a statement of a fact but a political assertion as well. That India lives also in its cities and towns, which contain 217 of its 860 million people, is yet to become a clear part of its political thinking and process. To a considerable extent, this perception of rural predominance is shared by other South Asian countries. This perception is a major factor underlying the issues of urban governance in these countries.

However there are significant demographic and economic changes that challenge this traditional perception. Approximately 62 percent of the world's total urban population increase during the decade from 1980 to 1990 occurred in Asia, with nearly one third from the South Asian countries. Future urban increases will be even more significant. By 2020, it is estimated that half of Asia's projected population of 4.5 billion will be living in urban areas. Two thirds of this urban growth will be in the six countries of Bangladesh, China, India, Indonesia, Japan, and Pakistan.

The economic changes are already quite significant. The structure of employment shows a steady decline in the share of agriculture from 83 percent in 1961 to 61 percent in 1981 in China, from 82 to 64 percent in Thailand, from 71 to 66 percent in India, and from 86 to 58 percent in Bangladesh. Although the increase in manufacturing and industry have been modest, the rise in the share of services has been prominent, accounting for nearly one third of the employment in these countries.

Globalization and liberalization of economies have very significant impacts for the cities of the region. "Asian Tigers" is now a part of contemporary vocabulary, but what the Tiger implies for the environment, the poor, or the social fabric of the terrain they prowl, are least understood. An Asian Development Bank's estimate shows that resource flows into the developing countries of Asia averaged US $75 billion per year and amounted to one half of the net resource flows to all developing countries. In the competition for a share of these flows, clearly there will be winners and losers. Yet, with the possible exception of China, Korea, and a few others, urban governments in the Asian countries are not conscious partners or players in the process of economic change. Most cities are, as yet, unprepared to seek and better utilize the capital and technology flows that globalization implies for improvement and maintenance of urban infrastructure.

The spread and depth of urban poverty in the midst of apparent economic growth is another formidable challenge. Although there may be an overall decline in the prevalence of urban poverty, considerable numbers of people are still below the poverty line. Here again urban governments have remained largely unengaged.

Megacity growth is another significant feature of Asian urbanization. In 1970 only 8 cities had populations of more than five million people, as compared with 31 cities only twenty years later. By the end of the twentieth century, most of the world's megacities will be in Asia. Some will be in the less urbanized and significantly poorer countries that are least able to mobilize the financial and other resources needed to manage such large agglomerations. The metropolitan city is no longer a Western phenomenon. Furthermore, many of the Asian metropolises are extended metropolitan regions, sprawling over several traditional jurisdictions, with different terrain and across large geographical areas. The structure of government in these metropolitan cities, such as they are, are more complex and incongruous in comparison to many Western cities. A metropolitan view of urban development, management, or governance has eluded most of these cities and its creation remains a formidable challenge.

Governance

The extent and effectiveness of the decentralization initiatives, in various Asian countries need to be assessed against these challenges and tasks. It is also important to understand the background, characteristics, and broad structure of the urban local authorities in these countries.

These bodies for the most part have been creatures of higher level governments. Whatever might have been the historical antecedents of local self-government in Asia, the city or the municipal government as presently constituted has been the product of colonial administrations or has been fashioned after Western models. For instance municipalities in South Asia and Malaysia have followed the British pattern. In Indonesia, city administration is partly fashioned after the Dutch model. Provincial and city governments in the Philippines are a hybrid of the Spanish and American systems. Perhaps what sets the British system apart is the division between the so called "deliberative" and "executive" wings of a municipal government. The elected head of a municipality was expected to preside over the municipal council, which made municipal laws and regulations and determined the taxes. The executive head would usually be a civil servant appointed by the provincial or the national government, in whom most of the executive powers of the city would be vested. In many South Asian cities this official would be called the commissioner and, in cities such as Bombay, would exercise considerable powers. This type of an internal structure, probably inspired by Montesque's philosophy of separation of powers, also reflected a bias against politics and an effort to keep the local government "neutral."

"All politics," according to Tip O'Neil, the former Speaker of the U.S. House of Representatives, "is local." To the British colonial, however, all politics was national and even that, only to the extent permitted by the colonial masters who carefully defined the limits of the national political arena. When entry into that arena was restricted, the doors to popular participation at the local level opened a little more. Local self-government was thus both a concession to national political aspirations and a means of containing them. However, despite some ups and down, the process mobilize a wide range of political leadership and local talent. Local self-government was indeed perceived and also proclaimed to be the "cradle of democracy." At the national level and across South and East Asia, cities were headed by personalities, such as Jawaharlal Nehru, who later became national leaders.

Decentralization Efforts

However, independence brought about an unexpected change to urban governments in these countries. National leaders, prompted by a variety of considerations such as national sovereignty, need to mobilize resources and organize basic services on a larger than municipal scale. Unfortunately the instrument devised to achieve these laudable objectives was rather "Cromwellian," a policy of "throwing the rascals out." Supersession or the removal of an elected municipal body and administration of the city directly by an official of the provincial or national government thus emerged as a dubious but distinct Asian contribution to the science of urban governance.

The question then arises, are national and local political aspirations often in conflict with each other? Is local self government in general and city governments in particular subservient to provincial and national governments? As a corollary, do local governments flourish more in periods of authoritarian rule at the national levels? The following examples will illustrate this issue.

In India, since independence (particularly in the 1960s and 1970s), at any given time nearly one half of the elected municipal bodies have been under supersession, regardless of which political party held power at the Center or the States. The city of Madras with a population of 4 million has not had elections for 23 years.

In Nepal, the partyless "Panchayat" system of the 1970s, with indirectly elected members at the local, district, and national levels and the Decentralisation Act of 1982 were initiatives of the government during the period when the king ruled the country directly.

In Pakistan, the initiatives for empowering cities and holding elections on a regular basis were more prominent during the time of the military regime. In Bangladesh, the creation of elected subdistrict committees (the Upazila Parishads) is credited to a President who had seized power in a military coup. Considered a major step towards decentralization, this set-up was subsequently abolished by democratically elected governments.

Decentralization and democracy at the national level appear to have gone through an inverse relationship in the South Asian countries. In the past two to three years, however, some major changes have been initiated in some. Fiscal decentralization in the Philippines has resulted in the devolution of approximately one half of national revenues to local authorities; it has also enlarged the scope of their functions. In Vietnam, there has been a conscious attempt to promote people's organizations and decentralize decision making and the implementation of development programs. Indonesian cities continue to witness an impressive growth of local NGOs and community groups involved in city management. In Bangladesh, city governments in the capital of Dhaka and three other main cities have been reorganized and function under directly elected mayors.

In 1992, India amended its constitution to stipulate mandatory elections in all urban and rural local bodies, mandatory finance commission in each state, mandatory reservation of one third of the seats in all local body councils for women, and mandatory district planning committees. Elections have already been held in most of the states and, when completed, approximately 400,000 elected functionaries will be released into the body politic.

The Impact of Decentralization

It is too early to predict what changes will take place in the political chemistry as a result of these developments, but in the interim a number of important issues need to be addressed. One is the functional domain of the municipalities. In most Asian countries, there is considerable ambivalence on this point. Although the constitution or the framework legislation may indicate certain functions to be patently municipal, in actual fact the position may be different. For example, water supply is identified as an obligatory function of the municipalities in 16 states in India, but in all of them the function is discharged by parastate organizations that are not answerable to the municipalities. City improvement schemes, transportation, and programs for poverty alleviation may not even figure in the list of municipal functions. Planning and development authorities created by state governments that perform housing or real estate development functions are another feature of South Asia cities that are outside the municipal reach.

Fiscal responsibility is another largely unanswered issue in many Asian cities. Expenditure on major items of infrastructure is usually met by higher levels of government, but in comparison to the needs, woefully short. Overall outlays for urban development activities has been 6 to 8 percent in Pakistan (1993–1998), 3 percent in Bangladesh (1990–1995), and 3 percent in India. Of the combined revenue base of the Center, States, and Municipalities, the share of the last category is no more than 2.9 percent as of 1993/1994. Municipalities in this region have an extremely narrow and inelastic tax base and have to rely on very high rates of taxation.This, in turn, leads to large-scale evasion.

Without a corresponding change in the devolution of resources and the assignment of tax powers, and an enabling framework to help the municipalities gain access to private capital, any initiative towards decentralization is reduced to political rhetoric.

Yet the recognition of cities as an entities on their own and the assurance of elections are a major source of hope in South Asian. The reservation of seats for women and less-powerful groups and the provision for direct election of mayors in some states are bold initiatives. Elections may often be exercises in legitimacy, but they are also a first and major step towards accountability.

Conclusion

As cities expand and spill over traditional boundaries, they are no longer homogeneous societies. Indeed social heterogeneity is considered a positive feature of cities. In the face of globalization that heterogeneity will be further accentuated. Cities will need to perceive and define roles at the macrolevel as well as microlevel. Communities and neighborhoods will need to devise ways to cope with the pressures of daily needs. The Barangays in Manila, the Kampungs in Indonesia, the Mohallas or Bustees in India, and the Katchi Abadis in Pakistan are all inspiring examples of community activism in organizing basic services at the local level and in dealing with the pressures of poverty. Yet there are not many successes to relate in scaling up these efforts to the city level. The hierarchical arrangement envisaged in the Indian constitutional amendment of ward committees, zonal committees, and the municipality of the city is one approach, but even this arrangement will not be able to capture the variety of social and political groups in a city. At the city level, there has to be a flexible and participatory framework, but one that will not succumb to fragmented pressures. In any system of governance and in searching a place for the city, this could be one of the critical questions.

Section 1 Citizens, New Technologies, and Ethics

Ilhan Tekeli

Citizens in all parts of the world are experiencing significant technological, social, and political transformations. These transformations are eroding the classic concepts and values that have traditionally guided our actions.

At present, an intensive debate is occurring about how to define this transformation and describe the changes it may bring about for society. This section of *Cities Fit for People* examines three scenarios for dealing with the dimensions of this developing transformation.

From an Industrial to an Information Society

The first scenario is the transition from an industrial to information society. In the late 1960s, the industrial world began the creation of the information society. Significant developments in the field of micro-electronics, innovations in computer technology and telecommunications, the introduction of new materials and conductors, and the formation of the new field of robotics have increased the speed and capacity of data processing, as well as the ability to transfer and access information. Developments in CAD and CAM have merged the fields of production, capital, and technology.[1] The means of production, which, in the industrial world, were traditionally labor intensive, have become, in the information age, intellectual activities.

The networks developed by the information society has created "cyberspace," a vast web of telecommunications whose fixed points are computers. The traffic is information and the vehicles that navigate its highways are software packages, sometimes known as knowbots.[2] As the expansion of cyberspace facilitates the diffusion of information, countries trying to maintain their dominance in the field of industrial production want to gain control of these developments. The result is a new kind of mercantilism.[3] The innovations in data processing and communications are not only supporting industrial production, but are also affecting individual lives. Although cyberspace can potentially emancipate individuals, different types of control mechanisms tend to transform people into dummy terminals bound to these networks. Thus, individuals are faced with the danger of isolation, instead of the reality of emancipation.

From Mass Production to Flexible Production

The second scenario is the transformation from the "Fordist mode" of industrial production to a flexible mode of production. In the Fordist mode of production, mass production, using economies of scale, are accomplished with product specific machinery and the benefits of the Taylorist work ethic. The production process is divided into simple, routine jobs and rigid jobs. This division, which rationalizes the use of only a limited number of skilled laborers, created the division of jobs into white collar and blue collar. During the Fordist stage, labor organized into unions. As a result of the efforts of organized labor and in response to increasing levels of purchasing power, the Keynesian welfare state emerged.

The recent transition from a mass to a more flexible production process is occurring because of new market conditions and new technological developments. In developed economies, the demand for mass-produced goods is decreasing. Different interests and tastes have created small-market niches. The information society, with its all-purpose machinery and its CAD/CAM capabilities, has made diversified production in small quantities economically feasible. This functional flexibility has increased the efficiency of small- and medium-sized enterprises, which tend to gather in specific places to share services. Because this process requires well-trained labor, unemployment among unskilled labor is a serious problem.

In addition, the current transformation also includes extensive subcontracting arrangements. This process increases the power of capital, which controls production, decreases the share of labor in the allocation of added value, and lowers the possibility that labor will organize.[4] As the productivity of labor increases because of new production methods, companies needed fewer employees. At the same time, societies cannot spare sufficient resources to support the growing welfare state. Instead, a larger proportion of created resources are allocated to rapid technological development and to financing production.

The third scenario is the current globalization process. Because of new innovations in information, telecommunications, and transportation technologies, the world is becoming smaller, and developments in distant places more directly affect each other. Geographical distance no longer has a negative impact on the formation of relationships. The current globalization process has resulted in an increase in international trade, capital movements and investments, determination of prices by world markets, and the internationalization of companies. The citizen entrepreneur, who is successful, must now take external market conditions into account. Economic competitiveness requires an understanding of ongoing developments throughout the world. Because of new patterns for the flow of capital and goods, states are losing, to a great extent, their basic economic regulatory functions. The nation–states are facing the need to continuously redefine their sovereignty.

At the discourse level, globalization is an optimistic state of worldwide integration that would potentially lead to the diffusion of welfare conditions. However, the present modes of globalization are resulting in the exclusion of a large part of the world's citizens. Globalization, in fact, is taking place largely in the developed parts of the world.

The Role of Space

The transition to an information society and to flexible modes of production, along with the process of globalization, is changing the experiences of individuals in a multidimensional way. To some extent, these changes also make territorial forms of control ineffective in the formation of social control mechanisms. In addition, the nature of competition and cooperation in society is changing. As a result, these changes are having important repercussions for the redistribution of the world's population and capital.

David Harvey defines this transformation as time and space compression. "Mass television ownership coupled with satellite communication makes it possible to experience a rush of images from different spaces almost simultaneously, collapsing the world's spaces into a series of images on television screens."[5] In other words, live experiences are being replaced by simulations.

The characteristics of space, which inhibit the formation of relationships and flows of people and capital, are losing their importance because of technological developments. The decreasing importance of distance does not mean that space has entirely lost its importance. In this new world of intense competition, the diminishing importance of distance also means that the enterprises are no longer protected from competition. For this reason, minor advantages provided by a specific location gain importance. Such factors as low-cost labor, the existence of connections to infrastructural networks, and the external economies of concentration may make a particular location more attractive to businesses. Therefore, the information society has its own characteristics of spatial organization.

The most important change that affects spatial organization in an information society and a globalized world is probably the change in the nature of space itself. Space has evolved into a relationship network. Living in an information society means being connected to this relationship network. An inability to connect can lead to exclusion from the system. This exclusion adds a new dimension of inequality to those already present. For those who participate in this network, cyberspace means living in a different world. Cyberspace is a "metacommunity," where words, human relationships, data, wealth, status, and power are made manifest by people using computer-mediated technology.[6] Participants become "netizens" (Internet citizens). Because of the way the network was created, it is a community of relationships between equal partners. Naturally, the new mercantilists would like to change this order by establishing strict control over this network. Only time will tell if they will succeed. These networks transcend national boundaries. Although network identities still cannot compete with national identities, there is now growing recognition of such a possibility, as well as the possibility of creating a cyberdemocracy within network communities. The major infrastructural projects of the twenty-first century will be the creation of fiberoptic digital information highways.

From Continuous Space to Network Space

The switch from continuous space to network space results means that present control mechanisms are replaced with new ones. In continuous space, control is established by boundaries and territories. For example. those born within the boundaries of a nation–state are socialized so that they acquire a particular national identity. In industrial society, the mode of control is territorial and a hierarchical order of settlements is an important control. However, in a system of networks, territorial control cannot be established based on a stable settlement hierarchy. Different units of the system can supersede the control of the hierarchical settlement pattern by forming relationships beyond traditional territorial boundaries and by creating dynamics that cannot be easily controlled by nation–states. In this case, the capacity of settlements to integrate into the world system gains importance, and economic policies are directed towards activating the local dynamics in addition to establishing regulations for the entire nation.

Conceptualizing space in the form of networks and establishing control through these networks is a major change, but it does not mean that there will be no size differentiation among settlements. Size differentiation will be produced in this new spatial structure by a new set of mechanisms. When settlements are conceptualized as nodes of different networks, it may lead to the conclusion that localities will possess no internal integration. However, the development of relationships between settlements does not make the construction of integration within settlements unnecessary. It would be proper to consider these nodes as settlements possessing the capacity of forming autonomous relationships through global networks.[7]

The transformation of world space into cyberspace creates new opportunities and reasons for both spatial dispersion and spatial concentration. In other words, the distribution of labor and capital in space is redefined. The possibilities offered by the information society on the one hand and the flexible mode of production on the other hand enable large firms to form subcontracting relations with a large number of small firms. These firms can easily disperse into different regions of the world as a result of the spatial dispersion of production activities. It is a mistake to claim that globalization leads to spatial dispersion. Parallel to this dispersion, some control functions tend to become more centralized. As a result, cities that possess global control functions are emerging. These cities are places where processes are coordinated and complex specialized services are produced to fulfill the requirements of dispersed and fragmented production process. The two most critical functions are the financial market and innovations in goods and technology. Changes in the nature of the finance sector, especially after the 1980s, have affected the structure of these world cites. A large number of financial service innovations have increased the importance of small finance firms. Therefore, world cites can no longer be described in relation to big companies. The global and innovative services offered by small firms are critical in explaining the global importance of these settlements.[8]

Clearly, developments in communications have given rise to both dispersion and concentration processes within the global community. The nature of this spatial redistribution is still evolving.

Population Dynamics

As we approach the twenty-first century, the population dynamics of developing countries are expected to determine the fate of global settlement. In some developed countries, population growth is below the level necessary for self-generation. In contrast, developing countries still have a high population and urbanization growth rate. By the beginning of the next century, there will be 21 megacities with populations of more than 10 million; 18 of these will be in developing countries.[9] Today, in developing countries, more than one half of the urban population lives in 360 cities that have a population of 1.5 million and more. With the new century, the number of such cities is expected to reach 520. This means that approximately one fourth of the world's population will be gathered in these cities.[10] Moreover, by the year 2001, 80 percent of the GNP in developing countries will be created in the cities. Although the cities are the source of economic dynamics, approximately one fourth of the people live below the level of absolute poverty. Today, income inequality is a reality that cannot be ignored. The income of the most affluent 20 percent of the world's population is equal to 150 times the income of the poorest 20 percent.[11] It is not expected that this trend will change in the short term.

These new forms of settlement are not direct consequences of such transformations as globalization, flexible production, and the transition to an information society. They are more the consequence of the success in realizing these transformations that have occurred in some parts of the world, but not others. Classifying large urban areas of the world according to the size of their populations is misleading. It would be more appropriate to classify and differentiate these areas according to their degree of control, capital accumulation, internal integration, and articulation within the world system. For example, the characteristics of large agglomerations in developed countries are different from those in undeveloped countries. In the former, the articulation to global networks is high, the functional dependencies within and between settlements are developed, infrastructure and production capital per capita and, in turn, productivity and income per capita, are strong. They also possess strong power of control. In contrast, the developing countries have a relatively low level of articulation to global networks; they lack functional internal integration, and comprise large marginal segments of the world. In addition, the infractructure and production capital per capita is low. In turn, productivity per capital is low, and their degree of control is weak. It would be proper to differentiate between these two types of locations by defining the former as "world cities" and the latter as "overgrown cities."

New Dimensions of Settlements

Currently, two features of settlement systems are emphasized. The first is the conceptualization of settlements in the form of point distribution. The second is the qualitative differentiation of settlements, which are represented as point distributions, within the confines of the urban–rural dichotomy. To what extent is this mode of representation sufficient to explain the ongoing transformation? What kind of deviations would emerge in the development of policies that are designed to solve those problems that emerge throughout the transformation of settlements?

Two essential processes could be described as part of the current mode of spatial reorganization. The first is modernization in a very wide context; the second is the spatial redistribution of people. These two processes are related. Existing cities have been expanding and new ones are being formed while adapting to the conditions of industrialization and modernization. People who live in these urban areas will possess the personality characteristics and values that a modern society needs.

Although such a conceptualization is sufficient for understanding and controlling certain process of industrial society within the domain of nation–states, it is insufficient in the information society, in which the notion of the nation–state is being superseded. A new mode of conceptualization is necessary to explain the ongoing formation of settlement systems in the world.

In the face of current realities, the concept of spatial distribution of population alone is not sufficient to explain new settlement systems. The explanation must also account for the spatial redistribution of capital and the intensity and network characteristics of external relationships. These factors must be related to the spatial formations that they acquire during the process of transformation to an information society.

The globalization process is accompanying the transformation to the information society and the world is becoming a unified system of settlement that are closely related through network relationships. All settlements must therefore be conceptualized with reference to this unity, which can appropriately be called "a globalized network of settlements."

Urbanization has significant societal consequences in the industrial society of nation–states. As a result, it involves a meaningful transformation process. Thus, the urbanization rate can also be a measure of modernization and development.

The process of urbanization, which is meaningful within the context of the transformation to an industrial society, is not as significant in the transformation to an information society. Although the process of urbanization is largely completed and has thus lost its distinguishing characteristic, it has no reference to globalization nor its societal consequences. Thus, even though the urbanization process remains significant for certain countries, it is increasingly a concept that should be undermined. At the same time, the rate of globalization should be emphasized because of its role in the transformation to a single globalized network of settlements.

In conceptualizing settlements as separate cities in the era of industrial society, the size of a city is valuable in explaining the characteristics of settlements. In this context, the size of a city can indicate the degree of differentiation and variety of its activities, as well as its rank in the hierarchical order of central places. In this era, territorial control is main tool in establishing societal control. Furthermore, this type of territorial control is influential in forming the identities of citizens. In the context of the world as a "globalized network of settlements," however, the size of a city loses its importance as a variable and is replaced by the degree of a settlement's connection to the network. Relative location is more important than absolute location in a tightly connected world. In this case, a higher ranking settlement cannot control the set of relationships of all lower ranking places, as the latter can establish independent relationships by using the opportunities created by the network. Thus the cost and time of transacting information is more important in human decision making than absolute distances between places. Territorial control will cease to be a tool of societal control; territorial identities will be replaced by network identities.

Making predictions on the emerging structure does not lead to the conclusion that we should be contented with these changes and tolerate them as being unavoidable. This, in fact, runs against human nature. The level of technology achieved within the process of human development does not inevitably determine the structure of society and its settlements. The developing technology does not imprison human beings within a certain type of social structure. On the contrary, it increases the range of possible social structures that can emerge, although these structures depend, to a great extent, on the type of governance prevalent in the world, as well as on the evolution of social movements and social criticism.

The world is experiencing transformations have not just in the fields of communication and production, but also in the use of political power. The arguments about what the "good" is in society, how it is determined, what we mean by rationality, which interventions can be accepted as legitimate for the development of society are also changing. Determining what the "good" is in society depends on the consensus that emerges as a result of mutual interaction. Technical instrumental rationality is replaced by communicative rationality. This may, or may not, be a positive step in the direction of democratization. Because the mass media are influential in the establishment of the new world consensus, they can be viewed as techniques to control change. The dynamics of the change in the information society are created by social movements. Indeed, we are living in an era of social movements.[12] The ecological movement has effectively dictated values that conflict with the short-term interests of powerful groups in society. For example, sustainable development is now accepted as a fundamental value to human beings. Similarly, the social movements related to human rights parallel the emphasis that civil society has given to them as universal values. On the other hand, the redefinitions of "good" and "legitimate" by these movements is by no means a completed process. This is indeed a neverending process. The concepts put forward by social movements will always remain on the agenda, because they are determined by social struggle rather than technical means.

The evaluation of settlement patterns and big agglomerations during the current global transformation will be based on the consensus stimulated by social movements. The major challenge faced by the world is not these big agglomerations, but rather the establishment of new settlement ethic based on social movements.

The Good Society

A good settlement system has the following three main characteristics: livability, sustainability, and equity.

Livability

This principle is established by performance criteria on which there is a widespread consensus. The specification of such a principle is appropriate because its content adapts to changes over time and its realization depends on local conditions and cultural relativity. Naturally, an adequate definition of the major characteristics of a livable settlement is an issue that should be argued in greater detail. However, what we are basically considering here is the necessity of supporting it with human rights. Human rights, when expressed in general, are at the level of abstract principles. The actualization of these rights manifests itself at the level of settlements. Therefore, the principle of livable settlements becomes a human rights issue expressed in on a concrete level. Universality of human rights could establish a firm foundation for the livability principle in the globalizing world.

Sustainable Development

The second principle with respect to the necessary characteristics of a good settlement is the concept of sustainability. "Sustainable development is development that meets the needs of the present without compromising the ability of future generations to meet their own needs."[13] Once the principle of meeting the needs of future generations is accepted, the necessity of maintaining and preserving the ecological balances and not destroying natural resources is clearly acknowledged. In other words, the definition of sustainability is closely linked to the principle of livability.

Sustainability, even in its narrowest sense, is a principle of justice among generations. A mode of thought that emphasizes justice throughout generations is obliged to have this sensitivity within the same generation. For this reason, when the principle of sustainability was first identified, the concept of equity was considered just as important as that of ecological balance. On the other hand, in practice, the equity dimension of sustainability has been neglected. Therefore, equity is proposed as the third principle of a good settlement system.

Equity

The concept of equity has been on the agenda of human beings since the French Revolution. It is vital for the sustainability and livability of societies. "Equity argues that, if their basic needs are met with fairness, each woman and man regardless of ethnicity, race, religion, political, or other preference will feel more able and secure, being freed to contribute to the community and to honor the rights of others. Continued injustice and exclusion can breed selfish, antisocial, and counterproductive behavior, which eventually destroy the civic spirit."[14] Equity is generally defined with reference to individuals. This approach will be insufficient when settlement systems are concerned because the inequality among individuals is reproduced and maintained by means of spatial inequalities. There are substantial inequalities among nations, regions, and settlements – and even within settlements. The destiny of a child born in a low-income district of an underdeveloped settlement of an underdeveloped region is determined to a great extent by the place of birth. For this reason, the principle of equity cannot be defined only by reference to individuals; the realization of equity among individuals is closely linked to the realization of spatial equity.

Conclusion

It is possible to suggest three principles for the proper way to ensure livable, sustainable, and equity-oriented settlement systems, with the values elaborated by social movements. These are (1) civic engagement, (2)enablement, and (3) good governance. These three principles complement each other as parts of a coherent approach.

Civic engagement stresses that all women and men have basic rights, but must also accept an obligation to protect the rights of others and to contribute actively to the common good. It is not possible to have a livable settlement without a sense of civic engagement. The individuals in a society can achieve civic engagement when they become citizens by retreating from considering only their own interests. As a result, solidarity may emerge in society. Emphasizing civic engagement only for a settlement is not sufficient in the face of the globalizing world. It is rather necessary to bear the responsibilities at the global level.

This is also necessary for overcoming the distinction between self and society, which legitimizes the nihilistic dualism making us people who float between inclination and duty. Despite the substantial opportunities for autonomy in modern societies, those opportunities have not translated into substantive possibilities for individual or collective self-determination. This leads us to the enablement principle. If a life cannot be good unless self chosen, the conditions and possibilities of choice must be available.[15]

The strategy of enabling individuals gains importance when the solutions found in societies are related to its ability to mobilize the potentials of various actors and to fulfill its own responsibilities rather than relate them to the power of central authorities. Enabling can be realized, on one hand, by developing the actors' generalized capacity and, on the other hand, by providing a welcoming environment. The actors' generalized capacity can be developed by improving their accessibility to political power, financial position, and information and technology. On the other hand, the openness of the environment can be improved by abolishing the restrictive nature of laws and regulations, providing the opportunity for access to information, and increasing the sensitivity of the environment toward those who want to improve their capacity.

Enablement should not be interpreted as an ordinary principle of deregulation. It should be considered as a principle necessary for citizenship in a democratic polity that is itself an ethical form of life through which we realize individual our collective self-determination.

The intended characteristics of a good settlement cannot be realized solely through civic engagement and enabling strategies. For the actions of participants to achieve their goals, guidance becomes a critical factor. This function is presently called governance. It is used to suggest a new form of relationship between society and government and indicates the transfer of the balance of responsibilities in guiding society from the state to the civil society. It emphasizes the process of coregulation in a system with a large number of actors.[16] As governance draws attention to a flexible structure that includes all of the nongovernmental actors who have the power to guide, it also emphasizes such principles as democracy, transparency, accountability, pluralism, and subsidarity.[17] Once government is replaced by a governance system with a large number of actors, the planning approach will also have to be replaced with an emancipatory planning approach.

Territorial extension of communication, economic interaction, and environmental pollution have greatly increased the need for horizontal coordination of policy. The increasing importance of network-like forms of coordination between the public and private sectors creates the impossibility for intervention by a goal-directed central authority. Thus the increasing demand for a new mode of public governance that will codirect in a network environment the activities many separate actors, with different and opposing interests and more or less independent positions. Governance is possible if each actor has the capacity for self-regulation. Thus, transition from current government systems to the governance structures will require a long process of social learning.

Notes

1. Manuel Castells, *The informational City.* Oxford: Blackwell, 1989, pp. 1-32.
2. Michael Batty and Bob Barri, "The Electronic Frontier," *Futures,* 1994, 26(7): pp. 699-712,
3. Michael R. Ogden, "Politics in a Parallel Universe," *Futures,* 1994, 26(7): 724.
4. Michael Storper and Bennett Harrison, "Flexibility, Hierarchy and Regional Development: The Changing Structure of Industrial Production Systems and Their Forms of Governance in the 1990s." *Research Policy,* 1991, 20: 407-427.
5. David Harvey, *The Condition of Postmodernity.* Oxford: Blackwell, 1990, p. 293.

6. Michael R. Ogden, "Cyberspace in a Parallel Universe." *Futures,* 1994, 26(7): 714-715.
7. G. Dematteis: "Global Networks. Local Cities," IGU Conference an Urban Systems and Urban Development.
8. Saskia Sassen, *The Global City.* Princeton University Press, 1991, pp. 1-15.
9. Eugene Linden, "Megacities," *Time,* 1993, 2 (Jan 11).
10. Carl Bartone, "Environmental Challenge in Third World Cities," *Journal of American Planners Association,* 57(1): 111.
11. The Hague Report, *Sustainable Development,* 1992.
12. Ernest Sternberg, "Transformations: The Eight New Ages of Capitalism," *Futures,* 1993, 25(10).
13. World Commission on Environment and Development, *Our Common Future.* Oxford: Oxford University Press, 1987, p. 43.
14. Preparatory Committee for the United Nations Conference on Human Settlements, "Draft Statement of Principles and Commitments and Global Plan of Action," A/Conf.165 PC.214, Jan. 16th, 1995, p. 5.
15. J. M. Bernstein, *Recovering Ethical Life.* London: Routledge, 1995, pp. 88-135.
16. Jan Kooiman, ed., *Modern Governance.* London: Sage, 1993, pp. 1-6.
17. Adrian Leftwich: "Governance, Democracy and Development in the Third World," *Third World Quarterly,* 1993, 14(3): 605.

Section 2 Cities, New Technologies, and Globalization

Fu-chen Lo

The population explosion and massive rural to urban migration in the developing countries during the second half of the twentieth century are among the key determinants of the rapid growth of the third world cities. In addition, policies and measures to promote economic development and industrialization in the developing countries have been transforming predominantly agricultural and rural societies to more industrialized and urbanized societies in a relatively short period. The growth and structural transformation of the third world cities are integral parts of national development. Furthermore, global economic integration, increased international trade, capital flows, telecommunication, new waves of technologies, and shifts in the comparative advantage of production continue to play a central role in integrating major urban centers and shaping the spatial organization of national economics at the world level. At the center of this global economic integration and structural adjustments is the interlinkage of megacities and other major metropolises, which form a world city system.

The rise and slow-down of OPEC cities; the debt burden of Latin American metropolises; the collapse of commodity prices and stagnation of import-substitution industries in African urban centers; and the rising role of Tokyo and other Asian cities as new, dominant trade and financial centers in East Asia and the world economy clearly demonstrate how the major metropolitan centers in the world have been affected by the current economic adjustments. During the 1980s, the world economy underwent a series of economic upheavals, in addition to the trend of globalization and a new wave of technologies that have changed the configuration of megacities and defined new conditions for their transformation in the early twenty-first century. The new technoeconomic paradigm is in the process of replacing the old production paradigm and reshaping the major metropolitan centers in both developed and developing countries.

Lewis Mumford wrote in 1961 that the "megalopolis is fast becoming a universal form, and the dominant economy is a metropolitan economy, in which no effective enterprise is possible without a close tie to a big city." Whether they should be called megalopolises, megacities, or world cities, their role at the world or national levels is increasingly associated with their economic capacity and external linkages, as the world economy has increased its interdependency during the post-World War II period.

The Impacts of Structural Adjustments

Global structural adjustments that occurred in the 1980s continue to transform the world economy into a clear pattern of tripolar development that consists of the European Community (EC), North America, and the fast growing Pacific Rim of Asia. This is accompanied by slow growth, or pockets of stagnation, in the third world economies of Africa, Latin America, the Middle East, and other low-income countries. The process of uneven growth and regionalization of world economic development is not a short-term phenomenon; it is mid- to long-term in scale and structural in nature, particularly to the developing world.

One of the key issues in the world economy today is the unresolved third world debt. Despite many efforts at debt rescheduling and negotiations, the net capital outflow to the industrialized countries is likely to continue for some time. The Latin American NICs, namely Brazil, Mexico, and Argentina, undertook heavy investments in the import-substitution industries and rapid expansion of the public sector during the commodity boom of the 1970s. The debt to GNP ratio in these countries reached 75 percent, yet the composition of manufacturing exports still remained at below 40 percent. In Africa, the debt to GNP ratio reached 55 percent in the late 1980s. The sub-Saharan countries, in particular, have been most seriously affected by widespread poverty and economic stagnation. The OPEC and Middle East bloc have also been experiencing a negative current account balance. On the other hand, the share of OPEC bloc oil production has also dropped to less than 40 percent against the share of non-OPEC bloc production. This trend has been further aggravated by a sharp devaluation of the U.S. dollar against other major currencies in the early 1980s.

In view of the regionalization of the world economy, the Asia–Pacific countries tend to be more economically complementary than competitive. The economies of East and Southeast Asia, which include Japan, the Asian NICs, ASEAN, and China, are at different stages of economic development. The shifting comparative advantage and the potential of a large market are positive contributory factors for future regional economic restructuring. The structural interdependency developed in the past decades, particularly in East and Southeast Asia, has been further strengthened in recent years, with East Asia as the highest growth region in the world.

Primary Commodities

The current third world debts and economic stagnation are largely attributed to the collapse of prices of oil and other primary commodities in the early 1980s. The relative prices of manufacturing goods increased against sharp declines in the petroleum and nonfuel commodity price index. As most of the developing countries are heavily dependent on commodity exports for their foreign exchange earnings to support their industrialization, the collapse of commodity prices has led to serious economic crises in Africa, Latin America, the OPEC bloc, and other commodity exporting developing countries.

Shares of fuels and nonfuel primary commodities in world trade declined from 43.5 percent in 1980 to 28.4 percent in 1987. This trend is reflected in the sharp declines in the imports (9 percent) of developed countries and exports (25 percent) of developing countries. This has dramatically changed North–South trade relations and worsened the terms of commodity trade and the external debt repayment schedules for those countries now facing serious debt problems.

Most seriously affected are the African countries. As their industrialization started much later than that of Latin America and Asia, more than half of the African countries are more than 90 percent dependent on primary commodity exports. Yet their import-substitution industries remain at a relatively early stage of development and are not ready to replace commodity exports. The Latin American bloc has a more serious debt problem because of rapid industrialization and heavy expenditures in the public sector during the period of commodity boom and intensive external borrowings.

Another possible structural problem is the trend of a long-term decline of material inputs in the developed economies. For instance, in Japan it was estimated that only 50 to 60 percent of resource inputs in nominal terms is required to produce the same level of GNP as a decade ago. A declining share of material inputs in products has been spreading across most of the high-value trade manufacturing products, including automobiles, machinery, and electronic goods. Microelectronics and communication, robotics technology, biotechnology, and new materials have gradually become the fast growth and dominating sectors in the developed countries and in some of the newly industrialized economies. And those sectors are basically resource saving in nature.

In view of these structural changes, commodity trade may increase in the course of increasing South–South trade, but the world economy may be entering a period of gradual disintegration of the commodity economy and of the industrial economy in the long run.

New Economic Configurations

The trade patterns that emerged among East Asian countries and between them and the United States and the EC resulted from the rapid industrialization of the 1970s and 1980s in the Asian countries. Two basic processes occurred during the period: (1) adjustments at the global economic level: the changing comparative advantage in manufactured goods among the advanced industrialized countries (i.e., the United States, the EC, and Japan, and (2) adjustments in East and Southeast Asia leading to their changing comparative advantage, sometimes referred as the "flying geese" pattern of development. This includes the shift from light manufactures to durable consumer goods and machinery products in the Asian NIEs and from dominating raw material exports to a new beginning of increasing share of manufacturing exports in ASEAN. Also evident is the emerging division of labor among Japan, NIEs, and ASEAN, with the creation of a new industrial belt within the global economy. The emergence of this area has been induced by worldwide structural adjustments and industrial relocation.

These adjustments follow the changing dynamic comparative advantage of the United States, the EC, and the East Asian countries in different sectors in the industrialization process. In this process, latecomers appear to have successfully adopted a strategy of entering into those sectors in which they have a rising comparative advantage in some cost terms and importing technology over an already mature economy whose competitive advantage in that industry seems to be on the decline. They later begin to invest in new industrial products using new technology and know-how for which they have the innovative edge. This industrial restructuring and subsequent shifts in the positions of the economies involved in the global specialization and division of labor are not always smooth and involve frictions in adjustment and competition.

The situation in the late 1970s and early 1980s, however, reached a stage in which the East Asian industrial belt, the NICs, and ASEAN have become competitive with Japan for different items in light manufacturing and in exports to the United States and elsewhere. As a result of this and the oil shocks and adjustments in the years after the 1973 to 1983 period, when Japan began to develop and adopt resource-saving technology, Japan has relocated "sunset industries" to the NICs, as in the case of nondurable consumer goods and electrical products. At the same time, food processing and textiles have been relocated from the NIEs to ASEAN. In the 1990s, the NICs and ASEAN have to depend on cross-Pacific trade, namely to the United States and the EC, to sustain their export drive in consumer and light industry. Since the mid-1980s, Japan has also gradually become a major importer of the manufacturing exports of the NIEs and ASEAN.

This shift was made possible by the global restructuring that took place, particularly in the United States and the EC. The pent-up demand for consumer goods in the world's largest market, rising labor costs that induced the creation of off-shore production facilities, and the availability of cheap labor in East and Southeast Asia, as well as active promotion of foreign investments, have contributed to rapid growth in manufactured exports from East Asia to the United States and the EC. International relocation of industry through this product life cycle is well illustrated by Vernon. Hall and others have attributed the decline of Western European cities in the 1970s to the product cycle theory.

Although the flying geese pattern of industrialization has been applicable to light manufactured goods, it has not proceeded to the level of intermediate goods and heavy industries. As a result, the situation is complementary and trade in East Asia has been increasing. This structural interdependency is based on international input–output analysis. The strongest ties in Japanese intra- and interindustrial linkages are with the NICs and ASEAN in chemical products, metal products, machinery, transport equipment, and construction. The growth of this trade constitutes the major distinguishing feature of trade in the region. The trade in intermediate and heavy industries between Japan and the rest of the East Asian countries appears to have increased in recent years.

The role of transnational corporations in this trade and investment activity in the region has further strengthened the globalization of production in East Asia. The importance of technology, finance, and market channels can be increasingly observed from the activities of transnationals. In some industries, it becomes clear that effective transfer of technology does take place, as well does an increase in the spin-off effects of direct foreign investment in host economies. Enhanced intrafirm division of labor and the new decentralized forms of organization of production have been intensified with the East Asian countries as illustrated by the increasing momentum of the flows of direct foreign investment in recent years.

By comparing the trade specialization coefficients of Japan, the EC, and the United States, Japan's superior performance in all manufactured goods is clearly indicated. The United States has shown a negative index (as net importer) from the early 1980s. The EC as a whole has maintained a position of net exporter with a declining trend. During this period, the United States has suffered with the twin deficits and has reduced U.S.–Latin American trade and investments considerably, a clear sign of economic disintegration between the two. In Europe, intraregional trade shares have steadily increased from 45 percent in 1970 to more than 70 percent in 1988. In view of the gradual economic integration of a new Europe, it is expected that this trend will strengthen in the future. Cross-country inter- and intra-industrial linkage have not only strengthened trade relations between the countries, but has also facilitated economic linkage of cities between host and home countries in terms of flows of foreign direct investment, products services, and other related economic activities.

The New Wave of Technologies

In recent years there has been a revival of interest in the long waves of economic structural changes. Schumpeter and Kuznets have studied 60-year cycles of long waves of economic fluctuations with historical data that are often known as Kondratieff cycles. Innovation is seen as the fundamental impulse that sets and keeps the economic engine in motion. A wave of new technologies has been evident throughout last decade.

It was argued that from 1930s to 1980s, with the rise of Fordist mass production as the dominant paradigm, Britain had lost its preeminence to the United States and Germany, with Japan emerging as a latecomer. The major world cities in the industrial countries became the growth centers for superconsumer markets, mass production, financial services, and technology. Fordist mass production was based on full standardization of components. The United States had the advantage of cheap energy resources and the requisite technology to tap mass markets. Increasingly, these world cities were the centers of hierarchical control of multinational affiliates around the globe. The speed and flexibility of air and automobile transportation allowed the world city greater power and influence over government and business.

The Fordist mass production paradigm coincided with the post-World War II industrial development of most of the third world countries. This was also the era of mass production and consumption. The availability of relatively cheap and abundant resources resulted a massive build-up in production capacity. The economies of both the North and South were becoming increasingly interdependent, with cross-border movements of raw materials, goods, capital, and technology. The major cities began to assist in the processes of globalization and integration of national economies.

Many of the developing nations embarked on import-substitution industrialization financed through the export earnings of primary products, such as oil, timber, and other natural resources exploitations. Many of these import-substitution industries suffer today from the technological obsolescence based on the old technologies adopted before the lost decade of 1980s. Furthermore, the sharp decline in the relative prices of commodities vis-à-vis manufactured goods in the mid-1980s has further aggravated the import-substitution industrialization strategy of many developing countries. The crossroads of the old and new technologies is evident in many industries where there is increasing technological fusion of the past and emerging technologies. The innovative combination of traditional mechanization with electronics is producing a new generation of factory automation, robotics, and numerical control machine tools. In office automation, the digitalization of telecommunications has rejuvenated such traditional products as cameras, business machines, mobile telephones, and other telecommunication equipment. A similar attempt is being made in the introduction of new materials and robotics in the automobile industry. These streams of new technologies are beginning to transcend a broad cross-section of industries in the old Fordist mass production paradigm. Developing countries trapped under the old regime are becoming less competitive, while advanced economies and the Asian NIEs are very focused on the next generation of technologies.

The Impacts of the New Technology

It has been argued that a new wave of technologies emerged in the period between the late-1980s and the 1990s with clusters of new innovations in (1) electronics, robotics, and telecommunications; (2) new materials; (3) biotechnology and life sciences, and maybe clean energy as a category that is becoming the leading growth sector in the world production system. The new paradigm is basically resource saving in nature, and it is capable of maximizing the diseconomies of scale and flexibility in production permitted by microelectronic "chip" technology.

The level of technological change is increasingly seen as the main determinant of structural change. The current microelectronics–new materials paradigm has challenged the Fordist mass production paradigm of massive resource utilization, especially high-energy consumption and scale economies of standardization. The application of microelectronics has minimized energy consumption, permitted flexible manufacturing, created new megasupplies and demands in many sectors, and invigorated many mature and declining sectors. This can be observed in many industries. Innovation and continuous technical change are used to create new growth markets as outdated products decline. The commercialization of many more new innovations based on this new technoeconomic paradigm awaits the economic incentives to create new megademands. According to a recent UN forecast, it is estimated that the potential from information technology will increase 10 times more in the next 10 years than in the past decades. World demand for computer services, for information technology systems was estimated to have grown 15 to 0 percent per year during the period from 1986 to 1995. Interestingly, the newly industrializing economies are projected to double their semiconductor production by the year 2000. Most notably, the Asian NIEs are investing heavily in high-technology industries in the new technoeconomic paradigm and are beginning to take a visible share in world trade.

Those megacities that have shown a greater potential to tap the new, rapidly growing knowledge-intensive industries have been able to rise in global prominence.

World Cities and the Shifting Technoeconomic Paradigm

During the 1980s and early 1990s, the world economy experienced a series of economic structural adjustments that changed the configuration of megacities and defined new conditions for their transformation in the early twenty-first century. The evolution of technology and product life cycle poses new challenges to the megacity's economic growth. Supply side policies of identifying industries with innovation and growth potential must be supported with investments in new infrastructure and services. The megacity in this context can be characterized by three trajectories: (1) the traditional megacity, (2) the network world city, and (3) the dominant world city.

The traditional megacity services the traditional manufacturing and agricultural sectors, which are often domestic market oriented. Among the cities in this trajectory are most of the those in South Asia and in the centrally planned economies, which have pursued very inward looking industrial policies in the past. They are less affected by the cyclical turns of the world economy and the advances in science and technology. In the traditional megacity, the tertiary sector is organized through vertical and hierarchical organizational forms mostly to meet market needs within national or regional boundaries. But even some of the traditional megacities are beginning to respond to the shifts in the technoeconomic paradigms. Despite inward looking strategies, New Delhi, Bombay, and Bangalore are participating in India's increasing software exports, which have been growing at 40 percent annually in recent years.

The network world city views the world as one open market and coordinates R&D, production, and marketing to achieve efficiency in the global industrial system. Many world cities in developing countries are host to branches of transnational corporations, as well to their domestic transnationals engaged in international trade and finance. Such firms are clustered in one or a few world cities in each developing country. The core industries include the Fordist mass production assembly type industries in consumer goods, household electronics, and automobiles, either induced under an import-substitution policy or as part of direct foreign investments. Increasingly, transnational corporations have created borderless regional and global operations to take advantage of their fast growth and dominant role in global trade and production.

The network world cities are greatly affected by the shifts in the technoeconomic paradigms. With European integration occurring with momentum, the European world cities may tend to strengthen their networks more on a regional basis. The fast growing East Asian economies are very dependent on world trade and, as such, their cities are very outward oriented despite being highly integrated with Japan. However, Latin American and African cities are tied to their primary commodities and debt burden, which lessen their integration into the fast growing sectors in the world city system. Furthermore, with the liberalization of capital and currency markets, the trade in this sector far exceeds by multiples of 10 the value of international trade in goods and services. In addition to the gradual separation of the commodity economy and the manufacturing economy since the 1980s, it is also evident that there is a departure in the separation of the "money economy" from the "real economy." World cities that are part of the world financial markets are gaining increasing prominence in the world city system through currency trade, transfers of short-term and long-term capital, and other forms of portfolio investments around the world financial markets.

The third mode, the dominant world city, is located mainly in the developed countries, but examples can be expected to emerge in a few newly industrializing countries. The dominant world city has some fundamental characteristics. First, it has become established as a predominant center of new innovations and technological diffusion. Second, it serves as the environment for the conglomeration of global, central managerial functions, including the headquarters of multinationals and international organizations. Third, it is a dominant world financial center. Fourth, it acts as the focal point of a network of other world cities. In the wake of new technologies that promote flexibility and transmission of information with great speed, these cities divest from complete centralization in management. Network relationships with autonomous regional and national organizations enable speedy decisions that quickly seize economic opportunities. The center provides consultative and expert services to its network. In the current economic environment, simple control and dissemination structures may be obsolete and incapable of responding to changing demand and technological conditions. As such, it may be increasingly difficult to define the boundary of a megacity by just national jurisdiction; rather, it may be more appropriately defined by its interactions with international networks.

As world economic gravity has shifted from a Pax Americana to a tripolar development, the role of the dominant megacities in Europe, the United States, and East Asia has also been adjusted accordingly.

Each one of the megacity models described could evolve into a higher order and adjust to the structural changes in the global economy. The rise of OPEC cities and some major cities in developing countries as result of the commodity boom in the mid-1970s and early 1980s has led to their integration into the financial and commodity capitals of the world. However, their inability to respond to new technologies and knowledge intensive industries, coupled with a subsequent downturn in primary commodity prices, have restricted these cities from evolving into the world city type. These cities seemed only to react to changes in relative factor prices to spur their growth and influence in the world city system. Similarly, Latin American and African megacities have been driven by their reliance on their import-substitution industries, resource exploitation, and export-crop agricultural economies, and have been seriously affected by the global adjustments of the 1980s. However, the cities of East Asia, as a result of the expansion in their export-oriented economies, have been able to move into the global mode. There is intense scanning of global markets and technologies by industrial organizations in East Asian cities through joint ventures and inflows of direct foreign investment. These cities had to serve their higher order needs by organizing and coordinating their vast economic and political relations. Tokyo is emerging as a dominant world city where complex and heterogeneous activities are organized in a systems approach and at the same time have the flexibility and spontaneity permitted by the new microelectronics and information intensive paradigm. Each megacity is dynamically interacting and evolving and the strategic allocation of megacity resources can alter the direction and speed of its evolution.

The New Functional City System

In the context of Pacific Asia, as the globalization of Japanese firms and FDI flows into the NIEs and ASEAN continued, the technological level of these countries further improved. This permitted the deepening of intrafirm trade and the division of labor between head offices and their subsidiaries abroad, thus effecting a greater division of labor between Japan and the concerned countries in the region. As a consequence, one dimension of the growing regional economic interdependence has been the devolution of power from the head office to overseas subsidiaries, although overall coordination and R&D functions firmly remain in headquarters in Japan.

What has emerged here is a "functional city system." The element that distinguishes this new city system from previous conceptual constructs is that what used to drive and sustain the growth of cities was their special advantages with respect to raw materials, location, or transportation endowments, all derived from their spatial relations to an immediate hinterland. In the "functional city system" identified here, it is the "functions" of a city that largely determine its role and importance nationally, regionally, and globally. In a borderless economy, these functions are spatially footloose and highly sensitive to cost factors and locales that are the most attractive for the generation of those functions. Thus, instead of a city system by population size, a linkage of cities through an important functional network tends to strengthen the external economic, social, and political relations of a given city within the network more than a city outside of the network. As the processes of globalization of production, capital markets, telecommunications systems, airlines and tourism, networks of transnational corporations, flows of new technology, investment and labor force are interwoven and superimposed one over another on major cities across the nations at the world regional level, the accumulation of different functions by a given city forms a foundation for its external linkage and economic strength of growth under the current world economic system. For instance, the populations of Singapore and Bangkok are smaller than that of Calcutta, but both Singapore and Bangkok are emerging as world cities because their functional linkages have expanded with the global economic integration and rapid growth of Pacific Asia.

One illustration of a new global production network of transnational corporations, Fujita and Ishii (1991) examined the locational behavior and spatial organization of some major electronics firms between 1975 and 1991 and have found as follows. Nine leading Japanese electronics firms increased their new production plants much more rapidly in overseas countries than in Japan. In particular, the share of East Asia is increasing, while those of North America and the EC are rather stable. this also implies that the share of the rest of the world is decreasing. However, their R&D facilities continue to be concentrated in the such metropolitan areas as Tokyo or Osaka, where many world headquarters are located. This observation also confirms a location theory well known in Japan that when production facilities are relocated and spread over a system of cities the "central managerial function" (Cheusu–Kanri–Kino) tends to concentrate in a major metropolis. The central managerial functions of a given firm include long-term strategic management, financial and legal decision making, long-term R&D strategy and new product development, information system, quality control, procurement, and overseas planning. In other words, the more a firm decentralizes its production network, the more the decision-making function tends to centralize. Many studies have confirmed that Tokyo's recent growth is basically attributable to the concentration of the world headquarters of Japanese firms spread across the world market. The spread of foreign direct investment from Japan has in fact created an ever stronger functional city system of manufacturing production over the world. One of the results of this trend is increasing network relations between Tokyo and a city system spread across NIEs, ASEAN, and the coastal area of Pacific Asia. In a much more limited scope, Korea, Taiwan, Hong Kong, Singapore, and ASEAN countries also have become the home countries of an increasing number of transnational corporations spread across the Asian cities and extending towards the rest of the world. All of this spontaneous growth of a network of industries has reinforced the functional linkage of the Asian cities with the rest of the world.

At another level, several economic hubs have emerged in the region that have essentially taken advantage of a certain complementarity, particularly of labor supply, across national boundaries. In case of involving synergetic relations between Hong Kong and the cities in the Zhujiang Delta, a large proportion of the manufacturing production in Hong Kong has been relocated to southern Guangdong in China. Approximately 3 to 5 million workers in this part of China are reportedly employed in factories funded, designed, and managed by Hong Kong entrepreneurs, taking full advantage of cheap local labor costs and land. The capital of Taiwan has also been attracted to this mode and locale of production, although much of it has been channeled though Hong Kong intermediaries because of the lack of direct contact between China and Taiwan. These three territories have the makings of a powerful growth triangle as they possess different strengths and experience.

By contrast, the Singapore Growth Triangle involves three sovereign nations, but essentially two paired relations centered on Singapore. Since the mid-1980s, Singapore has been seeking development outward because of its own structural change. It has found a spatial niche in developing industrial facilities, recreational facilities, hotels, and residential housing on a large scale in Johore and Batam, with far-reaching social and political implications. If economic agglomerations prove successful, more such growth hubs will emerge in Pacific Asia. There are more subregions in the region that are seriously exploring the possibilities of cooperative development.

At still another level, which tends to extend over a wider territory and is centered on a number of megacities, is the formation of urban corridors in many parts along the Western Pacific Rim. Each of these epitomizes the highest level of interconnectedness among the cities they encompass within the delineated limits as part of the regional restructured economy. The urban corridors identified are the Pan-Japan Sea Zone; Pan-Bohai Zone; South China Zone; Indo-China Peninsula Zone; Singapore Growth Triangle; and Jabotabek.

These urban corridors are at varying stages of formation, some exhibiting only incipient development, whereas others are quite advanced in form and connectivity. The best illustration of a mature urban corridor is the 1,500 km urban belt from Beijing to Tokyo via Pyongyang and Seoul connects 77 cities with more than 200,000 inhabitants each. More than 97 million urban dwellers live in this urban corridor, which, in fact, links four separate megalopolises in four countries in one.

A number of economic zones have been identified in Pacific Asia that, for geographic and other reasons, have been viewed as having a common interest in more rapid economic development. These are also regions where urban corridors are likely to develop in the future. If all these zones witness rapid development as advocated, it is not a far-fetched scenario that the coastal region of Pacific Asia will in the future be a continuous urban corridor stretching from Japan/North Korea to West Java (focused on Jabotabek). In China, the coastal cities have in effect linked an almost continuous corridor of rapidly developing areas from north to south, with the cities playing a catalyzing role in modernization and development and with tentacles of positive growth impulses reaching far to the inland provinces.

Conclusion

During past decades, the economic foundation of cities has been greatly determined by the (1) impacts of structural adjustment of the 1980s; (2) globalization and changing comparative advantage of production; and (3) new waves of technologies and formation of functional city systems.

First of all, because most of the developing countries are heavily dependent on commodity exports for their foreign exchange earnings to support their industrialization and job creation in the major urban centers, the increase in the price of manufactured goods against the sharp decline in primary commodity prices and the debt crises that emerged at that time seriously affected the economies of cities in Africa, Latin America, and other parts of the developing world in the 1980s. Many major cities are still suffering from the impacts of that lost decade.

At the same time, a new international division of labor emerged. Major developed countries have experienced a structural change in their economies, specifically, the increased domination of the service sector and the shift of blue collar jobs to the newly industrialized economies, particularly those in Pacific Asia. As a consequence, many manufacturing urban centers of the developed countries experienced high unemployment rates, particularly blue collar unemployment. A massive flow of foreign direct investment, together with relocations of manufacturing operations to the major cities in the newly industrialized countries, have benefited the economic growth of these cities in the Asia-Pacific region.

Furthermore, the new waves of technologies, particularly in electronics and telecommunications, new materials, biotechnology, and clean energy are beginning to be recognized as leading growth sectors in the world production system. Access to new technologies is likely to determine the vitality of urban economies in the future. Information technology also plays a key role in the networking of economic activities and cities. Globalization through functional networks of cities and differentiated roles dominated by selected city systems are an ongoing process in shaping the new economic configuration of global integration.

Globalization of productions and new waves of technology are shaping the future of the city system not only at the national/regional level but also at the global level. To avoid being marginalized in this process, the cities of tomorrow need to visualize their unique roles and positions in an integrated world city system.

Section 3 A New Development Paradigm: Informatic Technologies

Bernard Woods

The series of recent United Nations global conferences have defined in great detail the pressing challenges confronting humanity today and the need for new action by government, the private sector, and the international community. However, the same process has illustrated the extent to which solutions to these problems do not lie within the present context, or paradigm, for development.

New technologies and new funding mechanisms for making them accessible to people everywhere permit fundamental advances in traditional approaches and a new generation of development activity, investment, and employment. This creates a new context for empowering people and communities for their own development; for addressing the multidimensional nature of poverty; and stemming—even reversing—migration to cities in the future.

This section of *Cities Fit for People* briefly outlines the advances that are now possible; the profound implications of linking private sector capital and resources into achieving social and sustainable goals, and the opportunity and need for the international community to rearticulate the conclusions of the UN global conferences in the context of tomorrow.

Conventional thinking, policies, and approaches have brought global development to its present point. The World Summit on Social Development and the continuum of related United Nations global conferences have captured the worldwide recognition of the urgent need for new solutions, and an overriding priority for a focus on social development objectives. They further recognize that:

1. The objective of economic growth can no longer be regarded as the sole determinant of progress;
2. The primary threats facing peace and stability today are from turmoil within nations—emanating largely from population pressures, the unchecked growth of cities, and social degradation; and

3. Almost every country needs to find new sources of development funding and to break out from the traditional confines of public expenditure.

The Habitat II Conference has produced a prodigious list of commitments for governments to endorse. However, it does not define a basis for achieving those goals nor provide practical solutions for drawing private sector capital and resources into addressing the critical social dimension of the growth of cities in the future. The HABITAT Agenda defines the needs, but illustrates the absence in the present context for development of a large-scale and sustainable basis for achieving them.

Information Technology and New Opportunities

The move from the industrial to the information age provides an opportunity to advance beyond the limits of traditional approaches and institutional structures. The nature and capabilities of the technology have enormous potential for assisting people-centered approaches in future development. However, that potential has yet to be realized. Information highways and the growing sophistication of digital technologies, and of software in particular, are widening the gap between those people, small businesses, schools, communities, and others who can afford the technology and those who cannot. Investment in electronic highways and the Internet do not buy computers or any other equipment for people who cannot afford them. Something additional is needed to enable the full potential of the technology to be accessible and affordable for everyone.

This is now possible. The Copenhagen Declaration, following the World Summit on Social Development in March 1995, placed on the development agenda for the first time the relationship between social development, information technologies, and funding mechanisms, which can make the technologies accessible and affordable for all. This introduces a basis for a fundamental advance in global development—with a central focus on the development of people. The principles apply worldwide. We can create a new context as we enter the twenty-first century.

The full potential of the different communication technologies—radio, television satellites, telephones, cable, computers, and others—lies in combining their capabilities into integrated systems. This is possible as they all become digital. Computers can communicate in sound—as well as in pictures, symbols, graphics, numbers, and script. They can "talk" to illiterate people in their own languages, thereby enabling people of all ages and levels of education to use them. This capability of computers to communicate in sound has remained little developed, because illiterate people have not constituted a market for the technology. Every point on earth is now accessible, inexpensively, by two-way communication of digital information using radio and low-orbit satellites.

To date, there has been an emphasis on information, networks and data bases – mostly for large-scale commercial and governmental uses. Social applications call for an emphasis on software with which people can interact by entering their own information for their own purposes in their own time – in addition to accessing relevant information.

Isolated initiatives in communities in all parts of the world demonstrate the potential of the technology in a wide range of different applications. These show how the technology can empower people, small businesses, and communities, and transfer the initiative for development from outside sources to communities themselves. Few of these successes have spread widely as each one, on its own, has been unable to establish a basis for sustainable funding.

However, the experience demonstrates that information technologies have profound implications for new approaches in the major fields of application, namely learning, diagnosis, management (and government), physical planning, finance, entertainment, and communication. The technology provides new tools and solutions for enabling people and communities to help themselves, and for addressing the multidimensional nature of poverty. It has applications for the whole spectrum of Human Settlements goals – if it can be funded on a sustainable basis.

We can pay to use information technologies without having to own them. This new form of utility can make hardware, software, and information in digital form accessible to everyone on a pay-to-use basis – just as we currently pay to use electricity and water from utilities. Poor people, small businesses, schools, clinics, and other local institutions can all use the technology without having to own it. Poorer people can have access to the technology through community information/learning/business/communication/ entertainment centers. Community utilities are not a new technology; they are a new basis for approaching and funding the technology and its social applications. They follow from recognition that:

- The only practical way in which the technology can be made accessible and affordable for the poor is through a system that can spread the costs of the technology across all users. Revenue from use by wealthier users can be reallocated to permit use by poorer people and for social goals;
- Digital information and software can be treated like water. They can be gathered from distance sources, transferred to local storage, and used on demand. Use can be metered and charged for. Royalties for use can be paid to the software producers;
- Local needs for most software for social and many business purposes can be anticipated. The software can be decentralized to community resource centers overnight at very low cost and accessed at a fraction

of the cost and complexity of "on-line" (live) access to distant sources;

- The more users and uses that can be found for the same generic system, the lower its usage charges can become. Therefore it is in communities' interests to encourage use of the systems by all their members. Where use by the poor is funded from outside sources, that use can benefit the whole community by increasing usage and lowering usage rates for all users;
- As with conventional utilities, the new utilities supply, maintain, and upgrade hardware, charge regular access rates (like monthly telephone, electricity, and water service fees) and also charge for usage. It is in their economic interests to provide training for users and local help lines 24 hours a day to promote usage; and
- Public/private sector partnerships are needed to plan, fund, and operate community utilities. This introduces a basis for linking private sector funds and resources into delivering public services on a large scale for the first time.

Investment in information highways does not buy computers for poor people. The new utilities are locally owned and operated businesses that make hardware, software, and information accessible and affordable for users in the areas they serve. The utilities connect to, and increase use of, information highways—at whatever level of development those highways have reached. They make sustainable funding of the social uses of the technology possible on a large scale for the first time, and permit widespread replication of existing, successful experience.

Community utilities establish "community resource centers" in individual communities. These have very large storage and processing capability and make this and interactive software locally available at low cost. The "resource centers" are linked through information highways and central "gateways" to the Internet, the World Wide Web, Global Information Update, specialist networks, databases, and other sources of digital material.

Community utilities make no investment in their product (software producers and issuers of public information make it available to them) or in main distribution infrastructure (they can use existing telephone and cable networks and satellites). The utilities sell the use of information and software. These do not deplete with use. With no investment needed for their product or for its widespread distribution, and with that product not depleting with use, the new utilities can be profitable. By making the technology accessible to everyone and to businesses and institutions everywhere, they will open up the largest market there has ever been.

By making commitments of specific levels of future use of community utilities for governments' internal purposes and for education, health, local government, and other social goals, they can reduce the initial risk for private sector investment to establish the new utilities and to develop the hardware and software they can supply. The government of China is the first to do this. Other governments can do the same. Governments of poorer countries can seek assistance from UN agencies, Bretton Woods institutions, bilateral assistance, and major foundations to underwrite future usage.

New Markets for the Information

Bringing the poor into the information marketplace creates vast new markets for the telecommunication, cable, broadcasting, hardware, software, and entertainment industries. It is their market interests, and those of private financial sources, to participate in planning, establishing, and operating the new utilities through public/private sector partnerships.

Every country needs to invest to develop software production/adaptation and hardware production and/or assembly capability to achieve social development goals.

The potential of information technologies for empowering people and communities does not lie in the technologies themselves, but in their use. Through usage, people can create skills, employment, and wealth.

The technology can identify individual users by personal codes or cards. (Recognition by voice or facial heat profiles may be used in the future.) Through differential charges, revenue from use by the private sector, government, the military, and wealthier individuals, as well as for entertainment can be reallocated to permit use by poorer people, and for education, health, local management, and other social goals.

Most revenue for the utilities will come from business and industry, services, government agencies, wealthy individuals, entertainment and, increasingly, from small businesses and people working at home. In practice, utilities are likely to commence among easily identified concentrations of users (e.g., in local urban areas, mines, big plantations, large communities in irrigated areas, and universities) and then reach out to surrounding communities. Use by people in poorer areas will be made possible by revenue from the higher income areas.

Utility systems can deliver and record use of individual materials (e.g., for education, management, agriculture, machinery maintenance, health, banking, entertainment, and others). Differential charges can be made for different users and different uses. Thus the bill (or a portion of it) for use for instruction on credit and savings might go to participating banks; that for use of machinery maintenance software to suppliers of that machinery. Use by the poorest and the handicapped could go to

Trusts or Foundations sponsoring that use. The bill for use for primary education or basic health care for poorer categories of users can go to those ministries—and so on. In each case, the utilities still receive the revenue they need to be financially viable.

Governments and NGOs can promote usage by providing incentives for software production and/or allowing free or low-rate usage for social goals. They can also target certain groups (e.g., minorities, school dropouts, unmarried mothers and others). Similarly, private companies can make software freely accessible to promote new products or to maintain existing ones. The very poor can pay only nominal charges to use the technology. That use will, itself, generate economic activity and social benefits. The reallocation of revenue through differential user charges can be regarded as a social development tax—without a large intervening bureaucracy to administer it.

Conventional governmental approaches have funded the suppliers of information, knowledge, and assistance (e.g., as teachers, extension agents, and health workers). These approaches have failed to convey development investment to poorer people almost everywhere. Usage for specific purposes (e.g., education, health, small businesses, and parental guidance) can be delivered electronically to individual people in the form of allocations of usage time for specific purposes. In this way, for the first time, development funds can be channeled directly to people in need on a large scale.

This conversion of revenue into usage makes usage a commodity. Usage has a value. It can be transferred, measured, and monitored. The control of usage will be an electronic bookkeeping exercise, such as that for bank accounts and credit cards. These two features—(1) usage, a new commodity and (2) the capability of usage to create wealth—have profound implications for funding social development activities.

Advances in Thinking and Policies

Large and growing numbers of poor people at the periphery of the cash economy have remained beyond the reach of conventional approaches for economic and social development. Through their uses of information technologies from community utilities, they can acquire knowledge, skills, and access to information, services, and the entrepreneurial opportunities they need to become full participants in economic activity and democratic processes.

Implications of making the capabilities of information technologies accessible and affordable to everyone, and of drawing private sector capital and resources into doing so, include the following.

We can escape from the confines of public expenditure. Use of the utilities for learning, diagnosis, management, and other social objectives makes these revenue generating, and therefore economic, not just welfare, activities. Private sector funds and expertise can be drawn into activities which, until now, have been regarded as public sector roles.

The limitations of governments' existing organizational structures can be overcome. The technologies' seven major fields of application can be addressed as they apply across all activities, thus enabling new approaches to pervasive problems which fall across, rather than within, the domains of the traditional disciplines in which governments and aid agencies are organized and staffed.

Countries and donor agencies can recognize a "communication sector." The donor community and governments can invest in strengthening countries' communication processes for development within overall approaches in a "communication sector" (of which information highways and community utilities are subsets). Countries' can invest to develop this sector and its constituent communication systems and capacity in the same way that they have done to develop transportation systems.

Economic and structural adjustment theory can advance. Learning, job-related training, local management, and other social applications of technology can all become revenue generating. The social uses of integrated technology systems and making them accessible for the poor transforms the economic justification for investment in telecommunication, cable, and information highways.

Transformation, not just change, of conventional approaches is possible. The capabilities of the technology and funding mechanisms to make them accessible to everyone make transformation possible in all fields of application. This calls for a new generation of public policy in all these fields. No government yet has comprehensive policies for the social applications of digital technologies. This has allowed fragmented investments in technology as an "add-on" by every ministry and department of governments. Very few of these investments are sustainable independently. No one ministry can afford to own, operate, maintain, and upgrade integrated systems for its individual, limited purposes. Now, investment for all these uses can be coordinated within National Community Utility Programmes.

Any solution for poverty and related problems in cities will be short term unless, at the same time, it can stem rural to urban migration. The social applications of information technologies through community utilities have profound implications for improving living conditions and employment opportunities in small towns and rural areas. National community utility programs can serve comprehensive approaches to social development, environmental sustainability, and civil society goals in urban and rural areas. They hold great promise for stemming or even reversing migration to big cities.

Planning to introduce community utilities has begun in 14 countries. The Inter-American Development Bank is leading the multinational funding agencies in this new field by planning a new investment program to introduce community utilities with private sector support in the Latin American region. The European Union has already received funding requests to initiate community utility programs in four European countries. In every case, leadership for these has come from the private sector and NGOs—not from central governments.

Experience is showing that community utilities require new institutional structures and funding mechanisms; action at local, national, and international levels to create the environment of understanding needed for the advances they introduce; and critical seed funds to establish a focal point of responsibility in every country for involving suppliers and users, policy makers, local authorities, and the financial community in planning local and national community utility programs.

Conclusion

The principles outlined above apply worldwide. They create a new context in which fundamental advances in global development are possible. Driving forces in a new generation of people-centered development will be private sector market interests; the needs for governments everywhere to escape from the inherent confines of public expenditure; solutions for the social dimension of poverty alleviations and sustainability which are not possible in the present context, and demand from people, small businesses, and communities everywhere.

Section 4 Indicators for Citizens

Felix Dodds

In their recent book, *Global Dreams,* Richard Barnet and John Cavangh state that:

> The fundamental political conflict in the opening decades of the new century, we believe, will not be between nations or even between trading blocs but between the forces of globalization and the territorially based forces of local survival seeking to preserve and redefine community.[1]

In this uncertain world, citizens need ways to define their needs and their communities. Indicators are a way of doing that. Global indicators do not present a challenge to local communities, as the link with their own activities is too remote. Scientific and technical indicators are very often not accessible to ordinary people. Sustainable development indicators should not exist in a vacuum, but should be seen as a tool that can deliver change in the actions of both governments and individuals.

A New Vision

The challenges of the late 1990s clearly show the different times in which we live. We lack leaders or leadership that can shape the new world in a way that is meaningful to the majority. The move away from sovereignty of the nation–state to a more globalized world can be seen everywhere. National economies are becoming increasingly linked, leading to corporations that are larger than most nations.

These corporations are organized on a global scale, in which they lever considerable power and mobility. Yet, more than half of the world's people are without the money to buy much of anything. They are becoming shop window watchers in this new global marketplace that is increasing the gap between those who have and those who do not, and the accompanying sense of alienation. The disillusion with government and politicians and the fear of the "pace" of change is all adding to an attack on internationalism, whether it be the role of the European Union and the United Nations or the value of funding development aid.

However as the processes of globalization increase, a counteracting force is emerging—that of localism or communitarianism. More and more people are starting to adopt new approaches to work outside established economic and political structures.

The word community has been widely used over the past decade, but for the purposes of this discussion, the definition of community used by Herman Daly and John Cobb is more appropriate:

> a society should not call itself a community unless (i) there is extensive participation by its members in the decisions by which its life is governed, (ii) the society as whole takes responsibility for the members, and (iii) this responsibility includes respect for the diverse individuality of these members. By these definitions there can be a totalitarian society, but there can be no totalitarian community.[2]

A new form of governance—not government—is emerging—that of "stakeholders," or citizens. Local "stakeholders" in communities are linking together, whether they are local businesses, local authorities, non-governmental organizations, community-based organizations, or women's groups. Such groups that have an identified "stake" in the future of the community are coming together to create a vision for the future that has a set of goals and measurable benchmarks or indicators. This is an innovative approach that, if done well, enables a community to move forward together to ensure that decisions taken are based on a shared set of values. This would entail moving to a more sustainable community, working at a level that most people relate to and feel they have some influence over.

Policy makers now use the rhetoric of citizen or stakeholder approaches to such issues as finance, education, health, and social policy, as the new organizing model for society. As Tony Blair said in his speech in Singapore in February 1996:

> Successful companies invest, treat their employees fairly, value them as a resource not just of production but of creative innovation. . . . We cannot by legislation guarantee that a company will behave in a way conducive to truth and long-term commitment. But it is surely time to asses how we shift the emphasis in corporate ethos—from the company being a mere vehicle for the capital market—to be traded, bought and sold as a commodity; towards a vision of the company as a community of partnership in which each employee has a stake, and where a company's responsibilities are more clearly delineated.

The idea of involving the citizens has been with us for a while and was given a boost by the Brundtland Report and the Rio Summit. Rio designated nine stakeholders: local authorities, trade unions, business and industry, NGOs, women, youth, indigenous people, farmers, and scientists and academics. As Rio went beyond a focus on NGOs to develop a strategy for the involvement of much wider layers of society, it marked a clear recognition of the evolving reduced role of governments.

The growth of community activities can only become the bedrock of a new internationalism if people become more aware of the link between their actions and the global agenda. This will take time, as there needs to be a rebuilding of trust within the community and between "stakeholders" in those communities. At times we will not all agree, but when we disagree it will be from a position of a greater understanding. To facilitate this, we need a tool kit that will help to build practical links among these common concerns.

Global Indicators

The involvement of local stakeholders in the choice of the indicators that they feel are most relevant to them has had its own set of critics. But to quote Donella H. Meadows, writing about experiences in Seattle:

> The indicators a society chooses to report to itself about itself are surprisingly powerful. They reflect collective values and inform collective decisions. A nation that keeps a watchful eye on its salmon runs or the safety of its streets makes different choices than does a nation that is only paying attention to its GNP.
>
> The idea of citizens choosing their own indicators is something new under the sun—something intensely democratic.[3]

In short, indicators show we are moving in the right direction and have the capacity to be able to demonstrate tangible progress towards shared goals. One of the key instruments of our tool kit in the twenty-first century that will help us in mapping out the right path will be indicators. Since the Earth Summit in 1992, there has been considerable interest in the area of indicators.

The development of different types of indicators to measure progress and to achieve baseline information is a rapidly expanding area of innovation. Globally, a variety of institutions are involved in devising different sets of internationally and nationally comparable indicators. Chapter 40 of Agenda 21 on Information for Decision Making has been key to this development. It says:

> While considerable data already exist, as the various sectoral chapters of Agenda 21 indicate, more and different types of

> data need to be collected, at the local, provincial, national and international levels, indicating the status and trends of the planet's ecosystem, natural resources, pollution and socioeconomic variables.

Some of the same tensions between globalization and localism exist within the debate on indicators. These two approaches have been seen as opposing each other. Simplified they are classed as "a top-down or a bottom-up approach." Who should choose the indicators for a community? The UN? The Government? The Local Authority? The local stakeholders? A common view is that the process of building a framework of indicators for sustainable development should not be a top down exercise but a participatory one.[4]

At the international level, the Commission on Sustainable Development has established a target date of the year 2000 to have a set of indicators for the different chapters of Agenda 21, thereby creating an international set of indicators that countries should collect data for. UNSTAT have suggested a list that includes the quality of freshwater; the quality of marine water; and water treatment.[5]

The OECD, which has been working in this area for a considerable time, published its first set of indicators in 1991 and updated them in 1993.[6] They suggested core indicators such as climate change; ozone depletion; acidification; waste; fish resources; and soil degradation and erosion.

This approach is supported by a number of NGOs, such as the World Wide Fund for Nature (WWF) International, which is working with the New Economic Foundation that has already produced a set of indicators.[7] They have suggested, among others, overseas Development Assistance given or received as a percentage of GDP; mean years of schooling for females (expressed as a percentage); consumption of energy per capita and per unit of GDP (in ton of oil equivalent); population percentage living in absolute poverty; population percentage with access to safe water; urban and rural populations by percentage; and net rate of deforestation.

The British Government in March 1996 released its comprehensive report, *Indicators of Sustainable Development for the United Kingdom.*[8] The report stated we need indicators because:

> people are concerned about sustainable development and the environment. They need to be informed about the state of the environment and the economy and how and why they are changing, so that they can understand and monitor government policies, and see how their own personal actions may have an impact. Indicators are therefore needed in a form which is relevant to the general public and can be readily understood.

Local Indicators

At the same time another approach has taken root. This started in Jacksonville (with mainly quality of life indicators)[9] and Seattle (with sustainable development indicators)[10] in the United States in the late 1980s to early 1990s. Here a stakeholder approach has been piloted and was crucial to the whole developmental process.

The starting place for a discussion on sustainable cities in a globalized world should be what we are attempting to do within the city. This requires a goal against all indicators should measure progress. In the work in the Britain (piloted by the Local Government Management Board)[11] and within the United States, the inclination has been to use the UNEP definition of sustainable development: "[sustainable development is] improving the quality of life while living within the carrying capacity of supporting ecosystems."

Without an overarching goal, indicator work can at times be very abstract and leaves no clear feeling of understanding of goals. The definition leads to real clarity when expressed as a set of key sustainability factors.

Sustainability indicators attempt to integrate the important interactions among environmental protection, economic security, and social equity. As Environ, an independent environmental organization on sustainable development, said in their draft indicators report: "Sustainable development is about integrating the needs of environmental protection, social equity and economic opportunity into all decision making."[12]

Having agreed to a goal from which the indicators arise, a set of clear criteria for indicators should be developed. The criteria are that the indicators be easily understood by all stakeholders; related to the interests of one or more groups of stakeholders; measurable and meaningful; and on a scale at which action is possible.

Development and Use of Indicators

Getting the processes right to maximize the opportunities to be gained from well-functioning indicator programs, whatever their objectives, will take time. In the meantime it is important that programs/organizations continue to take existing information and use it effectively while highlighting the need for fresh approaches to data gathering and assessment. Informed experimentation is still the best way to move forward. It is vital that the "benchmarking" purpose of indicators is remembered in this planning process. The baseline measurements should allow judgments to be made on progress. In turn, these should lead to decisions on implementing policies or actions that will lead to change. Some current indicator work has concentrated on collecting data without informing policy making.

Again Seattle's approach is worth reviewing. Here, the city has set up a process that feeds back the results of the community derived indicator work into reviewing the City of Seattle's Comprehensive Plan. If the indicator is going in the wrong direction then the Comprehensive Plan implementation is revised to ensure that the indicator results feed into changes of policy.

Given the multitude of organizations that have an interest in improved shelter and better urban conditions, the task of collecting information for the indicators will benefit from agencies adopting a more participatory approach. For example, the coordinating organization, which is likely to be a local authority, uses a "stakeholder approach" to choose which indicators could be measured, to identify likely sources of information, and to allocate responsibilities for data collection, maintenance, and reporting.

Such an approach would ease the burden on local authority staff and widen the pool of expertise. It should encourage cross-sector partnerships and collaboration on data gathering, and might prevent duplication of resource use among different agencies collecting the same data. Enhanced stakeholder participation is also desirable given that sustainability is a term with many interpretations that depend on values and objectives. Underpinning all of this is the need to raise general awareness of the sustainability issue, and in particular, shelter and urban issues across different sectors. A citizen's approach shares knowledge and expertise and should, on a city level, lead to an active process whereby suggestions of necessary refinements and additions can be received over time.

Conclusion

Globalization is having an enormous effect but it does not need to all be destructive. It is true that present the balance is in the wrong direction, but we do have in our hands the possibility of developing sustainable economies and sustainable cities. The move toward a solution agenda, the sharing of good practice, and the development of partnerships or stakeholder approaches does give us hope.

In the area of indicators one of the important questions is whether it is possible to build a generic process; one that could apply to any indicators not only for collecting information but ensuring that follow-up action occurs. Is there another approach to having extensive lists of indicators, the relevance of which may not be immediately recognized? Is it really feasible to widen stakeholder participation? Is there another framework that would help draw out the key sustainability factors?

However all indicator programs are at an early stage of development implementation and the longer-term nature of indicators work needs to be borne in mind when making short-term assessments as to their worth. Processes must remain flexible.

Indicators are a useful tool, but they are no more than that. International comparisons between countries can be helpful, but a certain degree of caution has to be exercised when comparisons of this nature are made, because of differing measuring systems, starting points, and definitions. There is a role for including more qualitative indicators. Policies for action have to stem from the trends they reveal, and this is where adopting a participative approach in the choice and use of indicators is beneficial. Enhanced awareness of the complexity and interlinkages between issues and their relationship to sustainability is crucial. A sustainable future is about shared responsibilities for action. Perhaps our challenge is summed up by Senator Robert Kennedy when he said (1968):

> We have not solved our problems, but we are committed to finding solutions, and most important, the country has turned away, I hope forever, from whose hearts are dry as summer dust, those who feel that the poor are evil, that security is weakening, and that every person should fend for themselves.
>
> If we fail to dare if we fail not to try, the next generation will harvest our indifference; a world we did not want a world we did not choose—but a world we could have made better, by caring more for the results of our labor.

That generation failed therefore the challenge is even great today than in 1968. We can not afford to fail.[13]

Notes

1. Richard Barnet and John Cavanagh, *Global Dreams: Imperial Corporations and the New World Order.* New York: Simon & Schuster, 1994.
2. Herman Daly and John Cobb, *For the Common Good: Redirecting the Economy Towards Community, the Environment and Sustainable Future.* London: Green Print, Merlin Press, 1990.
3. Donella H. Meadows, *Sustainable Seattle.* Seattle: Metrocenter YMCA, 909 Fourth Avenue, 1993.
4. Jonas Rabinovitch, *Indicators Intersessional Convened by Belgium and Costa Rica.* UNDP, 1995.
5. UNSTAT, *Key Indicators and Indices of Sustainable Development,* (1993)
6. OECD, *Environmental Data Compendium.* Paris, 1993.
7. WWF/NEF, *Indicators for Action,* 1994.
8. UK Government, *Indicators of Sustainable Development,* March 1996.
9. Sustainable Seattle, *Indicators of Sustainable Community.* Seattle, 1993.
10. Jacksonville Chamber of Commerce, *Life in Jacksonville: Quality Indicators for Progress.* Jacksonville, Nov. 1993.

11. Local Government Management Board (Consultants: United Nations Association; NEF; Touche Ross), *Sustainable Indicators Research Project.*
12. ENVIRON, *The Vision of Leicester 2020: Indicators and Leicester.* Leicester, 1995
13. Jack Newfield, *Robert Kennedy.* New York: Plume, 1988.

Section 1 A Success Story of Urban Planning: Curitiba*

Jonas Rabinovitch

As late as the end of the nineteenth century, even a visionary like Jules Verne could not imagine a city with more than a million inhabitants. Yet, by the year 2010 more than 500 such concentrations will dot the globe, 26 of them with more than 10 million people. Indeed, for the first time in history more people now live in cities than in rural areas.

Most modern cities have developed to meet the demands of the automobile. Private transport has affected the physical layout of cities, the location of housing, commerce, and industries, and the patterns of human interaction. Urban planners design around highways, parking structures and rush-hour traffic patterns. And urban engineers attempt to control nature within the confines of the city limits, often at the expense of environmental concerns. Cities traditionally deploy technological solutions to solve a variety of challenges, such as drainage or pollution.

Curitiba, the capital of Paraná state in southeastern Brazil, has taken a different path. One of the fastest-growing cities in a nation of urban booms, its metropolitan area mushroomed from 300,000 citizens in 1950 to 2.1 million in 1990. Curitiba's economic base has changed radically during this period: once a center for processing agricultural products, it has become an industrial and commercial powerhouse. The consequences of such rapid change are familiar to students of Third World development: unemployment, squatter settlements, congestion, and environmental decay. But Curitiba did not end up like many of its sister cities. Instead, although its poverty and income profile is typical of the region, it has significantly less pollution, a slightly lower crime rate and a higher educational level among its among its citizens.

* This section is drawn from an article originally written with Josef Leitman, then of the World Bank, for *Scientific American*. Reprinted with permission.

Designing with Nature

Why did Curitiba succeed where others have faltered? Progressive city administrations turned Curitiba into a living laboratory for a style of urban development based on a preference for public transportation over the private automobile, working with the environment instead of against it, appropriate rather than high-technology solutions, and innovation with citizen participation in place of master planning. This philosophy was gradually institutionalized during the late 1960s and officially adopted in 1971 by a visionary mayor, Jaime Lerner, who was also an architect and planner. The past 25 years have shown that it was the right choice, Rafael Greca, the current mayor, has continued the policies of past administrations and built on them.

One of Curitiba's first successes was in controlling the persistent flooding that plagued the city center during the 1950s and early 1960s. Construction of houses and other structures along the banks of streams and rivers had exacerbated the problem. Civil engineers have covered many streams, converting them into underground canals that made drainage even more difficult—additional drainage canals had to be excavated at enormous cost. At the same time, developers were building new neighborhoods and industrial districts on the periphery of the city without proper attention to drainage.

Beginning in 1966, the city set aside strips of land for drainage and put certain low-lying areas off-limits for building. In 1975, stringent legislation was enacted to protect the remaining natural drainage system. To make use of these areas, Curitiba turned many riverbanks into parks, building artificial lakes to contain floodwaters. The parks have been extensively planted with trees, and disused factories and other streamside buildings have been recycled into sports and leisure facilities. Buses and bicycle paths integrate the parks with the city's transportation system.

This "design with nature" strategy has solved several problems at the same time. It has made the costly flooding a thing of the past even while it allowed the city to forgo substantial new investments in flood control. Perhaps even more important, the use of otherwise treacherous floodplains for parkland has enabled Curitiba to increase the amount of green space per capita from half a square meter in 1970 to 50 today—during a period of rapid population growth.

Priority to Public Transportation

Perhaps the most obvious sign that Curitiba differs from other cities is the absence of a gridlocked center fed by overcrowded highways. Most cities grow in a concentric fashion, annexing new districts around the outside while progressively increasing the density of the commercial and business districts at their core. Congestion is inevitable, especially if most commuters travel from the periphery to the center in private automobiles. During the 1970s, Curitiba authorities instead emphasized growth along prescribed structural axes, allowing the city to spread out while developing mass transit that kept shops, workplaces, and homes readily accessible to one another. Curitiba's road network and public transportation system are probably the most influential elements accounting for the shape of the city.

Each of the five main axes along which the city has grown consists of three parallel roadways. The central road contains two express bus lanes flanked by local roads, one block away to either side run high-capacity one-way streets heading into and out of the central city. Land-use legislation has encouraged high-density occupation, together with services and commerce, in the areas adjacent to each axis.

The city augmented these spatial changes with a bus-based public transportation system designed for convenience and speed. Interdistrict and feeder bus routes complement the express bus lanes along the structural axes. Large bus terminals at the far ends of the five express bus lanes permit transfers from one route to another, as do medium-size terminals located approximately every two kilometers along the express routes. A single fare allows passengers to transfer from the express routes to interdistrict and local buses.

The details of the system are designed for speed and simplicity just as much as the overall architecture. Special raised tube bus stops, where passengers pay their fares in advance (as in a subway station), speed boarding, as do the two extrawide doors on each bus. This combination has cut total travel time by a third. Curitiba also runs double- and triple-length articulated buses that increase the capacity of the express bus lanes.

Ironically, the reasoning behind the choice of transportation technology was not only efficiency but also simple economics: to build a subway system would have cost roughly US $60 million to US $70 million per kilometer; the express bus highways came in at US $200,000 per kilometer, including the boarding tubes. Bus operation and maintenance were also familiar tasks that the private sector could carry out. Private companies, following guidance and parameters established by the city administration, are responsible for all mass transit in Curitiba. Bus companies are paid by the number of kilometers that they operate rather than by the number of passengers they transport, allowing a balanced distribution of bus routes and eliminating destructive competition.

As a result, average low-income residents of Curitiba spend only about 10 percent of their income on transport, which is relatively low for Brazil. Although the city has more than 500,000 private cars (more cars per capita than any Brazilian city except the capital, Brasilia), three quarters of all commuters—more than 1.3 million passengers a day—

take the bus. Per capita fuel consumption is 25 percent lower than in comparable Brazilian cities, and Curitiba has one of the lowest rates of ambient air pollution in the country.

Although the buses run on diesel fuel, the number of car trips they eliminate more than makes up for their emissions.

In addition to these benefits, the city has a self-financing public transportation system and avoided being saddled by debt to pay for the construction and operating subsidies that a subway system entails. The savings have been invested in other areas. Even old buses are used to provide transportation to parks or serve as mobile schools.

The implementation of the public transport system also allowed the development of a low-income housing program that provided some 40,000 new dwellings. Before implementing the public transportation system, the city purchased and set aside land for low-income housing near the Curitiba Industrial City, a manufacturing district founded in 1972, located approximately eight kilometers west of the city center. Because the value of land is largely determined by its proximity to transportation and other facilities, these “land stocks” made it possible for the poor to have homes with ready access to jobs in an area where housing prices would otherwise have been unaffordable. The Curitiba Industrial City now supports 415 companies that directly and indirectly generate one fifth of all jobs in the city; polluting industries are not allowed.

An Integrated Busways Design: Participation Through Incentives

Curitiba’s express bus system is designed as a single entity, rather than as disparate components of buses, stops, and roads. As a result, the busways borrow many features from the subway system that the city might otherwise have built, had it a few billion dollars to spare. Most urban bus systems require passengers to pay as they board, slowing loading. Curitiba’s raised tube bus stops eliminate this step; passengers pay as they enter the tube, and so the bus spends more of its time actually moving people from place to place.

Similarly, the city installed wheelchair lifts at bus stops rather than on board buses easing weight restrictions and simplifying maintenance – buses with built-in wheelchair lifts are notoriously trouble prone, as are those that “kneel” to put their boarding steps within reach of the elderly. The tube-stop lifts also speed boarding by bringing disabled passengers to the proper height before the bus arrives.

As with subways, the buses have a track dedicated entirely to their use. This right-of-way significantly reduces travel time compared with buses that must fight automotive traffic to reach their destinations. By putting concrete and asphalt above the ground instead of excavating to place steel rails underneath it, however, the city managed to achieve most of the goals that subways strive for at less than 5 percent of the initial cost.

Some of the savings have enabled Curitiba to keep its fleet of 2,000 buses owned by 10 private companies under contract to the city among the newest in the world. The average bus is only three years old. The city pays bus owners 1 percent of the value of a bus each month; after 10 years it takes possession of retired vehicles and refurbishes them as free park buses or mobile schools.

Companies are paid according to the length of the routes they serve rather than the number of passengers they carry, giving the city a strong incentive to provide service that increases ridership. Indeed, more than a quarter of Curitiba's automobile owners take the bus to work. In response to increased demand, the city has augmented the capacity of its busways by using extralong buses the equivalent of multicar subway trains. The biarticulated bus, in service since 1992, has three sections connected by hinges that allow it to turn corners. At full capacity, these vehicles can carry 270 passengers, more than three times as many as an ordinary bus.

The city managers of Curitiba have learned that good systems and incentives are as important as good plans. The city's master plan helped to forge a vision and strategic principles to guide future developments. The vision was transformed into reality, however, by reliances on the right systems and incentives, not on slavish implementation of a static document.

One such innovative system is the provision of public information about land. City Hall can immediately deliver information to any citizen about the building potential of any plot in the city. Anyone wishing to obtain or renew a business permit must provide information about the project's impacts on traffic, infrastructure needs, parking requirements and municipal concerns. Ready access to this information helps to avoid land speculation; it has also been essential for budgetary purposes, because property taxes are the city's main source of revenue.

Incentives have been important in reinforcing positive behavior. Owners of land in the city's historic district can transfer the building potential of their plots to another area of the city—a rule that works to preserve historic buildings while fairly compensating their owners. In addition, business in specified areas throughout the city can "buy" permission to build up to two extra floors beyond the legal limit. Payment can be made in the form of cash or land that the city then uses to fund low-income housing.

Incentives and systems for encouraging beneficial behavior also work at the individual level. Curitiba's Free University for the Environment offers practical short courses at no cost for homemakers, building superintendents, shopkeepers, and others to teach the environmental implications of the daily routines of even the most common place jobs. The courses, taught by people who have completed an appropriate training program, are a prerequisite for licenses to work at some jobs, such as taxi driving, but many other people take them voluntarily.

The city also funds a number of important programs for children, putting money behind the often empty pronouncements municipalities make about the importance of the next generation. The Paperboy/Papergirl Program gives part-time jobs to schoolchildren from low-income families; municipal day care centers serve four meals a day to some 12,000 children; and SOS Children provides a special telephone number for urgent communications about children under any kind of threat.

Curitiba has repeatedly rejected conventional wisdom that emphasizes technologically sophisticated solutions to urban woes. Many planners have contended, for example, that cities with more than a million people must have a subway system to avoid traffic congestion. Prevailing dogma also claims that cities that generate more than 1000 tons of solid waste a day need expensive mechanical garbage-separation plants. Yet Curitiba has neither.

The city has attacked the solid-waste issue from both the generation and collection sides. Citizens recycle paper equivalent to nearly 1,200 trees each day. The Garbage That Is Not Garbage initiative has drawn more than 70 percent of households to sort recyclable materials for collection. The Garbage Purchase program, designed specifically for low-income areas, helps to clean up sites that are difficult for the conventional waste-management system to serve. Poor families can exchange filled garbage bags for bus tokens, parcels of surplus food, and children's school notebooks. More than 34,000 families in 62 poor neighborhoods have exchanged over 11,000 tons of garbage for nearly a million bus tokens and 1,200 tons of surplus food. During the past three years, students in more than 100 schools have traded nearly 200 tons of garbage for close to 1.9 million notebooks. Another initiative, All Clean, temporarily hires retired and unemployed people to clean up specific areas of the city where litter has accumulated.

These innovations, which rely on public participation and labor-intensive approaches rather than on mechanization and massive capital investment, have reduced the cost and increased the effectiveness of the city's solid-waste management system. They have also conserved resources, beautified the city, and provided employment.

Conclusions

No other city has precisely the combination of geographic, economic, and political conditions that mark Curitiba. Nevertheless, its successes can serve as lessons for urban planners in both the industrial and the developing worlds.

Perhaps the most important lesson is that top priority should be given to public transportation rather than to private cars and to pedestrians rather than to motorized vehicles. Bicycle paths and pedestrian areas should be an integrated part of the road network and public transportation system. Whereas intensive road-building programs elsewhere have led paradoxically to even more congestion, Curitiba's slighting of the needs of private motorized traffic has generated less use of cars and has reduced pollution.

Curitiba's planners have also learned the solutions to urban problems are not specific and isolated, but rather interconnected. Any plan should involve partnerships among private-sector entrepreneurs, nongovernmental organizations, municipal agencies, utilities, neighborhood associations, community groups, and individuals. Creative and labor-intensive ideas—especially where unemployment is already a problem—can often substitute for conventional capital-intensive technologies.

We have found that cities can turn traditional sources of problems into resources. For example, public transportation, urban solid waste, and unemployment are traditionally considered problems, but they have the potential to become generators of new resources, as they have in Curitiba.

Curitiba's experiences teaches us crucial principle: there is no time like the present. Rather than trying to revitalize urban centers that have begun falling into decay, planners in already-large cities and those that have just started to grow can begin solving problems without waiting for top-down master plans or near fiscal collapse.

Section 2 The Case of Costa Rica

Fernando Zumbado

Geographic and historical factors may make Costa Rica a particular case in the developing world, because the country is characterized by a long period of peace, the absence of an army since 1948, a tradition of democratic institutions and culture, a small geographic size, and a small population. However, moving beyond these generalities, a specific analysis of the Costa Rican housing experience sheds light on a realizable means of improving the quality of life of populations everywhere, a dream still to come true.

Two major factors account for the positive results of the four-year housing program: (1) an enabling environment built on the framework of continued democratic governance, a restored and stable macroeconomy, housing sector institutions that integrated an agile financial system to facilitate widened access to housing solutions, and (2) participation of the people at the grass-roots level in the preparation of housing plans and their implementation. This unleashed their productive forces, inserting reality and concrete possibility into their hopes and dreams.

Developmental Model

Despite the vulnerability of an economy in a conflict affected region, Costa Rica can be described as a small, democratic, and peaceful country, with a high level of human development. Costa Rican social and economic development is firmly rooted in a relatively egalitarian past, which the abolition of the army only strengthened. It not only fostered greater freedom and liberty, but facilitated the shift in development focus to tasks necessary for better human development, including strengthening of the democratic system and the reform of the public sector. Present indicators of social development of the country are comparable to that of some industrialized nations.

By 1990 Costa Rica's population had reached 3 million, compared to less than 800,000 in 1948. As with a large part of Latin America, this country too experienced high population growth. The highest rates occurred at the beginning of the 1960s, reaching 3.7 percent annually, and then decreased to 2.5 percent annually. Sixty percent of the population lived in cities of 2,000 or more inhabitants in 1990, compared with only one third in 1950.

The average growth rate of the economy exceeded 6 percent annually in the period before to 1979, much above the population growth rate. Nonetheless, the economy began to deteriorate in 1979. Formal unemployment rates rose from 5.9 percent in 1980 to 9.4 percent two years later. Exports fell from just over US $1 billion in 1980 to US $870.4 million in 1982. In dollar terms, the GDP fell from 4.3 to 2.5 billion in the same period and, as a consequence, per capita income fell precipitously from US $1,947 to US $1,080. This represented a decline of 55 percent in only two years.

The public sector too found itself in a difficult situation, so much so that by 1982 the deficit represented 14 percent of GDP. The local currency lost its value and the country suffered an unprecedented increase in price levels, with inflation reaching 90.1 percent in 1982. The external debt reached 121.6 percent of GDP in that same year, while debt servicing accounted for 85 percent of the total value of exports.

The crisis obviously impinged on the traditions of family economy and its capacity to access the housing market. It widened the gap between the cost of a home and the ability to pay for one. Prices increased far more than salaries, and the purchasing power of the population fell. The poorer families were most affected by these factors.

It was precisely during the height of the economic crisis that a series of land invasions took place, unprecedented in Costa Rica's history. Never before had the country seen so many squatters fight so hard for so little, namely, the limited access to land and housing.

To confront the crisis, a Structural Adjustment Programme was applied. It proved to be a severe test for the democratic institutions of the country, which nevertheless survived. The economy began to stabilize and growth was resumed. Right in the midst of the adjustment period, an ambitious housing program was launched, with a building target of 80,000 units in the period from 1986 to 1990. This, despite adverse national economic and fiscal limitations and a threatening external political environment. The program was intended to make a positive contribution to the development of the country, and most importantly, a tangible improvement in the quality of life of the human beings, on whom everything, including democracy, so clearly depends.

Before the Program

The quantitative housing deficit estimated in 1985 totaled more than 120,000 housing units, which was equivalent to one quarter of the existing stock of 509,000 units. The shortage included nearly 90 percent of units that could only be classified as "severely deteriorated" or "not repairable." Of the total number of deteriorated housing units, more than three quarters were located in the rural areas.

The increasing cost of financing and the decrease in real income for more than one third of Costa Rican families meant that access to housing by the average family diminished by 50 percent between 1980 and 1985. Given existing income levels and confronted by the high cost of a prototype home and the financial restrictions of the mortgage market, 20 percent of the poorest families could only hope for a home improvement loan—and that only if they resided in the Metropolitan Area of San Jose. Not even that if they were rural residents. During the nine years prior to 1986, the country constructed an average of 15,000 units and provide for the improvement or expansion of another 2,000 units.

To eliminate the housing shortage by the year 2000, it was estimated that 31,000 units had to be built each year between 1986 and 2000. In other words, the rate of production had to double. In this context, it is noteworthy that despite the relative importance of the informal sector in contributing toward the housing stock, traditionally such production had been categorized as "substandard" or "not repairable." To government authorities, at least statistically, these units formed part of the problem and not the solution.

It was evident from the beginning that the program would go beyond the enumeration provided by mere statistics. The struggle for survival in the informal sector on the part of families within the lowest income strata generated a wealth of experience and a potential resource that could not be ignored. This input could be tapped. The poorest families not only constituted the principal target population to benefit from any new progress, but also served as a major input by active participation within the program.

The landscape of formal institutions before 1986, appeared relatively inflexible, perhaps as a result of the concentration of most sector activities in one entity. The efforts of this one "super" institution to perform as a regulatory entity, to set policies, to provide funding, to stimulate new construction systems, and to coordinate other entities resulted finally in much activity and little output.

With no financial incentives to offer and with housing usually a less rewarding activity, the only organizations with clout, such as the banks, tended to give minimal priority to central government resolutions. However, their independence and occasional duplication of efforts, made for poor use of scarce resources and often led to a diminution in the quality of services offered.

Credit financing for the purchase and construction of housing depended, almost solely, on the participation of the state commercial banks.

Such financing competed for resources used in the productive and commercial sectors. By the mid-1980s, the supply of housing had reached serious constraints, and bottlenecks in nearly every area were apparent.

To further compound the problem, those requesting credit had to satisfy stringent criteria and meet harsh financial guarantees. Gradually, this led to fewer and fewer families obtaining mortgages through the commercial banking system. A major crisis had enveloped the sector. The demand for housing was low because a family's lack of income could not transform its need for housing into demand, being effectively restricted from the mortgage markets. The supply of housing was limited because high unit costs, delays in bureaucratic processing, and lack of bridge finance restricted the production of new housing units to only the wealthiest quarter of the population.

Initial Stage of the Program

The target goal of building 80,000 housing units within a four-year period established by the National Housing Programme represented an increase of 35 percent over the annual production levels achieved in the best of times. Of even greater significance was the fact that the preponderance of the new units would meet the needs of the poorest sectors of the population – a reversal of previous trends. More than half of the population of Costa Rica was included in this sector.

The quantitative target was not the only goal. By the end of the program, an institutional structure had to be in place capable of financing the construction of 30,000 units per year. Furthermore, the latter target implied the need for comprehensive reforms in the housing sector to support the increased volumes of financing production.

At this juncture, the housing goals of Costa Ricans constituted a bold political challenge. More importantly, the materialization in terms of concrete responses and symbolic actions contributed to an awakening of the imagination and self-confidence in the forces of the community and of democratic participation. Furthermore, the program could no longer be considered in isolated terms, but rather as part of an overall policy that aimed at establishing peace in the region. Housing policy was to demonstrate that the overall peace and democracy for the region also meant building and dignifying human life for Costa Ricans, particularly of the poor.

Although new policies and programs were formulated, it was necessary to reach agreements with organized groups in order to channel their efforts in the most effective manner and to respond to priority requests. A social pact was created. This represented a departure on the part of a public sector accustomed to setting its own agenda. The social pact established a set of priorities that determined the order in which housing needs would be met. The government committed itself to the construction of 20,000 units for families belonging to the larger housing organizations. For their part, these groups agreed to refrain from further land encroachments and to actively promote community participation in the implementation of housing projects. Although negotiations and outcomes varied according to the different viewpoints, the final result proved to be highly positive and established the basis for a new relationship between the government and the needs of families and organized groups. The social pact allowed for the planning and implementation of housing programs within a more realistic context, a context that could be realized, to make dreams come true, at least in the area of housing.

The government decided to first implement a contingency plan labeled "Immediate Action," with the dual purpose of assisting with the on-site improvement of highly visible projects and with the transfer of families from precarious sites to safer settlements. A total of 4,500 families were included in this plan. A first disbursement was arranged from the National Commission on Emergencies, side-stepping typical bureaucratic requirements to demonstrate that the problem could not only be confronted, but also solved expeditiously. In this manner, the citizenry gradually began to understand that the government was indeed purposeful and serious in addressing its problems. This in turn generated the requisite sense of urgency and commitment on behalf of the poor, thereby giving them the faith and emotional wherewithal to help themselves, to believe that they could and that they indeed would. This nonmaterial dimension cannot be stressed enough.

The Immediate Action Plan, targeted to the urban population, was complemented by a Rural Housing Programme mainly funded by the Government of Canada. This program was later changed and acquired greater institutional feasibility as a Foundation. At the beginning, credits were authorized using subsidized interest rates ranging from 8 to 12 percent, depending on the income level of the rural family. After the creation of the National Housing Financial System, the program began to operate under the guidelines established for subsidies, and the Foundation became self-sufficient.

Access to Credits

The policies adopted constituted a set of measures whose key components were:

- The functional integration of the institutions in the sector.
- The stimulation of the private sector to participate in new ways.
- The increased participation of the population at the grass-roots level.
- The establishment of a formally integrated financial sector that could respond to the needs of all families requiring housing.

In November 1986, the Legislature approved the creation of the National Housing Financial system, which called for the establishment and operation of the Home Mortgage Bank (Banco Hipotecario de la Vivienda, BANHVI) to serve as the backbone of the system. The new institution received resources that had not been utilized earlier. This avoided both the imposition of new taxes and the increasing of public expenditures. However, it did provide, as required, the financial instrument necessary to build houses.

Notwithstanding the above, no amount of credit resources could obviate the need for a mechanism that could reach out to those normally excluded from the housing market. A policy of housing subsidies was accordingly developed. The new system was designed to generate a direct subsidy immediately over the cost of housing in order not to negatively affect the financial markets. Furthermore, the system guaranteed that each family would receive only the minimum that it needed to acquire a decent home. Subsidies constituted the complement of the resources that the different public and private institutions already channeled towards housing, so that these resources would be placed efficiently and provide for sound financial recovery. This policy became the cornerstone to substantially increase access to the large sectors of the population with lower incomes.

BANHVI is a second-tier banking institution. That is, it centralizes the resources and discounts mortgages. It deals not directly with the public, but rather with various types of financial intermediaries. These serve as the "windows" of the system and are responsible for channeling and organizing the demand, both as working capital for construction firms as well as mortgages for homeowners. "Authorized entities" dealing with the public include savings and loans organizations, credit and housing cooperatives, private and public commercial banks, and specialized public sector institutions that provide important funds for housing. The resources are organized in terms of whether or not the funds are subsidized, thus fitting into two main categories: (1) The Subsidy Fund for Housing (Fondo de Subsidio para la Vivienda, FOSUVI) or (2) The National Fund for Housing (Fondo Nacional de la Vivienda, FONAVI).

By December 1989, after only two years of operation, BANHVI had supervised the distribution of US $121 million, with nearly 66 percent channeled through FOSUVI and the remaining to fund FONAVI activities. The Bank used these resources to generate short-term loans, nearly all of which were destined to meet the working capital requirements of construction companies involved in major housing projects. Long-term funding of mortgages meant that families, individually or in organized groups, could purchase or build their homes.[1]

The subsidy administered through FOSUVI on behalf of the families in the lower income levels acted directly on the cost of housing, without affecting the operation of FONAVI, which was governed by financial market criteria. The subsidy operated through the family bond (bono familiar) is defined by a set of factors including total family income, size of the family, and the cost of the proposed housing solution. It was conceived as a long-term loan (with a maximum term of 25 years) without interest payments, and a period of grace of up to 15 years.

With lower incomes, the relative weight of the mortgage bonus increases within the total financing authorized. The subsidy covers the entire amount financed in the cases of families whose incomes fall below the minimum monthly wage. A basic credit is formalized as a first mortgage; the mortgage bonus is represented as a secondary mortgage. The combination of these two instruments produces an effect equivalent to differentiated interest rates, varying from 0 percent for the lowest income bracket to real market rates of interest for families at the highest income levels permitted by the legislation.

With these instruments in place, access to the housing market increased dramatically. The program could now reach 80 percent of Costa Rican families and in the case of the poorest two deciles of income, the benefits extended to the total amount financed. The analysis of the distribution of all full or partial subsidy financing registered as of May 1990, showed that 30 percent went to families whose monthly income did not exceed the minimum monthly salary, and another 40 percent to those families whose monthly income ranged between one and two minimum monthly salaries. More than 35,000 mortgage bonuses had been authorized by May 1990. The average housing units cost approximately US $5,000, with the value of the average subsidy estimated at half that amount. The monthly income of the families that received these benefits averaged approximately US $250.

People's Participation

In addition to creating a new financial system, housing policy also instigated a profound institutional reform that had implications for all the entities in the sector. The government assumed a new role, that of a facilitator, by promoting, orienting and creating a sense of urgency not only within itself, but also within others external to it. It became a catalyst, an active player in individual lives, not just in institutions. This of course required clear guidelines and procedures to achieve the requisite managerial efficiency.

The role of the private sector had to change from one responding primarily to the housing needs of the middle- and upper-income families to one catering to the lower ranges of the income scales. An incentive system was put in place to stimulate developers and builders by giving them resources in volumes not previously available. Greater efficiency was achieved by letting the private sector take the initiative in construction, whether it was a traditional construction firm or a newly formed cooperative of mothers.

In addition, an essential element of the system was an increase in the organization at the grass roots. This not only led to a reduction in costs but served to transform every cent invested by the public sector into much more, created by the joint effort of the families participating in the project. Community-based organizations became the driving force of the program, as they guaranteed that the resources made available were channeled to the areas of greatest need. In many instances the program was a tool to strengthen the people's ability to organize. In fact, so much so that in reality housing became a secondary by product; the strengthening and empowerment of local organizations became the primary result.

Changes were promoted in the institutional system to increase openness and stimulate the participation of the private construction sector as well as of community-based housing organizations. A new and small Ministry of Housing and Human Settlements facilitated the operation of primary decision levels. A National Sectorial Council acted as the senior level policy decision-making body, presided over by the Minister. An Executive Secretariat of Sectorial Planning was responsible for planning and operating the coordinating mechanisms. Task forces and project-specific groups were also established to serve as liaisons in the areas of physical planning, infrastructure and services, grass-roots organizations, financing, and technology innovation.

These mechanisms facilitated the active participation of municipalities, cooperatives, private building contractors, associations, committee and local boards, nonprofit organizations (both national and international), universities, and research institutions. On the one hand, these ensured a better use of programs and institutions, where feasible. On the other hand, new operating mechanisms were created, enhancing innovation and effectiveness in the search for new and improved solutions. A number of regional outlets were created so that local housing organizations could access the additional financial resources with the necessary training and orientation on the part of both "supply" and "demand."

Some changes in the roles of existing institutions include:

- The Instituto Nacional de Vivienda y Urbanismo (INVU, established in 1954) continued to assist the middle- and lower-income groups by encouraging the participation of construction companies.
- The Instituto Mixto de Ayuda Social (IMAS, created in 1972) concentrated on smaller housing projects (between 20 and 60 families) and favored family self-help construction modes of operation. The new subsidy policy multiplied its activity. While only 5,000 units

had been constructed during 16 years prior to 1986, IMAS evolved so that it could process 2,500 units annually by 1990.

- Savings and Loan associations highly increased their activities.
- Other organizations (education, public works, transportation, electric energy, water supply, and health) channeled resources to projects coordinated by the Ministry of Housing and Human Settlements.

New institutions complemented the traditional ones:

- The Special Housing Commission (Comisión Especial de Vivienda, CEV), covered emergency actions. By 1990 the CEV had invested more than US $40 million for a total of 7,253 finished units and another 10,000 in different stages of construction.
- The Costa Rica–Canada Rural Housing Foundation (Fundación de Vivienda Rural Costa Rica–Canada) channeled funds through agricultural production organizations (mainly cooperatives). Canadian funds (US $22 million) and resources from BANHVI allowed credits for a total of US $11.3 million in 3.5 years. Credits were given to families whose monthly incomes averaged approximately US $200, stimulating local organizations.
- The Foundation to Promote Housing (Fundación Promotora de Vivienda, FPV) assisted the efforts of families in the lowest-income sectors in urban areas within a concept of community development. The Foundation was granted US $6 million by the Government of Sweden as initial capital. The basic thrust of FPV is to provide the bridge loan financing necessary for the construction of small urban housing projects, including home improvement and small-scale community projects.
- The bamboo program introduced this material for housing construction on the basis of experience of Colombia. It received support from the United Nations (HABITAT and UNDP) and a US $7 million contribution from the Government of the Netherlands.

Achievements

The target of 80,000 housing units set as the goal for the program was surpassed: the total reached 85,821 in the period from May 8, 1986 to April 30, 1990. It represented a 43 percent increase in the volume of construction registered in the previous four-year administration. But more significantly, the distribution of units underscores the fact that mortgage credit markets integrated sectors of the population formerly excluded. A total of 23,171 units corresponded to families with less than US $210 per month, 20,598 to families in the US $210 to 420 per month bracket, and 42,052 to families with larger incomes (more than US $420 per month). During the period from 1986 to 1990, approximately US $500 million were channeled as financial resources.

With the creation of the Ministry of Housing and Human Settlements, an institutional system was established that could define and balance overall objectives. For the first time the State became a facilitator, not an implementing agency. BANHVI was in charge of the financial subsector and a set of subsidies allowed the channeling of funds to those most in need without affecting sound financial practices. Finally, financial intermediaries could deal directly with those demanding credit while simultaneously mobilizing national and foreign resources. External support amounted to approximately US $100 million.

Conclusion

Notwithstanding the above, perhaps the most important element of the program was the transformation of the housing sector into a national pastime, a symbol of what democracy could conquer and the constructive energies it could unleash. The majority sectors of the population seized the opportunities to fully participate in the improvement of their quality of life. They felt and acted empowered, in control of a destiny they had earlier written off. The effort and amount of resources that many poor families brought to the building of their homes, the energy of women exerting leadership roles to improve the future of their families, enriched individual and national life and created new organizational options. It was a process of inclusion.

A word of caution should be added considering the obstacles that still must be confronted and the difficulties that naturally emerged at the end of the four-year program. It must be pointed out that accessibility to housing has shown a long-term decline in the period from 1980 to 1990, not considering the "family bond." Also, and particularly since 1990, the quantity of funds transferred annually to the National Housing Financial System did not meet the requirements prescribed by law.

Other drawbacks stemmed from the urgency of providing shelter at the expense of creating environmental problems both in rural and urban areas. The pressures arose even in areas where improvements were made or new settlements were erected to reduce slums and squatter settlements, although they may have ameliorated the conditions in which many families lived. The weaknesses of local municipalities and the absence of administrative arrangements at the metropolitan level represent a challenge to putting in place sustainable solutions to urban problems.

Other issues too must be confronted. Social costs of increased housing must include those attributed to any land speculation as well as to the increases in the costs of materials and construction. The institutional system must also face the difficulties of handling increased loads. This needs better training, improved processing systems, and more appropriate management procedures.

There are many ways to evaluate a program as ambitious as the one described above. This one produced qualitative, as well as quantitative, results. It also contributed to sustainable human development in the country. The program involved thousands of Costa Ricans and assisted them in realizing their dream of having a house in which to make a home, of becoming first-class citizens with the power to change and construct, to value the previously undervalued or unvalued self, to expand their choices, and, most importantly perhaps, to feel part of a worthwhile whole, not as isolated islands standing by themselves.

Notes

1. By March 1990, the Bank was processing 1,500 credits monthly, of which 90 percent required a partial or total subsidy. For these credits, 75 percent of the resources were provided by BANHVI (45 percent from FOSUVI and 30 percent from FONAVI). The remaining 25 percent was contributed by the authorized entities (such as banks, savings and loan associations, or credit cooperatives).

Section 3 A Case of Partnership from Asia: Bombay

Nasser Munjee

The emergence of cities about two or three thousand years after agriculture was firmly established heralded a new form of socioeconomic entity which would be uniquely "human." It also created the great divide between the town and country—the one to be identified with the production of manufactured goods, commercial activities, and intellectual pursuits; the other with supplying the food and raw material for the survival of these new concentrations. Cities also quickly began to emerge as centers of political power around which several constituencies would quickly evolve. The concentrated environment would encourage social contact and the dissemination of information. In its wake would come a certain energy and innovation that was unlikely to be generated in a purely rural setting. This in turn would attract the additional people was necessary to fuel the economic activity that cities implied. The problem posed by the concentration of humankind had arrived.

As economic reforms sweep across Asia, much of their impact is felt in the cities. The emergent middle classes enter the consumption stream and many of their new demands, from two wheelers to golf courses, have immediate impact on city environments. A casual visitor to Bangkok, Manila, Jakarta, or Bombay cannot fail to notice the impact of unbridled growth on city infrastructure, manifested most visibly in traffic congestion, insufficient drainage and sewerage systems, inadequate health and education facilities, water shortages, brown outs, rising crime, and other failures in city management. Worse still, with larger rates of economic growth fueled by economic reform, cities are likely to face many pressures for expansion—wider and more intrusive transportation systems, condominiums, shopping plazas—all of which make major demands on city infrastructure. Stimulating economic growth through economic reforms linked to liberalization, without sufficient attention to city planning and urban development, is likely to prove a short-run phenomenon; infrastructure constraints are rapidly catching up to and obviating the entire process.

The Impact of Globalization

The marked increase in global interconnectedness, which began in the 1960s, has been especially pronounced in the 1990s. Much of this acceleration is directly linked to new technologies, the pace of globalization, the process of structural change, and the almost ubiquitous impact of modern communications. As capital and information are transmitted flawlessly and instantly over the globe, the nature of business enterprises, the development of a global labor market, and the changing face of credit and capital markets have all undergone irrevocable change. All of these activities are located in and have huge impacts on cities. Indeed, the new boundaries shift from national governments to cities, as the former begin to lose their control over key elements of the traditional economy. The competitive advantage of cities will increasingly begin to overtake that of nations as the key driving forces of economic development. These trends are especially apparent in the Asia Pacific region as the economies in the area have witnessed sustained and rapid growth over the past decade. By 1992, Japan, Singapore, Taiwan, Hong Kong, Malaysia, and Thailand all scored above the OECD average of world competitiveness. In the Asian context, cities have moved much more rapidly than expected from predominantly manufacturing-based to service-based economies.

What are the challenges that these trends pose for Asian cities? The first might be the rapid outward focus of cities in terms of their export potential (exports here include shipments to the rest of the country as well); the second would be a trend towards rural urbanization with improved transportation and telecommunication systems; the third would be the challenge of urban poverty, as jobs shift toward higher value added service activities from low value added extensive production processes; the fourth would be some combination of the impact of the above – rapid urbanization, the emergence of the megacity with enormous implications for the investment in and the management of the social and physical infrastructure.

The Need for Infrastructural Financing

Any sector's expansion is in direct relation to the efficiency with which it is financed; this is as true of industrial and rural development as of housing and urban growth. Investments in the social and physical infrastructure by local governments have been woefully insufficient to meet the pace of urban economic growth. Much of this deficiency stems from the financial arrangements that exist for investments in infrastructure renewal and addition. Urban finance, therefore, emerges as a key priority, a necessary though not sufficient condition, for policy planning. With economic liberalization proceeding rapidly, devolution of responsibility for public finance and decentralization of powers to local authorities for the provision of infrastructure has not been met by a similar devolution for the access to a resource base.

The reluctance of central governments to grant access to established sources of funds by lower-level authorities stems from the fear that too many resources now accessed at the central level would be crowded out by local authorities. This could affect central government budgets as well as make macroeconomic management much more complex. The issue, therefore, is much greater than just urban finance; it concerns the political issue of urban governance itself.

The agenda for political reform in India, for example, remains confused and finds expression in knee-jerk reactions to ongoing practices that have become accepted by no other legitimacy than being standard practice over a period of time. Overregulation and weak supervision of financial institutions, nonbank financial intermediaries, local authorities and subnational governments, and stock markets accelerate with renewed enthusiasm. In a modern, sophisticated, and increasingly globalizing economy with rapid communications, city governance institutions are likely to emerge, as one commentator has noted, as "the institutional dinosaurs of India's urban Jurassic Parks."

With changing economic circumstances and the rush to "marketization" in many cities of the developing world, issues of urban development and city finance must be viewed in the context of the strong interlinkages between macroeconomic policy and the city economy; the issue of institutional development and local authority finance; and the relationship between fiscal policy and urban development. Many of these forces came upon us so rapidly that a considered response to these new developments is still to be found in the upper reaches of macroeconomic policy, even though their effects are being felt almost immediately on the urban economy.

The recent World Bank Development Report of 1994 focused attention on *Infrastructure for Development.* In this important and timely report, the Bank stressed the need for efficiency in infrastructure delivery that responds to effective demand, while addressing the issues of poverty alleviation and environmental sustainability. Most developing countries have suffered from a supply-driven orientation undertaken by bureaucracies rather than service delivery as an industry. The lack of a commercial sense, driven by appropriate product definition and pricing, has led to a situation where objectives are confused, little financial autonomy or discipline practiced, customer satisfaction ignored, and indeed the quality and quantity of services provided predicated by a monopolistic supplier. The report, not surprisingly, recommends commercialization through competitive supply that would create a situation where users had a direct impact on the type, quality, and quantity of services to be provided and where the private sector would compete or indeed join as partners in the process of delivery. The major role of government would shift from provider to prudent regulator of the system, taking up only those elements in the nature of "public goods" that could not be operated by the market mechanism.

Whatever one may say about the theoretical issues of commercialization and competition, in the final analysis, the institutional setting is the critical factor that will determine its efficacy. Unfortunately, it is precisely this last process that is so difficult to extract from governments and their institutions, which are so used to creating legislative environments that are rhetorically socially oriented but in practice serve their own ends. The future of our cities depends on succeeding in putting this approach into practice, but how is it to be achieved?

The Impending Institutional Crisis

Although the issues posed by the relationship of urban governance and urban finance for institutional structuring are profound and complex, a second major factor connected with macroeconomic adjustment, will perhaps, be the major driving force for change. This factor is the fairly rapid dismemberment of the directed credit system in developing countries.

In a directed credit system, major development banks and financial institutions—including parastatals involved in housing and urban finance—have developed and functioned in a cushioned environment, with government guaranteed funding, channeled through the directed credit system, constituting the major resource base. Liberalization and the demise of the planned system of economic development necessitates the collapse of this directed flow of credit. This leads to a major crisis for the institutions that have for decades depended on the system. Market institutions are highly adapted to the market and used to attracting their own capital on the basis of their performance and profitability.

The problem essentially is particularly acute for dependent institutions, which are now forced to reestablish their "connectedness" to their overall financial environment with only one parameter—performance—finally determining success or failure. The economics and technology of the process is also gradually eroding the established advantages of specialist knowledge and capability; forcing a more holistic understanding of changing markets. Institutions will no longer be able to anchor themselves to particular markets, but will have to redefine their comparative advantages in a more holistic manner. The "customer" has emerged as a more transitory bird, who is able and willing to perch on the most attractive tree. Unfortunately many of the institutions particularly affected by this trend, are those that have traditionally been in the field of urban and housing finance. How this transition will be managed is a vital issue facing many developing economies.

The Urban Poor

At the most basic level, cities are about jobs: Nothing more; nothing less. Walking though recession-afflicted London a few years ago gave one a sense of what gainful employment really means even in a highly developed society. Lincoln Inn Field and the Strand were commandeered by the homeless living in cardboard boxes. In developing societies, this is an endemic feature, as those on the bottom rung of the informal sector struggle to survive. They come to the city seeking jobs, and they rely on the success of their endeavors in their income-generating capacity to extract themselves from their current economic position.

One of the major issues arising from rapid urbanization will be the concentration of wealth in the new sunrise industries and a growing disparity between rich and poor. Even though cities are the engines of growth, they are simultaneously the focus of impoverishment of millions of people. This is sometimes referred to as the "Dual City" those that participate in the formal economy and those that constitute the "underclass." This duality can be minimized by concentrating attention on the potentials of cities and how these might be harnessed effectively for its future prosperity.

Cities need to establish a fairly well-defined sense of direction for their future economic potentials in this globalizing, competitive world to ensure that they have the right mix of opportunities for both high and low value added labor. Competitive pressure may shift this mix between cities—financial centers concentrating on the former and processing centers on the latter—but, overall, cities need to work very closely with and align themselves to their comparative advantages. With the inevitable shift towards service industries, as economies and cities develop, city planners need to be mindful of initiating close dialogues with industry, commerce, and trade to ensure that sunrise activities are being facilitated and declining industries are being phased out in a manner that ensures absorption of labor in the new support industries that the changing economy will demand. Failure to do so is likely to have major impact on labor markets and the city economy as a whole.

The success of this process will depend heavily on the institutional structures that the city has in place to respond effectively to rapidly changing circumstances. Slow response times, political feuding, and other constraints can delay critical decision making at huge cost to the city. Managing cities through effective governance systems will be the key to long-term success and prosperity for all its citizen. So often it is poor management, a failure to respond to clear signals and outdated legislation, that is the root cause of urban poverty. The ultimate response is then social programs (sometimes heavily subsidized) to alleviate the major consequences of the failure of urban governance. Urban governance is perhaps the single most important factor that can transform cities into vibrant economic, social, and cultural centers without marginalizing vast segments of the population.

Although governance is the key issue, its twin pillars are land policies and urban finance. Land policy impinges on every single aspect of city strategy: the vision; the environment; the economy; the infrastructure; the heritage; housing; and the networking so crucial to any modern economy. Urban finance is the building block of the appropriate use of the city's resources to create a self sustaining cycle of city growth in alignment with its economic and social potential. Both depend very much on the nature of urban governance: bad policies can rarely be changed with ease unless the governance mechanism is conducive to progressive change. Local bodies will not be given sufficient powers to raise resources unless enlightened governance mechanisms exist that can conceptualize a capital market in which several players have a role. The Philippines is a good example of good governance in this regard.

Multisource Financing

Current debate on the provision of urban services has shifted away from "who provides what" to how effectively services are actually delivered. In a recent book that discusses these issues lucidly, Gabriel Roth quotes from Keynes, *The End of Laissez-Faire,* as follows: "The important thing for government is not to do things which individuals are doing already and to do them a little better or a little worse: but to do those things which are not done at all."

The broad generic framework under which these reforms are being initiated is one of decentralization. By which level of government or the public sector should services be provided? How much managerial and fiscal autonomy should be granted? How should fiscal gaps be bridged? Much disagreement exists today on these issues. In the final analysis it seems that there are no clear answers; no "optimal" level of decentralization or revenue base. Bahl and Linn in their book, *Urban Public Finance in Developing Countries* (1992), arrive at the following conclusions, which are worth quoting, regarding this important issue:

1. An optimum level of decentralisation is arrived at by weighing the tradeoff between maintaining central government flexibility for macro-economic management and improving the level and delivery systems of urban services.
2. Any success in this endeavour will require devolution of powers to local governments.
3. Local government taxes are most effective when their objective is to raise revenues, and they are kept simple administratively. Equity

and allocational issues should be addressed by higher levels of government.

4. User charges meet the criteria in #3 above and are an excellent source of revenue.
5. The source of revenue raising depends upon the expenditure responsibility. Inter-governmental transfers should not discourage local revenue raising efforts.
6. There are no 'optimal' forms of local governance; it depends on the objectives the national government wishes to achieve through sub national governments.

In other words governance has to move closer to the constituency it is supposed to serve.

Decentralized governance mechanisms with active citizen participation in local infrastructure investment and revenue raising is the critical building block to improved systems of city management. Partnerships are likely to be the way forward; not defining roles, but asking how effectively desired objectives could be fulfilled and then providing the mechanisms through which participation—not consensus—can be achieved. The contribution of industry and business in this process is vital, as they are in a position to anticipate trends and to strategize the businesses they manage. Close connection with city governance would provide leading indicators of the directions of change taking place and how the city ought to be responding to changed circumstances. Conceptualizing these lead indicators would be a powerful first step to creating the environment where partnerships can really work. These indicators could also measure the extent of urban competitiveness emerging in different regions and the impact of this trend on both the suppliers and consumers of infrastructure services. The competitive advantage of cities would need very careful consideration, as this could well be the key for future economic strategies and therefore of all citizen of the city. An initiative that began recently in the city of Bombay can be mentioned as a case study.

Bombay First

Bombay has begun an initiative based on London First—an attempt to create a nongovernment institution drawing both financial and human resources from the corporate sector—to focus attention on city issues. "Bombay First," as it is known, is creating a core competency on the strategic needs of the city and the methods by which implementation strategies can be put in place. It has already created a policy foundation capitalized at approximately US $1 million, with a Bombay First Society drawing its membership from key citizens of the city who have, over the years, contributed to the city debate in various fields of activity from the environment to financial infrastructure. It will be the latter who will outline the agenda of the institution and arrive at core strategies with the help of the foundation. Five key groups have been established: Land Use and Housing (the Vision Group); Transport; Telecommunications; Bombay as a Financial Centre; and Education and Training. Bombay First, it is hoped, will create an energy around which many interested groups will be able to assemble and create a constituency for change. If the experiment is a success, one hopes that many other cities will follow in its footsteps, thus bringing about a major agenda for urban development and city planning throughout the country. It is one method that can completely redesign city governance systems in tune with a changing environment.

Conclusion

When Pericles of Athens declared his city "thrown open to the world," one could hardly have imagined what this might one day come to mean. We are gradually, though inevitably, becoming citizen of the world through communication links that were hardly dreamed of a mere five years ago. True citizenship once meant being a member of a city; we have arrived at an age where the competitive advantage of nations might well be the attractiveness of their cities for business as well as pleasure. The housing citizen—whatever form of tenure that might entail—will emerge as the basic building block of civilized life in the modern technological age. The megacities of today pose a major challenge for new institutional and governance mechanisms that will need to evolve to ensure that those without shelter and basic services for dignified human existence are a condition of the past. As one commentator observed:

> The chief function of the city is to convert power into form, energy into culture, dead matter into the living symbols of art, biological reproduction into social creativity. The positive functions of the city cannot be performed without creating new institutional arrangements capable of coping with the vast energies modern man now commands: arrangements just as bold as those that originally transformed the overgrown village and its stronghold into the nucleated, highly organized city.

These words were written more than thirty-five years ago by Lewis Mumford in *Cities in History*. They have a resonance which we would all do well to heed as we approach the next millennium.

Section 4 The Case of China

Weiping Wu

The reform period after 1979 marks an accelerated rate of urbanization and urban development in China. Largely as a result of a shift in the country's urban policy, cities resumed their roles as the centers of growth and development. Urban population has expanded rapidly, at the same time the number of big cities has increased steadily. The rising level of urbanization has been driven mainly by migration (defined as movement across county/city boundaries), as natural population growth in cities is strictly controlled by the family planning policy. Some gross estimates put the number of rural migrants into cities at around 100 million in the country, and predict another 100 million redundant peasants by year 2000.[1] Others even assert that the trend in China represents "the largest quick urban immigration in all human history."[2] Large cities (defined as cities with populations of more than a half million, including megacities with populations of more than 1 million), particularly those along the east coast, have been the major recipients of such migrants.

Resembling other developing countries at a similar stage, these rural migrants are predominantly young males who have come to cities to engage in nonagricultural activities. They often settle in illegal peasant villages in urban peripheries. On the one hand, these migrants have contributed to the growth of cities, but on the other hand, they have also had unprecedented impact on cities in such areas as infrastructure, security, education, public health, and family planning.

This section of *Cities Fit for People* will document the magnitude of this migration and its impact on China's large cities. The focus, though, is to show the inability of the current system to properly accommodate the surging volume of rural migrants, particularly in terms of adequate urban services, and to explore some feasible solutions.

Urban Policy and Economic Reform

China's post-1949 and prereform urbanization and urban policy can best be characterized as: (1) discouraging the growth of large cities and encouraging the development of medium and small cities; (2) developing industrial and urban centers away from coastal areas; and (3) using a variety of administrative measures to control the general growth and distribution of cities. All the large cities were growing at a steady but unspectacular pace, particularly Shanghai, but medium cities were undergoing the fastest rate of growth. The population of Beijing, Tianjin, and some other large cities were less successfully contained. Such a urban policy was the result of Mao's antiurban vision which viewed cities as parasitic.

The control of urban population growth was mainly through the household registration. Introduced and implemented in 1958, the system of household registration was designed to control population mobility and in particular rural–urban migration. Individuals had to establish firm legal residence in one locality, often based on employment, and changes in their registration were usually done through their employers. A household registered as urban was entitled to job guarantees, low-priced food rations, public housing, education, and services. Such a system has acted as a highly effective barrier separating urban from rural and agricultural from nonagricultural populations.[3] Ironically, this system also aggravated the inequality between urban and rural residents in employment, income, education, housing, and social welfare. The household registration system is still in place today in large cities, whereas small towns and cities are beginning to abandon it with the permission of the central government. Temporary migrants in large cities, as against permanent migrants according to China's definition, are not allowed to change their resident status no matter how long they have been living in the destination cities. As a result, they are denied the access to and use of urban services.

Since 1979 what was initially a limited reform has grown gradually until it covers all facets of economic life in China.[4] In the earlier years, agriculture was the principal beneficiary and expanding farm output accounted for about one half of overall economic growth.[5] After 1983, the spread of reform brought industry to the forefront. Since then, it is the urban, industrial economy that is largely responsible for China's growth performance.[6] Despite its partial and gradual nature, the reform has now touched virtually all areas of the economy, from enterprise management, fiscal relations, and financial systems to trade and investment.

The economic reform has inevitably steered the nation's urban policy in a new direction. Compared to the Maoist era (1949–1979), major changes in urban policy include four important factors. First, the strict administrative measures used in the 1960s and 1970s to control urban growth, particularly of large cities, by restricting migration began to loosen up, largely as a result of the rising agricultural productivity.[7] But the policy guideline to control the growth of large cities and encourage that of medium and small cities remains. Second, cities were again considered centers of regional and national development, in contrast to the antiurban bias of previous decades. Third, the coastal region was recognized as the most promising growth area and a number of cities there have been offered preferential policies, which include fiscal incentives and administrative autonomy.[8] Last, strict central planning is gradually giving way to market forces, and cities are given more and more latitude in their development policy-making and processes.

Rising Level of Urbanization

For the period from 1964 to 1982, the official measure of urban population was "city and town" population—the aggregate of all nonagricultural population in the designated cities and towns. The 1982 census used a different methodology, which defined urban population as all city-proper residents in all districts of cities, regardless of agricultural or nonagricultural status. Because of the growing concern of about the large proportion of the agricultural population entering the urban count, the 1990 census used a more complex system, similar, in principle, to that used before 1982. Therefore, in official Chinese statistics, urban population refers to nonagricultural populations in cities (excluding city-administered counties) and towns, as against a broader definition that counts all city-proper residents, as well as the population in towns. The current classification of city size in China based on the nonagricultural population in the city proper (excluding city-administered counties) is:

Megacities = more than 1 million population
Large cities = 0.5 – 1 million
Medium cities = 0.2 – 0.5 million
Small cities = under 0.2 million

Before the reform, urban growth was slow because of the control on migration. Although the contribution of migration to urbanization in China is hard to estimate for that period, the fact that major population movements were in the other direction indicates that urban growth was largely a result of natural growth.[9] In fact, there were years when the aggregate urban population growth in the country was negative. For instance, urban population decreased from 101 million in 1961 to 89 million in 1965. It was not until the early 1970s that it regained its 1961 level.[10] The end result was a sharp divergence from a "normal" pattern of urbanization for about twenty years.[11]

Changes in postreform urban policy have brought about a steady increase in the urban population, largely as a result of rural to urban migration.[12] This trend toward accelerated urbanization can also be seen in the rapidly growing number of cities and towns. By 1991 there were 479 cities, a more than threefold increase from 1949 when there were only 122 cities in China. Before 1975, the urban population grew at an average annual rate of two percent; in 1980, a total of 191.4 million people lived in urban areas. This accounted for approximately 19.4 percent of the Chinese population. Urban population has been growing at a much faster rate since 1975, averaging more than 4 percent annually, and reached 333 million in 1993, with an urbanization level of about 28.1 percent.[13] If such a rate is sustained or perhaps accelerates, the urban population could reach 400 million by the end of this century, and 600 million during the second decade of the next century, accounting for 43 percent of China's projected population of 1.4 billion.[14]

Large cities have witnessed rapid expansion. In 1991, 61 large cities accounted for 30.9 percent of total urban population.[15] The aggregate gross domestic product (GDP) of these 61 large cities contributed 50 percent of the national urban total in 1991. Living standards are also higher in these cities, as measured in per capita GDP terms (Y4,869 or US $897 in 1991 compared with the urban average of Y3,057 or US $563). Consequently, large cities are now the most desirable places of residence and provide the best employment opportunities.

Population Mobility

The administration kept population mobility extremely low during the 1960s and 1970s through a system of food rationing and household registration.[16] What was particularly discouraged was rural to urban migration and movement to large cities from other urban areas. The rationale was an antiurban bias, which was reinforced by national defense considerations that pulled population and resources away from the coastal region where most large cities were located. The only large movements of population happened mostly in the 1960s as a result of redistributive policies, including the recruitment of city residents to work in rural areas and dispersion of millions of young people to work in inland and frontier areas.[17]

But policies on population mobility and rural–urban migration began to change once reforms filtered down in the mid-1980s. The people's communes were dissolved in 1983 and the system of tying peasants to the land was loosened. Food rationing and job allocation also became less effectively regulated than before the reform. Such changes were prompted largely by the rising surplus rural labor resulting from the increasing productivity in agricultural production. The mushrooming of township enterprises also encouraged more and more peasants to engage in industrial and commercial activities in market towns. In connection with this, the central government issued a circular in 1984 that permitted migration of peasants and their families to market towns.[18] This represented the first break in migration policy of strictly controlling rural to urban migration. As this happened, peasants did not confine their moves merely to market towns. The booming construction business in many cities has created a huge demand for manual labor, so some peasants have been allowed into cities to work on construction sites while others to run small shops.

Meanwhile, higher living standards and income levels in urban areas prove to be a strong pull factor for rural–urban migration.[19] Despite a rather equitable pattern of income distribution compared to many other developing countries, the gulf between rural and urban areas in China is still very big. In 1988, the estimated per capita disposable urban income was about two and half times that of rural areas.[20] For rural peasants, particularly the young, cities appeal to them as a whole different world of modern life. Moreover, as large cities are given leadership roles in the development of smaller urban areas and rural hinterlands, the expanding industrial, commercial, service, and construction activities demand more manpower than currently available from urban resident population.[21]

The Magnitude of the Rural–Urban Migration

The working of both the push and pull factors has significantly driven up population mobility, largely through rural–urban migration. It was reported that 60 percent of urban floating population in China at the turn of the 1990s was from the countryside and the rest from interurban flows.[22] Rural–urban migrants are different from others migrants. In most cases they are considered temporary migrants who cannot obtain household registration at the place of destination no matter how long they live there. A host of disadvantages followed, as they have no right to claim rationed food stuff, housing, education, and other urban amenities. The number of such temporary rural migrants increased drastically in the 1980s, and their aggregated numbers amounted to millions, with many concentrated in the largest cities.[23]

An estimated 50 million temporary migrants was reported for 1988 in cities. Specifically, the 23 megacities with populations of more than 1 million together had 10 million such migrants. Shanghai had the most, about 1.8 million, followed by Beijing and Guangzhou, each with about 1.1 million.[24] Given the size of the urban population in these cities (7.3, 6.8, and 3.5 million, respectively), migrants were contributing an additional one fourth to one third to the population. Another study reports that in the same year, Shanghai had about 2.1 million migrant population, and Beijing and Guangzhou each had about 1.3 million.[25]

The Living Conditions of Rural Migrants

Housing conditions for rural migrants in large cities are generally poor, largely because of the persistent shortage of housing. Thirty years of underinvestment in urban construction has left China's cities short of decent dwellings for permanent, registered residents. The surge of rural migrants aggravates the crisis. The results of a 1986 survey shows that migrants reported an increase in income, but a decline in the quality of their housing.[26] For those who come to cities to work in foreign enterprises or joint ventures, in Special Economic Zones (SEZs) and some coastal open cities, housing is usually provided by their employers in the form of dormitory rooms. But for others, options include either living at the workplace, which is done by most construction workers, or squatting on the fringe of cities. A common problem in many developing countries, squatting was never a concern in contemporary urban China because the strict household registration system had prevented large migration until the controls were significantly loosened in the reform period. For those who are not able to find work, public places such as railroad and bus stations become temporary shelters, an issue of disguised homelessness. Many also sleep in underground sewers, under highway passes, and in parks. It was reported that three tenths of migrant workers in Shanghai had no fixed dwellings during the mid-1980s.[27]

Because these migrants are not considered permanent residents, their access to urban facilities and services is extremely limited. What is available to them is confined to some basic housing and utilities provided by their employment enterprises. Dormitory rooms provided by foreign enterprises or joint ventures would be normally equipped with faucet water, sewers, sanitary facilities, and electricity. But for other migrants, infrastructure and other urban services are minimal. With the increasing influx of migrant families, the prospect of a generation of uneducated, unemployed children becoming a new underclass is a nightmare. Recently, some migrants set up curbside classrooms, causing embarrassed municipal officials to announce plans to establish one public school for migrants in Shanghai.[28]

The Impact of Rural Migrants

Rural migrants have become an important force for urban development in large cities, without which the booming construction business cannot be sustained and joint venture production cannot profit. Many cities have also relied on temporary migration as an alternative to permanent migration, because the former allows cities to meet their labor force and service needs and helps to reduce rural surplus labor, while allowing cities to avoid assuming responsibility for absorbing vast numbers of rural–urban migrants into their permanent population. The sheer magnitude of the influx, however, is causing more and more municipalities to adopt measures to slow it down. The effect can only be minimal, as long as the large rural–urban income gulf is intact. China's urban statistics still do not include this portion of the urban population.[28]

For large cities, temporary migrant population has created tremendous pressure on their capacities, infrastructure, and social order, although the impacts are unevenly distributed among cities. With the increase volume of migrants, many cities have difficulty providing sufficient infrastructure for everyone. The system of accessibility to urban infrastructure is also seriously challenged by the increasing number of migrants. Moreover, migrants aggravate the shortage of transportation facilities and housing, which routinely plague China's large cities. For instance, a 1987 survey of 25 megacities revealed that the addition of temporary migrants caused a drop in per capita road space from 3.91 to 3.26 square meters.[29]

In a number of large cities, patterns of residential segregation began to emerge as a result of the large influx of rural migrants. For instance, in Shanghai, the southeast part of the center city (the Nanhui district) has traditionally been the hub for migrants. Before 1949, it accommodated manual laborers and rickshaw drivers from northern Jiangsu. For years, the area had the highest population density and worst living conditions. The system of workplace-related residence, where housing is usually provided by working units and in most cases state enterprises, further aggravates the problem. In Guangzhou, four groups of residents can be distinguished: cadres, intellectuals, factory workers, and farmers. More than any other district, the center city Huangpu cluster has the highest concentration of factory workers.[30] In Beijing, expeasant urban villages have begun to spread in peripheral areas of the city. Such villages are often named after the provinces from where groups of migrants originate.

Social problems arise with the surging migrant influx. Some migrants have become security burdens to cities. In Shanghai, only 7 percent of crime was committed by nonregistered residents in 1983, and this portion rose to 31 percent in 1989. At the end of the 1980s, approximately 3 percent of temporary migrants had been arrested for crimes, compared to 1 percent among the permanently registered residents.[31] With no way to control child-bearing within the migrant population, which is free from household registration, there is an increasing number of out-of-plan children. Migrants away from home escape such control by rural governments. Neither do they come under the power of working units and neighborhood committees, which oversee family planning in urban areas.

With no easy access to decent housing and sanitary facilities, migrants may become health threats as carriers of contagious diseases. Many erect tents and shacks in urban peripheries, very often crowded and lacking in basic amenities. One telling sign is that outbreaks in infectious diseases, such as polio and malaria, which had been eradicated in urban areas, have resurfaced recently.[32] Quite often, such problems are blamed on the habits of rural migrants rather than inadequate infrastructure and services. The absence of a rental market or secondary market at affordable prices leaves cities with few options to accommodate migrant workers.

Temporary migrants may be a quick alternative to satisfy the growing demands for labor that resulted from changing economic conditions and growth. They are also an indication of the step toward the transformation of China into a freer society characterized by population mobility. To properly contain migrants and to prevent possible outbreaks of social disorder, China's large cities will need to address several important issues, including housing, education, health care, and access to other urban amenities. Cities will need to provide some kind of accommodation and basic services to migrant workers and their families.

Accommodating Rural Migrants

China has made significant progress in improving the quality of people's lives, particularly in urban areas. Both death rates and infant mortality rates have declined drastically since the founding of the Republic, reaching a level, in 1992, that was comparable to upper-middle income economies. However, there remained small pockets where both rates were still very high. China has done well in raising life expectancy to that of middle-income countries. It was also reported that the number of people living in absolute poverty in rural areas decreased substantially in the 1980s.[33] Depending on the future population growth and rate of accumulation, China should be able to double its living standard between 1990 and 2000 and become moderately comfortable.

On an aggregate level, China has made significant progress in building urban infrastructure. Most urban residents, excluding temporary migrants, have access to faucet water, electricity, and public transportation. The most usual source for faucet water is surface water drawn from rivers, lakes, and reservoirs. Such water is often processed to a quality good enough for domestic and industrial use, but not for drinking. Water supply coverage has already reached more than 90 percent in urban China, but only about 30 percent of water is recycled. There were no intercity highways in 1986, by 1992 there were over 1,100 kilometers of roads. By 1993, 7 percent of China's urban population had telephones. The rate was much higher in coastal open cities—over 50 percent in Shenzhen, a level similar to that of Hong Kong.

Municipal governments are responsible for providing a full range of infrastructure that serves urban residents, including local roads, public transportation, water and sewers, utilities, telecommunications, and environmental protection services. In addition to State provision of electricity, municipalities operate their own power plants. Municipal Construction Commissions, the main local institution overseeing urban construction matters, are in charge of the construction, maintenance, and financing of the urban infrastructure.[34] The provision of local environmental services, such as waste disposal facilities, is under the authority of Municipal Environmental Protection Bureaus. In addition, Municipal City Planning Bureaus and Land Administration Bureaus have the joint control of land use decisions, with the former planning for the use of municipal land and the latter in charge of the actual administration of land.

Cities use the household registration as a basis for providing services and maintaining infrastructure. Access to urban infrastructure has been determined by the urban resident status. Thus, the quantity of water, gas, and electricity supplies, public transportation vehicles, roads, and sewerage systems have all been supplied in accord with the number of registered permanent residents in the city.[35] To them, urban infrastructure is provided free, as is education. Public services are also priced low—housing, water, electricity, and gas have become welfare goods. Such a system, of course, would not be able to incorporate the growing demand for urban services generated by surging temporary migrants.

The operation of the centralized state planning system has also relied on a vast number of state working units, including state-owned enterprises, government agencies, and state-owned institutions. These units are not only the providers of employment, but more importantly of individual and collective welfare facilities. A major form of collective welfare is public housing, often equipped with household utilities. Household water, electricity, and sewers in public housing are also provided by these working units.

Under the welfare system instituted within state working units, enterprise welfare funds have been the main source of finance for housing and household utilities. Since 1979, state working units have been allowed to retain 20 percent of their after-tax profits as welfare funds.[36] These funds will provide for individual welfare benefits, such as heating and commuting allowances and collective welfare facilities, including housing, public utilities, and cultural and recreational facilities. Nominal charges are levied for using these collective facilities, so large shortfalls have to be made up from enterprise welfare funds. Units that have difficulty in building collective facilities, such as housing and daycare centers, can contribute to municipal funds and obtain uses of facilities built by municipal governments. Often such units issue allowance to their employees as compensation.

Before the reform, the overwhelming majority of the urban population worked for state-owned units that provided housing and related infrastructure. For small state-working units, municipal governments provided housing. Once a state employee obtained a housing unit, he or she automatically gained access to household utilities. This system remains intact today for the state sector, and still accounts for close to two thirds of urban employment. Since the reform, however, the size of the nonstate sector has been growing. For workers in the private sector, public housing is generally unavailable. The same is true for most temporary rural migrants in the cities.[37]

Feasible Solutions

Given the inability of the current system to provide adequate infrastructure for the entire urban population, what are large cities doing to accommodate the ever increasing migrant population? Most of them have done little more than come up with administrative measures to control the influx. Shenzhen, one of the five SEZs, was the first to do so, as it is by nature a city of migrants.[38] The municipal personnel bureau issues a quota each year for permanent migrants. Getting such a quota is now almost as hard as in Shanghai and Beijing. For temporary migrants who come to Shenzhen to work in the numerous foreign enterprises and joint ventures, they have to obtain a resident permit on an annual basis assuming their work contracts are extended. Those whose work contracts are terminated and cannot find other work are not allowed to stay. Guangzhou is starting to use a similar system. In Beijing, the approach is even stricter. For any temporary migrants to live in the city, not only they but also their employers need to obtain permits from the municipal government. But such administrative controls are in a way inevitable, as large cities are the most desirable destinations and, without controls, these cities will be swamped with migrants.

In Shenzhen SEZ and other small cities and town, authorities have adopted a measure to allow rural migrants to settle in their cities after paying fees for urban infrastructure construction.[39] In Shanghai, rural migrants, as unregistered residents, cannot use the city's services without paying impossibly large sums of money. It has been estimated that for Beijing each new member of the migrant population costs an additional Y40,000 of investment in nonproductive service facilities, including housing, education, health, and transportation. Underwriting the costs of coping with more than 1 million migrants was reported to be seriously interfering with efforts to develop satellite towns to divert the metropolitan population growth. Enterprises there have been asked to pay Y100,000 to the municipal government for each migrant employed, and each worker has to pay Y50,000.[40]

Of course, any workable solution would pose hefty financial burdens on large cities, if they are to handle the problem on their own. Until Beijing is willing to shoulder some of the financial burdens, cities will be likely to postpone the provision of urban services to migrants. At present, an unemployment benefit program is under consideration in some Chinese cities targeted at displaced workers from loss-making state enterprises. Some similar kind of social safety net mechanism will need to be devised for rural migrants and sponsored jointly by the central government and cities.

Privileges given to urban residents, including housing, welfare payments, subsidized public transportation, education, and medical services, may be reduced. Migrants may then be allowed to share and compete for government-provided services or facilities. Shenzhen SEZ's experience proves that the separation of individual social benefits from household registration is feasible. There, the various privileges related to urban registration that are granted at the expense of the government are not necessarily provided by the government. This is the basis on which Shenzhen has recruited outside workers. [41] Housing and facilities to accommodate many such workers are often provided by enterprises in Shenzhen.

So another option may lie in requiring nonstate enterprises or employers to provide basic housing and services to migrant workers, as state working units have already been doing. But this would not solve the problem for those migrants in between jobs or seeking employment. In Shanghai, for example, about one half of migrants had no fixed jobs during the mid 1980s. Administrative control of migrant registration based on employment may still be necessary. But the current mechanism to contain migrants through issuance of resident permits based on working permits is feasible only in the short term, as a large number of migrants tend to stay in cities for a prolonged period of time, and the need of their families, particularly their children, has to be accommodated.

If enterprises are required to provide migrant employees with housing and utilities, cities need to install a regulatory framework to oversee such provision. There is still a lack of regulatory framework in cities that ensures the quality of infrastructure services and utilities provided by enterprises. Often a unit with a large number of employees and, hence, a large budget could build and maintain facilities with higher quality. On the other hand, smaller enterprises, especially those relying on municipal governments to provide housing for their employees, often cannot afford to properly maintain existing facilities. They also have difficulty to fulfill the housing demand of their employees.

Adequate housing may be the most important service for rural migrants, because some basic household infrastructure and utilities are often provided with public housing, including faucet water, sewerage facilities, and electricity. To prevent the social disorders associated with an unchecked influx of temporary migrants, cities will have to provide some kind of accommodation, either by setting up a housing rental market or building public housing for rent at affordable prices. As many migrants have settled illegally in peripheral urban villages in some cities, their self-help initiatives in building shelters may be directed by the government in a more desirable fashion. Comparative research from other developing countries has suggested that ex-peasant urban villages have not become hotbeds of political unrest—at least not for the first generation of settlers.[42]

New infrastructure investments will certainly be needed. Private and foreign investment in infrastructure development is desirable. Although there may be some increased budget allocation for infrastructure investment from both central and local governments, the main source of incremental revenue is seen as higher user charges. But what is often missing in many cities' agenda is the simple improvement in efficiency of the existing infrastructure. Inefficient and wasteful infrastructure is found in many cities. This is partly the result of the administrative bureaucracy that often leads to longer turn-around time in the distribution of infrastructure. Both the central and local governments should give priority to increase the efficient use of existing infrastructure while adding new capacity.

Conclusion

As with many other developing countries experiencing rapid urbanization, rural migrants have flocked into China's large cities. Their magnitude is estimated to be on the millions, and that number is expected to grow as rising agricultural productivity renders more peasants redundant. The migrant population, on the one hand, provides cities with a large reserve of cheap, manual labor; on the other hand, it brings unprecedented social problems in the areas of housing, infrastructure, education, public health, and social order. The influx of peasants into urban areas, moreover, adds diversity and complexity to the preexisting demographic configuration. Their impacts on cities have grown so strong that municipal governments can no longer ignore their presence and are forced to provide accommodation.

The legacy of the household registration system and a "urban public goods regime,"[43] where a host of services and amenities were granted to urban residents free or on a highly subsidized basis, has made service provision to migrants a burdensome task for cities. The current system of providing housing, household utilities, urban infrastructure, and other services for urban residents is incapable of absorbing the growing number of rural migrants. Because state monopoly in the provision of urban infrastructure and services has already proven to be unsustainable, the surging migrant influx may actually be an impetus for some drastic reforms. Most importantly, privileges enjoyed by urban residents should be significantly reduced, and migrants may be allowed to compete for and contribute to urban services. For instance, cities, employers, and employees should all contribute, gradually changing the free housing provision to a paid, self-supported distribution. Of course such reforms will not be easy because they will upset many urban residents. But the ignoring the migrant population will only lead to even more explosive social problems.

Notes

1. Guang Hua Wan, "Peasant Flood in China: Internal Migration and Its Policy Determinants," *Third World Quarterly,* 1995, 16(2): 173–195; and Linda Wong, "China's Urban Migrants: The Public Policy Challenge," *Pacific Affairs,* 1994, 67(3): 335–355.
2. Lynn T. White III, "Migration and Politics on the Shanghai Delta," *Issues and Studies,* 1994, 30(9): 63.
3. See Si-ming Li, "Population Mobility and Urban and Rural Development in Mainland China," *Issues and Studies,* 1995, 31(9): 37–54.
4. Shahid Yusuf and Weiping Wu, "Prospering Coastal Cities: Shanghai, Tianjin and Guangzhou in the Era of Reform" (unpublished manuscript).
5. Agriculture, which until 1983 included rural industry, grew at an average annual rate of 7 percent between 1978 and 1984. This was responsible for 30 percent of overall growth. Thereafter it declined, averaging 4 percent per annum for the remainder of the 1980s. See World Bank, *Country Economic Memorandum – China,* 1990.
6. Between 1978 and 1993, industrial growth in China averaged 13 percent per annum.
7. R. J. R., *Urbanization in China: Town and Country in a Developing Economy, 1949–2000 AD.* London: Croom Helm, 1985.
8. These include the five Special Economic Zones (SEZs): Shenzhen, Zhuhai, Shantou, Xiamen, and Hainan; and fourteen coastal open cities: Dalian, Qinhuangdao, Tianjin, Qingdao, Yantan, Lianyungang, Nantong, Shanghai, Ningbo, Wenzhou, Fuzhou, Guangzhou, Beihai, and Zhanjiang.
9. A large-scale nationwide survey of urban migration in China was not carried out until 1986. See Lincoln H. Day and Ma Xia, eds., *Migration and Urbanization in China.* Armonk, NY: Sharpe, 1994.
10. State Statistical Bureau, *China: The Forty Years of Urban Development,* 1990.
11. Urban growth in developing countries seems to have followed a relatively smooth pattern since the late nineteenth century. It started slow, accelerated as the Industrial Revolution hit full stride, and then slowed down. As a group, cities in these countries achieved their peak rates of growth in the early 1970s, with an average annual growth rate of approximately 4 percent between 1960 and 1980. See Jeffrey G. Williamson, "Macro Dimensions of Third World City Growth: Past, Present and Future." Paper presented at the World Bank Annual Conference in Development Economics, 1991.
12. It was reported that more than three quarters of urban growth in China could be accounted for by migration, as well as reclassification

between 1980 and 1990. See UN, *State of Urbanization in Asia and the Pacific.* New York: United Nations Economic and Social Commission for Asia and the Pacific, 1993.

13. From China State Statistical Bureau, *China Statistical Yearbook,* 1994. As discussed earlier, the accounting of urban population in China is complicated by changes in the definition of cities and towns. The figures cited here are a rather conservative calculation. A more liberal estimate puts China's level of urbanization at close to 53 percent in 1990. See Kam Wing Chan, "Urbanization and Rural Urban Migration in China since 1982: A New Baseline," *Modern China,* 1994, 20(3): 243–281.

14. World Bank, *China: Urban Transport Issues.* Washington, DC: China and Mongolia Department, 1994.

15. Excluding city-administrated counties. See *China Urban Statistical Yearbook,* 1992.

16. Ma (1994) divides China's internal migration into three general periods: a first period of free migration (1949–1957), a second of restricted migration (1958–1984), and a third of half-free and half-restricted migration (since 1984). See Ma Xia, "Changes in the Pattern of Migration in Urban China," in Day and Ma, 1994.

17. See Thomas P. Bernstein, *Up to the Mountains and Down to the Villages: The Transfer of Youth from Urban to Rural China.* New Haven: Yale University Press, 1977. In spite of the strict control on population movement, it was never hard if one wanted to migrate from urban to rural areas or from large to small cities. In fact, many separated couples were united when one spouse was willing to make such a movement.

18. But the permission was not without conditions. For details, see Ma, 1994.

19. There are still debates among scholars about the sources of urban growth regarding migration. Some believe that unusually rapid rates of population growth put pressure on limited farm land, pushing landless labor into cities; others think that urban growth is promoted by unusually strong economic forces, pulling migrants into cities. See Williamson, 1991. In China's case, both the push and pull factors have been apparently at work in the reform period.

20. The Gini coefficient for China as a whole was estimated to be approximately 0.38, according to a 1988 study by the Research Program on the Chinese Economy. For urban areas as well as rural areas, it was 0.23 and 0.34 respectively. It was the rural–urban gulf that drove up the aggregate Gini coefficient, transcending geographical variations. See Keith Griffins and Zhao Renwei, eds., *The Distribution of Income in China.* New York: St. Martin's Press, 1993.

21. Weiping Wu, "Urban Development in China's Large Cities." In Economic Development Institute, *Metropolitan Development and Environmental Management in Asia.* Washington, DC: World Bank, 1996.

22. See Chan, 1994.
23. See Alice Goldstein and Shenyang Guo, "Temporary Migration in Shanghai and Beijing." *Studies in Comparative International Development,* 1992, 27(2): 39–56.
24. From Sidney Goldstein, "Urbanization in China, 1982–87: Effects of Migration and Reclassification." *Population and Development Review,* 1990, 16(4): 673–701.
25. See Chan, 1994.
26. The survey covered both rural–urban and urban–urban migrants. See Lin You Su and Lincoln H. Day, "The Economic Adjustment of Migrants in Urban Areas," in Day and Ma, 1994.
27. White, 1994.
28. See "An Urban Underclass in the Making?" *Business Week,* September 5, 1994.
29. Wong, 1994.
30. For details, see C. P. Lo, "Economic Reform and Socialist City Structure: A Case Study of Guangzhou, China," *Urban Geography,* 1994, 15(2): 128–149.
31. See White, 1994.
32. Wong, 1994.
33. Peter Nolan, *State and Market in the Chinese Economy: Essays on Controversial Issues.* London: Macmillan, 1993.
34. World Bank, *China: Second Shanghai Metropolitan Transport Project.* Washington, DC, 1993.
35. Weiping Wu, "Financing and Management of Urban Infrastructure in China." Paper prepared for the Center for Urban and Community Studies, University of Toronto, 1995.
36. Kate Hannan, *China, Modernization and the Goal of Prosperity: Government Administration and Economic Policy in the Late 1980s.* Cambridge: Cambridge University Press, 1995.
37. Wu, 1995.
38. Starting from a farming village of just thousands of residents, by 1991 it was a modern city with registered population of about 1.2 million.
39. See Yukun Wang, "China: Urban Development and Research Towards the Year 2000." In Richard Stern, ed., *Urban Research in the Developing World 1.* Toronto: Center for Urban and Community Studies, University of Toronto, 1994.
40. Li, 1995, and Sidney Goldstein, "The Impact of Temporary Migration on Urban Places: Thailand and China as Case Studies." In John D. Kasarda and Allan M. Parnell, eds., *Third World Cities: Problems, Policies, and Prospects.* Newsbury Park: Sage, 1993.
41. Keiko Wakabayashi, "Migration from Rural to Urban Areas in China," *The Development Economics,* 1990, 28(4): 503–523.
42. White, 1994.

43. Dorothy J. Solinger, "China's Urban Transients in the Transition from Socialism and the Collapse of the Communist 'Urban Public Goods Regime,'" *Comparative Politics*, 1995 (Jan.): 127.

Section 5 The Case of Accra

Nat Nuno-Amarteifio

The first European nation to touch the shores of Ghana was Portugal, which later built forts mainly along the shores of the Central province of Ghana. Other European nations, including Denmark, the Netherlands, and Britain, followed suit. Eventually, the British emerged as the main colonial power in the then Gold Coast. Formal colonization of Ghana began in 1844, when the British signed a treaty with the local chiefs. The latter agreed to become subjects of the British Queen, and the former promised protection against invasion by inland tribes. In the 1930s, the British introduced the system of indirect rule. Under this system, British officials governed the country with the assistance of local chiefs. Well-educated and qualified Africans were excluded.

During this period, senior posts in the administrative and legal services were the exclusive preserve of Europeans. This open discrimination frustrated educated Africans, whose discontent found expression in the rise of nationalistic activities. First came the formation of the Fante Confederation, which drew pressed for the takeover of the administration in the Gold Coast. Second was the Aborigines Rights Protection Society, was formed in 1897, which defeated the Government's Land Bill of 1898 and the Forest Bill of 1912. The Society was later destroyed through a misunderstanding between the local Chiefs and the educated Africans. During the colonial period, the attitude of the people toward the colonial government was one of distrust and fear. Infractions in the country were severally punished. People to a large extent had no say in the governance of the country. Modern political parties sprang up in 1947 and 1949 with the formation of the United Gold Convention (UGCC) and the Convention Peoples Party (CPP), respectively, to fight for independence.

Early Local Government

The earliest attempts at local administration during the colonial era involved native authorities—usually, a chief or some unit of local royalty that was not clearly defined. These native authorities were not very democratic; their members were hand-picked representatives of the British. Their main interest was to help the British colonial government, which had limited involvement with local administration, to administer law and order.

The Municipal Ordinance of 1859 established municipalities in the coastal towns of the Cold Coast. In 1943, a new Ordinance set up elected town councils for Accra, Kumasi, Sekondi-Takoradi, and Cape Coast. In 1953, the Municipal Councils Ordinance was passed. After Ghana gained independence, this was followed by the Local Government Act, 1961 (Act 54). All of this legislation maintained the distinction between central and local government institutions. The central government is based in the capital city of Accra, with branches at the local (district) level. The local institutions are based in well-defined localities.

At the local level, the central government bodies dealt with national concerns. Local government bodies were vested with authority specifically for local matters, and had grown up side by side with central government agencies that operated at the local level. They were required to provide municipal services and amenities in their localities.

The central government bodies had better qualified personnel, with management skills and professional expertise, than did the local government bodies. Similarly, while central government bodies had sufficient funds to undertake their programs, Local Government bodies were unable to raise funds to meet their obligations and attract able and competent officers. As a result, local government bodies only succeeded in creating for themselves an image of ineptitude and incompetence.

Before independence was finally achieved, commissions and committees inquired into the administration of the country. Their reports made extensive recommendations for the devolution of central administrative authority to the local levels.

After Independence

When Ghana became independent, the pattern of governance continued with few modification. Local initiative was not encouraged. The government alone decided where schools, clinics, and other facilities should be sited. All requests for development were channeled to Accra. Thus, the government was viewed as an assemblage of few persons elected to make decisions and impose them on the majority. People did not feel part of the government apparatus.

In 1966, the Ghana armed forces, with the active assistance of the police, overthrew the government of Nkrumah. The incoming administration, the National Liberation Council (NLC) introduced policies to slow down government expenditure and stabilize the currency. The NLC handed over the administration to the Progress Party government, which was overthrown in 1972, and the National Redemption Council (NRC) was ushered into power. In 1975 the NRC was designated the Supreme Military council (SMC), but it was overthrown in 1979 by J. J. Rawlings, who relinquished power to the Peoples National party after an election. Then in December 1981, Rawlings came to power again after unseating the existing government of Limann in a coup d'etat.

The Era of Restructuring

When the Provisional National Defence Council (PNDC) came into power in 1982, a number of policy decisions were made to alter this unfortunate pattern of governance. Earlier, the Akuffo–Addo Commission (1966), Mills-Odoi Commission (1967), and the Constituent Assembly (1969) had all made far-reaching recommendations aimed at comprehensive decentralization of the country's administrative system. Although most of these recommendations were accepted by previous governments, none went as far as bold initiative of the PNDC government in 1986.

The first major step of this initiative in the area of local government was to increase the number of local districts from 65 to 110. The reason was to make local government more effective and to spread development as far as possible throughout the country. The new system has a four-tier metropolitan (of which my City of one) assembly and a three-tier municipal/district assemblies structure. On the whole, there are three metropolitan assemblies, four municipal assemblies and one hundred and three district assemblies. A metropolitan assembly area has a population of about 250,000, municipal 95,000, and district 75,000.

Their main purposes can be summarized as follows:

- To become the pivotal point for administrative and development decision-making in the district and therefore to serve as the basic unit of government administration;
- To perform with deliberation, legislative as well as executive functions under law;
- To establish a monolithic structure that is responsible for integrating the political, administrative, and development support needed to achieve a more equitable distribution of power, wealth, and development in Ghana;
- To serve as the planning authority for the district.

Under the 1992 constitution, the essential features of Ghana's new decentralized system are as follows:

- Functions, powers, and responsibilities should be transferred from the central government to local government units;

- Measures should be taken to enhance the capacity of local government authorities to plan, initiate, coordinate, manage, and execute policies in matters affecting local people,
- Local government units should have a sound financial base, with adequate and reliable sources of revenue;
- Local government staff must be controlled by local authorities;
- There should be popular participation in local decision making.

Financing Local Government

The previous local governments were unable to perform their statutory duties adequately mainly because of a lack of funds. This shortcoming has now been rectified. The government has established policies to stimulate the generation of revenue to enable local bodies perform their functions efficiently. These revenues may be generated locally through rates, land fees, licenses, trading services, and miscellaneous sources, or by such central government transfers as grants-in-aid and ceded revenue (now replaced by the District Assembly Common Fund).

The constitution also provides for the establishment of a District Assembly Common Fund, which shall:

- Be allocated annually by parliament and shall amount to not less than five percent of the total revenues of Ghana. It is payable in quarterly installments and intended for development;
- Be distributed among district assemblies on the basis of a formula to be approved by parliament; and
- Be administered by a District Assemblies Common Fund Administrator The object of the Common Fund is to make available to the district assemblies additional resources for development.

Other financial arrangements include revenue from lotto operators, royalties on timber, the Minerals Development Fund, and grants-in-aid from agencies and companies operating in areas of the jurisdiction of the assemblies.

New Administrative Measures

Under the 1992 constitution, the NDC government of the Fourth Republic of Ghana has consciously strived to consolidate the gains of the new local government system. Community participation in local administration has grown by leaps and bounds, as the Sukura experience illustrates.

Sukura is a settlement in the west of Accra approximately 8 kilometers from the central business district with a population of 55,550 in 1992. It is a typical heterogeneous, low-income community, predominantly Muslim.

One local problem had been the construction of unauthorized structures on land allocated for public amenities. Efforts by the Accra metropolitan assembly to control this construction of unauthorized structures had been unsuccessful, in part because the assembly did not become involved until the structures were already in place. Under decentralization, the residents of Sukura have made a comparatively successful effort to rationalize the land-use pattern through the Town Development Council, which is in a position to stop encroachment before construction begins or is completed. As a result, structures in Sukura that have been moved, partially demolished, and, in some cases, never built. This approach benefited from the cooperation of the Sempe Chief, who agreed, at least in principle, to the concept of provided land for people whose structures were demolished, as well as from the a plan that makes the Accra metropolitan assembly the final authority. Finally, the process was partly stimulated by the community's desire to be included in the World Bank's funded Urban II project in Accra.

The lesson of Sukura is that it is possible for communities to work with relevant authorities to control the process of encroachment. This is a successful example of a preventive and "barefoot" approach to planning.

The District Assemblies

District assemblies are enjoined to establish departments and organizations to perform functions previously under the jurisdiction of central government agencies. The ministries in Accra exist only to establish overall policy and offer professional advice. These organizations include the Ghana Education Service, Town and Country Planning Department, Public Works Department, Ghana Library Board, Controller and Accountant-General's Department, mention a few. This decentralization policy envisions that the staff of the district assembly will become officers of the district assembly. The one exception is the District Coordinating Director. The officers include civil servants and public officers who are employees of the decentralized organizations. This arrangement is supposed to ensure that the district assemblies have qualified staff.

The new experiment has introduced the widespread use of laypeople of various nonlegal backgrounds to serve under a qualified lawyer to speed up the administration of justice. Some of these people are retired social workers, teachers, and police officers. A Community Tribunal ensures that justice is observed as much as possible. The tribunals are vested with authority to try all cases, both criminal and civil. Revenues derived from the tribunals are to be shared by the Judicial Service and the local district assembly.

The Planning System

The decentralization policy necessitated a change ill the national planning process. It is now a decentralized "bottom-up" instead of a centralized "top-Down" system. A composite budget system has been introduced to complement the decentralized planning system. It is structured to give district assemblies control over their budgets. This has included the creation of a merged District Treasury System, the establishment of District Tender Boards, and the decentralization of contract awards and payments.

The empowerment of local residents to participate in the running of their affairs has contributed greatly to peace and stability in the country. Government has been brought to the doorstep of residents. Through the bottom-up approach to planning, ordinary residents feel confident in providing input in the district planning process. Some public-spirited business executives have even gone the extra step of funding clinics and schools in their communities without any prompting from government. The self-help spirit has been sustained by the decentralization process.

The Accra Experience

Accra City was established in 1898 as the Accra Town Council under the Town Council Ordinance of 1894. In 1944 a constitution was promulgated that raised the elected membership of the Town Council to seven, with the Gold Coast government appointing five and the Ga Native Authority appointing two. In 1953, a new constitution raised Accra's status to that of a municipality. The membership of its council was then increased from 14 to 31. The Wards had 27 representatives and the Ga Traditional Authority four.

After Ghana became independent in 1957, an amendment the 1953 constitution made the council totally representative. To accelerate decentralization, six area councils were created under the New Local Government System in 1974. Although created to be autonomous, in practical terms they relied wholly on the Head Office of the Council.

The New Local Government Law of 1988 gave a new lease on life to the Area Councils (now designated Sub-Metropolitan District Councils). The six Sub-District Councils were reorganized to number 25 to 30 members, including all of the elected assemblymen and women who represented the sub-district together with appointed members resident in the area. A total of 21 town councils undertake simple local community responsibilities.

To enhance the decentralization process, each sub-metro has been authorized to retain 25 percent of all rates and taxes collected in its jurisdiction for its administration and development budget. The revenue and other funds entering the coffers of the sub-metro offices have heightened their sense of responsibility. As a result, a number of community-initiated projects have been launched to improve the general well-being of the people at the grass-roots level. Some of the sub-metro offices used their funds to renovate local conveniences for the benefit of the floating population and those with inadequate toilet facilities.

Other sub-metro offices entered into joint venture agreements with estate developers to erect new office buildings. These activities generated enthusiasm among assembly members and other appointed officials, who see themselves as part of their local governments and as active agents of development.

Conclusion

The National Defence Council government has demonstrated great faith in the decentralization program. It ensures the timely release of vital funds through the Common Fund Administrator to the structures created at the local level.

The initiative shown by the people of Sukura is being duplicated in other areas. The Korle Gonno Town Council, with the Ablekuma Sub-Metro last year stopped a development project initiated by a local church. The council claimed that it had not been consulted before the project commenced on a plot of land belonging to the community. After a series of meetings, the impasse was resolved and the dispute settled amicable. Work resumed and the project is nearing completion.

This kind of active participation by community residents in development programs was previously the exception, rather than the rule. Such a reaction would have been ruthlessly suppressed during the colonial period. Even after independence, this kind of activity would not have been countenanced. At that time, government was regarded with awe. However, because of increased awareness, the majority of residents in Accra are now voluntarily contributing in various ways to the development of the cityœ.

Section 6 Three Stages of Globalization: Mombasa

Ali A. Mazrui

Mombasa is Kenya's second city. To that extent it may be worth considering whether second cities generally deserve their own theoretical framework. Do we need to study second cities as special entities? Is Montreal a second city to Toronto? Is Melbourne a second city to Sidney? Should we approach that subject in a different manner?

However Mombasa is also a kind of global city, although it is small as global cities go. It is the second largest city not only in Kenya, but in East Africa. But we are still talking about a city of less than a million people. It is the largest seaport of the region, and one of the oldest urban centers in Eastern Africa. It has been around for quite a while. The nature of its globalization had three, fairly distinct and different, phases. Within each of those phases, there were sub-phases or stages.

First we must bear in mind that Africa as a whole is culturally intermediate between Europe and Asia. There are parts of Africa that are more "occidental" than any part of Asia. Then there are parts of North Africa and parts of South Africa that are more Europeanized than you will find elsewhere on the Asian continent. On the other hand there are parts of Africa that have more in common with Asia than have any parts of Europe. Islam, for example, is older in parts of Africa than it is in most of Asia. And, Christianity is older in Ethiopia than it is in most of Western Europe. This essential intermediate position that Africa enjoys between the occident and the orient is captured in the story of Mombasa. This is part of the story of this African city on the Indian Ocean.

As indicated, Mombasa's history as a city can be divided into three distinct phases. The Afro-Oriental phase was the period when Mombasa was a small cultural arena in which traditions from West Asia and South Asia interacted with African traditions in search of new cultural configurations. This period covered several hundred years, during most of which Mombasa was known as Mvita.

The second historical period was the Afro-Occidental phase during which Mombasa was at last "discovered" by Europeans. First, the Portuguese and later the British initiated the process of reorienting Mombasa away from its traditional links with Asia and more toward a new relationship with Europeans and with Western culture.

The third phase of Mombasa's history is currently in progress—the Afro-global phase, during which the city feels the pull of both East and West. The old transition from being a city–state to being the main port of a nation–state has now greater global repercussions for Mombasa and its people.

The Afro-Oriental Phase

Three related factors conditioned the origins of the Afro-Oriental phase. One factor was that Mombasa lay in the path of the monsoon winds and was therefore reachable by trading sailing ships from parts of Asia using those winds.[1] Secondly, Mombasa itself had a natural harbor that could accommodate those ships, as well as serve as the basis for a nautical and shipbuilding tradition of its own. And thirdly, Mombasa was relatively near the Arabian peninsula and was soon to interact culturally, as well as commercially, with the land that gave birth to the Muslim religion. Mombasa became one of Islam's entry points into eastern Africa.

As a result of this configuration of factors, the multiculturalization of Mombasa began quite early. Consumption patterns felt the cultural influences that came with the trading traffic of the monsoons. From Arabia and other ports of Asia came expensive porcelain and plates, brass decorated wooden chests, silks, and finery.[2] In East Africa, these were sometimes paid for in ivory, copra, and animal skins. There was also a limited trade in slaves.

At the more popular level of consumption culture, the Afro-Oriental phase of Mombasa's history produced the increasing use of seasonings and spices in the local cuisine. New spices were imported into Mombasa from Asia and innovative, syncretic, and eclectic cuisine developed among the Coastal people generally, combining elements of African, Indian, and Arab food cultures.

It was during the Afro-Oriental phase that rice became the staple diet of the people of Mombasa and the surrounding coastline. Although the vocabulary of ordinary rice dishes remained completely African (*mpunga* for unhusked rice, *mchele* for uncooked rice, and *wali* for cooked rice), dishes for special occasions had such borrowed words as *biriyani* and *pilau* from South Asia. One the other hand, the names of the individual spices used in preparing these quasi-Indian dishes were more likely to be words borrowed from Arabic rather than from any Indian language (*bizari* for curry powder and *thumu* for garlic, for example).

The Afro-Oriental phase also witnessed changes in the musical culture of Mombasa and the coastal areas. In addition to the traditional African drums, the small Indian drum *(tabla)* found its way into the coastal range of musical instruments. In time the Arabian string instrument, the *Ud*, also entered Swahili culture. So did the dancing drums with small bells attached known as *matari*. Indeed, in some Islamic denominations at the Coast the *matari* were even used in the mosque in accompaniment to certain lively praise songs in honor of the Prophet Muhammad. More traditionalist Muslim theologians strongly disapproved of the use of drums in the mosque or for any religious purpose.[3]

The flute in Coastal music was a child of all three traditions—African, Arab, and Indian—reinforcing each other. But the "Orientalization" of Mombasa music was still increasing.[4]

Over time even the tunes of Swahili songs became strongly influenced by Arab music (especially Egyptian), on one side, and Indian music, on the other. At its worst, some so-called Swahili composers simply plagiarized the music of some Indian songs and substituted Swahili lyrics. Fortunately, there always remained a hard-core Swahili tradition, which tried to remain authentic against all comers from the Orient![5]

But the most profound changes which came from Asia into Mombasa concerned, first, religion and, secondly, language. Islam came to Eastern Africa while the Prophet Muhammad was still alive. But Islam's first African home was not Mombasa, but a part of Ethiopia. Persecuted Muslims from Arabia arrived in Abyssinia in quest of asylum during the Prophet of Islam's own lifetime. Because of that fact some have argued that the Hijjra from Arabia to Africa was almost as early, and in a few respects almost as symbolic, as the Prophet's own Hijjra from Mecca to Medina. With the African Hijjra (migration for asylum), a seed was being planted which, by the end of the twentieth century, had turned Africa into the first continent to have an absolute Muslim majority.

Not long after the death of the Prophet Muhammad, Islam spread to that part of eastern Africa now known as Mombasa. Mosques were being built in this part of East Africa before they were constructed in parts of what is now the Middle East. Islam in Mombasa is older than Islam in Istanbul and the rest of Turkey. It may be older than Islam in Islamabad and the rest of Pakistan. Is it older than Islam in parts of what is now the Arab world itself? Certainly parts of the Maghreb in North Africa (such as Morocco) were probably penetrated by Islam later than Mombasa, although much of this is in the arena of historical calculation rather than confirmation.

Before long the arrival of Islam in Mombasa and its surrounding areas affected diverse areas of the cultural experience of the people.[6] Marriage and kinship relations were changed profoundly, as were the rules of inheritance and succession. African indigenous norms were often in competition with the Islamic rules. In some cases syncretism was the result; in some cases the indigenous norms still had an edge; but increasingly the Afro-Oriental phase of Mombasa's history witnessed the gradual triumph in precolonial Mombasa of the Islamic rules of marriage, kinship, inheritance, and succession.

The arrival of Islam in Mombasa also had a profound impact on dress culture. The concept of nakedness was completely redefined for both men and women, with practical consequences for forms of attire for each gender. The *kanzu* entered the scene for men (the long outer garment) and subsequently became religion-neutral in Uganda, where both Christians and Muslims accepted it as a kind of national dress. (In Kenya the *kanzu* was still associated with Muslims.)

In Mombasa the womenfolk developed the black *buibui* for outdoor use, intended not only to veil their faces but also to deny shape to their bodies. The *buibui* was worn by Muslim woman of Mombasa only out of doors when they visited relatives or went grocery shopping. The shapelessness of the garment was part of Islam's quest for female modesty in public places. "In public do not emphasize the curves! Conscience begins with avoidance of temptation!" This is a strong Islamic premise. It profoundly affected dress culture in Mombasa during the Afro-Oriental phase.

The arrival of Islam in Mombasa also affected architecture, initially with the minaret and the architectural culture of the mosque. The homes of the people of Mombasa increasingly felt the influence of Islamic conceptions of gender segregation, the court yard, the use of tiles and clay in construction, and the place of prayer for women and with the ablution washroom attached to it.

And then the winds of the Western world were at last felt in Mombasa. East was East and West was West, but the twain were indeed about to meet in the African city of Mombasa.

The Afro-Occidental Phase

In the process of the Westernization or Occidentalization of Mombasa, there was always one Western power at the epicenter. Again three phases are identifiable. There is the phase when Portugal was the Western epicenter, virtually unchallenged. There was also the more comprehensive phase of European colonialism during which Britain was the epicenter of the Western presence in Kenya as a whole and in Mombasa. And thirdly, there is now the postcolonial phase when the epicenter of the Western world as a whole is the United States—and Mombasa has inevitably felt that shift in power and influence.

Vasco da Gama was virtually the first European to disembark in Mombasa. That was in April 1498. The sailors of Mombasa and the rest of this African coast helped him in his efforts to find his way to Calicut in India. Although the people of Mombasa did not realize it at the time, Vasco da Gama was also preparing the ground for the Portuguese imperial incursion into Eastern Africa.

The Portuguese later came with warships and sought to build coastal African colonies to service their trading fleets in the Orient. In Mombasa they subsequently built Fort Jesus, a fortress to defend and monopolize the old harbor, and from which they sought to rule Mombasa and its environment.

How was Mombasa "Westernized" in this Portuguese phase? For one thing, architecture was partly influenced by the Portuguese, as they built some of their own homes, which were emulated by the locals. The Portuguese language also had an impact on local languages. To the present day the Swahili words for slippers *(sapatu)*, female undergarment *(shimizi)*, and a certain water kettle *(kindirinya)* are originally derived from the Portuguese language. The old Mombasa dialect even used the metaphor *mreno* (Portuguese person) to mean any kind of aristocrat.

Perhaps the most enduring cultural impact of the Portuguese was on the food culture of Mombasa, and subsequently, of East Africa as a whole. Because of Portugal's links with the so-called New World of the Americas, the Portuguese in East Africa eventually brought maize and potatoes which assumed increasing importance in the diet of the local people.

In time many of the indigenous people of the Coast (such as the Giriama) adopted *ugali* or maize meal (powdered dry maize) as their staple food—a trend that subsequently spread to the hinterland of Kenya. The Waswahili of Mombasa continued to use rice as the staple, but they increased the use of potatoes as supportive diet and for minor meals of the day. Maize on the cob and *ugali* were also used for variation.

The Portuguese impact on the cuisine of Mombasa did not endure, except perhaps in the case of some desserts and puddings—an influence which was later reinforced by the British.[7]

Westernization under the Portuguese also meant the Westernization of warfare for the first time in Mombasa. The use of gunpowder, cannons, and guns entered a new phase in the city's history. Later on this became a case of "nemesis" for the Portuguese—the use of Western-style weapons to drive them out of Mombasa.

But clearly the most far-reaching period of the Westernization of Mombasa was under British rule from the late nineteenth century until December 1963. British colonial policy for Mombasa was far more comprehensive than Portuguese. British policy included the building of primary and secondary schools for local children, the establishment of a legal system for the society as a whole, the demarcation of Kenya as a future nation–state and an elaborate system of accountability within a global British Empire.

Within every twenty-four hours the children of Mombasa crossed civilizations several times. They might speak Swahili (or Kiswahili) at home, take Arabic or Islamic lessons at the mosque, watch Indian films some weekends, and be forced to speak English all the time at school.

Of these several civilizations under the British Raj, there was no doubt which was on the ascendancy in Mombasa. Western civilization exerted increasing influence at school, at the Kilindini harbor, in the new films at local cinemas, and as a direct result of the influence of British power.

The English language was implanted to a degree that the Portuguese language never was during Portugal's occupation of Mombasa. A school syllabus for British-style education was established linked to an empirewide system based on examinations set by the University of Cambridge in England. Schoolteachers in Mombasa included increasing numbers of men and women from the United Kingdom sent out to serve the British empire. Of course the white missionaries were also active, seeking to spread the Christian gospel through missionary schools, church services, and medical clinics bearing the cross.

The British helped to spread literacy not only in the English language, but also in select indigenous languages in what became Kenya. In Mombasa the relevant indigenous language was Swahili (or Kiswahili). In the first half of the twentieth century newspapers began to appear in both languages in Mombasa. The *Mombasa Times*, published daily in English, was the most influential newspaper in the city. It was edited and run by Europeans. But other racial groups in Mombasa (African, Arab, and Indian) developed weekly or monthly publications of their own in diverse languages. The languages was diverse, but the tradition of newspapers and weekly periodicals in any language reflected a process of Westernization.

Under British rule Kenya became a white-settler colony. The colonial power encouraged large-scale white immigration to farm in the very fertile soils of what were overtly called "the white highlands." Although these highlands were several hundred miles away from Mombasa, there is no doubt that the transformation of Kenya into a white-settler colony had profound implications for Mombasa.

Although Mombasa was an ancient city, it was bypassed in order to build the capital of Kenya closer to the White Highlands. Nairobi was rapidly developed from a minor train stop on the Uganda railway into a growing African metropolis. By the second half of the twentieth century Nairobi had outstripped Mombasa in size. What saved Mombasa from shrinking into insignificance was its continuing strategic value as the most important port in East Africa, regardless of where the Kenya capital was.

Mombasa and other parts of Kenya became Westernized in more basic ways as well. Dress among the younger generation borrowed more and more from the West. Manners, etiquette, and even forms of boasting became influenced by Western norms.

Above all the colonial mentality looked towards the imperial metropole for a general standard of life and culture. Caliban sought the guidance of Prospero. The British way of life was for a while the ultimate standard of civilization to the colonized. Mombasa was in the shadow of this mental dependency.

And then the emulation of British ways included British standards of democratic life. Colonial rule was undemocratic—the imperial power was hoisted by its own petard. Nationalists in Mombasa and other parts of Kenya started demanding "One Man, One Vote." British standards of democracy by the second half of the twentieth century meant universal adult suffrage, leading to full independence. By mid-December 1963 Mombasa was the proud port of independent Kenya. The old style colonialism was over.

It was during this postcolonial period that the epicenter of Westernization in Mombasa shifted from British to American. The shift was neither sharp nor total. After all, Britain and the United States were themselves close allies and were both English-speaking powers. Nevertheless, in the postcolonial world in Kenya, capitalism mattered more than colonial ties. And the leader of the capitalist world was obviously the United States.

American influence in determining the prices of Kenya's agricultural products (especially coffee and tea), American influence with the World Bank and the International Monetary Fund, and American influence among the community of aid-donors generally contributed to this shift from Britannic Westernization to Americo-centric Westernization. This is quite apart from the expanding trade, aid, and investment relations between the United States and Kenya.

Further American influences came through the increasing impact of American music, television programs, cinemas, and magazines which were making major cultural inroads into Mombasa and Nairobi. Young people also responded to American dress styles, particularly jeans and T-shirts.

The American genius in fast food also affected Mombasa streets and restaurants. The hamburger had arrived on the African side of the Indian Ocean. So had Kentucky Fried Chicken or its equivalent. Competing with African, Arab, and Indian snacks of old, there were now these new fast minimeals from the food culture of the United States. Popular cuisine among the young in Mombasa was becoming partly Americanized. The United States was clearly the new epicenter of this new burst of postcolonial Westernization.

From this westernizing phase of Mombasa's historical experience (the Afro-Occidental phase), it is an easy transition to the Afro-globalist phase. It is to this even more wide-ranging stage of Mombasa's historical evolution that we must now turn.

The Afro-Global Phase

Three forces contributed to the globalization of Mombasa—war, tourism, and international politics. The wars ranged from World War II to the Mau Mau insurrection in Kenya. Tourism went back to the days of Theodore Roosevelt. International politics included the repercussions of the Cold War.

Of course, there were earlier stages in the globalization of Mombasa. The first two phases themselves themselves were on a global scale. But there were other trends in the process.

Mombasa as a major seaport acquired additional significance during World War II. It became important both in the defeat of Italy in the earlier phases of the war and in transporting African troops to Burma in the war against Japan. Mombasa was also important simply in relation to the flow of goods between Africa and Europe during that critical wartime period.

Ironically, Mombasa had been fought over so often because of its strategic importance that its ancient name, Mvita, means Isle of War. In the twentieth century, Mombasa once again became Mvita, the Isle of War, but in a vastly different sense.

It has been estimated that about five hundred thousand (half a million) African soldiers from British colonies alone served in World War II. They fought not only in the Horn of Africa and North Africa, but also in Italy and Axis-occupied ports of the fertile crescent. Africa's heaviest casualties were in the war in Burma against the Japanese. A large proportion of those African soldiers sailed from Mombasa.

Almost none of those African soldiers who fought in World War II were ever allowed to rise above the rank of sergeant. They almost always had higher superior white officers. And while the contributions of Australians, New Zealanders, and other Commonwealth combatants have repeatedly been celebrated (including during the 1994 D-Day extravaganza), very little tribute has even been paid to the African heroes and martyrs of World War II. Mombasa was to many of those African soldiers what Portsmouth was to the soldiers who invaded Normandy on June 6, 1944—a point of departure on a momentous military mission.

When Italy's Eastern African empire of Ethiopia and Eritrea was overrun by the British, Mombasa was used to accommodate many Italian prisoners of war, both men and women. Some of the earliest interracial dating experienced by the local African population in Mombasa was the dating between Mombasa men and the Italian women detained in Mombasa during World War II. That interracial dating must itself be counted as a stage in the globalization of Mombasa. Before World War II, sex between blacks and whites in Kenya was a crime.

Later on Mombasa acquired a new value because of its relationship to the Suez Canal. After World War II, Egyptian nationalists were putting increasing pressure on the British to vacate their military base near the Suez Canal. After the Egyptian revolution of 1952, these nationalist pressures against the British military presence in Egypt became irresistible. Mombasa in combination with Aden in Yemen acquired additional significance in British strategic calculations. The two ports constituted the fall-back position after the loss of the Egyptian military prize.

Mombasa was being further absorbed into the strategic politics of the world. Unfortunately for British planners, the year of the Egyptian revolution was also the year of the outbreak of the Mau Mau war in Kenya. Both events unleashed forces that evicted the British from both countries. The British were subjected to the same militant fate in Aden.

The Mau Mau war in Kenya was itself a globalizing experience. It gave the colonial politics of Kenya much more publicity than it had ever had before. And the name "Jomo Kenyatta" became a household name in distant ports of the world. Although the war was fought mainly in central Kenya rather than at the Coast, it did of course affect Mombasa and must be seen as part of the wider forces of globalization at work. Of course, the British authorities also used Mombasa to bring in British troops, planes, and ammunition for the war against the Mau Mau nationalists. In the end it was a victory of the vanquished. The Mau Mau were defeated militarily, but their political cause of Black rule in Kenya prevailed. Kenya became independent in December 1963.

After Jimmy Carter was elected president of the United States in 1976, Mombasa acquired military significance to the United States for a while. The American concept of a Rapid Deployment Force in defense of the oil routes and the oil resources included a cluster of seaports that could be used by U.S. ships either for refueling or for "morale-boosting" holidays for the servicemen and women who were guarding the approaches to the Red Sea and the Persian Gulf.

Before long the beginnings of an American military base began to be established in Mombasa. American naval ships stopped periodically during the 1980s and American serviceman disembarked. The shops, nightclubs, hawkers, and whorehouses learnt the skills of catering for visiting American servicemen. Mombasa was absorbed into the more militarized side of the Cold War.

Tourism as a globalizing experience in Kenya is, in a sense, older than war. In the first half of the century Mombasa was the main point of entry for all overseas tourists, but the Coast of Kenya was only a minor part of the attraction of the country at that stage. The big attraction for European and North American tourists in the first half of the century was the great safari—traveling into the bush tracking wild animals either to photograph or to kill them. These were the days of animals' trophies—the most ambitious being leopard skins, elephant tusks, or the head of a lion. The white hunters came through Mombasa and left with their trophies through Mombasa. It was of course an age before the tourist airbus. One of the earliest tourists in Kenya this century was U.S. President Theodore Roosevelt (1858–1919).

In the second half of the twentieth century Mombasa became more than simply a point of entry for tourists. The port and the Kenya Coast as a whole became a major part of the attraction of the country. Some of the major beach hotels were built in Mombasa—as were expensive beach chalets for longer-term rent. The safari and the wild beasts were still a major part of Kenya's tourist package, but the beaches and Mombasa's own very distinctive cultural mixture had become independent additional attractions for visitors.

By the 1980s hunting in Kenya was outlawed—but the old style safari hunters had become only a tiny percentage of the tourists in any case.

With the coming of the jet age, Mombasa's importance as a point of entry for tourists had drastically declined—but Mombasa's significance a major tourist attraction had risen dramatically. The globalization of Mombasa has continued unabated.

The question arises whether the tourist globalization of Mombasa neutralized the previous Afro-orientalization of the city. It is true that Westernization had itself inevitably been partly at the expense of both African and Oriental ways. The new globalization is an ally of Westernization, and both have continued to corrode both African and Oriental legacies in Mombasa.

As the city has learned to cater to Western tourists and to American service personnel, the pleasures of the evening have become increasingly Westernized. More nightclubs, dance halls, bars, and Western-style restaurants have opened. The old rhythms of African drums, the Arab *ud* and the Indian *tabla* and sitar have been giving way to the aggressive guitars and drums of the Western world. Indeed, African music itself has become substantially Westernized in the last twenty years.

One cruel irony is whether what would otherwise have been the relentless Westernization of Mombasa even in the process of globalization is now being slowed down by the fears generated by Acquired Immune Deficiency Syndrome (AIDS). Certainly sexual liberation as an aspect of Westernization has become more circumspect in Mombasa in the 1990s. And the tourists who used to come from Western Europe in search of "white beaches, the blue ocean, and black sex" have become much more careful about this third component. So have their former Black partners, who regard white folks as the original carriers of AIDS into Africa.

It is one of the ironies of history that cultural Westernization in Mombasa is being slowed down partly because of the fear of AIDS. The African and Oriental cultures of Mombasa may be the accidental beneficiaries of a terrible disease. The Bible used historical floods and famines to tell a moral story. One day historians may use AIDS to draw definitive cultural conclusions.

When did international politics begin the globalization of Mombasa? Again this is a process that inevitably includes some of the previous phases of Mombasa's historical experience. Certainly the anticolonial struggle in Kenya became an experience in international politics. The name of Tom Mboya, the most prominent Kenyan politician after Jomo Kenyatta in the 1950s, became widely known in many circles in the United States, as well as Great Britain. He lectured widely in both countries in defense of the Black nationalist cause in Kenya. Mboya was definitely an eloquent illustration of how internationalism contributed to globalization.

In the 1950s Mombasa was important in Mboya's rise to national prominence in Kenya. He was a trade union leader who became involved in the dock strike in Mombasa of the 1950s. His combined talents for aggression and negotiation propelled him to national visibility. It was from within the ranks of trade unionism that he then entered wider anticolonial politics.

After independence the Cold War also became a major factor in the globalization of Mombasa. Although Jomo Kenyatta had been denounced by the British as a "leader into darkness and death," and had suffered as a "Mau Mau" detainee, he emerged from prison ready to forgive and forget. He became one of Kenya's leading Anglophiles, and took the country firmly into the capitalist camp in the Cold War.

However, Mombasa as a port was serving more than just Kenya. Uganda under Milton Obote attempted a "Move to the Left" ideologically and had tense relations with Kenya. Uganda needed Mombasa to export and import goods. Its relations with Kenya sometimes tempted Uganda to explore alternative points of access to the sea. Unfortunately for Uganda, Mombasa was still by far the best outlet to the sea.

Uganda under Idi Amin was, in domestic policy, capitalist. But its foreign policy grew increasingly anti-Western and pro-Soviet. There were also problems with the Kenya government, which sometimes included Kenyan threats to withhold the port services of Mombasa for Uganda. Here a paradox emerged. Mombasa's role as a service for East Africa as a whole was sometimes compromised by the wider regional and global politics. The Cold War cast its shadow on Mombasa directly and through interstate rivalries in East Africa.

Globalization of Mombasa was also influenced by the United Nations and its agencies. Certainly the United Nations High Commission for Refugees needed Mombasa for some of the problems of refugees from Somalia—including refugee camps in Mombasa. The United Nations' Environmental Programmes' (UNEP's) global headquarters were in Nairobi. UNEP's concerns included oceanic ones in Mombasa and elsewhere at the Kenya Coast. The location of UNEP in Nairobi, as the first UN agency to have its headquarters in Africa, inevitably increased UNEP's consciousness of its own immediate environment, including the debate about pollution in the Indian Ocean from Kenya. How culpable is Mombasa in relation to the pollution of the sea?

Africa's internationalization meant has also brought about Africa's inter-Africanization. During World War II Mombasa experienced what were perhaps its first visitors from West Africa—the soldiers from the Gold Coast (now Ghana). Mombasa also experienced white South Africans during World War II in uniform, on their way to battle areas elsewhere.

The inter-Africanization of East Africa has reached new levels since the 1940s. Since Kenya has become one of the leading diplomatic and conference centers of Africa, Mombasa has inevitably been a Pan-African beneficiary.

But no city exists independently of the state and nation to which it belongs. The state to which Mombasa now belongs is, of course, Kenya. Although the City has gone through three stages toward globalization, Kenya as a state has had a somewhat different transition. The national and state dilemmas have had implications for Mombasa.

Between the Atlantic and the Indian Ocean

Kenya is an Indian Ocean power (through Mombasa) which has been behaving as if it were an Atlantic power (through Nairobi). Perhaps of all African countries, Kenya evolved the most wide-ranging relationships with the leading countries of Western Europe and North America. For a while Kenya was the darling of the West, not only because of its tourist attractions, but also because of its strategic importance. Ironically, Kenya's strategic value to the West was precisely because Kenya was an Indian Ocean power. It was located along one of the great sea routes of the world and was also in close proximity to the oil reserves of the Middle East. It was a potential staging place for the rapid deployment of Western forces in a critical area of the globe. It was vital that Kenya remained pro-Western.

A paradox emerged. While the West flirted with Kenya because of its location on the Indian Ocean, Western flirtations turned Kenya's eyes away from the Indian Ocean. This country became excessively Western oriented and inadequately attentive to its Asian neighbors. The

West embraced Kenya partly because the West valued the Indian Ocean; Kenya embraced the West and turned its back on the Indian Ocean. Mombasa was part and parcel of the paradox.

But now the honeymoon is over. Kenya's intimate embrace of the Western world at the expense of all other relationships has at last to be reviewed. Kenya is a country which in the past was lukewarm about Pan-Africanism, hostile to the People's Republic of China, profoundly distrustful of the Arabs, indifferent towards India, and cool towards the Soviet Union (or Russia). For the bulk of the first 23 years of KANU rule, Kenya's most intimate allies were the Western powers (and Israel). Kenya was often amply rewarded by these particular friends.

Now that the cold war is over, the West has itself reviewed its own relationship with Kenya. Many Western countries have decided that they no longer have to humor the present KANU government simply because it is anticommunist. Western governments have at long last become friends of the cause of democracy in Kenya. Their pressures helped to force President Daniel arap Moi to accept the principle of multipartyism, although we must not underestimate the prior impact of domestic democratic pressures on President Moi's change of mind.

Whether KANU or some other party comes to power after the multiparty election, it is time that Kenya too embarked on a fundamental review of its wider global options. Just as Kenya is now of lesser strategic value to the West with the end of the cold war, so should the West become less fundamental to Kenya's global design in the wake of those wider developments.

On the ocean front in Mombasa, Kenya faces the Asian world rather than the European. Until the 1990s Kenya was far more sensitive to the imperatives of history (the history of being an excolony of Britain) than to the imperatives of geography (proximity to Asia and the Middle East). It is time to redress this imbalance between postcolonial historical continuities and the older dictates of geographic proximity. Firstly, Kenya has to recognize the fact that it is indeed an Indian Ocean power. In the past Kenya has tended to regard its own South Asian population at home as a historic liability (Indian immigrants in colonial Kenya go back beyond the building of the railway line to Uganda at the beginning of the century). Kenya should now learn to recognize its Asian population not as a politicohistorical liability, but as an economicogeographical asset.

The Kenya Coast is so culturally Indianized that the food culture of the Waswahili uses a lot of Indian spices, and the music of the Coast Province shows evidence of South Asian impact. This cultural influence of South Asia in Kenya could be converted into diplomatic currency in Kenya's economic relations with India, Pakistan, and Bangladesh. Trade between Kenya and those countries could also be enhanced if careful thought was given to the nature of economic exchange for the future.

Kenya is geographically close to the Arab world; it shares borders with two members of the Arab league (Sudan and Somalia); Kenya is itself the most stable country in Eastern Africa; it has a culturally Arabized population among its citizens (the Waswahili, the Somali and the other Muslims of Kenya); it has been economically prosperous since independence; it has exported both skilled and semiskilled human power to the Arab world since its independence.

Future Kenya governments will have to review their relations with the Arab world as a whole in order to improve them further. In population the bulk of the Arab world is within Africa. The largest Arab country in population is Egypt. The largest country in Africa in square miles is Arabized Sudan, with which Kenya shares a border.

Conclusion

Kenya may consolidate its role as an Indian Ocean power through Mombasa—without losing all the Western gains it made when it behaved like an Atlantic power through Nairobi. The new equilibrium can indeed be accomplished. But it will need a new political will, a greater sense of history and a deeper sensibility to geography.

Much older than Kenya as a country is of course Mombasa as a city. Kenya is a twentieth-century political entity; Mombasa is a phenomenon of at least a millennium. Just as Mombasa is an ancient city while Kenya is a young nation, Mombasa is a global city while Kenya is still grappling with its basic dilemma between the geographical contiguities of the Indian Ocean and the historical continuities of the Atlantic legacy.

Notes

1. See N. Chittick and R. I. Rotberg, eds., *East Africa and the Orient.* New York: Africana Press, 1975, and B. A. Datoo, "Influence of Monsoons on Movements of Dhows along the East African Coast," *East African Geographical Review,* 1974, 12: 23–33.
2. See, for example, C. Sassoon, *Chinese Porcelain in Fort Jesus.* Mombasa: National Museum of Kenya, 1975.
3. See R. Skene, "Arab and Swahili Dances and Ceremonies," *Journal of the Royal Anthropological Institute* (London), 1917, 47: 413–434.
4. See T. O. Ranger, *Dance and Society in Eastern Africa, 1890–1970: The Beni Ngoma.* London: Heinemann, 1975.
5. See, for example, Je de V N d. Allen "Ngoma: Music and Dance." In Mtoro bin Mwinyi Bakara, ed., *The Customs of the Swahili People: The Desturi za Waswahili.* Berkeley: University of California Press, 1981, pp. 233–46.

6. See, for example, R. L. Pouwels, *Horn and Crescent: Cultural Change and Traditional Islam on the East African Coast, 800–1900.* Cambridge: Cambridge University Press, 1987.

7. See J. Strandes, *The Portuguese period in East Africa.* Nairobi: East African Literature Bureau, 1961.

Section 7 The Impact of Transition: Hungary

Gyula Bora

At the end of the twentieth century, the globalization process will continue, although its quantitative and qualitative aspects are likely to change. The rapid growth of the world's population is a fact that results in considerable controversy, particularly because a considerable part of humanity lives in deplorable conditions. Science and technology offer few solutions to world problems. Among the questions that will face the new millennium are whether housing conditions can be improved, an adequate number of new jobs created, and infrastructure can keep pace with demand. In this globalizing world, it might be better to look for answers on a regional level.

At present, the countries of Central and Eastern Europe are undergoing radical political, economic, and social transformations. This process is unprecedented in world history. The one-party system has been changed into a democratic political structure; the centrally planned economy, based predominantly on state ownership, has changed into a market economy based on private ownership. This section of *Cities Fit for People* analyzes how the conditions of urbanization have changed in one state of East–Central Europe, namely Hungary. It discusses how new urbanization policies have replaced so-called socialist urban development, which had been implemented over four decades.

Did the Transition Disrupt Urbanization Trends?

Urbanization arrived later in East-Central Europe than in the West in large part because the Industrial Revolution, which is a major factor in urbanization, was slower in starting. Although urbanization was noticeable at the beginning of the twentieth century, the years after World War I did not favor faster urban development. This was particularly characteristic of Hungary.

A change began in the late 1960s with new centrally controlled social and economic policies. The goals included accelerated urbanization through the development of specific types of settlements and changes in the settlement pattern throughout the country. To implement the latter policy, a 1971 plan classified the settlements into a rigid hierarchical system, which specified which settlements would be developed into towns and further ranked existing towns into developmental categories. According to the plan, small settlements in rural areas were not to be further developed and distinctions in the development plans for existing towns appeared unjustified. Because of the economic hardships of the 1980s, as well as increasing opposition to the plan, it became impractical to implement.

The state, however, could make and implement decisions almost without control. Macroeconomic processes were built on a financial system in which the overwhelming part of gross domestic product was collected as part of the state budget. The state then allocated funds in accordance with already established priorities. The state's policies on urban development were based on the fact that town institutions, included public utilities, schools, and health and cultural institutions, were state owned. Towns earned little independent revenue; funding for maintenance and development were assigned from the state budget. Toward the end of this period, one change occurred—local housing and infrastructure projects were funded by local residents. The rent of state-owned dwellings and the costs of town services were less than the real operating costs. Thus, maintenance required state subsidies, which only increased the dependence of these settlements on the state government.

The state used direct and indirect methods to influence urbanization. One direct method was the use of development funds as a bargaining mechanism; an indirect method was linking housing and infrastructure investments with the locations of new industrial plants.

The process of urbanization was closely connected with economic growth (the urban population increased at an annual rate of 1.8 to 2.2 percent). Similarly, as in other East-Central European countries, the main source was rural–urban migration. Among the motives for migration were new jobs and a wider range of services.

In Hungary, the urban population has risen from 37 percent in 1950 to 61 percent in 1990. This was above average for East-Central Europe, but below that of Western Europe. As a result, most Hungarian towns were able to grow. In most towns, employment was already service rather than industry based. The proportion of those employed in agriculture fell to a minimum in towns, except for traditional market towns in the countryside. As long as economic growth did not stagnate, the towns were the prime movers of economic growth and the main suppliers for the country's population. The towns became information centers as new technology was introduced. Finally, towns became the centers for human capital, because they were home to institutions of higher education and scientific development.

However, urbanization also had negative effects, such as pressure on the infrastructure, increased environmental pollution, and the perennial shortage of housing. From the social aspect, however, the most serious problem was that the one-party system had dissolved all civil organizations. The town leadership break off all dialogue with the local population, eliminating any real support for town policies.

The political, economic, and social changes of the late 1980s resulted in changes in the process of urbanization. Since then, urbanization has slowed down, at least in the short run, to an annual increase of approximately one percent.

Changes In the Process of Urbanization

The major change of the late 1980s is the formation of democratic society with a market economy. This meant the restoration of representative government, as well as economic liberalization and privatization. Prices, once established centrally by the state, are now determined by market conditions.

The transition has affected urbanization in several ways. The state has been replaced by a parliamentary democracy of many parties. The centralized role of the state is now minimal. As a result, managing settlements has also become democratic. The council system has been replaced by the election of local authorities. Candidates for local governing bodies are put up by parties, but independent candidates may run as well. All local authorities are legally equal.

Local authorities of settlements, as well as towns, are independent economic units. The paternalistic role of the state is a thing of the past; local authorities exercise substantial autonomy in managing their revenues, which consist of centrally financed support for maintenance and development; part of personal income tax revenues; and other revenues based on local taxes and property income. Because of the sluggish economy, structural adjustments, and only mild economic growth, the earning power of local authorities is rather limited and varies from settlement to settlement.

The most important change in social conditions was the revival of civil organizations and the creation of new ones for environmental protection and town development. Self-governance now means a combination of elected governing bodies and civil organizations.

As a result of the economic crisis, depressed areas have evolved throughout the country. The northeastern part of the country, where heavy industry used to dominate, is experiencing high unemployment. The opposite is occurring in the capital, Budapest, and in the western part of the country in the vicinity of the Austrian border. These areas are home to new ventures and foreign capital investments, because they have better transportation facilities, a higher level of infrastructure, more sophisticated telecommunications links, and a more adaptable labor force. These towns are able to lay the foundations for sustainable development and their unemployment rate is below the national average.

In many towns, the number of inhabitants is decreasing, as people who once migrated from villages are being motivated by unemployment to return to their former homes. In addition, the process of migration itself has slowed down. In Budapest, the increase in the older population is presenting a problem. Pensioners constitute one fourth of the population, the birth rate declined, rural migration decreased, and many people moved to healthier settlements in the agglomerating zone. At the same time, the number of residents in many medium- and small-sized towns is growing at a higher rate than in large towns.

Further, the increase in some negative aspects of urban rate is alarming. Mention can here be made of growing juvenile delinquency, homelessness, impoverishment, deviant populations, unemployment, and slums.

However, one positive change, although not in all settlements, is the extension and increase in the level of infrastructure. Many more households are now connected to telephones, gas supplies, and sewerage facilities.

Local authorities can point to several indications of economic revival, including new businesses, competition for development funds, the implementation of infrastructure projects, and the organization of cultural events and exhibitions. These factors improve the ability of town to attract tourists and thus their ability to develop while drawing on their own resources. These should serve as a stimulus to local governing bodies in a number of stagnant towns.

New Policies of Urban Development

During this transition period, Hungary must lay the foundations for policies and institutions based on a market economy. Urban—and in a wider context, regional–development must also be viewed in this context.

Hungary's new policy of urban development is self-organizing management, which if turns out to be successful, will provide sound operation and development policies for the growing number of smaller settlements. Is such a policy necessary? There is every indication now that development will result in significant differentiation among towns. Because the conditions and opportunities of development vary from town to town, competition will evolve for domestic and foreign capital as well as for development funds. Each town will want an increasing number of businesses and institutions so that local revenues will rise.

Self-organizing management requires a new kind of management philosophy that includes active entry into the market and the "selling" of the town in a figurative sense. For example, some towns offer real estate of establish industrial parks to attract businesses that will result in the creation of new jobs.

There will be an increasing reliance on local authorities, to that application of the subsidiarity concept will spread. Subsidiarity implies a decentralization process, in which specific duties are assigned to the lowest level at which they can be performed efficiently and successfully. Development is, of course, the responsibility of both local and national authorities, which need to cooperate on issues of finance and business organization. Thus, the state should formulate the principles and control the means of urban and regional development, but the control must be closely connected to local interests. Great emphasis needs to be placed on local initiatives. According to the completion principle, money from different sources should complement each other for the purposes of settlement and regional development. Central support should be provided for local development only if the towns contribute their own funds to the fulfillment of the given task. Only the most disadvantaged settlements would be exempt from this rule.

The new legal bases of settlement development were laid out in the recently passed Regional Development Act. Because regional development is both spontaneous and planned, the act focuses on the mechanism of the market economy and the need to revitalize towns in depressed areas and backward regions. The act also reckons with the use of operating funds to subsidize the implementation of particular or well-defined tasks in infrastructure development and environmental protection.

Conclusion

Hungary is a small country of 93,000 square kilometers and a population of 10.3 million that is decreasing. The population of Budapest itself is 2 million; only 8 towns have a population between 100,000 and 200,000 inhabitants. Although there are 3,168 local authorities, the system is rather dismembered.

Budapest is the largest city in East-Central Europe because its favorable geographical location makes it the center of European transportation routes. As a sophisticated city, it can offer a wide range of services. Under the former regime, when socialist countries struggled with constant commodity shortages, it was the most frequented shopping center in the region. It is also an important center of tourism. The capital's institutions, including many government institutions, have built up important global networks of relationships. Transition must also mean openness, and openness has taken on a new meaning. In addition to the flow of goods, it now refers also to the flow of information and cultural developments.

In the future, Hungary needs to improve its infrastructure and search for solutions to the problems of housing shortages and unemployment. Hungarian policy is aimed at entry into the European Union as soon as possible. That would enable Hungary to become a more active participant in the process of globalization.

Section 8 Building Blocks for a Better World: From Vancouver to Istanbul

Üner Kırdar

Almost twenty years since the first United Nations conference on Human Settlements, held in Vancouver, Canada in 1976, world leaders again faced the question of making communities humane places to live. The Second United Nations Conference on Human Settlements (Habitat II) was held in Istanbul, Turkey, 3–14 June 1996. Labeled the "City Summit," by the former Secretary-General of the United Nations, this meeting completed the current cycle of UN global conferences held in the 1990s.

It was the culminating event in an unprecedented continuum of global forums convened by the United Nations on the doorstep of the twenty-first century. These conferences have successfully drawn up an agenda of action for the next millennium to make our planet a safe, healthy, just, and sustainable place. It started with the Children's Summit and has stretched to the Earth Summit (Rio), the International Conference on Human Rights (Vienna), the International Conference on Population and Development Cairo), the World Summit on Social Development (Copenhagen), and the Fourth World Conference on Women and Development (Beijing).

This event provided a major opportunity to synthesize the important outcomes of all previous global undertakings of the 1990s and maybe to sensitize world leaders and public opinion to the crucial economic and social issues associated with rapid urban population growth.

For me, Habitat II was a source of personal nostalgic and sentimental feelings. It was sentimental because the Conference took place in my hometown, Istanbul, and in the Conference Hall named after my late father, Dr. Lutfi Kırdar, who was Istanbul's mayor for 15 years during the 1940s and 1950s. It was nostalgic because I served as the Secretary of the first Habitat Conference in Vancouver. Finally, it was a special challenge in as much as I served as the Special Representative of the Secretary-General of Habitat II in coordinating the work of the Conference. Because of this special situation, one question frequently put to me was how Habitat II differed from Habitat I. Although the answer is not easy or simple, I can venture to identify seven main distinctions between the two conferences and, more specifically, between the global conferences of the 1970s and those of the 1990s convened by the United Nations.

Growing Interdependence and Interlinkages

During the 1970s, nearly every year, the United Nations convened a conference, each in a new area of interest: environment, population, food, status of women, Habitat, employment, water, desertification, science, and technology. These conferences elevated issues of primarily national concern to the global level. They alerted governments to the need to cooperate with one another and to take joint policy actions, but mostly in a fragmented and sectoral manner. During that decade, based on the recommendations of each conference, hardly a year went by without the establishment of one or two independent UN bodies, normally structured as separate intergovernmental organs, with a special secretariat and a related voluntary fund.

The last two decades, however, have taught us that the world is increasingly confronted with issues that affect humanity as a whole. Revolutionary changes in world affairs, spurred on by the globalization of markets, have shown that developmental, societal, and ecological problems cannot be solved merely by fragmented and sectoral initiatives alone. Their solutions require well-defined multidisciplinary, interlinked, and comprehensive approaches, with underpinning intellectual depth, vision, and long-term commitments.

We have learned that peace, economy, environment, social justice, and democracy are integral parts of the whole. Without peace, human energies cannot be productively employed. Without economic growth, there can be no sustained, broad-based improvement in material well-being or ecological balance. Without protection of the environment, the basis of human survival is eroded. Without societal justice, mounting inequalities threaten social cohesion. And, without political participation in freedom, development remains fragile and perpetually at risk.

Thus, it became an imperative that the Global Plan of Action adopted by "the City Summit" draw strength from a decade of UN conferences. It pressed as a whole the challenges that will confront the world community in the twenty-first century. It provided a more holistic and humane message about global problems and about the cooperative solutions they require.

The Developmental Dimension

The 1970s conferences, including the Habitat I Conference, dealt mainly with issues related to their respective sectoral concerns. The relationships between these issues and with the development process were not adequately considered. During the past two decades, we have become more cognizant that global peace and security cannot be achieved unless cooperation also deals with the threats that stem from failures in economic and social development and lack of tangible human progress. Therefore, each of the conferences of the 1990s has adopted a strong developmental dimension. Furthermore, this dimension has been more "people oriented." Development is no longer evaluated by how much growth, but what type of growth occurs. We have learned, for example, that a choice cannot be made between economic growth and environmental protection. True development can only be achieved through a balanced and integrated set of social, economic, and ecological policies. This new model of development may be called "Sustainable Human Development." It is a development model that not only conserves the nature, but places "people" at the very center of all concerns. It protects both human life and ecological life; develops human capabilities and provides opportunities for people to make maximum contributions to their own and societal development. It is a model which is pro-people, pro-nature, and pro-society. It is participatory and community based. It aims to mobilize all sectors of the civil society.

The Commonality of Interests

Rooted, as they were, in the geopolitics of the Cold War, the UN global conferences of the 1970s were strongly dominated by confrontations between the so-called industrialized countries and developing countries. The issues dealt with by the conferences were considered as problems primarily affecting the poor nations. And, therefore, the negotiations were specifically targeted to define what the North should do for the South.

During the last two decades, however, we have seen a widening gap between the rich and the poor, not only among, but also within, nations. We have noticed that in each country, in each city, and in each village, there is a proverbial "North" and "South." Today, unchecked population and urban growth, increasing poverty, crime, numbers of juvenile delinquents and street children, environmental decline, homelessness, unemployment, drugs, and societal disintegration are very much social and economic ills affecting all societies of the East, West, North, and South. The results of unmanaged urban development during the last two decades since the conference in Vancouver has reduced standards of living, damaged education quality, and considerably reduced health services.

At present, therefore, there is a mutuality of and similarity in the interests of all countries in finding tangible solutions to these issues. All countries have, or should have, equal concerns in searching for shared solutions to common problems.

The Oneness of Economic and Social Goals

If, in the 1970s, the UN Conferences did not adequately consider the close relationship existing between the sectoral issues and their developmental dimensions, during the 1980s, another basic lesson was overlooked—namely that the economic and the social spheres are one. They are complementary and mutually supporting. Too much "social equity" without adequate "economic growth" may lead to bankruptcy, and too much "economic growth" without sufficient "social equity" can lead to social disorder. Therefore, a package of integrated economic and social policies is essential for the maintenance of political and social peace.

The UN Global Conferences of the 1990s finally recognized this necessity and incorporated it in their global plans of action designed to implement sustainable human development policies.

The Reorientation of Policies

It has been conventional wisdom until recently that development requires active government involvement in the productive sectors of the economy, as in the establishment of government-owned enterprises, in providing subsidies to the private sector and in protecting industries engaged in import substitution. While these policies did result in economic growth in some countries up to the mid-1970s, for the most part, the experiences have been ones of stagnating growth, production failures, and very little improvement in standards of living.

Such empirical consequences have in turn led to a new thinking and fresh reorientation of the role and policies of governments. The emerging consensus at present is that the governments should do less in those areas where market forces work more efficiently. This does not necessarily mean less government, but a different form and or a better governance.

Facilitation, enabling instead of providing policies, regulation, and monitoring today have become major functions of governments in a market-driven economy. This reorientation of roles and policies of the governments are becoming much more apparent in the global plans of action of the 1990s UN global conferences, when compared with those of the 1970s.

A Partnership with New Actors

The UN conferences of the 1970s operated under the premise that global problems are primarily interstate issues and could, therefore, be solved mainly through negotiations between governments and their policy coordinators. However, during the last two decades, governments and international governmental organizations learned they are no longer the sole actors. Helped by remarkable new advances in information and communication technologies, the private sector (multinational corporations), nongovernmental organizations, media networks, professional associations, and civic groups are today playing a very dynamic role in shaping important global strategies, according to their own rules, priorities, and values. The emergence of these new actors in global relations has created a need for a redefinition of roles, functions, and obligations in responding to new global challenges.

Both the preparatory process, as well as the Habitat II Conference itself have explicitly recognized this important advance and sought active involvement and broad participation for all relevant actors: local governments, academics, professionals, foundations, the private sector, labor unions, and nongovernmental and community-based organizations. Through such broad-based participation, all actors of civil society had a role to play in finding and implementing the required solutions.

A Bottom-Up Approach

The 1970s conferences were generally prepared through a top-down process. Policies were formulated at the global level through international intergovernmental committees, with the expectations that they would be implemented at local, national, and regional levels. Eventually, however, the shortcomings of such approaches became apparent. Therefore, during the 1990s, in the preparatory process of many conferences, especially for Habitat II, a bottom-up approach was used to ensure a broad-based participation in policy formation, at all levels.

In many countries, national committees were established to prepare country reports and national plans of action. These committees were usually composed of the representatives of local governments, NGOs, professional organizations, universities, chambers of commerce and industries, trade unions, and other stakeholders. Thus, Habitat II sought to be a catalyst for improved local governance and policy making on a global basis that is broad-based, transparent, democratic, and equitable.

Conclusion

At the doorstep of the twenty-first century, the UN convened a series of very important global conferences on hitherto neglected and pressing problems facing humanity. These conferences have had an overall objective to influence national and international policies, by gathering scientific evidence, establishing partnerships among different members of civil society, mobilizing public opinion, recommending lines of action, and focusing the attention of world political leaders. They aimed at making our planet a safer, healthier, more just and sustainable place. These conferences have successfully drawn blueprints for human action for the next millennium. They have also left a legacy to the UN for the future, a legacy of sustainable human social, economic, and environmental development.

It is now widely accepted that the major challenges faced by the human race can only be met through multilateral action, and that the most logical place for such action is the UN. Paradoxically, at the very moment when this recognition is becoming widespread, there are growing doubts about the capability of the UN to meet these challenges. Yet the ability of the organization to master the awesome challenges confronting humanity now depends largely on the political will and support of its member states. We can no longer operate through the shortsighted and inward-looking internal politics that our shrinking planet has shown to be obsolete.

We must now learn to live with a global perspective. Humanity is a part of a complex planetary system and global issues affecting our lives must be the concern of all people and nations. There should be a change in the attitude that global issues are only the responsibility of others, unless, in the short term, they affect our own national constituencies.

The world community has the ability, means, and chance to turn the many threats of today into opportunities for human progress tomorrow. But it needs new vision, long-term perspectives, and bold leadership to succeed.

Contributors

Kofi A. Annan, Secretary-General, United Nations, New York

Philip Allott, Trinity College, Cambridge University, Cambridge, UK

Nezar AlSayyad, Executive Director, Center for Environmental Design Research, University of California, Berkeley

Nancy Barry, President, Women's World Banking, New York

Pii Elina Berghäll, United Nations University/World Institute for Development and Economic Research (WIDER), Helsinki

Gyula Bora, Professor, Department of Economic Geography, Budapest University of Economic Sciences, Budapest

Sylvia Chant, Department of Geography, London School of Economics, London

Michael A. Cohen, Senior Adviser, Environmentally Sustainable Development, Office of the Vice President, World Bank, Washington DC

Felix Dodds, Co-ordinator, UNED/UK Committee, London

Hazem El-Beblawi, Executive Secretary, United Nations Eonomic & Social Commission for Western Asia, Amman

Louis Emmerij, Special Advisor to the President, Inter-American Development Bank, Washington, DC

Herbert Girardet, Director, Middlesex University, Footprint Films, Professor Environment of Planning, London

William Gorham, President, The Urban Institute, Washington, DC

Isabelle Hentic, Urban Specialist, Policy Strategic Planning and Operation, Canadian International Development Agency, Quebec

Noeleen Heyzer, Director, United Nations Development Fund for Women, New York

Reino Hjerppe, Principal Academic Officer, United Nations University/World Institute for Development and Economic Research (WIDER), Helsinki

Inge Kaul, Director, Office of Development Studies, United Nations Development Programme, New York

Celina Kawas, Women's World Banking, New York

Azizur Rahman Khan, Professor, Department of Economics, University of California, Riverside

G. Thomas Kingley, The Urban Institute, Washington, DC

Üner Kırdar, Senior Adviser to the Administrator of UNDP, New York

Flora Lewis, Syndicated Columnist, *Herald Tribune* and *New York Times,* Paris

Fu-chen Lo, Deputy Director, United Nations University, Tokyo

Ali A. Mazrui, Director, Institute of Global and Cultural Studies, State University of New York, Binghamton

Diana Mitlin, Human Settlements Program, International Institute for Environment and Development, London

Valentine M. Moghadam, Independent Consultant, The Saratoga, Washington, DC.

Deborah Moldow, Representative to the United Nations, The World Peace Prayer Society, New York

Nasser Munjee, Executive Director, Housing Development Finance Corporation Ltd., Bombay

Wally N'Dow, Assistant Secretary-General, United Nations Center for Human Settlements, Nairobi; Secretary-General, Habitat II Conference

Amar Nuno-Amarteifio, Mayor of Accra, Accra Metropolitan Assembly, Accra

Jonas Rabinovitch, Senior Urban Development Advisor, BPPS/UNDP, New York

Samir Radwan, Director, Development and Technical Cooperation Department, International Labour Office, Geneva

K. C. Siva Rama Krishnan, Visiting Professor, Centre for Policy Research, Honorary Advisor, National Foundation for India, New Delhi

Gustav Ranis, Professor, Economic Growth Center, Department of Economics, Yale University, New Haven

Sixto K. Roxas, Vice Chairman, Foundation for Community Organization and Management Technology, Foundation for the Philippino Environment, Quezon City

David Satterthwaite, Human Settlements Program, International Institute for Environment and Development, London

Mihály Simai, Former Director, United Nations University/World Institute for Development and Economic Research (WIDER), Helsinki

James Gustave Speth, Administrator, United Nations Development Programme, New York

Frances Stewart, Director, Queen Elizabeth House, International Development Centre, Oxford

Paul Streeten, Professor Emeritus, Boston University, Spencertown

Ilhan Tekeli, Professor, Faculty of Architecture, Middle East Technical University, Ankara

Mariken Vaa, Senior Researcher, Institute for Social Research, Oslo

Jorge Wilheim, Former Deputy Secretary-General of Habitat II Conference, United Nations Center for Human Settlements, Nairobi

Bernard Woods, International Consultant, Elephant House, Kent

Weiping Wu, Assistant Professor, Department of Urban Studies and Planning, Virginia Commonwealth University, Richmond

Fernando Zumbado, Regional Director, Regional Bureau for Latin American and the Caribbean, UNDP, New York; Former Minister of Planning & Housing of Costa Rica

About the Editor

Üner Kırdar is Senior Adviser to the Administrator of the United Nations Development Programme.

Born in Turkey on 1 January 1933, he graduated from the Faculty of Law, Istanbul, undertook postgraduate studies at the London School of Economics, and received his Ph.D. from Jesus College, University of Cambridge, England.

Dr. Kırdar has served the United Nations system in various capacities, including Secretary of the Preparatory Committee and United Nations Conference on Human Settlements (1974-1976), Secretary of the Group of Experts on the Structure of the United Nations System (1975), and a Senior Officer for Inter-Agency Affairs in the Office of the United Nations Secretary-General (1972-1977). He was the Director of the Division of External Relations and Secretary to the Governing Council Secretariat of UNDP from 1980 to 1991.

He has been the main architect of the UNDP Development Study Programme and has organized several seminars, round-table meetings, lectures, and discussion groups attended by high-level national and international policy makers.

He has also held senior positions in the Ministry of Foreign Affairs of Turkey, including Director for International Economic Organizations and Deputy Permanent Representative of Turkey to the United Nations Office at Geneva.

Dr. Kırdar is the author of the book, *Structure of UN Economic Aid to Underdeveloped Countries* (1966; 1968). He is an editor or coeditor and contributor to *Human Development: The Neglected Dimension* (1986); *Human Development, Adjustment and Growth* (1987); *Managing Human Development* (1988); *Development and People* (1989); *Equality of Opportunity Within and Among Nations* (1977); "Human Resources Development: Challenge for the '80s," *Crisis of the '80s* (1983); "Impact of IMF Conditionality on Human Conditions." *Adjustment with Growth* (1984); *the Lingering Debt Crisis* (1985); *Change: Threat or Opportunity?*

(five volumes, 1991), *A World Fit for People* (1994); and *People: From Impoverishment to Empowerment* (1995).